# ELEMENTARY ALGEBRA

**Grades 5 - 6**

## by Marcia Dana

Carson-Dellosa Publishing Company, Inc.
Greensboro, North Carolina

# Credits

**Editor:** Amy Gamble
**Layout Design:** Tiara Reynolds
**Inside Illustrations:** J.J. Rudisill
**Cover Design:** Annette Hollister-Papp
**Cover Illustrations:** Annette Hollister-Papp

ISBN 1-59441-194-8

# Table of Contents

# Introduction

This book focuses on many of the early algebra concepts described in the NCTM Algebra strand. The activities in this book are designed to expand students' mathematical understanding, particularly in the area of algebra. A variety of developmentally appropriate activities will help students become familiar with the following elementary algebra skills:

- number and shape patterns
- skip counting
- functions
- equality and inequality
- writing equations
- solving equations
- properties of numbers
- mathematical relationships
- graphs and tables
- change
- variables

Each concept is presented in an easy-to-understand way that is intended to be both interesting and fun for students. This book can be a valuable tool in helping students achieve growth in their mathematical development.

# Crisscross Patterns

**Extending Patterns**

## Directions:

Shade in the shapes in each row to continue the pattern.

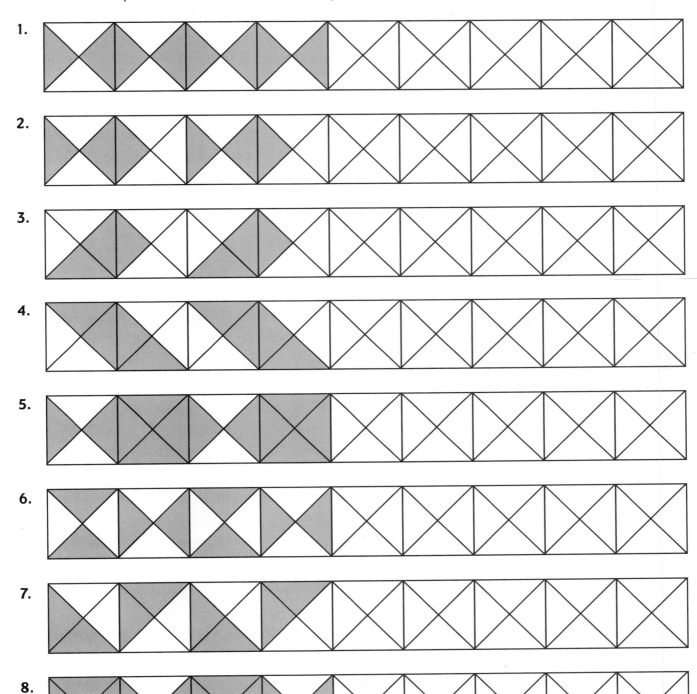

## Connect the Dots

 **Extending Patterns**

### Directions:
Connect dots in each row to continue the pattern as far as you can.

1.

2.

3.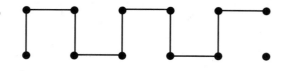

4.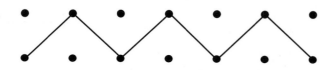

5.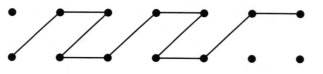

6.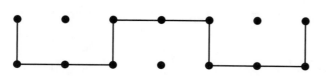

7.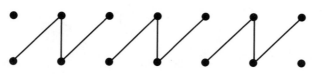

8.

# Name That Pattern!

**Identifying Patterns**

## Directions:

Find the rule for the pattern in each row. Continue the pattern and write the rule on the blank. The first one has been done for you.

**Pattern Rule**

1. (7) (10) (13) (16) (19) (22) (25) (28) (31) (34)  __+ 3__

2. (50) (48) (46) (44) (42) (40) (38) ( ) ( ) ( )  _____

3. (28) (33) (38) (43) (48) (53) (58) ( ) ( ) ( )  _____

4. (20) (28) (36) (44) (52) (60) (68) ( ) ( ) ( )  _____

5. (50) (46) (42) (38) (34) (30) (26) ( ) ( ) ( )  _____

6. (86) (96) (106) (116) (126) (136) (146) ( ) ( ) ( )  _____

7. (100) (92) (84) (76) (68) (60) (52) ( ) ( ) ( )  _____

8. (24) (35) (46) (57) (68) (79) (90) ( ) ( ) ( )  _____

9. (80) (75) (70) (65) (60) (55) (50) ( ) ( ) ( )  _____

10. (154) (144) (134) (124) (114) (104) (94) ( ) ( ) ( )  _____

11. (16) (36) (56) (76) (96) (116) (136) ( ) ( ) ( )  _____

12. (200) (185) (170) (155) (140) (125) (110) ( ) ( ) ( )  _____

## Jumbo Patterns

**Identifying Patterns**

**Directions:**
Figure out each pattern rule and complete the pattern.

**Rule**

| | | | | | | | | |
|---|---|---|---|---|---|---|---|---|
| _____ | 1. | 25 | 50 | 75 | 100 | _____ | _____ | _____ _____ |
| _____ | 2. | 7 | 22 | 37 | 52 | _____ | _____ | _____ _____ |
| _____ | 3. | 15 | 45 | 75 | 105 | _____ | _____ | _____ _____ |
| _____ | 4. | 17 | 67 | 117 | 167 | _____ | _____ | _____ _____ |
| _____ | 5. | 5 | 80 | 155 | 230 | _____ | _____ | _____ _____ |
| _____ | 6. | 53 | 153 | 253 | 353 | _____ | _____ | _____ _____ |
| _____ | 7. | 25 | 135 | 245 | 355 | _____ | _____ | _____ _____ |
| _____ | 8. | 6 | 156 | 306 | 456 | _____ | _____ | _____ _____ |
| _____ | 9. | 200 | 375 | 550 | 725 | _____ | _____ | _____ _____ |
| _____ | 10. | 250 | 500 | 750 | 1,000 | _____ | _____ | _____ _____ |
| _____ | 11. | 1,000 | 1,500 | 2,000 | 2,500 | _____ | _____ | _____ _____ |
| _____ | 12. | 1,235 | 2,235 | 3,235 | 4,235 | _____ | _____ | _____ _____ |
| _____ | 13. | 750 | 1,500 | 2,250 | 3,000 | _____ | _____ | _____ _____ |
| _____ | 14. | 148 | 348 | 548 | 748 | _____ | _____ | _____ _____ |
| _____ | 15. | 100 | 425 | 750 | 1,075 | _____ | _____ | _____ _____ |

# More Jumbo Patterns

**Directions:**
Figure out each pattern rule and complete the pattern.

**Rule**

_____ 1. 1,000   950   900   850   _____ _____ _____ _____

_____ 2. 1,000   990   980   970   _____ _____ _____ _____

_____ 3. 1,000   900   800   700   _____ _____ _____ _____

_____ 4. 1,000   975   950   925   _____ _____ _____ _____

_____ 5. 1,100   950   800   650   _____ _____ _____ _____

_____ 6. 1,000   986   972   958   _____ _____ _____ _____

_____ 7. 1,000   925   850   775   _____ _____ _____ _____

_____ 8. 1,000   965   930   895   _____ _____ _____ _____

_____ 9. 1,000   875   750   625   _____ _____ _____ _____

_____ 10. 1,000   904   808   712   _____ _____ _____ _____

_____ 11. 4,750   4,250   3,750   3,250   _____ _____ _____ _____

_____ 12. 5,000   4,800   4,600   4,400   _____ _____ _____ _____

_____ 13. 2,000   1,750   1,500   1,250   _____ _____ _____ _____

_____ 14. 8,263   7,263   6,263   5,263   _____ _____ _____ _____

_____ 15. 2,000   1,775   1,550   1,325   _____ _____ _____ _____

# Patterns with Fractions

**Identifying Patterns**

## Directions:

Find the rule for the pattern in each row. Continue the pattern and write the rule on the blank. The first one has been done for you.

**Pattern Rule**

1. $\frac{1}{2}$ · 1 · $1\frac{1}{2}$ · 2 · $2\frac{1}{2}$ · 3 · $3\frac{1}{2}$ · 4 · $4\frac{1}{2}$ · 5    $+\frac{1}{2}$ _____

2. $\frac{1}{2}$ · $1\frac{1}{2}$ · $2\frac{1}{2}$ · $3\frac{1}{2}$ · $4\frac{1}{2}$ · $5\frac{1}{2}$ · $6\frac{1}{2}$ · ○ · ○ · ○    _____

3. $\frac{1}{3}$ · $\frac{2}{3}$ · 1 · $1\frac{1}{3}$ · $1\frac{2}{3}$ · 2 · $2\frac{1}{3}$ · ○ · ○ · ○    _____

4. $\frac{1}{3}$ · $2\frac{1}{3}$ · $4\frac{1}{3}$ · $6\frac{1}{3}$ · $8\frac{1}{3}$ · $10\frac{1}{3}$ · $12\frac{1}{3}$ · ○ · ○ · ○    _____

5. $\frac{1}{3}$ · 1 · $1\frac{2}{3}$ · $2\frac{1}{3}$ · 3 · $3\frac{2}{3}$ · $4\frac{1}{3}$ · ○ · ○ · ○    _____

6. $\frac{1}{4}$ · $\frac{2}{4}$ · $\frac{3}{4}$ · 1 · $1\frac{1}{4}$ · $1\frac{2}{4}$ · $1\frac{3}{4}$ · ○ · ○ · ○    _____

7. $\frac{1}{4}$ · $\frac{3}{4}$ · $1\frac{1}{4}$ · $1\frac{3}{4}$ · $2\frac{1}{4}$ · $2\frac{3}{4}$ · $3\frac{1}{4}$ · ○ · ○ · ○    _____

8. $\frac{1}{4}$ · 1 · $1\frac{3}{4}$ · $2\frac{2}{4}$ · $3\frac{1}{4}$ · 4 · $4\frac{3}{4}$ · ○ · ○ · ○    _____

9. $\frac{1}{5}$ · $\frac{3}{5}$ · 1 · $1\frac{2}{5}$ · $1\frac{4}{5}$ · $2\frac{1}{5}$ · $2\frac{3}{5}$ · ○ · ○ · ○    _____

10. $\frac{1}{5}$ · $\frac{4}{5}$ · $1\frac{2}{5}$ · 2 · $2\frac{3}{5}$ · $3\frac{1}{5}$ · $3\frac{4}{5}$ · ○ · ○ · ○    _____

11. $\frac{1}{2}$ · 2 · $3\frac{1}{2}$ · 5 · $6\frac{1}{2}$ · 8 · $9\frac{1}{2}$ · ○ · ○ · ○    _____

12. $\frac{1}{3}$ · $1\frac{2}{3}$ · 3 · $4\frac{1}{3}$ · $5\frac{2}{3}$ · 7 · $8\frac{1}{3}$ · ○ · ○ · ○    _____

Name _____     Date _____

# More Patterns with Fractions

Identifying Patterns

**Directions:**
Write the rule for each pattern at the top of the page. Continue each pattern at the bottom of the page.

**Pattern Rule**

1. $10$    $9\frac{1}{2}$    $9$    $8\frac{1}{2}$    $8$    $7\frac{1}{2}$       _____

2. $12\frac{1}{2}$   $11\frac{1}{2}$   $10\frac{1}{2}$   $9\frac{1}{2}$   $8\frac{1}{2}$   $7\frac{1}{2}$       _____

3. $6$    $5\frac{2}{3}$    $5\frac{1}{3}$    $5$    $4\frac{2}{3}$    $4\frac{1}{3}$       _____

4. $10$    $9\frac{1}{3}$    $8\frac{2}{3}$    $8$    $7\frac{1}{3}$    $6\frac{2}{3}$       _____

5. $8\frac{1}{4}$    $7\frac{3}{4}$    $7\frac{1}{4}$    $6\frac{3}{4}$    $6\frac{1}{4}$    $5\frac{3}{4}$       _____

• • • • • • • • • • • • • • • • • • • • • • • • • • • • • • • • • • • • • • • • • • • •

6. $10$    $9\frac{1}{2}$    $9$    $8\frac{1}{2}$    ____   ____   ____   ____   ____

7. $12\frac{1}{2}$   $11\frac{1}{2}$   $10\frac{1}{2}$   $9\frac{1}{2}$    ____   ____   ____   ____   ____

8. $6$    $5\frac{2}{3}$    $5\frac{1}{3}$    $5$    ____   ____   ____   ____   ____

9. $10$    $9\frac{1}{3}$    $8\frac{2}{3}$    $8$    ____   ____   ____   ____   ____

10. $8\frac{1}{4}$    $7\frac{3}{4}$    $7\frac{1}{4}$    $6\frac{3}{4}$    ____   ____   ____   ____   ____

Name _____     Date _____

## Patterns with Decimals

**Directions:**
Figure out each pattern rule and complete the pattern.

**Rule**

_____     1. 1.0     1.1     1.2     1.3     ____ ____ ____ ____

_____     2. 0.8     1.0     1.2     1.4     ____ ____ ____ ____

_____     3. 0.5     1.0     1.5     2.0     ____ ____ ____ ____

_____     4. 1.0     2.1     3.2     4.3     ____ ____ ____ ____

_____     5. 0.2     1.7     3.2     4.7     ____ ____ ____ ____

_____     6. 1.00    1.02    1.04    1.06    ____ ____ ____ ____

_____     7. 0.15    0.30    0.45    0.60    ____ ____ ____ ____

_____     8. 0.25    0.50    0.75    1.00    ____ ____ ____ ____

_____     9. 3.0     2.9     2.8     2.7     ____ ____ ____ ____

_____     10. 4.0    3.8     3.6     3.4     ____ ____ ____ ____

_____     11. 15.0   13.9    12.8    11.7    ____ ____ ____ ____

_____     12. 15.0   13.5    12.0    10.5    ____ ____ ____ ____

_____     13. 0.50   0.47    0.44    0.41    ____ ____ ____ ____

_____     14. 3.00   2.85    2.70    2.55    ____ ____ ____ ____

_____     15. 5.00   4.75    4.50    4.25    ____ ____ ____ ____

# Jersey Patterns

**Directions:**
Write the missing numbers in each pattern. Write the pattern rule in the blank.

**1.** Decimal Dolphins _____

1.4  1.8  2.2  ____  3.0  ____

**2.** Fraction Falcons _____

1  ____  $1\frac{2}{3}$  2  $2\frac{1}{3}$  ____

**3.** Plus Porcupines _____

____  2.5  4.0  5.5  ____  8.5

**4.** Minus Macaws _____

6.0  ____  ____  5.1  4.8  4.5

**5.** Tenth Terriers _____

3.0  2.9  ____  2.7  2.6  ____

**6.** Half Hounds _____

2  ____  3  $3\frac{1}{2}$  4  ____

**7.** Hundredth Hawks _____

1.00  0.99  0.98  ____  ____  0.95

**8.** Fourth Ferrets _____

____  $4\frac{3}{4}$  $4\frac{1}{2}$  $4\frac{1}{4}$  ____  $3\frac{3}{4}$

**9.** Third Thrushes _____

2  $2\frac{2}{3}$  $3\frac{1}{3}$  ____  $4\frac{2}{3}$  ____

**10.** Addition Aardvarks _____

3.0  ____  ____  4.5  5.0  5.5

**11.** Subtraction Sharks _____

10  $8\frac{1}{2}$  7  ____  4  ____

**12.** Double Ducks _____

3  $5\frac{1}{3}$  $7\frac{2}{3}$  ____  ____  $14\frac{2}{3}$

**13.** Take-Away Tigers _____

3.00  ____  ____  2.55  2.40  2.25

**14.** Math Monarchs _____

____  7.2  8.4  9.6  10.8  ____

**15.** Arithmetic Antelopes _____

$\frac{1}{4}$  ____  $1\frac{3}{4}$  $2\frac{1}{2}$  $3\frac{1}{4}$  ____

**16.** Number Newts _____

____  0.010  0.009  0.008  0.007  ____

# Counting by Fractions

**Skip Counting**

## Directions:
Follow the directions to complete each pattern.

**1.** Count by halves.  $\frac{1}{2}$  $\frac{2}{2}$  $\frac{3}{2}$  $\frac{4}{2}$  — — — — — — — —

**2.** Rewrite as mixed numbers.  $\frac{1}{2}$  1  $1\frac{1}{2}$  2  ___ ___ ___ ___ ___ ___ ___ ___

**3.** Count by thirds.  $\frac{1}{3}$  $\frac{2}{3}$  $\frac{3}{3}$  $\frac{4}{3}$  — — — — — — — —

**4.** Rewrite as mixed numbers.  $\frac{1}{3}$  $\frac{2}{3}$  1  $1\frac{1}{3}$  ___ ___ ___ ___ ___ ___ ___ ___

**5.** Count by fourths.  $\frac{1}{4}$  $\frac{2}{4}$  $\frac{3}{4}$  $\frac{4}{4}$  — — — — — — — —

**6.** Rewrite as mixed numbers.  $\frac{1}{4}$  $\frac{2}{4}$  $\frac{3}{4}$  1  ___ ___ ___ ___ ___ ___ ___

**7.** Rewrite and reduce.  $\frac{1}{4}$  $\frac{1}{2}$  $\frac{3}{4}$  1  ___ ___ ___ ___ ___ ___ ___

**8.** Count by fifths.  $\frac{1}{5}$  — — — — — — — — —

**9.** Rewrite as mixed numbers.  ___ ___ ___ ___ ___ ___ ___ ___

**10.** Count by sixths.  $\frac{1}{6}$  — — — — — — — — —

**11.** Rewrite as mixed numbers.  ___ ___ ___ ___ ___ ___ ___ ___

**12.** Rewrite and reduce.  ___ ___ ___ ___ ___ ___ ___ ___

Elementary Algebra • CD-104106

# Plenty of Pattern Pals

**Extending Patterns**

## Directions:

Sometimes a pattern is made of two patterns put together. Look at the example, then complete the patterns below.

**Example:**  **+5, –3 Pattern**

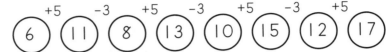

⁺⁵ ⁻³ ⁺⁵ ⁻³ ⁺⁵ ⁻³ ⁺⁵
( 6 ) ( 11 ) ( 8 ) ( 13 ) ( 10 ) ( 15 ) ( 12 ) ( 17 )

**Pattern Pal**

1. __+2__ , __+5__    ⁺²( 1 ) ⁺⁵( 3 ) ⁺²( 8 ) ( ) ( ) ( ) ( ) ( )

2. __+3__ , __+10__    ⁺³( 4 ) ⁺¹⁰( 7 ) ⁺³( 17 ) ( ) ( ) ( ) ( ) ( )

3. __–2__ , __–4__    ⁻²( 80 ) ⁻⁴( 78 ) ⁻²( 74 ) ( ) ( ) ( ) ( ) ( )

4. __–5__ , __–1__    ⁻⁵( 90 ) ⁻¹( 85 ) ⁻⁵( 84 ) ( ) ( ) ( ) ( ) ( )

5. __+2__ , __–3__    ⁺²( 50 ) ⁻³( 52 ) ⁺²( 49 ) ( ) ( ) ( ) ( ) ( )

6. __–4__ , __+10__    ⁻⁴( 30 ) ⁺¹⁰( 26 ) ⁻⁴( 36 ) ( ) ( ) ( ) ( ) ( )

7. __+10__ , __–1__    ⁺¹⁰( 12 ) ⁻¹( 22 ) ⁺¹⁰( 21 ) ( ) ( ) ( ) ( ) ( )

8. __–8__ , __+20__    ⁻⁸( 10 ) ⁺²⁰( 2 ) ⁻⁸( 22 ) ( ) ( ) ( ) ( ) ( )

9. __+3__ , __–6__    ⁺³( 30 ) ⁻⁶( 33 ) ⁺³( 27 ) ( ) ( ) ( ) ( ) ( )

10. __–10__ , __+5__    ⁻¹⁰( 50 ) ⁺⁵( 40 ) ⁻¹⁰( 45 ) ( ) ( ) ( ) ( ) ( )

11. __+7__ , __–2__    ⁺⁷( 30 ) ⁻²( 37 ) ⁺⁷( 35 ) ( ) ( ) ( ) ( ) ( )

12. __–5__ , __+6__    ⁻⁵( 25 ) ⁺⁶( 20 ) ⁻⁵( 26 ) ( ) ( ) ( ) ( ) ( )

# Identifying Pattern Pals

**Identifying Patterns**

**Directions:**
On the left, write what pattern pals make each pattern. Remember to tell whether they are plus or minus.

**Pattern Pal**

1. _____, _____  ③ ⑤ ⑫ ⑭ ㉑ ㉓ ㉚ ㉜

2. _____, _____  ⑧ ⑬ ⑪ ⑯ ⑭ ⑲ ⑰ ㉒

3. _____, _____  ⑥⓪ ⑤⑦ ⑤② ④⑨ ④④ ④① ③⑥ ③③

4. _____, _____  ⑩ ⑥ ⑫ ⑧ ⑭ ⑩ ⑯ ⑫

5. _____, _____  ㉒⓪ ㉚⓪ ⑧⓪ ⑨⓪ ①④⓪ ①⑤⓪ ②⓪⓪ ②①⓪

6. _____, _____  ⑤⓪ ⑥② ⑤② ⑥④ ⑤④ ⑥⑥ ⑤⑥ ⑥⑧

7. _____, _____  ②⓪⓪ ①⑨⑧ ①⑧③ ①⑧① ①⑥⑥ ①⑥④ ①④⑨ ①④⑦

8. _____, _____  ①⑤⓪ ①④⓪ ①④② ①③② ①③④ ①②④ ①②⑥ ①①⑥

9. _____, _____  ①⓪⓪ ①②⑤ ②②⑤ ②⑤⓪ ③⑤⓪ ③⑦⑤ ④⑦⑤ ⑤⓪⓪

10. _____, _____  ①⓪⓪ ①⑤⓪ ①②⓪ ①⑦⓪ ①④⓪ ①⑨⓪ ①⑥⓪ ②①⓪

11. _____, _____  ①⑤⓪ ①④⓪ ①④② ①③② ①③④ ①②④ ①②⑥ ①①⑥

12. _____, _____  ⑤⓪ ④⑤ ⑦⑤ ⑦⓪ ①⓪⓪ ⑨⑤ ①②⑤ ①②⓪

# Mighty Multiplication Patterns

**Multiplication Patterns**

## Directions:
Continue each pattern by multiplying according to the pattern rule.

**Pattern Rule**

1. x 2    ( 1 ) x2 ( 2 ) x2 ( 4 ) x2 ( ) x2 ( ) x2 ( ) x2 ( ) x2 ( )

2. x 2    ( 3 ) x2 ( 6 ) x2 ( ) x2 ( ) x2 ( ) x2 ( ) x2 ( ) x2 ( )

3. x 2    ( 5 ) x2 ( 10 ) x2 ( ) x2 ( ) x2 ( ) x2 ( ) x2 ( ) x2 ( )

4. x 3    ( 1 ) x3 ( 3 ) x3 ( ) x3 ( ) x3 ( ) x3 ( ) x3 ( ) x3 ( )

5. x 3    ( 2 ) x3 ( 6 ) x3 ( ) x3 ( ) x3 ( ) x3 ( ) x3 ( ) x3 ( )

6. x 4    ( 1 ) x4 ( 4 ) x4 ( ) x4 ( ) x4 ( ) x4 ( ) x4 ( ) x4 ( )

7. x 4    ( 2 ) x4 ( 8 ) x4 ( ) x4 ( ) x4 ( ) x4 ( ) x4 ( ) x4 ( )

8. x 5    ( 1 ) x5 ( 5 ) x5 ( ) x5 ( ) x5 ( ) x5 ( ) x5 ( ) x5 ( )

9. x 10   ( 1 ) x10 ( 10 ) x10 ( ) x10 ( ) x10 ( ) x10 ( ) x10 ( ) x10 ( )

10. x 10  ( 2 ) x10 ( 20 ) x10 ( ) x10 ( ) x10 ( ) x10 ( ) x10 ( ) x10 ( )

# Dare to Divide

**Division Patterns**

**Directions:**
These patterns are all made by dividing each number in half (or by 2). Complete the pattern and try to do the math in your head.

1. 56    28    _____    _____

2. 64    32    _____    _____

3. 200    100    _____    _____

4. 1,000    500    _____    _____

5. 400    _____    _____    _____

6. 144    _____    _____    _____

7. 600    _____    _____    _____

8. 192    _____    _____    _____

9. 800    _____    _____    _____

10. 320    _____    _____    _____

11. 1,600    _____    _____    _____

12. 2,000    _____    _____    _____

13. 2,400    _____    _____    _____

14. 3,000    _____    _____    _____

15. 4,000    _____    _____    _____

16. 5,000    _____    _____    _____

# Growing Patterns

**Extending Patterns**

## Directions:
Skip count to create the pattern rule, then continue each pattern below.

1.   count by 1    (2) +1 (3) +2 (5) +3 ( ) +4 ( ) +5 ( ) +6 ( ) +7 ( )

2.   count by 2    (2) +2 (4) +4 (8) +6 ( ) +8 ( ) +10 ( ) +12 ( ) +14 ( )

3.   count by 2    (1) +2 (3) +4 (7) +6 ( ) +8 ( ) +10 ( ) +12 ( ) +14 ( )

4.   count by 2 (odd)  (1) +1 (2) +3 (5) +5 ( ) +7 ( ) +9 ( ) +11 ( ) +13 ( )

5.   count by 2 (odd)  (2) +1 (3) +3 (6) +5 ( ) +7 ( ) +9 ( ) +11 ( ) +13 ( )

6.   count by 3    (1) +3 (4) +6 ( ) +9 ( ) +12 ( ) +15 ( ) +18 ( ) +21 ( )

7.   count by 3    (3) +3 (6) +6 ( ) +9 ( ) +12 ( ) +15 ( ) +18 ( ) +21 ( )

8.   count by 4    (4) +4 (8) +8 ( ) +12 ( ) +16 ( ) +20 ( ) +24 ( ) +28 ( )

9.   count by 4    (1) +4 (5) +8 ( ) ( ) ( ) ( ) ( ) ( )

10.  count by 5    (1) +5 (6) +10 ( ) ( ) ( ) ( ) ( ) ( )

11.  count by 5    (2) +5 (7) +10 ( ) ( ) ( ) ( ) ( ) ( )

12.  count by 5    (5) +5 (10) +10 ( ) ( ) ( ) ( ) ( ) ( )

13.  count by 10   (10) +10 (20) +20 ( ) ( ) ( ) ( ) ( ) ( )

14.  count by 10   (1) +10 (11) +20 ( ) ( ) ( ) ( ) ( ) ( )

# Chilly Patterns

**Extending Patterns**

## Directions:

Follow these patterns below zero. Write the missing numbers in each pattern at the top of the page. Then, tell the pattern rule for each pattern at the bottom of the page.

rule: −1    **1.** __2__ __1__ __0__ __−1__ ____ ____ ____ ____

rule: −2    **2.** __10__ __8__ __6__ __4__ ____ ____ ____ ____

rule: −3    **3.** __20__ __17__ __14__ __11__ ____ ____ ____ ____

rule: −4    **4.** __20__ __16__ __12__ __8__ ____ ____ ____ ____

rule: −2    **5.** __11__ __9__ __7__ __5__ ____ ____ ____ ____

rule: −3    **6.** __7__ __4__ __1__ __−2__ ____ ____ ____ ____

rule: −5    **7.** __20__ __15__ __10__ __5__ ____ ____ ____ ____

rule: −5    **8.** __17__ __12__ __7__ __2__ ____ ____ ____ ____

rule: −10   **9.** __35__ __25__ __15__ __5__ ____ ____ ____ ____

_____    **10.** __12__ __9__ __6__ __3__ __0__ __−3__ __−6__ __−9__

_____    **11.** __18__ __13__ __8__ __3__ __−2__ __−7__ __−12__ __−17__

_____    **12.** __15__ __11__ __7__ __3__ __−1__ __−5__ __−9__ __−13__

_____    **13.** __36__ __26__ __16__ __6__ __−4__ __−14__ __−24__ __−34__

_____    **14.** __21__ __14__ __7__ __0__ __−7__ __−14__ __−21__ __−28__

_____    **15.** __5__ __3__ __1__ __−1__ __−3__ __−5__ __−7__ __−9__

## Warmer Patterns

**Extending Patterns**

**Directions:**
Follow these patterns below zero. Write the missing numbers in each pattern at the top of the page. Then, tell the pattern rule for each pattern at the bottom of the page.

rule: +1    **1.**  -2    -1    0    1    ___    ___    ___    ___

rule: +2    **2.**  -10   -8   -6   -4   ___    ___    ___    ___

rule: +3    **3.**  -12   -9   -6   -3   ___    ___    ___    ___

rule: +4    **4.**  -20   -16  -12  -8   ___    ___    ___    ___

rule: +5    **5.**  -30   -25  -20  -15  ___    ___    ___    ___

rule: +2    **6.**  -11   -9   -7   -5   ___    ___    ___    ___

rule: +3    **7.**  -10   -7   -4   -1   ___    ___    ___    ___

rule: +6    **8.**  -20   -14  -8   -2   ___    ___    ___    ___

rule: +10   **9.**  -35   -25  -15  -5   ___    ___    ___    ___

_____    **10.**  -15   -11  -7   -3   1    5    9    13

_____    **11.**  -7    -5   -3   -1   1    3    5    7

_____    **12.**  -21   -14  -7   0    7    14   21   28

_____    **13.**  -30   -21  -12  -3   6    15   24   33

_____    **14.**  -25   -14  -3   8    19   30   41   52

_____    **15.**  -6    -3   0    3    6    9    12   15

## Make Your Own Patterns

Creating Patterns

### Directions:

Make up your own patterns. First, write a pattern rule for each pattern. Then, fill in the blanks to make the patterns follow the rules. Try to use some fractions, decimals, and negative numbers. Also, be sure to write some plus patterns and some minus patterns.

**Rule**

_____     1. _____  _____  _____  _____  _____  _____  _____  _____

_____     2. _____  _____  _____  _____  _____  _____  _____  _____

_____     3. _____  _____  _____  _____  _____  _____  _____  _____

_____     4. _____  _____  _____  _____  _____  _____  _____  _____

_____     5. _____  _____  _____  _____  _____  _____  _____  _____

_____     6. _____  _____  _____  _____  _____  _____  _____  _____

_____     7. _____  _____  _____  _____  _____  _____  _____  _____

_____     8. _____  _____  _____  _____  _____  _____  _____  _____

_____     9. _____  _____  _____  _____  _____  _____  _____  _____

_____     10. _____  _____  _____  _____  _____  _____  _____  _____

_____     11. _____  _____  _____  _____  _____  _____  _____  _____

_____     12. _____  _____  _____  _____  _____  _____  _____  _____

_____     13. _____  _____  _____  _____  _____  _____  _____  _____

_____     14. _____  _____  _____  _____  _____  _____  _____  _____

Name _____  Date _____

# Squaring and Cubing Numbers

## Directions:

Squaring a number is the same as multiplying it by itself. Cubing a number is the same as multiplying it by itself twice. Complete the charts and answer the questions below.

| Number Squared | 1 x 1 | 2 x 2 | 3 x 3 | 4 x 4 | 5 x 5 | 6 x 6 | 7 x 7 | 8 x 8 | 9 x 9 | 10 x 10 |
|---|---|---|---|---|---|---|---|---|---|---|
| Answer | 1 | 4 | 9 | 16 | | | | | | |

**1.** Difference between answers    3    5    7    ____  ____  ____  ____  ____  ____

**2.** What pattern or patterns do you see in the answers and the differences? _____

_____

_____

**3.** What would the answer to 13 x 13 be? Use the pattern in the differences to help you. _____

. . . . . . . . . . . . . . . . . . . . . . . . . . . . . . . . . . . . . . . . . . . .

| Number Cubed | 1 x 1 x 1 | 2x2x2 | 3x3x3 | 4x4x4 | 5x5x5 | 6x6x6 | 7x7x7 | 8x8x8 | 9x9x9 | 10x10x10 |
|---|---|---|---|---|---|---|---|---|---|---|
| Answer | 1 | 8 | 27 | 64 | | | | | | |

**4.** Difference between answers    7    19    37    ____  ____  ____  ____  ____  ____

**5.** Difference between the differences    12    18    ____  ____  ____  ____  ____

**6.** What pattern or patterns do you see in the answers and the differences? _____

_____

_____

_____

## Add to Forty

### Directions:

Write different combinations of numbers that add up to 40. Since the order of the addends doesn't matter, 38 + 1 + 1, 1 + 38 + 1, and 1 + 1 + 38 do not count as different combinations. Do not use zero. Use patterns to help.

_____ + _____ + _____ = 40

_____ + _____ + _____ = 40

_____ + _____ + _____ = 40

_____ + _____ + _____ = 40

_____ + _____ + _____ = 40

_____ + _____ + _____ = 40

_____ + _____ + _____ = 40

_____ + _____ + _____ = 40

_____ + _____ + _____ = 40

_____ + _____ + _____ = 40

_____ + _____ + _____ = 40

_____ + _____ + _____ = 40

_____ + _____ + _____ = 40

_____ + _____ + _____ = 40

_____ + _____ + _____ = 40

_____ + _____ + _____ = 40

_____ + _____ + _____ = 40

_____ + _____ + _____ = 40

_____ + _____ + _____ = 40

_____ + _____ + _____ = 40

Elementary Algebra • CD-104106

# Dreaming of Differences

**Writing Equations**

**Directions:**
Write different ways to make the differences given in each box. Do not use zero. Use patterns to help.

**1. Difference of 5**

_____ − _____ = 5

_____ − _____ = 5

_____ − _____ = 5

_____ − _____ = 5

_____ − _____ = 5

_____ − _____ = 5

_____ − _____ = 5

_____ − _____ = 5

**2. Difference of 50**

_____ − _____ = 50

_____ − _____ = 50

_____ − _____ = 50

_____ − _____ = 50

_____ − _____ = 50

_____ − _____ = 50

_____ − _____ = 50

_____ − _____ = 50

**3. Difference of 500**

_____ − _____ = 500

_____ − _____ = 500

_____ − _____ = 500

_____ − _____ = 500

_____ − _____ = 500

_____ − _____ = 500

_____ − _____ = 500

_____ − _____ = 500

**4. Difference of 0.5**

_____ − _____ = 0.5

_____ − _____ = 0.5

_____ − _____ = 0.5

_____ − _____ = 0.5

_____ − _____ = 0.5

_____ − _____ = 0.5

_____ − _____ = 0.5

_____ − _____ = 0.5

## Multiplication Fact Patterns

Writing
Equations

**Directions:**
Continue each pattern to learn an easy way to multiply by 6, 7, 8, and 9.

---

**1.  Sly Sixes**

$1 \times 6 = (1 \times 5) + 1$ ___6___
$2 \times 6 = (2 \times 5) + 2$ ___12___
$3 \times 6 = (3 \times 5) + 3$ ___18___
$4 \times 6 = (4 \times 5) + 4$ ___24___
$5 \times 6 =$ _____ _____
$6 \times 6 =$ _____ _____
$7 \times 6 =$ _____ _____
$8 \times 6 =$ _____ _____
$9 \times 6 =$ _____ _____
$10 \times 6 =$ _____ _____
$11 \times 6 =$ _____ _____

**2.  Slippery Sevens**

$1 \times 7 = (1 \times 5) + 2$ _____
$2 \times 7 = (2 \times 5) + 4$ _____
$3 \times 7 = (3 \times 5) + 6$ _____
$4 \times 7 =$ _____ _____
$5 \times 7 =$ _____ _____
$6 \times 7 =$ _____ _____
$7 \times 7 =$ _____ _____
$8 \times 7 =$ _____ _____
$9 \times 7 =$ _____ _____
$10 \times 7 =$ _____ _____
$11 \times 7 =$ _____ _____

**3.  Elusive Eights**

$1 \times 8 = (1 \times 10) - 2$ _____
$2 \times 8 = (2 \times 10) - 4$ _____
$3 \times 8 = (3 \times 10) - 6$ _____
$4 \times 8 =$ _____ _____
$5 \times 8 =$ _____ _____
$6 \times 8 =$ _____ _____
$7 \times 8 =$ _____ _____
$8 \times 8 =$ _____ _____
$9 \times 8 =$ _____ _____
$10 \times 8 =$ _____ _____
$11 \times 8 =$ _____ _____

**4.  Naughty Nines**

$1 \times 9 = (1 \times 10) - 1$ _____
$2 \times 9 = (2 \times 10) - 2$ _____
$3 \times 9 = (3 \times 10) - 3$ _____
$4 \times 9 =$ _____ _____
$5 \times 9 =$ _____ _____
$6 \times 9 =$ _____ _____
$7 \times 9 =$ _____ _____
$8 \times 9 =$ _____ _____
$9 \times 9 =$ _____ _____
$10 \times 9 =$ _____ _____
$11 \times 9 =$ _____ _____

# Mountains of Multiplying

## Directions:

Fill in the blanks in the mountains to make each equation true and different. You must use numbers greater than 9. Try to use patterns.

___ x 10 = ____
___ x 10 = ____
___ x 10 = ____
___ x 10 = ____
___ x 10 = ____
___ x 10 = ____
___ x 10 = ____
___ x 10 = ____
___ x 10 = ____

___ x 100 = ____
___ x 100 = ____
___ x 100 = ____
___ x 100 = ____
___ x 100 = ____
___ x 100 = ____
___ x 100 = ____
___ x 100 = ____
___ x 100 = ____

___ x 1,000 = ____
___ x 1,000 = ____
___ x 1,000 = ____
___ x 1,000 = ____
___ x 1,000 = ____
___ x 1,000 = ____
___ x 1,000 = ____
___ x 1,000 = ____
___ x 1,000 = ____

___ x 0.1 = ____
___ x 0.1 = ____
___ x 0.1 = ____
___ x 0.1 = ____
___ x 0.1 = ____
___ x 0.1 = ____
___ x 0.1 = ____
___ x 0.1 = ____
___ x 0.1 = ____

___ x 0.01 = ____
___ x 0.01 = ____
___ x 0.01 = ____
___ x 0.01 = ____
___ x 0.01 = ____
___ x 0.01 = ____
___ x 0.01 = ____
___ x 0.01 = ____
___ x 0.01 = ____

___ x 0.001 = ____
___ x 0.001 = ____
___ x 0.001 = ____
___ x 0.001 = ____
___ x 0.001 = ____
___ x 0.001 = ____
___ x 0.001 = ____
___ x 0.001 = ____
___ x 0.001 = ____

# Discovering Division Patterns

**Writing Equations**

## Directions:

Fill in the blanks to make each equation true and different. Use patterns to help.

_____ ÷ _____ = 10          _____ ÷ _____ = 100

_____ ÷ _____ = 10          _____ ÷ _____ = 100

_____ ÷ _____ = 10          _____ ÷ _____ = 100

_____ ÷ _____ = 10          _____ ÷ _____ = 100

_____ ÷ _____ = 10          _____ ÷ _____ = 100

_____ ÷ _____ = 10          _____ ÷ _____ = 100

_____ ÷ _____ = 10          _____ ÷ _____ = 100

_____ ÷ _____ = 10          _____ ÷ _____ = 100

_____ ÷ _____ = 10          _____ ÷ _____ = 100

_____ ÷ _____ = 10          _____ ÷ _____ = 100

_____ ÷ _____ = 10          _____ ÷ _____ = 100

_____ ÷ _____ = 10          _____ ÷ _____ = 100

_____ ÷ _____ = 10          _____ ÷ _____ = 100

_____ ÷ _____ = 10          _____ ÷ _____ = 100

Name _____   Date _____

## Dividing Thirty

**Directions:**

First, write the whole number answers that you know. Then, use a calculator to help with the remaining problems. Write the complete answers that the calculator shows. Do not round off. Then, answer the questions below.

30 ÷ 1 = _____          30 ÷ 16 = _____

30 ÷ 2 = _____          30 ÷ 17 = _____

30 ÷ 3 = _____          30 ÷ 18 = _____

30 ÷ 4 = _____          30 ÷ 19 = _____

30 ÷ 5 = _____          30 ÷ 20 = _____

30 ÷ 6 = _____          30 ÷ 21 = _____

30 ÷ 7 = _____          30 ÷ 22 = _____

30 ÷ 8 = _____          30 ÷ 23 = _____

30 ÷ 9 = _____          30 ÷ 24 = _____

30 ÷ 10 = _____         30 ÷ 25 = _____

30 ÷ 11 = _____         30 ÷ 26 = _____

30 ÷ 12 = _____         30 ÷ 27 = _____

30 ÷ 13 = _____         30 ÷ 28 = _____

30 ÷ 14 = _____         30 ÷ 29 = _____

30 ÷ 15 = _____         30 ÷ 30 = _____

**1.** What whole numbers are factors of 30?   _____ _____ _____ _____ _____ _____ _____ _____

**2.** What whole numbers have answers that stop at tenths?   _____   _____   _____   _____

**3.** What whole numbers have answers that stop at hundredths?   _____   _____

**4.** What whole number has an answer that stops at thousandths?   _____

**5.** Which whole numbers have answers that repeat a single digit to the right of the decimal?

_____     _____     _____

**6.** Which whole numbers have answers that repeat two digits to the right of the decimal?

_____     _____

## Place Value Patterns

**Using Patterns**

### Directions:

First, try to solve each equation using patterns to help. Then, check yourself with a calculator.

| | | |
|---|---|---|
| 6 x 10,000 = _____ | 25 x 10,000 = _____ | 0.4 x 10,000 = _____ |
| 6 x 1,000 = _____ | 25 x 1,000 = _____ | 0.4 x 1,000 = _____ |
| 6 x 100 = _____ | 25 x 100 = _____ | 0.4 x 100 = _____ |
| 6 x 10 = _____ | 25 x 10 = _____ | 0.4 x 10 = _____ |
| 6 x 1 = _____ | 25 x 1 = _____ | 0.4 x 1 = _____ |
| 6 x 0.1 = _____ | 25 x 0.1 = _____ | 0.4 x 0.1 = _____ |
| 6 x 0.01 = _____ | 25 x 0.01 = _____ | 0.4 x 0.01 = _____ |
| 6 x 0.001 = _____ | 25 x 0.001 = _____ | 0.4 x 0.001 = _____ |
| 6 x 0.0001 = _____ | 25 x 0.0001 = _____ | 0.4 x 0.0001 = _____ |
| 6 x 0.00001 = _____ | 25 x 0.00001 = _____ | 0.4 x 0.00001 = _____ |
| 5 ÷ 10,000 = _____ | 32 ÷ 10,000 = _____ | 0.9 x 10,000 = _____ |
| 5 ÷ 1,000 = _____ | 32 ÷ 1,000 = _____ | 0.9 x 1,000 = _____ |
| 5 ÷ 100 = _____ | 32 ÷ 100 = _____ | 0.9 x 100 = _____ |
| 5 ÷ 10 = _____ | 32 ÷ 10 = _____ | 0.9 x 10 = _____ |
| 5 ÷ 1 = _____ | 32 ÷ 1 = _____ | 0.9 x 1 = _____ |
| 5 ÷ 0.1 = _____ | 32 ÷ 0.1 = _____ | 0.9 x 0.1 = _____ |
| 5 ÷ 0.01 = _____ | 32 ÷ 0.01 = _____ | 0.9 x 0.01 = _____ |
| 5 ÷ 0.001 = _____ | 32 ÷ 0.001 = _____ | 0.9 x 0.001 = _____ |
| 5 ÷ 0.0001 = _____ | 32 ÷ 0.0001 = _____ | 0.9 x 0.0001 = _____ |
| 5 ÷ 0.00001 = _____ | 32 ÷ 0.00001 = _____ | 0.9 x 0.00001 = _____ |

Name _____  Date _____

# Sundae Patterns

**Using Patterns**

### Directions:
Make different sundaes by using different ice cream flavors and different toppings. You may only use one ice cream flavor and one topping per sundae.

**Example:**

| Ice Cream | Toppings |
|-----------|----------|
| Vanilla | Fudge |
| Strawberry | Nuts |

     **4 possible sundaes**

**Try this:**

| Ice Cream | Toppings |
|-----------|----------|
| Vanilla | Fudge |
| Strawberry | Nuts |
| Chocolate | |

Fill in the chart below about the number of possible sundaes, then answer the questions. Look for patterns.

| Sundae options | 1 topping | 2 toppings | 3 toppings | 4 toppings | 5 toppings |
|----------------|-----------|------------|------------|------------|------------|
| 1 flavor | 1 | 2 | | | |
| 2 flavors | 2 | 4 | | | |
| 3 flavors | 3 | 6 | | | |
| 4 flavors | 4 | | | | |
| 5 flavors | 5 | | | | |

1. How many possible sundaes can 4 ice cream flavors and 5 toppings make? _____

2. How many possible sundaes can 6 ice cream flavors and 6 toppings make? _____

3. The chart above looks like part of another chart you are familiar with. What chart is that?

_____

4. How many possible sundaes can 10 ice cream flavors and 10 toppings make? _____

5. If there are 5 ice cream flavors and 35 possible sundaes, how many toppings must there be?

_____

6. If there are 8 toppings and 72 possible sundaes, how many ice cream flavors must there be?

_____

7. If there are 32 ice cream flavors and 15 toppings, how many possible sundaes can be made?

_____

## Brownie Batches

### Directions:

There are a lot of brownie combinations that can be made. Fill in the letters for the different flavors of batter and the different special ingredients to determine the possible combinations. Then, answer the questions below.

1.  **C**hocolate batter with **N**uts, **R**aisins, or **M**arshmallows
    How many possible kinds of brownies are there?_____

    | C |
    |---|
    | N |

    |  |
    |---|
    |  |

    |  |
    |---|
    |  |

2.  **C**hocolate or **B**utterscotch batter with **N**uts, **R**aisins, or **M**arshmallows
    How many possible kinds of brownies are there?_____

    | C |
    |---|
    |   |

    | C |
    |---|
    |   |

    | C |
    |---|
    |   |

    |  |
    |---|
    |  |

    |  |
    |---|
    |  |

    |  |
    |---|
    |  |

3.  **C**hocolate, **B**utterscotch, or **V**anilla batter with **N**uts, **R**aisins, or **M**arshmallows
    How many possible kinds of brownies are there?_____

    | C |
    |---|
    | N |

    | C |
    |---|
    | R |

    | C |
    |---|
    | M |

    (You draw the rest.)

4.  **C**hocolate or **V**anilla batter with **N**uts, **R**aisins, or **M**arshmallows and **W**hite or **P**ink frosting
    How many possible kinds of brownies are there?_____

    | W |
    |---|
    | C |
    | N |

    | W |
    |---|
    | C |
    | R |

    | W |
    |---|
    | C |
    | M |

    (You draw the rest.)

5.  **C**hocolate or **B**utterscotch batter with **N**uts, **R**aisins, or **M**arshmallows and **W**hite, **P**ink, or **Y**ellow frosting
    How many possible kinds of brownies are there?_____

    | W |
    |---|
    | C |
    | N |

    | W |
    |---|
    | C |
    |   |

    | W |
    |---|
    |   |
    |   |

    (You draw the rest.)

Name _____        Date _____

# Mystery Weights

**Directions:**
Each balance has two sets of weights that are balanced. Fill in the table to show the possible amounts of weight on each balance, and write a ratio to describe the relationship between the square weight and the circle weight. Then, answer the questions.

**Example:**

| ■ | 1 | 2 | 3 | 4 | 5 | 6 | 7 | 8 |
|---|---|---|---|---|---|---|---|---|
| ● | 2 | 4 | 6 | 8 | 10 | 12 | 14 | 16 |

**ratio**
1 to 2

**1.**

| ■ | 1 | 2 | 3 | 4 | 5 | 6 | 7 | 8 |
|---|---|---|---|---|---|---|---|---|
| ● | 3 | 6 |   |   |   |   |   |   |

**ratio**
___ to ___

What pattern do you see in the circle row? _____

If there are 10 squares, how many circles are there? _____

If there are 27 circles, how many squares are there? _____

**2.**

| ■ | 2 | 4 | 6 | 8 | 10 | 12 | 14 | 16 |
|---|---|---|---|---|---|---|---|---|
| ● | 4 |   |   |   |   |   |   |   |

**ratio**
___ to ___

What pattern do you see in the circle row? _____

If there are 20 squares, how many circles are there? _____

If there are 60 circles, how many squares are there? _____

**3.**

| ■ | 2 | 4 | 6 | 8 |   |   |   |   |
|---|---|---|---|---|---|---|---|---|
| ● | 3 |   |   |   |   |   |   |   |

**ratio**
___ to ___

What pattern do you see in the circle row? _____

If there are 20 squares, how many circles are there? _____

If there are 90 circles, how many squares are there? _____

**4.**

| ■ | 5 | 10 | 15 | 20 |   |   |   |   |
|---|---|---|---|---|---|---|---|---|
| ● | 3 |   |   |   |   |   |   |   |

**ratio**
___ to ___

What pattern do you see in the circle row? _____

If there are 50 squares, how many circles are there? _____

If there are 60 circles, how many squares are there? _____

               Elementary Algebra • CD-104106

# Tic-Tac-Ratio

**Ratios**

## Directions:
Fill in the missing Os and numbers in each chart. Then, write the ratio.

**1.** For every X, there are 2 Os.   The ratio of X to O is _____ to _____.

| X | X X | X X X | X X X X | X X X X X | X X X X X X | . . . | 10 Xs | 20 Xs |
|---|-----|-------|---------|-----------|-------------|-------|-------|-------|
| O O | | | | | | . . . | ____Os | ____Os |

**2.** For every X, there are 3 Os.   The ratio of X to O is _____ to _____.

| X | X X | X X X | X X X X | X X X X X | X X X X X X | . . . | 10 Xs | 100 Xs |
|---|-----|-------|---------|-----------|-------------|-------|-------|--------|
| O O O | | | | | | . . . | ____Os | ____Os |

**3.** For every 2 Xs, there are 3 Os.   The ratio of X to O is _____ to _____.

| X X | X X X X | X X X X X X | X X X X X X X X | . . . | 10 Xs | 20 Xs | 100 Xs |
|-----|---------|-------------|-----------------|-------|-------|-------|--------|
| O O O | | | | . . . | ____Os | ____Os | ____Os |

**4.** For every X, there are 4 Os.   The ratio of X to O is _____ to _____.

| X | X X | X X X | X X X X | X X X X X | . . . | 10 Xs | 15 Xs | 100 Xs |
|---|-----|-------|---------|-----------|-------|-------|-------|--------|
| O O O O | | | | | . . . | ____Os | ____Os | ____Os |

**5.** For every 3 Xs, there are 4 Os.   The ratio of X to O is _____ to _____.

| X X X | X X X X X X | X X X X X X X X X | X X X X X X X X X X X | . . . | 15 Xs | 30 Xs | 60 Xs |
|-------|-------------|-------------------|-----------------------|-------|-------|-------|-------|
| O O O O | | | | . . . | ____Os | ____Os | ____Os |

# Cats and Kittens

**Using Patterns**

## Directions:

Carly and her friend used a tree diagram to show how many stray cats could be produced from female cats that aren't spayed. They started with one female cat that had 4 kittens: 2 male and 2 female. They based their chart on the assumption that each female cat produced would not be spayed and would have 4 kittens: 2 male and 2 female. Use the diagram to fill in the missing numbers in the charts and answer the questions below.

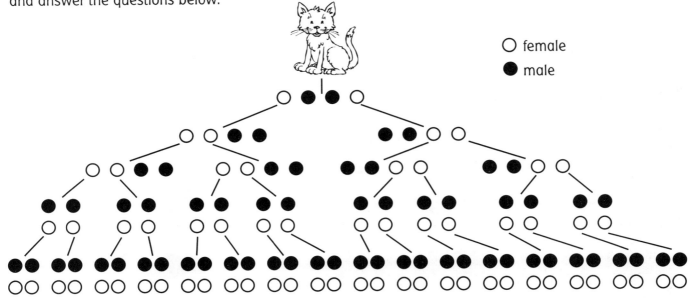

○ female
● male

1.

| Generation | 1 | 2 | 3 | 4 | 5 |
|---|---|---|---|---|---|
| Number of kittens | 4 | | | | |

2. What pattern do you see in the bottom row of the table from question 1? _____

3. Using the pattern, project how many kittens would be born in the next generations.

| Generation | 1 | 2 | 3 | 4 | 5 | 6 | 7 | 8 | 9 | 10 |
|---|---|---|---|---|---|---|---|---|---|---|
| Number of kittens | 4 | | | | | | | | | |

4. Add the number of kittens in all 10 generations to find out how many descendents the original cat would have if none of her female descendents were spayed. _____

5. How many descendents would the original cat have had if she had been spayed? _____

**Name** _____    **Date** _____

# Diagonal Patterns

## Directions:

Draw diagonal lines from corner to corner in each figure below. Then, complete the table and answer the questions.

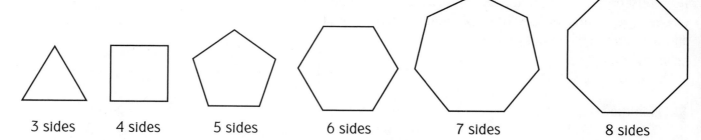

| 3 sides | 4 sides | 5 sides | 6 sides | 7 sides | 8 sides |

1.

| sides | 3 | 4 | 5 | 6 | 7 | 8 |
| --- | --- | --- | --- | --- | --- | --- |
| diagonals | 0 | | | | | |

2. What pattern do you see in the number of diagonals? _____
_____

3. In the 5-sided figure, how many diagonals are drawn to each corner? _____
   In the 6-sided figure, how many diagonals are drawn to each corner? _____
   In the 7-sided figure, how many diagonals are drawn to each corner? _____
   In the 8-sided figure, how many diagonals are drawn to each corner? _____

4. In the 5-sided figure, if there are 2 diagonals drawn from each corner and there are 5 corners, why aren't there 10 diagonals? _____
   _____
   _____

5. If you multiply the number of corners in a figure times the number of diagonals at each corner, what do you have to do to find out how many diagonals are in that figure? _____

6. The number of corners in the figure times the number of diagonals drawn from each corner divided by 2 should equal the number of diagonals in the figure. Try it:

   $(4 \times 1) \div 2 =$ _____    $(5 \times 2) \div 2 =$ _____    $(6 \times 3) \div 2 =$ _____    $(7 \times 4) \div 2 =$ _____    $(8 \times 5) \div 2 =$ _____

7. Use the formula to figure out the number of diagonals in a 9-sided and a 10-sided figure.

   9 sides _____    10 sides _____

Name _____ Date _____

# Building a Pyramid

### Directions:

Alf and Ralph were building a flat pyramid shape using dominoes. They placed the dominoes in the pattern shown, starting at the top. Then, they tried to figure out how many dominoes they would need if they followed this pattern for 20 rows. Help Alf and Ralph fill in their chart, find a pattern, and solve their problem.

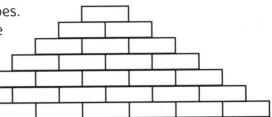

**1.** Fill in the chart through 7 rows.

| Number of rows | 1 | 2 | 3 | 4 | 5 | 6 | 7 | 8 | 9 | 10 | 11 | 12 |
|---|---|---|---|---|---|---|---|---|---|---|---|---|
| Total dominoes | 1 | 3 | 6 | | | | | | | | | |

**2.** Fill in the pattern for the totals.

**3.** Describe the pattern. _____

_____

**4.** Now, use the pattern to complete the chart above.

**5.** Look for a pattern between the rows and the dominoes. Finish the pattern started below.

$1 \times 1 = 1$          $5 \times \underline{\hspace{1cm}} = \underline{\hspace{1cm}}$          $9 \times \underline{\hspace{1cm}} = \underline{\hspace{1cm}}$

$2 \times 1\frac{1}{2} = 3$          $6 \times \underline{\hspace{1cm}} = \underline{\hspace{1cm}}$          $10 \times \underline{\hspace{1cm}} = \underline{\hspace{1cm}}$

$3 \times 2 = 6$          $7 \times \underline{\hspace{1cm}} = \underline{\hspace{1cm}}$          $11 \times \underline{\hspace{1cm}} = \underline{\hspace{1cm}}$

$4 \times 2\frac{1}{2} = 10$          $8 \times \underline{\hspace{1cm}} = \underline{\hspace{1cm}}$          $12 \times \underline{\hspace{1cm}} = \underline{\hspace{1cm}}$

**6.** What pattern did Alf and Ralph find? _____

With the help of their math teacher, they found out that for any number of rows they could figure out the total using this equation:

$$\text{total} = \frac{\text{number of rows} + 1}{2} \times \text{number of rows}$$

They checked it for 12 rows:    $\text{total} = \frac{12 + 1}{2} \times 12 = \frac{13}{2} \times 12 = 78$

**7.** Try the formula for 20 rows. What total do you get? _____

Name _____    Date _____

## Picturing Equations

**Directions:**
Write eight equations about each picture.

**Example:**

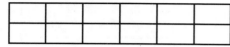

$6 \times 2 = 12$    $2 \times 6 = 12$    $12 = 6 \times 2$
$12 = 2 \times 6$    $12 \div 6 = 2$    $12 \div 2 = 6$
$2 = 12 \div 6$    $6 = 12 \div 2$

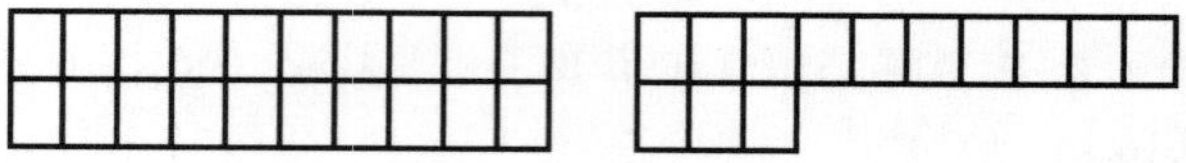

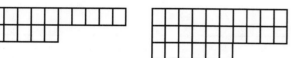

$20 + 13 = 33$    $13 + 20 = 33$    $33 = 20 + 13$
$33 = 13 + 20$    $33 - 13 = 20$    $33 - 20 = 13$
$20 = 33 - 13$    $13 = 33 - 20$

**1.**

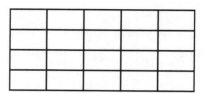

_____    _____

_____    _____

_____    _____

_____    _____

**2.**

_____    _____

_____    _____

_____    _____

_____    _____

**3.**

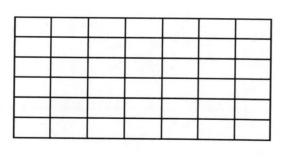

_____    _____

_____    _____

_____    _____

_____    _____

**4.**

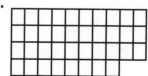 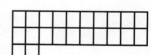

_____    _____

_____    _____

_____    _____

_____    _____

 Elementary Algebra • CD-104106

Name ______________________ Date ______________

# Picturing Equations Again

Modeling Equations

**Directions:**
Draw a picture to go with each equation.

| | |
|---|---|
| **1.** $6 \times 5 = 30$ | **2.** $8 + 7 = 15$ |
| **3.** $36 \div 9 = 4$ | **4.** $20 - 6 = 14$ |
| **5.** $30 = 15 + 15$ | **6.** $48 = 12 \times 4$ |
| **7.** $25 = 35 - 10$ | **8.** $7 = 56 \div 8$ |

Name ______________________________ Date ________________

# Books, Magazines, and Equations

Writing Equations

**Directions:**
Circle the equations that are true about each story.

**1.** Terry has W detective comic books. She gets V more. Now, she has U comic books.

$W + V = U$ $W \times V = U$ $W - V = U$ $W \div V = U$

$U - W = V$ $V - U = W$ $U = V + W$ $V = W \times U$

**2.** Maria has A stacks of fashion magazines. There are B magazines in each stack. She has C magazines altogether.

$A + B + C$ $A \times B = C$ $A - B = C$ $A \div B = C$

$C = B \times A$ $C = B - A$ $B = C \div A$ $B + C = A$

**3.** Matt has M fantasy comic books. He gives away N of them. Now, he has L left.

$M + N = L$ $M - N = L$ $M \times N = L$ $M \div N = L$

$L = N - M$ $M = L \times N$ $N = M - L$ $M = N + L$

**4.** Karl has R sports magazines. He puts T on each shelf. He uses S shelves.

$R + T = S$ $R - T = S$ $R \times T = S$ $R \div T = S$

$R = S - T$ $R = S \times T$ $R = T - S$ $S = R \div T$

**5.** Reese has D animal books. She puts them on two shelves. She puts E on one shelf and F on the other shelf.

$D + E = F$ $D - E = F$ $D \times E = F$ $D \div E = R$

$D = E + F$ $D = E \times F$ $D = E - F$ $E = D - F$

## Sports Stories

### Directions:

Write an equation for each story.

1.   During a softball game, Dinah (D) caught 2 more fly balls than Holly (H).

     equation: _____

2.   During their baseball tournament, Leroy (L) had 3 fewer hits than Art (A).

     equation: _____

3.   Marcos (M) shot baskets with his little sister LaToya (L). He made 10 more baskets
     than she did.

     equation: _____

4.   Eric (E) shot baskets with his big sister Keisha (K). She made twice as many baskets
     as he did.

     equation: _____

5.   Madison (M) and her friend Fran (F) made 24 saves together during a volleyball tournament.

     equation: _____

6.   During the hockey season, Guy (G) scored 4 fewer goals than his brother Rick (R).

     equation: _____

7.   At the end of the football season, the Hilldale Hornets (H) had scored 3 times as many
     points as the Riverview Raccoons (R).

     equation: _____

8.   During a basketball game, Nadia (N) scored more than her friend Kim (K), but the difference
     between their scores was only 1 point.

     equation: _____

9.   When the baseball statistics were compiled, Kirk (K) found that he had struck out 8 more times
     than his friend Joe (J).

     equation: _____

10.  Patty (P) scored half as many points as her friend Taylor (T) during their volleyball tournament.

     equation: _____

11.  Lonnie (L) carried the ball for 20 fewer yards than Chris (C) during their first football game.

     equation: _____

12.  Vera (V) and her brother Darnell (D) made a total of 154 baskets during their basketball practice.

     equation: _____

Name _____ Date _____

# Gummy Equations

**Writing and Solving Equations**

## Directions:

Write an equation about each story. Then, answer the questions.

1. Adrian (A) has some gummy pandas. Roy (R) has some too. Together, they have 20.

   equation: _____

   If Adrian has 7, how many does Roy have? _____

   If Roy has 5, how many does Adrian have? _____

2. Tom has 30 gummy dolphins. He puts them in B bags with E in each bag.

   equation: _____

   If Tom uses 6 bags, how many will be in each bag? _____

   If Tom puts 10 in each bag, how many bags will he use? _____

3. Velma has 40 gummy dinosaurs. She eats D dinosaurs. Now, she has L left.

   equation: _____

   If Velma eats 15, how many does she have left? _____

   If Velma has 20 left, how many did she eat? _____

4. Anne has 25 gummy apples. Some are red (R), and some are green (G).

   equation: _____

   If 17 are red, how many are green? _____

   If 13 are green, how many are red? _____

5. Waldo has some gummy lemons (G). They are in 6 bags with E in each bag.

   equation: _____

   If Waldo has 7 in each bag, how many does he have in all? _____

   If Waldo has 48 gummy lemons, how many are in each bag? _____

6. Polly arranged her gummy whales in 8 rows. There are E in each row. She has W altogether.

   equation: _____

   If Polly has 72, how many are in each row? _____

   If Polly puts 5 in each row, how many does she have altogether? _____

Name ______________________________ Date ______________

## Age Old Questions

Writing and Solving Equations

**Directions:**
Write an equation about each story. Then, answer the questions.

**1.** John (J) is twice as old as Sarah (S). equation: ______________

If John is 12, how old is Sarah? ______________

If Sarah is 10, how old is John? ______________

**2.** Danielle (D) is 4 years older than Ashley (A). equation: ______________

If Danielle is 10, how old is Ashley? ______________

If Ashley is 9, how old is Danielle? ______________

**3.** Teddy (T) is 5 years younger than Albert (A). equation: ______________

If Teddy is 6, how old is Albert? ______________

If Albert is 15, how old is Teddy? ______________

**4.** Mr. Johnson (J) is 10 years older than Ms. Tyler (T). equation: ______________

If Mr. Johnson is 35, how old is Ms. Tyler? ______________

If Ms. Tyler is 43, how old is Mr. Johnson? ______________

**5.** Shirelle (S) is 3 times as old as Ben (B). equation: ______________

If Shirelle is 9, how old is Ben? ______________

If Ben is 5, how old is Shirelle? ______________

**6.** Pam (P) is 25 years younger than her mother (M). equation: ______________

If Pam is 24, how old is her mother? ______________

If Pam's mother is 65, how old is Pam? ______________

**7.** Cara (C) is 10 years younger than Jake (J). equation: ______________

If Cara is 12, how old is Jake? ______________

If Jake is 16, how old is Cara? ______________

**8.** Mr. Polk (P) is half as old as his father (F). equation: ______________

If Mr. Polk is 30, how old is his father? ______________

If Mr. Polk's father is 76, how old is Mr. Polk? ______________

Name _____     Date _____

## Puzzling Pet Problems

**Directions:**
Circle the correct expression for each problem.

1. Alan has 3 more cats than Tori. If n stands for Tori's cats, what represents Alan's cats?

   n + 3          3 − n          n − 3          n x 3

2. Lucinda has 3 fewer gerbils than Pearl. If n stands for Pearl's gerbils, what represents Lucinda's gerbils?

   n + 3          n − 3          n ÷ 3          n x 3

3. Lewis has twice as many hamsters as Julian. If n stands for Julian's hamsters, what represents Lewis's hamsters?

   2 + n          2 ÷ n          n − 2          2 x n

4. Trina has half as many fish as Robert. If n stands for Robert's fish, what represents Trina's fish?

   n ÷ 2          2 ÷ n          n + 2          n x 2

5. Devon has 15 fewer mice than Tad. If n stands for Tad's mice, what represents Devon's mice?

   15 − n          n − 15          n + 15          n x 15

6. Pedro's family has 3 times as many dogs as Lily's family. If n stands for Lily's family's dogs, what represents Pedro's family's dogs?

   n ÷ 3          n x 3          n + 3          n − 3

7. LaQuisha's family has a third as many pets as her Aunt Ruth's family. If n stands for Aunt Ruth's family's pets, what represents LaQuisha's family's pets?

   n − 3          n + 3          n x 3          n ÷ 3

Write the correct expression for each problem. Let n stand for the unknown number.

8. sum of a number and 16 _____

9. 35 decreased by a number _____

10. 50 decreased by a number _____

11. a number decreased by 17 _____

12. product of 7 and a number _____

13. 150 added to a number _____

14. a number divided by 10 _____

15. product of a number and 25 _____

Name _____     Date _____

# Sharing Pencils

**Directions:**
For each problem, write an equation, fill in the table, and answer the questions.

---

**1.** Ron got pencils (P) with his name on them for his birthday. He used up 3 of them, then he had some left (L).

equation: _____

| P | L |
|---|---|
| 3 | |
| 4 | |
| 5 | |
| 6 | |
| 7 | |
| 8 | |
| 9 | |
| 10 | |
| 11 | |
| 12 | |
| 13 | |
| 14 | |
| 15 | |

**A.** If Ron got 11 pencils, how many did he have left?

_____

**B.** If Ron had 13 pencils left, how many did he get?

_____

**C.** If Ron got 100 pencils, how many did he have left?

_____

**D.** If Ron had 57 pencils left, how many did he get?

_____

---

**2.** Sheila got some holographic pencils (H). She gave away some (S), then she had 15 left.

equation: _____

| H | S |
|---|---|
| 15 | |
| 16 | |
| 17 | |
| 18 | |
| 19 | |
| 20 | |
| 21 | |
| 22 | |
| 23 | |
| 24 | |
| 25 | |
| 26 | |
| 27 | |

**A.** If Sheila got 25 pencils, how many did she give away?

_____

**B.** If Sheila gave away 12 pencils, how many did she get?

_____

**C.** If Sheila got 100 pencils, how many did she give away?

_____

**D.** If Sheila gave away 25 pencils, how many did she get?

_____

---

**3.** Barbara got 30 pencils decorated with cats. She gave away some (S) and kept the rest (R).

equation: _____

| S | R |
|---|---|
| 0 | |
| | |
| | |
| | |
| | |
| | |
| | |

**A.** If Barbara gave away 8 pencils, how many did she keep?

_____

**B.** If Barbara kept 19 pencils, how many did she give away?

_____

**C.** If Barbara gave away 15 pencils, how many did she keep?

_____

**D.** If Barbara kept 2 pencils, how many did she give away?

_____

---

**4.** Demetrius got 48 football team pencils. He gave his brother some (B) and kept the rest (R).

equation: _____

| B | R |
|---|---|
| 0 | |
| | |
| | |
| | |
| | |
| | |
| | |

**A.** If Demetrius gave his brother 10 pencils, how many did he keep?

_____

**B.** If Demetrius kept 40 pencils, how many did he give away?

_____

**C.** If Demetrius gave his brother 25 pencils, how many did he keep?

_____

**D.** If Demetrius kept 5 pencils, how many did he give away?

_____

---

Name _____     Date _____

# Measuring Length

## Directions:

Complete the chart for each set of length equivalencies, write an equation, and answer the questions.
The first one has been started for you.

**1.**

| Feet (F) | 1 | 2 | 3 | 4 | 5 | 6 | 7 | 8 |
|---|---|---|---|---|---|---|---|---|
| Inches (I) | 12 | 24 | 36 | 48 | 60 | 72 | 84 | 96 |

equation: I = ___12 x F___

How many inches are in 20 feet? _____

How many feet do 120 inches make? _____

**2.**

| Yards (Y) | 1 | 2 | 3 | 4 | 5 | 6 | 7 | 8 |
|---|---|---|---|---|---|---|---|---|
| Feet (F) | 3 | | | | | | | |

equation: F = _____

How many feet are in 100 yards? _____

How many yards do 30 feet make? _____

**3.**

| Meters (M) | 1 | 2 | 3 | 4 | 5 | 6 | 7 | 8 |
|---|---|---|---|---|---|---|---|---|
| Centimeters (C) | 100 | | | | | | | |

equation: C = _____

How many centimeters are in 50 meters? _____

How many meters do 900 centimeters make? _____

**4.**

| Yards (Y) | 1 | 2 | 3 | 4 | 5 | 6 | 7 | 8 |
|---|---|---|---|---|---|---|---|---|
| Inches (I) | 36 | | | | | | | |

equation: I = _____

How many inches are in 10 yards? _____

How many yards do 396 inches make? _____

**5.**

| Kilometers (K) | 1 | 2 | 3 | 4 | 5 | 6 | 7 | 8 |
|---|---|---|---|---|---|---|---|---|
| Meters (M) | 1,000 | | | | | | | |

equation: M = _____

How many meters are in 10 kilometers? _____

How many kilometers do 12,000 meters make? _____

 Elementary Algebra • CD-104106

Name _____  Date _____

# Measuring Time

**Directions:**
Complete the following tables and equations. Then, answer the questions.

**1.**

| Minutes (M) | 1 | 2 | 3 | 4 | 5 | 6 | 7 | 8 |
|---|---|---|---|---|---|---|---|---|
| Seconds (S) | 60 | | | | | | | |

equation: S = _____

**2.**

| Days (D) | 1 | 2 | 3 | 4 | 5 | 6 | 7 | 8 |
|---|---|---|---|---|---|---|---|---|
| Hours (H) | 24 | | | | | | | |

equation: H = _____

**3.**

| Weeks (W) | 1 | 2 | 3 | 4 | 5 | 6 | 7 | 8 |
|---|---|---|---|---|---|---|---|---|
| Days (D) | 7 | | | | | | | |

equation: D = _____

**4.**

| Hours (H) | 1 | 2 | 3 | 4 | 5 | 6 | 7 | 8 |
|---|---|---|---|---|---|---|---|---|
| Minutes (M) | 60 | | | | | | | |

equation: M = _____

5. How many seconds are in 8 minutes? _____

6. How many days are in 7 weeks? _____

7. How many minutes are in 5 hours? _____

8. How many hours are in 6 days? _____

9. How many weeks do 42 days make? _____

10. How many days do 192 hours make? _____

11. How many hours do 420 minutes make? _____

12. How many seconds are in 10 minutes? _____

13. How many days are in 10 weeks? _____

14. How many minutes are in 10 hours? _____

15. How many hours are in 10 days? _____

16. How many weeks do 77 days make? _____

17. How many minutes do 720 seconds make? _____

18. How many days do 480 hours make? _____

19. How many hours do 660 minutes make? _____

Name _____    Date _____

## Measuring Money

### Directions:

Complete the following tables and equations. Then, answer the questions.

**1.**

| Dimes (D) | 1 | 2 | 3 | 4 | 5 | 6 | 7 | 8 |
|---|---|---|---|---|---|---|---|---|
| Nickels (N) | 2 | | | | | | | |

equation: N = _____

**2.**

| Quarters (Q) | 1 | 2 | 3 | 4 | 5 | 6 | 7 | 8 |
|---|---|---|---|---|---|---|---|---|
| Nickels (N) | 5 | | | | | | | |

equation: N = _____

**3.**

| Dollars (D) | 1 | 2 | 3 | 4 | 5 | 6 | 7 | 8 |
|---|---|---|---|---|---|---|---|---|
| Quarters (Q) | 4 | | | | | | | |

equation: Q = _____

**4.**

| Dimes (D) | 1 | 2 | 3 | 4 | 5 | 6 | 7 | 8 |
|---|---|---|---|---|---|---|---|---|
| Pennies (P) | 10 | | | | | | | |

equation: P = _____

**5.**

| Dollars (D) | 1 | 2 | 3 | 4 | 5 | 6 | 7 | 8 |
|---|---|---|---|---|---|---|---|---|
| Nickels (N) | 20 | | | | | | | |

equation: N = _____

**6.**

| Quarters (Q) | 1 | 2 | 3 | 4 | 5 | 6 | 7 | 8 |
|---|---|---|---|---|---|---|---|---|
| Pennies (P) | 25 | | | | | | | |

equation: P = _____

**7.** How many nickels are in 8 dimes? _____

**8.** How many quarters are in 6 dollars? _____

**9.** How many nickels are in 5 dollars? _____

**10.** How many quarters do 40 nickels make? _____

**11.** How many dimes do 70 pennies make? _____

**12.** How many quarters do 125 pennies make? _____

**13.** How many nickels are in 10 quarters? _____

**14.** How many pennies are in 20 dimes? _____

**15.** How many pennies are in 10 quarters? _____

**16.** How many dimes do 30 nickels make? _____

**17.** How many dollars do 40 quarters make? _____

**18.** How many dollars do 200 nickels make? _____

# Many Measurements

Equality

## Directions:

Draw lines to connect equal amounts. Write the answers in the blanks.

| | |
|---|---|
| **1.** 1 foot = 12 inches | **2.** 7 days = 1 week |

**1.**

1 foot = 12 inches

| | |
|---|---|
| 2 feet | 5 feet |
| 36 inches | 3 feet |
| 60 inches | 120 inches |
| 10 feet | 24 inches |

4 feet = _____ inches

_____ feet = 84 inches

**2.**

7 days = 1 week

| | |
|---|---|
| 4 weeks | 70 days |
| 35 days | 28 days |
| 10 weeks | 5 weeks |
| 56 days | 8 weeks |

14 days = _____ weeks

_____ days = 7 weeks

**3.**

60 minutes = 1 hour

| | |
|---|---|
| 2 hours | 10 hours |
| 240 minutes | 120 minutes |
| 5 hours | 300 minutes |
| 600 minutes | 4 hours |

3 hours = _____ minutes

_____ hours = 360 minutes

**4.**

1 year = 12 months

| | |
|---|---|
| 3 years | 36 months |
| 96 months | 60 months |
| 5 years | 8 years |
| 72 months | 6 years |

7 years = _____ months

_____ years = 120 months

**5.**

1 meter = 100 centimeters

| | |
|---|---|
| 3 meters | 7 meters |
| 1,000 centimeters | 800 centimeters |
| 8 meters | 300 centimeters |
| 700 centimeters | 10 meters |

4 meters = _____ centimeters

_____ meters = 1,100 centimeters

**6.**

1 yard = 3 feet

| | |
|---|---|
| 3 yards | 4 yards |
| 12 feet | 9 feet |
| 5 yards | 7 yards |
| 21 feet | 15 feet |

6 yards = _____ feet

_____ yards = 30 feet

**7.**

1,000 meters = 1 kilometer

| | |
|---|---|
| 2,000 meters | 5 kilometers |
| 10 kilometers | 8,000 meters |
| 8 kilometers | 10,000 meters |
| 5,000 meters | 2 kilometers |

6,000 meters = _____ kilometers

_____ meters = 4 kilometers

**8.**

4 quarters = 1 dollar

| | |
|---|---|
| 12 quarters | 6 dollars |
| 10 dollars | 40 quarters |
| 24 quarters | 60 quarters |
| 15 dollars | 3 dollars |

16 quarters = _____ dollars

_____ quarters = 5 dollars

# Animal Speeds

**Equality**

## Directions:

Speed can be figured out by using this equation: speed = distance ÷ time (S = D ÷ T).
Write two other equations that are equal to S = D ÷ T.   D = _____    T = _____
Use these equations to complete the chart. Then, answer the questions below.

|     | Animal | Distance in Miles | Time in Hours | Speed in Miles per Hour |
|-----|--------|-------------------|---------------|-------------------------|
| 1.  | human | 50 | 2.5 | 20 |
| 2.  | greyhound | 117 | | 39 |
| 3.  | elephant | | 2 | 26 |
| 4.  | lion | 125 | 2.5 | |
| 5.  | racehorse | 50 | | 40 |
| 6.  | tortoise | 1 | 2 | |
| 7.  | black mamba | | 1.8 | 20 |
| 8.  | giraffe | 80 | 2.5 | |
| 9.  | spider | | 2 | 1.17 |
| 10. | cheetah | 195 | 3 | |
| 11. | pig | 16.5 | | 11 |
| 12. | cat | 36 | 1.2 | |
| 13. | zebra | | 2.5 | 40 |
| 14. | snail | 0.15 | 5 | |
| 15. | pronghorn antelope | | 1.5 | 60 |
| 16. | grizzly bear | 45 | | 30 |
| 17. | chicken | 4.5 | 0.5 | |
| 18. | rabbit | | 2 | 35 |

19. Which animal on this chart is the fastest? _____

20. Which animal on this chart is the slowest? _____

Name ______________________________ Date ____________________

# Perimeter and Area

**Mathematical Relationships**

**Directions:**
Find the perimeter and area of each rectangle. Then, answer the questions below about the rectangles. Refer to a rectangle by its letter.

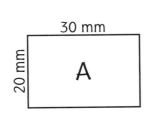

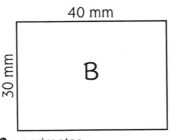

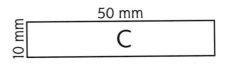

**1.** perimeter ____________
area ____________

**2.** perimeter ____________
area ____________

**3.** perimeter ____________
area ____________

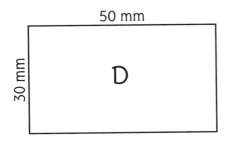

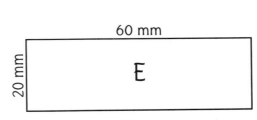

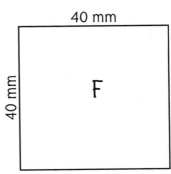

**4.** perimeter ____________
area ____________

**5.** perimeter ____________
area ____________

**6.** perimeter ____________
area ____________

**7.** Which rectangle has the largest area? ______ The smallest? ______

**8.** Which rectangles have the largest perimeter? ______, ______, ______ The smallest? ______

**9.** Which rectangles have equal perimeters? ______, ______, ______

**10.** Which rectangles have equal areas? ______, ______

**11.** Does the rectangle with the smallest perimeter have the smallest area? ____________

**12.** What is the difference between the largest perimeter and the smallest? ____________

**13.** What is the difference between the largest area and the smallest? ____________

Name _____  Date _____

# The Cookie Cart

**Writing and Solving Equations**

## Directions:
For each problem, write two equations and answer the questions.

**1.** Casey (C) bought 8 more cookies than his friend Alex (A).

    If Casey bought 16 cookies, how many cookies did Alex buy? _____

    If Alex bought 5 cookies, how many cookies did Casey buy? _____

    C = _____

    A = _____

**2.** Melody (M) bought twice as many cookies as her sister Gina (G).

    If Melody bought 12 cookies, how many cookies did Gina buy? _____

    If Gina bought 4 cookies, how many cookies did Melody buy? _____

    M = _____

    G = _____

**3.** Chocolate chip cookies (C) cost 10¢ more than peanut butter cookies (P).

    If chocolate chip cookies cost 25¢, how much do
peanut butter cookies cost? _____

    If peanut butter cookies cost 25¢, how much do
chocolate chip cookies cost? _____

    C = _____

    P = _____

**4.** Sugar cookies (S) cost 5¢ less than lemon cookies (L).

    If sugar cookies cost 20¢, how much do lemon cookies cost? _____

    If lemon cookies cost 18¢, how much do sugar cookies cost? _____

    S = _____

    L = _____

**5.** Frosted cookies (F) cost 3 times as much as plain cookies (P).

    If frosted cookies cost 21¢, how much do plain cookies cost? _____

    If plain cookies cost 10¢, how much do frosted cookies cost? _____

    F = _____

    P = _____

**6.** Mr. Anderson (A) bought cookies for his class. Mrs. Delafield (D) bought
20 more cookies for her class.

    If Mr. Anderson bought 50 cookies, how many cookies did
Mrs. Delafield buy? _____

    If Mrs. Delafield bought 65 cookies, how many cookies did
Mr. Anderson buy? _____

    A = _____

    D = _____

**7.** Vince (V) bought 12 fewer cookies than Julia (J).

    If Vince bought 10 cookies, how many cookies did Julia buy? _____

    If Julia bought 30 cookies, how many cookies did Vince buy? _____

    V = _____

    J = _____

**8.** Monster cookies (M) cost 4 times as much as regular cookies (R).

    If monster cookies cost 80¢, how much do regular cookies cost? _____

    If regular cookies cost 15¢, how much do monster cookies cost? _____

    M = _____

    R = _____

Name ______________________________ Date ______________

# Shaping Up with Equations

**Mathematical Relationships**

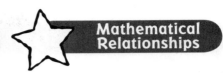

**Directions:**
Circle the equations that are true about the pictures.

**1.**

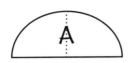

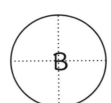

| | | | |
|---|---|---|---|
| $A > B$ | $C + A = B$ | $C < A + B$ | $C + C + C + C = B$ |
| $B > C$ | $B > A + C$ | $C = B - A$ | $B + B > C$ |
| $C + C = A$ | $B - C = A$ | $B - A > C$ | $A = B - A$ |
| $A \neq C$ | $B = A + A$ | $A > B + C$ | $A + A = B - C$ |

**2.**

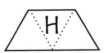

| | | | |
|---|---|---|---|
| $F > H$ | $G + H = F$ | $G = H - F$ | $G = F - H$ |
| $G = H$ | $F + H = G$ | $H = G + G + G$ | $H - G = F$ |
| $G < F$ | $H = F - G$ | $F < H + H$ | $F + G < H$ |
| $G \neq H$ | $G + G > F$ | $G + G > H$ | $F = G + G + G + G$ |

**3.**

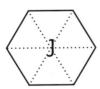

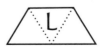

| | | | |
|---|---|---|---|
| $K < L$ | $L + L = J$ | $K + J < L$ | $L + K \neq J$ |
| $K > L$ | $K + L < J$ | $J = K + K + K$ | $L = K + K$ |
| $J > K$ | $L = J - K$ | $L - K = J$ | $J < L + L$ |
| $J < L$ | $K + K > L$ | $J - L = L$ | $K + K + K = L + L$ |

# CD Collections

**Solving Word Problems**

## Directions:
Each person has some rock CDs (R), some hip-hop CDs (H), and some pop CDs (P). Use the clues to figure out how many of each kind of CD each person has.

---

**1. LaQuisha's collection**
3 rock
2 more hip-hop
12 in all

R = ___   H = ___   P = ___

**2. Pedro's collection**
6 rock
2 fewer hip-hop
15 in all

R = ___   H = ___   P = ___

**3. Ruth's collection**
5 hip-hop
equal rock and pop
13 in all

R = ___   H = ___   P = ___

---

**4. Tony's collection**
4 rock
twice as many pop
18 in all

R = ___   H = ___   P = ___

**5. Lita's collection**
10 pop
half as many rock
20 in all

R = ___   H = ___   P = ___

**6. Dan's collection**
15 in all
1 more rock than pop
1 less hip-hop than pop

R = ___   H = ___   P = ___

---

**7. Richard's collection**
4 pop
3 times as many rock
half as many hip-hop
as pop

R = ___   H = ___   P = ___

**8. Shelly's collection**
8 hip-hop
half as many rock
twice as many pop
as hip-hop

R = ___   H = ___   P = ___

**9. Evita's collection**
7 rock
2 fewer pop
3 times as many hip-hop
as pop

R = ___   H = ___   P = ___

---

**10. Adam's collection**
16 in all
half are pop
one-fourth are rock

R = ___   H = ___   P = ___

**11. Ivy's collection**
20 in all
one-fourth are hip-hop
one-fifth are pop

R = ___   H = ___   P = ___

**12. Lou's collection**
24 in all
one-third are pop
one-half are rock

R = ___   H = ___   P = ___

---

**13. Steve's collection**
50 in all
one-fifth are rock
one-half are hip-hop

R = ___   H = ___   P = ___

**14. Xena's collection**
12 rock
twice as many hip-hop
2 fewer pop than hip-hop

R = ___   H = ___   P = ___

**15. Annie's collection**
30 in all
equal rock and pop
one-fifth are hip-hop

R = ___   H = ___   P = ___

---

Name _____     Date _____

## Weighty Problems

### Directions:
Write an equation to go with each balance. Then, figure out how much A, B, and C equal.

**1.**

_____ $A + A = 12$ _____     _____     _____

A = _____

B = _____

C = _____

• • • • • • • • • • • • • • • • • • • • • • • • • • • • • • • • • • • • •

**2.**

_____     _____     _____

A = _____

B = _____

C = _____

• • • • • • • • • • • • • • • • • • • • • • • • • • • • • • • • • • • • •

**3.**

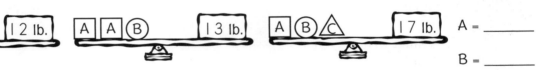

_____     _____     _____

A = _____

B = _____

C = _____

• • • • • • • • • • • • • • • • • • • • • • • • • • • • • • • • • • • • •

**4.**

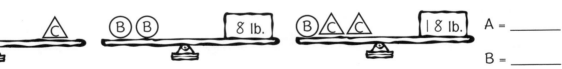

_____     _____     _____

A = _____

B = _____

C = _____

• • • • • • • • • • • • • • • • • • • • • • • • • • • • • • • • • • • • •

**5.**

_____     _____     _____

A = _____

B = _____

C = _____

Name ______________________ Date ______________

# You Be the Storyteller

Writing Word Problems

**Directions:**
Write a story to go with each equation.

1. $A + B = 50$ ______________________

2. $100 - C = D$ ______________________

3. $E = F \times 6$ ______________________

4. $G \div H = 5$ ______________________

5. $J - K = 2$ ______________________

6. $L = M + 10$ ______________________

7. $N \times P = 60$ ______________________

8. $Q = R \div 3$ ______________________

Name ______________________________ Date ______________

# Balancing Big Numbers

Mathematical Relationships

**Directions:**
Circle all of the true equations. Try not to do any calculating.

1. 250 + 250 = 400 + 100
2. 250 + 450 = 600 + 50
3. 275 + 125 = 200 + 100 + 75
4. 575 + 425 = 900 + 100
5. 425 + 175 = 175 + 425
6. 380 + 380 = 600 + 160
7. 350 + 350 = 600 + 50
8. 195 + 395 = 200 + 390
9. 560 + 240 = 600 + 260
10. 850 + 375 = 900 + 350
11. 730 + 270 = 800 + 200
12. 975 + 225 = 1,000 + 200
13. 850 − 225 = 825 − 200
14. 500 − 150 = 400 − 50
15. 910 − 260 = 700 − 60
16. 425 − 175 = 300 − 150
17. 650 − 350 = 550 − 250
18. 775 − 240 = 500 − 35
19. 895 − 275 = 900 − 280
20. 900 − 350 = 600 − 50
21. 1,000 − 540 = 500 − 40
22. 1,000 − 75 = 900 + 25
23. 1,500 + 250 = 1,700 + 250
24. 1,200 + 800 = 1,000 + 1,000
25. 1,725 + 175 = 100 + 1,800
26. 1,500 + 1,500 = 2,000 + 500
27. 2,500 + 2,500 = 4,000 + 1,000
28. 5,000 − 1,500 = 4,000 − 500

## Brain Twister

**Mathematical Relationships**

**Directions:**

Fill in each circle with the sign for equal or not equal. Try not to do any calculating.

1. 6 x 8 ◯ 3 x 2 x 8

2. 16 – 0 ◯ 15 – 0

3. 40 – 30 ◯ 30 – 40

4. 8 x 10 ◯ 4 x 20

5. 9 x 11 ◯ 11 x 9

6. 20 – 10 ◯ 21 – 11

7. 25 + 35 ◯ 35 + 25

8. 36 ÷ 9 ◯ 9 ÷ 36

9. 28 ÷ 7 ◯ 28 ÷ 4

10. 2 x 3 x 5 ◯ 5 x 3 x 3

11. 6 x 5 x 2 ◯ 5 x 2 x 6

12. 15 + 16 ◯ 14 + 17

13. 32 ÷ 32 ◯ 50 ÷ 50

14. 6 + 8 + 5 ◯ 8 + 5 + 6

15. 6 x 10 ◯ 3 x 3 x 10

16. 30 ÷ 6 ◯ 15 ÷ 3

17. 5 x 0 ◯ 65 x 0

18. 9 x 7 ◯ 7 x 3 x 3

19. 80 ÷ 5 ◯ 80 ÷ 4

20. 35 + 36 ◯ 37 + 38

21. 70 – 0 ◯ 70 + 0

22. 7 x 8 ◯ 9 x 7

23. 26 + 30 ◯ 27 + 31

24. 8 x 1 ◯ 8 ÷ 1

25. 35 – 8 ◯ 34 – 9

26. 17 + 63 ◯ 63 + 18

27. 8 x 5 ◯ 2 x 2 x 2 x 5

28. 6 x 3 x 2 x 7 ◯ 12 x 7

Name _____   Date _____

# Number Families

**Mathematical Relationships**

## Directions:
Eight different equations can be written about each set of numbers. Write all eight for each set.

**Examples:**

6, 7, 13

$6 + 7 = 13$    $13 - 7 = 6$
$7 + 6 = 13$    $13 - 6 = 7$
$13 = 6 + 7$    $6 = 13 - 7$
$13 = 7 + 6$    $7 = 13 - 6$

5, 20, 4

$5 \times 4 = 20$    $20 \div 5 = 4$
$4 \times 5 = 20$    $20 \div 4 = 5$
$20 = 5 \times 4$    $4 = 20 \div 5$
$20 = 4 \times 5$    $5 = 20 \div 4$

**1.**        15, 40, 25

_____   _____
_____   _____
_____   _____
_____   _____

**2.**        9, 8, 72

_____   _____
_____   _____
_____   _____
_____   _____

**3.**        50, 125, 75

_____   _____
_____   _____
_____   _____
_____   _____

**4.**        160, 8, 20

_____   _____
_____   _____
_____   _____
_____   _____

**5.**        11, 99, 9

_____   _____
_____   _____
_____   _____
_____   _____

**6.**        16, 0, 16

_____   _____
_____   _____
_____   _____
_____   _____

Name ______________________ Date ______________

# Times Shortcuts

Mathematical Relationships

**Directions:**
Circle the true equation or equations in each box. Try not to do any calculating.

| | |
|---|---|
| **1.**<br>$6 \times 6 = (5 \times 6) + 6$<br>$6 \times 6 = (3 \times 6) + (3 \times 6)$ | **2.**<br>$7 \times 6 = (3 \times 6) + (4 \times 6)$<br>$7 \times 6 = (5 \times 7) + 6$ |
| **3.**<br>$7 \times 7 = (4 \times 7) + (3 \times 7)$<br>$7 \times 7 = (5 \times 7) + 10$ | **4.**<br>$8 \times 7 = (4 \times 7) + (4 \times 7)$<br>$8 \times 7 = (5 \times 7) + (3 \times 7)$ |
| **5.**<br>$6 \times 8 = (4 \times 6) + (4 \times 6)$<br>$6 \times 8 = (3 \times 8) + (3 \times 8)$ | **6.**<br>$8 \times 8 = (4 \times 4) + (4 \times 4)$<br>$8 \times 8 = (5 \times 8) + (3 \times 8)$ |
| **7.**<br>$6 \times 9 = (5 \times 9) + 9$<br>$6 \times 9 = (3 \times 9) + (3 \times 6)$ | **8.**<br>$9 \times 7 = (7 \times 10) - 7$<br>$9 \times 7 = (5 \times 7) + (4 \times 7)$ |
| **9.**<br>$8 \times 9 = (8 \times 10) - 8$<br>$8 \times 9 = (4 \times 9) + (4 \times 9)$ | **10.**<br>$9 \times 9 = (10 \times 9) - 9$<br>$9 \times 9 = (4 \times 9) + (4 \times 9)$ |
| **11.**<br>$10 \times 11 = (10 \times 10) + 10$<br>$10 \times 11 = (10 \times 1) + (10 \times 1)$ | **12.**<br>$8 \times 12 = (8 \times 10) + (8 \times 2)$<br>$8 \times 12 = (6 \times 8) + (6 \times 8)$ |
| **13.**<br>$9 \times 13 = (10 \times 13) - 13$<br>$9 \times 13 = (10 \times 13) - 9$ | **14.**<br>$7 \times 14 = (7 \times 7) + (7 \times 7)$<br>$7 \times 14 = (7 \times 10) + (7 \times 4)$ |
| **15.**<br>$8 \times 15 = (7 \times 15) + 8$<br>$8 \times 15 = (8 \times 10) + (8 \times 5)$ | **16.**<br>$9 \times 25 = (9 \times 20) + (9 \times 5)$<br>$9 \times 25 = (10 \times 25) - 25$ |

Name _____ Date _____

# Hunting for Hundreds

Writing Equations

## Directions:
Make each equation different. Do not use zero. Try to use patterns.

### 1. Adding to 100

$100 = $ _____ + _____     $100 = $ _____ + _____     $100 = $ _____ + _____ + _____

$100 = $ _____ + _____     $100 = $ _____ + _____     $100 = $ _____ + _____ + _____

$100 = $ _____ + _____     $100 = $ _____ + _____     $100 = $ _____ + _____ + _____ + _____

$100 = $ _____ + _____     $100 = $ _____ + _____     $100 = $ _____ + _____ + _____ + _____

$100 = $ _____ + _____     $100 = $ _____ + _____     $100 = $ _____ + _____ + _____ + _____

### 2. Subtracting to 100

$100 = $ _____ – _____     $100 = $ _____ – _____     $100 = $ _____ – _____

$100 = $ _____ – _____     $100 = $ _____ – _____     $100 = $ _____ – _____

$100 = $ _____ – _____     $100 = $ _____ – _____     $100 = $ _____ – _____

$100 = $ _____ – _____     $100 = $ _____ – _____     $100 = $ _____ – _____

$100 = $ _____ – _____     $100 = $ _____ – _____     $100 = $ _____ – _____

### 3. Multiplying to 100

$100 = $ _____ x _____     $100 = $ _____ x _____     $100 = $ _____ x _____ x _____

$100 = $ _____ x _____     $100 = $ _____ x _____     $100 = $ _____ x _____ x _____

$100 = $ _____ x _____     $100 = $ _____ x _____     $100 = $ _____ x _____ x _____

$100 = $ _____ x _____     $100 = $ _____ x _____     $100 = $ _____ x _____ x _____ x _____

### 4. Dividing to 100

$100 = $ _____ ÷ _____     $100 = $ _____ ÷ _____     $100 = $ _____ ÷ _____

$100 = $ _____ ÷ _____     $100 = $ _____ ÷ _____     $100 = $ _____ ÷ _____

$100 = $ _____ ÷ _____     $100 = $ _____ ÷ _____     $100 = $ _____ ÷ _____

$100 = $ _____ ÷ _____     $100 = $ _____ ÷ _____     $100 = $ _____ ÷ _____

**Name** _____   **Date** _____

# The Fabulous Factor Factory

## Directions:

The Factor Factory produces products and their factors. Take the factors out of their boxes and write them in the correct pairs.

**1.** **Product of 60**

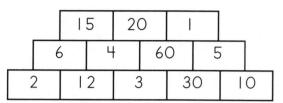

60 = _____ x _____      60 = _____ x _____

60 = _____ x _____      60 = _____ x _____

60 = _____ x _____      60 = _____ x _____

**2.** **Product of 84**

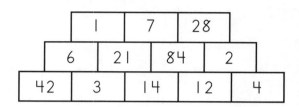

84 = _____ x _____      84 = _____ x _____

84 = _____ x _____      84 = _____ x _____

84 = _____ x _____      84 = _____ x _____

**3.** **Product of 96**

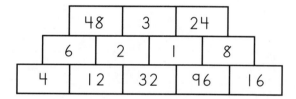

96 = _____ x _____      96 = _____ x _____

96 = _____ x _____      96 = _____ x _____

96 = _____ x _____      96 = _____ x _____

**4.** **Product of 120**

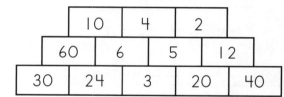

120 = _____ x _____      120 = _____ x _____

120 = _____ x _____      120 = _____ x _____

120 = _____ x _____      120 = _____ x _____

**5.** **Product of 200**

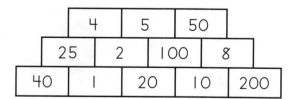

200 = _____ x _____      200 = _____ x _____

200 = _____ x _____      200 = _____ x _____

200 = _____ x _____      200 = _____ x _____

**6.** **Product of 500**

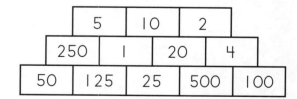

500 = _____ x _____      500 = _____ x _____

500 = _____ x _____      500 = _____ x _____

500 = _____ x _____      500 = _____ x _____

Name _____     Date _____

# More of the Fabulous Factor Factory

Factors

**Directions:**
The Factor Factory produces products and their factors. Take the factors out of their crates and write them in the correct pairs.

**1.    Product of 144**

| 36 | 16 | 3 | 4 |
| 18 | 12 | 144 | |
| 9 | 2 | 8 | 72 |
| 24 | 12 | 1 | |
| 6 | 48 | | |

144 = _____ x _____
144 = _____ x _____
144 = _____ x _____
144 = _____ x _____
144 = _____ x _____
144 = _____ x _____
144 = _____ x _____
144 = _____ x _____

**2.    Product of 300**

| 25 | 150 | 3 | 6 |
| 2 | 30 | 50 | |
| 12 | 75 | 5 | 10 |
| 100 | 4 | 60 | |
| 15 | 20 | | |

300 = _____ x _____
300 = _____ x _____
300 = _____ x _____
300 = _____ x _____
300 = _____ x _____
300 = _____ x _____
300 = _____ x _____
300 = _____ x _____

**3.    Product of 400**

| 2 | 5 | 100 | 80 |
| 40 | 16 | 1 | |
| 10 | 25 | 200 | 20 |
| 8 | 20 | 4 | |
| 400 | 50 | | |

400 = _____ x _____
400 = _____ x _____
400 = _____ x _____
400 = _____ x _____
400 = _____ x _____
400 = _____ x _____
400 = _____ x _____
400 = _____ x _____

**4.    Product of 800**

| 100 | 80 | 2 | 20 |
| 10 | 16 | 200 | |
| 5 | 400 | 8 | 50 |
| 25 | 32 | 160 | |
| 40 | 4 | | |

800 = _____ x _____
800 = _____ x _____
800 = _____ x _____
800 = _____ x _____
800 = _____ x _____
800 = _____ x _____
800 = _____ x _____
800 = _____ x _____

**5.    Product of 1,000**

| 1 | 25 | 4 | 50 |
| 10 | 250 | 2 | |
| 100 | 20 | 5 | 500 |
| 8 | 1,000 | 125 | |
| 40 | 200 | | |

1,000 = _____ x _____
1,000 = _____ x _____
1,000 = _____ x _____
1,000 = _____ x _____
1,000 = _____ x _____
1,000 = _____ x _____
1,000 = _____ x _____
1,000 = _____ x _____

**6.    Product of 600**

| 5 | 15 | 6 | 50 |
| 120 | 25 | 40 | |
| 3 | 12 | 100 | 75 |
| 200 | 24 | 8 | |
| 4 | 150 | | |

600 = _____ x _____
600 = _____ x _____
600 = _____ x _____
600 = _____ x _____
600 = _____ x _____
600 = _____ x _____
600 = _____ x _____
600 = _____ x _____

 Elementary Algebra • CD-104106

## Product Puzzles

**Factors**

**Directions:**
Find pairs of factors that make the product. Shade the box when you use a number. When you finish, all of the numbered boxes should be shaded.

### 1. Product of 1,600

1,600 = _____ x _____

1,600 = _____ x _____    1,600 = _____ x _____

1,600 = _____ x _____    1,600 = _____ x _____

1,600 = _____ x _____    1,600 = _____ x _____

1,600 = _____ x _____    1,600 = _____ x _____

1,600 = _____ x _____    1,600 = _____ x _____

| 1,600 | 40 | 320 | 25 | 8 | 50 |
|---|---|---|---|---|---|
| 16 | 1 | 160 | 800 | 5 | 200 |
| 64 | 80 | 100 | 32 | 20 | 2 |
| 10 | 4 | 400 | 40 | | |

### 2. Product of 1,500

1,500 = _____ x _____    1,500 = _____ x _____

1,500 = _____ x _____    1,500 = _____ x _____

1,500 = _____ x _____    1,500 = _____ x _____

1,500 = _____ x _____    1,500 = _____ x _____

1,500 = _____ x _____    1,500 = _____ x _____

1,500 = _____ x _____    1,500 = _____ x _____

| 30 | 750 | 125 | 25 | 75 | 4 |
|---|---|---|---|---|---|
| 100 | 10 | 1 | 5 | 15 | 250 |
| 1,500 | 50 | 500 | 375 | 60 | 12 |
| 6 | 3 | 150 | 20 | 2 | 300 |

### 3. Product of 1,200

1,200 = _____ x _____

1,200 = _____ x _____    1,200 = _____ x _____

1,200 = _____ x _____    1,200 = _____ x _____

1,200 = _____ x _____    1,200 = _____ x _____

1,200 = _____ x _____    1,200 = _____ x _____

1,200 = _____ x _____    1,200 = _____ x _____

1,200 = _____ x _____    1,200 = _____ x _____

1,200 = _____ x _____    1,200 = _____ x _____

| 8 | 400 | 24 | 80 | 150 | 2 |
|---|---|---|---|---|---|
| 48 | 4 | 300 | 6 | 30 | 100 |
| 120 | 20 | 50 | 3 | 15 | 25 |
| 5 | 200 | 16 | 240 | 60 | 10 |
| 1 | 40 | 1,200 | 12 | 75 | 600 |

# Figure the Factors

**Directions:**
Figure out as many pairs of factors as there are equations. Look for patterns.

**1.  Product of 100**

100 = _____ x _____

100 = _____ x _____

100 = _____ x _____

100 = _____ x _____

100 = _____ x _____

**2.  Product of 1,000**

1,000 = _____ x _____

1,000 = _____ x _____

1,000 = _____ x _____

1,000 = _____ x _____

1,000 = _____ x _____

1,000 = _____ x _____

1,000 = _____ x _____

1,000 = _____ x _____

**3.  Product of 10,000**

10,000 = _____ x _____

10,000 = _____ x _____

10,000 = _____ x _____

10,000 = _____ x _____

10,000 = _____ x _____

10,000 = _____ x _____

10,000 = _____ x _____

10,000 = _____ x _____

10,000 = _____ x _____

**4.  Product of 100,000**

100,000 = _____ x _____

100,000 = _____ x _____

100,000 = _____ x _____

100,000 = _____ x _____

100,000 = _____ x _____

100,000 = _____ x _____

100,000 = _____ x _____

100,000 = _____ x _____

100,000 = _____ x _____

# Factor-Factor-Product Designs

**Factors**

**Directions:**
In each shape, connect two factors and their product to make a triangle. Make all possible triangles in each shape.

1.
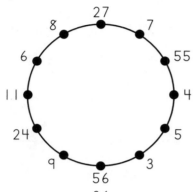

2.
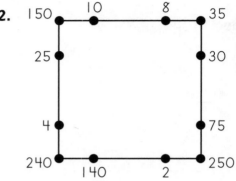

3.
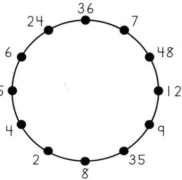

4.
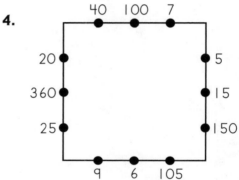

5.
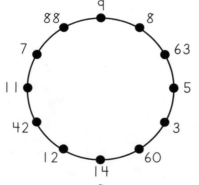

6.
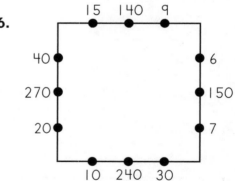

7.
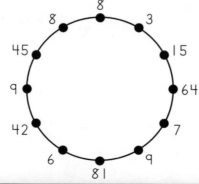

8.
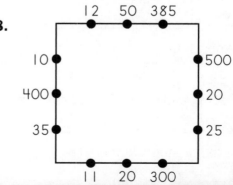

Elementary Algebra • CD-104106

Name _____ Date _____

# Factors and Multiples

**Directions:**
Fill in the Venn diagram with the numbers 1–50. List numbers that do not belong in any set in the outside set. Then, answer the questions below.

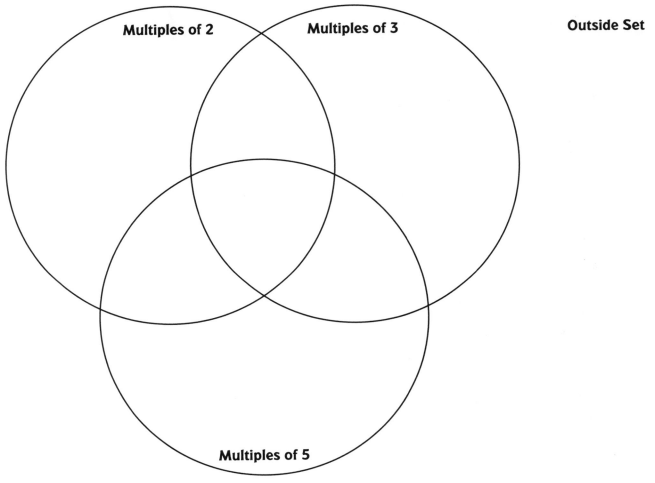

**Multiples of 2**   **Multiples of 3**   **Outside Set**

**Multiples of 5**

1. What numbers are in the intersection of multiples of 2 and multiples of 3?
   _____ How are they alike? _____

2. What numbers are in the intersection of multiples of 2 and multiples of 5?
   _____ How are they alike? _____

3. What numbers are in the intersection of multiples of 3 and multiples of 5?
   _____ How are they alike? _____

4. What is this pattern?   6, 12, 18, 24, 30, 36, 42, 48
   _____

5. Describe the numbers in the outside set.
   _____

Name _____     Date _____

# Think of a Number

## Directions:

Write at least one number that matches each description.

1.  I am even.
    I am a multiple of 10.
    I am greater than 100 but less than 200.

    _____

2.  I am odd
    I am a multiple of 7.
    I am greater than 60 but less than 100.

    _____

3.  I am even.
    I am a multiple of 6 and of 4.
    I am greater than 60 but less than 100.

    _____

4.  I am odd
    I am a multiple of 5 and of 3.
    I am less than 50.

    _____

5.  I am even.
    I am a multiple of 4 and of 3.
    I am greater than 60 but less than 100.

    _____

6.  I am odd
    I am a multiple of 9 and of 5.
    I am less than 100.

    _____

7.  I am even.
    I am a factor of 48 and of 72.
    I am not 2.

    _____

8.  I am odd
    I am a factor of 78.
    I am also a factor of 52.

    _____

9.  I am even.
    I am a factor of 96 and of 60.
    I am not 2.

    _____

10. I am odd
    I am a factor of 46.
    I am also a factor of 92.

    _____

11. I am even.
    I am a factor of 112 and of 64.
    I am not 2 or 4.

    _____

12. I am odd
    I am a factor of 85.
    I am also a factor of 34.

    _____

13. I am a prime number.
    I am greater than 80 but less than 100.

    _____

14. I a prime number.
    I am greater than 100 but less than 120.

    _____

Name _____   Date _____

# Division Dilemmas

★ **Writing Equations**

## Directions:
Fill in the blanks in these equations to make them true. Do not use 1.

$63 \div \underline{\hspace{1cm}} = \underline{\hspace{1cm}}$

$48 \div \underline{\hspace{1cm}} = \underline{\hspace{1cm}}$

$56 \div \underline{\hspace{1cm}} = \underline{\hspace{1cm}}$

$35 \div \underline{\hspace{1cm}} = \underline{\hspace{1cm}}$

$72 \div \underline{\hspace{1cm}} = \underline{\hspace{1cm}}$

$85 \div \underline{\hspace{1cm}} = \underline{\hspace{1cm}}$

$100 \div \underline{\hspace{1cm}} = \underline{\hspace{1cm}}$

$120 \div \underline{\hspace{1cm}} = \underline{\hspace{1cm}}$

$144 \div \underline{\hspace{1cm}} = \underline{\hspace{1cm}}$

$125 \div \underline{\hspace{1cm}} = \underline{\hspace{1cm}}$

$96 \div \underline{\hspace{1cm}} = \underline{\hspace{1cm}}$

$112 \div \underline{\hspace{1cm}} = \underline{\hspace{1cm}}$

$124 \div \underline{\hspace{1cm}} = \underline{\hspace{1cm}}$

$135 \div \underline{\hspace{1cm}} = \underline{\hspace{1cm}}$

$84 \div \underline{\hspace{1cm}} = \underline{\hspace{1cm}}$

$78 \div \underline{\hspace{1cm}} = \underline{\hspace{1cm}}$

$95 \div \underline{\hspace{1cm}} = \underline{\hspace{1cm}}$

$81 \div \underline{\hspace{1cm}} = \underline{\hspace{1cm}}$

$92 \div \underline{\hspace{1cm}} = \underline{\hspace{1cm}}$

$110 \div \underline{\hspace{1cm}} = \underline{\hspace{1cm}}$

$116 \div \underline{\hspace{1cm}} = \underline{\hspace{1cm}}$

$150 \div \underline{\hspace{1cm}} = \underline{\hspace{1cm}}$

$136 \div \underline{\hspace{1cm}} = \underline{\hspace{1cm}}$

$140 \div \underline{\hspace{1cm}} = \underline{\hspace{1cm}}$

$175 \div \underline{\hspace{1cm}} = \underline{\hspace{1cm}}$

$200 \div \underline{\hspace{1cm}} = \underline{\hspace{1cm}}$

$180 \div \underline{\hspace{1cm}} = \underline{\hspace{1cm}}$

$225 \div \underline{\hspace{1cm}} = \underline{\hspace{1cm}}$

**Name** _____  **Date** _____

# Quotient Quandary

**Investigating Division**

## Directions:

Make your way through the maze from start to finish. You may only go through boxes that have quotients of 5. Shade your path as you go.

| **Start**<br>10 ÷ 2 | 70 ÷ 10 | 80 ÷ 16 | 90 ÷ 18 | 30 ÷ 6 | 40 ÷ 4 | 186 ÷ 62 | 176 ÷ 44 |
|---|---|---|---|---|---|---|---|
| 45 ÷ 9 | 63 ÷ 7 | 150 ÷ 30 | 96 ÷ 16 | 100 ÷ 20 | 184 ÷ 23 | 92 ÷ 23 | 98 ÷ 14 |
| 200 ÷ 40 | 30 ÷ 5 | 35 ÷ 7 | 144 ÷ 24 | 50 ÷ 10 | 168 ÷ 56 | 124 ÷ 31 | 182 ÷ 26 |
| 20 ÷ 4 | 40 ÷ 5 | 60 ÷ 12 | 90 ÷ 6 | 95 ÷ 19 | 40 ÷ 8 | 204 ÷ 51 | 204 ÷ 34 |
| 85 ÷ 17 | 65 ÷ 13 | 125 ÷ 25 | 105 ÷ 15 | 90 ÷ 15 | 75 ÷ 15 | 108 ÷ 12 | 184 ÷ 46 |
| 60 ÷ 20 | 75 ÷ 5 | 102 ÷ 17 | 128 ÷ 32 | 175 ÷ 25 | 15 ÷ 3 | 126 ÷ 21 | 180 ÷ 45 |
| 80 ÷ 5 | 48 ÷ 8 | 72 ÷ 18 | 200 ÷ 50 | 210 ÷ 35 | 55 ÷ 11 | 25 ÷ 5 | 198 ÷ 33 |
| 36 ÷ 6 | 64 ÷ 16 | 100 ÷ 25 | 126 ÷ 18 | 72 ÷ 12 | 108 ÷ 27 | 210 ÷ 42 | **Finish**<br>70 ÷ 14 |

Name _____ Date _____

## Compare to One-Half

**Directions:**

Fill in the blanks with fractions to make comparisons. Try to use patterns when possible.

| Less than $\frac{1}{2}$ | Equal to $\frac{1}{2}$ | Greater than $\frac{1}{2}$ |
|---|---|---|
| $\frac{1}{2} >$ ___ | $\frac{1}{2} =$ ___ | $\frac{1}{2} <$ ___ |
| $\frac{1}{2} >$ ___ | $\frac{1}{2} =$ ___ | $\frac{1}{2} <$ ___ |
| $\frac{1}{2} >$ ___ | $\frac{1}{2} =$ ___ | $\frac{1}{2} <$ ___ |
| $\frac{1}{2} >$ ___ | $\frac{1}{2} =$ ___ | $\frac{1}{2} <$ ___ |
| $\frac{1}{2} >$ ___ | $\frac{1}{2} =$ ___ | $\frac{1}{2} <$ ___ |
| $\frac{1}{2} >$ ___ | $\frac{1}{2} =$ ___ | $\frac{1}{2} <$ ___ |
| $\frac{1}{2} >$ ___ | $\frac{1}{2} =$ ___ | $\frac{1}{2} <$ ___ |
| $\frac{1}{2} >$ ___ | $\frac{1}{2} =$ ___ | $\frac{1}{2} <$ ___ |
| $\frac{1}{2} >$ ___ | $\frac{1}{2} =$ ___ | $\frac{1}{2} <$ ___ |
| $\frac{1}{2} >$ ___ | $\frac{1}{2} =$ ___ | $\frac{1}{2} <$ ___ |
| $\frac{1}{2} >$ ___ | $\frac{1}{2} =$ ___ | $\frac{1}{2} <$ ___ |
| $\frac{1}{2} >$ ___ | $\frac{1}{2} =$ ___ | $\frac{1}{2} <$ ___ |

# Ordering Fractions

**Investigating Fractions**

**Directions:**
Circle numbers according to the directions.

| | | |
|---|---|---|
| **1. numbers less than $\frac{1}{2}$** | **2. numbers greater than $\frac{1}{2}$** | **3. numbers equal to $\frac{1}{2}$** |

**1. numbers less than $\frac{1}{2}$**

$\frac{4}{5}$    0.1    1.2    $\frac{2}{6}$

$\frac{5}{6}$    $\frac{1}{3}$    0.6

0.25    $\frac{5}{8}$    $\frac{1}{4}$

$\frac{2}{5}$    0.07

0.065

0.4    $\frac{3}{4}$

$\frac{2}{3}$    $\frac{2}{8}$

0.51

**2. numbers greater than $\frac{1}{2}$**

$\frac{3}{4}$    0.51    $\frac{2}{3}$

$\frac{5}{12}$

2.5    0.062

$\frac{3}{8}$    0.05    $\frac{10}{10}$

$\frac{2}{5}$    0.5    $\frac{1}{3}$    $\frac{3}{5}$

$\frac{5}{8}$    $\frac{7}{12}$    $\frac{1}{4}$

0.98    0.75

**3. numbers equal to $\frac{1}{2}$**

$\frac{3}{6}$    $\frac{50}{100}$    $\frac{6}{12}$

0.5    $\frac{5}{100}$

$\frac{15}{30}$    0.50

5.0    $\frac{5}{10}$    1.5

$\frac{5}{12}$    0.500    $\frac{3}{7}$

$\frac{4}{8}$    $\frac{6}{6}$    $\frac{4}{10}$    $\frac{2}{4}$

**4. numbers less than 1**

$\frac{4}{5}$    $\frac{9}{9}$    $\frac{4}{12}$

1.25    0.99    0.75

3.2    $\frac{1}{2}$    $1\frac{1}{2}$

$1\frac{2}{3}$    1.00

0.5

$\frac{4}{3}$    $\frac{6}{8}$    0.11    $1\frac{1}{10}$

**5. numbers greater than 1**

1.1    0.99    $\frac{1}{2}$

1.0    2.5    1.01

3.8

$\frac{1}{3}$    $\frac{11}{10}$    $1\frac{1}{2}$

0.7

$1\frac{2}{3}$    $\frac{6}{5}$    1.75

$\frac{9}{10}$    $\frac{4}{3}$    $3\frac{1}{8}$

1.5

**6. numbers equal to 1**

0.99    $\frac{6}{6}$    0.01

$\frac{1}{10}$    $\frac{5}{6}$    1.0

$\frac{5}{5}$    1.0000

$\frac{4}{3}$    $\frac{1}{5}$    0.1

1.00    1.5    $\frac{100}{100}$    $\frac{4}{4}$

$\frac{3}{3}$    1.000    $1\frac{1}{2}$

Name ______________________________ Date ______________

# Getting a Feel for Fractions

Investigating Fractions

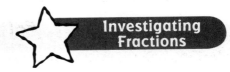

**Directions:**
Follow the directions in each section below.

Write >, <, or = in each circle.

1. $\frac{3}{2}$ ◯ 0.5
2. 1 ◯ $\frac{2}{3}$
3. $1\frac{1}{4}$ ◯ 1.5
4. 3.5 ◯ $3\frac{1}{2}$
5. $\frac{4}{10}$ ◯ 0.5
6. $\frac{6}{7}$ ◯ 1
7. 1.5 ◯ $1\frac{1}{3}$
8. 0.1 ◯ $\frac{1}{10}$
9. 0.1 ◯ $\frac{1}{2}$
10. $\frac{1}{2}$ ◯ $\frac{2}{4}$
11. $2\frac{1}{2}$ ◯ 2.5
12. 0.6 ◯ $\frac{6}{10}$
13. 1.25 ◯ $1\frac{1}{4}$
14. 0.07 ◯ $\frac{7}{10}$

Write each row of numbers in order from least to greatest.

15. $\frac{1}{2}$, 0.6, $\frac{1}{4}$ ____, ____, ____
16. 1, $\frac{1}{3}$, $\frac{1}{9}$ ____, ____, ____
17. 0.75, 0.075, 7.5 ____, ____, ____
18. 0.25, $\frac{1}{2}$, 1.5 ____, ____, ____
19. 4.1, 3.2, $3\frac{1}{2}$ ____, ____, ____
20. $\frac{1}{2}$, $\frac{5}{6}$, $\frac{2}{3}$ ____, ____, ____
21. $1\frac{1}{2}$, 1.4, 1.04 ____, ____, ____
22. 0.1, 1.0, $\frac{1}{2}$ ____, ____, ____
23. $\frac{1}{5}$, $\frac{1}{4}$, $\frac{1}{2}$ ____, ____, ____
24. 1.5, 0.15, 15 ____, ____, ____
25. $2\frac{1}{2}$, 2.51, $2\frac{1}{4}$ ____, ____, ____
26. $\frac{4}{10}$, 0.05, 0.41 ____, ____, ____
27. $\frac{3}{4}$, $\frac{5}{12}$, $\frac{14}{15}$ ____, ____, ____
28. 0.8, 0.08, $\frac{8}{16}$ ____, ____, ____

# The Amazing One-Half Maze

**Investigating Fractions**

## Directions:

Make your way through the maze from start to finish. You may only go through boxes that have numbers equal to one-half. Shade your path as you go.

| Start $\frac{1}{2}$ | $\frac{3}{4}$ | $\frac{9}{18}$ | $\frac{80}{160}$ | $\frac{15}{30}$ | $\frac{7}{8}$ | $\frac{6}{11}$ | $\frac{12}{23}$ |
|---|---|---|---|---|---|---|---|
| $\frac{20}{40}$ | $\frac{45}{91}$ | $\frac{50}{100}$ | $\frac{16}{30}$ | $\frac{8}{16}$ | $\frac{4}{9}$ | $\frac{7}{15}$ | $\frac{25}{51}$ |
| $\frac{2}{4}$ | $\frac{40}{80}$ | $\frac{18}{36}$ | $\frac{50}{99}$ | $\frac{14}{28}$ | $\frac{6}{13}$ | $\frac{12}{25}$ | $\frac{150}{400}$ |
| $\frac{5}{11}$ | $\frac{9}{14}$ | $\frac{40}{90}$ | $\frac{17}{35}$ | $\frac{3}{6}$ | $\frac{26}{50}$ | $\frac{32}{63}$ | $\frac{80}{170}$ |
| $\frac{2}{3}$ | $\frac{90}{180}$ | $\frac{7}{14}$ | $\frac{500}{1,000}$ | $\frac{75}{150}$ | $\frac{4}{7}$ | $\frac{6}{10}$ | $\frac{8}{17}$ |
| $\frac{50}{150}$ | $\frac{25}{50}$ | $\frac{100}{250}$ | $\frac{6}{21}$ | $\frac{83}{160}$ | $\frac{4}{8}$ | $\frac{51}{102}$ | $\frac{45}{90}$ |
| $\frac{5}{6}$ | $\frac{5}{10}$ | $\frac{12}{24}$ | $\frac{10}{20}$ | $\frac{250}{500}$ | $\frac{100}{200}$ | $\frac{2}{5}$ | $\frac{6}{12}$ |
| $\frac{20}{48}$ | $\frac{35}{71}$ | $\frac{5}{9}$ | $\frac{21}{50}$ | $\frac{300}{700}$ | $\frac{15}{31}$ | $\frac{74}{150}$ | **Finish** $\frac{24}{48}$ |

# Finish the Equation

## Directions:

Fill in the blanks in each equation to make it true. Do not use 0 or 1.

_____ x 4 = _____          _____ = _____ x 3

_____ x 5 = _____          _____ = _____ x 14

16 x _____ = _____          _____ = 7 x _____

8 x _____ = _____          _____ = 9 x _____

_____ x _____ = 50          80 = _____ x _____

_____ x _____ = 75          120 = _____ x _____

_____ x _____ = 108          _____ = 12 x _____

_____ ÷ 2 = _____          _____ = _____ ÷ 4

_____ ÷ 3 = _____          _____ = _____ ÷ 15

80 ÷ _____ = _____          _____ = 60 ÷ _____

24 ÷ _____ = _____          _____ = 30 ÷ _____

_____ ÷ _____ = 2          4 = _____ ÷ _____

_____ ÷ _____ = 10          12 = _____ ÷ _____

_____ ÷ 20 = _____          150 = _____ ÷ _____

# Equation Enigmas

**Writing Equations**

## Directions:

Write four equations for each box: addition, subtraction, multiplication, and division. You may not use the same number twice. The numbers must be touching each other at a side or corner. Circle the numbers that go together.

**Example**

$$6 + 4 = 10$$
$$15 - 8 = 7$$
$$2 \times 9 = 18$$
$$30 \div 5 = 6$$

**1.**

| 3 | 5 | 8 | 10 |
|---|---|---|----|
| 2 | 18 | 9 | 4 |
| 25 | 5 | 5 | 6 |

_____
_____
_____

**2.**

| 20 | 7 | 7 | 42 |
|----|---|---|----|
| 11 | 49 | 6 | 17 |
| 9 | 7 | 9 | 8 |

_____
_____
_____

**3.**

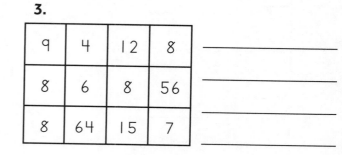

| 9 | 4 | 12 | 8 |
|---|---|----|---|
| 8 | 6 | 8 | 56 |
| 8 | 64 | 15 | 7 |

_____
_____
_____

**4.**

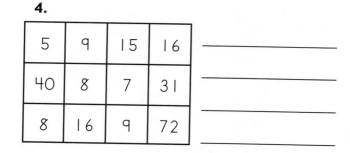

| 5 | 9 | 15 | 16 |
|---|---|----|----|
| 40 | 8 | 7 | 31 |
| 8 | 16 | 9 | 72 |

_____
_____
_____

**5.**

| 35 | 15 | 50 | 4 |
|----|----|----|---|
| 35 | 2 | 80 | 35 |
| 70 | 20 | 25 | 60 |

_____
_____
_____

**6.**

| 90 | 3 | 15 | 75 |
|----|---|----|----|
| 30 | 40 | 90 | 12 |
| 40 | 80 | 5 | 60 |

_____
_____
_____

**7.**

| 65 | 75 | 5 | 45 |
|----|----|---|----|
| 80 | 35 | 45 | 15 |
| 15 | 90 | 70 | 2 |

_____
_____
_____

Elementary Algebra • CD-104106

Name _____     Date _____

# All Operations

**Directions:**
For each pair of numbers, find the sum, difference, product, and quotient. All answers should be positive whole numbers.

| | Numbers | Sum | Difference | Product | Quotient |
|---|---|---|---|---|---|
| 1. | 5, 10 | | | | |
| 2. | 10, 20 | | | | |
| 3. | 5, 15 | | | | |
| 4. | 15, 30 | | | | |
| 5. | 5, 25 | | | | |
| 6. | 10, 50 | | | | |
| 7. | 25, 100 | | | | |
| 8. | 20, 40 | | | | |
| 9. | 25, 75 | | | | |
| 10. | 20, 100 | | | | |
| 11. | 20, 80 | | | | |
| 12. | 100, 100 | | | | |
| 13. | 2, 100 | | | | |
| 14. | 10, 200 | | | | |
| 15. | 5, 500 | | | | |

## Select the Signs

**Number Relationships**

### Directions:

In each box, use one of each of these signs to complete a true equation: +, −, x, ÷.

| | |
|---|---|
| **1.** 25 ◯ 5 = 20 <br> 25 ◯ 5 = 5 <br> 25 ◯ 5 = 30 <br> 25 ◯ 5 = 125 | **2.** 50 ◯ 2 = 100 <br> 50 ◯ 2 = 52 <br> 50 ◯ 2 = 25 <br> 50 ◯ 2 = 48 |
| **3.** 100 ◯ 10 = 10 <br> 100 ◯ 10 = 90 <br> 100 ◯ 10 = 1,000 <br> 100 ◯ 10 = 110 | **4.** 500 ◯ 50 = 550 <br> 500 ◯ 50 = 25,000 <br> 500 ◯ 50 = 450 <br> 500 ◯ 50 = 10 |
| **5.** 200 ◯ 25 = 5,000 <br> 200 ◯ 25 = 8 <br> 200 ◯ 25 = 175 <br> 200 ◯ 25 = 225 | **6.** 150 ◯ 15 = 135 <br> 150 ◯ 15 = 165 <br> 150 ◯ 15 = 10 <br> 150 ◯ 15 = 2,250 |
| **7.** 1,000 ◯ 250 = 750 <br> 1,000 ◯ 250 = 250,000 <br> 1,000 ◯ 250 = 1,250 <br> 1,000 ◯ 250 = 4 | **8.** 500 ◯ 250 = 2 <br> 500 ◯ 250 = 125,000 <br> 500 ◯ 250 = 250 <br> 500 ◯ 250 = 750 |
| **9.** 400 ◯ 100 = 40,000 <br> 400 ◯ 100 = 300 <br> 400 ◯ 100 = 500 <br> 400 ◯ 100 = 4 | **10.** 120 ◯ 6 = 126 <br> 120 ◯ 6 = 20 <br> 120 ◯ 6 = 114 <br> 120 ◯ 6 = 720 |

Name _____    Date _____

# Be a Math Detective

## Directions:

To figure out the mysterious number partners, make a list to see which numbers fit both descriptions. Write the number partners in the boxes.

**Example:**

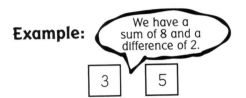

We have a sum of 8 and a difference of 2.

| 3 | 5 |

| sum of 8 | difference |
|---|---|
| 0 + 8 | 8 |
| 1 + 7 | 7 |
| 2 + 6 | 4 |
| 3 + 5 | 2 |
| 4 + 4 | 0 |

1. 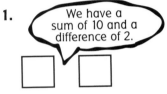 We have a sum of 10 and a difference of 2.

| sum of 10 | difference |
|---|---|
| | |

2.  We have a sum of 11 and a difference of 5.

| sum of 11 | difference |
|---|---|
| | |

3. We have a sum of 12 and a difference of 0.

| sum of 12 | difference |
|---|---|
| | |

4.  We have a sum of 13 and a difference of 5.

| sum of 13 | difference |
|---|---|
| | |

5. 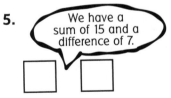 We have a sum of 15 and a difference of 7.

| sum of 15 | difference |
|---|---|
| | |

6. 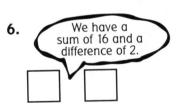 We have a sum of 16 and a difference of 2.

| sum of 16 | difference |
|---|---|
| | |

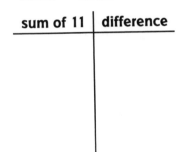
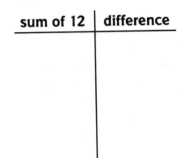

Name _____  Date _____

# Who Are We?

## Directions:

Use the clues to figure out the number partners.

1.
Our sum is 14.
Our product is 48.

2.
Our sum is 12.
Our product is 35.

3.
Our sum is 12.
Our product is 32.

4.
Our sum is 12.
Our product is 27.

5.
Our sum is 14.
Our product is 45.

6.
Our sum is 16.
Our product is 60.

7.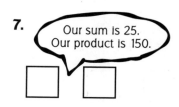
Our sum is 25.
Our product is 150.

8.
Our sum is 24.
Our product is 144.

9.
Our sum is 35.
Our product is 250.

10.
Our difference is 2.
Our product is 15.

11.
Our difference is 2.
Our product is 24.

12.
Our difference is 3.
Our product is 40.

13.
Our difference is 0.
Our product is 81.

14.
Our difference is 5.
Our product is 50.

15.
Our difference is 3.
Our product is 54.

16. Our difference is 3.
Our product is 28.

17.
Our difference is 11.
Our product is 42.

18.
Our difference is 10.
Our product is 200.

Name _____     Date _____

# Be a Math Magician

**Directions:**
Make the correct number partners appear in the spaces below.

1.  sum of 10
    quotient of 4

    ☐ ☐

2.  sum of 16
    quotient of 3

    ☐ ☐

3.  sum of 15
    quotient of 2

    ☐ ☐

4.  sum of 9
    quotient of 2

    ☐ ☐

5.  sum of 5
    quotient of 4

    ☐ ☐

6.  sum of 6
    quotient of 1

    ☐ ☐

7.  sum of 12
    quotient of 2

    ☐ ☐

8.  sum of 20
    quotient of 3

    ☐ ☐

9.  sum of 42
    quotient of 5

    ☐ ☐

10. difference of 2
    quotient of 2

    ○ ○

11. difference of 8
    quotient of 5

    ○ ○

12. difference of 4
    quotient of 3

    ○ ○

13. difference of 6
    quotient of 2

    ○ ○

14. difference of 12
    quotient of 5

    ○ ○

15. difference of 12
    quotient of 4

    ○ ○

16. difference of 9
    quotient of 4

    ○ ○

17. difference of 7
    quotient of 8

    ○ ○

18. difference of 0
    quotient of 1

    ○ ○

# Make Your Own Math

**Number Relationships**

## Directions:

Pick two numbers and fill in the two clues about them. Record your numbers at the bottom of the page. Fold the bottom under so that it cannot be seen and have a friend try to figure out your numbers. Then, check your friend's answers.

1.  **sum of** _____

    **difference of** _____

    ☐ ☐

2.  **sum of** _____

    **product of** _____

    ☐ ☐

3.  **sum of** _____

    **quotient of** _____

    ☐ ☐

4.  **difference of** _____

    **sum of** _____

    ☐ ☐

5.  **difference of** _____

    **product of** _____

    ☐ ☐

6.  **difference of** _____

    **quotient of** _____

    ☐ ☐

7.  **product of** _____

    **sum of** _____

    ☐ ☐

8.  **product of** _____

    **difference of** _____

    ☐ ☐

9.  **product of** _____

    **quotient of** _____

    ☐ ☐

10. **quotient of** _____

    **sum of** _____

    ☐ ☐

11. **quotient of** _____

    **difference of** _____

    ☐ ☐

12. **quotient of** _____

    **product of** _____

    ☐ ☐

- - - - - - - - - - - - - - - - - - - - - - - - - - - - - - - - - - - -

**Answers**

1.                    2.                    3.

4.                    5.                    6.

7.                    8.                    9.

10.                   11.                   12.

Name ______________________________ Date ____________________

# Troubling Triangles

**Writing Equations**

**Directions:**
Fill in the blanks for each number sentence with numbers from the triangle. A number may be used more than once.

**Example:**

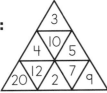

3 + 7 = 12 − 2

4 x 2 = 3 + 5

20 − 10 = 20 ÷ 2

**1.**

___ + ___ = ___ − ___

___ x ___ = ___ + ___

___ − ___ = ___ ÷ ___

**2.**

___ + ___ = ___ − ___

___ x ___ = ___ + ___

___ − ___ = ___ ÷ ___

**3.**

___ + ___ = ___ − ___

___ x ___ = ___ + ___

___ − ___ = ___ ÷ ___

**4.**

___ + ___ = ___ − ___

___ x ___ = ___ + ___

___ − ___ = ___ ÷ ___

**5.**

___ + ___ = ___ − ___

___ x ___ = ___ + ___

___ − ___ = ___ ÷ ___

**6.**

___ + ___ = ___ − ___

___ x ___ = ___ + ___

___ − ___ = ___ ÷ ___

**7.**

___ + ___ = ___ − ___

___ x ___ = ___ + ___

___ − ___ = ___ ÷ ___

**8.**

___ + ___ = ___ − ___

___ x ___ = ___ + ___

___ − ___ = ___ ÷ ___

**9.**

___ + ___ = ___ − ___

___ x ___ = ___ + ___

___ − ___ = ___ ÷ ___

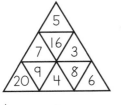

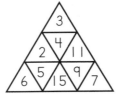

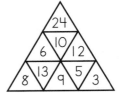

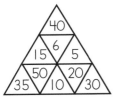

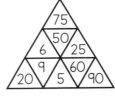

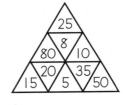

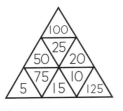

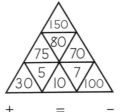

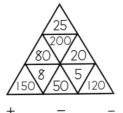

Name ______________________ Date ______________

# Mystery Signs

Number Relationships

**Directions:**
Fill in the circles in the equations with any of these signs so that the equations are true: +, −, x, ÷.

1. 20 ◯ 4 = 12 ◯ 4
2. 7 ◯ 2 = 18 ◯ 2
3. 5 ◯ 4 = 12 ◯ 8
4. 15 ◯ 5 = 30 ◯ 10
5. 16 ◯ 4 = 24 ◯ 4
6. 24 ◯ 6 = 9 ◯ 2
7. 12 ◯ 2 = 4 ◯ 2
8. 6 ◯ 4 = 20 ◯ 10
9. 18 ◯ 9 = 18 ◯ 2
10. 8 ◯ 3 = 6 ◯ 4
11. 20 ◯ 8 = 4 ◯ 7
12. 6 ◯ 2 = 60 ◯ 5
13. 8 ◯ 3 = 30 ◯ 6
14. 30 ◯ 6 = 20 ◯ 4
15. 40 ◯ 5 = 4 ◯ 2
16. 28 ◯ 7 = 12 ◯ 8
17. 50 ◯ 50 = 10 ◯ 10
18. 60 ◯ 40 = 100 ◯ 5
19. 10 ◯ 5 = 100 ◯ 50
20. 75 ◯ 5 = 20 ◯ 5
21. 40 ◯ 5 = 20 ◯ 10
22. 20 ◯ 5 = 32 ◯ 8

Name _____     Date _____

# Fun with Fours

**Number Relationships**

## Directions:

Working from left to right, fill in the circles with +, −, x, or ÷ to make the given answer. You may need to add parentheses to comply with the order of operations.

**Example:**     (4 ( + ) 4) ( ÷ )4   makes 2

1.   4 ( ) 4 ( ) 4   makes 32

2.   4 ( ) 4 ( ) 4   makes 20

3.   4 ( ) 4 ( ) 4   makes 64

4.   4 ( ) 4 ( ) 4   makes 5

5.   4 ( ) 4 ( ) 4   makes −3

6.   4 ( ) 4 ( ) 4   makes $\frac{1}{4}$

7.   4 ( ) 4 ( ) 4   makes −4

8.   Two different ways:

4 ( ) 4 ( ) 4   makes 12

4 ( ) 4 ( ) 4   makes 12

9.   Two different ways:

4 ( ) 4 ( ) 4   makes 0

4 ( ) 4 ( ) 4   makes 0

10.   Four different ways:

4 ( ) 4 ( ) 4   makes 4

4 ( ) 4 ( ) 4   makes 4

4 ( ) 4 ( ) 4   makes 4

4 ( ) 4 ( ) 4   makes 4

         Elementary Algebra • CD-104106

Name ______________________ Date ______________

# Square Stumpers

Solving Number Problems

**Directions:**
Figure out what number each letter stands for. The rows add up to the numbers on the right. The columns add up to the numbers along the bottom.

**1.**

| | | | |
|---|---|---|---|
| A | B | B | 21 |
| A | 5 | B | 18 |
| A | A | 3 | 13 |
| 15 | 18 | 19 | |

A = ____

B = ____

**2.**

| | | | |
|---|---|---|---|
| 10 | 6 | D | 22 |
| D | D | 8 | 20 |
| 4 | E | E | 22 |
| 20 | 21 | 23 | |

D = ____

E = ____

**3.**

| | | | |
|---|---|---|---|
| F | G | 9 | 16 |
| H | 8 | F | 19 |
| 5 | G | G | 11 |
| 16 | 14 | 16 | |

F = ____

G = ____

H = ____

**4.**

| | | | |
|---|---|---|---|
| J | K | 8 | 30 |
| 6 | 8 | K | 24 |
| J | L | 12 | 39 |
| 30 | 33 | 30 | |

J = ____

K = ____

L = ____

**5.**

| | | | | |
|---|---|---|---|---|
| 15 | P | Q | 20 | 95 |
| 35 | M | 15 | 25 | 105 |
| 20 | 25 | N | 15 | 100 |
| N | 15 | 30 | P | 120 |
| 110 | 105 | 110 | 95 | |

M = ____

N = ____

P = ____

Q = ____

**6.**

| | | | | |
|---|---|---|---|---|
| U | 25 | 20 | 40 | 160 |
| 20 | 45 | R | 15 | 140 |
| 10 | S | 15 | U | 150 |
| T | 30 | 35 | 10 | 130 |
| 160 | 150 | 130 | 140 | |

R = ____

S = ____

T = ____

U = ____

Name ______________________ Date ______________

# Tricky Truths

Mathematical Relationships

**Directions:**
Circle the true equations below. N stands for any number except zero.

1. $N \times 1 = N$
2. $4 + N \neq N + 4$
3. $0 \times N = 0$
4. $N \div 1 = N$
5. $0 + N = N$
6. $N - N = 0$
7. $N \div N \neq 1$
8. $N + 6 = 6 + N$
9. $1 \times N \neq N$
10. $N - N = 1$
11. $N + 0 = N$
12. $N \div 1 = 1 + N$
13. $N - 0 \neq N$
14. $0 \div N = 0$
15. $N + 0 = 1 + N$
16. $N \times 0 = 0$
17. $N \times 1 = 1 + N$
18. $N - 0 = N$
19. $1 \times N = N$
20. $N \times 0 \neq 0$
21. $N \div N = 1$
22. $0 \times N = 1$
23. $0 + N \neq N$
24. $0 \div N = N$

## Tackle These Equations

### Directions:

Solve each equation. Get a touchdown in each box by circling the equation that has an answer of 6.

---

**1. Addition**

$75 + \underline{\hspace{1cm}} = 100$

$\underline{\hspace{1cm}} + 91 = 100$

$113 + \underline{\hspace{1cm}} = 120$

$95 + 95 = \underline{\hspace{1cm}}$

$150 = \underline{\hspace{1cm}} + 142$

$112 = \underline{\hspace{1cm}} + 56$

$75 = 69 + \underline{\hspace{1cm}}$

$\underline{\hspace{1cm}} = 88 + 72$

**2. Subtraction**

$100 - 92 = \underline{\hspace{1cm}}$

$\underline{\hspace{1cm}} - 10 = 170$

$150 - \underline{\hspace{1cm}} = 144$

$200 - \underline{\hspace{1cm}} = 130$

$75 = 100 - \underline{\hspace{1cm}}$

$\underline{\hspace{1cm}} = 230 - 223$

$43 = \underline{\hspace{1cm}} - 7$

$125 = 250 - \underline{\hspace{1cm}}$

---

**3. Multiplication**

$15 \times \underline{\hspace{1cm}} = 150$

$\underline{\hspace{1cm}} \times 5 = 125$

$8 \times \underline{\hspace{1cm}} = 240$

$\underline{\hspace{1cm}} \times 50 = 300$

$140 = \underline{\hspace{1cm}} \times 20$

$96 = \underline{\hspace{1cm}} \times 12$

$175 = 35 \times \underline{\hspace{1cm}}$

$\underline{\hspace{1cm}} = 20 \times 20$

**4. Division**

$100 \div 5 = \underline{\hspace{1cm}}$

$75 \div \underline{\hspace{1cm}} = 25$

$99 \div \underline{\hspace{1cm}} = 11$

$160 \div 20 = \underline{\hspace{1cm}}$

$30 = 180 \div \underline{\hspace{1cm}}$

$\underline{\hspace{1cm}} = 144 \div 36$

$50 = \underline{\hspace{1cm}} \div 4$

$\underline{\hspace{1cm}} = 210 \div 30$

---

## Times for Thought

**Mathematical Relationships**

**Directions:**
Fill in each circle with = or ≠. Try not to do any computing.

1.  10 x 40 ◯ 20 x 20

2.  20 x 30 ◯ 20 x 20

3.  5 x 100 ◯ 5 x 5 x 25

4.  30 x 30 ◯ 9 x 100

5.  5 x 2 x 100 ◯ 2 x 500

6.  10 x 50 ◯ 500 x 1

7.  10 x 50 ◯ 25 x 15

8.  60 x 10 ◯ 300 x 2

9.  10 x 30 ◯ 10 x 10 x 3

10.  20 x 40 ◯ 20 x 20 x 10

11.  5 x 5 x 4 ◯ 5 x 4 x 5

12.  5 x 20 ◯ 20 x 4

13.  20 x 40 ◯ 20 x 20 x 2

14.  200 x 10 ◯ 20 x 10 x 5

15.  100 x 10 ◯ 1,000 x 2

16.  30 x 40 ◯ 40 x 30

17.  40 x 30 ◯ 8 x 6 x 25

18.  10 x 50 ◯ 25 x 20

19.  30 x 20 ◯ 10 x 10 x 30

20.  5 x 5 x 4 ◯ 20 x 4

21.  6 x 50 ◯ 3 x 2 x 25

22.  40 x 30 ◯ 8 x 5 x 6

23.  30 x 30 ◯ 5 x 6 x 10

24.  60 x 8 ◯ 8 x 6 x 10

Name ______________________________ Date ______________

# Freaky Factors

Number Relationships

**Directions:**
The factors are missing in the equations below. Figure out what they must be to make the equations true. You may only use these numbers: 2, 3, 4, 5. You may use the numbers more than once in an equation.

**1.** ____ x ____ x ____ = 20

**2.** ____ x ____ x ____ = 18

**3.** ____ x ____ x ____ = 16

**4.** ____ x ____ x ____ = 36

**5.** ____ x ____ x ____ = 50

**6.** ____ x ____ x ____ = 30

**7.** ____ x ____ x ____ = 27

**8.** ____ x ____ x ____ = 32

**9.** ____ x ____ x ____ = 24

**10.** ____ x ____ x ____ = 100

**11.** ____ x ____ x ____ = 45

**12.** ____ x ____ x ____ = 40

**13.** ____ x ____ x ____ = 64

**14.** ____ x ____ x ____ = 60

**15.** ____ x ____ x ____ = 80

**16.** ____ x ____ x ____ = 75

**17.** ____ x ____ x ____ = 48

**18.** ____ x ____ x ____ = 125

Name ______________________________ Date ______________

# Using Inverse Operations

Solving Equations

**Directions:**

Solve these equations using inverse operations. Then, check your work.

**Example:**

$$\begin{aligned} 2n + 4 &= 10 \\ -4 &\quad -4 \\ 2n &= 6 \\ \div 2 &\quad \div 2 \\ n &= \underline{3} \end{aligned}$$

check $(3 \times 2) + 4 = 10$

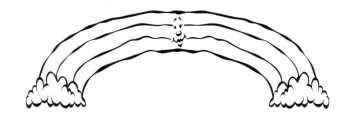

| | | |
|---|---|---|
| **1.** $3n + 2 = 11$<br>n = _____<br>check ______________ | **2.** $2n - 3 = 15$<br>n = _____<br>check ______________ | **3.** $20 + 2n = 34$<br>n = _____<br>check ______________ |
| **4.** $4n - 5 = 11$<br>n = _____<br>check ______________ | **5.** $7 + 5n = 17$<br>n = _____<br>check ______________ | **6.** $2n \div 3 = 4$<br>n = _____<br>check ______________ |
| **7.** $21 = 3n + 6$<br>n = _____<br>check ______________ | **8.** $19 = 3 + 2n$<br>n = _____<br>check ______________ | **9.** $5 = 8n - 3$<br>n = _____<br>check ______________ |
| **10.** $15 = 3n \div 2$<br>n = _____<br>check ______________ | **11.** $16 = 5n - 4$<br>n = _____<br>check ______________ | **12.** $22 = 6n - 8$<br>n = _____<br>check ______________ |

Name _____     Date _____

# Arithmewoman vs. Algebraman

## Directions:
Circle the person's name who has the correct solution to the equation.

1.  $n - 30 = 5$
    Arithmewoman says 35.
    Algebraman says 25.

2.  $75 = 25 + n$
    Arithmewoman says 100.
    Algebraman says 50.

3.  $3n = 30$
    Arithmewoman says 10.
    Algebraman says 90.

4.  $40 = 5n$
    Arithmewoman says 8.
    Algebraman says 200.

5.  $n + 9 = 50$
    Arithmewoman says 59.
    Algebraman says 41.

6.  $5 = 50 - n$
    Arithmewoman says 55.
    Algebraman says 45.

7.  $n \div 3 = 10$
    Arithmewoman says 30.
    Algebraman says 13.

8.  $6 = 120 \div n$
    Arithmewoman says 720.
    Algebraman says 20.

9.  $2n + 3 = 15$
    Arithmewoman says 6.
    Algebraman says 9.

10.  $23 = 3n + 5$
    Arithmewoman says 28.
    Algebraman says 6.

11.  $6 + 3n = 18$
    Arithmewoman says 8.
    Algebraman says 4.

12.  $4 = 2n - 6$
    Arithmewoman says 10.
    Algebraman says 5.

13.  $20 - 2n = 8$
    Arithmewoman says 6.
    Algebraman says 7.

14.  $8 = 5n - 2$
    Arithmewoman says 2.
    Algebraman says 1.

15.  $6n - 1 = 17$
    Arithmewoman says 5.
    Algebraman says 3.

16.  $20 = 4 + 4n$
    Arithmewoman says 5.
    Algebraman says 4.

Name _____   Date _____

## Many Answers

**Directions:**
On the line beside each equation, write what numbers n can be to make a true equation.

**Example:**

$6 + 4 > n$     _any number less than 10_

$6 + 4 < n$     _any number greater than 10_

$6 + 4 = n$     _10_

**1.**   $5 + n > 12$ _____

     $5 + n < 12$ _____

     $5 + n = 12$ _____

**2.**   $9 - n > 3$ _____

     $9 - n < 3$ _____

     $9 - n = 3$ _____

**3.**   $n - 4 > 5$ _____

     $n - 4 < 5$ _____

     $n - 4 = 5$ _____

**4.**   $5 \times 9 > n$ _____

     $5 \times 9 < n$ _____

     $5 \times 9 = n$ _____

**5.**   $n \times 7 > 28$ _____

     $n \times 7 < 28$ _____

     $n \times 7 = 28$ _____

**6.**   $6 \times n > 18$ _____

     $6 \times n < 18$ _____

     $6 \times n = 18$ _____

# Write Your Own Equations

**Mathematical Relationships**

## Directions:

Read an equation. Write three equations about the same relationship.

**Example:**   $A + B = C$       $\underline{B + A = C}$   $\underline{C - B = A}$   $\underline{B = C - A}$

1.    $D + E = F$                 _____    _____    _____

2.    $G - H = J$                 _____    _____    _____

3.    $K \times L = M$            _____    _____    _____

4.    $N \div P = Q$              _____    _____    _____

5.    $R = S + T$                 _____    _____    _____

6.    $U = V - W$                 _____    _____    _____

7.    $X = Y \times Z$            _____    _____    _____

8.    $A = B \div C$              _____    _____    _____

9.    $D + E = 10$                _____    _____    _____

10.   $F - G = 12$                _____    _____    _____

11.   $H \times J = 50$           _____    _____    _____

12.   $K \div L = 6$              _____    _____    _____

# Equations and Their Relatives

## Directions:

Neither A nor B is zero or negative. If A + B = C, which equations are always true? Circle them.

| | | | |
|---|---|---|---|
| A = A | A = C − B | C + B < A | A − B = A − B |
| B = C | A = B − C | C + B > A | A + B = C + B |
| A > B | C − A = B | C + A < B | A + B = B + A |
| B > A | B − C = A | C + A > B | A − B = C + B |
| C > A | A − B = C | A + B < C | A + B = C − B |
| C < B | C = B + A | A + B > C | A + B < C + B |

• • • • • • • • • • • • • • • • • • • • • • • • • • • • • • • • • • • • • •

## Directions:

Neither D nor E is zero or one, or is negative. If D x E = F, which equations are always true? Circle them.

| | | | |
|---|---|---|---|
| D > E | E x D = F | E x F > D | D x E = E x D |
| D < F | F ÷ E = D | D x E > F | D x F = E x F |
| D = E | E ÷ F = D | F ÷ E > D | D x E x F = F x E x D |
| F > E | F = D x E | D ÷ E < F | F ÷ E = F ÷ E |
| E = F | F x E = D | D x F > E | F ÷ D = F ÷ E |
| E > F | E = F ÷ D | F ÷ D < E | F x F > E x E |

Name ______________________ Date ______________

# Choose Your Answer

Solving Equations

**Directions:**
Solve each equation. Find the solution below and shade it in. Use each solution once.

1. 3 + 7 = _____ x 5
2. 6 + 3 = _____ ÷ 4
3. 9 + _____ = 6 + 6
4. 7 x _____ = 10 + 11
5. 15 − 7 = 4 + _____
6. _____ ÷ 5 = 40 ÷ 10
7. 5 x 4 = 12 + _____
8. 2 x 15 = _____ − 4
9. 20 − _____ = 9 x 2
10. _____ + 9 = 6 x 5
11. 50 ÷ 5 = 3 + _____
12. 42 ÷ _____ = 15 − 8
13. _____ x 6 = 2 x 12
14. 3 x 8 = _____ + 10
15. 10 − 4 = 48 ÷ _____
16. 16 ÷ _____ = 40 ÷ 5
17. 35 ÷ _____ = 12 − 7
18. 20 − _____ = 24 ÷ 2
19. 15 + _____ = 9 x 4
20. 24 + 24 = 4 x _____
21. _____ x 4 = 32 ÷ 2
22. 14 + 26 = _____ x 8
23. 20 − 8 = _____ + 5
24. 16 − 8 = 72 ÷ _____

| | | | | | | | | | | | |
|---|---|---|---|---|---|---|---|---|---|---|---|
| 7 | 8 | 3 | 14 | 21 | 4 | 7 | 12 | 2 | 34 | 4 | 5 |
| 9 | 21 | 2 | 36 | 2 | 8 | 6 | 4 | 3 | 20 | 7 | 8 |

# Complete Each Equation

Writing Equations

**Directions:**

Fill in the blanks to make true equations. Do not use zero or one. Make each equation different.

1. ___ + ___ = ___ + ___

   ___ + ___ = ___ + ___

   ___ + ___ = ___ + ___

2. ___ + ___ = ___ − ___

   ___ + ___ = ___ − ___

   ___ + ___ = ___ − ___

3. ___ + ___ = ___ x ___

   ___ + ___ = ___ x ___

   ___ + ___ = ___ x ___

4. ___ + ___ = ___ ÷ ___

   ___ + ___ = ___ ÷ ___

   ___ + ___ = ___ ÷ ___

5. ___ − ___ = ___ − ___

   ___ − ___ = ___ − ___

   ___ − ___ = ___ − ___

6. ___ − ___ = ___ x ___

   ___ − ___ = ___ x ___

   ___ − ___ = ___ x ___

7. ___ − ___ = ___ ÷ ___

   ___ − ___ = ___ ÷ ___

   ___ − ___ = ___ ÷ ___

8. ___ x ___ = ___ x ___

   ___ x ___ = ___ x ___

   ___ x ___ = ___ x ___

9. ___ x ___ = ___ ÷ ___

   ___ x ___ = ___ ÷ ___

   ___ x ___ = ___ ÷ ___

10. ___ ÷ ___ = ___ ÷ ___

    ___ ÷ ___ = ___ ÷ ___

    ___ ÷ ___ = ___ ÷ ___

Name ______________________________ Date ______________

# Letter Puzzles

Solving Equations

**Directions:**
Solve the equations to figure out what number each letter stands for.

| | |
|---|---|
| **1.**<br>$A + A + A + A = 100$<br>$A + B = 30$<br>$B + B + C + C + C = 40$<br><br>A = _____ B = _____ C = _____ | **2.**<br>$D + E + F = 80$<br>$E + E + E = 75$<br>$F + E + E = 65$<br><br>D = _____ E = _____ F = _____ |
| **3.**<br>$G + H = 120$<br>$H - I = 40$<br>$G + G + G + G + G = 250$<br><br>G = _____ H = _____ I = _____ | **4.**<br>$J = K + L$<br>$50 = J - 30$<br>$195 = J + J + K$<br><br>J = _____ K = _____ L = _____ |
| **5.**<br>$75 = P + N$<br>$40 = M - N$<br>$45 = N + 30$<br><br>M = _____ N = _____ P = _____ | **6.**<br>$75 = R - S$<br>$75 = 3 \times S$<br>$170 = R + Q$<br><br>Q = _____ R = _____ S = _____ |
| **7.**<br>$T = 4 \times V$<br>$T - U = 30$<br>$80 = V + 60$<br><br>T = _____ U = _____ V = _____ | **8.**<br>$Z \div 4 = Y$<br>$W + Y + Y = Z$<br>$60 = Z - 40$<br><br>W = _____ Y = _____ Z = _____ |

Name ______________________________ Date ______________

# Watch Out for Negative Numbers!

Solving Equations

**Directions:**
Fill in the table for each equation. Then, tell what pattern you see in the △ numbers.

**Example:** 8 + □ = 12 − △

pattern −1

| □ | 0 | 1 | 2 | 3 | 4 | 5 | 6 | 7 | 8 | 9 | 10 |
|---|---|---|---|---|---|---|---|---|---|---|---|
| △ | 4 | 3 | 2 | 1 | 0 | −1 | −2 | −3 | −4 | −5 | −6 |

**1.** 2 x □ = 12 − △

pattern ________

| □ | 0 | 1 | 2 | 3 | 4 | 5 | 6 | 7 | 8 | 9 | 10 |
|---|---|---|---|---|---|---|---|---|---|---|---|
| △ | | | | | | | | | | | |

**2.** 3 x □ = 6 + △

pattern ________

| □ | 0 | 1 | 2 | 3 | 4 | 5 | 6 | 7 | 8 | 9 | 10 |
|---|---|---|---|---|---|---|---|---|---|---|---|
| △ | | | | | | | | | | | |

**3.** 2 + □ = 8 + △

pattern ________

| □ | 0 | 1 | 2 | 3 | 4 | 5 | 6 | 7 | 8 | 9 | 10 |
|---|---|---|---|---|---|---|---|---|---|---|---|
| △ | | | | | | | | | | | |

**4.** 4 x □ = 10 − △

pattern ________

| □ | 0 | 1 | 2 | 3 | 4 | 5 | 6 | 7 | 8 | 9 | 10 |
|---|---|---|---|---|---|---|---|---|---|---|---|
| △ | | | | | | | | | | | |

**5.** 3 + □ = 6 − △

pattern ________

| □ | 0 | 1 | 2 | 3 | 4 | 5 | 6 | 7 | 8 | 9 | 10 |
|---|---|---|---|---|---|---|---|---|---|---|---|
| △ | | | | | | | | | | | |

**6.** 6 x □ = 5 + △

pattern ________

| □ | 0 | 1 | 2 | 3 | 4 | 5 | 6 | 7 | 8 | 9 | 10 |
|---|---|---|---|---|---|---|---|---|---|---|---|
| △ | | | | | | | | | | | |

**7.** 3 x □ = 9 − △

pattern ________

| □ | 0 | 1 | 2 | 3 | 4 | 5 | 6 | 7 | 8 | 9 | 10 |
|---|---|---|---|---|---|---|---|---|---|---|---|
| △ | | | | | | | | | | | |

# Watch Out for Fractions!

**Solving Equations**

## Directions:

Fill in the table for each equation. Then, tell what pattern you see in the △ numbers.

**Example:** $1 + \square = 2 \times \triangle$

pattern ___+ $\frac{1}{2}$___

| □ | 0 | 1 | 2 | 3 | 4 | 5 | 6 | 7 | 8 | 9 | 10 |
|---|---|---|---|---|---|---|---|---|---|---|---|
| △ | $\frac{1}{2}$ | 1 | $1\frac{1}{2}$ | 2 | $2\frac{1}{2}$ | 3 | $3\frac{1}{2}$ | 4 | $4\frac{1}{2}$ | 5 | $5\frac{1}{2}$ |

**1.** $6 - \square = 2 \times \triangle$

pattern _____

| □ | 0 | 1 | 2 | 3 | 4 | 5 | 6 | 7 | 8 | 9 | 10 |
|---|---|---|---|---|---|---|---|---|---|---|---|
| △ | | | | | | | | | | | |

**2.** $8 + \square = 3 \times \triangle$

pattern _____

| □ | 0 | 1 | 2 | 3 | 4 | 5 | 6 | 7 | 8 | 9 | 10 |
|---|---|---|---|---|---|---|---|---|---|---|---|
| △ | | | | | | | | | | | |

**3.** $4 + \square = 4 \times \triangle$

pattern _____

| □ | 0 | 1 | 2 | 3 | 4 | 5 | 6 | 7 | 8 | 9 | 10 |
|---|---|---|---|---|---|---|---|---|---|---|---|
| △ | | | | | | | | | | | |

**4.** $5 - \square = 5 \times \triangle$

pattern _____

| □ | 0 | 1 | 2 | 3 | 4 | 5 | 6 | 7 | 8 | 9 | 10 |
|---|---|---|---|---|---|---|---|---|---|---|---|
| △ | | | | | | | | | | | |

**5.** $3 + \square = 2 \times \triangle$

pattern _____

| □ | 0 | 1 | 2 | 3 | 4 | 5 | 6 | 7 | 8 | 9 | 10 |
|---|---|---|---|---|---|---|---|---|---|---|---|
| △ | | | | | | | | | | | |

**6.** $12 - \square = 3 \times \triangle$

pattern _____

| □ | 0 | 1 | 2 | 3 | 4 | 5 | 6 | 7 | 8 | 9 | 10 |
|---|---|---|---|---|---|---|---|---|---|---|---|
| △ | | | | | | | | | | | |

**7.** $10 + \square = 6 \times \triangle$

pattern _____

| □ | 0 | 1 | 2 | 3 | 4 | 5 | 6 | 7 | 8 | 9 | 10 |
|---|---|---|---|---|---|---|---|---|---|---|---|
| △ | | | | | | | | | | | |

Name _____     Date _____

# Solving Two Equations

**Directions:**
Complete the table for the first equation. Circle the values that will also work for the second equation. Then, write the x and y values in the blanks.

**Example:**   $x + y = 12$   $x = 7$

$x - y = 2$   $y = 5$

| x | 0 | 1 | 2 | 3 | 4 | 5 | 6 | 7 | 8 | 9 | 10 |
|---|---|---|---|---|---|---|---|---|---|---|----|
| y | 12 | 11 | 10 | 9 | 8 | 7 | 6 | 5 | 4 | 3 | 2 |

1.   $x + 10 = y$   $x = $ ____

$2x = y$   $y = $ ____

| x | 0 | 1 | 2 | 3 | 4 | 5 | 6 | 7 | 8 | 9 | 10 |
|---|---|---|---|---|---|---|---|---|---|---|----|
| y |   |   |   |   |   |   |   |   |   |   |    |

2.   $6x = 2y$   $x = $ ____

$y + x = 16$   $y = $ ____

| x | 0 | 1 | 2 | 3 | 4 | 5 | 6 | 7 | 8 | 9 | 10 |
|---|---|---|---|---|---|---|---|---|---|---|----|
| y |   |   |   |   |   |   |   |   |   |   |    |

3.   $x - 5 = y$   $x = $ ____

$2y + 1 = x$   $y = $ ____

| x | 0 | 1 | 2 | 3 | 4 | 5 | 6 | 7 | 8 | 9 | 10 |
|---|---|---|---|---|---|---|---|---|---|---|----|
| y |   |   |   |   |   |   |   |   |   |   |    |

4.   $5x = y$   $x = $ ____

$x + y = 30$   $y = $ ____

| x | 0 | 1 | 2 | 3 | 4 | 5 | 6 | 7 | 8 | 9 | 10 |
|---|---|---|---|---|---|---|---|---|---|---|----|
| y |   |   |   |   |   |   |   |   |   |   |    |

5.   $y + 3 = x$   $x = $ ____

$x = 2y$   $y = $ ____

| x | 0 | 1 | 2 | 3 | 4 | 5 | 6 | 7 | 8 | 9 | 10 |
|---|---|---|---|---|---|---|---|---|---|---|----|
| y |   |   |   |   |   |   |   |   |   |   |    |

6.   $2x = y$   $x = $ ____

$x + y = 18$   $y = $ ____

| x | 0 | 1 | 2 | 3 | 4 | 5 | 6 | 7 | 8 | 9 | 10 |
|---|---|---|---|---|---|---|---|---|---|---|----|
| y |   |   |   |   |   |   |   |   |   |   |    |

Name _____    Date _____

**Functions**

## Directions:

Math Mansion is a strange square house made entirely of numbers and symbols. Numbers enter Math Mansion at one corner and follow a path. When they come out at the opposite corner, they are changed. There are many different paths they can follow. Write the new number each number is changed into after following the path.

**Example:**

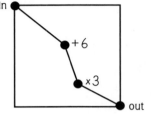

**On this path, if 5 goes in, 33 comes out.**
**(5 + 6 = 11; 11 x 3 = 33)**
**On this path, if 10 goes in, 48 comes out.**
**(10 + 6 = 16; 16 x 3 = 48)**

**1.**
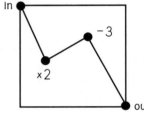

5 in, ____ out
10 in, ____ out
2 in, ____ out
−2 in, ____ out

**2.**
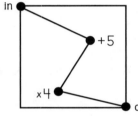

10 in, ____ out
2 in, ____ out
$\frac{1}{2}$ in, ____ out
1.5 in, ____ out

**3.**
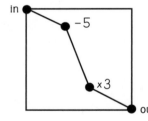

10 in, ____ out
20 in, ____ out
2 in, ____ out
6.5 in, ____ out

**4.**
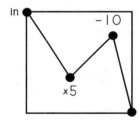

2 in, ____ out
8 in, ____ out
0.2 in, ____ out
50 in, ____ out

**5.**
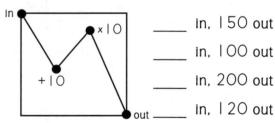

____ in, 150 out
____ in, 100 out
____ in, 200 out
____ in, 120 out

**6.**
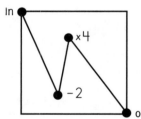

____ in, 12 out
____ in, 24 out
____ in, 32 out
____ in, 0 out

**7.**
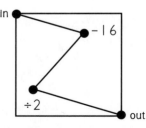

____ in, 4 out
____ in, 7 out
____ in, 13 out
____ in, 53 out

**8.**
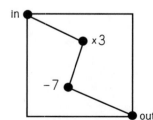

____ in, 2 out
____ in, 17 out
____ in, −1 out
____ in, 143 out

       **Elementary Algebra • CD-104106**

Name _____    Date _____

# More Marvelous Math Mansions

**Functions**

## Directions:

Draw the path each number must have followed through Math Mansion. Each path goes through two dots.

**1.**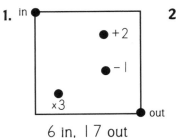

6 in, 17 out

**2.**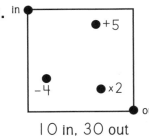

10 in, 30 out

**3.**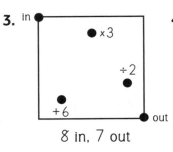

8 in, 7 out

**4.**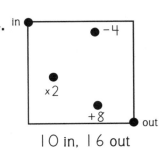

10 in, 16 out

**5.**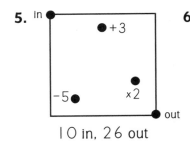

10 in, 26 out

**6.**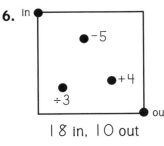

18 in, 10 out

**7.**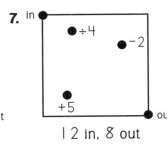

12 in, 8 out

**8.**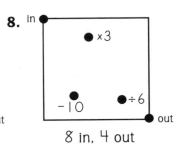

8 in, 4 out

**9.**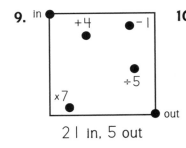

21 in, 5 out

**10.**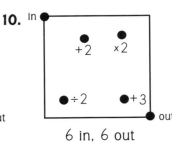

6 in, 6 out

**11.**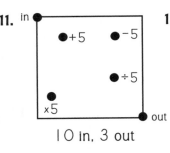

10 in, 3 out

**12.**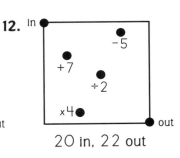

20 in, 22 out

**13.**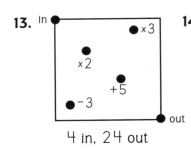

4 in, 24 out

**14.**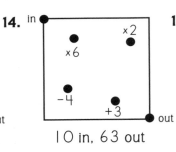

10 in, 63 out

**15.**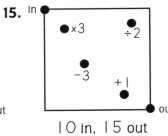

10 in, 15 out

**16.**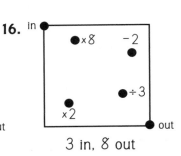

3 in, 8 out

# Mystery Graph

## Directions:
Locate each point on the graph with a dot and label the dot with the given letter. Then, connect the dots according to the directions below to reveal a mystery picture.

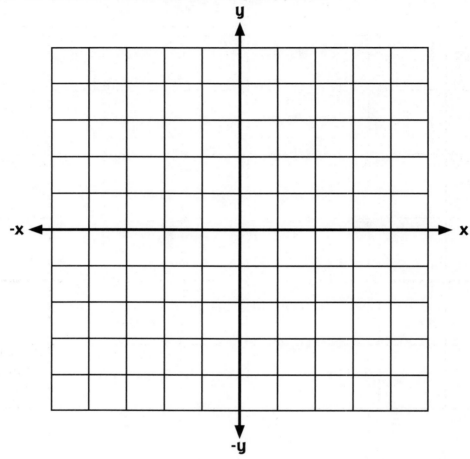

**A** (1, 3)   **B** (2, 4)   **C** (2, 3)   **D** (4, 2)   **E** (4, −1)
**F** (2, −2)   **G** (−2, −2)   **H** (−4, −1)   **I** (−4, 2)   **J** (−2, 3)
**K** (−2, 4)   **L** (−1, 3)   **M** (−2, 1)   **N** (0, 0)   **O** (2, 1)
**P** (−3, 0)   **Q** (3, 0)   **R** (−2, −1)   **S** (2, −1)   **T** (2, 2)
**U** (1, 2)   **V** (1, 1)   **W** (−1, 1)   **X** (−1, 2)   **Y** (−2, 2)

**Connect:**   A→B→C→D→E→F→G→H→I→J→K→L→A
**Connect:**   N→M, N→P, N→R, N→O, N→Q, N→S
**Connect:**   T→U→V→T
**Connect:**   W→X→Y→W

What is the mystery picture? _____

**Name** _____ **Date** _____

# A Map of Storybook Hills

**Directions:**
Write the ordered pair coordinate for each place shown on the map.

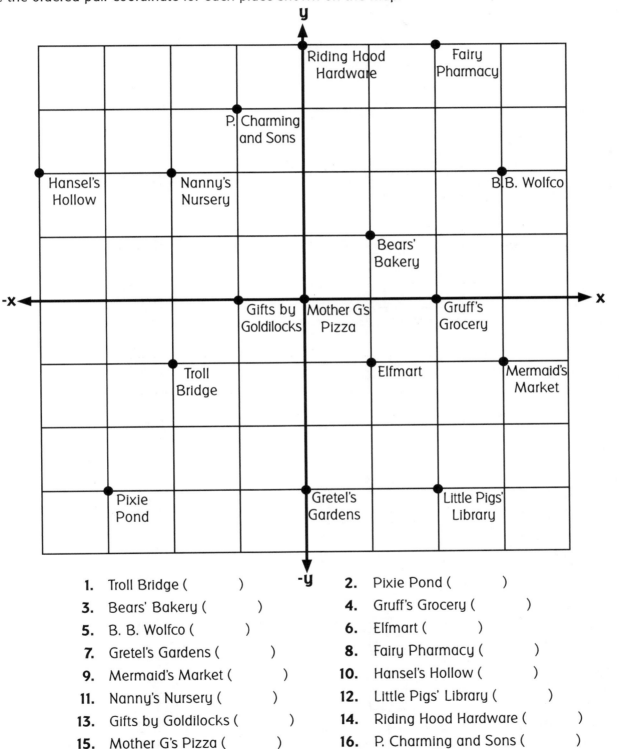

1. Troll Bridge ( )
2. Pixie Pond ( )
3. Bears' Bakery ( )
4. Gruff's Grocery ( )
5. B. B. Wolfco ( )
6. Elfmart ( )
7. Gretel's Gardens ( )
8. Fairy Pharmacy ( )
9. Mermaid's Market ( )
10. Hansel's Hollow ( )
11. Nanny's Nursery ( )
12. Little Pigs' Library ( )
13. Gifts by Goldilocks ( )
14. Riding Hood Hardware ( )
15. Mother G's Pizza ( )
16. P. Charming and Sons ( )

# Fast Food Graphs

## Directions:

Write an equation to go with each story. Fill in the tables for the given x values. Then, graph the equation.

**1.** Together, Irv (x) and Shane (y) bought 9 burgers.

equation: _____

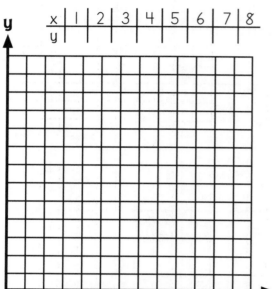

| x | 1 | 2 | 3 | 4 | 5 | 6 | 7 | 8 |
|---|---|---|---|---|---|---|---|---|
| y |   |   |   |   |   |   |   |   |

**2.** Steph had (x) toppings on her sundae. Emma (y) had 4 more toppings than Steph.

equation: _____

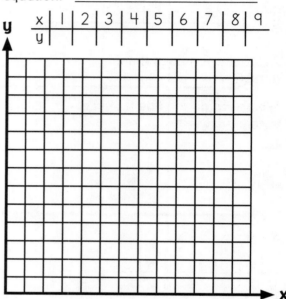

| x | 1 | 2 | 3 | 4 | 5 | 6 | 7 | 8 | 9 |
|---|---|---|---|---|---|---|---|---|---|
| y |   |   |   |   |   |   |   |   |   |

**3.** Charlie bought some tacos (x). He ate 3 and had (y) left.

equation: _____

| x | 4 | 5 | 6 | 7 | 8 | 9 | 10 | 11 | 12 |
|---|---|---|---|---|---|---|----|----|----|
| y |   |   |   |   |   |   |    |    |    |

**4.** Yin ordered fries (x). Candace ordered some (y) also. Yin had 2 more orders than Candace.

equation: _____

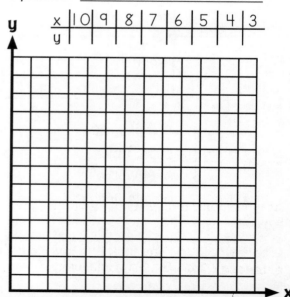

| x | 10 | 9 | 8 | 7 | 6 | 5 | 4 | 3 |
|---|----|---|---|---|---|---|---|---|
| y |    |   |   |   |   |   |   |   |

Name _____   Date _____

# Graphing Equations

Graphing Equations

**Directions:**
Fill in the tables for the given x values. Then, graph them and answer the questions.

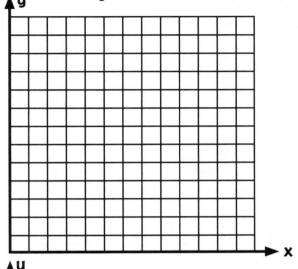

1. **x** + 2 = **y**

| x | 0 | 1 | 2 | 3 | 4 | 5 | 6 | 7 | 8 |
|---|---|---|---|---|---|---|---|---|---|
| y |   |   |   |   |   |   |   |   |   |

**At what point does the line intersect the y axis? (        )**

**Where would the line intersect the x axis if you extended it? (        )**

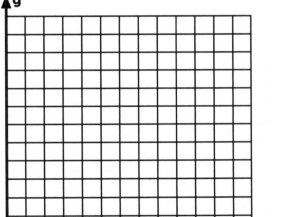

2. **x** + **y** = 6

| x | 0 | 1 | 2 | 3 | 4 | 5 | 6 |
|---|---|---|---|---|---|---|---|
| y |   |   |   |   |   |   |   |

**At what point are x and y equal?**
**(        )**

**What would y be if x = −2?**

_____

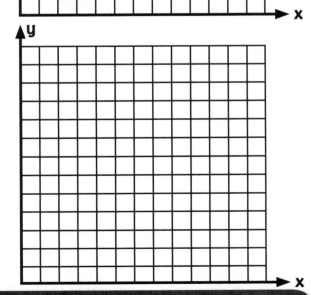

3. **x** − **y** = 4

| x | 4 | 5 | 6 | 7 | 8 | 9 | 10 |
|---|---|---|---|---|---|---|----|
| y |   |   |   |   |   |   |    |

**At what point does the line intersect the x axis? (        )**

**Where would the line intersect the y axis if you extended it? (        )**

     **Elementary Algebra • CD-104106**

# More Graphing Equations

## Directions:

Fill in the table for the given x values, then graph the equation.

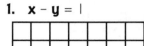

| x | 7 | 6 | 5 | 4 | 3 | 2 | 1 | 0 | -1 | -2 | -3 |
|---|---|---|---|---|---|---|---|---|----|----|----|
| y |   |   |   |   |   |   |   |   |    |    |    |

**1.  x – y = 1**

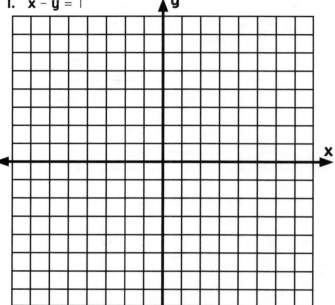

| x | -2 | -1 | 0 | 1 | 2 | 3 | 4 | 5 | 6 | 7 | 8 |
|---|----|----|---|---|---|---|---|---|---|---|---|
| y |    |    |   |   |   |   |   |   |   |   |   |

**2.  x + y = 3**

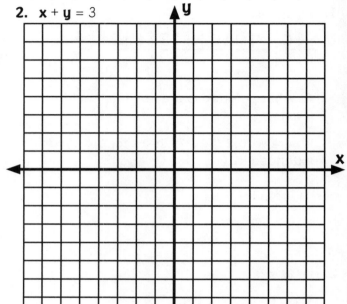

| x | -4 | -3 | -2 | -1 | 0 | 1 | 2 | 3 | 4 | 5 |
|---|----|----|----|----|---|---|---|---|---|---|
| y |    |    |    |    |   |   |   |   |   |   |

**3.  x = y**

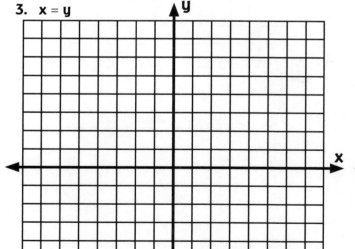

| x | -4 | -3 | -2 | -1 | 0 | 1 | 2 | 3 | 4 |
|---|----|----|----|----|---|---|---|---|---|
| y |    |    |    |    |   |   |   |   |   |

**4.  2x = y**

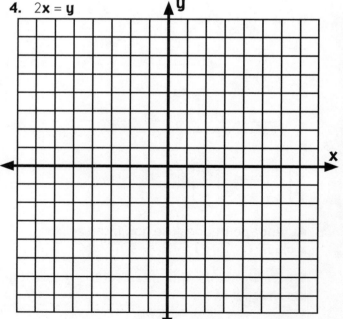

## What Is the Rule?

**Functions**

### Directions:

Look at each table. Figure out what rule is being used to relate x to y. Fill in the missing numbers for x and y. You may need to use inverse operations.

1.

| x | 1 | 2 | 6 |  | 10 |  | 15 | 40 |  |
|---|---|---|---|---|---|---|---|---|---|
| y | 3 | 4 |  | 10 |  | 14 |  | 50 | 100 |

Rule: _____

2.

| x | 1 | 5 | 10 |  | 15 |  |  | 35 | 70 | 100 |
|---|---|---|---|---|---|---|---|---|---|---|
| y | −3 | 1 | 6 | 9 |  | 20 | 28 |  |  |  |

Rule: _____

3.

| x | 5 | 7 | 10 |  | 20 |  | 30 |  |  | 100 |
|---|---|---|---|---|---|---|---|---|---|---|
| y | 15 | 21 | 30 | 45 |  | 75 |  | 150 | 225 |  |

Rule: _____

4.

| x | 4 | 10 | 16 |  | 30 |  |  | 70 |  | 150 |
|---|---|---|---|---|---|---|---|---|---|---|
| y | 2 | 5 | 8 | 10 |  | 20 | 25 |  | 50 |  |

Rule: _____

5.

| x | −20 | −1 | 7 | 10 | 23 |  | 56 |  | 81 |  |
|---|---|---|---|---|---|---|---|---|---|---|
| y | −11 | 8 | 16 |  |  | 43 |  | 75 |  | 105 |

Rule: _____

6.

| x | 10 | 20 | 30 |  | 60 |  | 95 |  | 110 |  |
|---|---|---|---|---|---|---|---|---|---|---|
| y | −15 | −5 | 5 | 15 |  | 48 |  | 80 |  | 100 |

Rule: _____

# Fascinating Functions

**Functions**

## Directions:
Use each function table to find the value of y.

1.
| x | y |
|---|---|
| 0 | 3 |
| 1 | 6 |
| 2 | 9 |
| 3 | 12 |
| 4 | 15 |

If x = 6,
**y** = ___.

2.
| x | y |
|---|---|
| 0 | 5 |
| 1 | 6 |
| 2 | 7 |
| 3 | 8 |
| 4 | 9 |

If x = 6,
**y** = ___.

3.
| x | y |
|---|---|
| 0 | 10 |
| 1 | 8 |
| 2 | 6 |
| 3 | 4 |
| 4 | 2 |

If x = 5,
**y** = ___.

4.
| x | y |
|---|---|
| 0 | 6 |
| 1 | 8 |
| 2 | 10 |
| 3 | 12 |
| 4 | 14 |

If x = 8,
**y** = ___.

5.
| x | y |
|---|---|
| 0 | 5 |
| 1 | 10 |
| 2 | 15 |
| 3 | 20 |
| 4 | 25 |

If x = 7,
**y** = ___.

6.
| x | y |
|---|---|
| 0 | 2 |
| 1 | 1 |
| 2 | 0 |
| 3 | -1 |
| 4 | -2 |

If x = 6,
**y** = ___.

7.
| x | y |
|---|---|
| 0 | 6 |
| 1 | 9 |
| 2 | 12 |
| 3 | 15 |
| 4 | 18 |

If x = 8,
**y** = ___.

8.
| x | y |
|---|---|
| 0 | 3 |
| 1 | 7 |
| 2 | 11 |
| 3 | 15 |
| 4 | 19 |

If x = 6,
**y** = ___.

9.
| x | y |
|---|---|
| 0 | 3 |
| 1 | 1 |
| 2 | -1 |
| 3 | -3 |
| 4 | -5 |

If x = 6,
**y** = ___.

10.
| x | y |
|---|---|
| 0 | 1 |
| 1 | 7 |
| 2 | 13 |
| 3 | 19 |
| 4 | 25 |

If x = 6,
**y** = ___.

11.
| x | y |
|---|---|
| 0 | 21 |
| 1 | 31 |
| 2 | 41 |
| 3 | 51 |
| 4 | 61 |

If x = 8,
**y** = ___.

12.
| x | y |
|---|---|
| 0 | -8 |
| 1 | -6 |
| 2 | -4 |
| 3 | -2 |
| 4 | 0 |

If x = 10,
**y** = ___.

# Formidable Functions

**Functions**

## Directions:
Circle the equation that goes with each table.

**1.**

| x | y |
|---|---|
| 0 | 3 |
| 1 | 4 |
| 2 | 5 |
| 3 | 6 |
| 4 | 7 |
| 5 | 8 |

$3x = y$
$x + 3 = y$
$x - 3 = y$
$2x + 1 = y$

**2.**

| x | y |
|---|---|
| 1 | 9 |
| 2 | 8 |
| 3 | 7 |
| 4 | 6 |
| 5 | 5 |
| 6 | 4 |

$10 - x = y$
$x + 8 = y$
$x - y = 8$
$4x = y$

**3.**

| x | y |
|---|---|
| 5 | 0 |
| 6 | 1 |
| 7 | 2 |
| 8 | 3 |
| 9 | 4 |
| 10 | 5 |

$y = 2x$
$x - y = 5$
$x + y = 5$
$2x + y = 3$

**4.**

| x | y |
|---|---|
| 4 | 0 |
| 5 | 1 |
| 6 | 2 |
| 7 | 3 |
| 8 | 4 |
| 9 | 5 |

$x + 4 = y$
$y - 4 = x$
$2x = y$
$x = y + 4$

**5.**

| x | y |
|---|---|
| 1 | 2 |
| 2 | 4 |
| 3 | 6 |
| 4 | 8 |
| 5 | 10 |
| 6 | 12 |

$y = 2x$
$x + 1 = y$
$2y = x$
$y - 2 = x$

**6.**

| x | y |
|---|---|
| 0 | 0 |
| 1 | 3 |
| 2 | 6 |
| 3 | 9 |
| 4 | 12 |
| 5 | 15 |

$y - x = 2$
$x + y = 4$
$y + 2x = 3$
$y = 3x$

**7.**

| x | y |
|---|---|
| 8 | 0 |
| 9 | 1 |
| 10 | 2 |
| 11 | 3 |
| 12 | 4 |
| 13 | 5 |

$x + y = 8$
$x + 3 = y$
$x - y = 8$
$y = 8x$

**8.**

| x | y |
|---|---|
| 0 | 20 |
| 1 | 19 |
| 2 | 18 |
| 3 | 17 |
| 4 | 16 |
| 5 | 15 |

$x + 20 = y$
$x + y = 20$
$y - x = 20$
$4x = y$

**9.**

| x | y |
|---|---|
| 0 | 8 |
| 1 | 9 |
| 2 | 10 |
| 3 | 11 |
| 4 | 12 |
| 5 | 13 |

$x + y = 8$
$y = x + 2$
$y = x + 8$
$y = 2x$

**10.**

| x | y |
|---|---|
| 0 | 1 |
| 1 | 5 |
| 2 | 9 |
| 3 | 13 |
| 4 | 17 |
| 5 | 21 |

$x + 4 = y$
$4x = y$
$y - 4 = x$
$4x + 1 = y$

**11.**

| x | y |
|---|---|
| 0 | 6 |
| 1 | 8 |
| 2 | 10 |
| 3 | 12 |
| 4 | 14 |
| 5 | 16 |

$x + 7 = y$
$x + y = 9$
$2x + 6 = y$
$y - x = 7$

**12.**

| x | y |
|---|---|
| 0 | 1 |
| 1 | 4 |
| 2 | 7 |
| 3 | 10 |
| 4 | 13 |
| 5 | 16 |

$3x + 1 = y$
$x + 3 = y$
$y - 3 = x$
$3x = y$

## Tough Tables

**Functions**

### Directions:
Match each table with an equation. Write the matching equation under the table. Each equation will be used once.

**1.**

| x | y |
|---|---|
| 0 | 12 |
| 1 | 11 |
| 2 | 10 |
| 3 | 9 |
| 4 | 8 |

_____

**2.**

| x | y |
|---|---|
| 12 | 8 |
| 11 | 7 |
| 10 | 6 |
| 9 | 5 |
| 8 | 4 |

_____

**3.**

| x | y |
|---|---|
| 0 | -2 |
| 1 | 1 |
| 2 | 4 |
| 3 | 7 |
| 4 | 10 |

_____

**4.**

| x | y |
|---|---|
| 3 | 1 |
| 4 | $1\frac{1}{3}$ |
| 5 | $1\frac{2}{3}$ |
| 6 | 2 |
| 7 | $2\frac{1}{3}$ |

_____

**5.**

| x | y |
|---|---|
| 0 | 5 |
| 1 | 6 |
| 2 | 7 |
| 3 | 8 |
| 4 | 9 |

_____

**6.**

| x | y |
|---|---|
| 1 | -1 |
| 3 | 0 |
| 5 | 1 |
| 7 | 2 |
| 9 | 3 |

_____

**7.**

| x | y |
|---|---|
| 6 | 0 |
| 7 | 1 |
| 8 | 2 |
| 9 | 3 |
| 10 | 4 |

_____

**8.**

| x | y |
|---|---|
| 1 | 2 |
| 2 | 4 |
| 3 | 6 |
| 4 | 8 |
| 5 | 10 |

_____

**9.**

| x | y |
|---|---|
| 2 | -6 |
| 3 | -4 |
| 4 | -2 |
| 5 | 0 |
| 6 | 2 |

_____

**10.**

| x | y |
|---|---|
| 0 | 3 |
| 1 | 5 |
| 2 | 7 |
| 3 | 9 |
| 4 | 11 |

_____

**11.**

| x | y |
|---|---|
| 2 | 0 |
| 4 | $\frac{1}{2}$ |
| 6 | 1 |
| 8 | $1\frac{1}{2}$ |
| 10 | 2 |

_____

**12.**

| x | y |
|---|---|
| 0 | 4 |
| 1 | 5 |
| 2 | 6 |
| 3 | 7 |
| 4 | 8 |

_____

### Equations

$2x = y$

$x - y = 4$

$x - 6 = y$

$y - x = 4$

$2x + 3 = y$

$x = 4y + 2$

$3x - 2 = y$

$x + y = 12$

$2x - y = 10$

$x = 3y$

$x = 2y + 3$

$x + 5 = y$

Elementary Algebra • CD-104106

Name _____   Date _____

# You Be the Mathematician

**Writing Equations**

**Directions:**

Think up your own equations using x and y. Fill in the table for each and answer the questions. Graph each on a separate piece of paper.

1. equation _____

| x | 0 | 1 | 2 | 3 | 4 | 5 | 6 | 7 | 8 | 9 | 10 |
|---|---|---|---|---|---|---|---|---|---|---|----|
| y |   |   |   |   |   |   |   |   |   |   |    |

   Are any of the values for y fractions? _____
   Are any of the values for y negative numbers? _____

2. equation _____

| x | 0 | 1 | 2 | 3 | 4 | 5 | 6 | 7 | 8 | 9 | 10 |
|---|---|---|---|---|---|---|---|---|---|---|----|
| y |   |   |   |   |   |   |   |   |   |   |    |

   Are any of the values for y fractions? _____
   Are any of the values for y negative numbers? _____

3. equation _____

| x | 0 | 1 | 2 | 3 | 4 | 5 | 6 | 7 | 8 | 9 | 10 |
|---|---|---|---|---|---|---|---|---|---|---|----|
| y |   |   |   |   |   |   |   |   |   |   |    |

   Are any of the values for y fractions? _____
   Are any of the values for y negative numbers? _____

4. equation _____

| x | 0 | 1 | 2 | 3 | 4 | 5 | 6 | 7 | 8 | 9 | 10 |
|---|---|---|---|---|---|---|---|---|---|---|----|
| y |   |   |   |   |   |   |   |   |   |   |    |

   Are any of the values for y fractions? _____
   Are any of the values for y negative numbers? _____

5. equation _____

| x | 0 | 1 | 2 | 3 | 4 | 5 | 6 | 7 | 8 | 9 | 10 |
|---|---|---|---|---|---|---|---|---|---|---|----|
| y |   |   |   |   |   |   |   |   |   |   |    |

   Are any of the values for y fractions? _____
   Are any of the values for y negative numbers? _____

6. equation _____

| x | 0 | 1 | 2 | 3 | 4 | 5 | 6 | 7 | 8 | 9 | 10 |
|---|---|---|---|---|---|---|---|---|---|---|----|
| y |   |   |   |   |   |   |   |   |   |   |    |

   Are any of the values for y fractions? _____
   Are any of the values for y negative numbers? _____

7. equation _____

| x | 0 | 1 | 2 | 3 | 4 | 5 | 6 | 7 | 8 | 9 | 10 |
|---|---|---|---|---|---|---|---|---|---|---|----|
| y |   |   |   |   |   |   |   |   |   |   |    |

   Are any of the values for y fractions? _____
   Are any of the values for y negative numbers? _____

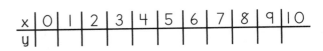

Name _____  Date _____

# Growing Up Triangular

**Directions:**
Fill in the table about the perimeters and areas of the equilateral triangles below. Complete the table by using patterns. Then, answer the questions.

A   B   C 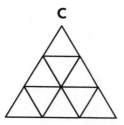  D 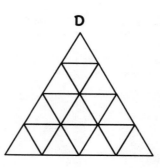  E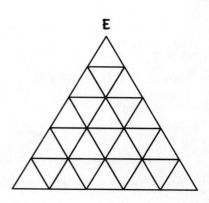

| | Length of a Side in Units | Perimeter in Units | Area in △ s |
|---|---|---|---|
| A | 1 | 3 | 1 |
| B | 2 | | |
| C | 3 | | |
| D | 4 | | |
| E | 5 | | |
| | 6 | | |
| | 7 | | |
| | 8 | | |
| | 9 | | |
| | 10 | | |

1. What pattern do you notice about the perimeters in the table? _____
_____

2. What pattern do you notice about the areas in the table? _____
_____

3. In which triangle are the perimeter and the area equal? _____

4. If the sides of one of these triangles were each 12 units, what would the perimeter and area be?

   perimeter: _____  area: _____

5. Which grows faster on this table: the perimeter or the area? _____

6. What do you multiply the length of a side by to get the perimeter?

   perimeter = _____ x length of a side

7. What do you multiply the length of a side by to get the area in △ s? _____

8. If the sides of a triangle are each 100 units, what would the perimeter and area be?

   perimeter: _____  area: _____

Name _____     Date _____

# Growing Up Square

**Investigating Change**

**Directions:**

Fill in the table about the perimeters and areas of the squares below. Complete the table by using patterns. Then, answer the questions.

**A**   **B**   **C**   **D**   **E**   **F**

 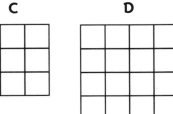 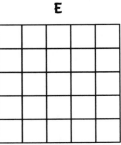

| | Length of a Side in Units | Perimeter in Units | Area in Square Units |
|---|---|---|---|
| **A** | 1 | 4 | 1 |
| **B** | 2 | | |
| **C** | 3 | | |
| **D** | 4 | | |
| **E** | 5 | | |
| **F** | 6 | | |
| | 7 | | |
| | 8 | | |
| | 9 | | |
| | 10 | | |

1. What pattern do you notice about the perimeters in the table? _____
_____

2. What pattern do you notice about the areas in the table? _____
_____

3. In which square are the perimeter and the area equal? _____

4. If the sides of one of these squares were each 12 units, what would the perimeter and area be?

perimeter: _____     area: _____

5. Which grows faster on this table: the perimeter or the area? _____

6. What do you multiply the length of a side by to get the perimeter?

perimeter = _____ x length of a side

7. What do you multiply the length of a side by to get the area in square units? _____

8. If the sides of a square are each 100 units, what would the perimeter and area be?

perimeter: _____     area: _____

Name _____     Date _____

# Multiplying Critters

## Directions:

Complete the table for each critter and answer the questions.

**Triffids** are made of triangles (T) and arms (A).
They can join together to make larger triffids.

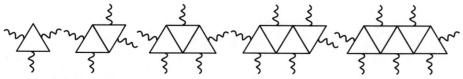

| T | A |
|---|---|
| 1 | 3 |
| 2 |   |
| 3 |   |
| 4 |   |
| 5 |   |

1.  Which equation tells how the triangles and arms are related?

    $T + A = 4$     $T + 2 = A$     $2T + 1 = A$     $A - 1 = T$

2.  If a triffid has 10 triangles, how many arms does it have? _____

**Riffids** are made of rhombuses (R) and arms (A).
They can join together to make larger riffids.

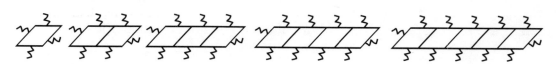

| R | A |
|---|---|
| 1 | 4 |
| 2 |   |
| 3 |   |
| 4 |   |
| 5 |   |

1.  Which equation tells how the rhombuses and arms are related?

    $R + 3 = A$     $A - 3 = R$     $3R + 1 = A$     $2R + 2 = A$

2.  If a riffid has 20 rhombuses, how many arms does it have? _____

**Piffids** are made of pentagons (P) and arms (A).
They can join together to make larger piffids.

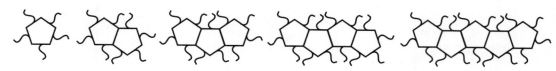

| P | A |
|---|---|
| 1 | 5 |
| 2 |   |
| 3 |   |
| 4 |   |
| 5 |   |

1.  Which equation tells how the pentagons and arms are related?

    $P + 4 = A$     $A - 2P = 2$     $3P + 2 = A$     $3P + 1 = A$

2.  If a piffid has 15 pentagons, how many arms does it have? _____

Name _____  Date _____

## Building Space Stations

**Directions:**
Here are some space station models. Complete the table for each model type and answer the questions.

**Space Station A** is made of one circular part (C) and 3 arms (A). The basic model can be connected to others to make larger stations.

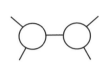 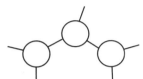 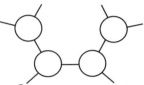

1. What pattern do you see in the number of arms? _____

2. If a space station of this kind has 6 circular parts, how many arms will it have? _____

3. Which equation will help you find the number of arms (A) if you know the number of circular parts (C)?

   C + 2 = A          2 x C = A          (2 x C) + 1 = A

4. If a space station was made with 100 circular parts, how many arms would it have? _____

| number of circles | number of arms |
|---|---|
| 1 | 3 |
| 2 | 5 |
| 3 | |
| 4 | |
| 5 | |
| 6 | |

**Space Station B** is made of one circular part (C) and 4 arms (A). The basic model can be connected to others to make larger stations.

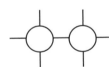 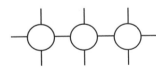 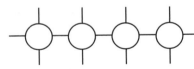

1. What pattern do you see in the number of arms? _____

2. If a space station of this kind has 6 circular parts, how many arms will it have? _____

3. Which equation will help you find the number of arms (A) if you know the number of circular parts (C)?

   C + 3 = A          3 x C = A          (3 x C) + 1 = A

4. If a space station was made with 100 circular parts, how many arms would it have? _____

| number of circles | number of arms |
|---|---|
| 1 | 4 |
| 2 | 7 |
| 3 | |
| 4 | |
| 5 | |
| 6 | |

Name _____   Date _____

# Patterns in a Line

**Directions:**

For each shape shown below, complete the table, choose the appropriate equation, and answer the questions.

## Perimeter and Triangles

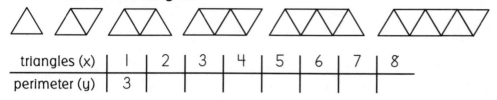

**Equation Choices**

$y + 2 = x$

$x + 2 = y$

$2x = y$

$x - y = 2$

| triangles (x) | 1 | 2 | 3 | 4 | 5 | 6 | 7 | 8 |
|---|---|---|---|---|---|---|---|---|
| perimeter (y) | 3 | | | | | | | |

1. If a shape like these had 10 triangles, what would its perimeter be? _____

2. If a shape like these had a perimeter of 50, how many triangles would it have? _____

## Perimeter and Squares

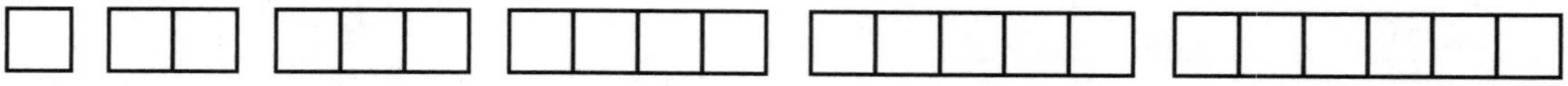

**Equation Choices**

$x + 3 = y$

$y - 4 = x$

$2x + 2 = y$

$2x = y$

| squares (x) | 1 | 2 | 3 | 4 | 5 | 6 | 7 | 8 |
|---|---|---|---|---|---|---|---|---|
| perimeter (y) | 4 | | | | | | | |

1. If a shape like these had 10 squares, what would its perimeter be? _____

2. If a shape like these had a perimeter of 30, how many squares would it have? _____

## Perimeter and Hexagons

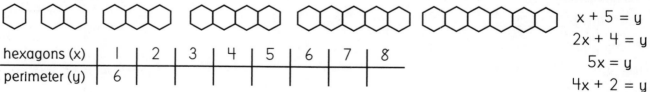

**Equation Choices**

$x + 5 = y$

$2x + 4 = y$

$5x = y$

$4x + 2 = y$

| hexagons (x) | 1 | 2 | 3 | 4 | 5 | 6 | 7 | 8 |
|---|---|---|---|---|---|---|---|---|
| perimeter (y) | 6 | | | | | | | |

1. If a shape like these had 10 hexagons, what would its perimeter be? _____

2. If a shape like these had a perimeter of 82, how many hexagons would it have? _____

## Page 5

1.
2.
3.
4.
5.
6.
7.
8.

## Page 6

1.
2.
3.
4.
5.
6.
7.
8.

## Page 7

1. 28, 31, 34; +3
2. 36, 34, 32; –2
3. 63, 68, 73; +5
4. 76, 84, 92; +8
5. 22, 18, 14; –4
6. 156, 166, 176; +10
7. 44, 36, 28; –8
8. 101, 112, 123; +11
9. 45, 40, 35; –5
10. 84, 74, 64; –10
11. 156, 176, 196; +20
12. 95, 80, 65; –15

## Page 8

1. +25; 125; 150; 175; 200
2. +15; 67; 82; 97; 112
3. +30; 135; 165; 195; 225
4. +50; 217; 267; 317; 367
5. +75; 305; 380; 455; 530
6. +100; 453; 553; 653; 753
7. +110; 465; 575; 685; 795
8. +150; 606; 756; 906; 1,056
9. +175; 900; 1,075; 1,250; 1,425
10. +250; 1,250; 1,500; 1,750; 2,000
11. +500; 3,000; 3,500; 4,000; 4,500
12. +1,000; 5,235; 6,235; 7,235; 8,235
13. +750; 3,750; 4,500; 5,250; 6,000
14. +200; 948; 1,148; 1,348; 1,548
15. +325; 1,400; 1,725; 2,050; 2,375

## Page 9

1. –50; 800; 750; 700; 650
2. –10; 960; 950; 940; 930
3. –100; 600; 500; 400; 300
4. –25; 900; 875; 850; 825
5. –150; 500; 350; 200; 50
6. –14; 944; 930; 916; 902
7. –75; 700; 625; 550; 475
8. –35; 860; 825; 790; 755
9. –125; 500; 375; 250; 125
10. –96; 616; 520; 424; 328
11. –500; 2,750; 2,250; 1,750; 1,250
12. –200; 4,200; 4,000; 3,800; 3,600
13. –250; 1,000; 750; 500; 250
14. –1,000; 4,263; 3,263; 2,263; 1,263
15. –225; 1,100; 875; 650; 425

## Page 10

1. 4  $4\frac{1}{2}$  5; $+\frac{1}{2}$
2. $7\frac{1}{2}$  $8\frac{1}{2}$  $9\frac{1}{2}$; +1
3. $2\frac{2}{3}$  3  $3\frac{1}{3}$; $+\frac{1}{3}$
4. $14\frac{1}{3}$  $16\frac{1}{3}$  $18\frac{1}{3}$; +2
5. 5  $5\frac{2}{3}$  $6\frac{1}{3}$; $+\frac{2}{3}$
6. 2  $2\frac{1}{4}$  $2\frac{2}{4}$; $+\frac{1}{4}$
7. $3\frac{3}{4}$  $4\frac{1}{4}$  $4\frac{3}{4}$; $+\frac{1}{2}$
8. $5\frac{2}{4}$  $6\frac{1}{4}$  7; $+\frac{3}{4}$
9. 3  $3\frac{2}{5}$  $3\frac{4}{5}$; $+\frac{2}{5}$
10. $4\frac{2}{5}$  5  $5\frac{3}{5}$; $+\frac{3}{5}$
11. 11  $12\frac{1}{2}$  14; $+1\frac{1}{2}$
12. $9\frac{2}{3}$  11  $12\frac{1}{3}$; $+1\frac{1}{3}$

## Page 11

1. $-\frac{1}{2}$
2. –1
3. $-\frac{1}{3}$
4. $-\frac{2}{3}$
5. $-\frac{1}{2}$
6. 8  $7\frac{1}{2}$  7  $6\frac{1}{2}$  6
7. $8\frac{1}{2}$  $7\frac{1}{2}$  $6\frac{1}{2}$  $5\frac{1}{2}$  $4\frac{1}{2}$
8. $4\frac{2}{3}$  $4\frac{1}{3}$  4  $3\frac{2}{3}$  $3\frac{1}{3}$
9. $7\frac{1}{3}$  $6\frac{2}{3}$  6  $5\frac{1}{3}$  $4\frac{2}{3}$
10. $6\frac{1}{4}$  $5\frac{3}{4}$  $5\frac{1}{4}$  $4\frac{3}{4}$  $4\frac{1}{4}$

## Page 12

1. +0.1; 1.4, 1.5, 1.6, 1.7
2. +0.2; 1.6, 1.8, 2.0, 2.2
3. +0.5; 2.5, 3.0, 3.5, 4.0
4. +1.1; 5.4, 6.5, 7.6, 8.7
5. +1.5; 6.2, 7.7, 9.2, 10.7
6. +0.02; 1.08, 1.10, 1.12, 1.14
7. +0.15; 0.75, 0.90, 1.05, 1.20
8. +0.25; 1.25, 1.50, 1.75, 2.00
9. –0.1; 2.6, 2.5, 2.4, 2.3
10. –0.2; 3.2, 3.0, 2.8, 2.6
11. –1.1; 10.6, 9.5, 8.4, 7.3
12. –1.5; 9.0, 7.5, 6.0, 4.5
13. –0.03; 0.38, 0.35, 0.32, 0.29
14. –0.15; 2.40, 2.25, 2.10, 1.95
15. –0.25; 4.00, 3.75, 3.50, 3.25

**Page 13**

1. +0.4; 2.6, 3.4
2. +$\frac{1}{3}$; 1$\frac{1}{3}$ , 2$\frac{2}{3}$
3. +1.5; 1.0, 7.0
4. -0.3; 5.7, 5.4
5. -0.1; 2.8, 2.5
6. +$\frac{1}{2}$; 2$\frac{1}{2}$, 4$\frac{1}{2}$
7. -0.01; 0.97, 0.96
8. -$\frac{1}{4}$ ; 5, 4
9. +$\frac{2}{3}$ ; 4, 5$\frac{1}{3}$
10. +0.5; 3.5, 4.0
11. -1$\frac{1}{2}$; 5$\frac{1}{2}$ , 2$\frac{1}{2}$
12. +2$\frac{1}{3}$; 10, 12$\frac{1}{3}$
13. -0.15; 2.85, 2.7
14. +1.2; 6, 12
15. +$\frac{3}{4}$; 1, 4
16. -0.001; 0.012, 0.011

**Page 14**

1. $\frac{5}{2}$ $\frac{6}{2}$ $\frac{7}{2}$ $\frac{8}{2}$ $\frac{9}{2}$ $\frac{10}{2}$ $\frac{11}{2}$ $\frac{12}{2}$
2. 2$\frac{1}{2}$ 3 3$\frac{1}{2}$ 4 4$\frac{1}{2}$ 5 5$\frac{1}{2}$ 6
3. $\frac{5}{3}$ $\frac{6}{3}$ $\frac{7}{3}$ $\frac{8}{3}$ $\frac{9}{3}$ $\frac{10}{3}$ $\frac{11}{3}$ $\frac{12}{3}$
4. 1$\frac{2}{3}$ 2 2$\frac{1}{3}$ 2$\frac{2}{3}$ 3 3$\frac{1}{3}$ 3$\frac{2}{3}$ 4
5. $\frac{5}{4}$ $\frac{6}{4}$ $\frac{7}{4}$ $\frac{8}{4}$ $\frac{9}{4}$ $\frac{10}{4}$ $\frac{11}{4}$ $\frac{12}{4}$
6. 1$\frac{1}{4}$ 1$\frac{2}{4}$ 1$\frac{3}{4}$ 2 2$\frac{1}{4}$ 2$\frac{2}{4}$ 2$\frac{3}{4}$ 3
7. 1$\frac{1}{4}$ 1$\frac{1}{2}$ 1$\frac{3}{4}$ 2 2$\frac{1}{4}$ 2$\frac{1}{2}$ 2$\frac{3}{4}$ 3
8. $\frac{2}{5}$ $\frac{3}{5}$ $\frac{4}{5}$ $\frac{5}{5}$ $\frac{6}{5}$ $\frac{7}{5}$ $\frac{8}{5}$ $\frac{9}{5}$ $\frac{10}{5}$ $\frac{11}{5}$ $\frac{12}{5}$
9. $\frac{1}{5}$ $\frac{2}{5}$ $\frac{3}{5}$ $\frac{4}{5}$ 1 1$\frac{1}{5}$ 1$\frac{2}{5}$ 1$\frac{3}{5}$ 1$\frac{4}{5}$ 2 2$\frac{1}{5}$ 2$\frac{2}{5}$
10. $\frac{2}{6}$ $\frac{3}{6}$ $\frac{4}{6}$ $\frac{5}{6}$ $\frac{6}{6}$ $\frac{7}{6}$ $\frac{8}{6}$ $\frac{9}{6}$ $\frac{10}{6}$ $\frac{11}{6}$ $\frac{12}{6}$
11. $\frac{1}{6}$ $\frac{2}{6}$ $\frac{3}{6}$ $\frac{4}{6}$ $\frac{5}{6}$ 1 1$\frac{1}{6}$ 1$\frac{2}{6}$ 1$\frac{3}{6}$ 1$\frac{4}{6}$ 1$\frac{5}{6}$ 2
12. $\frac{1}{6}$ $\frac{1}{3}$ $\frac{1}{2}$ $\frac{2}{3}$ $\frac{5}{6}$ 1 1$\frac{1}{6}$ 1$\frac{1}{3}$ 1$\frac{1}{2}$ 1$\frac{2}{3}$ 1$\frac{5}{6}$ 2

**Page 15**

1. 10, 15, 17, 22, 24
2. 20, 30, 33, 43, 46
3. 72, 68, 66, 62, 60
4. 79, 78, 73, 72, 67
5. 51, 48, 50, 47, 49
6. 32, 42, 38, 48, 44
7. 31, 30, 40, 39, 49
8. 14, 34, 26, 46, 38
9. 30, 24, 27, 21, 24
10. 35, 40, 30, 35, 25
11. 42, 40, 47, 45, 52
12. 21, 27, 22, 28, 23

**Page 16**

1. +2, +7
2. +5, -2
3. -3, -5
4. -4, +6
5. +10, +50
6. +12, -10
7. -2, -15
8. -10, +2
9. +25, +100
10. +50, -30
11. -10, +2
12. -5, +30

**Page 17**

1. 8; 16; 32; 64; 128
2. 12; 24; 48; 96; 192; 384
3. 20; 40; 80; 160; 320; 640
4. 9; 27; 81; 243; 729; 2,187
5. 18; 54; 162; 486; 1,458; 4,374

**Page 17 (cont.)**

6. 16; 64; 256; 1,024; 4,096; 16,384
7. 32; 128; 512; 2,048; 8,192; 32,768
8. 25; 125; 625; 3,125; 15,625; 78,125
9. 100; 1,000; 10,000; 100,000; 1,000,000; 10,000,000
10. 200; 2,000; 20,000; 200,000; 2,000,000; 20,000,000

**Page 18**

1. 14; 7
2. 16; 8
3. 50; 25
4. 250; 125
5. 200; 100; 50
6. 72; 36; 18
7. 300; 150; 75
8. 96; 48; 24
9. 400; 200; 100
10. 160; 80; 40
11. 800; 400; 200
12. 1,000; 500; 250
13. 1,200; 600; 300
14. 1,500; 750; 375
15. 2,000; 1,000; 500
16. 2,500; 1,250; 625

**Page 19**

1. 8, 12, 17, 23, 30
2. 14, 22, 32, 44, 58
3. 13, 21, 31, 43, 57
4. 10, 17, 26, 37, 50
5. 11, 18, 27, 38, 51
6. 10, 19, 31, 46, 64, 85
7. 12, 21, 33, 48, 66, 87
8. 16, 28, 44, 64, 88, 116
9. 13, 25, 41, 61, 85, 113
10. 16, 31, 51, 76, 106, 141
11. 17, 32, 52, 77, 107, 142
12. 20, 35, 55, 80, 110, 145
13. 40, 70, 110, 160, 220, 290
14. 31, 61, 101, 151, 211, 281

**Page 20**

1. -2, -3, -4, -5
2. 2, 0, -2, -4
3. 8, 5, 2, -1
4. 4, 0, -4, -8
5. 3, 1, -1, -3
6. -5, -8, -11, -14
7. 0, -5, -10, -15
8. -3, -8, -13, -18
9. -5, -15, -25, -35
10. -3
11. -5
12. -4
13. -10
14. -7
15. -2

**Page 21**

1. 2, 3, 4, 5
2. -2, 0, 2, 4
3. 0, 3, 6, 9
4. -4, 0, 4, 8
5. -10, -5, 0, 5
6. -3, -1, 1, 3
7. 2, 5, 8, 11
8. 4, 10, 16, 22
9. 5, 15, 25, 35
10. +4
11. +2
12. +7
13. +9
14. +11
15. +3

**Page 22**

Answers will vary.

## Page 23
Number Squared 1, 4, 9, 16, 25, 36, 49, 64, 81, 100
1. 9, 11, 13, 15, 17, 19    2. Answers will vary.    3. 169
Number Cubed 1, 8; 27; 64; 125; 216; 343; 512; 729; 1,000
4. 61, 91, 127, 169, 217, 271    5. 24, 30, 36, 42, 48, 54
6. Answers will vary.

## Pages 24–25
Answers will vary.

## Page 26
1. (5 x 5) + 5; 30
   (6 x 5) + 6; 36
   (7 x 5) + 7; 42
   (8 x 5) + 8; 48
   (9 x 5) + 9; 54
   (10 x 5) + 10; 60
   (11 x 5) + 11; 66

2. 7, 14, 21
   (4 x 5) + 8; 28
   (5 x 5) + 10; 35
   (6 x 5) + 12; 42
   (7 x 5) + 14; 49
   (8 x 5) + 16; 56
   (9 x 5) + 18; 63
   (10 x 5) + 20; 70
   (11 x 5) + 22; 77

3. 9, 18, 27
   (4 x 10) – 4; 36
   (5 x 10) – 5; 45
   (6 x 10) – 6; 54
   (7 x 10) – 7; 63
   (8 x 10) – 8; 72
   (9 x 10) – 9; 81
   (10 x 10) – 10; 90
   (11 X 10) – 11; 99

4. 8, 16, 24
   (4 x 10) – 8; 32
   (5 x 10) – 10; 40
   (6 x 10) – 12; 48
   (7 x 10) – 14; 56
   (8 x 10) – 16; 64
   (9 x 10) – 18; 72
   (10 x 10) – 20; 80
   (11 x 10) – 22; 88

## Pages 27–28
Answers will vary.

## Page 29
30; 15; 10; 7.5; 6; 5; 4.2857142; 3.75; 3.$\overline{3}$, 3; 2.$\overline{72}$;
2.5; 2.3076923; 2.1428571; 2; 1.875; 1.7647058;
1.$\overline{6}$; 1.5789473; 1.5; 1.4285714; 1.$\overline{36}$; 1.3043478;
1.25; 1.2; 1.1538461; 1.$\overline{1}$; 1.0714285; 1.0344827; 1
1. 1, 2, 3, 5, 6, 10, 15, 30    2. 4, 12, 20, 25
3. 8, 24    4. 16
5. 9, 18, 27    6. 11, 22

## Page 30
| | | |
|---|---|---|
| 60,000 | 250,000 | 4,000 |
| 6,000 | 25,000 | 400 |
| 600 | 2,500 | 40 |
| 60 | 250 | 4 |
| 6 | 25 | 0.4 |
| 0.6 | 2.5 | 0.04 |
| 0.06 | 0.25 | 0.004 |
| 0.006 | 0.025 | 0.0004 |
| 0.0006 | 0.0025 | 0.00004 |
| 0.00006 | 0.00025 | 0.000004 |

| | | |
|---|---|---|
| 0.0005 | 0.0032 | 9,000 |
| 0.005 | 0.032 | 900 |
| 0.05 | 0.32 | 90 |
| 0.5 | 3.2 | 9 |
| 5 | 32 | 0.9 |
| 50 | 320 | 0.09 |
| 500 | 3,200 | 0.009 |
| 5,000 | 32,000 | 0.0009 |
| 50,000 | 320,000 | 0.00009 |
| 500,000 | 3,200,000 | 0.000009 |

## Page 31
FV; NV; FS; NS; FC; NC
2 toppings: 8, 10; 3 toppings: 3, 6, 9, 12, 15;
4 toppings: 4, 8, 12, 16, 20; 5 toppings: 5, 10, 15, 20, 25
1. 20 sundaes
2. 36 sundaes
3. multiplication table
4. 100 sundaes
5. 7 toppings
6. 9 ice cream flavors
7. 480 sundaes

## Page 32
1. 3 kinds: CR, CM
2. 6 kinds: CN, CR, CM, BN, BR, BM
3. 9 kinds: BN, BR, BM, VN, VR, VM
4. 12 kinds: WVN, WVR, WVM, PCN, PCR, PCM, PVN, PVR, PVM
5. 18 kinds: WBN, WBR, WBM, PCN, PCR, PCM, PBN, PBR, PBM, YCN, YCR, YCM, YBN, YBR, YBM

## Page 33
1. circles: 9, 12, 15, 18, 21, 24; ratio: 1 to 3; count by 3s, 30 circles, 9 squares
2. circles: 8, 12, 16, 20, 24, 28, 32; ratio: 1 to 2 or 2 to 4 count by 4s, 40 circles, 30 squares
3. squares: 10, 12, 14, 16; circles: 6, 9, 12, 15, 18, 21, 24; ratio: 2 to 3; count by 3s, 30 circles, 60 squares
4. squares: 25, 30, 35, 40; circles: 6, 9, 12, 15, 18, 21, 24; ratio: 5 to 3; count by 3s, 30 circles, 100 squares

## Page 34
1. 1 to 2; 4, 6, 8, 10, 12, 20, 40
2. 1 to 3; 6, 9, 12, 15, 18, 30, 300
3. 2 to 3; 6, 9, 12, 15, 30, 150
4. 1 to 4; 8, 12, 16, 20, 40, 60, 400
5. 3 to 4; 8, 12, 16, 20, 40, 80

## Page 35
1. 8, 16, 32, 64    2. number is doubling
3. 8; 16; 32; 64; 128; 256; 512; 1,024; 2,048
4. 4,092    5. 0

## Page 36
1. 2, 5, 9, 14, 20
2. Answers will vary.
3. 2, 3, 4, 5
4. Answers will vary.
5. ÷2
6. 2, 5, 9, 14, 20
7. (9 x 6) ÷ 2 = 27; (10 x 7) ÷ 2 = 35

## Page 37
1. and 4. 10, 15, 21, 28, 36, 45, 55, 66, 78
2. +5: 15; +6: 21; +7: 28
3. Answers will vary.
4. 10, 15, 21, 28, 36, 45, 55, 66, 78
5. 5 x 3 = 15; 6 x $3\frac{1}{2}$ = 21; 7 x 4 = 28; 8 x $4\frac{1}{2}$ = 36;
   9 x 5 = 45; 10 x $5\frac{1}{2}$ = 55; 11 x 6 = 66; 12 x $6\frac{1}{2}$ = 78
6. Answers will vary.
7. 210

## Page 38
1. 26 + 15 = 41; 15 + 26 = 41; 41 = 26 + 15; 41 = 15 + 26;
   41 – 26 = 15; 41 – 15 = 26; 15 = 41 – 26; 26 = 41 – 15
2. 4 x 5 = 20; 5 x 4 = 20; 20 = 4 x 5; 20 = 5 x 4; 20 ÷ 4 = 5;
   20 ÷ 5 = 4; 5 = 20 ÷ 4; 4 = 20 ÷ 5
3. 6 x 7 = 42; 7 x 6 = 42; 42 = 6 x 7; 42 = 7 x 6; 42 ÷ 6 = 7;
   42 ÷ 7 = 6; 7 = 42 ÷ 6; 6 = 42 ÷ 7
4. 38 + 22 = 60; 22 + 38 = 60; 60 = 38 + 22; 60 = 22 + 38;
   60 – 38 = 22; 60 – 22 = 38; 22 = 60 – 38; 38 = 60 – 22

## Page 39
Pictures will vary.

## Page 40
1. W + V = U, U – W = V, U = V + W
2. C = B x A, A x B = C, B = C ÷ A
3. M – N = L, N = M – L, M = N + L
4. R = S x T, R ÷ T = S, S = R ÷ T
5. D = E + F, D – E = F, E = D – F

## Page 41
Any equivalent equation is correct.
1. D = 2 + H
2. L = A – 3
3. M = L + 10
4. K = 2 x E
5. M + F = 24
6. G = R – 4
7. H = 3 x R
8. N – K = 1
9. K = J + 8
10. P = T ÷ 2
11. L = C – 20
12. V + D = 154

## Page 42
Any equivalent equation is correct.
1. A + R = 20; 13 gummy pandas; 15 gummy pandas
2. B x D = 30; 5 gummy dolphins; 3 bags
3. 40 – E = L; 25 gummy dinos; 20 gummy dinos
4. R + G = 25; 8 gummy apples; 12 gummy apples
5. G = 6 x E; 42 gummy lemons; 8 gummy lemons
6. 8 x E = W; 9 gummy whales; 40 gummy whales

## Page 43
Any equivalent equation is correct.
1. J = 2 x S; 6 years old; 20 years old
2. D = 4 + A; 6 years old; 13 years old
3. T = A – 5; 11 years old; 10 years old
4. J = 10 + T; 25 years old; 53 years old
5. S = 3 x B; 3 years old; 15 years old
6. P = M – 25; 49 years old; 40 years old
7. C = J – 10; 22 years old; 6 years old
8. P = F ÷ 2; 60 years old; 38 years old

## Page 44
Any equivalent equation is correct.
1. n + 3
2. n – 3
3. 2 x n
4. n ÷ 2
5. n – 15
6. n x 3
7. n ÷ 3
8. n + 16
9. 35 – n
10. 50 – n
11. n – 17
12. 7 x n
13. n + 150
14. n ÷ 10
15. n x 25

## Page 45
Any equivalent equation is correct.
1. L: 0, 1, 2, 3, 4, 5, 6, 7, 8, 9, 10, 11, 12; P – 3 = L
   A. 8 pencils B. 16 pencils C. 97 pencils D. 60 pencils
2. S: 0, 1, 2, 3, 4, 5, 6, 7, 8, 9, 10, 11, 12; H – S = 15
   A. 10 pencils B. 27 pencils C. 85 pencils D. 40 pencils
3. S: 1, 2, 3, 4, 5, 6, 7, 8, 9, 10, 11, 12; R: 30, 29, 28, 27,
   26, 25, 24, 23, 22, 21, 20, 19, 18; 30 – S = R
   A. 22 pencils B. 11 pencils C. 15 pencils D. 28 pencils
4. B: 1, 2, 3, 4, 5, 6, 7, 8, 9, 10, 11, 12; R: 48, 47, 46,
   45, 44, 43, 42, 41, 40, 39, 38, 37, 36; 48 – B = R
   A. 38 pencils B. 8 pencils C. 23 pencils D. 43 pencils

## Page 46
1. 240 inches; 10 feet
2. 6, 9, 12, 15, 18, 21, 24; F = 3 x Y; 300 feet; 10 yards
3. 200, 300, 400, 500, 600, 700, 800; C = 100 x M;
   5,000 centimeters; 9 meters
4. 72, 108, 144, 180, 216, 252, 288; I = 36 x Y;
   360 inches; 11 yards
5. 2,000; 3,000; 4,000; 5,000; 6,000; 7,000; 8,000
   10,000 meters; 12 kilometers

## Page 47
1. S: 120, 180, 240, 300, 360, 420, 480; S = M x 60
2. H: 48, 72, 96, 120, 144, 168, 192; H = D x 24
3. D: 14, 21, 28, 35, 42, 49, 56; D = W x 7
4. M: 120, 180, 240, 300, 360, 420, 480; M = H x 60
5. 480 seconds
6. 49 days
7. 300 minutes
8. 144 hours
9. 6 weeks
10. 8 days
11. 7 hours
12. 600 seconds
13. 70 days
14. 600 minutes
15. 240 hours
16. 11 weeks
17. 12 minutes
18. 20 days
19. 11 hours

## Page 48

1. N: 4, 6, 8, 10, 12, 14, 16; N = D x 2
2. N: 10, 15, 20, 25, 30, 35, 40; N = Q x 5
3. Q: 8, 12, 16, 20, 24, 28, 32; Q = D x 4
4. P: 20, 30, 40, 50, 60, 70, 80; P = D x 10
5. N: 40, 60, 80, 100, 120, 140, 160; N = D x 20
6. P: 50, 70, 100, 125, 150, 175, 200; P = Q x 25
7. 16 nickels
8. 24 quarters
9. 100 nickels
10. 8 quarters
11. 7 dimes
12. 5 quarters
13. 50 nickels
14. 200 pennies
15. 250 pennies
16. 15 dimes
17. 10 dollars
18. 10 dollars

## Page 49

1. 2 feet = 24 inches; 36 inches = 3 feet; 60 inches = 5 feet; 10 feet = 120 inches; 48 inches; 7 feet
2. 4 weeks = 28 days; 35 days = 5 weeks; 10 weeks = 70 days; 56 days = 8 weeks; 2 weeks; 49 days
3. 2 hours = 120 minutes; 240 minutes = 4 hours; 5 hours = 300 minutes; 600 minutes = 10 hours; 180 minutes; 6 hours
4. 3 years = 36 months; 96 months = 8 years; 5 years = 60 months; 72 months = 6 years; 84 months; 10 years
5. 3 meters = 300 cm; 1,000 cm = 10 meters; 8 meters = 800 cm; 700 cm = 7 meters; 400 cm; 11 meters
6. 3 yards = 9 feet; 12 feet = 4 yards; 5 yards = 15 feet; 21 feet = 7 yards; 18 feet; 10 yards
7. 2,000 meters = 2 km; 10 km = 10,000 meters; 8 km = 8,000 meters; 5,000 meters = 5 km; 6 km; 4,000 meters
8. 12 quarters = 3 dollars; 10 dollars = 40 quarters; 24 quarters = 6 dollars; 15 dollars = 60 quarters; 4 dollars; 20 quarters

## Page 50

| | | | | |
|---|---|---|---|---|
| 2. 3 | 3. 52 | 4. 50 | 5. 1.25 | 6. 0.5 |
| 7. 36 | 8. 32 | 9. 2.34 | 10. 65 | 11. 1.5 |
| 12. 30 | 13. 100 | 14. 0.03 | 15. 90 | 16. 1.5 |
| 17. 9 | 18. 70 | 19. cheetah | 20. snail | |

## Page 51

1. 100 mm; 600 sq. mm
2. 140 mm; 1,200 sq. mm
3. 120 mm; 500 sq. mm
4. 160 mm; 1,500 sq. mm
5. 160 mm; 1,200 sq. mm
6. 160 mm; 1,600 sq. mm
7. F; C
8. D, E, F; A
9. D, E, F
10. B, E
11. no
12. 60 mm
13. 1,100 sq. mm

## Page 52

1. C = 8 + A; A = C – 8; 8; 13
2. M = G x 2; G = M ÷ 2; 6; 8
3. C = P + 10; P = C – 10; 15¢, 35¢
4. S = L – 5; L = S + 5; 25¢; 13¢
5. F = 3 x P; P = F ÷ 3; 7¢; 30¢
6. A = D – 20; D = 20 + A; 70; 45
7. V = J – 12; J = V + 12; 22; 18
8. M = 4 x R; R = M ÷ 4; 20¢; 60¢

## Page 53

1. C < A + B; B > C; B > A + C; B + B > C; C + C = A; B – A > C; A = B – A; A ≠ C; B = A + A; C + C + C = B
2. F > H; G + H = F; G = F – H; H = G + G + G; G < F; H = F – G; F < H + H; G ≠ H; F = G + G + G + G
3. K < L; L + L = J; L + K ≠ J; K + L < J; J = K + K + K; J > K; K + K > L; J – L = L; K + K + K = L + L

## Page 54

| | |
|---|---|
| 1. R = 3, H = 5, P = 4 | 2. R = 6, H = 4, P = 5 |
| 3. R = 4, H = 5, P = 4 | 4. R = 4, H = 6, P = 8 |
| 5. R = 5, H = 5, P = 10 | 6. R = 6, H = 4, P = 5 |
| 7. R = 12, H = 2, P = 4 | 8. R = 4, H = 8, P = 16 |
| 9. R = 7, H = 15, P = 5 | 10. R = 4, H = 4, P = 8 |
| 11. R = 11, H = 5, P = 4 | 12. R = 12, H = 4, P = 8 |
| 13. R = 10, H = 25, P = 15 | 14. R = 12, H = 24, P = 22 |
| 15. R = 12, H = 6, P = 12 | |

## Page 55

1. A + B = 10; B + C = 9; A = 6; B = 4; C = 5
2. A + A + A = 21; A + B = 16; A + C = B; A = 7; B = 9; C = 2
3. B + B + B + B = 12; A + A + B = 13; A + B + C = 17; A = 5; B = 3; C = 9
4. A + B = C; B + B = 8; B + C + C = 18; A = 3; B = 4; C = 7
5. B + B = C; C + C = 40; B + C = A; A = 30; B = 10; C = 20

## Page 56

Answers will vary.

## Page 57

The following problems should be circled: 1, 4, 5, 6, 8, 11, 12, 13, 14, 17, 19, 20, 21, 22, 24, 25, 27, 28

## Page 58

| | | | | |
|---|---|---|---|---|
| 1. = | 2. ≠ | 3. ≠ | 4. = | 5. = |
| 6. = | 7. = | 8. ≠ | 9. ≠ | 10. ≠ |
| 11. = | 12. = | 13. = | 14. = | 15. ≠ |
| 16. = | 17. = | 18. = | 19. ≠ | 20. ≠ |
| 21. = | 22. ≠ | 23. ≠ | 24. = | 25. ≠ |
| 26. ≠ | 27. = | 28. ≠ | | |

## Page 59

1. 15 + 25 = 40; 25 + 15 = 40; 40 = 15 + 25; 40 = 25 + 15; 40 − 15 = 25; 40 − 25 = 15; 25 = 40 − 15; 15 = 40 − 25
2. 9 × 8 = 72; 8 × 9 = 72; 72 = 9 × 8; 72 = 8 × 9; 72 ÷ 8 = 9; 72 ÷ 9 = 8; 9 = 72 ÷ 8; 8 = 72 ÷ 9
3. 50 + 75 = 125; 75 + 50 = 125; 125 = 50 + 75; 125 = 75 + 50; 125 − 50 = 75; 125 − 75 = 50; 75 = 125 − 50; 50 = 125 − 75
4. 8 × 20 = 160; 20 × 8 = 160; 160 = 8 × 20; 160 = 20 × 8; 160 ÷ 8 = 20; 160 ÷ 20 = 8; 20 = 160 ÷ 8; 8 = 160 ÷ 20
5. 11 × 9 = 99; 9 × 11 = 99; 99 = 11 × 9; 99 = 9 × 11; 99 ÷ 9 = 11; 99 ÷ 11 = 9; 11 = 99 ÷ 9; 9 = 99 ÷ 11
6. 16 + 0 = 16; 0 + 16 = 16; 16 = 16 + 0; 16 = 0 + 16; 16 − 0 = 16; 16 − 16 = 0; 16 = 16 − 0; 0 = 16 − 16

## Page 60

1. both equations circled
2. first equation circled
3. first equation circled
4. both equations circled
5. both equations circled
6. second equation circled
7. first equation circled
8. both equations circled
9. both equations circled
10. first equation circled
11. first equation circled
12. both equations circled
13. first equation circled
14. both equations circled
15. second equation circled
16. both equations circled

## Page 61

Answers will vary.

## Page 62

1. 15 × 4; 20 × 3; 1 × 60; 6 × 10; 5 × 12; 2 × 30
2. 1 × 84; 7 × 12; 28 × 3; 6 × 14; 21 × 4; 2 × 42
3. 48 × 2; 6 × 16; 3 × 32; 1 × 96; 24 × 4; 8 × 12
4. 10 × 12; 6 × 20; 4 × 30; 5 × 24; 2 × 60; 3 × 40
5. 4 × 50; 2 × 100; 5 × 40; 1 × 200; 25 × 8; 20 × 10
6. 5 × 100; 10 × 50; 2 × 250; 1 × 500; 20 × 25; 4 × 125

## Page 63

1. 36 × 4; 16 × 9; 3 × 48; 18 × 8; 12 × 12; 144 × 1; 2 × 72; 24 × 6
2. 25 × 12; 150 × 2; 3 × 100; 6 × 50; 30 × 10; 75 × 4; 5 × 60; 15 × 20
3. 2 × 200; 5 × 80; 100 × 4; 40 × 10; 16 × 25; 1 × 400; 20 × 20; 8 × 50
4. 100 × 8; 80 × 10; 2 × 400; 20 × 40; 16 × 50; 200 × 4; 5 × 160; 25 × 32
5. 1 × 1,000; 25 × 40; 4 × 250; 50 × 20; 10 × 100; 2 × 500; 5 × 200; 8 × 125
6. 5 × 120; 15 × 40; 6 × 100; 50 × 12; 25 × 24; 3 × 200; 75 × 8; 4 × 150

## Page 64

1. 1,600 × 1; 40 × 40; 320 × 5; 25 × 64; 8 × 200; 50 × 32; 16 × 100; 160 × 10; 800 × 2; 80 × 20; 4 × 400
2. 30 × 50; 750 × 2; 125 × 12; 25 × 60; 4 × 375; 100 × 15; 10 × 150; 1 × 1,500; 5 × 300; 250 × 6; 500 × 3; 75 × 20
3. 8 × 150; 400 × 3; 24 × 50; 80 × 15; 2 × 600; 48 × 25; 300 × 4; 6 × 200; 30 × 40; 100 × 12; 120 × 10; 20 × 60; 5 × 240; 16 × 75; 1 × 1,200

## Page 65

Answers will vary.

## Page 66

1. 8, 7, 56; 9, 3, 27; 6, 4, 24; 11, 5, 55
2. 2, 4, 8; 10, 25, 250; 2, 75, 150; 4, 35, 140; 8, 30, 240
3. 4, 9, 36; 6, 8, 48; 2, 12, 24; 7, 5, 35; 12, 4, 48; 2, 4, 8; 2, 24, 48; 4, 6, 24; 2, 6, 12
4. 40, 9, 360; 20, 5, 100; 7, 15, 105; 25, 6, 150
5. 9, 7, 63; 8, 11, 88; 3, 14, 42; 12, 5, 60
6. 10, 15, 150; 9, 30, 270; 20, 7, 140; 40, 6, 240
7. 8, 8, 64; 3, 15, 45; 9, 9, 81; 6, 7, 42
8. 12, 25, 300; 35, 11, 385; 10, 50, 500; 20, 20, 400

## Page 67

multiples of 2: all even numbers from 2–50
multiples of 3: 3, 6, 9, 12, 15, 18, 21, 24, 27, 30, 33, 36, 39, 42, 45, 48
multiples of 5: 5, 10, 15, 20, 25, 30, 35, 40, 45, 50
1. 6, 12, 18, 24, 30, 36, 42, 48; Answers will vary.
2. 10, 20, 30, 40, 50; Answers will vary.
3. 15, 30, 45; Answers will vary.
4. +6
5. Answers will vary.

## Pages 68–69

Answers will vary.

## Page 70

The correct path should go through: 10 ÷ 2; 45 ÷ 9; 200 ÷ 40; 20 ÷ 4; 85 ÷ 17; 65 ÷ 13; 125 ÷ 25; 60 ÷ 12; 35 ÷ 7; 150 ÷ 30; 80 ÷ 16; 90 ÷ 18; 30 ÷ 6; 100 ÷ 20; 50 ÷ 10; 95 ÷ 19; 40 ÷ 8; 75 ÷ 15; 15 ÷ 3; 55 ÷ 11; 25 ÷ 5; 210 ÷ 42; 70 ÷ 14

## Page 71

Answers will vary.

## Page 72

1. $0.1$, $\frac{1}{3}$, $\frac{2}{6}$, $0.25$, $0.07$, $\frac{1}{4}$, $\frac{2}{5}$, $0.4$, $0.065$, $\frac{2}{8}$

2. $\frac{3}{4}$, $0.51$, $\frac{2}{3}$, $2.5$, $\frac{10}{10}$, $\frac{3}{5}$, $\frac{5}{8}$, $\frac{7}{12}$, $0.98$, $0.75$

3. $\frac{3}{6}$, $\frac{6}{12}$, $\frac{50}{100}$, $0.5$, $0.50$, $\frac{15}{30}$, $\frac{5}{10}$, $0.500$, $\frac{2}{4}$, $\frac{4}{8}$

4. $\frac{4}{5}$, $\frac{4}{12}$, $0.99$, $0.75$, $\frac{1}{2}$, $0.5$, $\frac{6}{8}$, $0.11$

5. $1.1$, $2.5$, $1.01$, $3.8$, $\frac{11}{10}$, $1\frac{1}{2}$, $1\frac{2}{3}$, $\frac{6}{5}$, $1.75$, $\frac{4}{3}$, $1.5$, $3\frac{1}{8}$

6. $\frac{6}{6}$, $1.0$, $\frac{5}{5}$, $1.0000$, $1.00$, $\frac{4}{4}$, $\frac{100}{100}$, $\frac{3}{3}$, $1.000$

## Page 73

1. >  2. >  3. <  4. =  5. <
6. <  7. >  8. =  9. <  10. =
11. =  12. =  13. =  14. <

15. $\frac{1}{4}$, $\frac{1}{2}$, $0.6$   16. $\frac{1}{9}$, $\frac{1}{3}$, $1$

17. $0.075$, $0.75$, $7.5$   18. $0.25$, $\frac{1}{2}$, $1.5$

19. $3.2$, $3\frac{1}{2}$, $4.1$   20. $\frac{1}{2}$, $\frac{2}{3}$, $\frac{5}{6}$

21. $1.04$, $1.4$, $1\frac{1}{2}$   22. $0.1$, $\frac{1}{2}$, $1.0$

23. $\frac{1}{5}$, $\frac{1}{4}$, $\frac{1}{2}$   24. $0.15$, $1.5$, $15$

25. $2\frac{1}{4}$, $2\frac{1}{2}$, $2.51$   26. $0.05$, $\frac{4}{10}$, $0.41$

27. $\frac{5}{12}$, $\frac{3}{4}$, $\frac{14}{15}$   28. $0.08$, $\frac{8}{16}$, $0.8$

## Page 74

The path should go through: $\frac{1}{2}$ $\frac{20}{40}$ $\frac{2}{4}$ $\frac{40}{80}$ $\frac{18}{36}$ $\frac{50}{100}$ $\frac{9}{18}$ $\frac{80}{160}$ $\frac{15}{30}$ $\frac{8}{16}$ $\frac{14}{28}$ $\frac{3}{6}$ $\frac{75}{150}$ $\frac{500}{1,000}$ $\frac{7}{14}$ $\frac{90}{180}$ $\frac{25}{50}$ $\frac{5}{10}$ $\frac{12}{24}$ $\frac{10}{20}$ $\frac{250}{500}$ $\frac{100}{200}$ $\frac{4}{8}$ $\frac{51}{102}$ $\frac{45}{90}$ $\frac{6}{12}$ $\frac{24}{48}$

## Page 75

Answers will vary.

## Page 76

Any equivalent equation is correct.

1. $3 + 5 = 8$, $2 \times 9 = 18$, $25 \div 5 = 5$, $10 - 6 = 4$
2. $11 + 9 = 20$, $7 \times 7 = 49$; $42 \div 6 = 7$, $17 - 9 = 8$
3. $9 + 6 = 15$, $8 \times 8 = 64$, $56 \div 7 = 8$, $12 - 4 = 8$
4. $5 \times 8 = 40$, $9 + 7 = 16$, $72 \div 8 = 9$, $31 - 15 = 16$
5. $35 + 15 = 50$, $2 \times 35 = 70$, $80 \div 4 = 20$, $60 - 35 = 25$
6. $3 \times 30 = 90$, $40 + 40 = 80$, $60 \div 5 = 12$, $90 - 15 = 75$
7. $65 + 15 = 80$, $5 \times 15 = 75$, $90 - 45 = 45$, $70 \div 2 = 35$

## Page 77

1. 15, 5, 50, 2   2. 30, 10, 200, 2
3. 20, 10, 75, 3   4. 45, 15, 450, 2
5. 30, 20, 125, 5   6. 60, 40, 500, 5
7. 125; 75; 2,500; 4   8. 60, 20, 800, 2
9. 100; 50; 1,875; 3   10. 120; 80; 2,000; 5
11. 100; 60; 1,600; 4   12. 200; 0; 10,000; 1
13. 102, 98, 200, 50   14. 210; 190; 2,000; 20
15. 505; 495; 2,500; 100

## Page 78

1. –, ÷, +, x   2. x, +, ÷, –
3. ÷, –, x, +   4. +, x, –, ÷
5. x, ÷, –, +   6. –, +, ÷, x
7. –, x, +, ÷   8. ÷, x, –, +
9. x, –, +, ÷   10. +, ÷, –, x

## Page 79

1. 6, 4   2. 8, 3   3. 6, 6
4. 9, 4   5. 11, 4   6. 9, 7

## Page 80

1. 6, 8   2. 7, 5   3. 8, 4
4. 3, 9   5. 9, 5   6. 6, 10
7. 10, 15   8. 12, 12   9. 10, 25
10. 3, 5   11. 6, 4   12. 8, 5
13. 9, 9   14. 10, 5   15. 6, 9
16. 4, 7   17. 14, 3   18. 20, 10

## Page 81

1. 8, 2   2. 12, 4   3. 10, 5
4. 6, 3   5. 4, 1   6. 3, 3
7. 8, 4   8. 15, 5   9. 35, 7
10. 4, 2   11. 10, 2   12. 6, 2
13. 12, 6   14. 15, 3   15. 16, 4
16. 12, 3   17. 8, 1   18. any 2 = numbers

## Page 82

Answers will vary.

## Page 83

Answers may vary.

1. $8 + 7 = 20 - 5$; $4 \times 3 = 7 + 5$; $9 - 5 = 16 \div 4$
2. $3 + 4 = 9 - 2$; $7 \times 2 = 9 + 5$; $11 - 6 = 15 \div 3$
3. $9 + 3 = 24 - 12$; $6 \times 3 = 13 + 5$; $12 - 9 = 24 \div 8$
4. $10 + 5 = 30 - 15$; $5 \times 15 = 40 + 35$; $40 - 35 = 30 \div 6$
5. $25 + 5 = 90 - 60$; $5 \times 9 = 20 + 25$; $60 - 50 = 90 \div 9$
6. $25 + 15 = 50 - 10$; $5 \times 10 = 15 + 35$; $25 - 15 = 80 \div 8$
7. $75 + 15 = 100 - 10$; $5 \times 15 = 25 + 50$; $50 - 25 = 125 \div 5$
8. $70 + 5 = 150 - 75$; $5 \times 30 = 80 + 70$; $80 - 75 = 150 \div 30$
9. $50 + 20 = 150 - 80$; $5 \times 25 = 120 + 5$; $120 - 80 = 200 \div 5$

## Page 84

1. –, +   2. +, ÷   3. x, +
4. +, – or ÷, ÷   5. +, –   6. –, x
7. ÷, +   8. +, – or –, ÷   9. –, ÷
10. x, x   11. +, x   12. x, ÷
13. x, – or –, ÷   14. ÷, ÷, or –, +   15. ÷, x
16. ÷, –   17. +, x or –, –, or ÷, ÷
18. –, ÷   19. x, – or ÷, ÷   20. ÷, –
21. x, x   22. ÷, ÷

## Page 85
1. +, x
2. x, +
3. x, x
4. ÷, +
5. ÷, −
6. ÷, ÷
7. −, −
8. +, +; x, −
9. −, x; −, ÷
10. x, ÷; +, −; ÷, x; −, +

## Page 86
1. A = 5; B = 8
2. D = 6, E = 9
3. F = 4; G = 3; H = 7
4. J = 12; K = 10; L = 15
5. M = 30; N = 40; P = 35; Q = 25
6. R = 60; S = 50; T = 55; U = 75

## Page 87
The following equations should be circled: 1, 3, 4, 5, 6, 8, 11, 14, 16, 18, 19, 21

## Page 88
1. 25, 9, 7, 190, 8, 56, **6**, 160
2. 8, 180, **6**, 70, 25, 7, 50, 125
3. 10, 25, 30, **6**, 7, 8, 5, 400
4. 20, 3, 9, 8, **6**, 4, 200, 7

## Page 89
1. =
2. ≠
3. ≠
4. =
5. =
6. =
7. ≠
8. =
9. =
10. ≠
11. =
12. ≠
13. =
14. ≠
15. ≠
16. =
17. =
18. =
19. ≠
20. ≠
21. ≠
22. ≠
23. ≠
24. =

## Page 90
1. 2 x 5 x 2 = 20
2. 3 x 3 x 2 = 18
3. 2 x 2 x 4 = 16
4. 3 x 3 x 4 = 36
5. 2 x 5 x 5 = 50
6. 3 x 2 x 5 = 30
7. 3 x 3 x 3 = 27
8. 2 x 4 x 4 = 32
9. 2 x 3 x 4 = 24
10. 5 x 5 x 4 = 100
11. 3 x 3 x 5 = 45
12. 4 x 2 x 5 = 40
13. 4 x 4 x 4 = 64
14. 3 x 4 x 5 = 60
15. 4 x 4 x 5 = 80
16. 5 x 5 x 3 = 75
17. 4 x 4 x 3 = 48
18. 5 x 5 x 5 = 125

## Page 91
1. 3
2. 9
3. 7
4. 4
5. 2
6. 6
7. 5
8. 8
9. 1
10. 10
11. 4
12. 5
Students should show their work.

## Page 92
1. 35
2. 50
3. 10
4. 8
5. 41
6. 45
7. 30
8. 20
9. 6
10. 6
11. 4
12. 5
13. 6
14. 2
15. 3
16. 4

## Page 93
1. any number greater than 7; any number less than 7; 7
2. any number less than 6; any number greater than 6; 6
3. any number greater than 9; any number less than 9; 9
4. any number less than 45; any number greater than 45; 45
5. any number greater than 4; any number less than 4; 4
6. any number greater than 3; any number less than 3; 3

## Page 94
Answers will vary.

## Page 95
The following should be circled: A = A; A = C − B; C + B > A; A − B = A − B; C > A; C − A = B; C + A > B; A + B = B + A; C = B + A; A + B < C + B

D < F; E x D = F; E x F > D; D x E = E x D; F > E; F ÷ E = D; D ÷ E < F; D x E x F = F x E x D; F = D x E; D x F > E; F x F > E x E; E = F ÷ D

## Page 96
1. 2
2. 36
3. 3
4. 3
5. 4
6. 20
7. 8
8. 34
9. 2
10. 21
11. 7
12. 6
13. 4
14. 14
15. 8
16. 2
17. 7
18. 8
19. 21
20. 12
21. 4
22. 5
23. 7
24. 9

## Page 97
Answers will vary.

## Page 98
1. A = 25; B = 5; C = 10
2. D = 40; E = 25; F = 15
3. G = 50; H = 70; I = 30
4. J = 80; K = 35; L = 45
5. M = 55; N = 15; P = 60
6. Q = 70; R = 100; S = 25
7. T = 80; U = 50; V = 20
8. W = 50; Y = 25; Z = 100

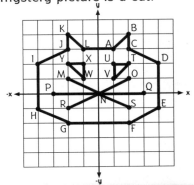
## Page 99

1. −2; 12, 10, 8, 6, 4, 2, 0, -2, -4, -6, -8
2. +3; -6, -3, 0, 3, 6, 9, 12, 15, 18, 21, 24
3. +1; -6, -5, -4, -3, -2, -1, 0, 1, 2, 3, 4
4. −4; 10, 6, 2, -2, -6, -10, -14, -18, -22, -26, -30
5. −1; 3, 2, 1, 0, -1, -2, -3, -4, -5, -6, -7
6. +6; -5, 1, 7, 13, 19, 25, 31, 37, 43, 49, 55
7. −3; 9, 6, 4, 0, -3, -6, -9, -12, -15, -18, -21

## Page 100

1. $-\frac{1}{2}$ ; 3, $2\frac{1}{2}$, 2, $1\frac{1}{2}$, 1, $\frac{1}{2}$, 0, $-\frac{1}{2}$, -1, $-1\frac{1}{2}$, -2
2. $+\frac{1}{3}$ ; $2\frac{2}{3}$, 3, $3\frac{1}{3}$, $3\frac{2}{3}$, 4, $4\frac{1}{3}$, $4\frac{2}{3}$, 5, $5\frac{1}{3}$, $5\frac{2}{3}$, 6
3. $+\frac{1}{4}$ ; 1, $1\frac{1}{4}$, $1\frac{2}{4}$, $1\frac{3}{4}$, 2, $2\frac{1}{4}$, $2\frac{2}{4}$, $2\frac{3}{4}$, 3, $3\frac{1}{4}$, $3\frac{2}{4}$
4. $-\frac{1}{5}$ ; 1, $\frac{4}{5}$, $\frac{3}{5}$, $\frac{2}{5}$, $\frac{1}{5}$, 0, $-\frac{1}{5}$, $-\frac{2}{5}$, $-\frac{3}{5}$, $-\frac{4}{5}$, -1
5. $+\frac{1}{2}$ ; $1\frac{1}{2}$, 2, $2\frac{1}{2}$, 3, $3\frac{1}{2}$, 4, $4\frac{1}{2}$, 5, $5\frac{1}{2}$, 6, $6\frac{1}{2}$
6. $-\frac{1}{3}$ ; 4, $3\frac{2}{3}$, $3\frac{1}{3}$, 3, $2\frac{2}{3}$, $2\frac{1}{3}$, 2, $1\frac{2}{3}$, $1\frac{1}{3}$, 1, $\frac{2}{3}$
7. $+\frac{1}{6}$ ; $1\frac{4}{6}$, $1\frac{5}{6}$, 2, $2\frac{1}{6}$, $2\frac{2}{6}$, $2\frac{3}{6}$, $2\frac{4}{6}$, $2\frac{5}{6}$, 3, $3\frac{1}{6}$, $3\frac{2}{6}$

## Page 101

1. x = 10, y = 20; 10, 11, 12, 13, 14, 15, 16, 17, 18, 19, **20**
2. x = 4, y = 12; 0, 3, 6, 9, **12**, 15, 18, 21, 24, 27, 30
3. x = 9, y = 4; -5, -4, -3, -2, -1, 0, 1, 2, 3, **4**, 5
4. x = 5, y = 25; 0, 5, 10, 15, 20, **25**, 30, 35, 40, 45, 50
5. x = 6, y = 3; -3, -2, -1, 0, 1, 2, **3**, 4, 5, 6, 7
6. x = 6, y = 12; 0, 2, 4, 6, 8, 10, **12**, 14, 16, 18, 20

## Page 102

1. 7, 17, 1, -7
2. 60, 28, 22, 26
3. 15, 45, -9, 4.5
4. 0, 30, -9, 240
5. 5, 0, 10, 2
6. 5, 8, 10, 2
7. 24, 30, 42, 22
8. 3, 8, 2, 50

## Page 103

1. x3, −1
2. +5, x2
3. +6, ÷2
4. x2, −4
5. +3, x2
6. ÷3, +4
7. ÷4, +5
8. x3, ÷6
9. +4, ÷5
10. ÷2, +3
11. +5, ÷5
12. +7, −5
13. x2, x3
14. x6, +3
15. x3, ÷2
16. x8, ÷3

## Page 104

The mystery picture is a cat.

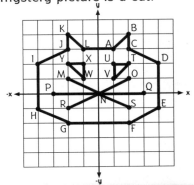

## Page 105

1. (-2, -1)
2. (-3, -3)
3. (1, 1)
4. (2, 0)
5. (3, 2)
6. (1, -1)
7. (0, -3)
8. (2, 4)
9. (3, -1)
10. (-4, 2)
11. (-2, 2)
12. (2, -3)
13. (-1, 0)
14. (0, 4)
15. (0, 0)
16. (-1, 3)

## Page 106

1. x + y = 9; 8, 7, 6, 5, 4, 3, 2, 1

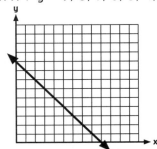

2. x + 4 = y; 5, 6, 7, 8, 9, 10, 11, 12, 13

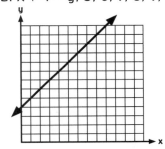

3. x − 3 = y; 1, 2, 3, 4, 5, 6, 7, 8, 9

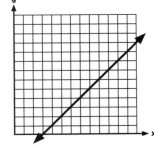

4. x − 2 = y; 8, 7, 6, 5, 4, 3, 2, 1

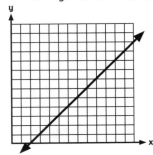

## Page 107

1. 2, 3, 4, 5, 6, 7, 8, 9, 10
   y (0, 2); (-2, 0)

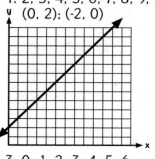

2. 6, 5, 4, 3, 2, 1, 0
   y (3, 3); 8

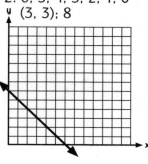

3. 0, 1, 2, 3, 4, 5, 6
   y (4, 0); (0, -4)

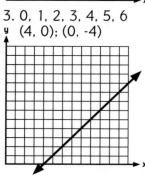

## Page 108

1. 6, 5, 4, 3, 2, 1, 0, -1,
   -2, -3, -4

2. 5, 4, 3, 2, 1, 0, -1, -2,
   -3, -4, -5

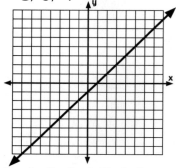

3. -4, -3, -2, -1, 0, 1, 2,
   3, 4, 5

4. -8, -6, -4, -2, 0, 2,
   4, 6, 8

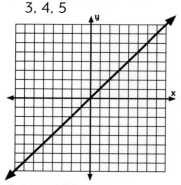
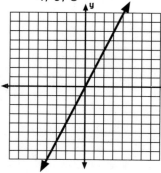

## Page 109

1. x: 8, 12, 48, 98; y: 8, 12, 17, 42; add 2 to x to get y
2. x: 13, 24, 32; y: 11, 31, 66, 96; subtract 4 from x to get y
3. x: 15, 25, 50, 75; y: 60, 90, 300; multiply x by 3 to get y
4. x: 20, 40, 50, 100; y: 15, 35, 75; divide x by 2 to get y
5. x: 34, 66, 96; y: 19, 32, 65, 90; add 9 to x to get y
6. x: 40, 73, 105, 125; y: 35, 70, 85; subtract 25 from x to get y

## Page 110

| | | | | | |
|---|---|---|---|---|---|
| 1. 21 | 2. 11 | 3. 0 | 4. 22 | 5. 40 | 6. -4 |
| 7. 30 | 8. 27 | 9. -9 | 10. 37 | 11. 101 | 12. 12 |

## Page 111

1. $x + 3 = y$     2. $10 - x = y$     3. $x - y = 5$
4. $x = y + 4$     5. $y = 2x$     6. $y = 3x$
7. $x - y = 8$     8. $x + y = 20$     9. $y = x + 8$
10. $4x + 1 = y$     11. $2x + 6 = y$     12. $3x + 1 = y$

## Page 112

1. $x + y = 12$     2. $x - y = 4$     3. $3x - 2 = y$
4. $x = 3y$     5. $x + 5 = y$     6. $x = 2y + 3$
7. $x - 6 = y$     8. $2x = y$     9. $2x - y = 10$
10. $2x + 3 = y$     11. $x = 4y + 2$     12. $y - x = 4$

## Page 113

Answers will vary.

## Page 114

table: 6, 4; 9, 9; 12, 16; 15, 25; 18, 36; 21, 49; 24, 64;
27, 81; 30, 100
1. counting by 3s     2. square of the length of side
3. C                  4. 36 units, 144 sq. units
5. area               6. 3
7. itself             8. 300 units; 10,000 sq. units

## Page 115

table: 8, 4; 12, 9; 16, 16; 20, 25; 24, 36; 28, 49; 32,
64; 36, 81; 40, 100
1. counting by 4s     2. square of the length of side
3. D                  4. 48 units, 144 sq. units
5. area               6. 4
7. itself             8. 400 units; 10,000 sq. units

## Page 116

**Triffids** arms: 4, 5, 6, 7; 1. $T + 2 = A$; 2. 12 arms
**Riffids** arms: 6, 8, 10, 12; 1. $2R + 2 = A$; 2. 42 arms
**Piffids** arms: 8, 11, 14, 17; 1. $3P + 2 = A$; 2. 47 arms

## Page 117

**A** arms: 7, 9, 11, 13
1. +2; 2. 13 arms; 3. $(2 \times C) + 1 = A$; 4. 201 arms
**B** arms: 10, 13, 16, 19
1. +3; 2. 19 arms; 3. $(3 \times C) + 1 = A$; 4. 301 arms

## Page 118

**Triangles** y: 4, 5, 6, 7, 8, 9, 10; $x + 2 = y$; 1. 12; 2. 48
**Squares** y: 6, 8, 10, 12, 14, 16, 18; $2x + 2 = y$; 1. 22; 2. 14
**Hexagons** y: 10, 14, 18, 22, 26, 30, 34; $4x + 2 = y$; 1. 42; 2. 20

# A2
LEVEL

# CHEMISTRY
## FOR CCEA A2 LEVEL

**COLOURPOINT**
EDUCATIONAL

# Wingfield Glassey

© 2017 Wingfield Glassey and Colourpoint Creative Ltd

ISBN: 978-1-78073-017-2

First Edition
First Impression

Layout and design: April Sky Design
Printed by: GPS Colour Graphics Ltd, Belfast

## The Author

Dr Wingfield Glassey teaches Chemistry at Friends' School Lisburn, and is an examiner for GCE AS and A2 Chemistry. Dr Glassey also maintains a professional interest in the teaching and learning of science, and has published scholarly articles in a number of peer-reviewed journals including *The Journal of Chemical Education*. He maintains a web site containing resources for A-Level Chemistry at http://wglassey.me.uk

## Copyright

**Colourpoint Educational**
*An imprint of Colourpoint Creative Ltd*
Colourpoint House
Jubilee Business Park
21 Jubilee Road
Newtownards
County Down
Northern Ireland
BT23 4YH

Tel:  028 9182 6339
Fax: 028 9182 1900
E-mail: sales@colourpoint.co.uk
Web site: www.colourpoint.co.uk

**Publisher's Note:** This book has been through a rigorous quality assurance process by an independent person experienced in the CCEA specification prior to publication. It has been written to help students preparing for the A2 Chemistry specification from CCEA. While Colourpoint Educational, the author and the quality assurance person have taken every care in its production, we are not able to guarantee that the book is completely error-free. Additionally, while the book has been written to closely match the CCEA specification, it is the responsibility of each candidate to satisfy themselves that they have fully met the requirements of the CCEA specification prior to sitting an exam set by that body. For this reason, and because specifications change with time, we strongly advise every candidate to avail of a qualified teacher and to check the contents of the most recent specification for themselves prior to the exam. Colourpoint Creative Ltd therefore cannot be held responsible for any errors or omissions in this book or any consequences thereof.

# CONTENTS

# Unit A2 1:

# Further Physical and Organic Chemistry

# 4.1 Energetics: Solids and Solutions

Previously, at AS Level, we used Hess's Law to determine enthalpy changes that could not be measured in the laboratory. In this section we examine how Hess's Law can be used to determine enthalpy changes for reactions involving solids and solutions.

## Lattice Enthalpy

**In this section we are learning to:**

- Explain what is meant by the lattice enthalpy of an ionic compound.
- Account for trends in the lattice enthalpies of ionic compounds.

An ionic compound is made up of cations and anions packed tightly in an ordered lattice. The ionic lattice in solid sodium chloride is illustrated in Figure 1. The compound is held together by strong attractive forces between oppositely charged ions in the lattice. The strength of the ionic bonding between the ions in the lattice is measured by the lattice enthalpy of the compound. The **lattice enthalpy** of an ionic compound, $\Delta_{latt}H$ is *the enthalpy change when one mole of an ionic compound is converted to gas phase ions.*

*Lattice enthalpy of sodium oxide:*
$$Na_2O_{(s)} \rightarrow 2Na^+_{(g)} + O^{2-}_{(g)} \quad \Delta H = \Delta_{latt}H(Na_2O)$$

*Lattice enthalpy for magnesium fluoride:*
$$MgF_{2(s)} \rightarrow Mg^{2+}_{(g)} + 2F^-_{(g)} \quad \Delta H = \Delta_{latt}H(MgF_2)$$

The lattice enthalpies for Group I and Group II fluorides in Figure 2a demonstrate that lattice enthalpy decreases as the metal ions get bigger and the distance between neighbouring ions increases down the group. The comparison also demonstrates that the lattice enthalpies of the Group II fluorides are significantly greater than the corresponding Group I fluorides. This results from greater attraction between neighbouring ions as the charge on the metal ions increases.

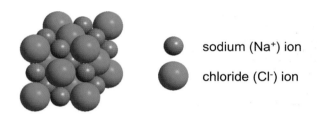

○ sodium (Na⁺) ion

○ chloride (Cl⁻) ion

*Figure 1: The ionic lattice in sodium chloride, NaCl. The sodium cations are surrounded by chloride anions and vice versa.*

Similarly, Figure 2b demonstrates that the lattice enthalpy of a Group II oxide is greater than that of the corresponding Group II fluoride as the charge on an oxide ($O^{2-}$) ion is greater than the charge on a fluoride ($F^-$) ion in the corresponding Group II fluoride. The effect of ion size and charge on the lattice enthalpy of an ionic compound is summarised in Figure 3.

**Exercise 4.1A**

1. The strength of the ionic bonding in compounds, such as magnesium fluoride and magnesium chloride, is related to the lattice enthalpy of the compound. Define the term *lattice enthalpy*.

   *(CCEA January 2011)*

2. Which one of the following equations represents the lattice enthalpy of sodium chloride?

   A   $NaCl_{(aq)} \rightarrow Na_{(g)} + Cl_{(g)}$
   B   $NaCl_{(aq)} \rightarrow Na^+_{(g)} + Cl^-_{(g)}$
   C   $NaCl_{(s)} \rightarrow Na^+_{(aq)} + Cl^-_{(aq)}$
   D   $NaCl_{(s)} \rightarrow Na^+_{(g)} + Cl^-_{(g)}$

   *(CCEA May 2012)*

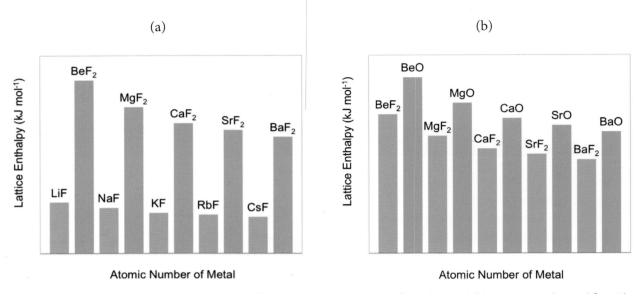

Figure 2: Comparison of the lattice enthalpy for (a) Group I and Group II fluorides, and (b) Group II oxides and fluorides.

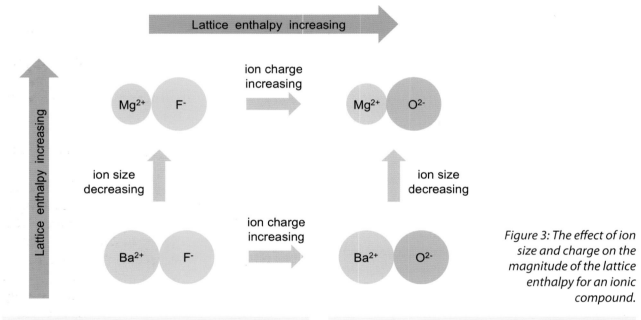

Figure 3: The effect of ion size and charge on the magnitude of the lattice enthalpy for an ionic compound.

3. Which one of the following equations represents the lattice enthalpy of calcium bromide?

A  $Ca_{(s)} + Br_{2(l)} \rightarrow CaBr_{2(s)}$

B  $CaBr_{2(s)} \rightarrow Ca_{(s)} + Br_{2(g)}$

C  $Ca^{2+}_{(g)} + 2Br^-_{(g)} \rightarrow CaBr_{2(g)}$

D  $CaBr_{2(s)} \rightarrow Ca^{2+}_{(g)} + 2Br^-_{(g)}$

(CCEA May 2009)

4. Values for the lattice enthalpies of the calcium halides are given in the following table.
(a) Explain why all of these values are positive.

(b) Suggest why the values of the lattice enthalpies for the calcium halides decrease as Group VII is descended.

| CaF$_2$ | CaCl$_2$ | CaBr$_2$ | CaI$_2$ |
|---|---|---|---|
| +2630 | +2258 | +2176 | +2074 |

(CCEA May 2015)

5. The lattice enthalpies for Group I chlorides are listed in the following table. Suggest why the lattice enthalpy decreases as you descend the group.

| Salt | Lattice enthalpy, kJ mol$^{-1}$ |
|---|---|
| Lithium chloride | 848 |
| Sodium chloride | 780 |
| Potassium chloride | 711 |
| Rubidium chloride | 685 |
| Caesium chloride | 661 |

*(CCEA January 2010)*

6. Suggest why the lattice enthalpies of the magnesium halides in the following table decrease.

| | Lattice enthalpy, kJ mol$^{-1}$ |
|---|---|
| Magnesium fluoride | +2913 |
| Magnesium bromide | +2097 |
| Magnesium iodide | +1944 |

*(Adapted from CCEA January 2009)*

7. (a) Write the equation for the lattice enthalpy of magnesium chloride. (b) Explain why the lattice enthalpy for sodium chloride is less than the lattice enthalpy for magnesium chloride.

*(CCEA June 2005)*

Before moving to the next section, check that you are able to:

- Define the *lattice enthalpy* of an ionic compound.
- Account for trends in the lattice enthalpies of ionic compounds in terms of the size and charge of the ions in the compounds.

## Born-Haber Cycles

In this section we are learning to:

- Construct a Born-Haber cycle for an ionic compound.

The lattice enthalpy of an ionic compound cannot be measured directly and must instead be calculated from enthalpy changes that can be measured. This is accomplished by using Hess's Law to construct a type of enthalpy diagram known as a **Born-Haber cycle**. The Born-Haber cycle for an ionic compound relates the enthalpy changes associated with forming the compound from its elements.

The **standard enthalpy of formation**, $\Delta_f H^\circ$ of a compound is *the enthalpy change when one mole of the compound is formed from its elements under standard conditions.*

$$Mg_{(s)} + Cl_{2(g)} \rightarrow MgCl_{2(s)} \qquad \Delta H = \Delta_f H^\circ$$

This is equivalent to first converting atoms of each element into gas phase atoms ($\Delta_{atoms}H$), and then into gas phase ions ($\Delta_{ions}H$), before finally using the gas phase ions to form the compound ($-\Delta_{latt}H$).

$$Mg_{(s)} + Cl_{2(g)} \rightarrow Mg_{(g)} + 2Cl_{(g)} \qquad \Delta H = \Delta_{atoms}H$$

$$Mg_{(g)} + 2Cl_{(g)} \rightarrow Mg^{2+}_{(g)} + 2Cl^-_{(g)} \qquad \Delta H = \Delta_{ions}H$$

$$Mg^{2+}_{(g)} + 2Cl^-_{(g)} \rightarrow MgCl_{2(s)} \qquad \Delta H = -\Delta_{latt}H$$

*Applying Hess's law gives:*
$$\Delta_f H^\circ = \Delta_{atoms}H + \Delta_{ions}H - \Delta_{latt}H \qquad \text{Equation 1}$$

This relationship can be represented in the form of a Born-Haber cycle. The Born-Haber cycle for $MgCl_2$ in given in Figure 4 and is similar to the Born-Haber cycles for other ionic compounds. The lattice enthalpy, $\Delta_{latt}H$ is endothermic as energy is needed to overcome the attractive forces between oppositely charged ions in the lattice. The enthalpy change $\Delta_{atoms}H$ is also endothermic as energy is required to break the bonds between the atoms in the elements. For most ionic compounds, the enthalpy change $\Delta_{ions}H$ is also endothermic as the energy needed to ionise the metal atoms is greater than the energy released on adding electrons to the non-metal atoms. In contrast, the standard enthalpy of formation, $\Delta_f H^\circ$ for an ionic compound is exothermic as the energy released when the ions bond to form the lattice is greater than the energy needed to break bonds in the elements.

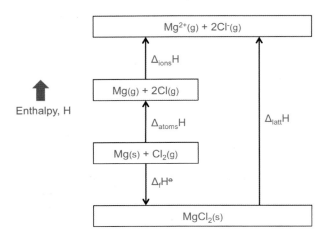

*Figure 4: A Born-Haber cycle for magnesium chloride, MgCl₂.*

### Forming Atoms from Elements

In the case of $MgCl_2$, $\Delta_{atoms}H$ is the enthalpy change when one mole of gas phase magnesium atoms and two moles of gas phase chlorine atoms are formed from magnesium and chlorine in their standard states: $Mg_{(s)}$ and $Cl_{2(g)}$.

*Forming magnesium atoms:*
$$Mg_{(s)} \rightarrow Mg_{(g)} \qquad \Delta H = \Delta_{atom}H(Mg)$$

*Forming chlorine atoms:*
$$Cl_{2(g)} \rightarrow 2Cl_{(g)} \qquad \Delta H = 2\Delta_{atom}H(Cl)$$

*Overall change:*
$$Mg_{(s)} + Cl_{2(g)} \rightarrow Mg_{(g)} + 2Cl_{(g)}$$
$$\Delta H = \Delta_{atoms}H = \Delta_{atom}H(Mg) + 2\Delta_{atom}H(Cl)$$

The **enthalpy of atomisation**, $\Delta_{atom}H$ of an element is *the enthalpy change when one mole of gas phase atoms are formed from the element in its standard state.*

. . . . . . . . . . . . . . . . . . . . . . . . . . . . . . . . . . . . . . . . . . . . . . . . . . . . . . . . . . . . .

### Worked Example 4.1i

Write the equation used to define the enthalpy of atomisation for (a) iron, (b) bromine and (c) phosphorus.

### Strategy

- Recall that atomisation is the process of turning atoms in their standard state into atoms in the gas phase.
- Recall that under standard conditions: iron is a

metal, bromine is a diatomic liquid and phosphorus is a molecular solid with formula $P_4$.

### Solution

(a) $Fe_{(s)} \rightarrow Fe_{(g)} \qquad \Delta H = \Delta_{atom}H(Fe)$

(b) $\frac{1}{2} Br_{2(l)} \rightarrow Br_{(g)} \qquad \Delta H = \Delta_{atom}H(Br)$

(c) $\frac{1}{4} P_{4(s)} \rightarrow P_{(g)} \qquad \Delta H = \Delta_{atom}H(P)$

. . . . . . . . . . . . . . . . . . . . . . . . . . . . . . . . . . . . . . . . . . .

> **Before moving to the next section, check that you are able to:**
>
> - Define the *standard enthalpy of formation* of an ionic compound.
> - Define the *enthalpy of atomisation* of an element.
> - Explain how Hess's Law can be used to relate the enthalpy of formation and lattice enthalpy of an ionic compound by constructing a Born-Haber cycle.

### Forming Ions from Atoms

In the case of $MgCl_2$, $\Delta_{ions}H$ corresponds to the enthalpy change when one mole of gas phase magnesium atoms are converted to $Mg^{2+}$ ions, and two moles of gas phase chlorine atoms are converted to $Cl^-$ ions.

*Forming magnesium ions:*
$$Mg_{(g)} \rightarrow Mg^{2+}_{(g)} \qquad \Delta H = \Delta_{ion}H(Mg)$$

*Forming chloride ions:*
$$2Cl_{(g)} \rightarrow 2Cl^-_{(g)} \qquad \Delta H = 2\Delta_{ion}H(Cl)$$

*Overall change:*
$$Mg_{(g)} + 2Cl_{(g)} \rightarrow Mg^{2+}_{(g)} + 2Cl^-_{(g)}$$
$$\Delta H = \Delta_{ions}H = \Delta_{ion}H(Mg) + 2\Delta_{ion}H(Cl)$$

The enthalpy change to form $Mg^{2+}$ ions from gas phase magnesium atoms, $\Delta_{ion}H(Mg)$ is the sum of the first and second ionisation energies (IE1 and IE2) for magnesium.

$$Mg_{(g)} \rightarrow Mg^+_{(g)} + e^- \qquad \Delta H = IE1(Mg)$$
$$Mg^+_{(g)} \rightarrow Mg^{2+}_{(g)} + e^- \qquad \Delta H = IE2(Mg)$$
$$Mg_{(g)} \rightarrow Mg^{2+}_{(g)} + 2e^- \qquad \Delta H = \Delta_{ion}H(Mg)$$
$$= IE1(Mg) + IE2(Mg)$$

The enthalpy change to form $Cl^-$ ions from gas phase chlorine atoms, $\Delta_{ion}H(Cl)$ is the first electron affinity for chlorine, EA1(Cl).

$$Cl_{(g)} + e^- \rightarrow Cl^-_{(g)} \qquad \Delta H = \Delta_{ion}H(Cl) = EA1(Cl)$$

The **first electron affinity** (EA1) of an element is *the enthalpy change when one mole of electrons is added to one mole of gas phase atoms to form gas phase ions with a charge of 1–.*

*First electron affinity for oxygen:*
$$O_{(g)} + e^- \rightarrow O^-_{(g)} \qquad \Delta H = EA1(O)$$

*First electron affinity for hydrogen:*
$$H_{(g)} + e^- \rightarrow H^-_{(g)} \qquad \Delta H = EA1(H)$$

The first electron affinity, EA1 for oxygen, fluorine and other electronegative elements is very exothermic. Less electronegative elements have a smaller EA1.

The **second electron affinity** (EA2) of an element is *the enthalpy change when one mole of electrons is added to one mole of gas phase ions with a charge of 1– to form gas phase ions with a charge of 2–.*

*Second electron affinity for chlorine:*
$$Cl^-_{(g)} + e^- \rightarrow Cl^{2-}_{(g)} \qquad \Delta H = EA2(Cl)$$

*Second electron affinity for oxygen:*
$$O^-_{(g)} + e^- \rightarrow O^{2-}_{(g)} \qquad \Delta H = EA2(O)$$

The second electron affinity, EA2 is endothermic as energy is required to overcome the repulsion when an electron is added to a negatively charged ion.

## Exercise 4.1B

1. Which one of the following reactions in the Born-Haber cycle for potassium iodide is exothermic?

   A   $KI_{(s)} \rightarrow K^+_{(g)} + I^-_{(g)}$

   B   $K_{(g)} \rightarrow K^+_{(g)} + e^-$

   C   $I_{2(g)} \rightarrow 2I_{(g)}$

   D   $I_{(g)} + e^- \rightarrow I^-_{(g)}$

   *(CCEA May 2008)*

2. Which one of the following has a positive enthalpy value?

   A   $Na_{(g)} \rightarrow Na_{(s)}$

   B   $Na^+_{(g)} + e^- \rightarrow Na_{(g)}$

   C   $O_{(g)} + e^- \rightarrow O^-_{(g)}$

   D   $O^-_{(g)} + e^- \rightarrow O^{2-}_{(g)}$

   *(CCEA June 2014)*

3. The energy produced when an electron is added to an isolated atom would be the highest for elements in:

   A   Group I

   B   Group III

   C   Group VII

   D   Group VIII

   *(CCEA January 2012)*

4. The lattice enthalpies for potassium chloride and potassium bromide are +710 kJ mol⁻¹ and +679 kJ mol⁻¹ respectively. (a) State three other enthalpy changes that would differ in the Born-Haber cycles for these compounds. (b) Explain why these enthalpy changes differ for each compound.

   *(CCEA May 2013)*

5. For which one of the following chlorides is it not possible to construct a Born-Haber cycle?

   A   AgCl        B   HCl

   C   RbCl        D   MgCl₂

   *(CCEA January 2007)*

Before moving to the next section, check that you are able to:

- Explain the changes that occur when gaseous atoms are converted to gaseous ions.
- Define the *first and second ionisation energies* of an element.
- Define the *first and second electron affinities* of an element.
- Recall the relationship between the electronegativity of an element and the size of EA1.
- Explain why EA2 is endothermic.

# Working with Born-Haber Cycles

## In this section we are learning to:

- Use a Born-Haber cycle to calculate enthalpy changes associated with the formation of an ionic compound.

## Calculating Lattice Enthalpy

While all Born-Haber cycles have the same basic form as the cycle for $MgCl_2$ in Figure 4, the individual enthalpy changes that make up $\Delta_{atoms}H$ and $\Delta_{ions}H$ may be organised or grouped differently, making the cycle appear more complex.

Often, the goal of constructing a Born-Haber cycle is to calculate the lattice enthalpy, $\Delta_{latt}H$ for an ionic compound. The relationship between $\Delta_fH^\circ$, $\Delta_{atoms}H$, $\Delta_{ions}H$ and $\Delta_{latt}H$ obtained by applying Hess's Law (Equation 1, page 7) can be rearranged to give an equation that can be used to calculate the lattice enthalpy (Equation 2, below).

Equation to calculate lattice enthalpy:
$$\Delta_{latt}H = \Delta_{atoms}H + \Delta_{ions}H - \Delta_fH^\circ \qquad \text{Equation 2}$$

## Worked Example 4.1ii

Magnesium chloride is an ionic compound. The Born-Haber cycle for the formation of magnesium chloride is shown in the following diagram.

(a) Name the energy changes X, Y and Z.

(b) Calculate the lattice enthalpy for magnesium chloride

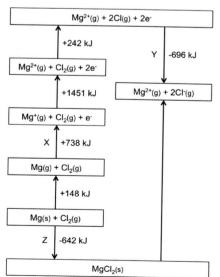

(CCEA May 2010)

### Strategy

- Use the definitions of $\Delta_{atom}H$, IE1, IE2 and EA1 to identify X, Y and Z.
- Combine the individual enthalpy changes to calculate $\Delta_{atoms}H$ and $\Delta_{ions}H$.
- Use the relationship between $\Delta_{latt}H$, $\Delta_{atoms}H$, $\Delta_{ions}H$ and $\Delta_fH^\circ$ (Equation 2) to calculate the lattice enthalpy.

### Solution

(a) X represents the first ionisation energy for magnesium.

Y represents twice the electron affinity of chlorine.

Z represents the enthalpy of formation of magnesium chloride.

(b) $\Delta_{atoms}H = \Delta_{atom}H(Mg) + 2\,\Delta_{atom}H(Cl)$
   $= 148 + 242 = 390 \text{ kJ mol}^{-1}$

   $\Delta_{ions}H = IE1(Mg) + IE2(Mg) + 2\,EA1(Cl)$
   $= 738 + 1451 + (-696) = 1493 \text{ kJ mol}^{-1}$

   $\Delta_{latt}H = \Delta_{atoms}H + \Delta_{ions}H - \Delta_fH^\circ$
   $= 390 + 1493 - (-642) = 2525 \text{ kJ mol}^{-1}$

### Exercise 4.1C

1   (a) Complete the Born-Haber cycle for magnesium fluoride shown in the following diagram.

(b) Use the data in the table to calculate the lattice enthalpy for magnesium fluoride.

|  | kJ mol⁻¹ |
|---|---|
| Standard enthalpy of formation for magnesium fluoride | −1123 |
| First electron affinity of fluorine | −348 |
| Atomisation enthalpy of fluorine | 79 |
| First ionisation enthalpy of magnesium | 736 |
| Second ionisation enthalpy of magnesium | 1450 |
| Atomisation enthalpy of magnesium | 150 |

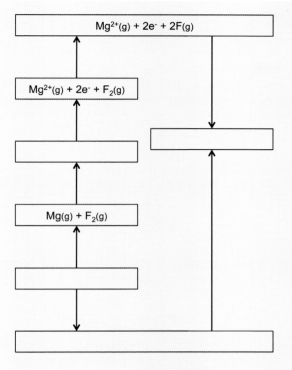

*(CCEA January 2011)*

2. The lattice enthalpy of magnesium chloride can be calculated using the following diagram.

(a) What name is given to this type of diagram?
(b) Identify the type of energy change that occurs in Steps 1, 2 and 3. (c) Use the information given below to calculate the lattice enthalpy of magnesium chloride.

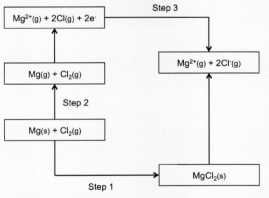

$Mg_{(s)} \rightarrow Mg_{(g)}$ $\qquad \Delta H = +149$ kJ mol$^{-1}$

$Mg_{(g)} \rightarrow Mg^{2+}_{(g)} + 2e^-$ $\quad \Delta H = +2240$ kJ mol$^{-1}$

$\frac{1}{2} Cl_{2(g)} \rightarrow Cl_{(g)}$ $\qquad \Delta H = +121$ kJ mol$^{-1}$

$Cl_{(g)} + e^- \rightarrow Cl^-_{(g)}$ $\qquad \Delta H = -364$ kJ mol$^{-1}$

$Mg_{(s)} + Cl_{2(g)} \rightarrow MgCl_{2(s)}$ $\Delta H = -642$ kJ mol$^{-1}$

*(CCEA January 2014)*

3. A Born-Haber cycle for potassium iodide is shown in the following diagram. The lattice enthalpy is labelled. Other enthalpy changes are shown by the letters A to E. (a) State which letter (A to E) represents:
(i) the standard enthalpy of formation of potassium iodide.
(ii) the first electron affinity of iodine.
(iii) the first ionisation energy of potassium.
(iv) the enthalpy of atomisation of potassium.

(b) Use the data in the table to calculate the lattice enthalpy of potassium iodide.

| Enthalpy change | A | B | C | D | E |
|---|---|---|---|---|---|
| $\Delta H$ / kJ mol$^{-1}$ | 89.5 | 420.0 | 106.6 | −295.4 | −327.6 |

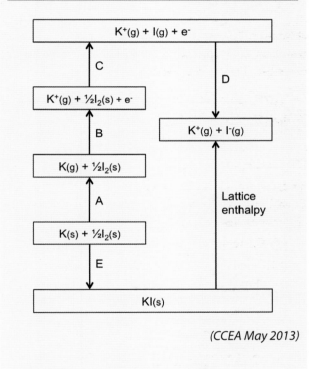

*(CCEA May 2013)*

**Calculating Other Enthalpy Changes**

The relationship between $\Delta_{latt}H$, $\Delta_{atoms}H$, $\Delta_{ions}H$ and $\Delta_f H^{\ominus}$ in Equation 2 can also be used to calculate one of the contributions to $\Delta_{atoms}H$ or $\Delta_{ions}H$ such as IE1 or EA1.

## Exercise 4.1D

1. (a) Complete the Born-Haber cycle for the formation of magnesium chloride in the following diagram. (b) Use the data in the table to calculate the electron affinity of chlorine.

| | kJ mol$^{-1}$ |
|---|---|
| Standard enthalpy of formation for magnesium chloride | −642 |
| Lattice enthalpy for magnesium chloride | 2493 |
| Atomisation enthalpy of chlorine | 121 |
| First ionisation enthalpy of magnesium | 736 |
| Second ionisation enthalpy of magnesium | 1450 |
| Atomisation enthalpy of magnesium | 150 |

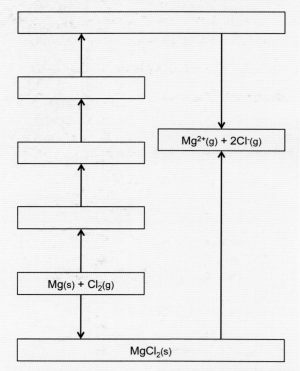

*(CCEA May 2011)*

2. Calcium could form the chlorides CaCl and CaCl$_3$. The following lattice enthalpies were calculated using the theoretical sizes of the ions.

$$CaCl_{(s)} \rightarrow Ca^+_{(g)} + Cl^-_{(g)} \qquad \Delta_{latt}H = +719 \text{ kJ}$$

$$CaCl_{2(s)} \rightarrow Ca^{2+}_{(g)} + 2Cl^-_{(g)} \qquad \Delta_{latt}H = +2218 \text{ kJ}$$

$$CaCl_{3(s)} \rightarrow Ca^{3+}_{(g)} + 3Cl^-_{(g)} \qquad \Delta_{latt}H = +4650 \text{ kJ}$$

(a) Use the thermodynamic values in the following table, together with the appropriate lattice enthalpy, to calculate the enthalpy of formation for CaCl$_{3(s)}$. (b) Use the enthalpy of formation to explain why CaCl$_3$ does not exist. (c) Explain why the lattice enthalpies increase from CaCl to CaCl$_2$ to CaCl$_3$.

| first ionisation energy of calcium | = +590 kJ mol$^{-1}$ |
|---|---|
| second ionisation energy of calcium | = +1145 kJ mol$^{-1}$ |
| third ionisation energy of calcium | = +4912 kJ mol$^{-1}$ |
| standard enthalpy of atomisation of chlorine | = +112 kJ mol$^{-1}$ |
| standard enthalpy of atomisation of calcium | = +178 kJ mol$^{-1}$ |
| electron affinity of chlorine | = −349 kJ mol$^{-1}$ |

*(CCEA May 2015)*

---

**Before moving to the next section, check that you are able to:**

- Identify the individual enthalpy changes used to construct a Born-Haber cycle.
- Complete the Born-Haber cycle for an ionic compound.
- Use a Born-Haber cycle to calculate one of the enthalpy changes associated with the formation of an ionic compound.

---

## Using Bond Enthalpy Values

In elements such as chlorine (Cl$_2$) and oxygen (O$_2$) the enthalpy of atomisation, $\Delta_{atom}H$ can be simply related to the bond enthalpy for the bonds in the element. *In this context the term bond enthalpy (E) refers to the energy needed to break one mole of bonds of a specified type in the element.*

*Breaking one mole of Cl-Cl bonds:*
$Cl_{2(g)} \rightarrow 2Cl_{(g)}$  $\Delta H = E(Cl\text{-}Cl) = 2\Delta_{atom}H(Cl)$

*Breaking one mole of O=O bonds:*
$O_{2(g)} \rightarrow 2O_{(g)}$  $\Delta H = E(O=O) = 2\Delta_{atom}H(O)$

In elements such as bromine the relationship between bond enthalpy, E and enthalpy of atomisation, $\Delta_{atom}H$ is more complex. The enthalpy of atomisation for bromine, $\Delta_{atom}H(Br)$ is the enthalpy change when one mole of atoms in liquid bromine are converted into gas phase atoms.

$Br_{2(l)} \rightarrow 2Br_{(g)}$  $\Delta H = 2\Delta_{atom}H(Br)$

This process is equivalent to vaporising one mole of liquid bromine, $Br_{2(l)}$ before breaking the Br-Br bonds in the bromine vapour, $Br_{2(g)}$ to form two moles of gas phase bromine atoms, $2Br_{(g)}$.

$Br_{2(l)} \rightarrow Br_{2(g)}$  $\Delta H = \Delta_{vap}H(Br)$

$Br_{2(g)} \rightarrow 2Br_{(g)}$  $\Delta H = E(Br\text{-}Br)$

(a)

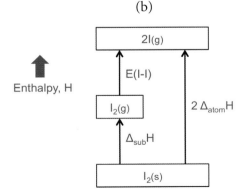

Apply Hess' s law:  $2\Delta_{atom}H = \Delta_{vap}H + E(Br\text{-}Br)$

(b)

Apply Hess's law:  $2\Delta_{atom}H = \Delta_{sub}H + E(I\text{-}I)$

*Figure 5: Hess cycles relating bond enthalpy and the enthalpy of atomisation for (a) bromine and (b) iodine.*

On defining the **enthalpy of vaporisation**, $\Delta_{vap}H$ to be *the enthalpy change when one mole of a liquid is converted to vapour*, the Hess cycle in Figure 5a can be used to relate the Br-Br bond enthalpy, E(Br-Br) to the enthalpy of atomisation for bromine, $\Delta_{atom}H(Br)$.

Similarly, on defining the **enthalpy of sublimation**, $\Delta_{sub}H$ to be *the enthalpy change when one mole of a solid is converted to vapour*, the Hess cycle in Figure 5b can be used to relate the I-I bond enthalpy, E(I-I) to the enthalpy of atomisation for iodine, $\Delta_{atom}H(I)$.

**Worked Example 4.1iii**

The partially completed Born-Haber cycle for sodium fluoride is shown in the following diagram.

(a) Complete the empty boxes in the cycle.

(b) Use the data in the table to calculate the lattice enthalpy for sodium fluoride.

|  | kJ mol⁻¹ |
|---|---|
| First ionisation energy of sodium | +496 |
| Enthalpy of atomisation of sodium | +107 |
| Bond enthalpy of fluorine | +158 |
| Electron affinity of fluorine | −333 |
| Enthalpy of formation of sodium fluoride | −574 |

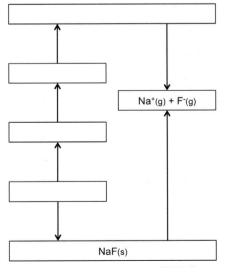

(CCEA January 2010)

### Strategy

- Use the definitions of bond enthalpy, $\Delta_{atom}H$, IE1 and EA1 to identify each step in the cycle.
- Combine the individual enthalpy changes to calculate $\Delta_{atoms}H$ and $\Delta_{ions}H$.
- Use the relationship between $\Delta_{latt}H$, $\Delta_{atoms}H$, $\Delta_{ions}H$ and $\Delta_fH^{\ominus}$ (Equation 2) to calculate the lattice enthalpy.

### Solution

(a)

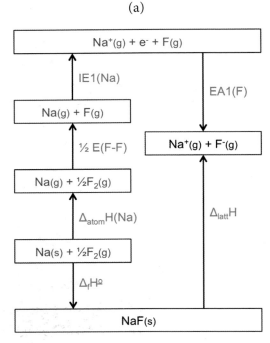

(b)

$$\Delta_{atoms}H = \Delta_{atom}H(Na) + \frac{1}{2}\,E(F{-}F)$$
$$= 107 + \frac{158}{2} = 186 \text{ kJ mol}^{-1}$$

$$\Delta_{ions}H = IE1(Na) + EA1(F) = 496 + (-333)$$
$$= 163 \text{ kJ mol}^{-1}$$

$$\Delta_{latt}H = \Delta_{atoms}H + \Delta_{ions}H - \Delta_fH^{\ominus}$$
$$= 186 + 163 - (-574)$$
$$= 923 \text{ kJ mol}^{-1}$$

### Exercise 4.1 E

1. The incomplete Born-Haber cycle for calcium chloride is shown below. (a) Complete the two empty boxes in the cycle. (b) Name the enthalpy change that is labelled X. (c) Use the values in the table to calculate the lattice enthalpy of calcium chloride.

|  | kJ mol⁻¹ |
|---|---|
| First ionisation energy of calcium | +590 |
| Second ionisation energy of calcium | +1146 |
| Enthalpy of atomisation of calcium | +190 |
| Bond enthalpy of chlorine | +242 |
| Electron affinity of chlorine | −348 |
| Enthalpy of formation of calcium chloride | −795 |

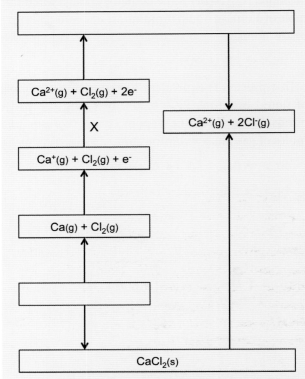

*(Adapted from CCEA May 2012)*

2. The partially completed Born-Haber cycle for rubidium chloride is shown below. (a) Complete the empty boxes in the cycle. (b) Use the data in the following table to calculate the enthalpy of formation for rubidium chloride.

|  | kJ mol⁻¹ |
|---|---|
| First ionisation energy of rubidium | +403 |
| Enthalpy of atomisation of rubidium | +81 |
| Bond enthalpy of chlorine ($Cl_2$) | +242 |
| Electron affinity of chlorine | −348 |
| Lattice enthalpy of rubidium chloride | +685 |

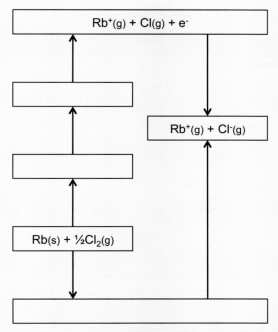

*(Adapted from CCEA January 2010)*

3. The Born-Haber cycle can be written in many different ways. One of those ways is shown in the following diagram. (a) Explain the meaning of the terms: $\Delta H_{diss}$, $\Delta H_{atom}$ and $I_{Mg}$. (b) Calculate the value of U for magnesium oxide. (c) Using the Born-Haber cycle explain why magnesium oxide is very stable. (d) Explain why a Born-Haber cycle cannot be constructed for phosphorus(V) oxide.

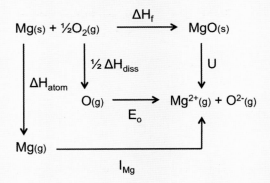

The values of the terms shown in the scheme are:
$\Delta H_f = -602$ kJ mol$^{-1}$, $\Delta H_{diss} = +498$ kJ mol$^{-1}$, $\Delta H_{atom} = +148$ kJ mol$^{-1}$, $I_{Mg} = +2189$ kJ mol$^{-1}$ and $E_o = +657$ kJ mol$^{-1}$.

*(CCEA January 2012)*

4. Calcium hydride is an ionic solid for which a Born-Haber cycle can be constructed as shown in the following diagram. (a) Write the electronic structures of the calcium and hydride ions. (b) State the value of the H-H bond enthalpy. (c) If the first ionisation enthalpy of calcium is 590 kJ mol$^{-1}$, calculate the second ionisation enthalpy. (d) Calculate the lattice enthalpy of calcium hydride.

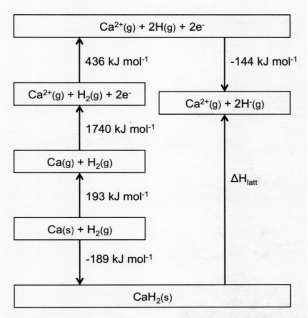

*(CCEA January 2008)*

5. Which one of the following is a correct statement about the Born-Haber cycle for a Group I halide?

A The enthalpy of atomisation of the metal is exothermic.

B The enthalpy of atomisation of the halogen is equal in value to the bond dissociation energy of the halogen.

C The first ionisation energy of the metal is endothermic.

D The electron affinity of the halogen is endothermic.

*(CCEA May 2003)*

6. Explain which element in Group VII has the lowest atomisation enthalpy.

*(CCEA May 2015)*

7. The Born-Haber cycle for calcium oxide is shown below. Which one of the following is a correct statement about the cycle?

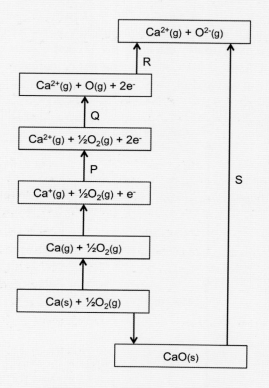

A   The electron affinity of oxygen is Q.

B   The second ionisation enthalpy of calcium is P.

C   The enthalpy of formation of calcium oxide is S.

D   The bond dissociation enthalpy of oxygen is R.

*(Adapted from CCEA May 2014)*

---

Before moving to the next section, check that you are able to:

- Use Hess's Law to relate the enthalpy of atomisation of an element to the bond enthalpy for the bonds in the element.

- Use Born-Haber cycles that make use of bond enthalpies to calculate enthalpy changes associated with the formation of an ionic compound.

## Dissolving Ionic Compounds

### In this section we are learning to:

- Explain what is meant by the enthalpy of solution and the hydration enthalpy of an ionic compound.
- Use Hess's Law to calculate enthalpy changes associated with the dissolving of an ionic compound.

---

### Enthalpy of Solution

When an ionic compound such as magnesium chloride, $MgCl_2$ dissolves in water the magnesium ions, $Mg^{2+}$ and chloride ions, $Cl^-$ break from the solid, and bond with water molecules to form **solvated ions**. The **ion-dipole bonds** that result from the attraction between an ion and the dipoles on surrounding water molecules are illustrated in Figure 6.

(a)

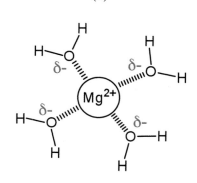

(b)

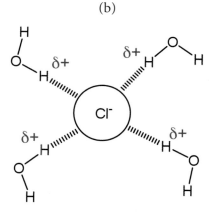

*Figure 6: (a) A solvated magnesium ion, $Mg^{2+}_{(aq)}$ and (b) a solvated chloride ion, $Cl^-_{(aq)}$ in an aqueous solution.*

(a)

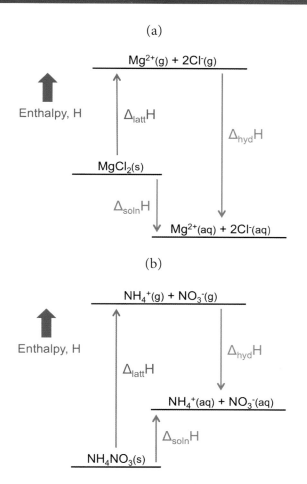

(b)

*Figure 7: An enthalpy diagram describing the relationship between the lattice enthalpy, $\Delta_{latt}H$ hydration enthalpy, $\Delta_{hyd}H$ and enthalpy of solution, $\Delta_{soln}H$ for (a) $MgCl_2$ and (b) $NH_4NO_3$.*

If we define the **enthalpy of solution**, $\Delta_{soln}H$ for a solute to be *the enthalpy change when one mole of the solute dissolves in a solvent*, the enthalpy of solution for magnesium chloride dissolving in water is defined by the change:

$$MgCl_{2(s)} \rightarrow Mg^{2+}{}_{(aq)} + 2Cl^-{}_{(aq)} \qquad \Delta H = \Delta_{soln}H$$

The enthalpy of solution can be endothermic or exothermic. The magnitude and sign of $\Delta_{soln}H$ is determined by the amount of energy needed to break apart the ions in the lattice, and the energy released when the ions become solvated. The energy needed to break apart the lattice corresponds to the lattice enthalpy of the compound, $\Delta_{latt}H$ and is defined by the change:

$$MgCl_{2(s)} \rightarrow Mg^{2+}{}_{(g)} + 2Cl^-{}_{(g)} \qquad \Delta H = \Delta_{latt}H$$

On defining the **enthalpy of hydration for a compound**, $\Delta_{hyd}H$ to be *the enthalpy change when the gas phase ions formed from one mole of the compound bond with water to form solvated ions*, the enthalpy of hydration for $MgCl_2$ is defined by the change:

$$Mg^{2+}{}_{(g)} + 2Cl^-{}_{(g)} \rightarrow Mg^{2+}{}_{(aq)} + 2Cl^-{}_{(aq)} \qquad \Delta H = \Delta_{hyd}H$$

*Applying Hess's Law gives:*
$$\Delta_{soln}H = \Delta_{latt}H + \Delta_{hyd}H \qquad \text{Equation 3}$$

The enthalpy diagram in Figure 7a reveals that the process of dissolving magnesium chloride is exothermic ($\Delta_{soln}H < 0$) as the energy needed to break apart lattice ($\Delta_{latt}H$) is less than the energy released when the ions are solvated ($\Delta_{hyd}H$). In contrast, the enthalpy diagram in Figure 7b reveals that the process of dissolving ammonium nitrate, $NH_4NO_3$ is endothermic ($\Delta_{soln}H > 0$) as the energy needed to break apart the lattice ($\Delta_{latt}H$) is greater than the energy released when the ions are solvated ($\Delta_{hyd}H$).

---

Before moving to the next section, check that you are able to:

- Explain what is meant by the *enthalpy of solution* and the *hydration enthalpy* of an ionic compound.
- Use Hess's Law to explain the relationship between the enthalpy of solution, the hydration enthalpy, and the lattice enthalpy of an ionic compound.

---

**Hydration Enthalpies for Ions**

The enthalpy of hydration of $MgCl_2$, $\Delta_{hyd}H(MgCl_2)$ is the enthalpy change when one mole of gas phase $Mg^{2+}$ ions and two moles of gas phase $Cl^-$ ions are hydrated to form solvated ions.

*Hydrating magnesium chloride:*
$Mg^{2+}{}_{(g)} + 2Cl^-{}_{(g)} \rightarrow Mg^{2+}{}_{(aq)} + 2Cl^-{}_{(aq)}$
$\Delta H = \Delta_{hyd}H(MgCl_2)$

On defining the **enthalpy of hydration for an ion** to be *the enthalpy change when one mole of gas phase ions bond with water to form solvated ions*, the enthalpy of hydration for a compound is obtained by adding the enthalpies of hydration for the ions formed from one mole of the compound. For example:.

*Hydrating magnesium ions:*

$Mg^{2+}_{(g)} \rightarrow Mg^{2+}_{(aq)}$ $\qquad \Delta H = \Delta_{hyd}H(Mg^{2+})$

*Hydrating chloride ions:*

$Cl^{-}_{(g)} \rightarrow Cl^{-}_{(aq)}$ $\qquad \Delta H = \Delta_{hyd}H(Cl^{-})$

*Hydrating magnesium chloride:*

$\Delta_{hyd}H(MgCl_2) = \Delta_{hyd}H(Mg^{2+}) + 2\Delta_{hyd}H(Cl^{-})$

### Worked Example 4.1iv

Magnesium chloride has a lattice enthalpy of 2493 kJ mol$^{-1}$ and an enthalpy of solution of –155 kJ mol$^{-1}$. If the enthalpy of hydration for Mg$^{2+}$ ions is –1920 kJ mol$^{-1}$ the enthalpy of hydration for Cl$^{-}$ ions is:

A   –728 kJ mol$^{-1}$

B   –364 kJ mol$^{-1}$

C   +364 kJ mol$^{-1}$

D   +728 kJ mol$^{-1}$

*(CCEA May 2011)*

### Strategy

- Use $\Delta_{soln}H = \Delta_{latt}H + \Delta_{hyd}H$ (Equation 3) to calculate $\Delta_{hyd}H$ for MgCl$_2$.

- Use $\Delta_{hyd}H$ for MgCl$_2$ and $\Delta_{hyd}H$ for Mg$^{2+}$ to calculate $\Delta_{hyd}H$ for Cl$^{-}$.

### Solution

$\Delta_{hyd}H = \Delta_{soln}H - \Delta_{latt}H = (-155) - 2493$
$\qquad = -2648$ kJ mol$^{-1}$

$2\Delta_{hyd}H(Cl^{-}) = \Delta_{hyd}H - \Delta_{hyd}H(Mg2+)$
$\qquad = (-2648) - (-1920) = -728$ kJ mol$^{-1}$

Answer B.

### Exercise 4.1F

1. Sodium chloride dissolves in water by an overall endothermic process. The NaCl$_{(s)}$ separates into its gaseous ions.

   $NaCl_{(s)} \rightarrow Na^{+}_{(g)} + Cl^{-}_{(g)}$ $\quad \Delta H_1 = +776$ kJ

   The gaseous ions then dissolve to form aqueous ions.

   $Na^{+}_{(g)} + Cl^{-}_{(g)} + aq \rightarrow Na^{+}_{(aq)} + Cl^{-}_{(aq)}$
   $\qquad\qquad\qquad\qquad \Delta H_2 = -771$ kJ

(a) What is the name for the enthalpy value $\Delta H_1$? (b) What is the name for the enthalpy value $\Delta H_2$? (c) $\Delta H_3$ is the enthalpy of solution. Draw a labelled diagram to show the relationship between $\Delta H_1$, $\Delta H_2$ and $\Delta H_3$.

*(CCEA January 2013)*

2. Magnesium chloride dissolves in water and has an enthalpy of solution of –155 kJ mol$^{-1}$. Define the term *enthalpy of solution*.

*(CCEA May 2011)*

3. The energy cycle for dissolving sodium fluoride in water is shown below. Which one of the following is the enthalpy change of solution for sodium fluoride?

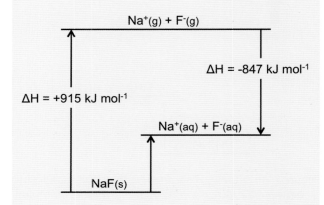

A   –68 kJ mol$^{-1}$

B   +68 kJ mol$^{-1}$

C   +847 kJ mol$^{-1}$

D   –847 kJ mol$^{-1}$

*(CCEA May 2015)*

4. Magnesium fluoride and magnesium chloride are both soluble in water. Magnesium chloride has an enthalpy of solution of –155 kJ mol$^{-1}$. (a) Using diagrams show how magnesium and fluoride ions interact with water molecules in an aqueous solution of magnesium fluoride. (b) Given that the enthalpies of hydration of magnesium ions and chloride ions are –1920 kJ mol$^{-1}$ and –364 kJ mol$^{-1}$ respectively, calculate the lattice enthalpy of magnesium chloride.

*(CCEA January 2011)*

5. (a) Write an equation, including state symbols, to represent potassium chloride dissolving in water. (b) The enthalpies of hydration for potassium ion and chloride ion are $-305$ kJ mol$^{-1}$ and $-384$ kJ mol$^{-1}$ respectively. The lattice enthalpy for potassium chloride is $710$ kJ mol$^{-1}$. Calculate the enthalpy change when one mole of potassium chloride is dissolved in water.

*(CCEA May 2013)*

6. Use the following enthalpy changes to determine the enthalpy of solution of calcium chloride, $CaCl_2$.

$\Delta_{latt}H(CaCl_2) = 2267$ kJ mol$^{-1}$

$\Delta_{hyd}H(Ca^{2+}) = -1651$ kJ mol$^{-1}$

$\Delta_{hyd}H(Cl^-) = -364$ kJ mol$^{-1}$

*(Adapted from CCEA May 2012)*

Before moving to the next section, check that you are able to:

- Use the enthalpy of hydration for individual ions to calculate the enthalpy of hydration of an ionic compound.
- Use Hess's Law to calculate enthalpy changes associated with the dissolving of an ionic compound.

# 4.2 Entropy and Free Energy

**CONNECTIONS**

- When liquids or gases mix, the particles in the mixture begin to diffuse and the entropy of the mixture increases.
- Salts dissolve because the free energy of the solution formed is less than the combined free energy of the salt and solvent.

## Why Reactions Occur

**In this section we are learning to:**

- Use the term entropy to describe the amount of disorder in a substance.
- Calculate the change in entropy, $\Delta S$ for a chemical reaction.
- Describe the extent to which the change in entropy, $\Delta S$ and the change in enthalpy, $\Delta H$ for a reaction can be used to determine if the reaction occurs.

In this section we consider the conditions necessary for a chemical reaction to occur when the reactants are mixed. We begin by developing the concept of entropy, and examine the extent to which the change in entropy that accompanies a reaction can be used to predict if the reaction occurs.

### Entropy

The **entropy** of a substance, S is a positive number and *is a measure of the amount of disorder in the substance.* The relative amount of entropy in solids, liquids and gases is illustrated in Figure 1. The particles in a solid move about fixed positions and, as a result, have very little entropy. In contrast, the particles in a liquid are able to move past each other,

frequently changing speed and direction. As a result, the entropy of a liquid or solution is greater than the entropy of a solid. The particles in a gas move much faster and change direction more often than the particles in liquids and solutions. As a result, the entropy of a gas is greater than the entropy of a liquid or solution.

The standard entropy values in Table 1 also illustrate the relative amount of entropy in solids, liquids and gases. The **standard entropy**, S° of a substance is defined to be *the amount of entropy in one mole of the substance under standard conditions.*

| | Substance | Formula | $S^\circ$ $(JK^{-1}mol^{-1})$ |
|---|---|---|---|
| Solids | Iron | $Fe_{(s)}$ | 27.3 |
| | Magnesium oxide | $MgO_{(s)}$ | 26.9 |
| | Quartz | $SiO_{2(s)}$ | 41.8 |
| Liquids and Solutions | Hydrochloric acid | $HCl_{(aq)}$ | 56.5 |
| | Water | $H_2O_{(l)}$ | 69.9 |
| | Potassium hydroxide | $KOH_{(aq)}$ | 91.6 |
| | Ammonia solution | $NH_{3(aq)}$ | 111.0 |
| Gases | Steam | $H_2O_{(g)}$ | 188.7 |
| | Oxygen | $O_{2(g)}$ | 205.0 |
| | Carbon dioxide | $CO_{2(g)}$ | 213.6 |

*Table 1: Standard entropy values, S° for solids, liquids and gases.*

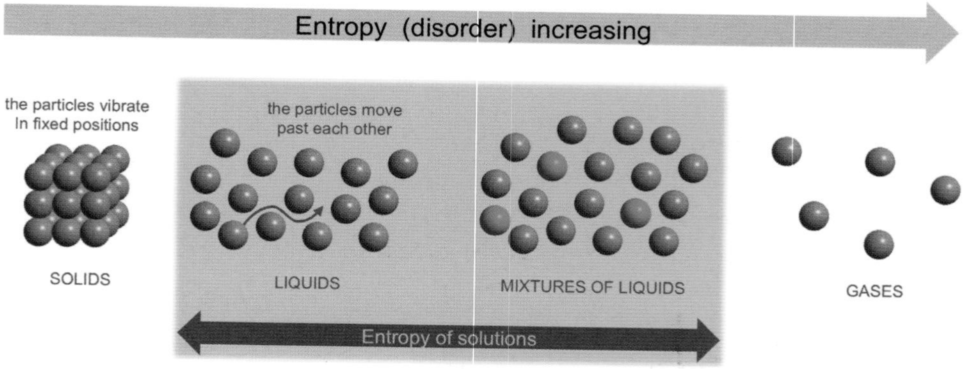

*Figure 1: Entropy in solids, liquids and gases.*

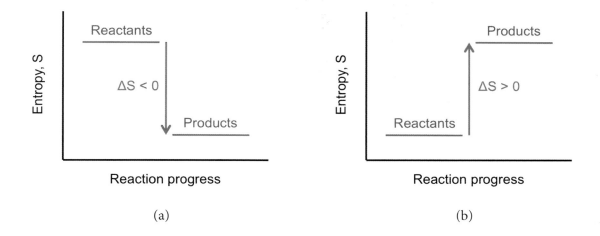

*Figure 2: Entropy diagram for a reaction with (a) $S_{reactants} > S_{products}$ and (b) $S_{reactants} < S_{products}$.*

The change in entropy, $\Delta S$ produced by a reaction is the difference between the total entropy of the products ($S_{products}$) and the total entropy of the reactants ($S_{reactants}$). The relationship between $S_{reactants}$, $S_{products}$ and the sign of $\Delta S$ for a reaction is summarised by the entropy diagrams in Figure 2.

If a reaction produces gases from substances with less entropy such as liquids and solids, $S_{products} > S_{reactants}$ and $\Delta S > 0$. For example, when calcium carbonate is heated, it decomposes to form calcium oxide and carbon dioxide.

$$CaCO_{3(s)} \rightarrow CaO_{(s)} + CO_{2(g)}$$

Calcium carbonate and calcium oxide are both solids and have similar standard entropy values. The entropy change for the reaction is approximately the amount of entropy gained by forming carbon dioxide.

$$S_{reactants} = S(CaCO_3) \quad and \quad S_{products} = S(CaO) + S(CO_2)$$

therefore $\Delta S = S(CaO) + S(CO_2) - S(CaCO_3)$
$$\approx S(CO_2) > 0$$

In contrast, if the reaction produces solids from substances with more entropy such as liquids and gases, $S_{products} < S_{reactants}$ and $\Delta S < 0$. For example, when magnesium burns in air it combines with oxygen to form magnesium oxide.

$$2Mg_{(s)} + O_{2(g)} \rightarrow 2MgO_{(s)}$$

Magnesium and magnesium oxide are both solids and have similar standard entropy values. The entropy change for the reaction is approximately the amount of entropy lost when oxygen reacts.

$$S_{reactants} = 2S(Mg) + S(O_2) \quad and \quad S_{products} = 2S(MgO)$$

therefore $\Delta S = 2S(MgO) - 2S(Mg) - S(O_2)$
$$\approx -S(O_2) < 0$$

**Worked Example 4.2i**

The combustion of butane, $C_4H_{10(g)}$ produces carbon dioxide and water vapour. (a) Write a balanced chemical equation for the reaction. Include state symbols. (b) Explain why $\Delta S$ is positive for the combustion of butane.

*Solution*

(a) $C_4H_{10(g)} + \dfrac{13}{2} O_{2(g)} \rightarrow 4CO_{2(g)} + 5H_2O_{(g)}$

(b) The entropy change, $\Delta S > 0$ as the reaction increases the amount of gas in the reaction mixture.

## Exercise 4.2A

1. The combustion of methane, $CH_{4(g)}$ produces carbon dioxide and water vapour. (a) Write a balanced chemical equation for the reaction. Include state symbols. (b) Explain why the value of $\Delta S$ for the combustion of methane is small.

2. Which one of the following reactions would give an increase in entropy?

   A    $N_{2(g)} + 3H_{2(g)} \rightarrow 2NH_{3(g)}$

   B    $2SO_{2(g)} + O_{2(g)} \rightarrow 2SO_{3(g)}$

   C    $H_{2(g)} + I_{2(g)} \rightarrow 2HI_{(g)}$

   D    $C_3H_{8(g)} + 5O_{2(g)} \rightarrow 3CO_{2(g)} + 4H_2O_{(g)}$

   *(CCEA May 2012)*

3. The molecules in an aqueous solution of hydrogen peroxide, $H_2O_{2(aq)}$ decompose to form oxygen gas. What is the sign of $\Delta S$ for the decomposition reaction? Explain your answer.

   $2H_2O_{2(aq)} \rightarrow 2H_2O_{(l)} + O_{2(g)}$

4. The entropy change, $\Delta S$ when sodium chloride dissolves to form an aqueous solution is $+43.4$ J K$^{-1}$ mol$^{-1}$. Explain the sign of $\Delta S$.

5. A precipitate of silver chloride is formed when a few drops of acidified silver nitrate solution are added to a solution containing chloride ions. The entropy change, $\Delta S$ for the precipitation reaction is $-33.0$ J K$^{-1}$ mol$^{-1}$. (a) Write an ionic equation for the precipitation reaction. Include state symbols. (b) Explain the sign of $\Delta S$ for the precipitation reaction.

6. Which one of the following reactions has the greatest increase in entropy?

   A    $X_{2(s)} + Y_{2(g)} \rightarrow 2XY_{(g)}$

   B    $P_{2(g)} + Q_{2(g)} \rightarrow 2PQ_{(g)}$

   C    $M_{(s)} + Z_{(s)} \rightarrow MZ_{(s)}$

   D    $2A_{2(g)} + B_{2(g)} \rightarrow 2A_2B_{(g)}$

   *(CCEA January 2013)*

---

**Before moving to the next section, check that you are able to:**

- Recall that entropy is a measure of the amount of disorder in a substance.
- Predict the sign of $\Delta S$ for a chemical reaction and explain your reasoning in terms of changes in the number and type of particles.

---

### Calculating Standard Entropy Changes

The entropy change for a chemical reaction, $\Delta S$ is obtained by subtracting the total entropy of the reactants, $S_{reactants}$ from the total entropy of the products, $S_{products}$.

$$\Delta S = S_{products} - S_{reactants} \qquad \text{Equation 1}$$

Equation 1 can be used to calculate the entropy change for a reaction under any conditions. If standard entropy values are used for the reactants and products, the change in entropy becomes the **standard entropy change**, $\Delta S^{\ominus}$ for the reaction (Equation 2) and represents *the change in entropy when the reaction is carried out under standard conditions.*

$$\Delta S^{\ominus} = S^{\ominus}_{products} - S^{\ominus}_{reactants} \qquad \text{Equation 2}$$

---

### Worked Example 4.2ii

The standard entropy change for the following reaction is 139 J K$^{-1}$ mol$^{-1}$. The standard entropies of $Fe_2O_{3\ (s)}$, $H_{2\ (g)}$ and $Fe_{(s)}$ are 90, 131 and 27 J K$^{-1}$ mol$^{-1}$ respectively. Calculate the standard entropy of steam.

$$Fe_2O_{3(s)} + 3H_{2(g)} \rightarrow 2Fe_{(s)} + 3H_2O_{(g)}$$

*(Adapted from CCEA May 2011)*

*Solution*

$S^{\ominus}_{reactants} = S^{\ominus}(Fe_2O_3) + 3S^{\ominus}(H_2) = 90 + 3(131)$
$= 483$ J K$^{-1}$

$S^{\ominus}_{products} = 2S^{\ominus}(Fe) + 3S^{\ominus}(H_2O) = 54 + 3S^{\ominus}(H_2O)$ J K$^{-1}$

$\Delta S^{\ominus} = S^{\ominus}_{products} - S^{\ominus}_{reactants} = 3S^{\ominus}(H_2O) - 429$
$= 139$ J K$^{-1}$

Solving gives $S^{\ominus}(H_2O) = 189$ J K$^{-1}$ mol$^{-1}$

## Exercise 4.2B

1. The standard entropies of $N_2O_{4(g)}$ and $NO_{2(g)}$ are 304.2 and 240.0 J $K^{-1}$ $mol^{-1}$. (a) Calculate the standard entropy change, $\Delta S°$ for the decomposition reaction $N_2O_{4(g)} \rightarrow 2NO_{2(g)}$. (b) Explain the sign of $\Delta S°$.

2. The standard entropies of $CO_{(g)}$, $O_{2(g)}$ and $CO_{2(g)}$ are 197.6, 205.0 and 213.6 J $K^{-1}$ $mol^{-1}$ respectively. (a) Calculate the standard entropy change, $\Delta S°$ for the reaction $2CO_{(g)} + O_{2(g)} \rightarrow 2CO_{2(g)}$. (b) Explain the sign of $\Delta S°$.

3. The standard entropies of $Fe_2O_{3(s)}$, $Al_{(s)}$, $Al_2O_{3(s)}$ and $Fe_{(s)}$ are 87.4, 28.3, 50.9 and 27.3 J $K^{-1}$ $mol^{-1}$ respectively. (a) Calculate the standard entropy change, $\Delta S°$ for the reaction $Fe_2O_{3(s)} + 2Al_{(s)} \rightarrow Al_2O_{3(s)} + 2Fe_{(s)}$. (b) Explain the size of $\Delta S°$.

---

Before moving to the next section, check that you are able to:

- Recall the meaning of $\Delta S$ and $\Delta S°$ for a reaction.
- Use the entropies of the reactants and products to calculate the entropy change for a reaction.

---

## Why Reactions Occur

Reactions that occur under one set of conditions may no longer be feasible if the reaction conditions change. For example, the scenarios in Figure 3 demonstrate that the melting of ice is only feasible above 0°C.

The entropy change for the melting of ice, $\Delta S = S_{water} - S_{ice} > 0$ at temperatures above and below 0°C. As a result the sign of the entropy change, $\Delta S$ cannot be used to explain why ice only melts above 0°C, and we must look for an alternative measure that can explain why the melting of ice is only feasible above 0 °C.

Similarly, when an ionic compound such as ammonium nitrate dissolves in water, the entropy change is positive ($\Delta S > 0$) as the ions break away from the solid and are able to move freely throughout the solution. In the case of ammonium nitrate the dissolving process is endothermic ($\Delta H > 0$) and the temperature of the solution decreases as the solid dissolves.

*Dissolving ammonium nitrate in water:*
$$NH_4NO_{3(s)} \rightarrow NH_4^{+}{}_{(aq)} + NO_3^{-}{}_{(aq)}$$

✓ entropy increases ($\Delta S > 0$)
✓ endothermic ($\Delta H > 0$)
✓ feasible at 20°C

(a)

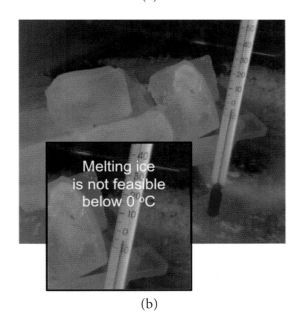

(b)

*Figure 3: The melting of ice is (a) feasible at temperatures above 0 °C and (b) not feasible at temperatures below 0 °C*

**Dissolving ammonium nitrate, NH$_4$NO$_3$ in water is feasible at room temperature**

The temperature drops as the solid dissolves

(a)

**Dissolving sodium Hydroxide, NaOH in water is feasible at room temperature**

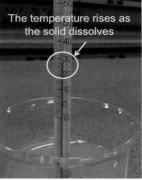

The temperature rises as the solid dissolves

(b)

*Figure 4: (a) Dissolving ammonium nitrate, NH$_4$NO$_3$ in water is endothermic. (b) Dissolving sodium hydroxide, NaOH in water is exothermic.*

In contrast, when sodium hydroxide dissolves, the temperature of the solution increases as the dissolving process is exothermic ($\Delta H < 0$).

*Dissolving sodium hydroxide in water:*
$NaOH_{(s)} \rightarrow Na^+_{(aq)} + OH^-_{(aq)}$

✓ entropy increases ($\Delta S > 0$)
✓ exothermic ($\Delta H < 0$)
✓ feasible at 20 °C

Together these examples demonstrate that the sign of $\Delta H$ for a reaction cannot be used to determine if the reaction will occur.

In order to determine if a reaction is feasible we must instead consider the change in Free Energy, $\Delta G$ for the reaction.

Before moving to the next section, check that you are able to:

- Recall that the sign of $\Delta S$ and $\Delta H$ cannot be used to determine if a reaction is feasible.
- Recall that the change in free energy, $\Delta G$ for a reaction can be used to determine if a reaction is feasible.

## Determining if a Reaction Occurs

**In this section we are learning to:**

- Explain how the free energy change for a reaction, $\Delta G$ can be used to determine if the reaction occurs.
- Calculate the free energy change, $\Delta G$ and standard free energy change, $\Delta G°$ for a reaction.
- Calculate the temperature at which a reaction becomes feasible, or stops being feasible.
- Determine the effect of temperature on the value of $\Delta G$ for a reaction.

### Free Energy

The change in free energy that accompanies a chemical reaction, $\Delta G$ is the difference between the total free energy of the reactants, $G_{reactants}$ and the total free energy of the products, $G_{products}$.

$$\Delta G = G_{products} - G_{reactants}$$

A chemical reaction is **feasible** if *the free energy change for the reaction, $\Delta G < 0$.* Conversely, a reaction is not feasible, and will not occur, if the free energy change for the reaction, $\Delta G > 0$.

The Free Energy diagrams in Figure 5 illustrate the relationship between $G_{reactants}$ and $G_{products}$ for reactions that are feasible and reactions that are not feasible.

It therefore follows that ice melts above 0 °C as the free energy change for melting ice is negative ($\Delta G < 0$) when the temperature is above 0 °C. Similarly it follows that ice does not melt below 0 °C as the free energy change for melting ice is positive ($\Delta G > 0$) when the temperature is below 0 °C.

If a mixture of ice and water is maintained at exactly 0 °C, as in Figure 6, a dynamic equilibrium between ice and water is established as $\Delta G = 0$ for the melting of ice (and the freezing of water) at this temperature.

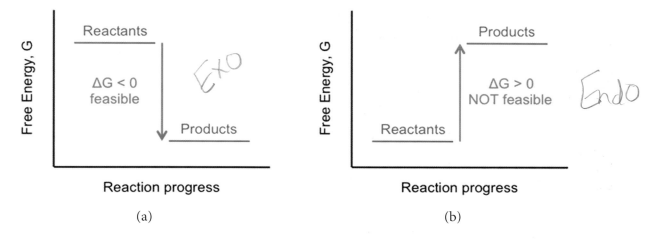

Figure 5: Free energy diagram for (a) a reaction that is feasible, and (b) a reaction that is not feasible.

Figure 6: The dynamic ice-water equilibrium in a mixture of ice and water at 0 °C (273 K).

---

**Before moving to the next section, check that you are able to:**

- Use the sign of ΔG to determine if a reaction is feasible.
- Recall that an equilibrium can be established when the change in free energy for the reaction, ΔG = 0.

---

### Calculating Free Energy Changes

The free energy change for a reaction, ΔG is related to the enthalpy change for the reaction, ΔH, the entropy change for the reaction, ΔS and the temperature at which the reaction occurs, T.

> *Free energy change:*
> $$\Delta G = G_{products} - G_{reactants} = \Delta H - T\Delta S$$

If a reaction occurs under standard conditions, the free energy change is referred to as the **standard free energy change**, ΔG° for the reaction and is related to the standard enthalpy change, ΔH° and standard entropy change, ΔS° for the reaction.

> *Standard free energy change:*
> $$\Delta G° = \Delta H° - T\Delta S°$$

When calculating free energy changes the temperature at which a reaction occurs, T must be expressed in units of Kelvin.

> Temperature in Kelvin = Temperature in °C + 273
> *For example:*
> - 25 °C corresponds to 25 °C + 273 = 298 K
> - 268 K corresponds to 268 K – 273 = –5 °C

It is also necessary to ensure that the units for G, H and S are the same. Changes in free energy (ΔG) and enthalpy (ΔH) are usually expressed in units of kJ mol⁻¹. Changes in entropy (ΔS) are much smaller and are usually expressed in units of J K$^{-1}$ mol$^{-1}$. As a result $\Delta S$ should be converted to have units of kJ K$^{-1}$ mol$^{-1}$, so that T$\Delta S$ has units of kJ mol$^{-1}$, before using $\Delta H$ and T$\Delta S$ to calculate $\Delta G$.

Alternatively, $\Delta H$ could be converted to have units of J mol$^{-1}$, before combining $\Delta H$ and T$\Delta S$ (which already has units of J mol$^{-1}$) to calculate $\Delta G$ in units of J mol$^{-1}$.

## Worked Example 4.2iii

The standard enthalpy change and standard entropy change for the decomposition of calcium carbonate are $\Delta H° = +178$ kJ mol$^{-1}$ and $\Delta S° = +161$ J K$^{-1}$ mol$^{-1}$. Calculate the standard free energy change, $\Delta G°$ for the reaction at 25 °C.

$$CaCO_{3(s)} \rightarrow CaO_{(s)} + CO_{2(g)}$$

*(Adapted from CCEA May 2010)*

### Strategy

- Convert $\Delta S°$ to kJ K$^{-1}$ mol$^{-1}$ and 25 °C to Kelvin.
- Use the equation $\Delta G° = \Delta H° - T\Delta S°$ to calculate $\Delta G°$.

### Solution

(a) $\Delta S° = 0.161$ kJ K$^{-1}$ mol$^{-1}$ and T = 25 °C + 273 = 298 K

(b) $\Delta G° = \Delta H° - T\Delta S° = 178 - (298)(0.161)$ = 130 kJ mol$^{-1}$

## Exercise 4.2C

1. The entropy change, $\Delta S$ for the formation of calcium chloride, $CaCl_2$ is $-152$ J K$^{-1}$ mol$^{-1}$. Using a suitable calculation, state and explain whether or not the formation of calcium chloride is feasible at 298 K. The enthalpy of formation of calcium chloride is $-795$ kJ mol$^{-1}$.

*(Adapted from CCEA May 2012)*

2. When solid ammonium carbonate is added to ethanoic acid a large volume of gas is produced and the temperature of the reaction mixture drops. (a) Write the equation for the reaction. (b) Explain the meaning of the term *feasible*. (c) Explain why this reaction is both endothermic and feasible.

*(Adapted from CCEA January 2012)*

3. The formation of ammonium carbonate is being investigated as a possible method to remove carbon dioxide from combustion processes. $\Delta G = -25$ kJ mol$^{-1}$ and $\Delta H = -170$ kJ mol$^{-1}$ for the reaction. Use the data provided to calculate the temperature at which the process operates.

$$CO_{2(g)} + 2NH_{3(g)} + H_2O_{(l)} \rightarrow (NH_4)_2CO_{3(aq)}$$

| | CO$_2$ | H$_2$O | (NH$_4$)$_2$CO$_3$ | NH$_3$ |
|---|---|---|---|---|
| Entropy, J K$^{-1}$ mol$^{-1}$ | +214 | +70 | +220 | +192 |

*(Adapted from CCEA January 2012)*

4. The hydrogen cyanide used in the manufacture of methyl methacrylate is produced by the Degussa process in which ammonia reacts with methane in the presence of a platinum catalyst. (a) Name the industrial sources of methane and ammonia. (b) Use the following bond energies to calculate $\Delta H$ for the reaction. (c) The entropy change for the reaction is +125 J mol$^{-1}$ K$^{-1}$. Suggest why the entropy change is positive and calculate the temperature at which the $\Delta G$ value is zero.

$$NH_{3(g)} + CH_{4(g)} \rightarrow HCN_{(g)} + 3H_{2(g)}$$

| Bond | Bond energy (kJ mol$^{-1}$) |
|---|---|
| N-H | 391 |
| C-H | 413 |
| C≡N | 887 |
| H-H | 436 |

*(Adapted from May 2015)*

5. The enthalpy of formation for $CaCl_{(s)}$ is $-178$ kJ mol$^{-1}$ whilst that for $CaCl_{2(s)}$ is $-796$ kJ mol$^{-1}$. (a) Calculate the enthalpy change for the reaction: $2CaCl_{(s)} \rightarrow CaCl_{2(s)} + Ca_{(s)}$. (b) Explain why the term T$\Delta S$ may be neglected when predicting the feasibility of this reaction.

*(CCEA May 2015)*

6. The reaction of carbon, oxygen, nitrogen and hydrogen to form urea is shown below. When allowed to remain in contact for several years no urea is detected.

$$C_{(s)} + \frac{1}{2} O_{2(g)} + N_{2(g)} + 2H_{2(g)} \leftrightharpoons CO(NH_2)_{2(s)}$$

The thermodynamic values for the reaction are:

$$\Delta_f H = -333 \text{ kJ mol}^{-1} \text{ and } \Delta G = -205 \text{ kJ mol}^{-1}$$

Which one of the following is the reason for the lack of formation of urea?

A The enthalpy change of formation is greater than the free energy change.

B The equilibrium constant for the reaction is very low.

C The entropy change for the reaction is positive.

D The activation energy for the reaction is very high.

*(CCEA May 2015)*

---

**Before moving to the next section, check that you are able to:**

- Recall the meaning of $\Delta G$ and $\Delta G^\oplus$ for a reaction.
- Calculate $\Delta G$ and $\Delta G^\oplus$ for a reaction.
- Calculate the temperature at which a reaction becomes feasible, or stops being feasible.

---

## The Effect of Temperature on $\Delta G$

### Case 1: Reactions with $\Delta H > 0$ and $\Delta S > 0$

The size of the free energy change for a reaction, $\Delta G$ is determined by the temperature at which the reaction occurs. As a result, a reaction that is feasible at one temperature ($\Delta G < 0$) may not be feasible ($\Delta G > 0$) at a different temperature. Consider, for example, the dissociation of dinitrogen tetroxide, $N_2O_4$.

$$N_2O_{4(g)} \rightarrow 2NO_{2(g)}$$

The reaction is endothermic ($\Delta H > 0$) as energy is needed to break bonds in $N_2O_4$. The reaction also increases entropy ($\Delta S > 0$) by increasing the amount of gas in the reaction mixture as the reaction proceeds. As a result the enthalpy change, $\Delta H$ and the product $T\Delta S$ are both positive numbers. At low temperature $\Delta H$ is larger than $T\Delta S$ and the reaction is not feasible as $\Delta G = \Delta H - T\Delta S > 0$.

As the temperature increases, $T\Delta S$ becomes bigger until $T\Delta S = \Delta H$, and $\Delta G = 0$. Above this temperature $T\Delta S$ is bigger than $\Delta H$ and the reaction is feasible as $\Delta G = \Delta H - T\Delta S < 0$. The effect of temperature on $\Delta H$, $T\Delta S$ and $\Delta G$ for the reaction is illustrated in Figure 7. In this way the temperature at which $\Delta G = 0$ is the temperature above which the reaction is feasible, or equivalently the temperature below which the reaction stops being feasible.

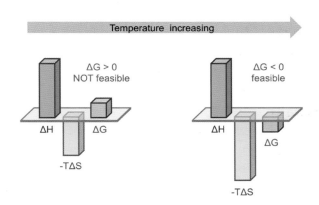

*Figure 7: The effect of temperature on $\Delta H$, $T\Delta S$ and $\Delta G$ for an endothermic process ($\Delta H > 0$) that generates entropy ($\Delta S > 0$). The reaction becomes feasible as temperature increases.*

### Case 2: Reactions with $\Delta H < 0$ and $\Delta S < 0$

The relationship between $\Delta H$, $T\Delta S$ and $\Delta G$ for a process in which $\Delta H$ and $\Delta S$ are both negative is shown in Figure 8. At low temperature the reaction is feasible as $T\Delta S$ is a small negative number and $\Delta G = \Delta H - T\Delta S < 0$. As the temperature increases $T\Delta S$ becomes larger until $T\Delta S = \Delta H$ and $\Delta G = \Delta H - T\Delta S = 0$. Above this temperature $T\Delta S$ is bigger than $\Delta H$ and the reaction is no longer feasible as $\Delta G > 0$.

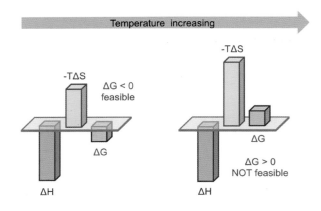

*Figure 8: The effect of temperature on ΔH, TΔS and ΔG for an exothermic process (ΔH < 0) that reduces entropy (ΔS < 0). The reaction stops being feasible as temperature increases.*

The temperature at which a reaction becomes feasible, or stops being feasible, can be calculated by using the values for $\Delta H$ and $\Delta S$ to calculate the temperature, T for which $\Delta G = \Delta H - T\Delta S = 0$.

⋯⋯⋯⋯⋯⋯⋯⋯⋯⋯⋯⋯⋯⋯⋯⋯⋯⋯⋯⋯

### Worked Example 4.2iv

Zinc is manufactured by the reduction of its oxide using carbon. Calculate the minimum temperature needed for the reaction to become feasible given that $\Delta H^\oplus = +237$ kJ mol$^{-1}$ and $\Delta S^\oplus = +190$ J K$^{-1}$ mol$^{-1}$ for the reaction.

$$ZnO_{(s)} + C_{(s)} \rightarrow Zn_{(s)} + CO_{(g)}$$

*(CCEA January 2010)*

### Strategy

- Convert $\Delta S^\oplus$ to kJ K$^{-1}$ mol$^{-1}$.
- Use the equation $\Delta G^\oplus = \Delta H^\oplus - T\Delta S^\oplus = 0$ to calculate T.

### Solution

$$T = \frac{\Delta H^\theta}{\Delta S^\theta} = \frac{237 \text{ kJ mol}^{-1}}{0.190 \text{ kJ K}^{-1} \text{ mol}^{-1}} = 1247 \text{ K}$$

$$= 1.25 \times 10^3 \text{ K}$$

⋯⋯⋯⋯⋯⋯⋯⋯⋯⋯⋯⋯⋯⋯⋯⋯⋯⋯⋯⋯

### Summary

*Case 1: ΔH > 0 and ΔS > 0*
The process is feasible <u>above</u> $T = \dfrac{\Delta H}{\Delta S}$

*Case 2: ΔH < 0 and ΔS < 0*
The process is feasible <u>below</u> $T = \dfrac{\Delta H}{\Delta S}$

### Case 3: Reactions with ΔH < 0 and ΔS > 0

If a reaction is exothermic ($\Delta H < 0$) and generates entropy ($\Delta S > 0$) the free energy change for the reaction, $\Delta G$ is obtained by subtracting a positive number (T$\Delta S$) from a negative number ($\Delta H$). As a result, $\Delta G = \Delta H - T\Delta S$ is negative at all temperatures, making the reaction feasible at all temperatures.

$$\Delta H < 0$$
$$\Delta G = \Delta H - T\Delta S$$

$\Delta G < 0$ at all T $\qquad$ $\Delta S > 0$ therefore T$\Delta S > 0$

### Case 4: Reactions with ΔH > 0 and ΔS < 0

In contrast, if a reaction is endothermic ($\Delta H > 0$) and reduces entropy ($\Delta S < 0$) the free energy change for the reaction, $\Delta G$ is obtained by subtracting a negative number (T$\Delta S$) from a positive number ($\Delta H$). As a result, $\Delta G = \Delta H - T\Delta S$ is positive at all temperatures, and the reaction is not feasible at any temperature.

$$\Delta H > 0$$
$$\Delta G = \Delta H - T\Delta S$$

$\Delta G > 0$ at all T $\qquad$ $\Delta S < 0$ therefore T$\Delta S < 0$

## Summary

Case 3: $\Delta H < 0$ and $\Delta S > 0$
The process is <u>feasible</u> ($\Delta G < 0$) at all temperatures.

Case 4: $\Delta H > 0$ and $\Delta S < 0$
The process is <u>not feasible</u> ($\Delta G > 0$) at all temperatures.

## Exercise 4.2D

1. Heat is produced when magnesium reacts with sulfuric acid. Which one of the following statements is true for the reaction?

$$Mg_{(s)} + H_2SO_{4(aq)} \rightarrow MgSO_{4(aq)} + H_{2(g)}$$

A $\Delta S$ is negative.

B $\Delta H$ is positive.

C $\Delta G$ is positive.

D The reaction is feasible at any temperature.

*(CCEA May 2011)*

2. A reaction is always feasible when:

A $\Delta H$ and $\Delta S$ are both positive.

B $\Delta H$ and $\Delta S$ are both negative.

C $\Delta H$ is positive and $\Delta S$ is negative.

D $\Delta H$ is negative and $\Delta S$ is positive.

*(Adapted from CCEA January 2014)*

3. (a) Use the data below to calculate $\Delta H^\circ$, $\Delta S^\circ$ and $\Delta G^\circ$ for the reduction of iron(III) oxide by carbon at 298 K. (b) Explain why the reaction is not feasible at 298 K. (c) Calculate the temperature above which this reaction is feasible.

$$2Fe_2O_{3(s)} + 3C_{(s)} \rightarrow 4Fe_{(s)} + 3CO_{2(g)}$$

| Substance | $\Delta_f H^\circ$ /kJ mol$^{-1}$ | $S^\circ$ /J K$^{-1}$ mol$^{-1}$ |
|---|---|---|
| $Fe_2O_3$ | −824.2 | 87.4 |
| C | 0.0 | 5.7 |
| Fe | 0.0 | 27.3 |
| $CO_2$ | −393.5 | 213.6 |

*(CCEA January 2011)*

4. (a) Use the enthalpies of combustion for ammonia and hydrogen to calculate the molar enthalpy of decomposition for ammonia:
$$2NH_{3(g)} \rightarrow N_{2(g)} + 3H_{2(g)}.$$

$$2NH_{3(g)} + \tfrac{3}{2}O_{2(g)} \rightarrow N_{2(g)} + 3H_2O_{(l)} \quad \Delta H = -766 \text{ kJ}$$
$$H_{2(g)} + \tfrac{1}{2}O_{2(g)} \rightarrow H_2O_{(l)} \qquad\qquad \Delta H = -286 \text{ kJ}$$

(b) Use the bond energies in the table to calculate the molar enthalpy of decomposition for ammonia.

| Bond | Bond enthalpy/kJ mol$^{-1}$ |
|---|---|
| H-H | 436 |
| N-H | 388 |
| N≡N | 944 |

(c) Use the entropy values in the table to calculate the entropy change for the molar decomposition of ammonia.

| Substance | Entropy value/J K$^{-1}$ mol$^{-1}$ |
|---|---|
| $N_{2(g)}$ | 191.6 |
| $H_{2(g)}$ | 130.7 |
| $NH_{3(g)}$ | 192.8 |

(d) State the equation which links $\Delta H$ and $\Delta S$ to $\Delta G$. (e) Explain what is meant by the term *feasible*. (f) Use the value of $\Delta H$ obtained by applying Hess's Law to calculate the temperature at which the reaction becomes feasible.

*(Adapted from CCEA May 2014)*

5. Gunpowder is a mixture of potassium nitrate, carbon and sulfur. The explosive effect of gunpowder is caused by the rapid production of a large volume of gas from a small mass of solid.

$$2KNO_{3(s)} + S_{(s)} + 3C_{(s)} \rightarrow K_2S_{(s)} + N_{2(g)} + 3CO_{2(g)}$$

(a) Use the following standard enthalpy of formation, $\Delta_f H^\circ$ values to calculate the enthalpy change for the explosion of gunpowder in kJ.

| Substance | $\Delta_f H^\circ$ /kJ mol$^{-1}$ |
|---|---|
| KNO$_3$ | −493 |
| K$_2$S | −418 |
| CO$_2$ | −394 |

(b) Use the following standard entropy, S° values to calculate the standard entropy change for the explosion of gunpowder. (c) Explain why this reaction is feasible at all temperatures.

| Substance | $S^\circ$ /J K$^{-1}$ mol$^{-1}$ |
|---|---|
| KNO$_3$ | 172 |
| S | 32 |
| C | 5.7 |
| K$_2$S | 115 |
| N$_2$ | 191 |
| CO$_2$ | 214 |

*(Adapted from CCEA May 2013)*

6. The Water Gas reaction is used to produce hydrogen. Standard thermodynamic data for the reactants and products is given in the table.

$$CO_{(g)} + H_2O_{(g)} \rightarrow CO_{2(g)} + H_{2(g)}$$

| | Standard enthalpy of formation (kJ mol$^{-1}$) | Standard molar entropy (J K$^{-1}$ mol$^{-1}$) |
|---|---|---|
| CO$_{(g)}$ | −110.5 | 197.9 |
| H$_2$O$_{(g)}$ | −241.8 | 188.7 |
| CO$_{2(g)}$ | −393.5 | 213.6 |
| H$_{2(g)}$ | 0 | 114.6 |

(a) Why is the standard enthalpy of formation of hydrogen zero? (b) Calculate the standard enthalpy change of the reaction. (c) Calculate the standard entropy change of the reaction. (d) Calculate the temperature at which the reaction becomes feasible.

*(Adapted from CCEA January 2014)*

7. Ammonium nitrate decomposes on heating to form nitrogen(I) oxide and water. (a) Write the equation for this decomposition. (b) This reaction is exothermic and has a positive entropy change. Explain why this process is feasible at all temperatures.

*(CCEA May 2010)*

8. The reaction between citric acid and sodium hydrogencarbonate is endothermic.

$$C_6H_8O_7 + 3NaHCO_3$$
$$\rightarrow Na_3C_6H_5O_7 + 3CO_2 + 3H_2O$$

(a) Use the expression $\Delta G^\circ = \Delta H^\circ - T\Delta S^\circ$ to explain why the reaction is feasible despite being endothermic. (b) Explain the meaning of the symbol $\Delta S^\circ$.

*(Adapted from CCEA January 2010)*

9. (a) Explain the meaning of the term *entropy*. (b) Write an equation for the endothermic reaction between ammonium carbonate and ethanoic acid. (c) Explain why the reaction is feasible. (d) Explain whether reactions which have a negative entropy change and a positive enthalpy change are feasible or not.

*(Adapted from CCEA January 2013)*

---

Before moving to the next section, check that you are able to:

- Use the sign of ΔH and ΔS to determine if a reaction becomes feasible, or stops being feasible, when the temperature is increased.

# 4.3 Chemical Kinetics

Rate vs Conc allows determination of order.

Conc vs time shows initial Rate of Reaction

**CONNECTIONS**

- The shelf-life of foods, m … can be estimated by studying the kinetics of … er time.
- Kinetic models can be u … for the large-scale production of chemical…
- Kinetic studies can be u … n complex reactions such as the reactions that occu…

## Rate of Reaction

**In this section we are le…**

- Define the rate of a reac… which individual reactar… which individual products are formed.
- Distinguish between the rate, initial rate and average rate of a reaction.

### Defining Rate

The **rate of a reaction** *is a positive number that describes how quickly the concentrations of the reactants and products change during the reaction.* Consider the reaction that occurs between propanone and iodine in acidic solution.

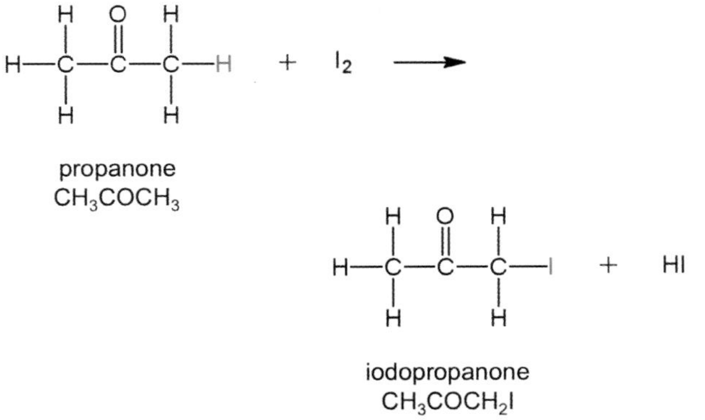


The rate of the reaction can be determined by plotting the concentration of propanone in the reaction mixture, $[CH_3COCH_3]$ against time and calculating the slope of the plot. The construction used to determine the rate at a time $t_0$ after the start of the reaction is shown in Figure 1a.

If during the reaction, the concentration of propanone changes by an amount, $\Delta[CH_3COCH_3]$ during a small interval of time, $\Delta t$ (where $\Delta t << 1$ second) the rate of reaction at this point in time during the reaction is defined as:

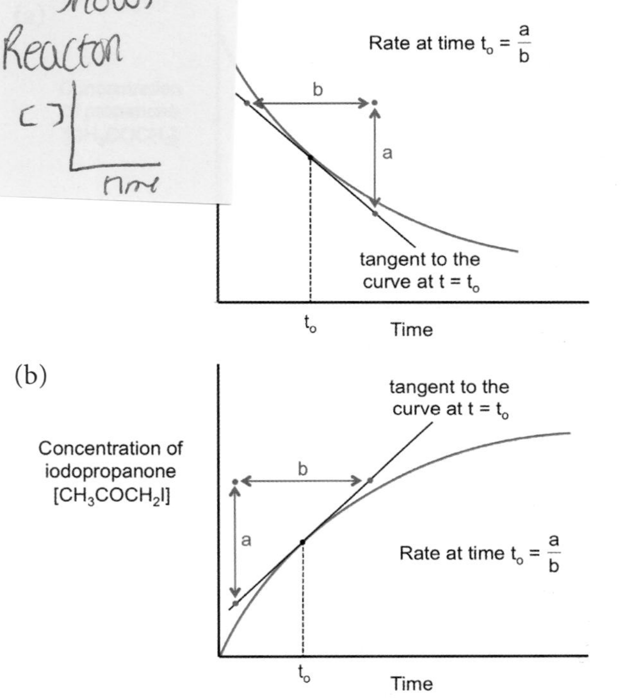


*Figure 1: Determining the rate of reaction at a time $t_o$ from a plot showing the concentration of (a) propanone against time and (b) iodopropanone against time.*

$$\text{Rate of reaction, } R = -\frac{\Delta[CH_3COCH_3]}{\Delta t}$$

Units: mol $dm^{-3}$ $s^{-1}$

The units of rate are concentration (mol $dm^{-3}$) divided by time (s). The negative sign is introduced to transform the negative change in concentration, $\Delta[CH_3COCH_3]$ into a positive number, and by so doing ensure that the rate of reaction, R is a positive number.

The rate of the reaction can also be determined by plotting the concentration of iodopropanone in the reaction mixture, $[CH_3COCH_2I]$ against time and calculating the slope of the plot. The construction used to determine the rate at a time $t_0$ after the start of the reaction is shown in Figure 1b.

If during the reaction, the concentration of iodopropanone changes by an amount, $\Delta[CH_3COCH_2I]$ during a small interval of time, $\Delta t$ the rate of reaction at this point in time during the reaction is defined as:

$$\text{Rate of reaction, } R = + \frac{\Delta[CH_3COCH_2I]}{\Delta t}$$

In this instance a negative sign is not required as the change in the concentration of iodopropanone, $\Delta[CH_3COCH_2I]$ is a positive number.

## Rates of Formation and Removal

The rate of a reaction is related to the rate at which reactants are used, and the rate at which products form. The nature of the relationship is determined by the chemical equation for the reaction. Consider, for example, the decomposition of aqueous hydrogen peroxide.

$$2H_2O_{2(aq)} \rightarrow 2H_2O_{(l)} + 1O_{2(g)}$$

According to the equation, two moles of water are formed for every mole of oxygen formed by the reaction. This means that water is formed *twice* as fast as oxygen, and is equivalent to stating that the **rate of formation** of water is *twice* the rate of formation of oxygen.

$$\text{Rate of formation of } O_2 = \frac{\Delta[O_2]}{\Delta t}$$

$$\text{Rate of formation of } H_2O = \frac{\Delta[H_2O]}{\Delta t} = 2\frac{\Delta[O_2]}{\Delta t}$$

The chemical equation also reveals that two moles of hydrogen peroxide decompose for every mole of oxygen formed. As a result hydrogen peroxide decomposes *twice* as fast as oxygen is formed, making the **rate of removal** of hydrogen peroxide *twice* the rate of formation of oxygen.

$$\text{Rate of removal of } H_2O_2 = -\frac{\Delta[H_2O_2]}{\Delta t} = 2\frac{\Delta[O_2]}{\Delta t}$$

Here again a negative sign is introduced to transform a decrease in the concentration of hydrogen peroxide, $\Delta[H_2O_2]$ into a positive number, and to ensure that the rate of removal of $H_2O_2$ is a positive number.

The rates of formation and removal are obtained by multiplying the rate of reaction by the moles of substance in the chemical equation.

Rate of formation of $O_2$ = 1 × Rate of reaction
Rate of formation of $H_2O$ = 2 × Rate of reaction
Rate of removal of $H_2O_2$ = 2 × Rate of reaction

### Worked Example 4.3i

Dinitrogen pentoxide, $N_2O_5$ decomposes when heated. When a sample of $N_2O_5$ with a concentration of 0.002 mol dm$^{-3}$ is heated the rate of disappearance of $N_2O_5$ is observed to be $1.1 \times 10^{-6}$ mol dm$^{-3}$ s$^{-1}$. Calculate (a) the rate of reaction and (b) the rate of formation of oxygen under these conditions.

$$2N_2O_{5(g)} \rightarrow 2N_2O_{4(g)} + O_{2(g)}$$

*(Adapted from CCEA May 2007)*

### Strategy

(a) Define the rate of reaction in terms of the disappearance of $N_2O_5$.

(b) Define the rate of reaction in terms of the formation of $O_2$.

### Solution

(a) Rate of reaction

$= \frac{1}{2} \times$ Rate of disappearance of $N_2O_5$

Rate of reaction $= \dfrac{1.1 \times 10^{-6}}{2}$

$= 5.5 \times 10^{-7}$ mol dm$^{-3}$ s$^{-1}$

(b) Rate of formation of $O_2$ = Rate of reaction
$= 5.5 \times 10^{-7}$ mol dm$^{-3}$ s$^{-1}$

### Exercise 4.3A

1. Aqueous hydrogen peroxide decomposes to form water and oxygen. The rate of decomposition is calculated to be $1.5 \times 10^{-3}$ mol dm$^{-3}$ s$^{-1}$. Calculate (a) the rate of reaction, and (b) the rate at which oxygen forms under these conditions.

$$2H_2O_{2(aq)} \rightarrow 2H_2O_{(l)} + O_{2(g)}$$

2. The rate of the reaction between propanone and bromine is calculated to be $2.94 \times 10^{-5}$ mol dm$^{-3}$ s$^{-1}$. Calculate: (a) the rate at which propanone reacts and (b) the rate at

which hydrogen bromide is formed under these conditions.

$$CH_3COCH_{3(aq)} + Br_{2(aq)}$$
$$\rightarrow CH_3COCH_2Br_{(aq)} + HBr_{(aq)}$$

3. The 'bromine clock' reaction proceeds according to the following equation. The rate of disappearance of bromide ion is observed to be $1.2 \times 10^{-4}$ mol dm$^{-3}$ s$^{-1}$. Calculate: (a) the rate of reaction, (b) the rate of disappearance of bromate(V) ion, $BrO_3^-$ and (c) the rate of formation of bromine under these conditions.

$$6H^+_{(aq)} + 5Br^-_{(aq)} + BrO_3^-_{(aq)} \rightarrow 3Br_{2(aq)} + 3H_2O_{(l)}$$

*(Adapted from CCEA January 2010)*

## Initial Rate

The **initial rate** of a reaction *is the rate when the reactants are mixed and the reaction begins (the rate at time, t=0)*. The initial rate of a reaction is a measure of how fast the reaction is, and *can be used to compare the rates of different chemical reactions*. The initial rate of a reaction can be obtained from a plot of concentration against time by using the constructions in Figure 2 to determine the slope of the graph at time, t=0.

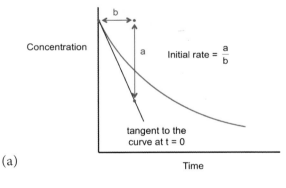

(a)

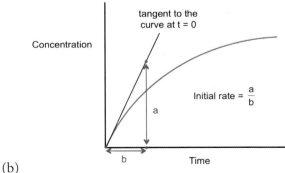

(b)

*Figure 2: Determining the initial rate for a reaction from a graph in which (a) concentration decreases with time and (b) concentration increases with time.*

## Average Rate

The **average rate** of a reaction is *the average speed at which the reactants are converted to products during the reaction*, and does not take account of the changes in rate that occur during the reaction. The construction used to determine the average rate of a reaction is shown in Figure 3.

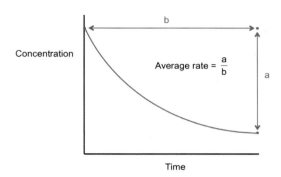

*Figure 3: The construction used to determine the average rate of a reaction.*

**Before moving to the next section, check that you are able to:**

- Explain how to obtain the rate of a reaction from a graph of concentration against time.
- Relate the rate of reaction to the rates at which products form and the rates at which reactants are used during a reaction.
- Obtain the initial rate of a reaction and the average rate of a reaction from a graph of concentration against time.

## Measuring Rates

**In this section we are learning to:**

- Recall experimental techniques to determine the rate of a chemical reaction.
- Describe how experimental techniques may be used to determine the rate of a chemical reaction.

In order to determine the initial rate of a reaction it is necessary to measure the amount of a particular reactant or product in the reaction mixture at intervals during the reaction. Changes in the amount of a reactant or product may be monitored by recording changes in the mass, colour, acidity or electrical conductivity of the reaction mixture.

## Measuring Gas Volume

The rate of a reaction can also be calculated by monitoring the rate at which gas is produced or used by reaction. For example, the amount of hydrogen gas produced by the reaction between magnesium and dilute hydrochloric acid can be monitored using a graduated syringe as shown in Figure 4.

$$Mg_{(s)} + 2HCl_{(aq)} \rightarrow MgCl_{2(aq)} + H_{2(g)}$$

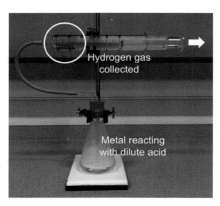

*Figure 4: Use of a graduated syringe to monitor the volume of gas produced during the reaction between magnesium and dilute hydrochloric acid.*

The (initial) rate of the reaction is determined by plotting the volume of gas produced against time and calculating the slope of the plot at time t=0.

## Measuring Change in Mass

The amount of gas produced by a reaction can also be monitored by using an electronic balance to record the drop in mass as the gas is released from the reaction mixture. The use of an electronic balance to monitor the loss of carbon dioxide during the reaction between marble chips (mostly $CaCO_3$) and dilute hydrochloric acid is shown in Figure 5.

$$CaCO_{3(s)} + 2HCl_{(aq)} \rightarrow CaCl_{2(aq)} + H_2O_{(l)} + CO_{2(g)}$$

*Figure 5: Use of an electronic balance to monitor the mass of the reaction mixture during the reaction between calcium carbonate and dilute hydrochloric acid. The cotton wool plug prevents loss of mass due to 'spray' from the reaction.*

The rate of the reaction between bromine and methanoic acid can be determined by monitoring the volume of carbon dioxide produced, or the drop in mass as carbon dioxide is released from the reaction mixture.

$$Br_{2(aq)} + HCOOH_{(aq)} \rightarrow 2Br^-_{(aq)} + 2H^+_{(aq)} + CO_{2(g)}$$

## Using Colorimetry

The rate of the reaction between bromine and methanoic acid can also be determined by colorimetry. In a colorimetry experiment the progress of the reaction is monitored by recording the amount of light of a particular wavelength absorbed by a substance in the reaction mixture as the reaction proceeds. In the case of the reaction between methanoic acid and bromine, the rate of the reaction can be determined by monitoring the amount of light absorbed by bromine in the reaction mixture as the reaction proceeds.

(a)

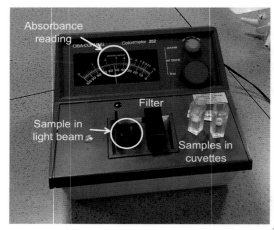

(b)

Group 7 Element is usually Colorimetry

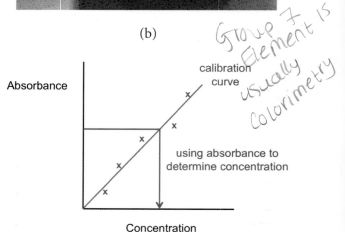

*Figure 6: (a) Using a colorimeter to measure the amount of light absorbed by a substance in a reaction mixture. (b) Using a calibration curve to convert absorbance to concentration.*

The amount of light absorbed by bromine is monitored by placing a sample of the reaction mixture in a colorimeter as shown in Figure 6a. The amount of light absorbed is recorded at intervals during the reaction and each reading converted to a concentration using a calibration curve as shown in Figure 6b. The initial rate of the reaction can then be determined by plotting the concentration of bromine against time and calculating the slope of the plot at time, t=0.

Substances that absorb visible light appear coloured. As a result, *colorimetry can often be used to study reactions in which one or more of the substances in the reaction mixture are coloured.*

### Worked Example 4.3ii

Methanoic acid undergoes an acid catalysed reaction with bromine. Suggest an experimental method to investigate the rate of this reaction.

$$Br_{2(aq)} + HCOOH_{(aq)} \rightarrow 2Br^-_{(aq)} + 2H^+_{(aq)} + CO_{2(g)}$$

*(Adapted from CCEA January 2010)*

### Strategy

Suitable methods include:

- Using colorimetry to monitor the amount of bromine in the reaction mixture.

- Using a graduated syringe to monitor the volume of gas produced during the reaction.

### Solution

Colorimetry can be used to measure the absorption of light by bromine in the reaction mixture. A calibration curve is then used to convert absorption to concentration. The initial rate of the reaction is obtained by plotting bromine concentration against time and calculating the slope of the tangent to the plot at t=0.

### Alternative answer

A graduated syringe can be used to measure the total volume of carbon dioxide produced at intervals during the reaction. The initial rate of the reaction can then be obtained by plotting the volume of carbon dioxide produced against time and calculating the slope of the tangent to the plot at t=0.

Colorimetry can also be used to determine the rate of the reaction between propanone and iodine in acidic solution.

$$CH_3COCH_{3(aq)} + I_{2(aq)} \rightarrow CH_3COCH_2I_{(aq)} + HI_{(aq)}$$

Iodine, $I_2$ gives the reaction mixture a brown colour which fades as the amount of iodine in the reaction mixture decreases. As a result, the amount of light absorbed by iodine can be monitored and used to determine the amount of iodine remaining at intervals during the reaction. The initial rate of reaction can then be determined by plotting the concentration of iodine against time and calculating the slope of the plot at time t=0.

### Measuring Conductivity

The rate of the reaction between propanone and iodine can also be determined by monitoring the electrical conductivity of the reaction mixture. The aqueous hydrogen iodide, $HI_{(aq)}$ produced in the reaction is a strong acid and dissociates to form hydrogen ($H^+$) ions and iodide ($I^-$) ions. The formation of ions increases the electrical conductivity of the reaction mixture. The increase in conductivity can be monitored by using a conductivity meter to measure the electrical conductivity of the reaction mixture at intervals during the reaction.

### Titration

The progress of the reaction between propanone and iodine can also be monitored by taking samples from the reaction mixture and halting the reaction occurring in the samples before titrating the hydrogen ($H^+$) ions in each sample against a standard alkali. The process of halting the reaction is known as 'quenching' and can be accomplished by quickly reacting the remaining reactants in the sample, or adding a large excess of solvent to dilute the reactants.

The amount of iodine present in the reaction mixture can also be determined by quenching a small sample of the reaction mixture, and titrating the iodine present in the sample against a standard solution of sodium thiosulfate, $Na_2S_2O_3$ using starch as an indicator. The starch forms a blue-black complex with iodine that is replaced by a colourless solution at the end point of the titration.

### Precipitation

Alternatively, the progress of the reaction between propanone and iodine could be monitored by taking samples from the reaction mixture, quenching the reaction, and adding an excess of acidified silver nitrate to precipitate the iodide ($I^-$) ions present in the sample as solid silver iodide, AgI. The amount of iodide ions present in the sample can then be determined by filtering the mixture and washing the precipitate with water before drying and weighing the precipitate.

### Worked Example 4.3iii

A chloroalkane is reacted with an aqueous solution of sodium hydroxide according to the following equation. (a) The rate of reaction can be investigated by monitoring the concentration of sodium hydroxide. Describe a titration method for carrying this out. (b) How would you use the results to determine the rate of reaction?

$$RCl + NaOH \rightarrow ROH + NaCl$$

*(CCEA May 2012)*

### Solution

(a) Take a small sample from the reaction mixture at regular intervals. Add an excess of water to quench the reaction, then titrate the solution against a standard solution of hydrochloric acid or sulfuric acid using phenolphthalein indicator.

(b) Plot the concentration of NaOH against time. The rate of the reaction can then be determined by drawing a tangent to the curve and calculating the slope of the tangent.

### Exercise 4.3B

1.  Propanone reacts with iodine in the presence of an acid. Which method would be the most suitable for investigating the rate of reaction?

    $$CH_3COCH_{3(aq)} + I_{2(aq)} \rightarrow CH_3COCH_2I_{(aq)} + HI_{(aq)}$$

    A   Colorimetry.

    B   Weighing the reaction vessel.

    C   Titrating samples with an acid.

    D   Using a graduated syringe.

    *(CCEA May 2011)*

2.  The following results were obtained in an experiment to determine the rate of reaction between persulfate ions and iodide ions in aqueous solution.

$$S_2O_8^{2-} + 2I^- \rightarrow 2SO_4^{2-} + I_2$$

| Concentration of $S_2O_8^{2-}$ /mol dm$^{-3}$ | Concentration of $I^-$ /mol dm$^{-3}$ | Initial rate /mol dm$^{-3}$ s$^{-1}$ |
|---|---|---|
| 0.050 | 0.050 | 0.18 |
| 0.100 | 0.050 | 0.36 |
| 0.100 | 0.100 | 0.72 |

Describe how you would use (a) titration and (b) precipitation to study the rate of the reaction. The concentration of one of the reactants or products will need to be measured with respect to time and can then be used to determine the rate of reaction.

*(Adapted from CCEA May 2014)*

Before moving to the next section, check that you are able to:

*   Identify a suitable experimental method to determine the rate of a chemical reaction.
*   Describe the experimental procedure used to determine the rate of a chemical reaction.

## Rate Equations

In this section we are learning to:

*   Use the rate equation for a reaction to determine how changing the composition of a reaction mixture affects the rate of the reaction.
*   Explain how the rate equation for a reaction can be determined graphically.

The **rate equation** for a chemical reaction *defines the relationship between the rate of reaction and the composition of the reaction mixture*. For example, the rate equation for the reaction between propanone and iodine in acidic solution reveals that the rate of reaction depends on the concentration of propanone, $[CH_3COCH_3]$ and the concentration of hydrogen ions, $[H^+]$ in the reaction mixture. The concentration of iodine, $[I_2]$ does not affect the rate of reaction.

*Chemical equation:*
$$CH_3COCH_3 + I_2 \rightarrow CH_3COCH_2I + HI$$

*Rate equation:*
Rate = $k [CH_3COCH_3] [H^+]$

The **rate constant**, k for a reaction is *a positive number that varies with temperature and defines the relationship between the rate of the reaction and the concentrations in the rate equation.*

The rate equation for reaction between iodine and propanone reveals that the rate of the reaction doubles when the concentration of propanone is doubled, or when the concentration of hydrogen ions in the reaction mixture is doubled.

$$\text{Rate} = k \, [CH_3COCH_3]^1 \, [H^+]^1$$
$$\underbrace{\quad}_{x2} \quad \underbrace{\qquad}_{x2}$$

$$\text{Rate} = k \, [CH_3COCH_3]^1 \, [H^+]^1$$
$$\underbrace{\quad}_{x2} \quad \underbrace{\quad}_{x2}$$

If both concentrations are doubled, the rate doubles and then doubles again to increase the rate by a factor of $2 \times 2 = 4$.

$$\text{Rate} = k \, [CH_3COCH_3]^1 \, [H^+]^1$$
$$\underbrace{\quad}_{2 \times 2 = x4} \quad \underbrace{\qquad}_{x2} \quad \underbrace{\quad}_{x2}$$

Similarly, if the concentration of propanone is doubled and the concentration of hydrogen ions increased by a factor of three, the rate increases by a factor of $2 \times 3 = 6$.

$$\text{Rate} = k \, [CH_3COCH_3]^1 \, [H^+]^1$$
$$\underbrace{\quad}_{2 \times 3 = x6} \quad \underbrace{\qquad}_{x2} \quad \underbrace{\quad}_{x3}$$

Given that iodine is a reactant, it is perhaps surprising that the rate of the reaction does not depend on the concentration of iodine in the reaction mixture. This is an indication that propanone and iodine have different roles in the reaction that cannot be distinguished from the chemical equation.

Comparing the chemical equation and rate equation for the reaction also provides insight into the role of hydrogen (H⁺) ion in the reaction. Hydrogen (H⁺) ion acts as a catalyst for the reaction. As the concentration of H⁺ ion increases, more collisions involve H⁺ ions and can take advantage of the lower energy pathway provided by the catalyst. As a result, more collisions are successful and the rate of reaction increases as the concentration of H⁺ ion increases.

## Exercise 4.3C

1. Methanoic acid undergoes an acid catalysed reaction with bromine. (a) Deduce the effect of doubling the initial concentration of bromine on the initial rate of reaction. (b) Deduce the overall effect of doubling the initial concentrations of bromine and methanoic acid on the rate of reaction.

$$Br_{2(aq)} + HCOOH_{(aq)} \rightarrow 2Br^-_{(aq)} + 2H^+_{(aq)} + CO_{2(g)} \quad \text{Rate} = k \, [Br_2] \, [HCOOH]$$

*(Adapted from CCEA January 2010)*

2. The rate law for the acid catalysed reaction between iodine and propanone is given below. (a) Deduce the effect of doubling the initial concentration of (i) propanone, (ii) iodine and (iii) acid on the initial rate of reaction. (b) Deduce the overall effect of doubling the initial concentrations of propanone and iodine on the rate of reaction.

$$CH_3COCH_3 + I_2 \rightarrow CH_3COCH_2I + HI \quad \text{Rate} = k \, [CH_3COCH_3] \, [H^+]$$

*(Adapted from CCEA May 2010)*

## Order of Reaction

The **order of a reaction** is *the sum of the powers to which the concentration terms are raised in the rate equation.* In the case of the reaction between propanone and iodine, the order of the reaction is $1+1 = 2$ and the reaction is described as *second order overall*.

$$\text{Rate} = k \, [CH_3COCH_3]^1 \, [H+]^1$$
$$\underbrace{\qquad\qquad}_{1 + 1 = 2 \quad \text{second order reaction}}$$

Similarly, the rate equation for the reaction between bromate(V) ion, $BrO_3^-$ and bromide ion, $Br^-$ in acidic solution reveals that the reaction is first order with respect to bromate(V) ion, $[BrO_3]^1$ first order with respect to bromide ion, $[Br^-]^1$ and second order with respect to hydrogen ion, $[H^+]^2$. As a result the order of the reaction is $1+1+2 = 4$ and the reaction is described as *fourth order overall*.

$$\text{Rate} = k \, [BrO_3^-]^1 \, [Br^-]^1 \, [H^+]^2$$
$$\underbrace{\qquad\qquad}_{1 + 1 + 2 = 4 \quad \text{fourth order reaction}}$$

The rate equations for the reactions in Table 1 demonstrate that the orders in a rate equation cannot be deduced from the chemical equation for the reaction.

| Order of Reaction | Reaction |
|---|---|
| Zero order | Decomposition of ammonia on a hot platinum wire: $2NH_3 \rightarrow N_2 + 3H_2$ Rate = k |
| First order | Hydrolysis of 2-bromo-2-methylpropane in dilute alkali: $C(CH_3)_3Br + OH^- \rightarrow C(CH_3)_3OH + Br^-$ Rate = k $[C(CH_3)_3Br]$ |
| Second order | Decomposition of nitrogen(IV) oxide: $2NO_2 \rightarrow 2NO + O_2$ Rate = k $[NO_2]^2$ Decomposition of hydrogen peroxide in the presence of aqueous potassium iodide: $2H_2O_2 \rightarrow 2H_2O + O_2$ Rate = k $[H_2O_2]$ $[I^-]$ |
| Third order | Oxidation of nitrogen(II) oxide in air: $2NO + O_2 \rightarrow 2NO_2$ Rate = k $[NO]^2$ $[O_2]$ |

Table 1: Examples of rate equations for zero, first, second and third order reactions.

## Graphical Determination of Order

If we include the concentration of each reactant in the rate equation for the reaction between propanone and iodine in acidic solution becomes:

Rate = k $[CH_3COCH_3]^1$ $[H^+]^1$ $[I_2]^0$

When written in this way the rate equation reveals that the reaction is first order with respect to propanone, $[CH_3COCH_3]^1$ first order with respect to hydrogen ion, $[H^+]^1$ and zero order with respect to iodine, $[I_2]^0$.

The first order relationship between the rate of reaction and the concentration of propanone in Figure 7a can be deduced by measuring the initial rate of reaction for a series of reactions in which the concentration of hydrogen ions and the concentration of iodine does not vary. Similarly, the first order relationship between the rate of the reaction and the concentration of hydrogen ions in

Figure 7a can be deduced by measuring the initial rate of reaction for a series of reactions in which the concentration of propanone and the concentration of iodine does not vary.

The plots in Figure 7a are characteristic of a first order relationship between rate and concentration. Similarly, the form of the relationship between the rate of the reaction and the concentration of iodine in Figure 7b is characteristic of a zero order relationship.

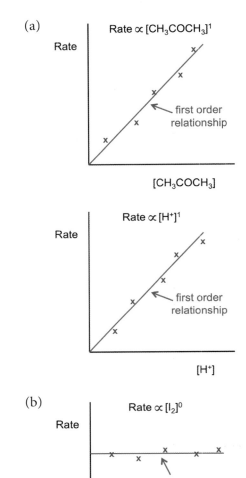

Figure 7: (a) The first order relationships between rate and concentration for propanone, $CH_3COCH_3$ and hydrogen ion, $H^+$. (b) The zero order relationship between rate and concentration for iodine, $I_2$.

The reaction between bromate(V) ion, $BrO_3^-$ and bromide, $Br^-$ in acidic solution can be used to illustrate a second order relationship between the rate of reaction and the concentration of a reactant.

*Chemical equation:*

$BrO_3^-{}_{(aq)} + 5Br^-{}_{(aq)} + 6H^+{}_{(aq)} \rightarrow 3Br_{2(aq)} + 3H_2O_{(l)}$

*Rate equation:*

$Rate = k [BrO_3^-] [Br^-] [H^+]^2$

The rate equation reveals that the reaction is first order with respect to bromate(V) ion, $[BrO_3^-]^1$ first order with respect to bromide, $[Br^-]^1$ and second order with respect to hydrogen ion, $[H^+]^2$. The plots used to deduce these first and second order relationships are shown in Figure 8.

(a)

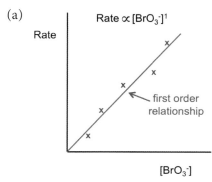

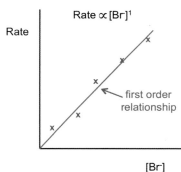

(b)

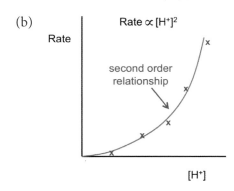

*Figure 8: (a) The first order relationships between rate and concentration for bromate(V) ion, $BrO_3^-$ and bromide ion, $Br^-$. (b) The second order relationship between rate and concentration for hydrogen ion, $H^+$.*

**Exercise 4.3D**

1. Which one of the following graphs shows a reaction that is first order with respect to reactant Z?

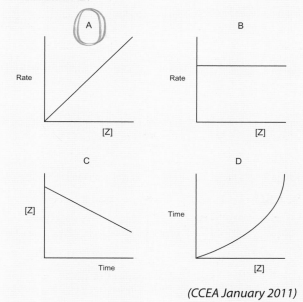

*(CCEA January 2011)*

2. The rate law for the acid catalysed reaction between iodine and propanone is given below.

$CH_3COCH_3 + I_2 \rightarrow CH_3COCH_2I + HI$

$Rate = k [CH_3COCH_3] [H^+]$

Sketch the form of the graph that would be obtained on plotting (a) $[CH_3COCH_3]$ against time and (b) Rate against $[CH_3COCH_3]$.

*(Adapted from CCEA May 2010)*

3. Acidified hydrogen peroxide oxidises iodide ions according to the following equation.

$H_2O_{2(aq)} + 2I^-{}_{(aq)} + 2H^+{}_{(aq)} \rightarrow I_{2(aq)} + 2H_2O_{(l)}$

(a) Name the reagent and the expected result to show that iodine is produced in the reaction.
(b) The reaction is first order with respect to iodide ions. Sketch the graph that would be obtained on plotting i) $[I^-]$ against time and ii) Rate against $[I^-]$.

*(Adapted from CCEA January 2014)*

4. Methanoic acid undergoes an acid catalysed reaction with bromine. Sketch the expected shape for the graph of (a) $[HCOOH]$ against time and (b) Rate against $[HCOOH]$.

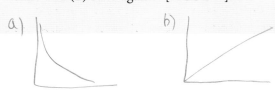

| Experiment | [CH$_3$COCH$_3$] (mol dm$^{-3}$) | [H$^+$] (mol dm$^{-3}$) | [I$_2$] (mol dm$^{-3}$) | Initial Rate (mol dm$^{-3}$ s$^{-1}$) |
|---|---|---|---|---|
| 1 | 0.33 | 0.32 | 3.32 | $3.87 \times 10^{-6}$ |
| 2 | 0.33 | 0.32 | 6.65 | $3.91 \times 10^{-6}$ |
| 3 | 0.67 | 0.32 | 6.65 | $7.95 \times 10^{-6}$ |
| 4 | 1.33 | 0.16 | 6.65 | $8.02 \times 10^{-6}$ |
| 5 | 1.33 | 0.32 | 6.65 | $1.61 \times 10^{-5}$ |

*Table 2: The effect of concentration on the initial rate of the reaction between propanone and iodine in acidic solution.*

$Br_{2(aq)} + HCOOH_{(aq)} \rightarrow 2Br^-_{(aq)} + 2H^+_{(aq)} + CO_{2(g)}$
Rate = k [Br$_2$] [HCOOH]

*(CCEA January 2010)*

5. Hydrogen peroxide decomposes to produce water and oxygen. The reaction is catalysed by bromide ions. Explain how you would use a gas syringe to follow this reaction in order to determine the rate of the reaction and hence the order of reaction with respect to hydrogen peroxide.

$2H_2O_{2(aq)} \rightarrow 2H_2O_{(l)} + O_{2(g)}$

*(Adapted from CCEA May 2015)*

---

Before moving to the next section, check that you are able to:

- Explain what is meant by the *rate equation* and the *rate constant* for a chemical reaction.
- Use the rate equation for a reaction to determine the effect of changing the concentration of one or more reactants on the rate of the reaction.
- Explain what is meant by *the order of a chemical reaction*.
- Describe how the order of reaction with respect to a reactant can be determined graphically.

---

**Determining Order from Initial Rate Measurements**

The order of reaction with respect to a reactant can be determined by measuring the effect of changing the concentration of the reactant on the initial rate of the reaction. Consider, once again, the acid catalysed reaction between propanone and iodine.

*Chemical equation:*
$CH_3COCH_3 + I_2 \rightarrow CH_3COCH_2I + HI$

*Rate equation:*
Rate = k [CH$_3$COCH$_3$]$^1$ [H$^+$]$^1$ [I$_2$]$^0$

The initial rates in Table 2 can be used to determine the order of reaction with respect to propanone, iodine and hydrogen ion.

The initial rates for Experiments 2 and 3 reveal that doubling the concentration of propanone approximately doubles the rate of reaction. This relationship demonstrates that the reaction is first order with respect to propanone.

Rate α [CH$_3$COCH$_3$]$^1$

Similarly, Experiments 4 and 5 reveal that the reaction is first order with respect to hydrogen ion as doubling the concentration of hydrogen ion doubles the rate.

Rate α [H$^+$]$^1$

In contrast, the initial rates for Experiments 1 and 2 reveal that doubling the concentration of iodine does not double the rate. This demonstrates that the order of reaction with respect to iodine is zero.

Rate α [I$_2$]$^0$

---

**Exercise 4.3E**

1. A chloroalkane is reacted with an aqueous solution of sodium hydroxide according to the following equation. (a) Deduce the order of the reaction with respect to (i) RCl and (ii) NaOH. (b) Deduce the rate equation.

$RCl + NaOH \rightarrow ROH + NaCl$

| Experiment | [RCl] (mol dm$^{-3}$) | [NaOH] (mol dm$^{-3}$) | Rate (mol dm$^{-3}$ s$^{-1}$) |
|---|---|---|---|
| 1 | $1.3 \times 10^{-3}$ | $9.0 \times 10^{-4}$ | 0.2 |
| 2 | $2.6 \times 10^{-3}$ | $9.0 \times 10^{-4}$ | 0.4 |
| 3 | $1.3 \times 10^{-3}$ | $1.8 \times 10^{-3}$ | 0.4 |

*(CCEA May 2012)*

2. The ionic equation for the alkaline hydrolysis of $C_4H_9Br$ is given below. Use the data in the following table to calculate the order of the reaction with respect to (a) $C_4H_9Br$ and (b) $OH^-$. Explain your reasoning in each case. (c) Write the rate equation for the reaction.

$$C_4H_9Br + OH^- \rightarrow C_4H_9OH + Br^-$$

| Experiment | Initial [C$_4$H$_9$Br] (mol dm$^{-3}$) | Initial [OH$^-$] (mol dm$^{-3}$) | Initial Rate (mol dm$^{-3}$ s$^{-1}$) |
|---|---|---|---|
| 1 | 0.02 | 0.02 | 40.0 |
| 2 | 0.01 | 0.02 | 20.0 |
| 3 | 0.03 | 0.04 | 60.0 |

*(CCEA May 2011)*

3. Acidified hydrogen peroxide oxidises iodide ions according to the following equation. The reaction is first order with respect to iodide ions.

$$H_2O_{2(aq)} + 2I^-_{(aq)} + 2H^+_{(aq)} \rightarrow I_{2(aq)} + 2H_2O_{(l)}$$

The table shows the initial rates for the reaction for different concentrations of hydrogen peroxide and hydrogen ions. (a) State the order of the reaction with respect to hydrogen peroxide and hydrogen ions. (b) State the rate equation for the reaction between $H_2O_2$ and acidified $I^-$ ions.

| Experiment | [H$_2$O$_{2(aq)}$] (mol dm$^{-3}$) | [H$^+_{(aq)}$] (mol dm$^{-3}$) | Initial rate $\times 10^{-6}$ (mol dm$^{-3}$ s$^{-1}$) |
|---|---|---|---|
| 1 | 0.00075 | 0.10 | 2.1 |
| 2 | 0.00150 | 0.10 | 4.2 |
| 3 | 0.00150 | 0.20 | 4.2 |

*(CCEA January 2014)*

4. The following results were obtained in an experiment to determine the rate of reaction between persulfate ions and iodide ions in aqueous solution.

$$S_2O_8^{2-} + 2I^- \rightarrow 2SO_4^{2-} + I_2$$

| Concentration of S$_2$O$_8^{2-}$ /mol dm$^{-3}$ | Concentration of I$^-$ /mol dm$^{-3}$ | Initial rate /mol dm$^{-3}$ s$^{-1}$ |
|---|---|---|
| 0.050 | 0.050 | 0.18 |
| 0.100 | 0.050 | 0.36 |
| 0.100 | 0.100 | 0.72 |

(a) Deduce the order of reaction with respect to each of the reactants. (b) Write the rate equation for the reaction. (c) Using this reaction explain what is meant by the overall order of a reaction.

*(CCEA May 2014)*

5. Use the initial rate data in the table to determine the rate equation for the bromination of propanone in acidic solution.

$$CH_3COCH_3 + Br_2 \rightarrow CH_3COCH_2Br + HBr$$

| Experiment | [CH$_3$COCH$_3$] (mol dm$^{-3}$) | [H$^+$] (mol dm$^{-3}$) | [Br$_2$] (mol dm$^{-3}$) | Initial Rate (mol dm$^{-3}$ s$^{-1}$) |
|---|---|---|---|---|
| 1 | 0.80 | 0.20 | 8.66 | $6.06 \times 10^{-6}$ |
| 2 | 0.80 | 0.20 | 4.33 | $6.07 \times 10^{-6}$ |
| 3 | 0.80 | 0.40 | 8.66 | $1.21 \times 10^{-5}$ |
| 4 | 1.60 | 0.20 | 8.66 | $1.23 \times 10^{-5}$ |

6. Use the data in the following table to deduce the rate equation for the reaction:

$$2A + B + 2C \rightarrow D + E + F$$

| [A] /mol dm$^{-3}$ | [B] /mol dm$^{-3}$ | [C] /mol dm$^{-3}$ | Rate of reaction /mol dm$^{-3}$ s$^{-1}$ |
|---|---|---|---|
| 1.0 | 0.50 | 0.40 | $1.8 \times 10^{-4}$ |
| 1.0 | 0.40 | 0.40 | $1.8 \times 10^{-4}$ |
| 1.0 | 0.30 | 0.20 | $9.0 \times 10^{-5}$ |
| 0.10 | 0.20 | 0.40 | $1.8 \times 10^{-5}$ |

*(Adapted from CCEA May 2015)*

Before moving to the next section, check that you are able to:

- Use initial rate measurements to determine the order of reaction with respect to a reactant.

## Rate Constants

**In this section we are learning to:**

- Calculate the rate constant for a reaction and determine its units.
- Explain how temperature and the presence of a catalyst affect the magnitude of the rate constant for a reaction.

### Calculating the Rate Constant

The value of the rate constant, k can be obtained by inserting values for the initial rate and the corresponding concentrations into the rate equation. For example, the data in Table 2 (page 40) can be used to determine the rate constant for the reaction between propanone and iodine in acidic solution.

Chemical equation:
$$CH_3COCH_3 + I_2 \rightarrow CH_3COCH_2I + HI$$

Rate equation:
$$Rate = k [CH_3COCH_3] [H^+]$$

Using the data from Experiment 1 (Table 2, page 40) gives:

$$k = \frac{Rate}{[CH_3COCH_3][H^+]} = \frac{3.87 \times 10^{-6}}{(0.33)(0.32)}$$

$$= 3.7 \times 10^{-5} \text{ mol}^{-1} \text{ dm}^3 \text{ s}^{-1}$$

Similarly, using the data from Experiment 3 (Table 2) gives:

$$k = \frac{Rate}{[CH_3COCH_3][H^+]} = \frac{7.95 \times 10^{-6}}{(0.67)(0.32)}$$

$$= 3.7 \times 10^{-5} \text{ mol}^{-1} \text{ dm}^3 \text{ s}^{-1}$$

The units for the rate constant are obtained by dividing the units for rate (mol dm$^{-3}$ s$^{-1}$) by the units for concentration raised to the order of the reaction, in this instance (mol dm$^{-3}$)$^2$ = mol$^2$ dm$^{-6}$. The expressions used to calculate the rate constant for a reaction and determine its units are summarised in Table 3 (page 43).

| Order of Reaction | Expression for the rate constant, k | Units for the rate constant, k |
|---|---|---|
| zero | $k = \text{Rate}$ | $\text{mol dm}^{-3}\,\text{s}^{-1}$ |
| first | $k = \dfrac{\text{Rate}}{\text{Concentration}}$ | $\dfrac{\text{mol dm}^{-3}\,\text{s}^{-1}}{\text{mol dm}^{-3}} = \text{s}^{-1}$ |
| second | $k = \dfrac{\text{Rate}}{\text{Concentration}^2}$ | $\dfrac{\text{mol dm}^{-3}\,\text{s}^{-1}}{\text{mol}^2\,\text{dm}^{-6}}$ $= \text{mol}^{-1}\,\text{dm}^3\,\text{s}^{-1}$ |
| third | $k = \dfrac{\text{Rate}}{\text{Concentration}^3}$ | $\dfrac{\text{mol dm}^{-3}\,\text{s}^{-1}}{\text{mol}^3\,\text{dm}^{-9}}$ $= \text{mol}^{-2}\,\text{dm}^6\,\text{s}^{-1}$ |

*Table 3: The expressions used to calculate the rate constant for a reaction and determine its units.*

## Exercise 4.3F

1. The rate of decomposition of ethanal at 500 °C is given by the equation: Rate = k [ethanal]². What are the units of k?

    A $s^{-1}$  
    B $\text{mol dm}^{-3}\,\text{s}^{-1}$  
    C $\text{mol}^{-1}\,\text{dm}^3\,\text{s}^{-1}$  
    D $\text{mol}^2\,\text{dm}^{-6}\,\text{s}^{-1}$

    *(CCEA January 2009)*

2. The rate equation for the reaction of hydrogen with nitrogen monoxide is Rate = k [H$_2$] [NO]². What are the units of the rate constant?

    A $\text{mol}^{-1}\,\text{dm}^3\,\text{s}^{-1}$  
    B $\text{mol dm}^{-3}\,\text{s}^{-1}$  
    C $\text{mol}^{-2}\,\text{dm}^{-6}\,\text{s}^{-1}$  
    D $\text{mol}^{-2}\,\text{dm}^6\,\text{s}^{-1}$

    *(CCEA January 2011)*

3. Calculate the rate constant for the reaction between persulfate ions and iodide ions in aqueous solution and state its units.

    $S_2O_8^{2-} + 2I^- \rightarrow 2SO_4^{2-} + I_2$

    Rate = k [S$_2$O$_8^{2-}$] [I$^-$]   $mol^{-1}\ dm^3\ s^{-1}$

| Concentration of S$_2$O$_8^{2-}$ /mol dm$^{-3}$ | Concentration of I$^-$ /mol dm$^{-3}$ | Initial rate /mol dm$^{-3}$ s$^{-1}$ |
|---|---|---|
| 0.050 | 0.050 | 0.18 |
| 0.100 | 0.050 | 0.36 |
| 0.100 | 0.100 | 0.72 |

*(Adapted from CCEA May 2014)*

## Factors Affecting the Rate Constant

### Temperature

The Maxwell-Boltzmann distributions in Figure 9 demonstrate that increasing the temperature of a reaction mixture increases the fraction of particles with at least the activation energy, $E_a$. As a result, more collisions involve particles with enough energy to react, and the number of successful collisions per second increases. This explains why, in general, the rate of a reaction increases as the temperature of the reaction mixture increases.

According to the rate equation, the increase in rate must be due to an increase in the rate constant, k. In this way we see that *the rate constant, k must increase as the temperature of the reaction mixture increases.*

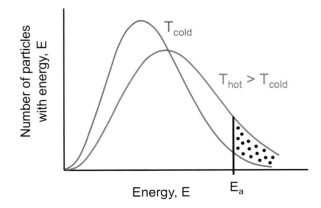

*Figure 9: The Maxwell-Boltzmann distribution for a reaction mixture at temperature $T_{cold}$, and temperature $T_{hot}$, where $T_{hot} > T_{cold}$. The shaded area represents the additional number of particles with energy greater than $E_a$ as the temperature increases from $T_{cold}$ to $T_{hot}$.*

### Adding a Catalyst

The Maxwell-Boltzmann distributions in Figure 10 demonstrate that adding a catalyst to a reaction mixture lowers the activation energy for the reaction from $E_a$ to $E_{cat}$. As a result, a greater fraction of particles in the reaction mixture have enough energy to react, and the number of successful collisions per second increases. This explains why adding a catalyst increases the rate of a chemical reaction.

According to the rate equation, the increase in rate on adding a catalyst must be due to an increase in the rate constant, k and it follows that *the rate constant for the reaction increases when a catalyst is used to lower the activation energy for the reaction.*

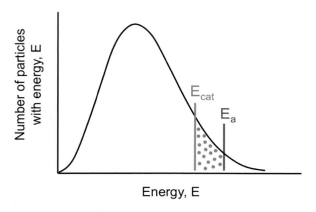

*Figure 10: The additional number of particles with enough energy to react (shaded) in the presence of a catalyst.*

### Exercise 4.3G

1. The rate law for the acid catalysed reaction between iodine and propanone is given below.

$$CH_3COCH_3 + I_2 \rightarrow CH_3COCH_2I + HI$$
$$Rate = k\,[CH_3COCH_3]\,[H^+]$$

The reaction is exothermic. (a) Construct an enthalpy diagram for the reaction, labelling both the catalysed and uncatalysed pathways. (b) Suggest what effect, if any, the use of a catalyst will have on the value of k for the reaction at a given temperature.

*Adding a catalyst will ↑ Rate Constant*

*(CCEA May 2010)*

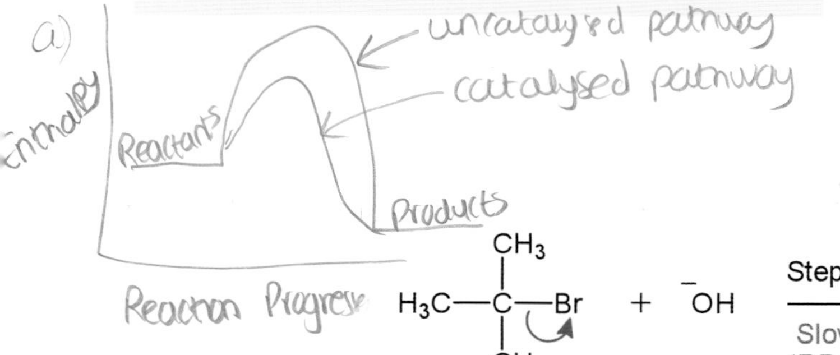

*a)*

*Enthalpy*

*Reactants*

*unratalysed pathway*

*catalysed pathway*

*Products*

*Reaction Progress*

*Rate Determining Step*

---

> Before moving to the next section, check that you are able to:
>
> - Use the rate equation to calculate the rate constant for a reaction and determine its units.
> - Explain why increasing the temperature of a reaction mixture or adding a catalyst to the reaction mixture increases the rate constant for the reaction.

## Determining Reaction Mechanisms

> **In this section we are learning to:**
>
> - Explain the relationship between the rate equation for a reaction and the mechanism of the reaction.

The rate equation for a reaction can be used to help determine the mechanism for the reaction. Consider, for example, the alkaline hydrolysis of 2-bromo-2-methylpropane.

*Hydrolysis of 2-bromo-2-methylpropane:*
$$C(CH_3)_3Br + OH^- \rightarrow C(CH_3)_3OH + Br^-$$
$$Rate = k\,[C(CH_3)_3Br]$$

The reaction proceeds by the two step mechanism shown in Figure 11. The first step involves the heterolytic fission of the C-Br bond to form a tertiary carbocation, $(CH_3)_3C^+$. Hydroxide ion then acts as a nucleophile by forming a coordinate bond with the electron-deficient carbon in the carbocation ($C^+$).

The rate of the reaction is determined by the speed of the **rate determining step (RDS)** which is, by

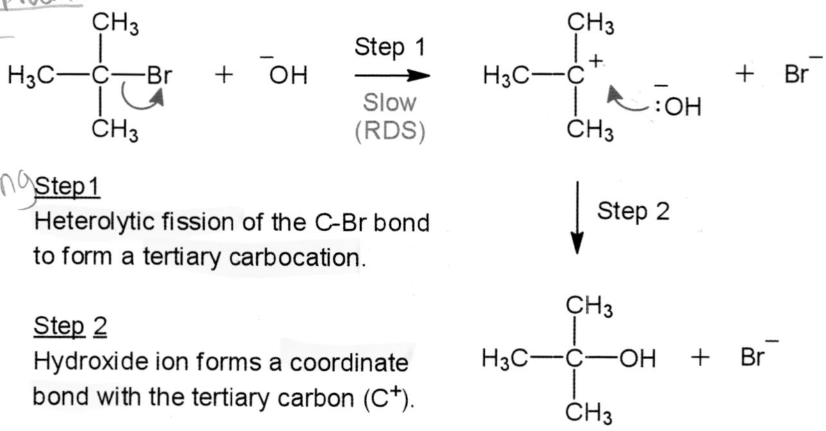

**Step 1**
Heterolytic fission of the C-Br bond to form a tertiary carbocation.

**Step 2**
Hydroxide ion forms a coordinate bond with the tertiary carbon ($C^+$).

*Tertiary Carbon*

*Figure 11: Mechanism for the alkaline hydrolysis of 2-bromo-2-methylpropane.*

definition, *the slowest step in the mechanism for the reaction.*

By defining the rate determining step in this way it follows that *only substances involved in the rate determining step appear in the rate equation and affect the rate of the reaction.* For instance, in the hydrolysis of 2-bromo-2-methylpropane (Figure 11), the first step in the mechanism must be rate determining as the hydroxide ions in the second step do not appear in the rate equation and are therefore not involved in the rate determining step.

The rate equation for the hydrolysis of 2-bromo-2-methylpropane has the same form as the rate equation for the hydrolysis of other tertiary halogenoalkanes, and is evidence that the mechanism is the same for the hydrolysis of all tertiary halogenoalkanes.

*Mechanism for the hydrolysis of a tertiary halogenoalkane, RX*

$RX + OH^- \rightarrow ROH + X^-$    Rate = k [RX]
                           where X = Cl, Br, I

Step 1  $RX \rightarrow R^+ + X^-$    (slow)

Step 2  $R^+ + OH^- \rightarrow ROH$

In contrast, the rate equation for the hydrolysis of 1-bromobutane and other primary halogenoalkanes suggests that both the halogenoalkane and hydroxide ion are involved in the rate determining step.

*Hydrolysis of 1-bromobutane:*

$CH_3(CH_2)_3Br + OH^- \rightarrow CH_3(CH_2)_3OH + Br^-$
Rate = k $[CH_3(CH_2)_3Br] [OH^-]$

The mechanism in Figure 12 is consistent with the rate equation and suggests that the reaction occurs in a single step. As hydroxide ion approaches the halogenoalkane it uses a lone pair to begin forming a coordinate bond with the electron-deficient carbon in the carbon-halogen bond ($C^{\delta+}$–$Br^{\delta-}$).

As the coordinate bond forms (C---OH) the carbon-halogen bond begins to break (C---Br). The process continues until the coordinate bond is fully formed (C-OH) and the carbon-halogen bond has undergone heterolytic fission to produce bromide ion. The intermediate structure (HO---C---Br) is referred to as a **transition state**. The transition state is not a stable substance and cannot be isolated as a compound.

The rate equation for the hydrolysis of 1-bromobutane has the same form as the rate equation for the hydrolysis of other primary halogenoalkanes,

(a)

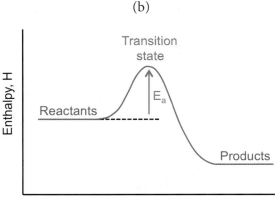

Transition State

(b)

Figure 12: (a) Mechanism for the alkaline hydrolysis of 1-bromobutane. Dashed lines (---) are used to indicate partially broken and partially formed bonds. (b) The location of the transition state on the reaction profile.

and is evidence that the mechanism is the same for the hydrolysis of all primary halogenoalkanes.

> *Mechanism for the hydrolysis of a primary halogenoalkane, RX*
>
> $RX + OH^- \rightarrow ROH + X^-$     (slow)
>
> Rate = k [RX] [OH$^-$]   where   X = Cl, Br, I

Hydroxide ion is a more effective **nucleophile** than water as it is more strongly attracted to the electron-deficient carbon atom (C$^{\delta+}$) in the carbon-halogen bond. As a result the hydrolysis of a primary halogenoalkane to form the corresponding alcohol (RX + H$_2$O $\rightarrow$ ROH + HX) is significantly faster when a small amount of alkali (containing OH$^-$) is added to the reaction mixture.

.................................................

**Worked Example 4.3iv**

Which one of the following is the order of decreasing nucleophilic reactivity of the three species?

A  OH$^-$ > H$_2$O > H$_3$O$^+$     B  OH$^-$ > H$_3$O$^+$ > H$_2$O

C  H$_2$O > H$_3$O$^+$ > OH$^-$     D  H$_2$O > OH$^-$ > H$_3$O$^+$

*(CCEA January 2013)*

**Strategy**

(a) The negatively charged hydroxide (OH$^-$) ion is a better nucleophile than water as it is attracted to an electron-deficient ($\delta+$) atom.

(b) Water is a better nucleophile than H$_3$O$^+$ ion as the H$_3$O$^+$ ion is repelled by an electron-deficient ($\delta+$) atom.

**Solution**

Answer A.

.................................................

**Exercise 4.3H**

1. Which one of the following statements is correct for the hydrolysis of a primary alkyl halide?

   A  A carbocation is formed.

   B  A positively charged transition state is formed.

   C  A negatively charged transition state is formed.

   D  The reaction is first order.

   *(CCEA January 2014)*

2. Draw a reaction mechanism for the hydrolysis of C$_4$H$_9$Br which is consistent with the following rate equation. Show the structure of C$_4$H$_9$Br clearly in your mechanism and identify the rate determining step.

   C$_4$H$_9$Br + OH$^-$ $\rightarrow$ C$_4$H$_9$OH + Br$^-$
   Rate = k [C$_4$H$_9$Br] [OH$^-$]

   *(CCEA May 2011)*

3. A chloroalkane is reacted with an aqueous solution of sodium hydroxide according to the following equation. (a) Name the mechanism of this reaction. (b) Classify RCl as a primary or tertiary chloroalkane giving a reason for your answer.

   RCl + NaOH $\rightarrow$ ROH + NaCl
   Rate = k [RCl] [NaOH]

   *(CCEA May 2012)*

4. Ethanal reacts with hydrogen cyanide to form a cyanohydrin.

   CH$_3$CHO + HCN $\rightarrow$ CH$_3$CH(OH)CN

   In the first step cyanide ion reacts with the carbonyl group to form an intermediate. This is the rate determining step. (a) Draw the structure of the intermediate. (b) Explain the meaning of the term *rate determining step*. (c) Write the rate equation and state the meaning of the symbol *k*. (d) State the order of the reaction.

   *(CCEA January 2012)*

5. Ethoxide ion, CH$_3$CH$_2$O$^-$ is a strong base. When 2-chloro-2-methylpropane is heated with a solution containing ethoxide ion it reacts to form 2-methylpropene.

   The rate equation for the reaction is Rate = k [C$_4$H$_9$Cl]. Propose a mechanism for the reaction that is consistent with the rate equation. Clearly identify the slow step in the mechanism.

6. Which one of the following would be a possible mechanism for the reaction between X and Y?

$$X + 2Y \rightarrow XY_2 \quad \text{Rate} = k\,[Y]^2$$

A   $X + Y \rightarrow XY$ (fast); $XY + Y \rightarrow XY_2$ (slow)
B   $Y + Y \rightarrow Y_2$ (slow); $Y_2 + X \rightarrow XY_2$ (fast)
C   $X + Y + Y \rightarrow XY_2$ (slow)
D   $X + Y \rightarrow XY$ (slow); $XY + Y \rightarrow XY_2$ (fast)

*only substances that involved in RDS appear in Rate Equation*

*(CCEA May 2010)*

7. The following is a proposed reaction mechanism for the formation of bromine from bromate ions. Write the overall equation for the reaction.

$$BrO_3^- + 2H^+ \rightarrow H_2BrO_3^+$$
$$Br^- + H_2BrO_3^+ \rightarrow Br_2O_2 + H_2O$$
$$Br_2O_2 + 4H^+ + 4Br^- \rightarrow 3Br_2 + 2H_2O$$

*(Adapted from CCEA January 2013)*

8. Acidified hydrogen peroxide oxidises iodide ions according to the following equation:

$$H_2O_{2(aq)} + 2I^-_{(aq)} + 2H^+_{(aq)} \rightarrow I_{2(aq)} + 2H_2O_{(l)}$$

The reaction takes place in two steps. The first step is rate determining and is:

$$H_2O_{2(aq)} + I^-_{(aq)} \rightarrow H_2O_{(l)} + IO^-_{(aq)}$$

(a) What is meant by the *rate determining step*?
(b) Suggest the equation for the second step in the reaction.

$$I^- + 2H^+ + IO^- \rightarrow I_2 + H_2O$$

*(CCEA January 2014)*

---

Before moving to the next section, check that you are able to:

- Explain what is meant by the *rate determining step (RDS)* of a reaction.
- Use the rate equation for a reaction to determine the form of the RDS in the mechanism for the reaction.
- Draw mechanisms for the alkaline hydrolysis of primary and tertiary halogenoalkanes and identify the RDS.
- Explain how the rate of a nucleophilic substitution reaction is affected by the ability of the nucleophile.

---

## Catalysis

**In this section we are learning to:**

- Identify a catalyst from its role in the mechanism for a reaction.

A **catalyst** is a substance that *speeds up a reaction by lowering the activation energy, and is not consumed by the reaction.* For example, in the absence of a catalyst the decomposition of aqueous hydrogen peroxide occurs very slowly.

$$2H_2O_{2(aq)} \rightarrow 2H_2O_{(l)} + O_{2(g)}$$

The reaction occurs much more quickly when a small volume of aqueous potassium iodide is added to the reaction mixture. The iodide, $I^-$ ions act as a catalyst by reacting with a molecule of hydrogen peroxide, $H_2O_2$ to form water and iodate(I) ions, $IO^-$. The iodate(I) ions then react with more hydrogen peroxide to form the remaining products of the reaction.

*Mechanism for the catalysed decomposition of hydrogen peroxide:*

$$2H_2O_{2(aq)} \rightarrow 2H_2O_{(l)} + O_{2(g)}$$
$$\text{Rate} = k\,[H_2O_2]\,[I^-]$$
$$\text{Step 1  } H_2O_{2(aq)} + I^-_{(aq)} \rightarrow H_2O_{(l)} + IO^-_{(aq)} \text{ (slow)}$$
$$\text{Step 2  } H_2O_{2(aq)} + IO^-_{(aq)} \rightarrow H_2O_{(l)} + O_{2(g)} + I^-_{(aq)}$$

The iodate(I) ions, IO- are an example of a **reaction intermediate** as they *are formed during the reaction and subsequently consumed by the reaction as it proceeds.*

The iodide, $I^-$ ions affect the rate of the reaction and therefore must appear in the rate equation. The rate equation reveals that $H_2O_2$ and $I^-$ are both involved in the rate determining (slow) step. The mechanism also clearly demonstrates that the catalyst, $I^-$ is regenerated in its original form as the reaction proceeds, and is therefore not used up by the reaction.

### Worked Example 4.3v

Ethanal reacts with hydrogen cyanide to form a cyanohydrin.

$$CH_3CHO + HCN \rightarrow CH_3CH(OH)CN$$

In the first step cyanide ion reacts with ethanal to form an intermediate. This is the rate determining step. The second step of the reaction involves adding $H^+$ to the intermediate formed in the first step.

Structure of the intermediate:

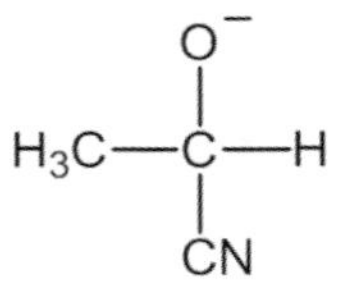

$$H_3C—\underset{\underset{CN}{|}}{\overset{\overset{O^-}{|}}{C}}—H$$

(a) Write the equation for the second step by reacting hydrogen cyanide with the intermediate. (b) Would you expect this to be a fast or slow step? Explain your answer. (c) Suggest how the equation for the second step could be used to show cyanide ion acting as a catalyst for the reaction.

*(Adapted from CCEA January 2012)*

### Solution

(a)

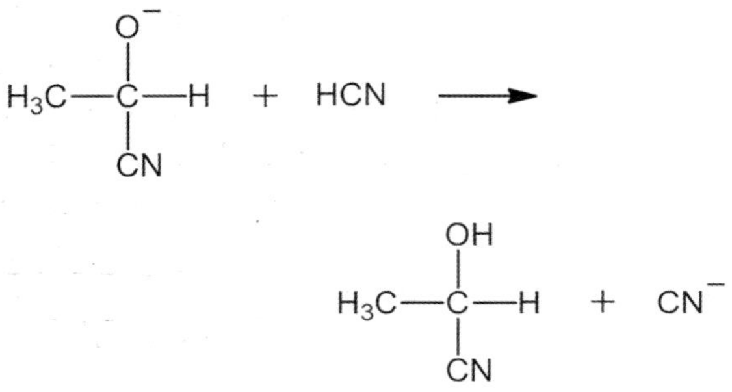

$$H_3C—\underset{\underset{CN}{|}}{\overset{\overset{O^-}{|}}{C}}—H \ + \ HCN \longrightarrow$$

$$H_3C—\underset{\underset{CN}{|}}{\overset{\overset{OH}{|}}{C}}—H \ + \ CN^-$$

(b) The second step would be fast as the intermediate was formed in the rate determining step.

(c) The cyanide ion from the first step is regenerated.

- - - - - - - - - - - - - - - - - - - - - - - - - - - - - - -

### Exercise 4.3l

1. Hydrogen peroxide decomposes to produce water and oxygen. The reaction is catalysed by bromide ions.

$$2H_2O_{2(aq)} \rightarrow 2H_2O_{(l)} + O_{2(g)}$$

The mechanism for the overall reaction is believed to take place in two steps as shown below.

Step 1 $H_2O_2 + Br^- \rightarrow H_2O + OBr^-$

Step 2 $H_2O_2 + OBr^- \rightarrow H_2O + Br^- + O_2$

The rate equation for the reaction is:
Rate $= k\,[H_2O_2]\,[Br^-]$

(a) Explain how the rate equation is related to the speeds of step 1 and step 2. (b) Explain which of the species in steps 1 and 2 can be regarded as a reactive intermediate. (c) State the overall order for this rate equation. (d) Using steps 1 and 2 explain why $Br^-$ is a catalyst. (e) Outline how you could determine the amount of bromide ion present in the reaction mixture at the end of the reaction.

*(Adapted from CCEA June 2015)*

---

Before moving to the next section, check that you are able to:

- Explain what is meant by the term *catalyst*.
- Identify a catalyst from its role in the mechanism for a reaction.

---

a) Rate equation reveals that Step 1 is slow and Step 2 is fast

b) The $OBr^-$ ion is a Reactive intermediate as it is formed during the Reaction and Consumed in a Subsequent step

c) Second order

d) $Br^-$ is a catalyst as it is a reactant in the Rate determining step and is regenerated in the course of the Reaction

e) Add an excess of silver nitrate solution, Filter the mixture and weigh the amount of solid silver Bromide Formed

# 4.4 Chemical Equilibrium

Previously we have used an **equilibrium constant**, $K_c$ to describe the composition of a mixture in which a state of dynamic equilibrium has been established.

| | Reversible reaction |
|---|---|
| | reactants $\rightarrow$ products |
| | products $\rightarrow$ reactants |

Dynamic equilibrium

reactants $\leftrightharpoons$ products

$$\frac{\text{Rate of forward}}{\text{reaction}} = \frac{\text{Rate of reverse}}{\text{reaction}}$$

In this section we consider how the properties of $K_c$ can be used to calculate a value of $K_c$. We also consider how the value of $K_c$ can be used to determine the amounts of individual reactants and products present in a dynamic equilibrium, and the initial amounts required to establish a dynamic equilibrium with a specific composition.

## Properties of $K_c$

**In this section we are learning to:**

- Deduce the form of the equilibrium constant, $K_c$ and the units for the value of $K_c$, for a dynamic equilibrium.
- Relate the values of Kc for the forward and reverse reactions that give rise to a dynamic equilibrium.

If an acidic solution containing chromate(VI) ions, $CrO_4^{2-}$ and dichromate(VI) ions, $Cr_2O_7^{2-}$ is allowed to reach a state of dynamic equilibrium, the concentration of chromate(VI) ion, $[CrO_4^{2-}]$ the concentration of dichromate(VI) ion, $[Cr_2O_7^{2-}]$ and the concentration of hydrogen ion, $[H^+]$ can be used to calculate the value of $K_c$ for the equilibrium.

$$2CrO_4^{2-}{}_{(aq)} + 2H^+{}_{(aq)} \leftrightharpoons Cr_2O_7^{2-}{}_{(aq)} + H_2O_{(l)}$$

$$K_c = \frac{[Cr_2O_7^{2-}]}{[CrO_4^{2-}]^2[H^+]^2}$$

Units for $K_c$ $\dfrac{(\text{mol dm}^{-3})}{(\text{mol dm}^{-3})^4} = \text{mol}^{-3}\,\text{dm}^9$

The equilibrium is shown in Figure 1a and reveals that, in alkali, the position of equilibrium shifts to the left, and the yellow colour of chromate(VI) ion, $CrO_4^{2-}$ dominates. Conversely Figure 1b reveals that, in acid, the position of equilibrium shifts to the right, and the orange colour of dichromate(VI) ion, $Cr_2O_7^{2-}$ dominates. In each case *the value of $K_c$ does not change on adding acid or alkali; the amount of each ion in the solution simply adjusts until a new equilibrium is established that is described by the same value of $K_c$.*

The concentration of water is not included in the expression for $K_c$ as water is the solvent for the reaction and its concentration does not change significantly when the position of equilibrium changes.

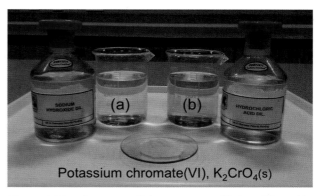

Potassium chromate(VI), $K_2CrO_4(s)$

*Figure 1: The chromate-dichromate equilibrium formed by dissolving potassium chromate(VI) in water. (a) The yellow colour of chromate(VI) ion, $CrO_4^{2-}$ dominates in alkaline solution. (b) The orange colour of dichromate(VI)ion, $Cr_2O_7^{2-}$ dominates in acidic solution.*

If we had instead defined the chromate-dichromate equilibrium by the equation:

$$Cr_2O_7^{2-}{}_{(aq)} + H_2O_{(l)} \leftrightarrows 2CrO_4^{2-}{}_{(aq)} + 2H^+{}_{(aq)}$$

the equilibrium constant would have been written:

$$K_c' = \frac{[CrO_4^{2-}]^2[H^+]^2}{[Cr_2O_7^{2-}]} = \frac{1}{K_c}$$

Units for $K_c'$ $\dfrac{(mol\,dm^{-3})^4}{(mol\,dm^{-3})} = mol^3\,dm^{-9}$

and it becomes necessary to specify how the chemical equation is written when talking about the equilibrium constant for a chemical reaction. The equilibrium constants in Table 1 demonstrate how the general form for $K_c$ given below can be used to construct the equilibrium constant for a **homogeneous reaction** in which *all of the reactants and products are in the same physical state.*

*Equilibrium Constant for a general equilibrium:*

General equilibrium $aA + bB \leftrightarrows cC + dD$

Equilibrium constant, $K_c = \dfrac{[C]^c\,[D]^d}{[A]^a\,[B]^b}$

Units for $K_c$ $\dfrac{(mol\,dm^{-3})^{c+d}}{(mol\,dm^{-3})^{a+b}}$

### Exercise 4.4A

1  The equilibrium constant, $K_c$ for the dissociation of hydrogen gas: $H_2{}_{(g)} \leftrightarrows H_{(g)} + H_{(g)}$ is very small. (a) Write an expression defining $K_c$ for the dissociation of hydrogen gas. (b) Calculate the value of $K_c$ for the dissociation of hydrogen gas if the equilibrium constant for the formation of hydrogen: $H_{(g)} + H_{(g)} \leftrightarrows H_2{}_{(g)}$ is $1 \times 10^{40}$ mol$^{-1}$ dm$^3$. (c) State the units of $K_c$ for the dissociation of hydrogen gas.

2  The water-gas shift reaction: $CO_{(g)} + H_2O_{(g)} \leftrightarrows CO_2{}_{(g)} + H_2{}_{(g)}$ increases the amount of hydrogen in synthesis gas, the term used to describe a mixture of hydrogen and carbon monoxide. (a) Define $K_c$ for the water-gas shift reaction and state the units of $K_c$. (b) Calculate the value of $K_c$ for the water-gas shift reaction if the equilibrium constant, K = 0.23 for the conversion of hydrogen to water: $CO_2{}_{(g)} + H_2{}_{(g)} \leftrightarrows CO_{(g)} + H_2O_{(g)}$.

Before moving to the next section, check that you are able to:

- Define $K_c$ for a homogeneous equilibrium.
- Use the expression for $K_c$ to deduce the units for $K_c$.
- Relate the values of $K_c$ for the forward and reverse reactions.

## Calculating K$_c$

In this section we are learning to:

- Calculate the value of the equilibrium constant, $K_c$ for a dynamic equilibrium given data that can be used to determine the composition of the equilibrium.

### Calculating K$_c$ from Concentrations

If the concentrations of the reactants and products in a dynamic equilibrium are specified, as in Worked

| Chemical Reaction | Equilibrium Constant | Units for $K_c$ |
|---|---|---|
| $N_2O_4{}_{(g)} \leftrightarrows 2NO_2{}_{(g)}$ | $K_c = \dfrac{[NO_2]^2}{[N_2O_4]}$ | $\dfrac{(mol\,dm^{-3})^2}{mol\,dm^{-3}} = mol\,dm^{-3}$ |
| $H_2{}_{(g)} + I_2{}_{(g)} \leftrightarrows 2HI_{(g)}$ | $K_c = \dfrac{[HI]^2}{[H_2][I_2]}$ | $\dfrac{(mol\,dm^{-3})^2}{(mol\,dm^{-3})^2} = no\,units$ |
| $2SO_2{}_{(g)} + O_2{}_{(g)} \leftrightarrows 2SO_3{}_{(g)}$ | $K_c = \dfrac{[SO_3]^2}{[SO_2]^2[O_2]}$ | $\dfrac{(mol\,dm^{-3})^2}{(mol\,dm^{-3})^3} = mol^{-1}\,dm^3$ |

*Table 1: Equilibrium constants constructed using the general form for $K_c$*

Example 4.4i, the value for $K_c$ can be obtained by entering the concentrations in the expression for $K_c$.

## Worked Example 4.4i

The following equilibrium is established when hydrogen fluoride is added to water. The concentrations of $HF_{(aq)}$ and $F^-_{(aq)}$ at equilibrium are found to be 0.0077 mol dm$^{-3}$ and 0.0023 mol dm$^{-3}$ respectively. Calculate the value of the equilibrium constant.

$$HF_{(aq)} \leftrightarrows H^+_{(aq)} + F^-_{(aq)}$$

*(CCEA June 2006)*

### Solution

The dissociation of HF produces one $H^+$ ion for every $F^-$ ion therefore $[H^+] = [F^-] = 0.0023$ mol dm$^{-3}$.

$$K_c = \frac{[H^+][F^-]}{[HF]} = \frac{(0.0023)(0.0023)}{(0.0077)}$$

$$= 6.9 \times 10^{-4} \text{mol dm}^{-3}$$

## Calculating $K_c$ from Amounts in Moles

If the amount of reactants and products in an equilibrium mixture is given in moles, as in Worked Example 4.4ii, the following equation should be used to convert amounts in moles to concentrations that can be used to calculate the value of $K_c$ for the equilibrium.

$$\text{Concentration} = \frac{\text{Moles}}{\text{Volume of equilibrium mixture}}$$

## Worked Example 4.4ii

Phosgene, $COCl_2$ is manufactured by passing carbon monoxide and chlorine through a bed of porous carbon which acts as a catalyst. A mixture containing 2 mol of carbon monoxide and 5 mol of chlorine is allowed to reach equilibrium in a 10 dm$^3$ vessel. At equilibrium, 1 mol of carbon monoxide remained. Calculate the equilibrium constant for the reaction under these conditions.

$$CO_{(g)} + Cl_{2(g)} \leftrightarrows COCl_{2(g)}$$

*(Adapted from CCEA January 2008)*

### Strategy

- Use the amount that reacts to calculate the moles present at equilibrium.
- Use the volume of the mixture and the moles at equilibrium to calculate $K_c$.

### Solution

According to the chemical equation 1 mol of CO reacts with 1 mol of $Cl_2$ to form 1 mol of $COCl_2$.

| | CO | + | Cl$_2$ | $\leftrightarrows$ | COCl$_2$ |
|---|---|---|---|---|---|
| Initial moles: | 2 | | 5 | | 0 |
| Change in moles: | −1 | | −1 | | +1 |
| Equilibrium moles: | 1 | | 4 | | 1 |

The moles at equilibrium are then used to calculate $K_c$:

$$K_c = \frac{[COCl_2]}{[CO][Cl_2]} = \frac{\left(\dfrac{1 \text{ mol}}{10 \text{ dm}^3}\right)}{\left(\dfrac{1 \text{ mol}}{10 \text{ dm}^3}\right)\left(\dfrac{4 \text{ mol}}{10 \text{ dm}^3}\right)} = 2.5 \text{ mol}^{-1} \text{dm}^3$$

If the number of molecules is the same on both sides of the equilibrium, as in Worked Example 4.4iii, the value of $K_c$ for the equilibrium can be calculated without knowing the volume of the equilibrium mixture.

## Worked Example 4.4iii

One mole of propanoic acid, one mole of methanol and two moles of water were mixed and allowed to reach equilibrium. At equilibrium 0.5 mole of methyl propanoate, $CH_3CH_2COOCH_3$ was present. Calculate $K_c$ for the reaction.

$$CH_3CH_2COOH + CH_3OH$$
$$\leftrightarrows CH_3CH_2COOCH_3 + H_2O$$

*(Adapted from CCEA May 2011)*

### Strategy

- Use the moles of product formed and the chemical equation to determine the moles at equilibrium.
- Use the moles at equilibrium to calculate $K_c$.

### Solution

According to the chemical equation 0.5 mol of propanoic acid reacts with 0.5 mol of methanol to form 0.5 mol of methyl propanoate and 0.5 mol of water.

| | $CH_3CH_2COOH$ + | $CH_3OH$ $\leftrightarrows$ | $CH_3CH_2COOCH_3$ + | $H_2O$ |
|---|---|---|---|---|
| Initial | 1.0 | 1.0 | 0.0 | 2.0 |
| Change | − 0.5 | − 0.5 | + 0.5 | + 0.5 |
| Equilibrium | 0.5 | 0.5 | 0.5 | 2.5 |

The moles at equilibrium are then used to calculate $K_c$:

$$K_c = \frac{[CH_3CH_2COOCH_3][H_2O]}{[CH_3CH_2COOH][CH_3OH]}$$

$$= \frac{\left(\dfrac{0.5\ mol}{V}\right)\left(\dfrac{2.5\ mol}{V}\right)}{\left(\dfrac{0.5\ mol}{V}\right)\left(\dfrac{0.5\ mol}{V}\right)} = 5 \text{ (no units)}$$

### Exercise 4.4B

1. Phosphorus pentachloride, $PCl_5$ vaporises and decomposes to form an equilibrium mixture. The equilibrium mixture is found to contain 1.1 mol of $PCl_3$, 1.1 mol of $Cl_2$ and 3.9 mol of $PCl_5$ when the equilibrium is established in a 10 $dm^3$ container at 300 °C. Calculate $K_c$ for the reaction under these conditions and state the units for $K_c$.

   $PCl_{5(g)} \leftrightarrows PCl_{3(g)} + Cl_{2(g)}$ $\Delta H = +91$ kJ $mol^{-1}$

   *(Adapted from CCEA May 2009)*

2. When 2.0 moles of sulphuryl chloride, $SO_2Cl_2$ were allowed to dissociate in a 5 $dm^3$ container, the equilibrium formed was found to contain 1.5 moles of chlorine. Calculate $K_c$ for the reaction and state the units of $K_c$.

   $SO_2Cl_{2(g)} \leftrightarrows SO_{2(g)} + Cl_{2(g)}$

   *(Adapted from CCEA May 2010)*

3. Tetrafluoroethene is produced from chlorodifluoromethane according to the equation:

   $2CHClF_{2(g)} \leftrightarrows C_2F_{4(g)} + 2HCl_{(g)}$ $\Delta H$ = +128 kJ $mol^{-1}$

   An equilibrium formed by placing 0.2 mol of chlorodifluoromethane in a 5 $dm^3$ flask was found to contain 0.04 mol of chlorodifluoromethane. Calculate $K_c$ for the reaction and state the units of $K_c$.

   *(CCEA January 2010)*

4. Ammonia is formed by the reaction of nitrogen with hydrogen at high temperature and pressure.

   $N_2 + 3H_2 \leftrightarrows 2NH_3$

   A mixture containing 100 mol of nitrogen and 300 mol of hydrogen produces 150 mol of ammonia at equilibrium when placed in a 200 $dm^3$ reaction vessel at high temperature. Calculate $K_c$ for the reaction and state the units of $K_c$.

   *(Adapted from CCEA January 2013)*

5. Hydrogen cyanide is manufactured by passing a mixture of ammonia and methane over a platinum catalyst.

   $NH_{3(g)} + CH_{4(g)} \leftrightarrows HCN_{(g)} + 3H_{2(g)}$

   When a mixture containing 0.2 mol of ammonia and 0.2 mol of methane is heated to 500 °C in a 1 $dm^3$ container, 0.1 mol of hydrogen cyanide and 0.3 mol of hydrogen are formed at one atmosphere pressure. Calculate the equilibrium constant, $K_c$ for the reaction under these conditions and state the units of $K_c$.

   *(CCEA January 2010)*

### Calculating $K_c$ from Amounts in Grams

If the amounts of reactants and products in an equilibrium mixture are given in grams or other unit of mass, as in Worked Example 4.4iv, they should be converted to amounts in moles, and then to concentrations that can be used to calculate the value of $K_c$ for the equilibrium.

### Worked Example 4.4iv

The ester pentyl ethanoate is formed from pentan-1-ol and ethanoic acid.

$$CH_3COOH + C_5H_{11}OH \leftrightarrows CH_3COOC_5H_{11} + H_2O$$

(a) Write an expression for the equilibrium constant, $K_c$ for this reaction. (b) 1.1 g of pentan-1-ol and 1.2 g of ethanoic acid were mixed. At equilibrium 0.6 g of ethanoic acid remained. Calculate the value of $K_c$.

*(CCEA May 2013)*

## Strategy

- Calculate the amount of ethanoic acid that reacted with pentan-1-ol.
- Calculate the moles of each reactant and product at equilibrium.
- Use the moles at equilibrium to calculate $K_c$.

## Solution

(a) $K_c = \dfrac{[CH_3COOC_5H_{11}][H_2O]}{[CH_3COOH][C_5H_{11}OH]}$

(b) Moles of ethanoic acid reacted

$= \dfrac{1.2\,g - 0.6\,g}{60\,g\,mol^{-1}} = 0.01\,mol$

Moles at equilibrium:

| | CH₃COOH | + | C₅H₁₁OH | ⇌ | CH₃COOC₅H₁₁ | + | H₂O |
|---|---|---|---|---|---|---|---|
| Initial | 0.02 | | 0.0125 | | 0.00 | | 0.00 |
| Change | −0.01 | | −0.01 | | +0.01 | | +0.01 |
| Equilibrium | 0.01 | | 0.0025 | | 0.01 | | 0.01 |

The moles at equilibrium are then used to calculate $K_c$:

$$K_c = \frac{\left(\dfrac{0.01}{V}\right)\left(\dfrac{0.01}{V}\right)}{\left(\dfrac{0.01}{V}\right)\left(\dfrac{0.0025}{V}\right)} = 4$$

## Exercise 4.4C

1. About one third of global ethanol production is via the direct hydration of ethene. When a mixture containing 35.0 g of ethene and 22.5 g of steam was allowed to react in a 1 dm³ reaction vessel at 300 °C the mixture was found to contain 32.0 g of ethanol at equilibrium. (a) Calculate the value of $K_c$ for this reaction. (b) State the units of $K_c$.

$C_2H_{4(g)} + H_2O_{(g)} \leftrightarrows C_2H_5OH_{(g)}$
$\Delta H = -46\,kJ\,mol^{-1}$

*(Adapted from CCEA January 2006)*

2. Ethyl ethanoate is prepared by reacting ethanol with ethanoic acid. A mixture containing 12.0 g of ethanoic acid, 9.2 g of ethanol and 18.0 g of water was allowed to reach equilibrium. The mixture was found to contain 0.133 moles of ethanoic acid at equilibrium. Calculate $K_c$ for the reaction.

$CH_3CH_2OH + CH_3COOH$
$\leftrightarrows CH_3COOCH_2CH_3 + H_2O$
*(Adapted from CCEA May 2003)*

3. Hydrogen gas for the Haber process is produced by reacting methane with steam. A mixture containing 120 g of methane and 108 g of steam was allowed to reach equilibrium in a 10 dm³ reaction vessel at 400 °C and 250 atm pressure. The mixture was found to contain 32 g of methane at equilibrium. Calculate the value of $K_c$ and state the units of $K_c$.

$CH_{4(g)} + H_2O_{(g)} \leftrightarrows CO_{(g)} + 3H_{2(g)}$
$\Delta H = +206\,kJ\,mol^{-1}$

*(Adapted from CCEA June 2005)*

## Calculating $K_c$ from the Extent of Reaction

The value of $K_c$ for a dynamic equilibrium can also be calculated by specifying the extent to which the reaction has occurred.

## Worked Example 4.4v

One mole of ozone gas is 30 % dissociated when placed in a 10 dm³ flask. Calculate the value of $K_c$ for the dissociation of ozone under these conditions and state the units of $K_c$.

$2O_{3(g)} \leftrightarrows 3O_{2(g)}$

*(CCEA May 2012)*

## Solution

Moles of ozone at equilibrium = 0.70 mol

Moles of oxygen formed = Moles of ozone

dissociated $\times \dfrac{3}{2} = 0.45\,mol$

$$K_c = \frac{\left(\dfrac{0.45}{10}\right)^3}{\left(\dfrac{0.70}{10}\right)^2} = 1.9 \times 10^{-2}\,mol\,dm^{-3}$$

## Exercise 4.4D

1. (a) Calculate $K_c$ for the reaction between hydrogen and iodine if 75 % of the hydrogen is converted to hydrogen iodide when equimolar amounts of hydrogen and iodine are allowed to reach equilibrium. (b) Explain why the volume of the container was not needed to calculate $K_c$. (c) Calculate $K_c$ for the reverse reaction at the same temperature.

$$H_{2(g)} + I_{2(g)} \rightleftharpoons 2HI_{(g)}$$

*(Adapted from CCEA May 2010)*

---

Before moving to the next section, check that you are able to:

- Calculate $K_c$ for a dynamic equilibrium given amounts present at equilibrium or reacting amounts.

## Using $K_c$ to Calculate Amounts

**In this section we are learning to:**

- Use $K_c$ to calculate amounts present at equilibrium, or the amounts needed to establish a dynamic equilibrium with a specified composition.

### Calculating Amounts at Equilibrium

The value of $K_c$ can be used to calculate the concentration of a reactant or product in a dynamic equilibrium.

#### Worked Example 4.4vi

The equilibrium constant, $K_c$ for the reaction $3O_{2(g)} \rightleftharpoons 2O_{3(g)}$ is $1.7 \times 10^{-56}$ mol$^{-1}$ dm$^3$ at 25 °C. Calculate the equilibrium concentration of ozone, $O_3$ in air at 25 °C if the concentration of oxygen in air is $8.0 \times 10^{-3}$ mol dm$^{-3}$ at 25 °C.

#### Solution

$$K_c = \frac{[O_3]^2}{[O_2]^3} = \frac{[O_3]^2}{(8.0 \times 10^{-3})^3} = 1.7 \times 10^{-56} \text{ mol}^{-1} \text{ dm}^3$$

Rearranging gives $[O_3] = \sqrt{(1.7 \times 10^{-56})(8.0 \times 10^{-3})^3}$
$= 9.3 \times 10^{-32}$ mol dm$^{-3}$

## Exercise 4.4E

1. Calculate the equilibrium concentration of nitrogen dioxide, $NO_2$ in mol dm$^{-3}$ if the concentration of dinitrogen tetroxide, $N_2O_4$ is 1.52 mol dm$^{-3}$ and $K_c = 1.0 \times 10^{-5}$ mol dm$^{-3}$ for the equilibrium between dinitrogen tetroxide and nitrogen dioxide at 300 K.

$$N_2O_{4(g)} \rightleftharpoons 2NO_{2(g)}$$

*(Adapted from CCEA June 2005)*

2. Ammonia is formed by the reaction of nitrogen with hydrogen at high temperature and pressure. Calculate the equilibrium concentration of $NH_3$ at 600 K if the equilibrium concentrations of nitrogen and hydrogen are 0.034 mol dm$^{-3}$ and 0.15 mol dm$^{-3}$. The equilibrium constant $K_c$ has the value 4.2 at 600 K.

$$N_2 + 3H_2 \rightleftharpoons 2NH_3$$

### Calculating Initial Amounts

The value of $K_c$ can also be used to calculate the amount of reactant needed to establish an equilibrium with a specific composition, or the amount of product formed in a reaction.

#### Worked Example 4.4vii

Propanone, $CH_3COCH_3$ reacts with hydrogen cyanide to form propanone cyanohydrin. The equilibrium constant, $K_c$ for the reaction is 30 dm$^3$ mol$^{-1}$ at 20 °C. Calculate the number of moles of hydrogen cyanide needed to produce 2 moles of propanone cyanohydrin at equilibrium, starting with a mixture containing 5 moles of propanone dissolved in 2 dm$^3$ of alcohol.

$$CH_3COCH_3 + HCN \rightleftharpoons CH_3C(OH)(CN)CH_3$$

*(Adapted from CCEA January 2002)*

#### Strategy

- Calculate the change in moles for each reactant and product.
- Use the expression for $K_c$ to find the initial moles of HCN.

## Solution

| | CH$_3$COCH$_3$ + | HCN ⇌ | CH$_3$C(OH)(CN)CH$_3$ |
|---|---|---|---|
| Initial | 5 | $x$ | 0 |
| Change | $-2$ | $-2$ | $+2$ |
| Equilibrium | 3 | $(x-2)$ | 2 |

$$K_c = \frac{[CH_3C(OH)(CN)CH_3]}{[CH_3COCH_3][HCN]} = \frac{\left(\dfrac{2}{V}\right)}{\left(\dfrac{3}{V}\right)\left(\dfrac{x-2}{V}\right)}$$

$$= 30 \text{ mol}^{-1} \text{ dm}^3$$

The volume of the reaction mixture, $V = 2 \text{ dm}^3$.

Solving gives $x = 2.04$ mol.

................................................................

### Exercise 4.4F

1. The ester ethyl ethanoate, $CH_3COOCH_2CH_3$ is formed when a mixture of ethanoic acid, $CH_3COOH$ and ethanol, $CH_3CH_2OH$ is heated.

$$CH_3COOH + CH_3CH_2OH \rightleftharpoons CH_3COOCH_2CH_3 + H_2O$$

(a) Write the expression for $K_c$. (b) Calculate the number of moles of ethanoic acid needed to convert 80% of the ethanol in the reaction mixture to ethyl ethanoate if the reaction mixture initially contains 2.5 mol of ethanol. The value of $K_c$ is 3.2 at the temperature of the reaction mixture.

---

**Before moving to the next section, check that you are able to:**

- Use the value of $K_c$ to calculate amounts present at equilibrium, or the initial amount of reactant needed to reach equilibrium.

# 4.5 Acid-Base Equilibria

## Brønsted-Lowry Theory

**In this section we are learning to:**

- Use Brønsted-Lowry theory to explain what is meant by the terms *acid* and *base*, and write equations for acid-base reactions.

The definitions of an acid and a base in Brønsted-Lowry theory can be used to describe many more reactions than simple theories in which an acid produces hydrogen ($H^+$) ions and a base produces hydroxide ($OH^-$) ions. On defining a **Brønsted-Lowry acid** to be *a molecule or ion that can donate a hydrogen ion to another molecule or ion,* the dissociation of a weak acid such as ethanoic acid becomes an acid-base reaction.

*The dissociation of ethanoic acid in water:*

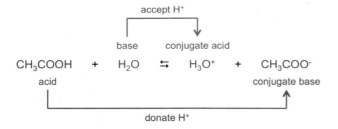

The forward reaction occurs when a molecule of ethanoic acid, $CH_3COOH$ acts as a Brønsted-Lowry acid by donating a hydrogen ($H^+$) ion to a water molecule. If we then define a **Brønsted-Lowry base** to be *a molecule or ion that can accept a hydrogen ion from another molecule or ion,* the water molecule becomes a Brønsted-Lowry base that accepts a hydrogen ion from ethanoic acid to form a hydronium ion, $H_3O^+$.

The reverse reaction can also be described as an acid-base reaction in which hydronium ion, $H_3O^+$ acts as a Brønsted-Lowry acid by donating a hydrogen

ion to ethanoate ion, $CH_3COO^-$. The hydronium ion is referred to as the **conjugate acid** of water as it is transformed into water by behaving as a Brønsted-Lowry acid. Similarly, ethanoate ion, $CH_3COO^-$ is referred to as the **conjugate base** of ethanoic acid, $CH_3COOH$ as it is transformed into ethanoic acid by behaving as a Brønsted-Lowry base.

*In Brønsted-Lowry theory an acid-base reaction involves two conjugate acid-base pairs: one pair consists of an acid and its conjugate base, the other consists of a base and its conjugate acid.* In the dissociation of ethanoic acid, water (a base) and hydronium ion (its conjugate acid) form a conjugate acid-base pair. The second conjugate acid-base pair consists of ethanoic acid (an acid) and ethanoate ion (its conjugate base).

Aqueous ammonia also contains acid-base conjugate pairs resulting from the dissociation of water molecules in the solution.

*The dissociation of water in aqueous ammonia:*

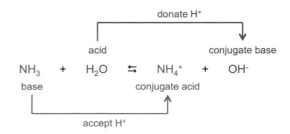

In this example water acts as a Brønsted-Lowry acid by donating a hydrogen ion to ammonia. In the reverse reaction ammonium ion, $NH_4^+$ acts as a Brønsted-Lowry acid by donating a hydrogen ion to hydroxide ion to form water.

### Hydronium Ion

A hydronium ion, $H_3O^+$ is formed when the oxygen atom in a water molecule uses a lone pair of electrons to form a coordinate bond with a hydrogen ion. Formation of the coordinate bond in $H_3O^+$ is illustrated in Figure 1.

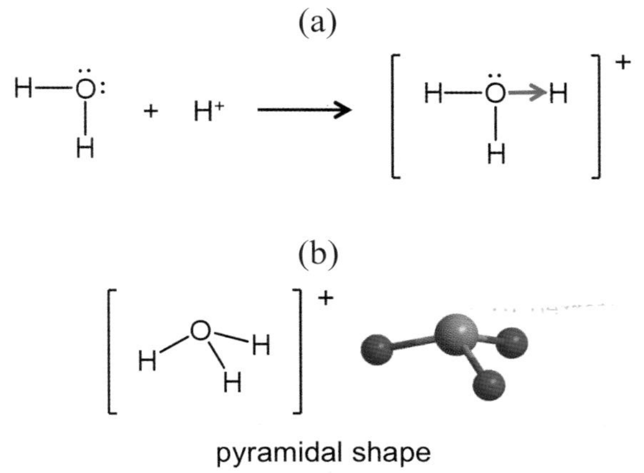

(a)

(b)

pyramidal shape

*Figure 1: (a) Formation of the coordinate bond in hydronium ion, $H_3O^+$. (b) The shape of a hydronium ion.*

When writing equations, hydronium ion is often represented by an aqueous hydrogen ion, $H^+_{(aq)}$. As a result, the partial dissociation of a weak acid such as HF can be represented by the formation of hydronium ions or hydrogen ions.

*The partial dissociation of hydrofluoric acid:*

to form *hydronium* ion
$$HF_{(aq)} + H_2O_{(l)} \rightleftharpoons H_3O^+_{(aq)} + F^-_{(aq)}$$

to form *hydrogen* ion
$$HF_{(aq)} \rightleftharpoons H^+_{(aq)} + F^-_{(aq)}$$

**Worked Example 4.5i**

Explain the reaction of calcium hydride with water in terms of the Brønsted-Lowry theory of acids and bases.        Acid

$$CaH_2 + 2H_2O \rightarrow Ca(OH)_2 + 2H_2$$

*(CCEA January 2008)*

**Strategy**

- Identify conjugate acid-base pairs.

**Solution**

Hydride ion ($H^-$) acts as a Brønsted-Lowry base by accepting a hydrogen ion from water to form hydrogen, $H_2$. Water acts as a Brønsted-Lowry acid by donating a hydrogen ion.

**Exercise 4.5A**

1. Sulfuric acid is described as a strong Brønsted-Lowry acid. What is meant by the term *Brønsted-Lowry acid*?

   *(CCEA June 2011)*

2. Which of the following is an acid-base conjugate pair?

   | | Acid | Conjugate Base |
   |---|---|---|
   | A | $H_2SO_4$ | $HSO_4^-$ |
   | B | $HSO_4^-$ | $H_3O^+$ |
   | C | $SO_4^{2-}$ | $HSO_4^-$ |
   | D | $HSO_4^-$ | $H_2SO_4$ |

   *(CCEA May 2007)*

3. What is the conjugate base of the acid $HCO_3^-$?

   A $CO_3^{2-}$     B $H_2CO_3$
   C $H_3O^+$     D $OH^-$

   *(CCEA May 2010)*

4. Which one of the following is the conjugate acid of the hydrogenphosphate(V) ion, $HPO_4^{2-}$?

   A $H_3PO_4$     B $H_3PO_4^-$
   C $H_2PO_4^-$     D $PO_4^{3-}$

   *(CCEA May 2013)*

5. Which one of the following reactions is the compound in bold type acting as an acid?

   A **NaH** $+ H_2O \rightarrow NaOH + H_2$
   B **NH$_3$** $+ H_2O \rightarrow NH_4^+ + OH^-$
   C **H$_2$O** $+ HCO_3^- \rightarrow CO_3^{2-} + H_3O^+$
   D **H$_2$O** $+ HPO_4^{2-} \rightarrow H_2PO_4^- + OH^-$

   *(Adapted from CCEA June 2006)*

6. Sulfuric acid reacts with nitric acid as follows:

   $$H_2SO_4 + HNO_3 \rightarrow H_2NO_3^+ + HSO_4^-$$

   Which one of the following is the role of $HNO_3$ in the reaction?

   A Conjugate acid of $H_2NO_3^+$
   B Conjugate acid of $HSO_4^-$
   C Conjugate base of $H_2NO_3^+$
   D Conjugate base of $HSO_4^-$

   *(CCEA May 2014)*

7. Hydrogen peroxide, $H_2O_2$ is a liquid which is more acidic than water having a pH of 6.2 when in a pure state and a pH of 4.5 when diluted with water. It ionises in water according to the following equation.

$$H_2O_{2(aq)} + H_2O_{(l)} \rightleftharpoons H_3O^+_{(aq)} + HO_2^-_{(aq)}$$

(a) Use the Brønsted-Lowry theory to identify both conjugate acid-base pairs in the hydrogen peroxide solution. (b) Using the equilibrium equation explain why diluting pure hydrogenperoxide decreases the pH value.

*(CCEA May 2015)*

---

Before moving to the next section, check that you are able to:

- Explain what is meant by the terms *acid*, *base*, *conjugate acid* and *conjugate base*.
- Identify conjugate acid-base pairs in acid-base reactions.
- Describe acid-base reactions in terms of the transfer of hydrogen ions between an acid and a base to form a conjugate acid and a conjugate base.

---

## Aqueous Solutions

### In this section we are learning to:

- Classify an aqueous solution as acidic, neutral or alkaline based on the relative amount of $H^+$ and $OH^-$ ions in the solution.
- Calculate the concentration of $H^+$ and $OH^-$ ions in aqueous solutions.

---

The term aqueous solution is used to refer to any solution in which water is the solvent. In an aqueous solution a very small number of water molecules dissociate to form ions. The extent to which the water molecules dissociate is described by the **ionic product of water**, $K_w$.

*In terms of hydronium ion:*

$$2H_2O_{(l)} \rightleftharpoons H_3O^+_{(aq)} + OH^-_{(aq)}$$
$$K_w = [H_3O^+][OH^-] = 1 \times 10^{-14} \text{ at } 25\,^\circ C$$

*Or equivalently in terms of hydrogen ion:*

$$H_2O_{(l)} \rightleftharpoons H^+_{(aq)} + OH^-_{(aq)}$$
$$K_w = [H^+][OH^-] = 1 \times 10^{-14} \text{ at } 25\,^\circ C$$

The ionic product, $K_w$ is an equilibrium constant, and behaves in exactly the same way as other equilibrium constants. The units of $K_w$ are $(mol\,dm^{-3})^2$ = $mol^2\,dm^{-6}$.

The dissociation of water to form $H^+$ and $OH^-$ ions is endothermic. As a result increasing the temperature of an aqueous solution increases $K_w$ as the forward reaction is used to absorb heat, shifting the position of the equilibrium to the right.

When comparing the size of $K_w$ at different temperatures it is often more convenient to compare the size of $pK_w$ at different temperatures.

$$pK_w = -\log_{10} K_w = -\log_{10}(1 \times 10^{-14}) = 14 \text{ at } 25\,^\circ C$$

### Exercise 4.5B

1. Which one of the following statements about $K_w$ is not correct?

   A $K_w$ has a value of $1 \times 10^{-14}$ at 25 °C

   B $pK_w = -\log K_w$

   C The units of $K_w$ are $mol\,dm^{-3}$

   D The value of $K_w$ changes with temperature

   *(CCEA May 2012)*

2. The pH of a solution depends on temperature as the ionic product of water varies with temperature. (a) Write an equation for the ionic product of water. (b) Deduce whether the dissociation of water is an exothermic or endothermic process. Explain your reasoning.

| Temperature /K | $K_w$ /mol$^2$ dm$^{-6}$ |
|---|---|
| 298 | $1.0 \times 10^{-14}$ |
| 333 | $5.6 \times 10^{-14}$ |

*(CCEA January 2009)*

The ionic product can be used to define solutions as acidic, alkaline or neutral in terms of the amount of hydrogen ions and hydroxide ions they contain.

$$K_w = [H^+][OH^-]$$

*Neutral solution at 25 °C:*

$[H^+] = 1 \times 10^{-7}$ and $[OH^-] = \dfrac{K_w}{[H^+]} = 1 \times 10^{-7}$
since $K_w = 1 \times 10^{-14}$ at 25 °C

*Acidic solution at 25 °C:*

$[H^+] > 1 \times 10^{-7}$ and $[OH^-] = \dfrac{K_w}{[H^+]} < 1 \times 10^{-7}$
since $K_w = 1 \times 10^{-14}$ at 25 °C

*Alkaline solution at 25 °C:*

$[H^+] < 1 \times 10^{-7}$ and $[OH^-] = \dfrac{K_w}{[H^+]} > 1 \times 10^{-7}$
since $K_w = 1 \times 10^{-14}$ at 25 °C

The concentration of hydrogen ions and hydroxide ions in acidic, alkaline and neutral solutions at 25 °C are illustrated in Figure 2.

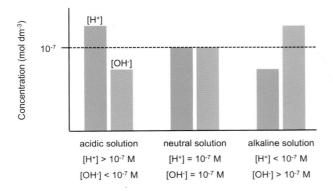

*Figure 2: The concentration of hydrogen (H⁺) ions and hydroxide (OH⁻) ions in acidic, neutral and alkaline solutions at 25 °C.*

### Worked Example 4.5ii

The concentration of hydrogen ions in a solution is $1 \times 10^{-6}$ mol dm$^{-3}$. What is the concentration of hydroxide ions in the solution?

  A  $1 \times 10^{-4}$ mol dm$^{-3}$

  B  $1 \times 10^{-7}$ mol dm$^{-3}$

  C  $1 \times 10^{-8}$ mol dm$^{-3}$

  D  $1 \times 10^{-14}$ mol dm$^{-3}$

*(CCEA January 2007)*

### Strategy

*   Assume the solution is at room temperature (25 °C).
*   Use the expression for $K_w$ and the value of $K_w$ at 25 °C to calculate $[OH^-]$.

### Solution

$K_w = [H^+][OH^-] = 1 \times 10^{-14}$ mol$^2$ dm$^{-6}$

$[OH^-] = \dfrac{K_w}{[H^+]} = \dfrac{1 \times 10^{-14}}{1 \times 10^{-6}} = 1 \times 10^{-8}$ mol dm$^{-3}$

Answer C.

---

**Before moving to the next section, check that you are able to:**

*   Write an expression for $K_w$ and recall the value of $K_w$ at 25 °C.
*   Predict and explain the effect of temperature on the value of $K_w$.
*   Use the concentration of H⁺ and OH⁻ ions in an aqueous solution to classify the solution as acidic, neutral or alkaline.
*   Use the value of $K_w$ to calculate the concentration of H⁺ and OH⁻ ions in an aqueous solution.

## Acid and Base Strength

**In this section we are learning to:**

*   Calculate the pH of acids and bases in aqueous solution.
*   Explain the relationship between pH and the acidity of an aqueous solution.

### The pH Scale

The acidity of a solution is determined by the concentration of hydrogen ions in the solution. The concentration of hydrogen ions in a solution is often very small and it becomes convenient to use a quantity known as pH to measure the acidity of the solution, where pH is defined by the equation:

$$pH = -\log_{10}[H^+]$$

### Worked Example 4.5iii

Calculate the pH of 0.2 mol dm$^{-3}$ hydrochloric acid solution.

### Strategy

*   Use the concentration of the acid to determine $[H^+]$.
*   Use $[H^+]$ to calculate the pH of the solution.

## Solution

| | HCl$_{(aq)}$ → | H$^+$$_{(aq)}$ + | Cl$^-$$_{(aq)}$ |
|---|---|---|---|
| Moles in 1 dm$^3$ | | | |
| before dissociation: | 0.2 | 0.0 | 0.0 |
| after dissociation: | 0.0 | 0.2 | 0.2 |

$$pH = -\log_{10}[H^+] = -\log_{10} 0.2 = 0.7$$

*The pH is rounded to one decimal place as [H$^+$] has one significant figure.*

*When calculating the pH of a solution the number of decimal places in the answer is the same as the number of significant figures in the value of [H$^+$].*

### Exercise 4.5C

1. Calculate the concentration of (a) hydrogen ions and (b) hydroxide ions in a 0.1 mol dm$^{-3}$ solution of hydrochloric acid at 25 °C.

2. Calculate the concentration of (a) hydroxide ions and (b) hydrogen ions in a 0.05 mol dm$^{-3}$ solution of sodium hydroxide at 25 °C.

3. Calculate the pH of 0.05 mol dm$^{-3}$ sulfuric acid assuming that one hydrogen atom per formula has completely dissociated to form hydrogensulfate(VI), HSO$_4^-$ ions.

$$H_2SO_{4(aq)} → H^+_{(aq)} + HSO_4^-{}_{(aq)}$$

4. Calculate the pH of the solution obtained by mixing 50.0 cm$^3$ of 1.00 mol dm$^{-3}$ sodium hydroxide solution with 49.0 cm$^3$ of 1.00 mol dm$^{-3}$ hydrochloric acid.

*(Adapted from CCEA June 2014)*

The equation to calculate the pH of a solution can also be used to calculate the concentration of hydrogen ions in a solution given the pH of the solution.

$$pH = -\log_{10}[H^+]$$
$$therefore\ [H^+] = antilog_{10}(-pH)$$

## Worked Example 4.5iv

Acid rain is formed when sulfur dioxide produced by the burning of fossil fuels dissolves in rain droplets in the atmosphere. Calculate the concentration of hydrogen ions in acid rain with a pH of 4.5.

### Strategy

- Calculate [H$^+$] by taking the inverse of the equation for pH.

### Solution

Taking the inverse log of pH $= -\log_{10}[H^+]$ gives [H$^+$] $=$ antilog$_{10}$(−pH).

Solving [H$^+$] $=$ antilog$_{10}$(−4.5) $= 3 \times 10^{-5}$ mol dm$^{-3}$

*[H$^+$] is rounded to one significant figure as the pH has one decimal place.*

*When calculating the concentration of hydrogen ions in a solution, [H$^+$] the number of significant figures in the answer is the same as the number of decimal places in the pH value.*

### Exercise 4.5D

1. In humans the pH of blood is maintained in the range 7.35 to 7.45. Calculate the concentration of hydrogen ions in blood with (a) a pH of 7.35 and (b) a pH of 7.45.

By defining pH in this way a solution with a low pH value has a higher concentration of hydrogen (H$^+$) ions, and is more acidic, than a solution with a higher pH value. Conversely, a solution with a high pH value will be less acidic (more alkaline), and have a lower concentration of H$^+$ ions, than a solution with a lower pH value.

| | Acidic solutions | | | Neutral solution | Alkaline solutions | |
|---|---|---|---|---|---|---|
| [H$^+$] | 2 | 10$^{-1}$ | 10$^{-4}$ | 10$^{-7}$ | 10$^{-10}$ | 10$^{-14}$ |
| pH | -0.3 | 1 | 4 | 7 | 10 | 14 |

Acidity increasing

Alkalinity increasing

Before moving to the next section, check that you are able to:

- Use the concentration of $H^+$ ions in a solution to calculate the pH of the solution.
- Use the pH of a solution to calculate the concentration of $H^+$ ions in the solution.
- Explain the relationship between the acidity of solutions and their pH values in terms of the concentration of $H^+$ ions in solution.

## Calculating the pH of an Alkali

*[handwritten: Kw For pH of an alkali]*

The equation for pH can also be used to calculate the pH of an alkaline solution by first calculating $[OH^-]$ and then using the equation for $K_w$ to calculate $[H^+]$.

$$pH = -\log_{10}[H^+] \text{ where } [H^+] = \frac{K_w}{[OH^-]}$$

### Worked Example 4.5v

Calcium oxide reacts with water to form calcium hydroxide. Calculate the pH of the solution formed when 0.020 mol of calcium oxide reacts with 100 cm³ of water at 25 °C. The ionic product, $K_w = 1.0 \times 10^{-14} \text{ mol}^2 \text{ dm}^{-6}$ at 25 °C.

### Strategy

- Use the chemical equation for the reaction to determine the concentration of hydroxide ion in the solution formed by the reaction.
- Use the ionic product, $K_w$ to calculate the concentration of hydrogen ions in the solution.

### Solution

$$CaO_{(s)} + H_2O_{(l)} \rightarrow Ca^{2+}_{(aq)} + 2OH^-_{(aq)}$$

Moles of hydroxide ions formed = $2 \times 0.020$
$= 0.040$ mol

$$\text{Concentration of hydroxide ions} = \frac{\text{Moles}}{\text{Volume}}$$

$$= \frac{0.040 \text{ mol}}{0.100 \text{ dm}^3} = 0.40 \text{ mol dm}^{-3}$$

$$[H^+] = \frac{K_w}{[OH^-]} = \frac{1.0 \times 10^{-14}}{0.40} = 2.5 \times 10^{-14} \text{ mol dm}^{-3}$$

$$pH = -\log_{10}[H^+] = -\log_{10}(2.5 \times 10^{-14}) = 13.60$$

Before moving to the next section, check that you are able to:

- Use the value of $K_w$ to calculate the pH of strong alkalis.

## Calculating the pH of a Weak Acid

*[handwritten: Ka For weak Acid]*

In order to calculate the pH of a weak acid it is first necessary to calculate the concentration of hydrogen ions produced by the partial dissociation of the acid. Carboxylic acids such as ethanoic acid, $CH_3COOH$ are weak acids. In aqueous solution the carboxyl group can dissociate to form a hydrogen ion which then combines with water to form a hydronium ion, $H_3O^+$.

*In terms of hydronium ion:*
$$CH_3COOH_{(aq)} + H_2O_{(l)} \leftrightarrows H_3O^+_{(aq)} + CH_3COO^-_{(aq)}$$

$$K_a = \frac{[H_3O^+][CH_3COO^-]}{[CH_3COOH]}$$

*Or equivalently in terms of hydrogen ion:*
$$CH_3COOH_{(aq)} \leftrightarrows H^+_{(aq)} + CH_3COO^-_{(aq)}$$

$$K_a = \frac{[H^+][CH_3COO^-]}{[CH_3COOH]}$$

The extent to which a weak acid dissociates is described by the **acid dissociation constant, $K_a$** for the acid. The acid dissociation constant is an equilibrium constant, and behaves in exactly the same way as other equilibrium constants. The units for $K_a$ are always mol dm⁻³ as the solvent (water) is not included when writing the equilibrium constant for a reaction in solution.

*Compounds with a large $K_a$ value dissociate more and are stronger acids than compounds with a smaller $K_a$ value.*

The expression for the acid dissociation constant, $K_a$ of a weak acid can be used to calculate the pH of the acid.

## Worked Example 4.5vi

The acid dissociation constant, $K_a$ for ethanoic acid is $1.74 \times 10^{-5}$ mol dm$^{-3}$. Calculate the pH of a 0.20 mol dm$^{-3}$ solution of ethanoic acid.

*(CCEA May 2011)*

### Strategy

- Write an expression for $K_a$ in terms of equilibrium concentrations.
- Use the value of $K_a$ to calculate the equilibrium concentration of H$^+$ ions.
- Use the equilibrium concentration of H$^+$ ions to calculate the pH of the acid.

### Solution

| | $CH_3COOH_{(aq)}$ $\rightleftharpoons$ | $H^+_{(aq)}$ + | $CH_3COO^-_{(aq)}$ |
|---|---|---|---|
| Moles in 1 dm$^3$ | | | |
| before dissociation: | 0.20 | | |
| after dissociation: | $0.20 - x$ | $x$ | $x$ |

*It is always safe to assume that the amount of dissociation (x) is small when compared with the concentration of the acid ie $(0.20 - x) \approx 0.20$.*

$$K_a = \frac{[H^+][CH_3COO^-]}{[CH_3COOH]} = \frac{(x)(x)}{(0.20 - x)} \approx \frac{x^2}{0.20}$$
$$= 1.74 \times 10^{-5}$$

Solving gives $x = [H^+] = 1.9 \times 10^{-3}$ mol dm$^{-3}$

$$pH = -\log_{10}[H^+] = -\log_{10}(1.9 \times 10^{-3}) = 2.72$$

### Exercise 4.5F

1. The acid dissociation constant, $K_a$ for propanoic acid, $CH_3CH_2COOH$ is $1.35 \times 10^{-5}$ mol dm$^{-3}$ at 25°C. (a) Write the expression for the acid dissociation constant of propanoic acid. (b) Calculate the pH of a 0.25 mol dm$^{-3}$ solution of propanoic acid.

   *(Adapted from CCEA January 2011)*

2. Methanoic acid, HCOOH is a weak acid. (a) Give the formula of the conjugate base of methanoic acid. (b) The $K_a$ of methanoic acid is $1.6 \times 10^{-4}$ mol dm$^{-3}$. Calculate the pH of 0.1 mol dm$^{-3}$ methanoic acid solution.

   *(CCEA January 2014)*

3. When dissolved in water nitric acid establishes the following equilibrium:

   $$HNO_{3(aq)} + H_2O_{(l)} \rightleftharpoons H_3O^+_{(aq)} + NO_3^-_{(aq)}$$

   Nitric acid is a strong acid with a dissociation constant of 40 mol dm$^{-3}$. (a) Calculate the pH of a 2.0 M solution of fully ionised nitric acid. (b) Using the dissociation constant of nitric acid calculate the pH of a 2.0 M solution of nitric acid. (c) Explain why the calculated pH values are different.

   *(CCEA June 2015)*

---

Before moving to the next section, check that you are able to:

- Write the acid dissociation constant, $K_a$ for a weak acid.
- Use the value of $K_a$ to calculate the pH of a weak acid.

---

## Polybasic acids

**In this section we are learning to:**

- Describe dissociation in acids that form more than one hydrogen ion.
- Calculate the pH of acids that dissociate to form more than one hydrogen ion.
- Use p$K_a$ as a measure of acid strength.

---

Hydrochloric acid, $HCl_{(aq)}$ nitric acid, $HNO_{3(aq)}$ and ethanoic acid, $CH_3COOH_{(aq)}$ are referred to as **monobasic acids** as they *are acids that dissociate to produce one hydrogen ion per formula.* In contrast, carbonic acid, $H_2CO_{3(aq)}$ sulfuric acid, $H_2SO_{4(aq)}$ and sulfurous acid, $H_2SO_{3(aq)}$ are examples of **polybasic acids** as they *are acids that dissociate to produce more than one hydrogen ion per formula.* The hydrogen atoms that dissociate to form hydrogen ions are referred to as **acidic hydrogen atoms**. The acidic hydrogen atoms in a number of common acids are identified in Table 1.

The extent to which each acidic hydrogen atom dissociates in a polybasic acid is described by a separate acid dissociation constant.

| Acidic Hydrogen Atoms per Formula | Strong Acids | Weak Acids |
|---|---|---|
| 1 | Hydrochloric acid, HCl<br>Nitric acid, $HNO_3$ | Hydrofluoric acid, HF<br>Ethanoic acid, $CH_3COOH$ |
| 2 | Sulfuric acid, $H_2SO_4$ | Sulfurous acid, $H_2SO_3$<br>Carbonic acid, $H_2CO_3$<br>Oxalic acid $\begin{array}{c}COOH\\ \vert \\ COOH\end{array}$ |
| 3 | | Phosphoric acid, $H_3PO_4$<br>Citric acid $\quad HO-\underset{\underset{CH_2COOH}{\vert}}{\overset{\overset{CH_2COOH}{\vert}}{C}}-COOH$ |

Table 1: Acidic hydrogen atoms in common acids.

First acid dissociation constant for carbonic acid:

$$H_2CO_{3(aq)} \leftrightarrows H^+_{(aq)} + HCO_3^-_{(aq)}$$

$$K_{a1} = \frac{[H^+][HCO_3^-]}{[H_2CO_3]} = 4.3 \times 10^{-7} \text{ mol dm}^{-3} \text{ at } 25\,°C$$

Second acid dissociation constant for carbonic acid:

$$HCO_3^-_{(aq)} \leftrightarrows H^+_{(aq)} + CO_3^{2-}_{(aq)}$$

$$K_{a2} = \frac{[H^+][CO_3^{2-}]}{[HCO_3^-]} = 5.6 \times 10^{-11} \text{ mol dm}^{-3} \text{ at } 25\,°C$$

In the case of carbonic acid $K_{a1}$ is approximately 10,000 times greater than $K_{a2}$. As a result most of the hydrogen ions in aqueous carbonic acid result from the first dissociation ($K_{a1}$), and hydrogen ions from the dissociation of hydrogencarbonate, $HCO_3^-$ ($K_{a2}$) can be neglected when calculating the pH of carbonic acid.

**Worked Example 4.5vii**

The first and second acid dissociation constants for carbonic acid, $H_2CO_3$ are $K_{a1} = 4.3 \times 10^{-7}$ mol dm$^{-3}$ and $K_{a2} = 5.6 \times 10^{-11}$ mol dm$^{-3}$. Calculate the pH of a 0.10 mol dm$^{-3}$ solution of carbonic acid.

**Strategy**

- $K_{a2} \ll K_{a1}$ therefore neglect the very few H$^+$ ions produced by the second dissociation ($K_{a2}$) when calculating the concentration of H$^+$ ions in the acid.

**Solution**

| | $H_2CO_{3\,(aq)}$ | $\leftrightarrows$ $H^+_{(aq)}$ | + $HCO_3^-_{(aq)}$ |
|---|---|---|---|
| Moles in 1 dm$^3$ before dissociation: | 0.10 | | |
| after dissociation: | $0.10 - x$ | $x$ | $x$ |

It is always safe to assume that the amount of dissociation ($x$) is small when compared with the concentration of the acid ie $(0.10 - x) \approx 0.10$.

$$K_{a1} = \frac{[H^+][HCO_3^-]}{[H_2CO_3]} = \frac{(x)(x)}{(0.10-x)} \approx \frac{x^2}{0.10}$$

$$= 4.3 \times 10^{-7}$$

Solving gives x = [H$^+$] = 2.1 × 10$^{-4}$ mol dm$^{-3}$

$$pH = -\log_{10}[H^+] = -\log_{10}(2.1 \times 10^{-4}) = 3.68$$

**Exercise 4.5G**

1. Sulfurous acid, $H_2SO_3$ is a polybasic acid. (a) Explain what is meant by the term *polybasic acid*. (b) Write an equation for the first acid dissociation of sulfurous acid. (c) Write an expression for the first acid dissociation constant of sulfurous acid, $K_{a1}$.

2. The first acid dissociation constant for sulfuric acid, $H_2SO_4$ is very large. The second acid dissociation constant, $K_{a2} = 1.2 \times 10^{-2}$ mol dm$^{-3}$. (a) Suggest why sulfuric acid is considered to be a strong acid. (b) Write an equation for the second acid dissociation of sulfuric acid. (c) Write an expression for the second acid dissociation constant of sulfuric acid, $K_{a2}$.

3. Phosphoric acid, $H_3PO_4$ is a weak acid. (a) Calculate the pH of a 0.10 mol dm$^{-3}$ solution of phosphoric acid. (b) Write an equation for the third acid dissociation of phosphoric acid. (c) Write an expression for the third acid dissociation constant of phosphoric acid, $K_{a3}$.

$$H_3PO_4 \text{(aq)} \rightleftharpoons H^+ \text{(aq)} + H_2PO_4^- \text{(aq)}$$
$$K_{a1} = 7.5 \times 10^{-3} \text{ mol dm}^{-3}$$

$$H_2PO_4^- \text{(aq)} \rightleftharpoons H^+ \text{(aq)} + HPO_4^{2-} \text{(aq)}$$
$$K_{a2} = 6.2 \times 10^{-8} \text{ mol dm}^{-3}$$

4. Citric acid is a weak tribasic acid found in citrus fruits. The first acid dissociation constant, $K_a$ for citric acid is $8.4 \times 10^{-4}$ mol dm$^{-3}$. (a) Write an equation for the first ionisation of citric acid in aqueous solution. (b) Write an expression for the first acid dissociation constant, $K_a$ for citric acid using RCOOH to represent citric acid. (c) Calculate the pH of a 0.1 mol dm$^{-3}$ solution of citric acid assuming only the first ionisation takes place.

CH$_2$COOH
|
HO — C — COOH        Citric acid
|
CH$_2$COOH

*(CCEA January 2010)*

---

Before moving to the next section, check that you are able to:

- Explain what is meant by the terms *monobasic acid* and *polybasic acid*.
- Write equations to describe acid dissociation in a polybasic acid, and expressions for the corresponding acid dissociation constants ($K_{a1}$, $K_{a2}$, ...).
- Calculate the pH of a polybasic acid.

## Comparing Acid Strength

The pK$_a$ of an acid is a measure of the strength of the acid and can be used to easily compare the strengths of different acids.

$$pK_a = - \log_{10} K_a$$

On defining pK$_a$ in this way the pK$_a$ value of an acid decreases, and becomes negative, as the acid becomes stronger.

| | Strong acid | Weak acids | | | Very weak acid |
|---|---|---|---|---|---|
| $K_a$ | $2.0 \times 10^6$ | $1.5 \times 10^{-2}$ | $7.5 \times 10^{-3}$ | $1.8 \times 10^{-5}$ | $4.3 \times 10^{-7}$ |
| $pK_a$ | -6.3 | 1.8 | 2.1 | 4.7 | 6.4 |

Acidity increasing ←

---

### Worked Example 4.5viii

Tartaric acid is one of several organic acids that have an important role in winemaking. The first pK$_a$ value for the ionisation of tartaric acid is 2.9. Calculate the pH of a 0.1 mol dm$^{-3}$ solution of tartaric acid. Assume only one H$^+$ dissociation.

O   OH H   O
‖    |   |   ‖
HO—C—C—C—C—OH        Tartaric acid
       |   |
       H   OH

*(CCEA May 2012)*

#### *Strategy*

- Calculate $K_{a1}$ from pK$_a$.
- Use $K_{a1}$ to calculate the concentration of H$^+$ ions.
- Calculate the pH of the acid.

#### Solution

$$K_{a1} = \text{antilog}_{10}(-pK_a) = \text{antilog}_{10}(-2.9)$$
$$= 1 \times 10^{-3} \text{ mol dm}^{-3}$$

| | $C_4H_6O_6$ (aq) | $\rightleftharpoons$ H$^+$(aq) | + $C_4H_5O_6^-$(aq) |
|---|---|---|---|
| Moles in 1 dm$^3$ | | | |
| before dissociation: | 0.1 | | |
| after dissociation: | 0.1 − $x$ | $x$ | $x$ |

$$K_{a1} = \frac{[H^+][C_4H_5O_6^-]}{[C_4H_6O_6]} = \frac{(x)(x)}{(0.1-x)} \approx \frac{x^2}{0.1}$$

$$= 1 \times 10^{-3}$$

Solving gives x = $[H^+]$ = $1 \times 10^{-2}$ mol dm$^{-3}$

pH = $-\log_{10}[H^+]$ = $-\log_{10}(1 \times 10^{-2})$ = 2.0

### Exercise 4.5H

1. When dissolved in water nitric acid establishes the following equilibrium.

   $$HNO_{3(aq)} + H_2O_{(l)} \rightleftharpoons H_3O^+_{(aq)} + NO_3^-_{(aq)}$$

   Nitric acid is a strong acid with a dissociation constant of 40 mol dm$^{-3}$. Calculate the pK$_a$ value for nitric acid.

   *(CCEA May 2015)*

2. Propanoic acid, $CH_3CH_2COOH$ has a pK$_a$ value of 4.87. Calculate the pH of a 0.05 M solution of the acid.

   *(Adapted from CCEA May 2010)*

3. Lactic acid, $CH_3CH(OH)COOH$ has a pK$_a$ value of 3.86 at 25 °C. Calculate the concentration of lactic acid in mg dm$^{-3}$ present in saliva which would produce a pH of 5.20.

   *(Adapted from CCEA January 2008)*

---

Before moving to the next section, check that you are able to:

- Explain the relationship between the pK$_a$ and acid strength.
- Use the pK$_a$ of an acid to calculate K$_a$ for the acid.

## Buffer Solutions

**In this section we are learning to:**

- Explain how a buffer solution resists changes in pH.

A **buffer solution** is *a solution that resists changes in pH that result from the addition of small amounts of acid or alkali to the solution.*

A buffer solution contains significant amounts of a weak acid (HA) and the conjugate base of the weak acid (A$^-$). A buffer solution is formed when sodium ethanoate, $CH_3COONa$, the sodium salt of ethanoic acid, dissolves in ethanoic acid. When sodium ethanoate dissolves it dissociates completely to form sodium ions and ethanoate ions, $CH_3COO^-$.

$$CH_3COONa_{(s)} \rightarrow CH_3COO^-_{(aq)} + Na^+_{(aq)}$$

Ethanoate ion, $CH_3COO^-$ is the conjugate base of ethanoic acid, $CH_3COOH$ and reacts with added hydrogen ions to form ethanoic acid.

$$CH_3COO^-_{(aq)} + H^+_{(aq)} \rightarrow CH_3COOH_{(aq)}$$

Ethanoic acid, $CH_3COOH$ is a weak acid. As a result very few of the ethanoic acid molecules in the buffer solution dissociate to form hydrogen ions. When a small amount of alkali is added hydroxide ions from the alkali react with ethanoic acid molecules in the buffer solution to form ethanoate ions, $CH_3COO^-$.

$$CH_3COOH_{(aq)} + OH^-_{(aq)} \rightarrow CH_3COO^-_{(aq)} + H_2O_{(l)}$$

In this way a solution containing significant amounts of ethanoic acid and ethanoate ion can function as a buffer by removing most of the hydrogen ions or hydroxide ions present when a small amount of acid or alkali is added to the buffer solution.

---

**BUFFER SOLUTIONS** contain a weak acid and the conjugate base of the weak acid.

- The weak acid (HA) removes added hydroxide ions:

  $$HA_{(aq)} + OH^-_{(aq)} \rightarrow A^-_{(aq)} + H_2O_{(l)}$$

- The conjugate base (A$^-$) removes added hydrogen ions:

  $$A^-_{(aq)} + H^+_{(aq)} \rightarrow HA_{(aq)}$$

---

### Worked Example 4.5ix

Methanoic acid, HCOOH is a carboxylic acid. A buffer solution is formed when sodium hydroxide solution is added to excess methanoic acid. Explain, using equations, how the solution formed acts as a buffer.

$$HCOOH_{(aq)} + NaOH_{(aq)} \rightarrow HCOONa_{(aq)} + H_2O_{(l)}$$

sodium methanoate

*(Adapted from CCEA January 2014)*

### Strategy

- Explain how the leftover methanoic acid can act to remove hydroxide ions from the solution and write an equation for the reaction.

- Explain how the methanoate ions (the conjugate base of methanoic acid) can act to remove hydrogen ions from the solution and write an equation for the reaction.

### Solution

The excess methanoic acid remaining in solution will react with added hydroxide ions to form methanoate ions.

$$HCOOH + OH^- \rightarrow HCOO^- + H_2O$$

Methanoate ions formed by the reaction between methanoic acid and sodium hydroxide will react with added hydrogen ions to form methanoic acid.

$$HCOO^- + H^+ \rightarrow HCOOH$$

### Exercise 4.5I

1. A buffer solution can be made by mixing propanoic acid and aqueous sodium propanoate. With the aid of relevant equations, explain how this buffer resists a change in pH when a small amount of acid is added.

   *(Adapted from CCEA May 2010)*

2. Ammonium ethanoate mixed with ethanoic acid can be used as a buffer solution. Use an equation to show how the buffer removes (a) added hydrogen ions and (b) added hydroxide ions.

   *(CCEA January 2012)*

3. A mixture of tartaric acid, $C_4H_6O_6$ and tartrate ion, $C_4H_5O_6^-$ acts as a buffer solution. Write equations to show how this buffer solution responds to (a) the addition of acid and (b) the addition of base.

   *(CCEA May 2012)*

4. Ammonium cyanide, $NH_4CN$ is a white crystalline solid. It is very soluble in water and the solution smells of almonds. The smell is associated with hydrogen cyanide gas.

Explain, using equations, how a solution of ammonium cyanide can be used as a buffer solution.

$$NH_4CN_{(aq)} \rightarrow NH_4^+{}_{(aq)} + CN^-{}_{(aq)}$$

*(CCEA May 2014)*

---

**Before moving to the next section, check that you are able to:**

- Identify a buffer solution as a solution containing a weak acid and the conjugate base of the weak acid.

- Explain using equations how the components of a buffer solution remove added $H^+$ ions and $OH^-$ ions from the buffer solution.

### Calculating the pH of a Buffer Solution

In a buffer solution consisting of a weak acid and its conjugate base, the concentration of the weak acid, [HA] and the concentration of its conjugate base, $[A^-]$ are related by the acid dissociation constant for the weak acid, $K_a$.

Partial dissociation of a weak acid, HA:

$$HA_{(aq)} \rightleftharpoons H^+{}_{(aq)} + A^-{}_{(aq)} \qquad K_a = \frac{[H^+][A^-]}{[HA]}$$

Changing the concentration of the weak acid, [HA] or its conjugate base, $[A^-]$ alters the concentration of hydrogen ions, $[H^+]$ in the buffer solution. As a result the pH of a buffer solution can be varied by altering the composition of the buffer. This makes it possible to prepare buffer solutions that can be used as solvents for reactions that must be carried out at a specific pH. For example, in humans, the pH of blood is maintained in the range 7.35 to 7.45 by a buffer consisting of carbonic acid, $H_2CO_3$ and hydrogencarbonate ions, $HCO_3^-$.

### Worked Example 4.5x

When a solution of ethanoic acid is partially neutralised using sodium hydroxide a buffer solution is formed. (a) Write an equation for the reaction which occurs when sodium hydroxide is added to ethanoic acid. (b) Calculate the pH of the buffer solution formed when 15.0 cm³ of a 0.20 mol dm⁻³ solution of sodium hydroxide is added to 25.0 cm³ of a 0.20 mol dm$^{-3}$ solution of ethanoic acid ($K_a = 1.74 \times 10^{-5}$ mol dm$^{-3}$).

*(CCEA May 2011)*

### Strategy

- Calculate the amount of salt formed and the amount of acid remaining when the acid reacts with sodium hydroxide.
- Calculate the concentration of the acid and its conjugate base in the buffer formed by the reaction.
- Use the value of $K_a$ to calculate [H$^+$] in the buffer solution.

### Solution

(a)   $CH_3COOH + NaOH \rightarrow CH_3COONa + H_2O$

(b) Moles of $CH_3COOH$ added
= 0.20 mol dm$^{-3}$ × 0.0250 dm$^3$ = $5.0 \times 10^{-3}$ mol

Moles of NaOH added = Moles of $CH_3COONa$ formed = $3.0 \times 10^{-3}$ mol

Moles of $CH_3COOH$ remaining = $2.0 \times 10^{-3}$ mol

$$[CH_3COOH] \text{ in buffer} = \frac{2.0 \text{ x } 10^{-3} \text{ mol}}{0.0400 \text{ dm}^3}$$
= 0.050 mol dm$^{-3}$

$[CH_3COO^-]$ in buffer = $[CH_3COONa]$

$$= \frac{3.0 \text{ x } 10^{-3} \text{ mol}}{0.0400 \text{ dm}^3} = 0.075 \text{ mol dm}^{-3}$$

$$[H^+] = \frac{K_a[CH_3COOH]}{[CH_3COO^-]}$$

$$= \frac{(1.74 \text{ x } 10^{-5})(0.050)}{(0.075)} = 1.2 \times 10^{-5} \text{ mol dm}^{-3}$$

$$pH = -\log_{10}[H^+] = -\log_{10}(1.2 \times 10^{-5}) = 4.92$$

----

### Exercise 4.5j

1. The acid dissociation constant, $K_a$ for propanoic acid is $1.35 \times 10^{-5}$ mol dm$^{-3}$. A buffer solution can be prepared by mixing a solution of propanoic acid with a solution of sodium propanoate. (a) What is meant by the term buffer solution? (b) Calculate the pH of the buffer solution formed when 300 cm$^3$ of a 0.25 mol dm$^{-3}$ solution of propanoic acid is mixed with 200 cm$^3$ of a 0.15 mol dm$^{-3}$ solution of sodium propanoate.

*(CCEA January 2011)*

2. Calculate the pH of a solution containing 6.0 g of ethanoic acid, $CH_3COOH$ ($K_a = 1.74 \times 10^{-5}$ mol dm$^{-3}$) and 2.0 g of sodium ethanoate, $CH_3COONa$ dissolved in 100 cm$^3$ of solution.

*(CCEA January 2010)*

3. Calculate the pH of the buffer formed by adding 2.0 g of sodium hydroxide to 500 cm$^3$ of 0.30 mol dm$^{-3}$ methanoic acid, HCOOH ($K_a = 1.6 \times 10^{-4}$ mol dm$^{-3}$).

*(Adapted from CCEA January 2014)*

4. What is the approximate pH of a buffer solution containing 0.20 mol of a weak monobasic acid ($pK_a = 4.8$) and 0.02 mol of the sodium salt of the acid?

     A 2.8   B 3.8   C 4.8   D 5.8

*(CCEA June 2015)*

5. Calculate how many grams of sodium ethanoate must be added to 500 cm$^3$ of 0.010 mol dm$^{-3}$ ethanoic acid ($K_a = 1.86 \times 10^{-5}$ mol dm$^{-3}$) to produce a buffer solution with a pH of 5.8.

*(Adapted from CCEA January 2009)*

----

Before moving to the next section, check that you are able to:

- Calculate the pH of a buffer with a specified composition.
- Calculate the composition of a buffer solution with a specified pH.

## Salt Formation and Hydrolysis

**In this section we are learning to:**

- Write equations for the neutralisation of monobasic and polybasic acids.
- Classify the salts formed in neutralisation reactions as acidic, basic or neutral.

----

### Neutralisation Reactions

The term **neutralisation** refers to *the reaction between an acid and a base to form a salt*. If an acid reacts with an excess of base, each hydrogen atom that is capable of dissociating from the acid to form a hydrogen ion will react.

Examples of neutralisation:

- $HCl_{(aq)} + KOH_{(aq)} \rightarrow KCl_{(aq)} + H_2O_{(l)}$
  Ionic equation: $H^+_{(aq)} + OH^-_{(aq)} \rightarrow H_2O_{(l)}$

- $H_2SO_{4(aq)} + 2NaOH_{(aq)} \rightarrow Na_2SO_{4(aq)} + 2H_2O_{(l)}$
  Ionic equation:
  $H^+_{(aq)} + HSO_4^-_{(aq)} + 2OH^-_{(aq)} \rightarrow SO_4^{2-}_{(aq)} + 2H_2O_{(l)}$

- $2HNO_{3(aq)} + Na_2CO_{3(aq)}$
  $\rightarrow 2NaNO_{3(aq)} + H_2O_{(l)} + CO_{2(g)}$
  Ionic equation:
  $2H^+_{(aq)} + CO_3^{2-}_{(aq)} \rightarrow H_2O_{(l)} + CO_{2(g)}$

- $CH_3COOH_{(aq)} + NaOH_{(aq)}$
  $\rightarrow CH_3COONa_{(aq)} + H_2O_{(l)}$
  Ionic equation:
  $CH_3COOH_{(aq)} + OH^-_{(aq)} \rightarrow CH_3COO^-_{(aq)} + H_2O_{(l)}$

- $HCl_{(aq)} + NH_{3(aq)} \rightarrow NH_4Cl_{(aq)}$
  Ionic equation: $H^+_{(aq)} + NH_{3(aq)} \rightarrow NH_4^+_{(aq)}$

### Worked Example 4.5xi

Antioxidants such as citric acid are added to food to prevent the oxidation of fats and oils. (a) Write an equation for the reaction of citric acid with excess sodium hydroxide solution. (b) Calculate the concentration of a citric acid solution in $g\,dm^{-3}$ if $25.0\,cm^3$ of solution reacted with $17.5\,cm^3$ of $0.10\,M$ sodium hydroxide solution.

$$\begin{array}{c} CH_2COOH \\ | \\ HO - C - COOH \\ | \\ CH_2COOH \end{array} \quad \text{Citric acid}$$

*(Adapted from CCEA May 2008)*

### Strategy

- Each carboxyl (-COOH) group reacts with sodium hydroxide to form a sodium salt and water.

### Solution

$$\text{(a) } \begin{array}{c} CH_2COOH \\ | \\ HO - C - COOH \\ | \\ CH_2COOH \end{array} + 3NaOH$$

$$\longrightarrow \begin{array}{c} CH_2COONa \\ | \\ HO - C - COONa \\ | \\ CH_2COONa \end{array} + 3H_2O$$

(b) Moles of NaOH reacted $= 0.10\,mol\,dm^{-3}$
$\times 0.0175\,dm^3 = 1.8 \times 10^{-3}\,mol$

Moles of citric acid in $25\,cm^3 = \dfrac{1}{3} \times$ Moles of NaOH reacted $= 6.0 \times 10^{-4}\,mol$

Molarity of citric acid $= 6.0 \times 10^{-4}\,mol$
$\times \dfrac{1000\,cm^3}{25\,cm^3} = 2.4 \times 10^{-2}\,mol\,dm^{-3}$

Concentration in $g\,dm^{-3} = 2.4 \times 10^{-2}\,mol\,dm^{-3}$
$\times 192\,g\,mol^{-1} = 4.6\,g\,dm^{-3}$

### Exercise 4.5K

1. Citric acid is a tribasic acid. (a) Suggest the meaning of *tribasic*. (b) Write the equation for the reaction of citric acid with excess calcium carbonate. (c) Citric acid is reformed when the calcium citrate formed is reacted with sulfuric acid. Write the equation for this reaction.

$$\begin{array}{c} CH_2COOH \\ | \\ HO - C - COOH \\ | \\ CH_2COOH \end{array} \quad \text{Citric acid}$$

*(CCEA January 2013)*

2. (a) Write an equation to show sulfur trioxide dissolving in water to form sulfuric acid, $H_2SO_4$. (b) Write an equation for the reaction of sulfuric acid with excess sodium hydroxide.

*(Adapted from CCEA January 2012)*

3. (a) Write an equation to show sulfur dioxide dissolving in water to form sulfurous acid, $H_2SO_3$. (b) Write an equation for the reaction of sulfurous acid with excess sodium hydroxide.

*(CCEA January 2012)*

3. Ethanedioic acid has the formula, $(COOH)_2$. Calculate the volume of $0.50\,M$ sodium hydroxide solution needed to completely neutralise $25.0\,cm^3$ of $0.250\,M$ aqueous ethanedioic acid.

$$\begin{array}{c} COOH \\ | \\ COOH \end{array} \quad \text{Ethanedioic acid}$$

*(Adapted from CCEA May 2010)*

Before moving to the next section, check that you are able to:

- Write equations for the neutralisation of monobasic and polybasic acids.

## Salt Hydrolysis

Salts such as sodium chloride are referred to as *neutral salts* as they dissolve in water to form a solution with a pH close to 7.

$$NaCl_{(aq)} \rightarrow Na^+_{(aq)} + Cl^-_{(aq)}$$

In contrast, sodium ethanoate is an example of a *basic salt* as it dissolves in water to form a solution with pH value above 7. The solution is alkaline as the ethanoate ions formed when the salt dissolves react with water to form hydroxide ions.

$$CH_3COO^-_{(aq)} + H_2O_{(l)} \rightarrow CH_3COOH_{(aq)} + OH^-_{(aq)}$$

The reaction of ethanoate ion with water is an example of **salt hydrolysis** as *the hydrolysis of water to form H+ or OH- ions occurs as the result of an aqueous ion reacting with water in the solution.* Salt hydrolysis also occurs when ammonium salts such as ammonium chloride, $NH_4Cl$ dissolve in water. In the case of ammonium chloride, $NH_4Cl$ the solution formed is acidic as ammonium ions in the solution donate a hydrogen ion to water to form hydronium ion, $H_3O^+$.

$$NH_4^+_{(aq)} + H_2O_{(l)} \rightarrow NH_3_{(aq)} + H_3O^+_{(aq)}$$

Ammonium chloride, $NH_4Cl$ is an example of an *acidic salt* as it dissolves in water to form a solution with a pH value below 7.

The ability of a salt to form an acidic, basic or neutral solution can be predicted by considering the relative strengths of the acid and base used to form the salt.

- An *acidic salt* is formed when a base reacts with a *stronger acid.*
- A *neutral salt* is formed when a strong acid reacts with a strong base, or a weak acid reacts with a weak base, as *the acid and base have similar strengths.*
- A *basic salt* is formed when an acid reacts with a *stronger base.*

pH of salt solution increasing →

| Acidic salt | Neutral salt | Basic salt |
|---|---|---|
| Acid stronger than base | Acid and base have equal strength | Base stronger than acid |

## Worked Example 4.5xii

Explain why a saturated solution of sodium sulfite has a pH of 9 and sodium sulfate solution has a pH of 7.

*(CCEA January 2012)*

### Strategy

- Explain how the pH of the salt solution is determined by the strength of the acid and base used to form the salt.

### Solution

Sodium sulfate, $Na_2SO_4$ is a neutral salt as it is the salt of a strong acid ($H_2SO_4$) and a strong base (NaOH). Sodium sulfite, $Na_2SO_3$ is a basic salt as it is the salt of a weak acid ($H_2SO_3$) and a strong base (NaOH).

## Exercise 4.5L

1. Which one of the following salts would produce a neutral solution when dissolved in water?

   A  Ammonium chloride

   B  Potassium chloride

   C  Potassium ethanoate

   D  Sodium carbonate

   *(CCEA May 2013)*

2. Which one of the following salts will dissolve to produce a solution with the highest pH?

   A  Ammonium chloride

   B  Ammonium ethanoate

   C  Sodium chloride

   D  Sodium ethanoate

   *(CCEA January 2014)*

3. Ammonium nitrate is produced by the reaction of ammonia with nitric acid. (a) Write the equation for this reaction. (b) State and explain whether an aqueous solution of ammonium nitrate is acidic, neutral or alkaline.

   *(CCEA May 2010)*

4. Suggest a value for the pH of the solution formed when calcium chloride is dissolved in water and explain your answer.

*(CCEA May 2012)*

5. Would a solution of sodium ethanoate be acidic, alkaline or neutral? Explain your answer.

*(CCEA May 2011)*

6. Potassium persulfate, $K_2S_2O_8$ is made by the oxidation of potassium sulfate using electricity. It is a salt of peroxysulfuric acid.

$HO-SO_2-O-O-SO_2-OH$     peroxysulfuric acid

(a) Suggest the structure of peroxysulfuric acid showing all of the bonds present. (b) Although peroxysulfuric acid is a powerful oxidising agent it is a weak acid. Explain whether a solution of potassium persulfate is acidic, alkaline or neutral.

*(CCEA May 2014)*

7. Aluminium oxide is a weaker base than sodium oxide, which is a strong base. Both react with nitric acid to form nitrate salts. Solutions of aluminium nitrate, sodium nitrate and ammonium nitrate have different pH values. Explain which one is acidic, which one is slightly acidic and which one is neutral.

*(Adapted from CCEA May 2015)*

8. An aqueous solution of ammonium chloride has a pH less than 7 because:

A   the ammonium ions donate protons to water molecules.

B   the chloride ions combine with hydrogen ions to form hydrochloric acid.

C   aqueous ammonium chloride is unstable and evolves ammonia gas leaving hydrochloric acid.

D   the ammonium ions combine with hydroxide ions to form ammonium hydroxide leaving an excess of hydrogen ions.

*(CCEA January 2009)*

---

Before moving to the next section, check that you are able to:

- Explain, with the aid of equations, why aqueous solutions of salts can be acidic, basic or neutral.
- Account for the acidic, basic or neutral nature of a salt in terms of the strength of the acid and base used to form the salt.

## Acid-Base Titrations

### In this section we are learning to:

- Use a titration curve to determine the equivalence point of an acid-base titration.
- Determine if an indicator is suitable for a particular acid-base titration.

---

In an acid-base titration the amount of acid or alkali in a measured amount of solution is determined by measuring the volume of a standard acid or alkali needed to reach the **equivalence point**, *the point at which the acid or alkali in the solution being titrated has been completely neutralised.* The equivalence point can be detected by adding a few drops of a suitable indicator to the solution as it is titrated, or by using an electronic pH meter to measure the pH of the solution as it is titrated.

The **titration curve** in Figure 3 is a *plot showing the pH of the solution being titrated (in the conical flask) against the volume of solution added from the burette.*

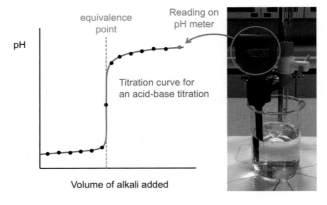

*Figure 3: Using an electronic pH meter to determine the equivalence point for the titration of an acid (in the conical flask) against a base (in the burette).*

## SASB Titrations

Neutralisation of a strong acid (SA) by a strong base (SB) is referred to as a strong acid - strong base (SASB) titration. The SASB reaction produces a neutral salt.

$$HCl_{(aq)} + NaOH_{(aq)} \rightarrow NaCl_{(aq)} + H_2O_{(l)}$$

strong acid    strong base      neutral salt

neutral solution
pH ≈ 7

The titration curve for the titration of a strong acid (in the conical flask) against a strong base (in the burette) in Figure 4 reveals that:

1. Before equivalence the neutral salt formed in the reaction does not affect the pH and the solution remains acidic.

2. At equivalence the pH rises sharply to around pH 7 as the last of the acid reacts with the base to form a solution of a neutral salt.

3. The pH continues to rise as more base is added and the solution becomes alkaline.

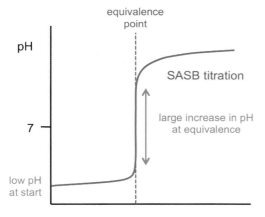

Figure 4: Titration curve for a strong acid - strong base (SASB) titration.

## WASB Titrations

Neutralisation of a weak acid (WA) by a strong base (SB) is referred to as a weak acid - strong base (WASB) titration. The WASB reaction produces a basic salt.

$$CH_3COOH_{(aq)} + NaOH_{(aq)} \rightarrow CH_3COONa_{(aq)} + H_2O_{(l)}$$

weak acid     strong base     basic salt

alkaline solution
pH > 7

The titration curve for the titration of a weak acid

(in the conical flask) against a strong base (in the burette) in Figure 5 reveals that:

1. The basic salt formed before equivalence increases the pH of the solution.

2. At equivalence the pH rises sharply to above pH 7 as the last of the acid reacts with the base to form a solution of a basic salt.

3. The pH then continues to rise steadily as more base is added and the solution becomes more alkaline.

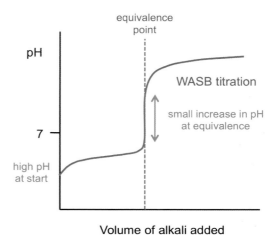

Figure 5: Titration curve for a weak acid - strong base (WASB) titration.

## WBSA Titrations

Neutralisation of a weak base (WB) by a strong acid (SA) is referred to as a weak base - strong acid (WBSA) titration. The WBSA reaction produces an acidic salt.

$$HCl_{(aq)} + NH_{3(aq)} \rightarrow NH_4Cl_{(aq)}$$

strong acid     weak base     acidic salt

(solution pH < 7)

The titration curve for the titration of a weak base (in the conical flask) against a strong acid (in the burette) in Figure 6 reveals that:

1. The acidic salt formed before equivalence decreases the pH of the solution.

2. At equivalence the pH drops sharply to below pH 7 as the last of the base reacts with the acid to form a solution of an acidic salt.

3. The pH then continues to decrease as more acid is added and the solution becomes more acidic.

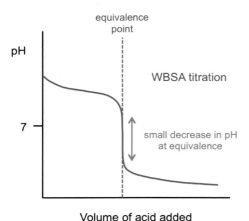

*Figure 6: Titration curve for a weak base - strong acid (WBSA) titration.*

### WAWB Titrations

Neutralisation of a weak acid (WA) by a weak base (WB) is referred to as a weak acid - weak base (WAWB) titration. The WAWB reaction produces a neutral salt.

$$CH_3COOH_{(aq)} + NH_{3(aq)} \rightarrow CH_3COONH_{4(aq)}$$

weak acid  weak base  neutral salt

(solution pH ≈ 7)

The titration curve for the titration of a weak acid (in the conical flask) against a weak base (in the burette) is shown in Figure 7. The rise in pH at the equivalence point is small, making it difficult to find an indicator that will change colour when the pH rises at equivalence. As a result it becomes difficult to accurately determine the equivalence point of a WAWB titration.

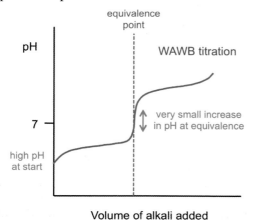

*Figure 7: Titration curve for a weak acid - weak base (WAWB) titration.*

### Exercise 4.5M

1. Which one of the following curves correctly shows the change in pH during the titration of 25.0 cm³ of 0.10 mol dm⁻³ sodium carbonate solution with 0.10 mol dm⁻³ nitric acid?

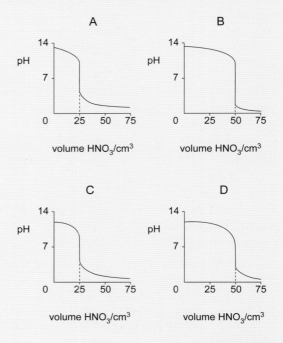

*(CCEA May 2015)*

2. Sketch the titration curve for the addition of 50 cm³ of 0.1 mol dm⁻³ sodium hydroxide solution to 25 cm³ of 0.1 mol dm⁻³ methanoic acid solution.

*(CCEA January 2014)*

3. (a) Draw the titration curve for the titration of aqueous ammonia with aqueous hydrocyanic acid, HCN₍aq₎, a weak acid. (b) Use the titration curve to explain why the titration is not normally carried out.

*(CCEA May 2014)*

Before moving to the next section, check that you are able to:

- Sketch the titration curve for an acid-base titration and identify the equivalence point on the sketch.
- Account for the principal features of acid-base titration curves.

## Indicator Choice

An indicator can be used to detect the equivalence point in an acid-base titration if it changes colour when the pH rises or falls sharply at the equivalence point. Acid-base indicators are weak acids; a solution of the indicator contains the acid form of the indicator (HIn) and its conjugate base (In⁻) in equilibrium.

> **Acid-base indicator (HIn)**
>
> $HIn_{(aq)} \rightleftharpoons H^+_{(aq)} + In^-_{(aq)}$

A compound can be used as an acid-base indicator if the acid form of the indicator (HIn) and its conjugate base (In⁻) produce different colours in solution. If the indicator is added to a solution that is sufficiently acidic, the position of the equilibrium moves to the left and the colour associated with the acid form (HIn) is observed.

$$HIn \rightleftharpoons H^+ + In^-$$

colour at low pH ← add acid — colour at high pH

If the pH is then increased the position of the equilibrium shifts to the right and the colour associated with the conjugate base (In⁻) is observed.

$$HIn \rightleftharpoons H^+ + In^-$$

colour at low pH — add base → colour at high pH

Most indicators change colour over a range of approximately 2 pH units. For example, the indicator phenolphthalein changes colour in the range pH 8–10.

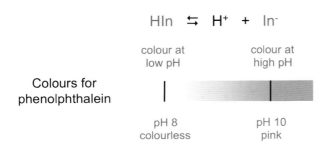

$$HIn \rightleftharpoons H^+ + In^-$$

colour at low pH — colour at high pH

Colours for phenolphthalein

pH 8 colourless — pH 10 pink

If the indicator is added to a solution with a pH below 8 the acid form of the indicator (HIn) dominates and the indicator is colourless. If the pH of the solution is then increased above pH 10 the conjugate base (In⁻) form of the indicator dominates and produces a pink colour in the solution.

The ability of phenolphthalein to change colour over the range pH 8–10 makes it suitable for use in SASB and WASB titrations as it changes colour when the pH rises sharply at equivalence. The use of phenolphthalein to detect the equivalence point of a WASB titration is illustrated in Figure 8a. In contrast, the titration curve for a WBSA titration in Figure 8b demonstrates that phenolphthalein cannot be used to detect the equivalence point of a WBSA titration as it changes colour before the equivalence point has been reached.

The equivalence point of a WBSA titration can however be detected using the indicator methyl orange.

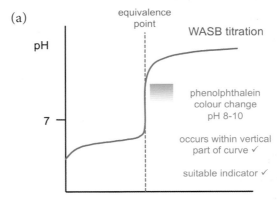

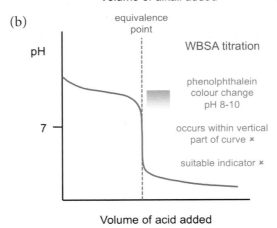

*Figure 8: (a) Using phenolphthalein to detect the equivalence point in a WASB titration. (b) Phenolphthalein cannot detect the equivalence point in a WBSA titration as it changes colour before the equivalence point.*

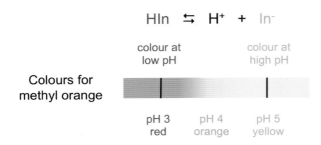

$$HIn \rightleftharpoons H^+ + In^-$$

colour at low pH    colour at high pH

Colours for methyl orange

pH 3 red    pH 4 orange    pH 5 yellow

The titration curve in Figure 9a demonstrates that methyl orange changes colour from yellow (In⁻ dominates) at pH 5 to red (HIn dominates) at pH 3 when the pH decreases sharply at equivalence. In contrast, the titration curve in Figure 9b demonstrates that methyl orange cannot detect the equivalence point of a WASB titration as it changes colour before the equivalence point is reached.

Together these examples demonstrate that *an acid-base indicator will only be suitable for use in a*

*particular titration if the indicator changes colour over a range of pH that lies within the vertical portion of the titration curve.*

The suitability of an indicator to detect the equivalence point of a SASB, WASB or WBSA titration can be determined by comparing the pH range over which it changes colour to the ranges given in Figure 10.

In contrast, the equivalence point of a WAWB titration cannot be determined using an acid-base indicator as the change in pH at equivalence is not sufficient to change the colour of the indicator.

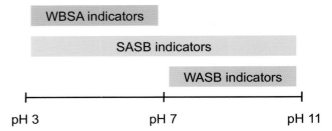

WBSA indicators

SASB indicators

WASB indicators

pH 3          pH 7          pH 11

*Figure 10: The pH ranges over which SASB, WASB and WBSA indicators change colour.*

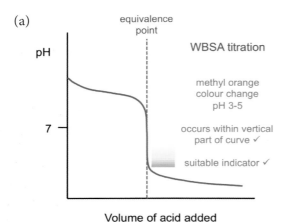

(a)

equivalence point

pH

WBSA titration

methyl orange colour change pH 3-5

7

occurs within vertical part of curve ✓

suitable indicator ✓

Volume of acid added

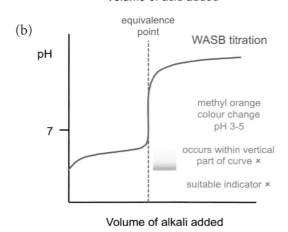

(b)

equivalence point

pH

WASB titration

methyl orange colour change pH 3-5

7

occurs within vertical part of curve ✗

suitable indicator ✗

Volume of alkali added

*Figure 9: (a) Using methyl orange to detect the equivalence point in a WASB titration. (b) Methyl orange cannot detect the equivalence point in a WASB titration as it changes colour before the equivalence point.*

## Worked Example 4.5xiii

Which one of the following indicators would be suitable for a titration between molar solutions of sulfuric acid and ammonia?

|   | Indicator | pH range |
|---|-----------|----------|
| A | malachite green | 0.2–1.8 |
| B | methyl yellow | 2.9–4.0 |
| C | thymolphthalein | 8.3–10.6 |
| D | alizarin yellow | 10.1–13.0 |

*(CCEA May 2010)*

### Strategy

- The indicator for a WBSA titration should change colour between pH 3 and pH 7.

### Solution

Answer B.

## Exercise 4.5N

1. Bromothymol blue is an indicator which changes colour over a pH range of 6.0–7.8. At pH 6.0 it is yellow, above pH 7.8 it is blue. The indicator can be considered a weak acid, HIn in equilibrium with the In$^-$ ion.

$$HIn \rightleftharpoons H^+ + In^-$$

(a) Identify the conjugate acid and base in the equilibrium. (b) Use the equilibrium to explain the colour changes that occur when acid and alkali are added separately to the indicator.

*(Adapted from CCEA May 2009)*

2. Which indicator is suitable to establish the end point when adding 0.1 M HCl to 0.1 M NH$_3$?

| | Indicator | pH range for colour change |
|---|---|---|
| A | salicyl yellow | 10.0–12.0 |
| B | thymol blue | 8.0–9.6 |
| C | bromothymol blue | 6.0–7.6 |
| D | malachite green | 0.2–1.8 |

*(Adapted from CCEA May 2007)*

3. Titration curves for the reaction of sulfuric acid with excess sodium hydroxide are shown in the following diagram. (a) Explain why the length of the vertical sections of the curves decreases as the concentration of the acid decreases. (b) Explain how you would choose a suitable indicator for the titration of 0.001 M sulfuric acid with 0.1 M NaOH.

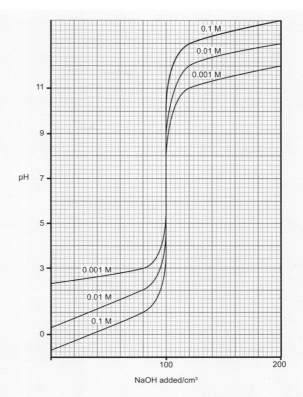

*(CCEA January 2012)*

4. The titration curve in the following diagram shows the change in pH when a 0.20 mol dm$^{-3}$ solution of sodium hydroxide is added to 25.0 cm$^3$ of a solution of propanoic acid of unknown concentration. (a) Write the equation for the neutralisation reaction which occurs. (b) Suggest a suitable indicator for the titration. Give the colour change and explain why the indicator is suitable. (c) Calculate the concentration of the propanoic acid.

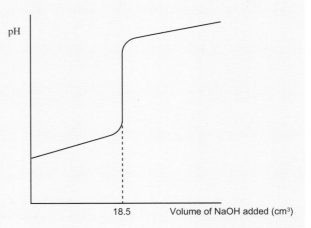

*(CCEA January 2011)*

5. The titration curve for the reaction of 0.1 M sulfuric acid with 0.2 M ammonia solution is shown below. (a) Write the equation for the reaction of sulfuric acid with ammonia. (b) Explain why ammonia is regarded as a Brønsted-Lowry base in this reaction. (c) Name a suitable indicator for the titration. (d) Using the titration curve, explain why this indicator is suitable.

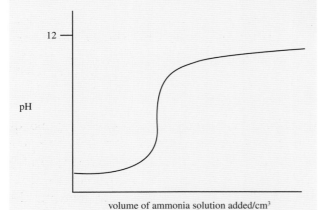

volume of ammonia solution added/cm³

*(CCEA January 2010)*

6. Ammonia reacts with ethanoic acid to form ammonium ethanoate. (a) Write an equation for the reaction. (b) Explain why it is not possible to measure an accurate end point in the titration of ammonia with ethanoic acid.

*(CCEA January 2010)*

7. Tartaric acid is one of several organic acids that have an important role in winemaking. A titration is carried out to determine the amount of tartaric acid in wine. A 25.0 cm³ portion of white wine from a 750 cm³ bottle is titrated against 0.20 mol dm⁻³ sodium hydroxide solution. 9.8 cm³ of sodium hydroxide is required to *completely* neutralise the acid. (a) Suggest a suitable indicator for the titration and explain your choice. (b) Calculate the mass of tartaric acid in the bottle of wine.

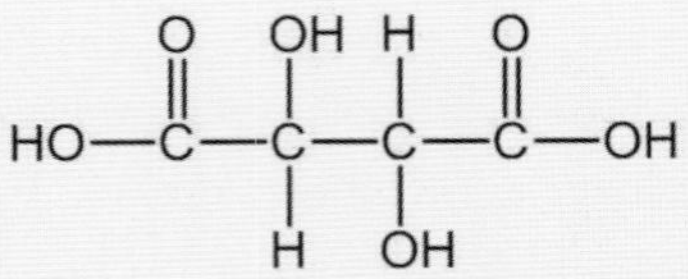

HO—C—C—C—C—OH    Tartaric acid

*(Adapted from CCEA May 2012)*

Before moving to the next section, check that you are able to:

- Explain why acid-base indicators change colour over a range of pH values.
- Select a suitable indicator for an acid-base titration and explain your reasoning.

# 4.6 Isomerism

**CONNECTIONS**

- Most of the C=C bonds in naturally occurring fats and oils have groups attached to the same side of the C=C bond in a *cis* arrangement.
- The compounds responsible for the aromas of caraway and spearmint are isomers of carvone, $C_{10}H_{14}O$.

## The Origins of Isomerism

**In this section we are learning to:**

- Distinguish between structural and geometric isomerism.
- Recognise geometric isomerism as a type of stereoisomerism.

**Isomers** are *compounds with the same formula that have a different arrangement of atoms within the compound.* The ability of a substance to form isomers is referred to as isomerism.

### Structural Isomerism

Structural isomerism gives rise to **structural isomers** which *are compounds with the same molecular formula that have different structural formulas.* For example, the compounds but-1-ene and but-2-ene are structural isomers of butene, $C_4H_8$ and are distinguished by the location of the C=C bond within the carbon chain.

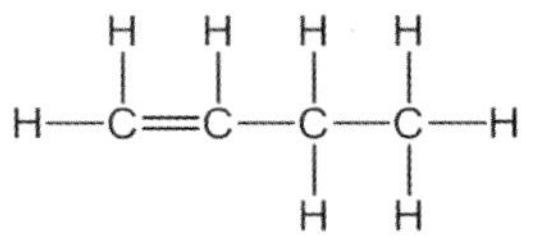

but-1-ene

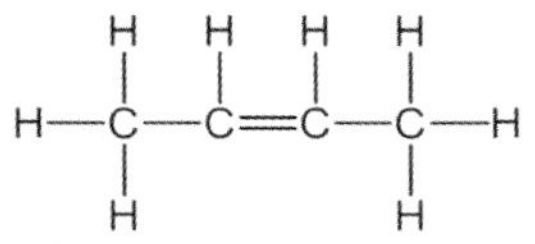

but-2-ene

**Exercise 4.6A**

1. Glucose and fructose are *structural isomers.* Explain what is meant by this term.

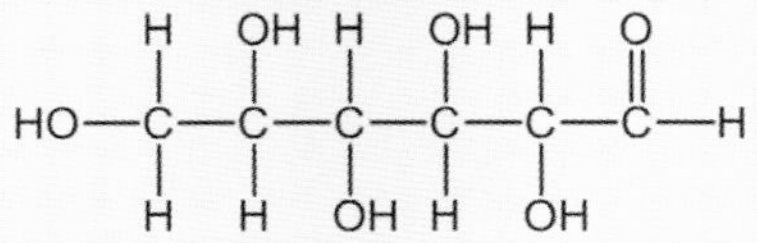

glucose

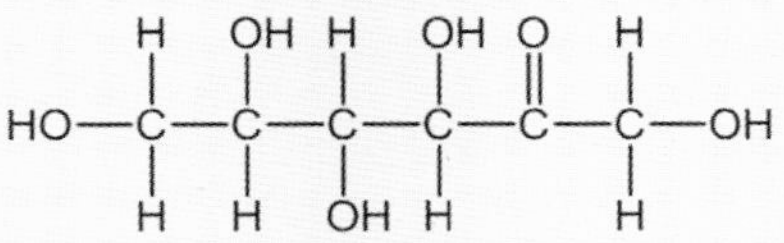

fructose

*(CCEA June 2012)*

2. Explain why ethyl ethanoate, $CH_3COOCH_2CH_3$ and butanoic acid, $CH_3CH_2CH_2COOH$ are isomers.

*(CCEA January 2003)*

### Stereoisomerism

Compounds containing one or more C=C bonds may also exist as **geometric isomers** which *have the same structural formula but a different arrangement of atoms in space as the molecule cannot rotate about the C=C bonds in the compound.* For example, the geometric (E-Z) isomers of but-2-ene, $CH_3CH{=}CHCH_3$ are distinguished by the relative positioning of the methyl ($-CH_3$) groups attached at opposite ends of the C=C bond.

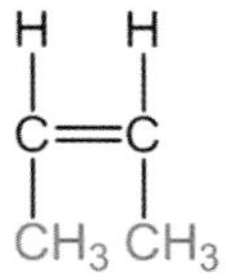

*Z*-but-2-ene

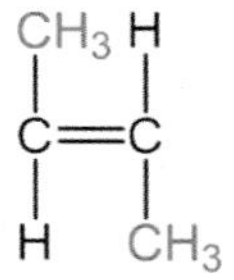

*E*-but-2-ene

In compounds such as but-1-ene, $CH_2{=}CHCH_2CH_3$ the presence of a double bond is not sufficient to generate geometric isomers *as each atom forming the double bond must be attached to two different groups of atoms.*

Geometric isomerism is a type of **stereoisomerism** as it *gives rise to isomers with the same structural formula that have a different arrangement of atoms in space.* The relationship between structural isomerism and stereoisomerism is summarised in Figure 1.

**Exercise 4.5B**

1. The E isomer of butenedioic acid is called fumaric acid and is produced naturally in the body. Explain why isomerism exists in this compound.

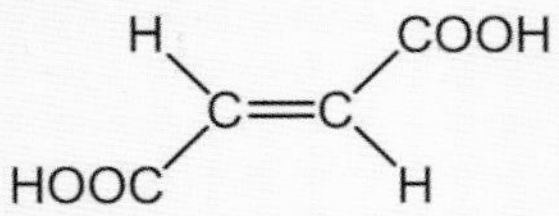

fumaric acid

*(Adapted from CCEA January 2014)*

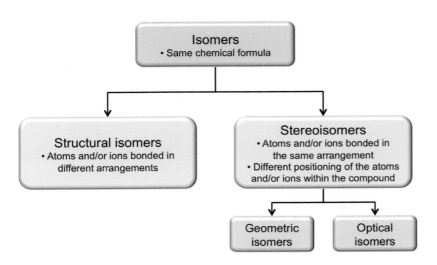

2. Explain why a compound with the formula $C_3H_6$ cannot have geometric isomers.

3. The compound $CH_3COCOOH$ can be formed by heating tartaric acid with potassium hydrogensulfate. Hydroxymaleic acid is formed in the process. Draw the E and Z isomers of hydroxymaleic acid.

$$HOOC-\underset{\underset{H}{|}}{C}=\underset{\underset{OH}{|}}{C}-COOH \qquad \text{hydroxymaleic acid}$$

*(CCEA January 2012)*

4. Draw the structural formula for each isomer with the formula $C_5H_{12}$.

5. Write the condensed formula for each structural isomer with the formula $C_5H_{10}$.

6. Draw the structural formula for each geometric isomer with the formula $C_5H_{10}$.

---

Before moving to the next section, check that you are able to:

- Explain the relationship between *structural isomers* and *stereoisomers*.
- Explain why geometric isomers are also stereoisomers.

## Optical Isomerism

**In this section we are learning to:**

- Explain the origin of optical isomerism in compounds and the relationship between the optical isomers of a compound.

---

Optical isomerism is a type of stereoisomerism that arises when a compound contains one or more asymmetric centres. The term **asymmetric centre** refers to *an atom bonded to four different groups of atoms in a tetrahedral arrangement*. Asymmetric centres are also known as chiral centres and impart a left or right 'handedness' to the compound. The carbon atom bonded to the hydroxyl (-OH) group in butan-2-ol is an example of an asymmetric centre. The tetrahedral arrangement of groups about the asymmetric centre in butan-2-ol is illustrated in Figure 2.

$$H-\underset{\underset{H}{|}}{\overset{\overset{H}{|}}{C}}-\underset{\underset{H}{|}}{\overset{\overset{OH}{|}}{\overset{*}{C}}}-\underset{\underset{H}{|}}{\overset{\overset{H}{|}}{C}}-\underset{\underset{H}{|}}{\overset{\overset{H}{|}}{C}}-H$$

(a)                              (b)

*Figure 2: (a) The structural formula for butan-2-ol. (b) The molecular structure of butan-2-ol. The asymmetric centre is labelled with an asterisk (\*).*

The left and right-handed forms of butan-2-ol in Figure 3 are referred to as **optical isomers** and *are non-superimposable mirror images of each other.* Optical isomers are also referred to as enantiomers.

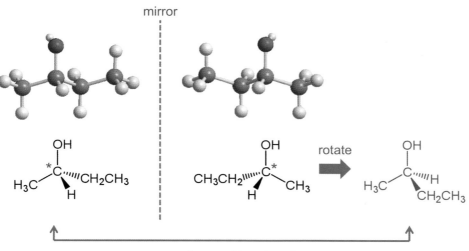

*Figure 3: The relationship between the optical isomers of butan-2-ol. The asymmetric centre is labelled with an asterisk (*).*

non-superimposable mirror images

## Worked Example 4.6i

There are a number of structural isomers with molecular formula $C_4H_9Br$. Only one contains an asymmetric centre and can exist as optical isomers. (a) What is meant by the term *asymmetric centre*? (b) Explain, in terms of structure, the meaning of the expression *optical isomers*. (c) Draw and name the structural isomer of $C_4H_9Br$ which contains an asymmetric centre. (d) Draw 3D representations of the two optical isomers of this structural isomer.

*(Adapted from CCEA May 2011)*

## Solution

(a) The term asymmetric centre refers to an atom with four different groups of atoms attached to it.

(b) Compounds are optical isomers if their structures are non-superimposable mirror images of each other.

(c) H—C—C—C—C—H   2-bromobutane

(b)

## Exercise 4.6C

1. Which one of the following molecules can exist as optical isomers?

   A  $(CH_3)_2C=CHCH_3$
   B  $CH_3CH_2CH(CH_3)CH=CH_2$
   C  $CH_3CH_2CH_2CH_2CH=CH_2$
   D  $CH_3CH_2CH_2CH_2CH=CHCH_3$

   *(CCEA January 2003)*

2. The compound $CH_2(OH)CH(CH_3)CH=CH_2$ has

   A  a trans isomer
   B  an E isomer
   C  no optical isomers
   D  two optical isomers

   *(CCEA January 2014)*

3. The number of stereoisomers for a compound with the structure $CH_3CHBrCH=CH_2$ is:

   |   | Geometric *(cis-trans)* | Optical |
   |---|---|---|
   | A | zero | zero |
   | B | zero | two |
   | C | two | zero |
   | D | two | two |

   *(CCEA May 2006)*

4. Ethane reacts with chlorine to form a variety of chlorinated hydrocarbons ranging from $C_2H_5Cl$ to $C_2Cl_6$. How many of the compounds formed have an asymmetric centre?   None

   *(Adapted from CCEA January 2012)*

5. Which one of the following does **not** contain an asymmetric centre?

   A CH₃CH(CH₃)CH₂CH₃ — 2 CH₃ groups
   B CH₃CH(OH)CH₂CH₃
   C CH₃CHClCH₂CH₃
   D CH₃CH(NH₂)CH₂CH₃

   *(CCEA January 2007)*

6. The compound CH₃COCOOH can be formed by heating tartaric acid with potassium hydrogensulfate. Label each asymmetric centre in a molecule of tartaric acid with an asterisk (*).

   HOOC—C—C—COOH    tartaric acid
   (with H, OH above and OH, H below)

   *(Adapted from CCEA January 2012)*

---

**Before moving to the next section, check that you are able to:**

- Recall that optical isomerism is due to the presence of one or more asymmetric centres in a compound.
- Identify asymmetric centres and draw the structures of optical isomers.
- Explain the relationship between the structures of optical isomers.

---

## Optical Activity

**In this section we are learning to:**

- Explain how optical activity can be used to identify optical isomers.
- Account for optical activity in the products of chemical reactions.

---

*The optical isomers of a compound have the same physical properties and can only be distinguished by their ability to rotate the plane of plane-polarised light.*

The term plane-polarised describes visible light, or other forms of electromagnetic radiation, whose vibrations occur in a single plane. When plane-polarised light is passed through a solution containing one optical isomer, the plane in which the vibrations occur is rotated as shown in Figure 4, and the solution is described as **optically active** as it *rotates the plane of plane-polarised light.*

A solution containing the same concentration of the other optical isomer rotates the plane of plane-polarised light by an equal amount in the opposite direction. As a result *the optical isomers of a compound can be distinguished by the direction they rotate the plane of plane-polarised light.*

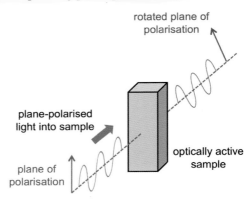

*Figure 4: Rotation of the plane of plane-polarised light by an optically active substance.*

In contrast, a substance is said to be optically inactive if *it does not rotate the plane of plane-polarised light.* A solution containing equal amounts of two optical isomers is known as a **racemic mixture** and will be optically inactive as *the optical isomers in the mixture rotate the plane of plane-polarised light by equal amounts in opposite directions.*

A racemic mixture is often formed when a chemical reaction produces a product containing one or more asymmetric centres. For example, the reduction of butanone, CH₃CH₂COCH₃ produces a racemic mixture containing both optical isomers of butan-2-ol as illustrated by Figure 5.

............................................................

### Worked Example 4.6ii

Ethanal, CH₃CHO reacts with hydrogen cyanide to form a cyanohydrin. The product is optically inactive. (a) Explain the meaning of the term *optically inactive*. (b) Draw the 3D structures of the two cyanohydrin isomers. (c) Explain why the cyanohydrin product is optically inactive.

H₃C—C(=O)—H  +  HCN  ⟶  H₃C—C(CN)(OH)—H

*(CCEA January 2012)*

### Solution

   (a)  A substance is optically inactive if it does not rotate the plane of plane-polarised light.

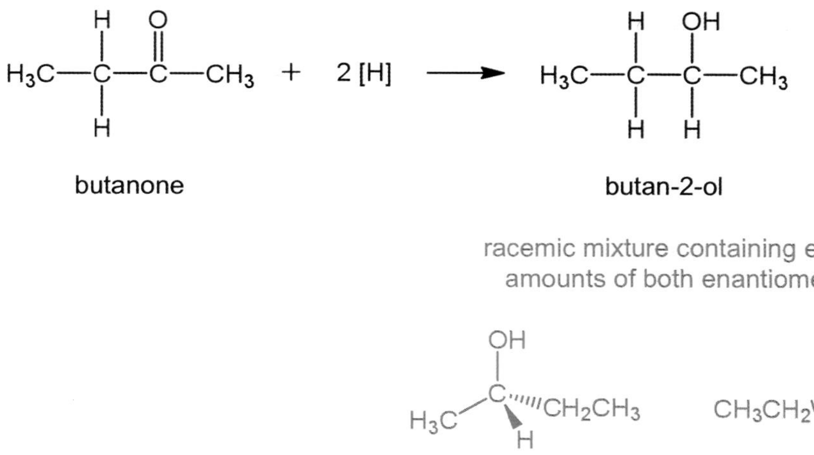

*Figure 5: Forming a racemic mixture containing equal amounts of butan-2-ol isomers.*

butanone    butan-2-ol

racemic mixture containing equal amounts of both enantiomers

(b)

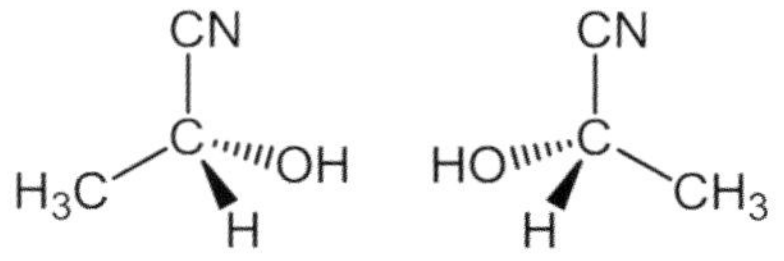

(c) The solution formed does not rotate the plane of plane-polarised light as the cyanohydrin isomers are formed in equal amounts.

- - - - - - - - - - - - - - - - - - - - - - - - - -

## Exercise 4.6D

1. Lactic acid, $CH_3CH(OH)COOH$ is a weak acid which builds up in muscles during exercise. The molecule is optically active. (a) Explain the term *optically active*. (b) Draw the 3D structures of the two optical isomers.

   *(Adapted from CCEA January 2010)*

2. How can the optical isomers of a compound be distinguished?

   *(CCEA May 2011)*

3. Acetoin is optically active. (a) Explain what is meant by the term *optically active*. (b) Explain, in terms of structure, why acetoin is optically active. (c) Draw the two optical isomers of acetoin. (d) Explain why a mixture of the two isomers of acetoin may not exhibit any optical activity.

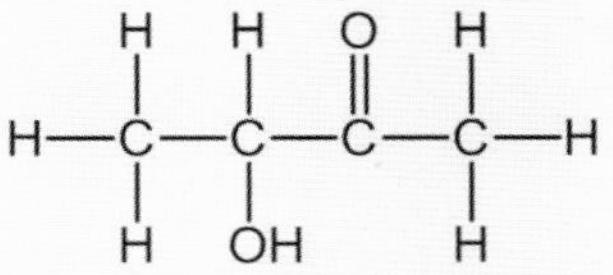

acetoin

*(CCEA May 2013)*

4. Tartaric acid exhibits optical activity. (a) Explain what is meant by the term *optical activity*. (b) Mark the asymmetric centre(s) on the structure of tartaric acid. (c) Explain why some samples of tartaric acid extracted from wine do not display optical activity.

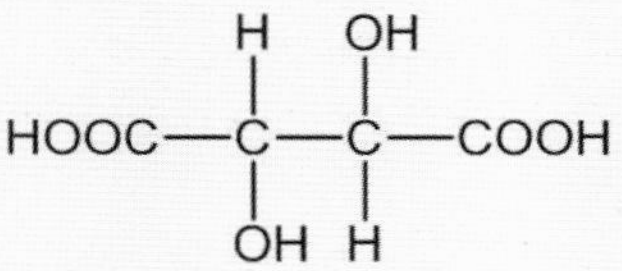

tartaric acid

*(CCEA May 2012)*

5. Lactic acid, $CH_3CH(OH)COOH$ extracted from muscle tissue exhibits optical isomerism while lactic acid obtained by the hydrolysis of 2-hydroxypropanenitrile, $CH_3CH(OH)CN$ does not. Suggest why lactic acid from the hydrolysis of 2-hydroxypropanenitrile will not rotate the plane of polarised light.

*(CCEA January 2006)*

Before moving to the next section, check that you are able to:

- Recall the effect of optical isomers on plane- polarised light and explain what is meant by *optical activity*.
- Explain how optical activity can be used to distinguish optical isomers.
- Account for the optical inactivity of a racemic mixture.

## Optical Isomers in Medicines

### In this section we are learning to:

- Recall the use of optical isomers in medicines.
- Explain, in terms of structure, why the therapeutic effects of a medicine are often associated with one optical isomer.

Many medicines contain optical isomers, or a racemic mixture of optical isomers. The therapeutic effects of the medicine are often due to the presence of one optical isomer as illustrated by the following examples.

### Thalidomide

The drug thalidomide was introduced in 1957 to treat morning sickness during pregnancy. It was soon withdrawn as it was found to cause severe birth defects in children whose mothers had used thalidomide during pregnancy.

Thalidomide

Thalidomide contains an asymmetric centre that gives rise to two optical isomers: R-thalidomide and S-thalidomide. The thalidomide tablets prescribed by doctors in the 1950s contained a racemic mixture of the isomers. The R-isomer was found to be effective in treating morning sickness and was also found to be an effective sedative. In contrast, the S-isomer was found to have none of the therapeutic effects attributed to the R-isomer, and was responsible for the limb deformities and other severe birth defects observed in children whose mothers had used thalidomide during pregnancy.

### Citalopram

The compound citalopram is an effective treatment for depression, and is administered in the form of tablets containing a racemic mixture of optical isomers. The therapeutic properties of citalopram are due solely to one isomer whose shape allows it to bond with receptor sites in the body. The binding of citalopram then signals an increase in the production of serotonin, a neurotransmitter found to be lacking in the brain tissue of people suffering from depression.

Citalopram

### Exercise 4.6E

1. The compound thalidomide has been found to be an effective treatment for several types of cancer. It contains an asymmetric centre and is administered in the form of tablets containing a racemic mixture of isomers. (a) Explain what is meant by the term *racemic mixture*. (b) Draw the structure of thalidomide and use an asterisk (*) to identify the location of the asymmetric centre in the structure. (c) Suggest, in terms of molecular shape, why only one isomer may be responsible for the therapeutic effects of thalidomide.

2. One optical isomer of the compound citalopram is responsible for its ability to treat severe depression. (a) Draw the structure of citalopram and use an asterisk (*) to identify the location of the asymmetric centre in the structure. (b) Suggest, in terms of molecular shape, why only one isomer is responsible for the therapeutic effects of citalopram.

### Before moving to the next section, check that you are able to:

- Explain, in terms of structure, why one optical isomer is often solely responsible for the therapeutic effects of a compound.

# 4.7 Carbonyl Compounds

**CONNECTIONS**

- Millions of tons of formaldehyde, acetone and other carbonyl compounds are produced each year by the chemical industry. They are used as solvents and as feedstock for the production of other chemicals.
- Many natural aromas are due to the presence of carbonyl compounds such as carvone (spearmint), vanillin (vanilla) and cinnamaldehyde (cinnamon) in plants.

The term carbonyl compound is used to describe a compound that contains a carbonyl (C=O) functional group bonded to one or more alkyl groups.

Carbonyl compounds
(R and R' are alkyl groups)

## Structure and Properties

**In this section we are learning to:**

- Classify carbonyl compounds as aldehydes and ketones.
- Account for the physical properties of carbonyl compounds in terms of bonding and structure.
- Use systematic (IUPAC) rules to name carbonyl compounds.

### Aldehydes

The term **aldehyde** refers to *a compound that contains a carbonyl (C=O) group in the form of a -CHO functional group.* Simple aldehydes are represented by the general formula RCHO where R represents an alkyl group.

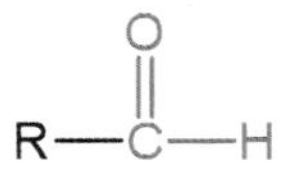

aldehyde
RCHO

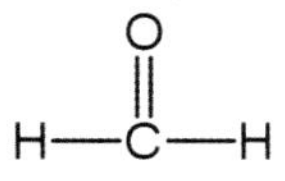

methanal (n=1)
HCHO

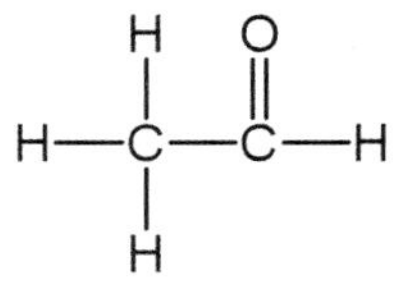

ethanal (n=2)
$CH_3CHO$

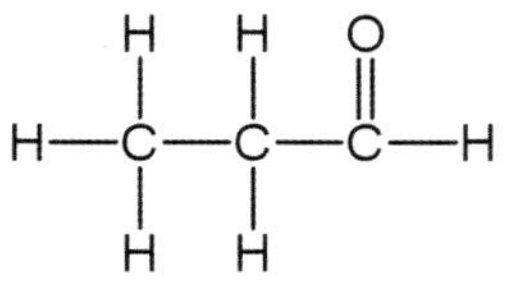

propanal (n=3)
$CH_3CH_2CHO$

The molecular formulas of simple aldehydes are obtained by setting n = 1, 2, 3 ... in the general formula $C_nH_{2n}O$.

In larger aldehydes the alkyl group (R) gives rise to structural isomers. For example, the aldehydes butanal and 2-methylpropanal are structural isomers.

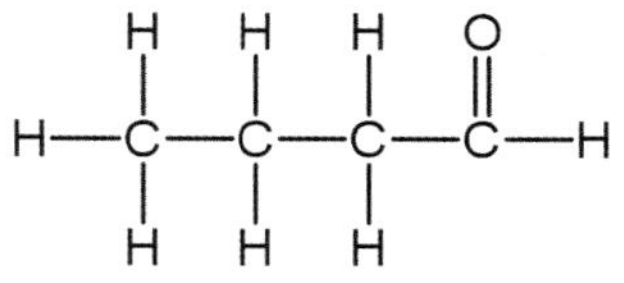

butanal
$CH_3CH_2CH_2CHO$

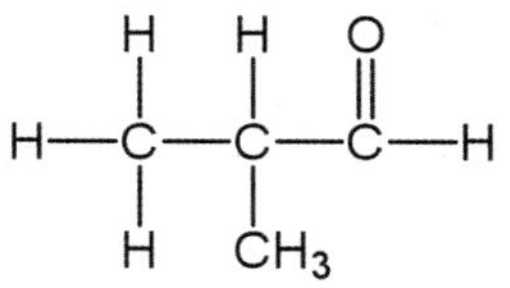

2-methylpropanal
$CH_3CH(CH_3)CHO$

**Exercise 4.7A**

1. Deduce the structures of all possible aldehydes with the molecular formula, $C_5H_{10}O$.
2. Deduce the number of aldehydes with the molecular formula $C_6H_{12}O$.

### Ketones

The term **ketone** refers to *a compound that contains a carbonyl (C=O) group in the form of a RCOR' functional group where R and R' each represent an alkyl group.* The molecular formulas of simple ketones are obtained by setting n = 3, 4, 5 ... in the general formula $C_nH_{2n}O$.

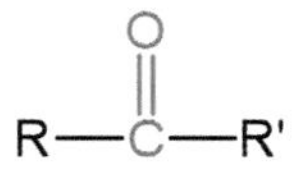

ketone
RCOR'

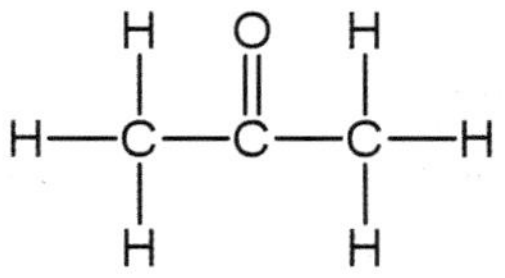

propanone (n=3)
$CH_3COCH_3$

butanone (n=4)
$CH_3CH_2COCH_3$

In larger ketones the position of the carbonyl (C=O) group within the carbon chain gives rise to structural isomers. For example, the ketones pentan-2-one and pentan-3-one are structural isomers.

pentan-2-one
$CH_3COCH_2CH_2CH_3$

pentan-3-one
$CH_3CH_2COCH_2CH_3$

Simple aldehydes and ketones with the same number of carbon atoms are structural isomers as they are both obtained from the general formula $C_nH_{2n}O$.

*Structural isomers with formula $C_3H_6O$:*

propanal, $CH_3CH_2CHO$
(aldehyde isomer)

propanone, $CH_3COCH_3$
(ketone isomer)

### Exercise 4.7B

1.  Deduce the structures of all possible ketones that are isomers of pentanal, $CH_3CH_2CH_2CH_2CHO$.

2.  Deduce the number of ketones with the molecular formula $C_6H_{12}O$.

Before moving to the next section, check that you are able to:

• Distinguish aldehydes and ketones by the functional groups they contain.

• Use the general formula $C_nH_{2n}O$ to generate the formulas of simple aldehydes and ketones.

• Demonstrate that aldehydes and ketones with the same number of carbon atoms are structural isomers.

### Physical Properties

The carbonyl (C=O) bond has a significant dipole and gives rise to attractive dipole forces between molecules. In simple aldehydes (RCHO) and ketones (RCOR') the remainder of the molecule is composed of nonpolar alkyl groups as shown in Figure 1. As a result simple aldehydes and ketones experience a combination of attractive dipole forces and van der Waals attraction between neighbouring molecules.

carbonyl group
(polar)

alkyl group
(non-polar)

*Figure 1: The partitioning of butanal into polar (carbonyl) and nonpolar (alkyl) regions.*

As molar mass increases an increase in van der Waals attraction between neighbouring molecules results in higher melting and boiling points as illustrated by the sequence of simple aldehydes in Figure 2.

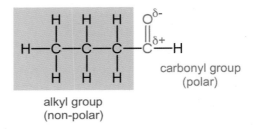

Van der Waals attraction increasing

| n | 1 | 2 | 3 | 4 |
|---|---|---|---|---|
| Formula | HCHO | $CH_3CHO$ | $C_2H_5CHO$ | $C_3H_7CHO$ |
| Boiling point (°C) | -19 | 21 | 49 | 75 |

Boiling point increasing

*Figure 2: The effect of van der Waals attraction on the boiling point of straight-chain aldehydes.*

The oxygen atom in the carbonyl group can also form hydrogen bonds with hydrogen atoms attached to electronegative (N, O and F) atoms in neighbouring molecules. As a result, aldehydes and ketones can form strong hydrogen bonds with solvents such as water as shown in Figure 3. The ability to form hydrogen bonds helps to explain why small carbonyl compounds such as ethanal, $CH_3CHO$ and propanone, $CH_3COCH_3$ are miscible with solvents such as water and ethanol.

As the alkyl groups in aldehydes and ketones get bigger, van der Waals attraction between neighbouring molecules dominates the other attractive forces between molecules to the extent that hexanal, $CH_3CH_2CH_2CH_2CH_2CHO$ will dissolve readily in nonpolar solvents such as hexane and is immiscible with water.

### Exercise 4.7C

1. Formaldehyde (methanal), HCHO is a colourless gas which is readily soluble in water. Explain why formaldehyde is soluble in water.

   *(CCEA January 2010)*

2. Explain why propanone, $CH_3COCH_3$ is much more soluble in water than heptan-2-one, $CH_3COCH_2CH_2CH_2CH_2CH_3$.

3. Acetoin is found in butter and is added to foods to give a buttery taste. Explain why acetoin is soluble in water.

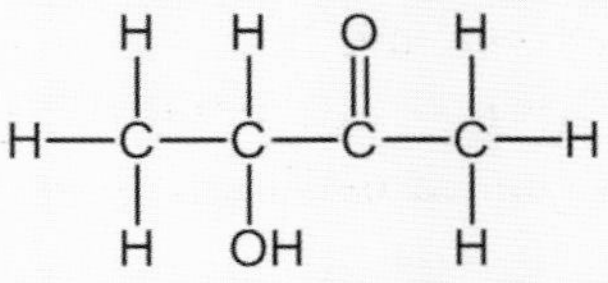

acetoin

*(CCEA May 2013)*

Before moving to the next section, check that you are able to:

- Describe the nature of the attractive forces between the molecules in aldehydes and ketones.
- Account for trends in the boiling points of aldehydes and ketones in terms of the attractive forces between molecules.
- Explain why aldehydes and ketones become less soluble in polar solvents such as water and ethanol as they get larger.

### Naming Aldehydes

The systematic (IUPAC) name for an aldehyde is based on the name of the parent straight-chain alkane. For example, the aldehyde pentanal is named using the prefix *pentan* as its structure is based on the chain of five carbon atoms in pentane, $CH_3CH_2CH_2CH_2CH_3$. The suffix *al* is then added to indicate that the compound is an aldehyde.

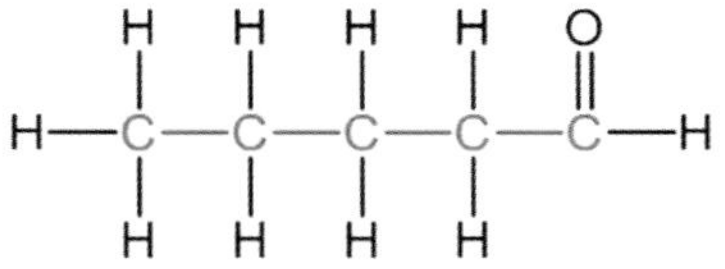

pentanal

The compounds 2-methylbutanal and 3-methylbutanal are structural isomers of pentanal. Both are named as butanals as their structure is based on the four carbon chain in butane, $CH_3CH_2CH_2CH_3$. The prefix *2-methyl* or *3-methyl* is then used to locate the methyl group on the carbon chain.

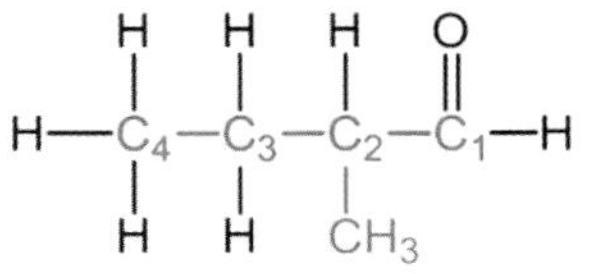

2-methylbutanal 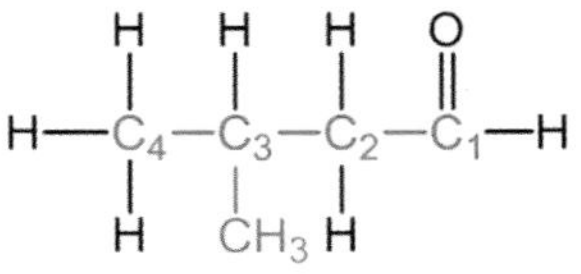        3-methylbutanal

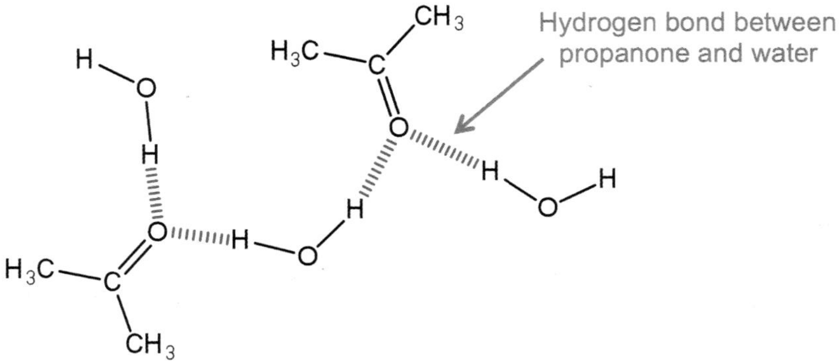

Hydrogen bond between propanone and water

*Figure 3: The formation of hydrogen bonds between propanone molecules and water molecules in aqueous propanone.*

The presence of additional groups on the carbon chain is then described by adding an additional prefix for each type of group. In 2-amino-3-hydroxybutanal the prefixes *2-amino* and *3-hydroxy* are used to locate an amino (-NH$_2$) group on the second carbon in the chain and a hydroxyl (-OH) group on the third carbon in the chain. As in other types of compound the prefixes are given in alphabetical order. In 3,3-dimethylbutanal the locations of the methyl groups are described by using the number prefix *di* to construct the prefix dimethyl.

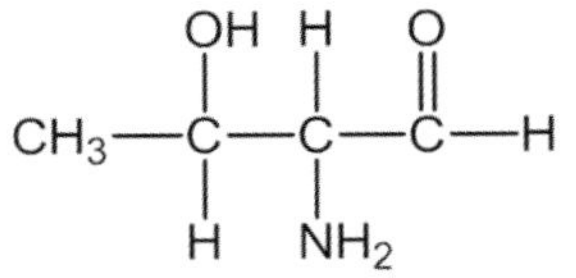

2-amino-3-hydroxybutanal 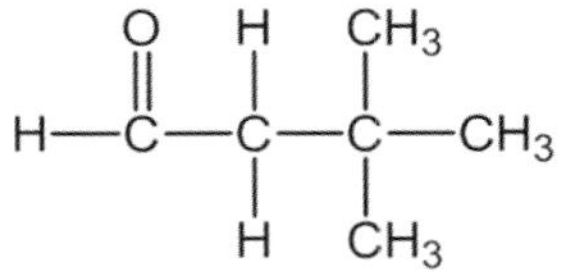    3,3-dimethylbutanal

An **enal** is *an aldehyde that contains a C=C bond in the carbon chain.* The compound 3-methylbut-2-enal is an enal and is a butenal as its structure is based on a butene. The prefix 3-methyl is used to locate the methyl group on the third carbon atom and the suffix *2-enal* is used to locate the C=C bond between the second pair of carbon atoms in the carbon chain.

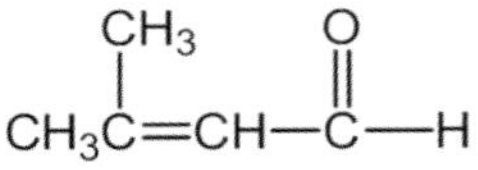

3-methylbut-2-enal

A **dienal** is *an aldehyde that contains two C=C bonds in the carbon chain.* The name of a dienal is based on the name of the parent diene. For example, hexa-2,4-dienal is named as a hexadienal as its structure is based on a hexadiene. The suffix *2,4-dienal* is used to locate C=C bonds between second and fourth pairs of carbon atoms in the carbon chain.

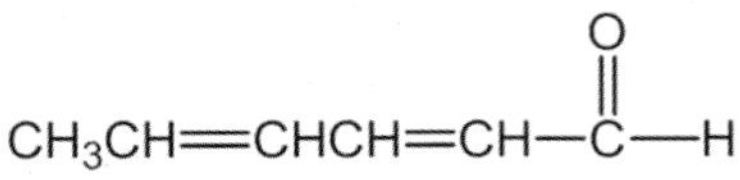

hexa-2,4-dienal

**Rules** for naming aldehydes (including enals):

1. The name of the compound is is based on the name of the parent alkane (suffix *al*) or alkene (suffix *enal*).

2. The number of C=C bonds in an enal is indicated by using the number prefixes *di, tri, tetra, ...* to generate suffixes such as *dienal* and *trienal*.

3. The location of each C=C bond is then added to produce suffixes such as *3-enal* and *3,5-dienal* where the carbon atoms are numbered from the aldehyde group.

4. The location of additional functional groups is then described by adding additional prefixes in alphabetical order.

**Exercise 4.7D**

1. Name the following aldehydes.

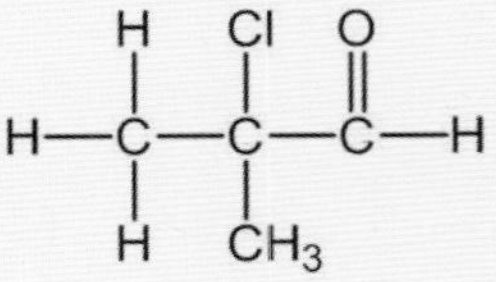

   (a) 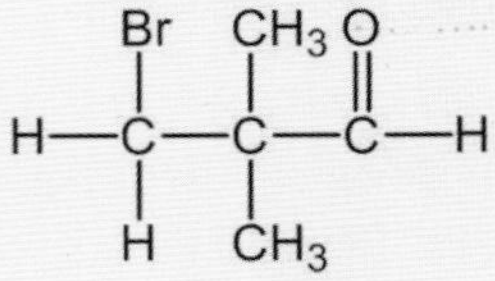                          (b)

2. Draw the structure of (a) 2-ethylbutanal and (b) 2-bromo-4-methylhexanal.

3. Name the following enals.

   (a)

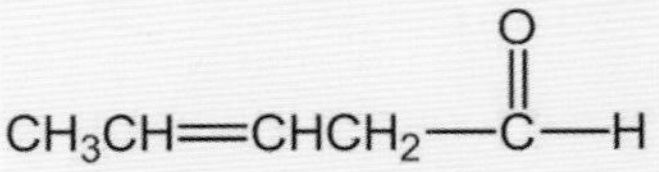

   (b)

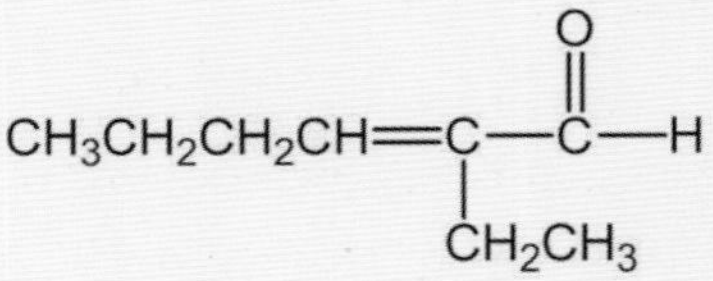

4. Name the following enals.

   (a)

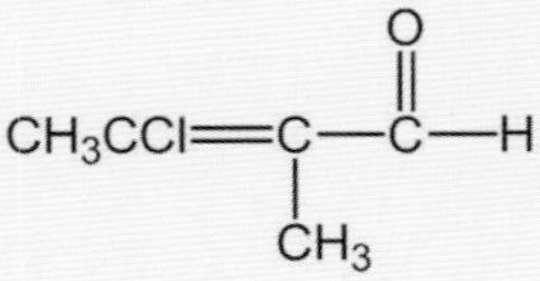

   (b)

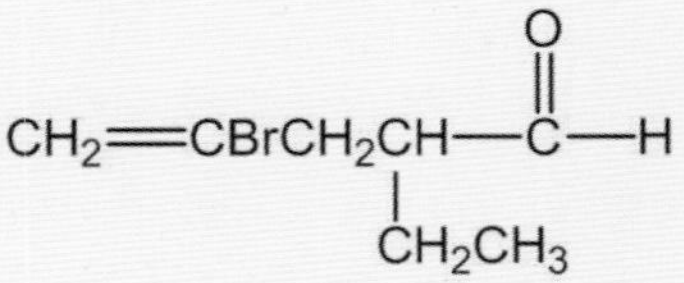

5. Draw the structural formula for all possible enals with the formula $C_4H_6O$. Label each isomer with its systematic name.

---

Before moving to the next section, check that you are able to:

- Use systematic rules to name aldehydes, enals and dienals.

---

### Naming Ketones

The systematic (IUPAC) name of a ketone is based on the name of the parent straight-chain alkane. The suffix *one* is added to indicate that the compound is a ketone. For example, the isomers pentan-2-one and pentan-3-one are named as pentanones as their structure is based on the chain of five carbon atoms in pentane, $CH_3CH_2CH_2CH_2CH_3$.

pentan-2-one

pentan-3-one

The location of the carbonyl (C=O) group within the carbon chain is described by the numbered suffix *2-one* or *3-one* where the carbon atoms are numbered from the end that generates the lowest number prefix.

pentan-2-one ✓

pentan-4-one ✗

---

The location of groups attached to the carbon chain is then described by adding additional prefixes in alphabetical order. For example, in *4-hydroxy-3-methylbutanone* the prefixes *4-hydroxy* and *3-methyl* are used to locate a hydroxyl group on the fourth carbon and a methyl group on the third carbon in the chain. The compound is named as a butanone as it is based on the four carbon chain in butane. When naming a butanone the location of the carbonyl group is not specified as the carbonyl can only be located on the second carbon.

4-hydroxy-3-methylbutanone

1-bromo-3,3-dimethylbutanone

An **enone** is *a ketone that contains a C=C bond in the carbon chain.* The compound 1-bromobut-3-en-2-one is an example of an enone. It is named as a butenone as its structure is based on a butene. The suffix *3-en-2-one* is used to locate the C=C bond between the third pair of carbon atoms and the carbonyl (C=O) group at the second carbon in the chain. The prefix *1-bromo* is then added to locate bromine on the first carbon atom in the chain.

1-bromobut-3-en-2-one

A **dienone** is *a ketone that contains two C=C bonds in the carbon chain.* The compound 6-bromohexa-3,5-dien-2-one is named as a hexadienone as its structure is based on a hexadiene. The suffix *3,5-dien-2-one* is used to locate C=C bonds between the third and fifth pair of carbon atoms and a C=O group at the second carbon in the chain. The prefix *6-bromo* is then added to locate bromine on the sixth carbon atom in the chain.

6-bromohexa-3,5-dien-2-one

**Rules** for naming ketones (including enones):

1. The name of the compound is based on the name of the parent alkane (suffix *one*) or alkene (suffix *enone*).

2. The location of the carbonyl group is described using a suffix such as *2-one* or *en-2-one* where the carbon atoms are numbered from the end that gives the lowest number in the suffix.

3. The number of C=C bonds in an enone is indicated by using the number prefixes *di*, *tri*, *tetra* ... to generate suffixes such as *dien-2-one* and *trien-2-one*.

4. The location of each C=C bond is then added to produce suffixes such as *3-en-2-one* and *3,5-dien-2-one*.

5. The location of additional functional groups is then described by adding additional prefixes in alphabetical order.

**Exercise 4.7E**

1. Acetoin is found in butter and is added to foods to give a buttery taste. State the systematic name for acetoin.

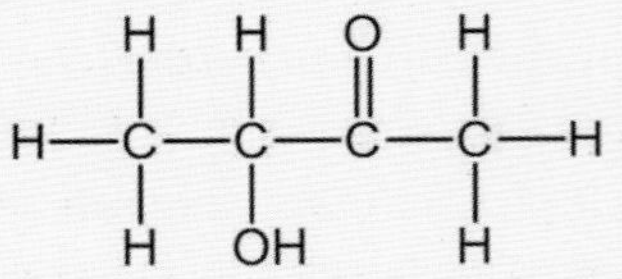

acetoin

*(CCEA May 2013)*

2. Name the following ketones.

(a)

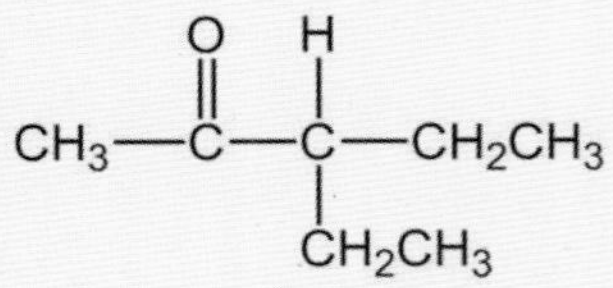

(b)

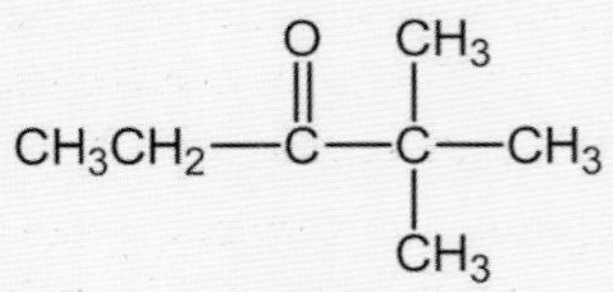

3. Draw the structure of (a) 1-chlorobutanone and (b) 3-chloro-3-methylbutanone.

4. Name the following enones.

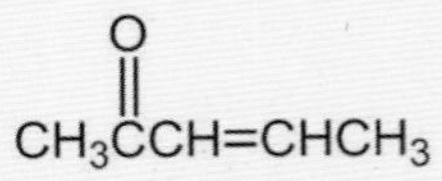

(a) 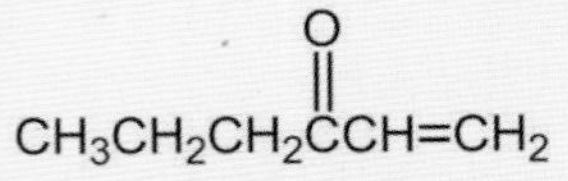  (b)

5. Name the following enones.

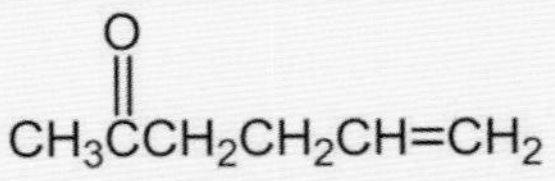

(a) 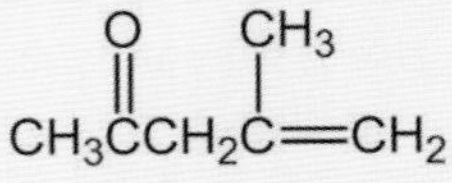  (b)

6. Draw the structures of (a) 5-methylhex-4-en-3-one and (b) 3-ethylhex-5-en-2-one.

Before moving to the next section, check that you are able to:

• Use systematic rules to name ketones, enones and dienones.

## Preparation

**In this section we are learning to:**

• Deduce the structure of the product when an alcohol is oxidised to a carbonyl compound, and write an equation for the reaction.

• Account for the observations when an alcohol is oxidised in terms of oxidation and reduction.

Aldehydes (RCHO) are prepared in the laboratory by partial oxidation of the corresponding primary alcohol (RCH$_2$OH).

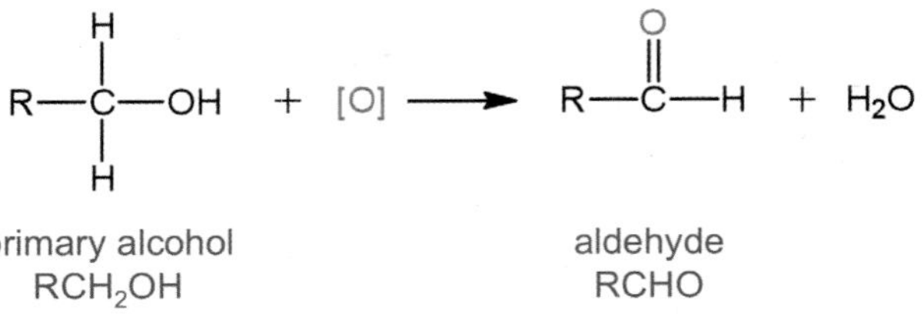

primary alcohol  aldehyde
RCH$_2$OH  RCHO

The aldehyde is formed by adding the alcohol to acidified potassium dichromate and distilling the mixture. If the mixture is instead refluxed the alcohol is completely oxidised to the corresponding carboxylic acid (RCOOH).

Acidified potassium dichromate solution contains dichromate ion, Cr$_2$O$_7^{2-}$. The dichromate ion contains chromium in an oxidation state of +6 and gives the solution its characteristic orange colour. As the reaction proceeds the orange colour of dichromate ion is replaced by the green colour of aqueous chromium(III) ions, $Cr^{3+}$ as chromium is reduced from an oxidation state of +6 in dichromate ion, to an oxidation state of +3.

$$Cr_2O_7^{2-}(aq) \ + \ 14H^+(aq) \ + \ 6e^-$$

orange solution

$$\rightarrow \ 2Cr^{3+}(aq) \ + \ 7H_2O(l)$$

green solution

Ketones (RCOR') are prepared in the laboratory by the partial oxidation of the corresponding secondary alcohol (RCH(OH)R').

secondary alcohol
RCH(OH)R'

ketone
RCOR'

Once formed the ketone cannot be oxidised further. As a result, the ketone can be formed by adding the alcohol to acidified potassium dichromate and refluxing the mixture. Oxidation of the alcohol by dichromate ion is again accompanied by a colour change from orange to green as the chromium in dichromate ion is reduced to form aqueous chromium(III) ions.

The oxidation of an alcohol to form the corresponding aldehyde or ketone can also be carried out using acidified potassium permanganate, $KMnO_4(aq)$. As the reaction proceeds the characteristic purple colour of permanganate ion, $MnO_4^-$ is replaced by a colourless solution containing manganese(II) ion, $Mn^{2+}$ as the manganese in permanganate ion is reduced from an oxidation state of +7 to an oxidation state of +2.

$$MnO_4^-(aq) \ + \ 8H^+(aq) \ + \ 5e^-$$

purple solution

$$\rightarrow \ Mn^{2+}(aq) \ + \ 4H_2O(l)$$

colourless solution

**Exercise 4.7F**

1. Which one of the following alcohols does not undergo oxidation when treated with warm acidified potassium dichromate(VI)?

   A  3-methylpentan-1-ol
   B  3-methylpentan-2-ol
   C  2-methylpentan-2-ol
   D  2-methylpentan-1-ol

   *(CCEA January 2007)*

2. (a) Write an equation for the reaction that occurs when a mixture of butan-1-ol and acidified potassium dichromate is distilled. (b) Explain why the mixture is distilled. (c) Draw and name the organic product of the reaction. (d) Explain the colour change that occurs in terms of the ions present in the solution.

3. (a) Draw and name the alcohol used to form 2-methylpentan-3-one by refluxing with acidified potassium permanganate. (b) Write an equation for the reaction.

   $CH_3CHCCH_2CH_3$    2-methylpentan-3-one
   $|$
   $CH_3$

4. Pyruvic acid, $CH_3COCOOH$ can be prepared by the oxidation of lactic acid, $CH_3CH(OH)COOH$ using silver oxide suspended in water. (a) Write the formula for silver oxide. (b) Write the equation for the formation of pyruvic acid from lactic acid using [O] to represent the oxidising agent.

   *(CCEA January 2012)*

Before moving to the next section, check that you are able to:

- Deduce the structure of the aldehyde formed when a primary alcohol is oxidised and use [O] to write an equation for the reaction.

- Deduce the structure of the ketone formed when a secondary alcohol is oxidised and use [O] to write an equation for the reaction.

- Account for the colour change observed when an alcohol is oxidised by acidified dichromate solution, and acidified permanganate solution, in terms of oxidation and reduction.

## Distinguishing Aldehydes and Ketones

**In this section we are learning to:**

- Describe the use of oxidising agents to distinguish aldehydes and ketones.

Oxidising agents such as acidified dichromate, acidified permanganate, Tollens' reagent and Fehling's solution can be used to distinguish between aldehydes and ketones.

### Reaction with Acidified Dichromate

When a mixture containing an aldehyde and acidified potassium dichromate is heated gently, the solution changes colour from orange to green as the aldehyde is oxidised to the corresponding carboxylic acid.

$$R-\overset{\overset{\displaystyle O}{\|}}{C}-H \ + \ [O] \ \longrightarrow \ R-\overset{\overset{\displaystyle O}{\|}}{C}-OH$$

aldehyde
RCHO

carboxylic acid
RCOOH

The colour change is shown in Figure 4 and occurs when the chromium in the dichromate ions, $Cr_2O_7^{2-}$ is reduced to form chromium(III) ion, $Cr^{3+}$.

$$Cr_2O_7^{2-}(aq) \ + \ 14H^+(aq) \ + \ 6e^-$$

orange solution

$$\rightarrow \ 2Cr^{3+}(aq) \ + \ 7H_2O(l)$$

green solution

In contrast, when a ketone is heated with acidified potassium dichromate, the mixture remains orange as the ketone cannot be oxidised further.

Hot water bath
(gentle heating)

*Figure 4: The colour change that occurs when an aldehyde is heated with acidified potassium dichromate.*

### Worked Example 4.7i

Describe how an acidified solution of potassium dichromate could be used to distinguish an aldehyde from a ketone.

*(Adapted from CCEA May 2011)*

### Strategy

- Describe how solutions of each compound are prepared and tested.
- State the result expected for each solution.

### Solution

Add acidified potassium dichromate to samples of the aldehyde and ketone in separate boiling tubes. Heat the mixtures gently using a water bath. The solution containing the aldehyde will change colour from orange to green. The solution containing the ketone will remain orange.

### Exercise 4.7G

1. Describe how an acidified solution of potassium dichromate could be used to distinguish propanal from propanone.

*(Adapted from CCEA May 2011)*

**Before moving to the next section, check that you are able to:**

- Explain how acidified potassium dichromate solution could be used to distinguish between an aldehyde and a ketone.
- Explain any observations in terms of oxidation and reduction.

### Using Tollens' Reagent

Aldehydes and ketones can also be distinguished by heating with Tollens' reagent; a colourless alkaline solution containing silver(I) ions, $Ag^+$ that behaves as a mild oxidising agent. When a mixture of an aldehyde and Tollens' reagent is heated gently using a water bath, the aldehyde is oxidised, and the silver(I) ions from Tollens' reagent are reduced to form a thin layer of silver on the side of the test tube as shown in Figure 5.

*Oxidation of an aldehyde:*
$RCHO + 3OH^- \rightarrow RCOO^- + 2H_2O + 2e^-$

*Reduction of silver(I) ion:*
$Ag^+ + e^- \rightarrow Ag$

In contrast, when a mixture of a ketone and Tollens' reagent is heated, the mixture remains colourless and a 'silver mirror' does not form as shown in Figure 5.

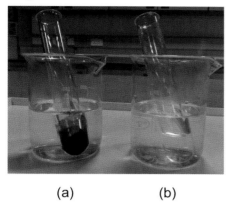

(a)                    (b)

*Figure 5: (a) Formation of a 'silver mirror' when an aldehyde is heated with Tollens' reagent. (b) The solution remains colourless when a ketone is heated with Tollens' reagent.*

### Worked Example 4.7ii

Butanal is a structural isomer of butanone. Describe, giving practical details, how you would carry out a chemical test to distinguish between samples of butanal and butanone.

*(CCEA January 2011)*

### Strategy

- Describe how solutions of each compound are prepared and tested.
- State the result expected for each solution.

### Solution

Add Tollens' reagent to samples of butanal (an aldehyde) and butanone (a ketone) in separate boiling tubes. Heat the mixtures gently using a water bath. When the mixture containing butanal is heated a silver mirror forms on the side of the boiling tube. When the mixture containing butanone is heated a silver mirror does not form.

### Exercise 4.7H

1. The following diagram shows how to distinguish between propanal and propanone. (a) State the metal ion present in Tollens' reagent. (b) State the functional group present in both propanal and propanone. (c) Explain why hot water is used. (d) State what is observed in separate experiments with (i) propanal and (ii) propanone.

*To speed up the Reaction*

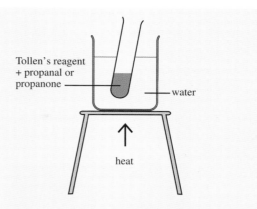

*(CCEA January 2007)*

2. Formaldehyde (methanal), HCHO is a reducing agent as illustrated by its reaction with Tollens' reagent. (a) Write an equation for the oxidation of formaldehyde using [O] to represent the oxidising agent. (b) Write the half-equation for the reduction of silver ions in Tollens' reagent. (c) What is observed during this reaction?

*(CCEA January 2010)*

3. Methanoic acid, HCOOH is a strong reducing agent as it can behave as an aldehyde. (a) Giving experimental details and observations describe the reaction between methanoic acid and Tollens' reagent. (b) Write the ionic equation for the reduction of the metal ion present in Tollens' reagent.

*(CCEA January 2014)*

---

Before moving to the next section, check that you are able to:

- Explain how Tollens' reagent can be used to distinguish between aldehydes and ketones.
- Explain any observations, including the formation of a silver mirror, in terms of oxidation and reduction.

---

### Reaction with Fehling's Solution

Aldehydes and ketones can also be distinguished by heating with Fehling's solution; an alkaline solution containing copper(II) ions, $Cu^{2+}$. The aqueous copper(II) ions give the solution a characteristic blue colour. When an aldehyde is heated with Fehling's solution the aldehyde is oxidised and copper(II) ions in the solution are reduced to form a red precipitate of copper(I) oxide, $Cu_2O$ as shown in Figure 6.

Oxidation of an aldehyde:

$$RCHO + 3OH^- \rightarrow RCOO^- + 2H_2O + 2e^-$$

Reduction of aqueous copper(II) ion:

$$2Cu^{2+} + 2OH^- + 2e^- \rightarrow Cu_2O + H_2O$$

In contrast, when a ketone is heated with Fehling's solution the ketone is not oxidised, a precipitate does not form, and the solution remains blue as shown in Figure 6.

(a)                    (b)

*Figure 6: (a) Formation of a red precipitate when an aldehyde is heated with Fehling's solution. (b) The solution remains blue when a ketone is heated with Fehling's solution.*

### Worked Example 4.7iii

Butanal is a structural isomer of butanone. Describe, giving practical details, how you would carry out a chemical test to distinguish between samples of butanal and butanone.

*(CCEA January 2011)*

### Strategy

- Describe how solutions of each compound are prepared and tested.
- State the result expected for each solution.

### Solution

Add Fehling's solution to samples of butanal (an aldehyde) and butanone (a ketone) in separate boiling tubes. Heat the solutions gently using a water bath. When the solution containing butanal is heated a red precipitate forms. When the mixture containing butanone is heated no change is observed.

### Exercise 4.7I

1. Pheromones are used as a chemical communication system by insects and were first isolated and identified in 1959. The isomers A and B are pheromones. (a) What is the systematic name for A? (b) Describe the use of Fehling's solution to distinguish between A and B stating any observations you would make. (c) The cabbage white butterfly can detect as little as $1.0 \times 10^{-13}$ g of B. Calculate the number of molecules in this amount of B.

$$CH_3CH_2CH_2COCH_3 \qquad CH(CH_3)_2CH_2CHO$$

A                              B

*(Adapted from CCEA May 2007)*

2. Glucose and fructose are both examples of 'reducing sugars'. (a) Name two functional groups present in both glucose and fructose. (b) Suggest why glucose and fructose are both reducing agents and state what would be observed with Fehling's solution. (c) Write the half-equation for the reduction that occurs when glucose reacts with Fehling's solution.

glucose

fructose

*(Adapted from CCEA May 2012)*

3. Which one of the following compounds is optically active and incapable of reducing Fehling's solution?

A  $CH_3CH(CH_3)CH_2CHO$
B  $CH_3CH(C_2H_5)COCH_3$
C  $CH_3CHClCH_2CHO$
D  $CH_3CH(CH_3)COCH_3$

*(CCEA January 2012)*

4. Some Scotch whiskies have the fragrance of cut grass. This smell is attributed to *cis* hex-3-enal, an unsaturated aldehyde. (a) Suggest a structure for *cis* hex-3-enal. (b) What would be observed if *cis* hex-3-enal is warmed with Fehling's solution.

*(CCEA May 2009)*

Before moving to the next section, check that you are able to:

- Explain how Fehling's solution can be used to distinguish between an aldehyde and a ketone.
- Explain any observations, including the formation of a red precipitate, in terms of oxidation and reduction.

## Reactions

**In this section we are learning to:**

- Describe the reactions of carbonyl compounds with reducing agents.
- Describe the addition of HCN to carbonyl compounds.

The oxidation of an alcohol to an aldehyde or ketone can be reversed by reacting aldehydes and ketones with lithium aluminium hydride, $LiAlH_4$; a reducing agent referred to as 'lithal'. When an aldehyde is refluxed with a solution of lithal in dry ether, the aldehyde is reduced to the corresponding primary alcohol.

aldehyde
RCHO

primary alcohol
$RCH_2OH$

Reducing agents such as lithal are a source of hydrogen, and can be simply represented by a hydrogen atom, [H] when writing chemical equations. The equation for the reduction of an aldehyde reveals that two equivalents of hydrogen (2[H]) are needed to reduce the aldehyde to the corresponding alcohol.

Similarly, when a ketone (RCOR') is refluxed with a solution of lithal in dry ether, the ketone is reduced to the corresponding secondary alcohol (RCH(OH)R').

ketone
RCOR'

secondary alcohol
RCH(OH)R'

Again two equivalents of hydrogen (2[H]) are needed to reduce the ketone to the corresponding alcohol.

### Exercise 4.7J

1. (a) Using [H] to represent the reducing agent write an equation for the reduction of butanone.
   (b) Write the systematic name of the product.

   *(Adapted from CCEA May 2011)*

2. Name the organic product formed when hexan-2-one reacts with lithal, $LiAlH_4$.

   *(Adapted from CCEA May 2008)*

3. Draw the structure of each isomer with the molecular formula $C_3H_6O$ that can be reduced by lithal to form an alcohol.

4. Which one of the following alcohols, all with molecular formula $C_5H_{12}O$, could **not** be produced by the reduction of an aldehyde or a ketone?

   A  2-methylbutan-1-ol
   B  2-methylbutan-2-ol
   C  3-methylbutan-1-ol
   D  3-methylbutan-2-ol

   *(CCEA January 2009)*

5. Butanone can be reduced using lithal. The product is optically inactive and dehydrates to give a mixture of but-1-ene and but-2-ene.
   (a) Using [H] to represent lithal, write a balanced equation for the reduction. (b) Name the product. (c) Give the meaning of the term *optically inactive*. (d) Suggest why the product is optically inactive.

   *(CCEA January 2011)*

6. Cholesterol is concentrated in the brain and spinal cord. It is present both as the free alcohol and as esters of organic acids.

   cholesterol

   (a) Cholesterol is a monohydric alcohol whereas glycerol is trihydric. Suggest the meaning of the term *monohydric*. (b) Explain whether cholesterol is a primary, secondary or tertiary alcohol. (c) Cholesterol can be converted to cholestan-3-one and then reduced as shown by the following flow scheme. Name the reagents A, B and C. (d) Cholesterol is not very soluble in water and cholestan-3-one is less soluble than cholesterol. Explain these solubilities.

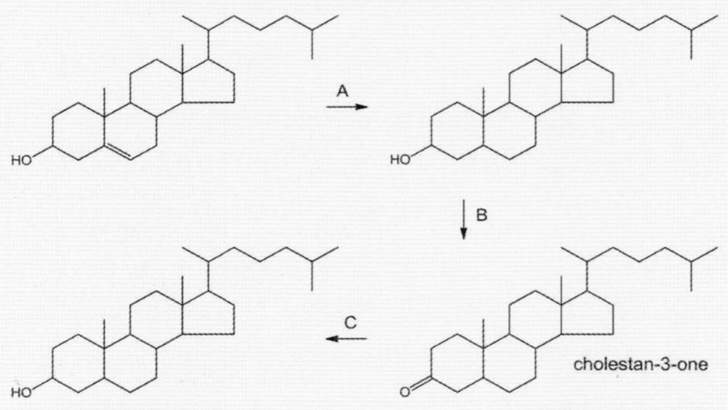

cholestan-3-one

*(CCEA May 2014)*

**Before moving to the next section, check that you are able to:**

- Deduce the product formed when a carbonyl compound is reduced to the corresponding alcohol and use [H] to write an equation for the reaction.

## Addition of HCN

Refluxing an aldehyde or ketone with an aqueous solution of sodium cyanide, NaCN and a small amount of sulfuric acid produces the corresponding hydroxynitrile.

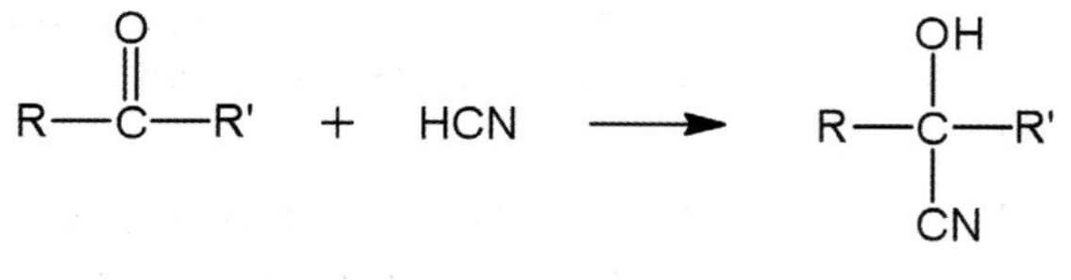

aldehyde/ketone
RCOR'

hydroxynitrile
RC(OH)(CN)R'

The hydroxynitrile contains a hydroxyl (-OH) group and a nitrile (-CN) group attached to the same carbon atom. The mechanism for the reaction is shown in Figure 7. In the first step cyanide ion, CN⁻ behaves as a nucleophile by using a lone pair of electrons to form a coordinate bond with the electron deficient carbon atom belonging to the carbonyl (C=O) group. As the coordinate bond forms, the

$\pi$-bond in the carbonyl (C=O) group undergoes heterolytic fission, with both electrons being given to the oxygen to form an anion.

The anion formed in the first step then reacts with the hydrogen ion from HCN to form the hydroxynitrile. This step is much faster than the first as the addition of a hydrogen ion (H⁺) does not involve the breaking of bonds, and is aided by the attraction between oppositely charged ions. As a result, the first step is the rate determining step (RDS), and the rate equation for the reaction involves only those species involved in the first step.

*Rate equation for the addition of HCN:*
Rate = k [RCOR'][CN⁻]

The addition of HCN to a carbonyl group is an example of a **nucleophilic addition** reaction as it involves cyanide ion, CN⁻ acting as a nucleophile, and results in the addition of HCN.

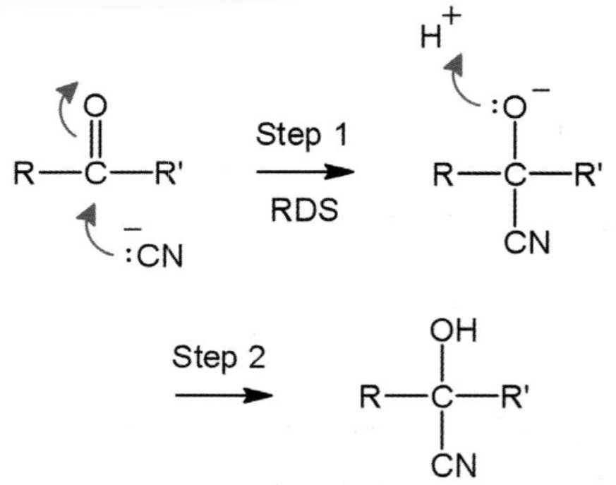

*Figure 7: Mechanism for the addition of HCN to the carbonyl (C=O) group in an aldehyde or ketone (RCOR').*

**Rules** for naming hydroxynitriles:

Add the suffix *nitrile* to the name of the parent alkane. Include the carbon atom in the nitrile (-CN) group when naming the parent alkane.

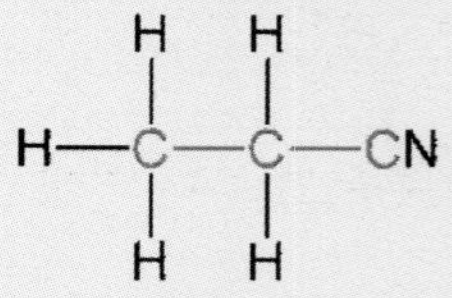

propanenitrile

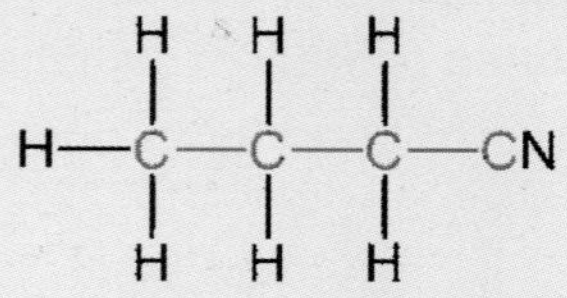

butanenitrile

Use a numbered prefix to describe the location of the hydroxyl (-OH) group on the carbon chain.

Number the carbon atoms from the nitrile group.

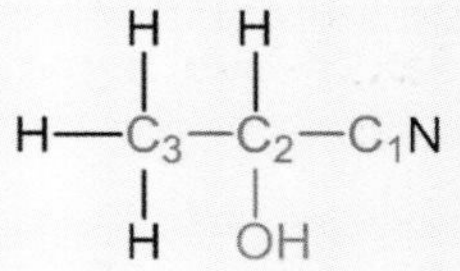

2-hydroxypropanenitrile 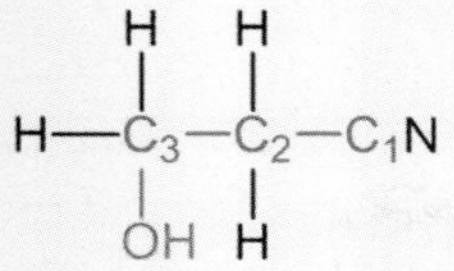  3-hydroxypropanenitrile

## Worked Example 4.7iv

2-hydroxypropanenitrile is formed by the reaction of hydrogen cyanide with ethanal. Draw a flow scheme to represent the mechanism for this reaction.

*(CCEA January 2006)*

### Solution

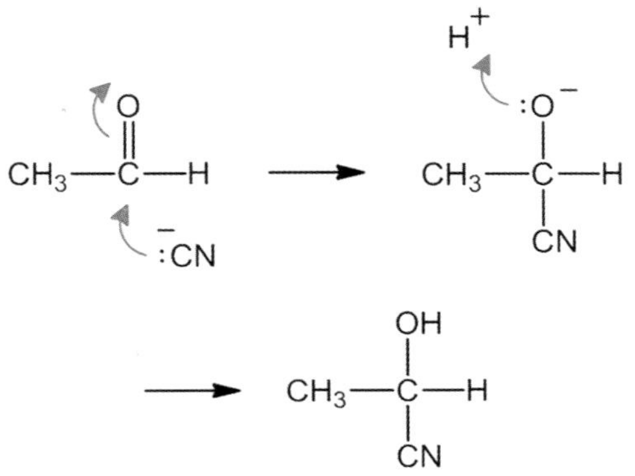

## Exercise 4.7K

1. (a) Explain why a carbonyl group is susceptible to attack by a nucleophile. (b) Draw a flow scheme to show the mechanism for the reaction of hydrogen cyanide with methanal.

*(CCEA January 2013)*

2. Which one of the following statements about the addition of hydrogen cyanide to the carbonyl group in an aldehyde or ketone is correct?

   A Cyanide ion acts as an electrophile.

   B The CO bond is polar before the cyanide ion approaches.

   C The oxygen atom in the intermediate has an incomplete octet.

   D The hydroxynitrile is nonpolar.

*(Adapted from CCEA May 2003)*

3. Draw a flow scheme to show the mechanism for the reaction between the sugar fructose (RCOR') and hydrogen cyanide.

*(CCEA May 2012)*

### Additional Problems

4. Butanone reacts with hydrogen cyanide to form a product that contains an asymmetric centre.

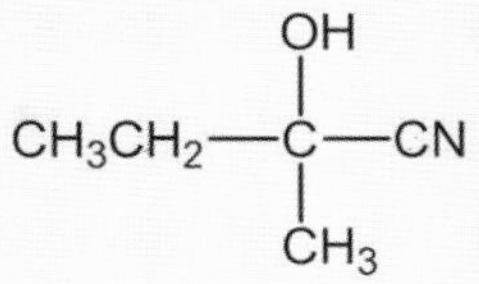

   (a) Write the systematic name of the product. (b) What type of stereoisomerism is shown by the product? (c) Draw the 3D representations of the stereoisomers. (d) Name the mechanism for the reaction. (e) Draw the mechanism for this reaction.

*(CCEA January 2011)*

5. The isomers of citral have a strong lemon odour and are found in the oils of several plants. (a) How are the isomers of citral related? (b) Draw the structure of the organic product formed when citral reacts with (b) LiAlH₄, (c) HCN and (d) an oxidising agent.

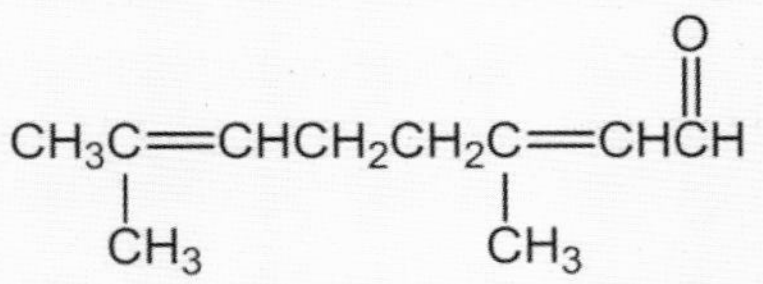

Before moving to the next section, check that you are able to:

- Draw and explain the mechanism for the addition of HCN to a carbonyl group.
- Name the hydroxynitrile formed by the addition of HCN to a simple aldehyde (RCHO) or ketone (RCOR').
- Explain why the addition of HCN to a carbonyl group is an example of nucleophilic addition.

## Identifying Aldehydes and Ketones

In this section we are learning to:

- Identify aldehydes and ketones by forming solid derivatives.

The identity of a particular aldehyde or ketone can be deduced by making a solid derivative of the compound; a solid compound 'derived from' the original compound by one or more chemical reactions. The identity of the original compound is then determined by comparing the melting point of the derivative to the melting point of derivatives made from known compounds. With the advent of chemical instrumentation, the original compound can also be identified by combining information from an instrumental analysis of the compound as described in Figure 8.

| Identifying a compound by derivative formation | Identifying a compound by instrumental analysis |
| --- | --- |
| Make a derivative of the unknown compound | Use the mass spectrum of the unknown compound to deduce: • the molecular mass • molecular fragments |
| Determine the melting point of the derivative | |
| | Use the infra-red spectrum of the unknown to deduce: • specific bonds present • functional groups present |
| Use the melting point to identify the derivative | |
| Identify the compound used to make the derivative | Determine the structure of the unknown compound |

*Figure 8: Identification of a compound by (a) making a derivative of the compound and (b) instrumental analysis of the compound.*

### Making Hydrazone Derivatives

The compound 2,4-dinitrophenylhydrazine (2,4-DNPH) reacts with aldehydes and ketones to form the corresponding 2,4-dinitrophenylhydrazone as shown in Figure 9.

| Structural formula for 2,4-dinitrophenylhydrazine | Skeletal formulas for 2,4-dinitrophenylhydrazine |
| --- | --- |

The formation of a hydrazone derivative is an example of a **condensation reaction** as a molecule of water is formed when the reactants combine to form the product.

The hydrazone derivatives formed by aldehydes and ketones are orange solids with melting points that can be determined using standard melting point apparatus as illustrated by Figure 10. If the hydrazone is pure it

will melt within a narrow range of temperature (typically 1–2 °C). Samples that contain impurities will melt over a broader range of temperature.

Having determined the melting point of the hydrazone, the identity of the aldehyde or ketone used to make the hydrazone can be confirmed by using data tables to compare the melting point of the hydrazone to the melting points of hydrazones made from a range of aldehydes and ketones.

### Worked Example 4.7v

Unknown ketones can be identified by reaction with 2,4-dinitrophenylhydrazine. (a) Draw the structure of the product formed when butanone reacts with 2,4-dinitrophenylhydrazine. (b) Describe the appearance of the organic product formed in the reaction. (c) Explain how the product can be used to confirm the identity of butanone.

*(Adapted from CCEA May 2011)*

### Solution

(a)

(b) An orange solid.

(c) The identity of butanone can be confirmed by comparing the melting point of the derivative formed in the reaction with the melting point of the 2,4-dinitrophenylhydrazine derivative of butanone given in data tables.

### Exercise 4.7L

1. Propanone reacts with 2,4-dinitrophenylhydrazine to form a solid derivative. (a) Draw the structure of the derivative. (b) Calculate the relative molecular mass of the derivative.

*(Adapted from CCEA May 2010)*

2. Which one of the following is a product formed between benzaldehyde, $C_6H_5CHO$ and 2,4-dinitrophenylhydrazine? *(continued)*

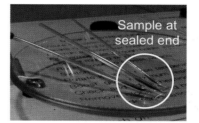

Figure 9: Forming a hydrazone derivative of an aldehyde or ketone.

A) $C_6H_5CHNNHC_6H_3(NO_2)_2$
B  $C_6H_5CH_2NNC_6H_3(NO_2)_2$
C  $C_6H_5CHNHNC_6H_3(NO_2)_2$
D  $C_6H_5CHNHNHC_6H_3(NO_2)_2$

*(CCEA January 2014)*

3. (a) Write an equation for the reaction of methanal with an excess of aqueous 2,4-dinitrophenylhydrazine. (b) The hydrazone derivative is formed using a solution that contains 37% methanal by mass. Calculate the mass of methanal solution needed to form 1.4 g of the hydrazone derivative assuming a 95% yield.

*(Adapted from CCEA May 2012)*

**Additional Problems**

4. The scheme below shows some of the reactions of acetoin. Complete the scheme to show the structure of the organic product for each reaction.

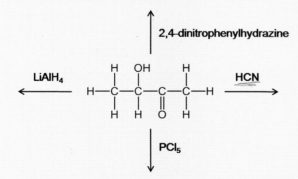

*(CCEA May 2013)*

5. The reaction of carbonyl compounds with amino compounds is used as a means of identifying the carbonyl compound. Initially, the reaction of carbonyl compounds with hydrazine, $NH_2NH_2$ was used.     *(continued)*

(a)

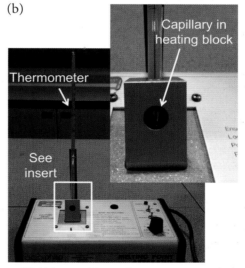

(b)

Figure 10: Using melting point apparatus to determine the melting point of a solid sample. (a) The sample is placed in a capillary tube sealed at one end. (b) The sample is then heated slowly in the melting point apparatus, and the range of temperature over which the sample melts recorded.

(a) Write the equation for the reaction of propanone with hydrazine. (b) Suggest the first step in the mechanism for the reaction. (c) Suggest, in terms of intermolecular forces, the advantages of using 2,4-dinitrophenylhydrazine over hydrazine, $NH_2NH_2$ when preparing derivatives of carbonyl compounds.

*(Adapted from CCEA January 2013)*

6. Hydroxylamine, NH$_2$OH may be used to form oximes which were also used for identification purposes. Write the equation for the condensation reaction of propanal with hydroxylamine.

*(CCEA January 2013)*

7. Technological methods have removed the need to form derivatives for identification purposes. Outline how they can be used to determine the identity of an organic compound.

*(CCEA January 2013)*

**Before moving to the next section, check that you are able to:**

- Deduce the structure of the 2,4-dinitrophenylhydrazone formed by an aldehyde or ketone, and write an equation for the reaction.

- Explain how the melting point of a 2,4-dinitrophenylhydrazone derivative can be used to identify the compound that was used to form the derivative.

- Explain how instrumental analysis can be used to deduce the structure of a compound.

## Preparation and Purification of Hydrazone Derivatives

The hydrazone derivative of a carbonyl compound is prepared by reacting the compound with an acidified solution of 2,4-dinitrophenylhydrazine dissolved in methanol (also known as Brady's Reagent). The hydrazone formed in the reaction is insoluble, and forms an orange coloured precipitate that is isolated from the reaction mixture by **vacuum filtration** as shown in Figure 11.

. . . . . . . . . . . . . . . . . . . . . . . . . . . . . . . . . . .

### Worked Example 4.7vi

An orange precipitate is formed when a few drops of propanal are added to a solution of 2,4-dinitrophenylhydrazine. The precipitate is then collected by vacuum filtration. (a) Describe, giving experimental details, how you would prepare a crude sample of the hydrazone derivative formed from propanal. (b) Explain, with the aid of a diagram, how vacuum filtration is carried out. (c) State why it is used in preference to normal (gravity) filtration.

### Solution

(a) Add a few drops of propanal to the solution in

(a) 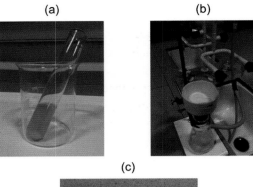 (b)

(c)

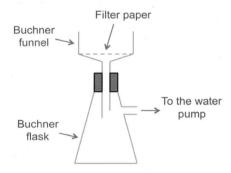

*Figure 11: (a) Formation of an insoluble hydrazone derivative. (b) Isolation of a hydrazone by vacuum filtration. (c) A hydrazone derivative obtained by vacuum filtration.*

a test tube. If crystals do not form add dilute sulfuric acid and warm the mixture. Cool the mixture using an iced-water bath then use vacuum filtration to obtain a crude sample of the hydrazone.

(b) Apparatus for vacuum filtration:

A Buchner funnel is placed into a Buchner flask and the sidearm of the flask connected to a water pump. The suction generated by the pump is then used to draw the reaction mixture through a damp filter paper placed in the funnel.

(c) Vacuum filtration is faster and dries the residue on the filter paper as it draws air through the Buchner funnel.

. . . . . . . . . . . . . . . . . . . . . . . . . . . . . . . . . . .

The crude hydrazone derivative is then purified by **recrystallisation** and the compound used to form the hydrazone identified by comparing the melting point of the pure hydrazone to the melting points of 2,4-dinitrophenylhydrazone derivatives in data tables.

## Worked Example 4.7vii

The identity of an unknown ketone was determined by preparing a solid derivative using 2,4-dinitrophenylhydrazine and determining the melting point of the purified product. (a) Describe how you would purify the solid derivative by recrystallisation using ethanol as a solvent. (b) Describe how the melting point of the purified solid would be determined experimentally. (c) What two effects would impurities have on the recorded melting point?

*(Adapted from CCEA January 2010)*

## Solution

(a) Dissolve the crude hydrazone in the minimum amount of hot ethanol. Filter the solution while hot, leave the filtrate to cool, and allow crystals to form. Filter the mixture, wash the solid hydrazone with a small amount of ethanol, then dry the solid in a low temperature oven or dessicator.

(b) Place a small amount of the solid in a capillary tube sealed at one end and slowly heat the sample in a melting point apparatus. Record the temperature when the solid begins to melt and the temperature when the solid finishes melting. Repeat to ensure the result is accurate.

(c) If the hydrazone contains impurities it will begin to melt at a lower temperature, and will melt over a broader range of temperature.

## Exercise 4.7M

1. Hydrazone derivatives are recrystallised using ethanol as a solvent. (a) Explain why hydrazones are soluble in ethanol and not in hexane. (b) Describe how you would recrystallise a hydrazone.

*(Adapted from CCEA May 2012)*

2. Giving full experimental details explain how you would determine the melting point of a hydrazone derivative.

*(Adapted from CCEA January 2013)*

3. Cinnamaldehyde can be identified by reaction with 2,4-dinitrophenylhydrazine to form a hydrazone. (a) Write the equation for this reaction showing the full structure of the hydrazone. (b) Explain how you would prepare

le of the purified hydrazone from ldehyde and use it to confirm the of the aldehyde.

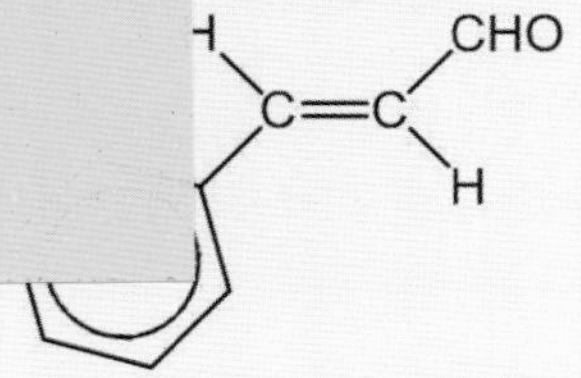

cinnamaldehyde

*(CCEA May 2006)*

4. The hydrazone shown below may be prepared by reacting excess aqueous 2,4-dinitrophenylhydrazine with butanone. Butanone is a liquid at room temperature with a density of $0.80 \text{ g cm}^{-3}$.

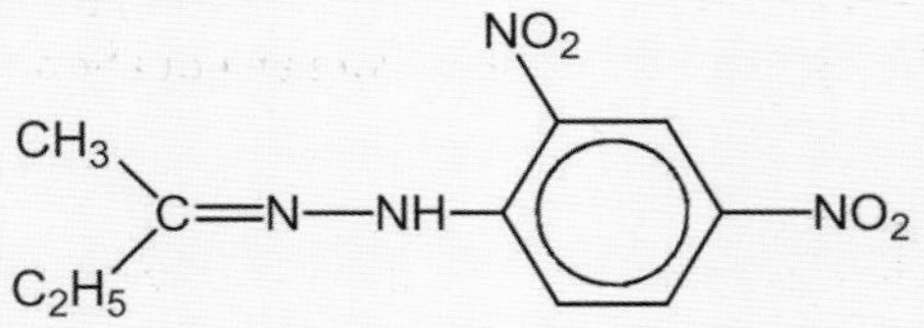

(a) Write the equation for the formation of the hydrazone. (b) Calculate the volume of butanone needed to form 5.4 g of the hydrazone assuming a 90% yield. (c) The hydrazone is formed as an orange precipitate which is collected by suction filtration using a Buchner flask. (i) Explain how 'Buchner filtration' is carried out. (ii) State why it is used in preference to normal filtration. (d) The solvent used to recrystallise the hydrazone is methanol. (i) Explain why the hydrazone is soluble in methanol and not in octane. (ii) Describe how you would recrystallise the hydrazone.

*(Adapted from CCEA May 2012)*

---

Before moving to the next section, check that you are able to:

- Describe the preparation of a pure, dry sample of a hydrazone derivative, including the use of vacuum filtration and recrystallisation.
- Describe how to determine the melting point of a hydrazone derivative and recall the effects of impurities on the melting point of a compound.
- Explain how the melting point of a hydrazone derivative can be used to identify the compound used to make the derivative.

# 4.8 Carboxylic Acids

**CONNECTIONS**
- Commercially important polymers such as Nylon and PET are synthesised from carboxylic acids.
- Many different types of cells use The Citric Acid Cycle to generate chemical energy from food. The process involves compounds derived from carboxylic acids with up to six carbon atoms.

## Structure and Properties

**In this section we are learning to:**

- Account for the physical properties of carboxylic acids in terms of bonding and structure.
- Use systematic (IUPAC) rules to name carboxylic acids.

### Structure and Bonding $C_nH_{2n}O_2$

A **carboxylic acid** is *a compound containing a carboxyl (-COOH) functional group.* Small carboxylic acids such as ethanoic acid, $CH_3COOH$ and propanoic acid, $CH_3CH_2COOH$ are colourless liquids and are miscible with water.

ethanoic acid, $CH_3COOH$   propanoic acid, $CH_3CH_2COOH$

In aqueous solution the carboxyl group partially dissociates to form hydrogen ions. The extent to which a carboxyl group dissociates is described by the acid dissociation constant, $K_a$ for the group.

*Acid dissociation in ethanoic acid:*
$$CH_3COOH \leftrightharpoons CH_3COO^- + H^+$$

$$K_a = \frac{[CH_3COO^-][H^+]}{[CH_3COOH]}$$

A **dicarboxylic acid** is *a compound containing two carboxyl groups.* Oxalic acid, $(COOH)_2$ is a dicarboxylic acid. The dissociation of each carboxyl group is described by an acid dissociation constant.

oxalic acid, $H_2C_2O_4$

*The first acid dissociation in oxalic acid:*

$$H_2C_2O_4 \leftrightharpoons HC_2O_4^- + H^+ \quad K_{a1} = \frac{[HC_2O_4^-][H^+]}{[H_2C_2O_4]}$$

*The second acid dissociation in oxalic acid:*

$$HC_2O_4^- \leftrightharpoons C_2O_4^{2-} + H^+ \quad K_{a2} = \frac{[C_2O_4^{2-}][H^+]}{[HC_2O_4^-]}$$

The formulas of simple carboxylic acids containing one carboxyl (COOH) group can be obtained by setting $n = 1, 2, ...$ in the general formula $C_nH_{2n}O_2$. The molecular structures and formulas for simple straight-chain carboxylic acids with n=1–6 are summarised in Table 1.

| n | Molecular Formula | Molecular Structure |
|---|---|---|
| 1 | $CH_2O_2$ | methanoic acid, HCOOH |
| 2 | $C_2H_4O_2$ | ethanoic acid, $CH_3COOH$ |
| 3 | $C_3H_6O_2$ | propanoic acid, $CH_3CH_2COOH$ |
| 4 | $C_4H_8O_2$ | butanoic acid, $CH_3CH_2CH_2COOH$ |
| 5 | $C_5H_{10}O_2$ | pentanoic acid, $CH_3CH_2CH_2CH_2COOH$ |
| 6 | $C_6H_{12}O_2$ | hexanoic acid, $CH_3CH_2CH_2CH_2CH_2COOH$ |

*Table 1: Molecular formulas and structures for simple straight-chain carboxylic acids.*

## Exercise 4.8A

1. Which one of the following is the formula of a simple carboxylic acid?

   A $C_4H_6O_2$   B $C_3H_6O$   C $C_3H_6O_2$   D $C_4H_8O$

2. A carboxylic acid was found to contain 58.7 % carbon, 9.8 % hydrogen and 31.5 % oxygen. Deduce the empirical formula of the acid.

   *(CCEA January 2010)*

---

**Before moving to the next section, check that you are able to:**

- Recall and use the general formula $C_nH_{2n}O_2$ to generate formulas for simple carboxylic acids.
- Draw the structures of simple carboxylic acids with up to six carbon atoms.
- Explain why carboxylic acids are weak acids.

---

## Solubility

The carboxyl (-COOH) group gives rise to dipole attraction and hydrogen bonding between neighbouring molecules. As a result, smaller acids such as ethanoic acid, $CH_3COOH$ and propanoic acid, $CH_3CH_2COOH$ are miscible with water and other liquids that can form hydrogen bonds. The formation of hydrogen bonds in ethanoic acid and aqueous ethanoic acid is shown in Figure 1.

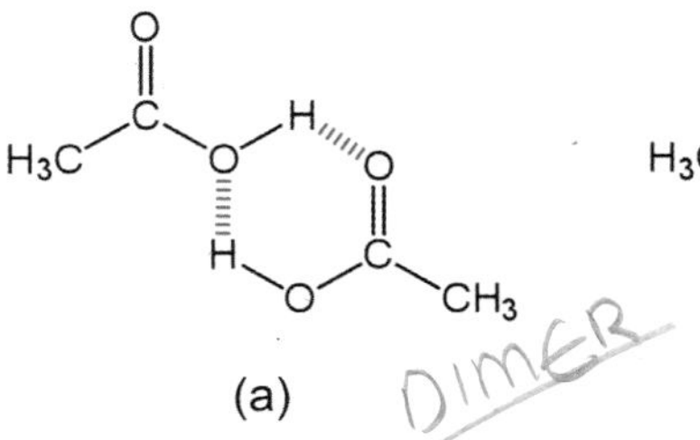

*Figure 1: The formation of hydrogen bonds between molecules in (a) ethanoic acid and (b) aqueous ethanoic acid.*

In a simple carboxylic acid the remainder of the molecule is comprised of a nonpolar alkyl group. The partitioning of propanoic acid, $CH_3CH_2COOH$ and pentanoic acid, $CH_3(CH_2)_3COOH$ into polar and nonpolar regions is illustrated in Figure 2. As the alkyl group becomes larger, the van der Waals attraction between molecules dominates to the extent that hexanoic acid, $CH_3(CH_2)_4COOH$ is only sparingly soluble in water.

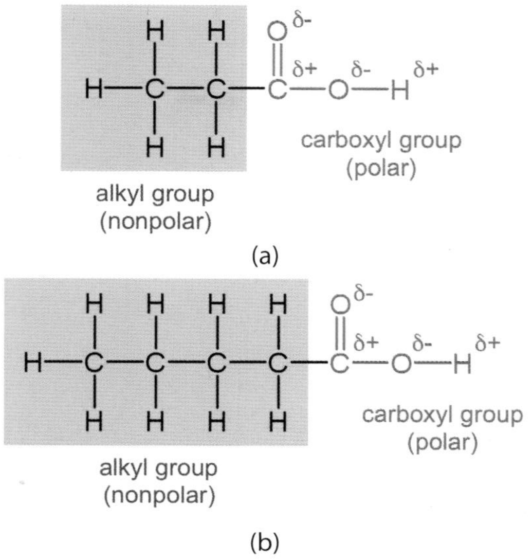

*Figure 2: Polar and nonpolar regions within molecules of (a) propanoic acid, $CH_3CH_2COOH$ and (b) pentanoic acid, $CH_3(CH_2)_3COOH$.*

## Exercise 4.8B

1. Pyruvic acid is miscible in water. (a) Explain the meaning of the term *miscible*. (b) Explain why pyruvic acid is miscible in water.

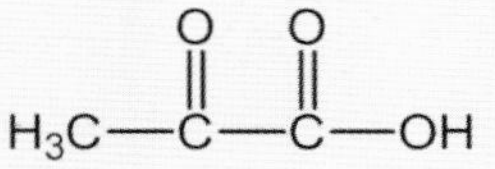

   *(Adapted from CCEA January 2012)*

2. Lauric acid, $C_{11}H_{23}COOH$ is the main acid found in coconut oil. It is a white solid at room temperature and is insoluble in water. Explain why ethanoic acid is soluble in water but lauric acid, $C_{11}H_{23}COOH$ is insoluble.

   *(CCEA May 2012)*

---

**Before moving to the next section, check that you are able to:**

- Explain, in terms of the forces between molecules, why carboxylic acids become less soluble in polar solvents as they get larger.

---

## Melting and Boiling Points

The boiling points of the simple straight-chain carboxylic acids in Figure 3 demonstrate that the van der Waals attraction between carboxylic acid molecules increases as the alkyl group gets bigger.

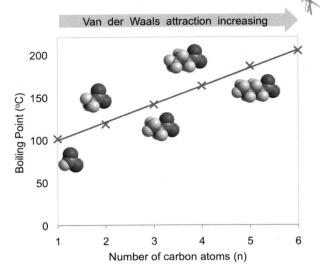

*Figure 3: The effect of increasing van der Waals attraction on the boiling points of simple straight-chain carboxylic acids.*

The corresponding melting points in Figure 4 reveal a similar trend amongst larger carboxylic acids. The melting points of small carboxylic acids such as ethanoic acid, $CH_3COOH$ are higher than expected as a result of strong hydrogen bonding between molecules in the solid. As the length of the carbon chain increases there are fewer hydrogen bonds in the solid, and van der Waals attraction increasingly becomes the dominant force between neighbouring molecules.

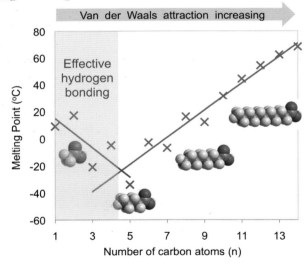

*Figure 4: The effect of increasing van der Waals attraction on the melting points of simple straight-chain carboxylic acids. The trend is disrupted by strong hydrogen bonding between molecules in the smaller acids.*

The formation of hydrogen bonds between neighbouring molecules also results in carboxylic acids having significantly higher boiling points than other carbonyl compounds with a similar mass such as aldehydes (RCHO), ketones (RCOR') and esters (RCOOR') that are unable to form hydrogen bonds between neighbouring molecules.

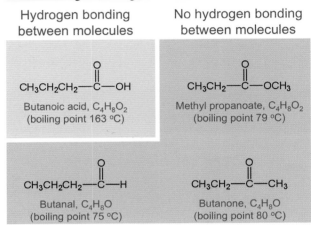

| Hydrogen bonding between molecules | No hydrogen bonding between molecules |
|---|---|
| Butanoic acid, $C_4H_8O_2$ (boiling point 163 °C) | Methyl propanoate, $C_4H_8O_2$ (boiling point 79 °C) |
| Butanal, $C_4H_8O$ (boiling point 75 °C) | Butanone, $C_4H_8O$ (boiling point 80 °C) |

## Exercise 4.8C

1. The carboxylic acids that occur in nature have straight chains and usually contain an even number of carbon atoms. The melting points of some of the acids are shown below. Explain why there is a gradual increase in the melting point of the acids.

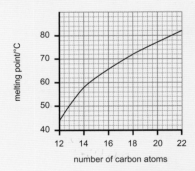

*(CCEA January 2013)*

2. Explain why ethanoic acid (boiling point 118 °C) has a much greater boiling point than ethanal, $CH_3CHO$ (boiling point 21 °C).

*(Adapted from CCEA June 2004)*

3. The boiling point of propanoic acid is 141 °C. Explain why the boiling point of the ester methyl propanoate, $CH_3CH_2COOCH_3$ is only 79 °C despite its higher molecular mass.

*(CCEA May 2010)*

Before moving to the next section, check that you are able to:

- Account for trends in the melting and boiling points of carboxylic acids in terms of the forces between molecules.

## Naming Carboxylic Acids

The systematic (IUPAC) name for a carboxylic acid is based on the name of the parent straight-chain alkane. For example, pentanoic acid is named using the prefix *pentan* as its structure is based on the chain of five carbon atoms in pentane, $CH_3CH_2CH_2CH_2CH_3$. The suffix *oic acid* is then added to indicate that the compound is a carboxylic acid.

pentanoic acid

The compounds 2-methylbutanoic acid and 2,2-dimethylpropanoic acid are structural isomers of pentanoic acid. The compound 2-methylbutanoic acid is named using the prefix *butan* as its structure is based on the chain of four carbon atoms in butane. The additional prefix *2-methyl* is then added to locate a methyl group on the second carbon atom. *In a carboxylic acid the carbon atoms are always numbered from the carboxyl (-COOH) end of the carbon chain.*

2-methylbutanoic acid
$CH_3CH_2CH(CH_3)COOH$

Similarly the compound 2,2-dimethylpropanoic acid is named using the prefix *propan* as its structure is based on the chain of three carbon atoms in propane. The additional prefix 2,2-dimethyl is then added to locate both methyl groups on the second carbon atom.

2,2-dimethylpropanoic acid
$C(CH_3)_3COOH$

The presence of additional groups on the carbon chain is described by adding an additional prefix for each type of group. In 2-amino-3-cyanopropanoic acid the prefixes *2-amino* and *3-cyano* are used to locate an amino ($-NH_2$) group on the second carbon and a cyano (-CN) group on the third carbon. *As in other types of compound the prefixes are given in alphabetical order.*

2-amino-3-cyanopropanoic acid
$CH_2(CN)CH(NH_2)COOH$

Similarly, in 5-hydroxy-4-oxopentanoic acid the prefixes *5-hydroxy* and *4-oxo* are used to locate a hydroxyl (-OH) group on the fifth carbon and an oxo (=O) group on the fourth carbon.

5-hydroxy-4-oxopentanoic acid
$CH_2(OH)COCH_2CH_2COOH$

The compound 3-chlorobut-2-enoic acid is considered a butenoic acid as its structure is based on but-2-ene. The prefix *3-chloro* is then added to locate chlorine (-Cl) on the third carbon atom in the carbon chain. Similarly, hexa-2,4-dienoic acid is named as a hexadienoic acid as its structure is based on a hexadiene. The suffix *2,4-dienoic acid* is then added to locate C=C bonds between the second and fourth pairs of carbon atoms in the carbon chain.

3-chlorobut-2-enoic acid
$CH_3CClCHCOOH$

$CH_3CH=CHCH=CHCOOH$

hexa-2,4-dienoic acid
$CH_3(CH)_4COOH$

**Rules for naming carboxylic acids:**

1. The name consists of a prefix followed by the suffix *oic acid* or *enoic acid*. The prefix is based on the name of the parent alkane (suffix *oic acid*) or alkene (suffix *enoic acid*).

2. The number of C=C bonds in the carbon chain is indicated by using the number prefixes *di*, *tri*, *tetra*, ... to generate suffixes such as *dienoic acid* and *trienoic acid*.

3. The location of each C=C bond is then added to generate suffixes such as *3-enoic acid* and *3,5-dienoic* acid where the carbon atoms are numbered from the carboxyl group.

4. The location of additional functional groups is then described by adding additional prefixes in alphabetical order.

**Exercise 4.8D**

1. Write the systematic name for (a) butyric acid, $CH_3CH_2CH_2COOH$ and (b) isobutyric acid, $CH_3CH(CH_3)COOH$.

2. Write the systematic name for (a) valeric acid, $CH_3(CH_2)_3COOH$ and (b) isovaleric acid, $CH_3CH(CH_3)CH_2COOH$.

3. The amino acids used to construct proteins belong to a class of compounds known as alpha amino acids. The general structure of an alpha amino acid is drawn below. Use the general structure to write the systematic name for each amino acid in the table.

General structure of an alpha amino acid

$$R-\underset{\underset{NH_2}{|}}{\overset{\overset{H}{|}}{C}}-COOH$$

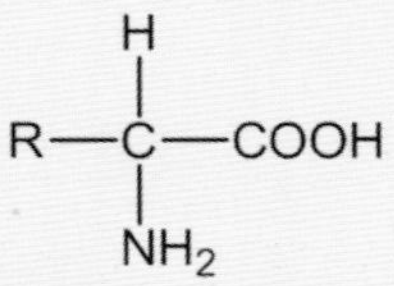

| | Amino Acid | Structure of -R |
|---|---|---|
| (a) | serine | $-CH_2OH$ |
| (b) | threonine | $-CH(OH)CH_3$ |
| (c) | ornithine | $-CH_2CH_2CH_2NH_2$ |
| (d) | lysine | $-CH_2CH_2CH_2CH_2NH_2$ |

4. Name the following carboxylic acids.

(a)

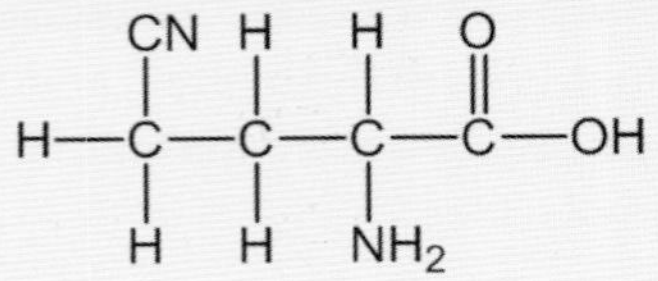

(b)

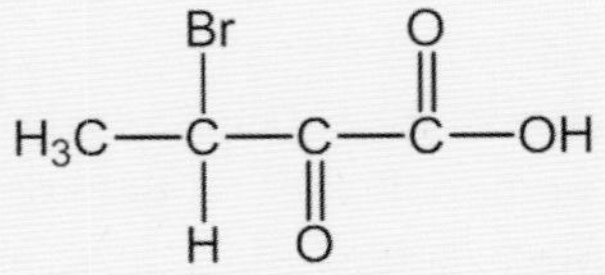

5. Name the following carboxylic acids.

(a)

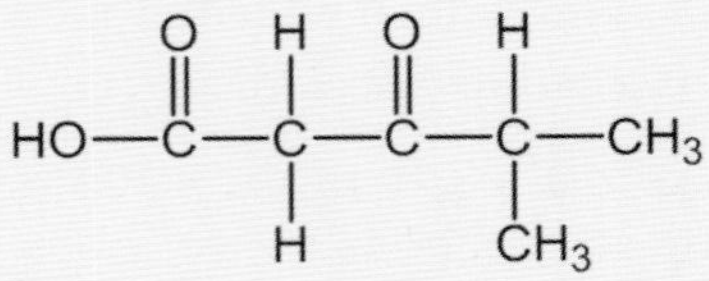

(b)

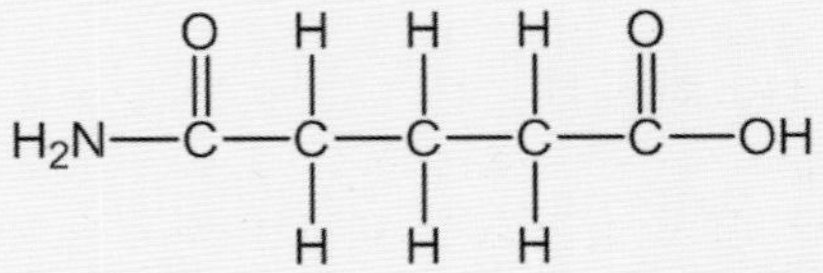

6. Draw and name the isomers of butenoic acid that arise from the positioning of the C=C bond in the molecule.

7. Draw the geometric isomers of pent-3-enoic acid.

8. Which one of the following is the correct formula for 4-chloro-2-methylpent-2-enoic acid?

A $CH_3CCl=CHCH(CH_3)COOH$
B $(CH_3)_2C=CHCHClCOOH$
C $CH_3CH_2CCl=C(CH_3)COOH$
D $CH_3CHClCH=C(CH_3)COOH$

*(CCEA January 2008)*

**Dicarboxylic Acids**

The name of a dicarboxylic acid is based on the name of the parent straight-chain alkane. The suffix *dioic acid* is then added to indicate that the compound is a dicarboxylic acid. For example, the structure of ethanedioic acid is based on the chain of two carbon atoms in ethane, $CH_3CH_3$.

COOH
|
COOH

ethanedioic acid
$(COOH)_2$

Similarly 2-chloro-3-hydroxybutanedioic acid is named as a butanedioic acid as its structure is based on the chain of four carbon atoms in butane. As in other carboxylic acids the additional prefix *2-chloro-3-hydroxy* is used to locate chlorine (-Cl) and a hydroxyl (-OH) group on the carbon chain.

$$HOOC-\overset{\overset{\displaystyle H}{|}}{\underset{\underset{\displaystyle Cl}{|}}{C}}-\overset{\overset{\displaystyle H}{|}}{\underset{\underset{\displaystyle OH}{|}}{C}}-COOH$$

2-chloro-3-hydroxybutanedioic acid
HOOCCHClCH(OH)COOH

If the compound contains a C=C bond in the carbon chain it is named after the parent alkene. For example, pent-2-enedioic acid is named as a pentenedioic acid as its structure is based on the five carbon chain in pent-2-ene. Similarly 2-aminohexa-2,4-dienedioic acid is named as a hexadienedioic acid as its structure is based on hexadiene.

HOOCCH=CHCH$_2$COOH

pent-2-enedioic acid
HOOC(CH)$_2$CH$_2$COOH

$$\overset{\overset{\displaystyle NH_2}{|}}{HOOCCH=CHCH=CCOOH}$$

2-aminohexa-2,4-dienedioic acid
HOOC(CH)$_3$C(NH$_2$)COOH

**Rules** for naming dicarboxylic acids:

1. The name of the parent alkane or alkene is followed by the suffix *dioic acid*.

2. The location of additional functional groups is then described by adding additional prefixes in alphabetical order.

**Exercise 4.8E**

1. The systematic name for succinic acid is butanedioic acid. Draw the structure of (a) 2,3-dihydroxysuccinic acid and (b) 2-hydroxy-3-oxosuccinic acid.

2. Name the following dicarboxylic acids.

(a)
$$HOOC-\overset{\overset{\displaystyle H}{|}}{\underset{\underset{\displaystyle NH_2}{|}}{C}}-\overset{\overset{\displaystyle CH_3}{|}}{\underset{\underset{\displaystyle H}{|}}{C}}-\overset{\overset{\displaystyle H}{|}}{\underset{\underset{\displaystyle H}{|}}{C}}-COOH$$

(b)
$$HOOC-\overset{\overset{\displaystyle O}{||}}{C}-\overset{\overset{\displaystyle H}{|}}{\underset{\underset{\displaystyle H}{|}}{C}}-\overset{\overset{\displaystyle H}{|}}{\underset{\underset{\displaystyle CH_3}{|}}{C}}-COOH$$

3. Draw and name the isomers of hexenedioic acid that arise from the positioning of the C=C bond in the molecule.

4. The compound (Z,Z)-3-chloromuconic acid is formed during the degradation of halogenated hydrocarbons by microorganisms. (a) Write the systematic name for 3-chloromuconic acid. (b) Draw the structure of (E,E)-3-chloromuconic acid.

(Z,Z)-3-chloromuconic acid

Before moving to the next section, check that you are able to:

- Use systematic (IUPAC) rules to name carboxylic acids, including compounds with one or more C=C bonds and up to two carboxyl groups.

## Preparation

### In this section we are learning to:

- Explain, with the aid of equations, how carboxylic acids are obtained by the oxidation of alcohols and aldehydes.
- Describe the preparation of a carboxylic acid from the corresponding primary alcohol.
- Explain, with the aid of equations, how carboxylic acids are obtained by the hydrolysis of esters and nitriles.

### Oxidation of Alcohols and Aldehydes

An aqueous solution of a carboxylic acid can be prepared by refluxing the corresponding primary alcohol or aldehyde with an oxidising agent such as acidified potassium dichromate or acidified potassium permanganate. The oxidising agent is a source of oxygen and can be represented by a single oxygen atom, [O] when writing the equation for the reaction.

$H_2SO_4$

$$R-\underset{\underset{H}{|}}{\overset{\overset{H}{|}}{C}}-OH \ + \ 2[O] \longrightarrow R-\overset{\overset{O}{\|}}{C}-OH \ + \ H_2O$$

primary alcohol
$RCH_2OH$

carboxylic acid
$RCOOH$

$$R-\overset{\overset{O}{\|}}{C}-H \ + \ [O] \longrightarrow R-\overset{\overset{O}{\|}}{C}-OH$$

aldehyde
$RCHO$

carboxylic acid
$RCOOH$

If a pure, dry sample of the acid is required, the carboxylic acid can be distilled from the aqueous reaction mixture.

### Worked Example 4.8i

The European paper wasp uses 3-methylbutanoic acid $(CH_3)_2CHCH_2COOH$ as a pheromone. Explain, giving experimental details, how a pure sample of 3-methylbutanoic acid could be prepared from the alcohol 3-methylbutan-1-ol.

*(CCEA June 2007)*

### Solution

Carefully add small amounts of concentrated sulfuric acid to a small amount of water in a round bottomed flask. Swirl and cool the mixture using an iced water bath after each addition. Dissolve potassium dichromate in the solution before adding small amounts of 3-methylbutan-1-ol to the mixture; swirling and cooling the mixture after each addition. Then add anti-bumping granules and reflux the mixture for an extended period. Allow the mixture to cool before rearranging the apparatus for distillation. Distil the reaction mixture and collect 3-methylbutanoic acid at its boiling point.

### Exercise 4.8F

1. Using [O] to represent an oxidising agent, write an equation for the oxidation of (a) propan-1-ol, $CH_3CH_2CH_2OH$ and (b) ethane-1,2-diol, $HOCH_2CH_2OH$ using an excess of the oxidising agent.

   *(Adapted from CCEA May 2011)*

2. Which one of the following contains a hydroxyl group that could be oxidised to form a carboxyl group?

   A propan-2-ol
   B 2-methylbutan-2-ol
   C 3-hydroxypropanoic acid
   D 2-hydroxybut-2-ene

3. Glycerol (glycerine) is the most common trihydric alcohol found in nature. (a) Write an equation for the reaction of glycerol with an oxidising agent, represented as [O], to form glyceric acid. (b) Suggest the systematic name for glyceric acid.

   $$\begin{array}{ll} CH_2OH & COOH \\ | & | \\ CHOH & CHOH \\ | & | \\ CH_2OH & CH_2OH \end{array}$$

   glycerol      glyceric acid

   *(Adapted from CCEA May 2014)*

4. (a) Explain, giving experimental details, how a pure sample of succinic acid could be prepared from butane-1,4-diol. (b) Using [O] to represent an oxidising agent, write an equation for the reaction.

   $$\begin{array}{ll} CH_2CH_2OH & CH_2COOH \\ | & | \\ CH_2CH_2OH & CH_2COOH \end{array}$$

   butane-1,4-diol      succinic acid

Before moving to the next section, check that you are able to:

- Use the symbol [O] to write equations for the oxidation of primary alcohols and aldehydes to the corresponding carboxylic acid.
- Explain, giving experimental details, how a pure, dry sample of a carboxylic acid is obtained from the corresponding primary alcohol or aldehyde.

## Hydrolysis of Nitriles

Carboxylic acids can also be produced by the hydrolysis of nitriles. When a nitrile is refluxed with dilute acid or dilute alkali the cyano (-CN) group in the nitrile is converted to a carboxyl (-COOH) group.

$$R-C\equiv N \ + \ 2H_2O \longrightarrow R-\overset{\overset{\displaystyle O}{\|}}{C}-OH \ + \ NH_3$$

nitrile           carboxylic acid
RCN            RCOOH

If the nitrile is refluxed with dilute hydrochloric acid the ammonia formed in the hydrolysis reacts with the acid to form the corresponding ammonium salt.

*Acid hydrolysis:*
$RCN + 2H_2O + HCl \rightarrow RCOOH + NH_4Cl$

If the nitrile is instead refluxed with an excess of dilute sodium hydroxide, the carboxylic acid formed in the hydrolysis (RCOOH) reacts with the alkali to form the corresponding salt (RCOONa). The carboxylic acid is then liberated from the salt by adding an excess of dilute hydrochloric acid.

*Alkaline hydrolysis:*
$RCN + H_2O + NaOH \rightarrow RCOONa + NH_3$

*Liberating the acid from the salt:*
$RCOONa + HCl \rightarrow RCOOH + NaCl$

### Exercise 4.8G

1. (a) Write an equation for the reaction that occurs when 3-oxobutanenitrile, $CH_3COCH_2CN$ is refluxed with dilute hydrochloric acid. (b) Draw the structure of the organic product formed.

2. Pyruvic acid, $CH_3COCOOH$ can be prepared by hydrolysis of 2-oxopropanenitrile. (a) Write an equation for the reaction that occurs when 2-oxopropanenitrile is refluxed with dilute sodium hydroxide. (b) Draw the structure of the organic product. (c) Explain how you would obtain pyruvic acid from the organic product.

$$H_3C-\overset{\overset{\displaystyle O}{\|}}{C}-CN \qquad \text{2-oxopropanenitrile}$$

Before moving to the next section, check that you are able to:

- Explain, with the aid of equations, how a carboxylic acid is obtained from the corresponding nitrile by hydrolysis using dilute acid or dilute alkali.

## Reactions

### In this section we are learning to:

- Describe the reactions of carboxylic acids with bases, alcohols, $PCl_5$ and $LiAlH_4$.
- Describe the reactions of acyl chlorides with nucleophiles.

### Salt Formation

A carboxylic acid (RCOOH) will react with a base to form a salt containing the corresponding **carboxylate ion** (RCOO⁻).

*Reaction with sodium hydroxide:*
$RCOOH_{(aq)} + NaOH_{(aq)} \rightarrow RCOONa_{(aq)} + H_2O_{(l)}$
Ionic equation: $RCOOH_{(aq)} + OH^-_{(aq)}$
$\rightarrow RCOO^-_{(aq)} + H_2O_{(l)}$

*Reaction with aqueous ammonia:*
$RCOOH_{(aq)} + NH_{3(aq)} \rightarrow RCOONH_{4(aq)}$
Ionic equation: $RCOOH_{(aq)} + NH_{3(aq)}$
$\rightarrow RCOO^-_{(aq)} + NH_4^+_{(aq)}$

*Reaction with sodium carbonate:*
$RCOOH_{(aq)} + Na_2CO_{3(aq)}$
$\rightarrow RCOONa_{(aq)} + H_2O_{(l)} + CO_{2(g)}$
Ionic equation: $RCOOH_{(aq)} + CO_3^{2-}_{(aq)}$
$\rightarrow RCOO^-_{(aq)} + H_2O_{(l)} + CO_{2(g)}$

Carboxylic acids also react with hydrogencarbonate salts to form carbon dioxide. *The formation of carbon dioxide on adding solid sodium carbonate or sodium hydrogencarbonate to an organic liquid can be used as a positive test for a carboxylic acid.*

Carboxylate salts have similar properties to other ionic compounds. The sodium, potassium and ammonium salts of carboxylic acids are white crystalline solids held together by strong attractive forces between oppositely changed ions. The names and formulas of several carboxylate salts are summarised in Table 2.

### Exercise 4.8H

1. Methanoic acid, HCOOH is present in nettle stings and ant bites. (a) Describe what you would observe when methanoic acid is added to aqueous sodium carbonate, giving an equation for the reaction. (b) Explain how the reaction could be used to test for the presence of a carboxylic acid.

*(Adapted from CCEA January 2014)*

2. The best known pentanoic acids are valeric acid and isovaleric acid. (a) State the systematic name for isovaleric acid. (b) Write the equation for the reaction of valeric acid with sodium carbonate. (c) Explain how you would reform valeric acid from the aqueous solution.

$$CH_3CH_2CH_2CH_2COOH$$
valeric acid

$$CH_3\overset{\overset{\displaystyle CH_3}{|}}{C}HCH_2COOH$$
isovaleric acid

*(CCEA January 2005)*

3. Draw the structure of the organic product formed when oxalic acid, $(COOH)_2$ reacts with an excess of (a) $Na_2CO_3$ and (b) $NH_3$.

$$\overset{\displaystyle COOH}{\underset{\displaystyle COOH}{|}}$$
oxalic acid

*(Adapted from CCEA June 2005)*

**Before moving to the next section, check that you are able to:**

- Deduce the structure and formula of the carboxylate salt formed when a carboxylic acid reacts with a base.
- Write equations for the reactions of carboxylic acids with bases, including sodium carbonate and ammonia.

### Esterification

The term **esterification** is used to describe *a reaction in which an ester is formed.* Carboxylic acids can be converted to an ester by refluxing the carboxylic acid with an alcohol and a small amount of concentrated sulfuric acid.

| Parent Acid | Carboxylate Ion | Carboxylate Salt |
|---|---|---|
| $CH_3CH_2COOH$ propanoic acid | $CH_3CH_2-\overset{\overset{\displaystyle O}{\|\|}}{C}-O^-$ propanoate ion $CH_3CH_2COO-$ | $CH_3CH_2-\overset{\overset{\displaystyle O}{\|\|}}{C}-ONH_4$ ammonium propanoate $CH_3CH_2COONH_4$ |
| $CH_3COOH$ ethanoic acid | $CH_3-\overset{\overset{\displaystyle O}{\|\|}}{C}-O^-$ ethanoate ion $CH_3COO-$ | $\left(CH_3-\overset{\overset{\displaystyle O}{\|\|}}{C}-O\right)_2 Mg$ magnesium ethanoate $(CH_3COO)_2Mg$ |
| $(COOH)_2$ ethanedioic acid | $^-O-\overset{\overset{\displaystyle O}{\|\|}}{C}-\overset{\overset{\displaystyle O}{\|\|}}{C}-O^-$ ethanedioate ion $(COO)_2^{2-}$ | $\left(\overset{\displaystyle COO}{\underset{\displaystyle COO}{|}}\right)Ca$ calcium ethanedioate $(COO)_2Ca$ |

Table 2: The names and formulas of carboxylate salts.

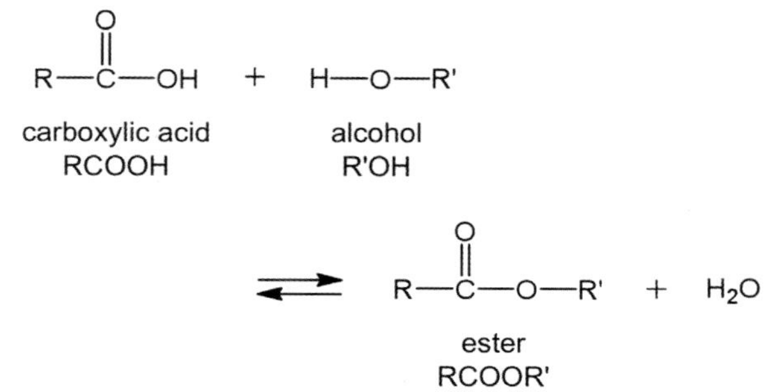

carboxylic acid   alcohol
RCOOH      R'OH

ester
RCOOR'

In this way an **ester** is 'derived' from a carboxylic acid and is referred to as a derivative of a carboxylic acid. The hydrogen ions from the concentrated sulfuric acid increase the rate of the reaction by acting as a catalyst. The concentrated sulfuric acid also increases the yield of ester by removing water from the reaction mixture, shifting the position of equilibrium to the right.

If the carboxylic acid contains two or more carboxyl (-COOH) groups, each carboxyl group reacts to form an ester.

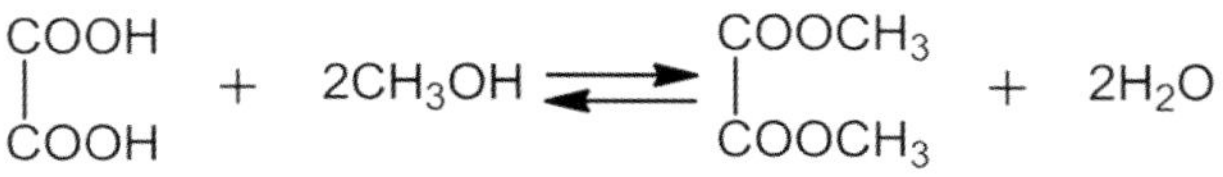

### Exercise 4.8I

1. (a) Write the equation for the reaction of pentanoic acid with ethanol. (b) State two ways by which the rate of esterification can be increased.

*(Adapted from CCEA January 2005)*

2. Methacrylic acid is an important intermediate in the manufacture of the polymer Perspex, poly(methyl methacrylate).

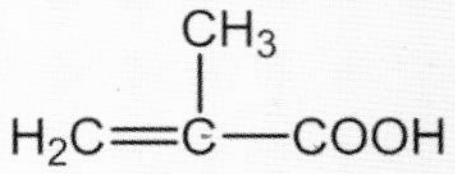

methacrylic acid 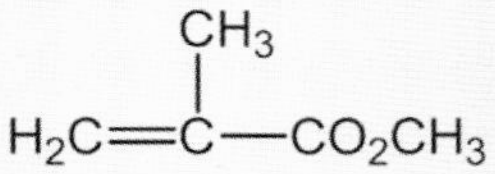        methyl methacrylate

(a) Suggest a systematic name for methacrylic acid. (b) Name the reactant and catalyst needed to convert methacrylic acid into methyl methacrylate. (c) What is the general name given to this type of reaction.

*(Adapted from CCEA May 2015)*

3. When lactic acid, $CH_3CH(OH)COOH$ is heated it forms compounds known as lactides. The lactide A is a dimer and the lactide B is a polymer. (a) Explain why the formation of lactide B from lactic acid could be regarded as esterification. (b) Write an equation for the formation of lactide A from lactic acid.

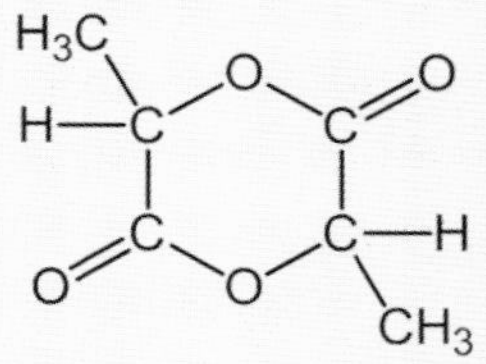

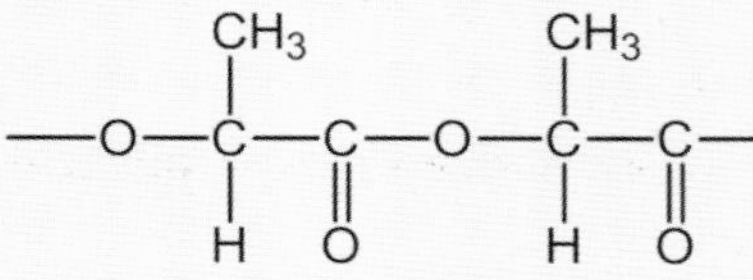

*(CCEA January 2004)*

4. The E isomer of butenedioic acid is called fumaric acid and is produced naturally in the body. The ester diethyl fumarate is used in the treatment of psoriasis. (a) Write the equation for the formation of diethyl fumarate from fumaric acid and ethanol. (b) State one condition which is necessary to carry out this reaction. (c) Name the catalyst for the reaction.

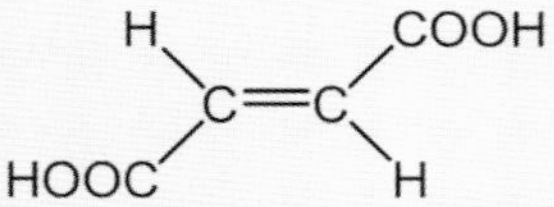

fumaric acid

*(CCEA January 2014)*

Before moving to the next section, check that you are able to:

- Write an equation for the esterification of a given carboxylic acid and deduce the structure of the ester formed.
- Explain the role of concentrated sulfuric acid in esterification reactions.

## Forming Acyl Chlorides

Phosphorus(V) chloride, $PCl_5$ is a white solid that reacts vigorously with carboxylic acids to form the corresponding **acyl chloride** (RCOCl).

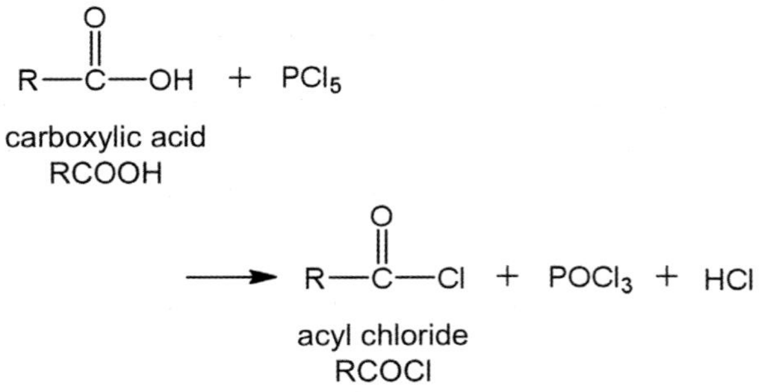

$$R—\overset{\overset{\displaystyle O}{\|}}{C}—OH \ + \ PCl_5$$

carboxylic acid
RCOOH

$$\longrightarrow \ R—\overset{\overset{\displaystyle O}{\|}}{C}—Cl \ + \ POCl_3 \ + \ HCl$$

acyl chloride
RCOCl

The reaction is exothermic and must be carried out in a fume cupboard as it produces a pungent smelling gas (HCl).

*The addition of phosphorus(V) chloride can be used to test for a carboxylic acid as the HCl gas produced by the reaction turns damp blue litmus paper red and produces white fumes when it contacts the vapour produced by concentrated ammonia solution.*

### Exercise 4.8J

1. Write the equation for the reaction between phosphorus pentachloride and ethanoic acid.

   *(CCEA May 2009)*

2. (a) Give two observations for the reaction between phosphorus(V) chloride and 3- methylbutanoic acid. (b) Write an equation for the reaction.

   *(CCEA May 2007)*

3. Draw the structure of the organic product formed when oxalic acid, $(COOH)_2$ reacts with an excess of $PCl_5$.

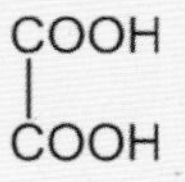

   COOH
   |          oxalic acid
   COOH

   *(Adapted from CCEA June 2005)*

Acyl chlorides (RCOCl) are derivatives of carboxylic acids. The carbon atom in the carbonyl group is very electron deficient and is readily attacked by nucleophiles. The resulting nucleophilic substitution reactions can be used to form a range of carboxylic acid derivatives as shown in Figure 5.

### Exercise 4.8K

1. Nucleophilic substitution occurs when ethanoyl chloride, $CH_3COCl$ is refluxed with sodium cyanide. (a) Write an equation for the reaction. (b) State and explain the role of cyanide ion, $CN^-$ in the reaction.

2. Acyl chlorides react vigorously with alcohols to form esters. Hydrogen chloride is the only other product of the reaction. (a) Write an equation for the reaction of propanoyl chloride, $CH_3CH_2COCl$ with ethanol. (b) State and explain the role of the alcohol in the reaction.

3. Acyl chlorides react vigorously with ammonia to form the corresponding amide, $RCONH_2$. Hydrogen chloride formed in the reaction then reacts with ammonia to form ammonium chloride, $NH_4Cl$. (a) Write an equation for the formation of ethanamide, $CH_3CONH_2$ from the corresponding acyl chloride. Assume the acyl chloride is added to an excess of ammonia. (b) Explain why the reaction is an example of nucleophilic substitution.

General structure
of an amide

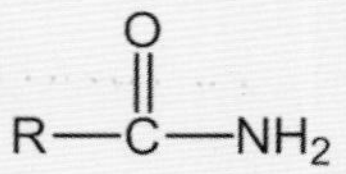

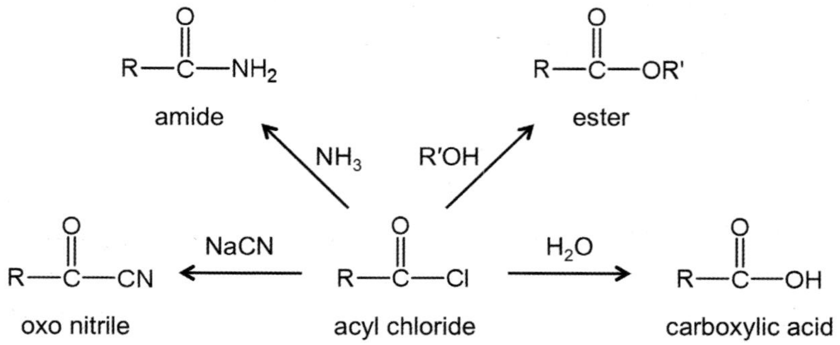

$$R—\overset{\overset{\displaystyle O}{\|}}{C}—NH_2$$

*Figure 5: Formation of carboxylic acid derivatives by nucleophilic substitution of an acyl chloride.*

Before moving to the next section, check that you are able to:

- Write an equation for the reaction that occurs when a carboxylic acid reacts with PCl$_5$ and deduce the structure of the product.
- Explain why acyl chlorides undergo nucleophilic substitution and deduce the structure of the product formed.

## Reduction

Lithium aluminium hydride or 'lithal', LiAlH$_4$ is a powerful reducing agent and will add hydrogen to a compound by attacking carbonyl (C=O) groups and other functional groups containing an electron-deficient carbon atom (C$^{\delta+}$). Lithal will not add hydrogen atoms to C=C bonds and other groups that do not contain an electron-deficient atom. As a result, if a carboxylic acid is refluxed with a solution of lithal in dry ether, the acid is reduced to the corresponding primary alcohol.

$$R\overset{\overset{\displaystyle O}{\|}}{-C}-OH \ + \ 4[H] \longrightarrow R-\overset{\overset{\displaystyle H}{|}}{\underset{\underset{\displaystyle H}{|}}{C}}-OH \ + \ H_2O$$

carboxylic acid · · · · · · · · · primary alcohol
RCOOH · · · · · · · · · · · · · · · · RCH$_2$OH

### Worked Example 4.8ii

Which one of the following compounds is formed when the acid CH$_3$COCH(CHO)COOH is reduced with excess lithium aluminium hydride?

A  CH$_3$COCH(CH$_2$OH)$_2$

B  CH$_3$COCH(CHO)CH$_2$OH

C  CH$_3$CHOHCH(CHO)CH$_2$OH

D  CH$_3$CHOHCH(CH$_2$OH)$_2$

*(CCEA January 2013)*

### Strategy

- Lithal will reduce carboxyl (-COOH), aldehyde (-CHO) and oxo (=O) groups to a hydroxyl (-OH) group.

### Solution

Structure of the product:
$$H_3C-\overset{\overset{\displaystyle OH}{|}}{\underset{\underset{\displaystyle H}{|}}{C}}-\overset{\overset{\displaystyle CH_2OH}{|}}{\underset{\underset{\displaystyle H}{|}}{C}}-CH_2OH$$

Answer D.

### Exercise 4.8L

1. (a) Write the equation for the reaction of propanoic acid with LiAlH$_4$. (b) Draw the structure of the organic product.

    *(Adapted from CCEA May 2010)*

2. Which one of the following substances is formed when CH$_3$CH=CHCH=CHCH$_2$COOH is heated with *excess* lithium aluminium hydride?

    A  CH$_3$CH$_2$CH$_2$CH$_2$CH$_2$CH$_2$COOH
    B  CH$_3$CH=CHCH=CHCH$_2$CH$_2$OH
    C  CH$_3$CH=CHCH=CHCH$_2$CHO
    D  CH$_3$CH$_2$CH$_2$CH$_2$CH$_2$CH$_2$CH$_2$OH

    *(CCEA May 2015)*

3. Pyruvic acid, CH$_3$COCOOH reacts as a ketone and a carboxylic acid. (a) Write the equation for the reaction of pyruvic acid with lithium aluminium hydride. (b) Draw the structure of the organic product. (c) Name the organic product.

    *(Adapted from CCEA January 2012)*

4. Which one of the following compounds can be reduced to form a product which can exist as optical isomers?

    A  Butan-2-one
    B  Hex-2-ene
    C  Propanal
    D  *Trans*-butenedioic acid

    *(CCEA May 2014)*

5. Lauric acid, C$_{11}$H$_{23}$COOH is the main acid found in coconut oil. It is a white solid at room temperature and is insoluble in water. (a) Describe a chemical test to prove that lauric acid is an acid. (b) Write an equation for the reduction of lauric acid to the corresponding alcohol. Use [H] to represent the reducing agent. (c) Name a suitable reducing agent for the reduction of lauric acid.

    *(CCEA May 2012)*

Before moving to the next section, check that you are able to:

- Recall that lithal will reduce a carboxyl (-COOH) group to a hydroxyl group.
- Deduce the structure of the product when lithal is used to reduce a carboxylic acid and use the symbol [H] to write an equation for the reaction.

# 4.9 Esters

## Structure and Properties

**In this section we are learning to:**

• Account for the physical properties of esters in terms of bonding and structure.
• Use systematic (IUPAC) rules to name esters.

### Structure

An ester, RCOOR' is a derivative of a carboxylic acid. The structure of an ester is obtained by replacing the hydrogen in the carboxyl (-COOH) group of the parent carboxylic acid with an alkyl group (R').

Ester                Carboxylic acid

Simple esters such as ethyl ethanoate and methyl propanoate are colourless oily liquids with a fruity odour. They are found in natural oils and are often used as flavourings or ingredients in perfumes. The physical properties and reactions of esters are determined by the properties of the ester linkage (-COO-) in the molecule.

ethyl ethanoate
$CH_3COOCH_2CH_3$

methyl propanoate
$CH_3CH_2COOCH_3$

*An ester that contains one ester linkage (-COO-) is referred to as a monoester.* The molecular formulas of monoesters (RCOOR') can be obtained by setting n = 1, 2, 3 ... in the general formula $C_nH_{2n}O_2$. The location of the ester linkage within the carbon chain gives rise to structural isomers. Ethyl ethanoate, $C_4H_8O_2$ and methyl propanoate, $C_4H_8O_2$ are structural isomers; they have the same molecular formula and differ only in the location of the ester linkage within the carbon chain.

**Exercise 4.9A**

1. Which one of the following is the formula of a monoester?

   A $C_3H_6O$   B $C_3H_8O_2$   C $C_2H_4O_2$   D $C_2H_4O$

2. Draw the structure of all possible monoesters with the formula $C_3H_6O_2$.

Before moving to the next section, check that you are able to:

• Recall and use the general formula $C_nH_{2n}O_2$ to generate molecular formulas for monoesters.
• Deduce the structure of all possible monoesters with a given molecular formula.

### Solubility

The carbon-oxygen bonds in an ester are polar and give rise to a molecular dipole. The remainder of the molecule is comprised of nonpolar alkyl groups.

Origin of the molecular dipole in an ester

molecular dipole

The ester linkage (-COO-) cannot be used to form hydrogen bonds between the molecules in an ester. As a result the molecules in an ester experience a combination of dipole attraction and van der Waals attraction. In contrast, the oxygen atoms in the ester linkage can hydrogen bond with the hydrogen atoms in solvents such as water and ethanol as illustrated in Figure 1. The formation of hydrogen bonds results in small esters such as ethyl methanoate, $HCOOCH_2CH_3$ and ethyl ethanoate, $CH_3COOCH_2CH_3$ being moderately soluble in water. As the molar mass of the ester increases, the van der Waals attraction between molecules increases to the extent that ethyl propanoate $CH_3CH_2COOCH_2CH_3$ is only slightly soluble in water.

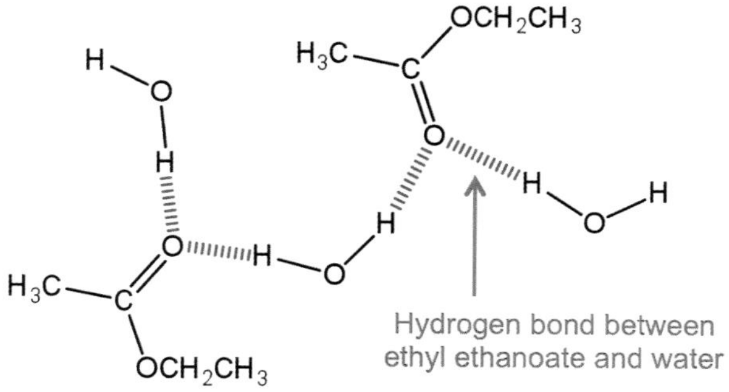

Figure 1: The formation of hydrogen bonds between ethyl ethanoate molecules and water molecules in aqueous ethyl ethanoate.

### Exercise 4.9B

1. The esters ethyl propanoate and ethyl lactate are liquids. (a) Explain, with reference to intermolecular forces, why ethyl propanoate has a very low solubility in water while ethyl lactate is miscible with water. (b) Explain what is meant by *miscible*.

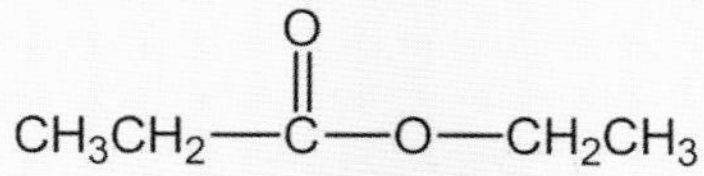

ethyl propanoate

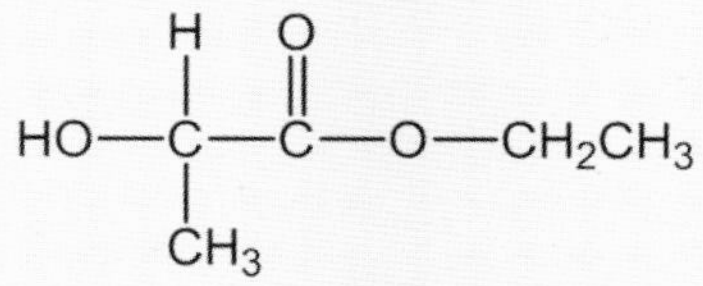

ethyl lactate

2. Compounds A and B are cyclic esters. Compound A is an oily liquid with a boiling point of 204 °C. Compound B is also an oily liquid and is used as an ingredient in insect repellents. With reference to intermolecular forces suggest why compound A is miscible in water and compound B is insoluble in water.

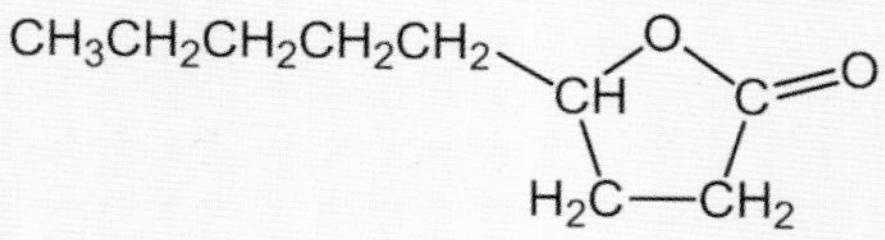

Before moving to the next section, check that you are able to:

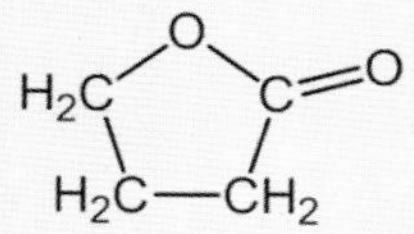

- Explain, in terms of the forces between molecules, why esters become less soluble in polar solvents as they get larger.

### Boiling Point

As the molar mass of the ester increases, van der Waals attraction between the molecules increases, and results in an increase in boiling point as demonstrated by the boiling points of the ethanoate esters ($CH_3COOR$) in Table 1.

| Molecular Structure | Molar Mass (g mol$^{-1}$) | Boiling Point (°C) |
|---|---|---|
| $CH_3COOCH_3$ methyl ethanoate | 74 | 57 |
| $CH_3COOCH_2CH_3$ ethyl ethanoate | 88 | 77 |
| $CH_3COOCH_2CH_2CH_3$ propyl ethanoate | 102 | 102 |
| $CH_3COOCH_2CH_2CH_2CH_3$ butyl ethanoate | 116 | 126 |
| $CH_3COOCH_2CH_2CH_2CH_2CH_3$ pentyl ethanoate | 130 | 147 |
| $CH_3COOCH_2CH_2CH_2CH_2CH_2CH_3$ hexyl ethanoate | 144 | 169 |

Table 1: The effect of increasing molar mass on the boiling point of simple ethanoate esters ($CH_3COOR$).

The magnitude of the molecular dipole produced by the ester linkage (-COO-) is comparable to the magnitude of the molecular dipole generated by the carbonyl (C=O) group in an aldehyde or ketone. As a result the magnitude of the attractive forces between the molecules in an ester is similar to the magnitude of the attractive forces between the molecules in an aldehyde or ketone with a similar molar mass. It therefore follows that the boiling point of an ester will be similar to the boiling point of an aldehyde or ketone with a similar molar mass.

Methyl ethanoate, $C_3H_6O_2$
(boiling point 57 °C)

Propanone, $C_3H_6O$
(boiling point 56 °C)

### Exercise 4.9C

1. The esters amyl acetate and pentyl hexanoate are sweet-smelling oily liquids. Amyl acetate is found in banana oil and pentyl hexanoate is found in pineapples. With reference to intermolecular forces explain why the boiling point of pentyl hexanoate is higher than the boiling point of amyl acetate.

$$CH_3COO(CH_2)_4CH_3$$
amyl acetate (boiling point 149 °C)

$$CH_3(CH_2)_4COO(CH_2)_4CH_3$$
pentyl hexanoate (boiling point 226 °C)

2. Dihydrofuranone, $C_4H_6O_2$ is a cyclic ester. It is an oily liquid with a boiling point of 204 °C and is miscible in water. With reference to intermolecular forces suggest why the boiling point of dihydrofuranone is significantly higher than the boiling point of the ester ethyl ethanoate.

dihydrofuranone (boiling point 204 °C)

ethyl ethanoate (boiling point 77 °C)

3. Compounds A and B are cyclic esters. With reference to intermolecular forces suggest why the boiling point of compound B is lower than the boiling point of compound A.

Compound A
(boiling point 204 °C)

Compound B
(boiling point 122 °C)

Before moving to the next section, check that you are able to:

- Account for trends in the boiling point of esters in terms of the forces between molecules.

### Naming Esters

The systematic (IUPAC) name for an ester consists of a prefix to describe the alkyl group attached to the ester linkage (-COOR') followed by the name of the carboxylate ion formed by the parent carboxylic acid. For example, ethyl ethanoate is an *ethanoate* ester as it is a derivative of ethanoic acid.

ethanoic acid
$CH_3COOH$

ethyl ethanoate
$CH_3COOC_2H_5$

The prefix *ethyl* is added to describe the ethyl group attached to the ester linkage. Similarly, the name propyl ethanoate is used to refer to the propyl ester of ethanoic acid.

ethanoic acid
$CH_3COOH$

propyl ethanoate
$CH_3COOC_3H_7$

Additional prefixes can then be used to locate additional groups attached to the carbon chain in the alkyl group. For example, in 1-methylethyl ethanoate, the prefix *1-methyl* is used to locate a methyl group on the first carbon within the ethyl group attached to the ester linkage. Similarly, in 2-methylpropyl ethanoate, the prefix *2-methyl* is used to locate a methyl group on the second carbon atom within the propyl group attached to the ester linkage.

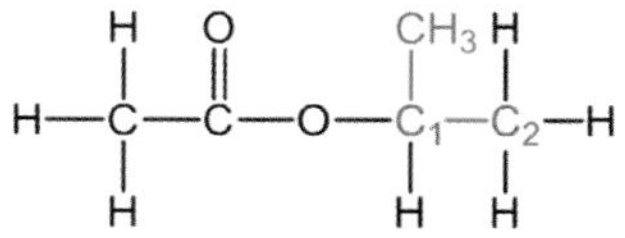

1-methylethyl ethanoate

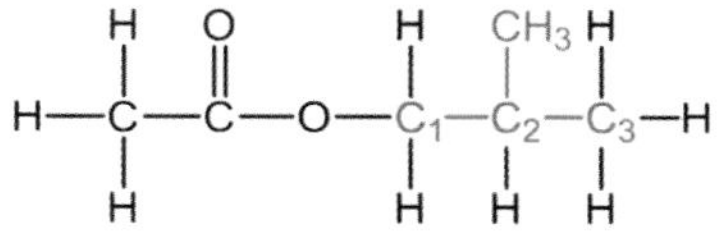

2-methylpropyl ethanoate

## Worked Example 4.9i

Write the systematic names for the esters A and B.

A $CH_3CH(OH)CH_2COOCH_3$

B $CH(CH_3)_2CH(OH)COOCH_2CH_3$

### Strategy

- Compound A is the methyl ester of 3-hydroxybutanoic acid:

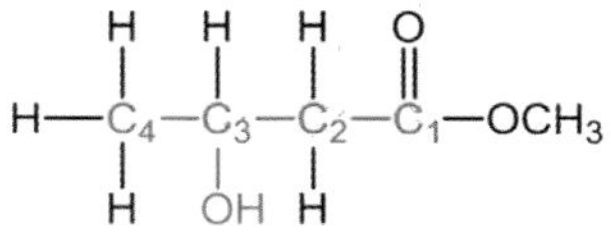

- Compound B is the ethyl ester of 2-hydroxy-3-methylbutanoic acid:

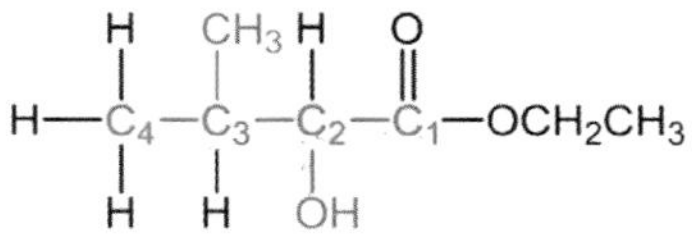

### Solution

Ester A is methyl 3-hydroxybutanoate.

Ester B is ethyl 2-hydroxy-3-methylbutanoate.

---

**Rules** for naming esters:

1. The name of the alkyl group attached to the ester linkage (-COOR') is followed by the name of the carboxylate ion formed by the parent carboxylic acid.

2. Additional prefixes are used to locate groups attached to the carbon chain in the alkyl group.

3. The carbon atoms in the alkyl group are numbered from the ester linkage.

## Exercise 4.9D

1. Which one of the following is the molecular formula of methyl propanoate?

   A $CH_3CH_2COOCH_3$

   B $C_2H_4O$

   C $C_4H_8O_2$

   D $HCOOCH_2CH_2CH_3$

   *(CCEA January 2014)*

2. Which one of the following molecules has a different empirical formula from that of aldol, $CH_3CHOHCH_2CHO$?  $C_4H_8O_2$

   A Ethanal

   B Butanoic acid

   C Methyl propanoate

   D Propanoic acid

   *(CCEA May 2015)*

3. Amyl acetate and isoamyl acetate are found in banana oil. Write the systematic name for (a) amyl acetate and (b) isoamyl acetate.

   $CH_3COO(CH_2)_4CH_3$     $CH_3COOCH_2CH_2CH(CH_3)_2$
      amyl acetate         isoamyl acetate

4. Which one of the following is not an isomer of the ester $CH_3CO_2CH(CH_3)_2$?

   A propyl ethanoate

   B butyl methanoate

   C pentanoic acid

   D ethyl ethanoate

   *(CCEA January 2009)*

5. Draw and name all possible esters of propanoic acid with the molecular formula $C_6H_{12}O_2$.

6. Draw the structure of 2-methylpropyl 3-hydroxybutanoate.

7. Leucic acid is produced when the amino acid leucine is metabolised in muscle tissue. Write the systematic name for the methyl ester of leucic acid.

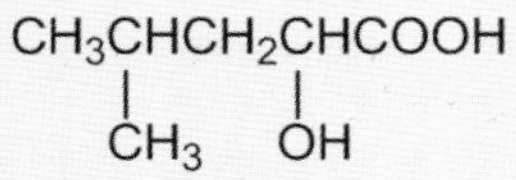

leucic acid

Before moving to the next section, check that you are able to:

- Deduce the systematic name for esters, including esters formed from substituted carboxylic acids and substituted alcohols.

## Preparation

**In this section we are learning to:**

- Deduce the structure of the ester formed when an alcohol reacts with a carboxylic acid or an acid chloride, and write an equation for the reaction.
- Describe the preparation of an ester from the corresponding carboxylic acid.
- Explain the reaction conditions used to form an ester from a carboxylic acid, and the advantages of forming esters from acyl chlorides.

### Esters from Simple Alcohols

#### Forming the Ester

Refluxing a carboxylic acid with an alcohol in the presence of a small amount of concentrated sulfuric acid results in a dynamic equilibrium:

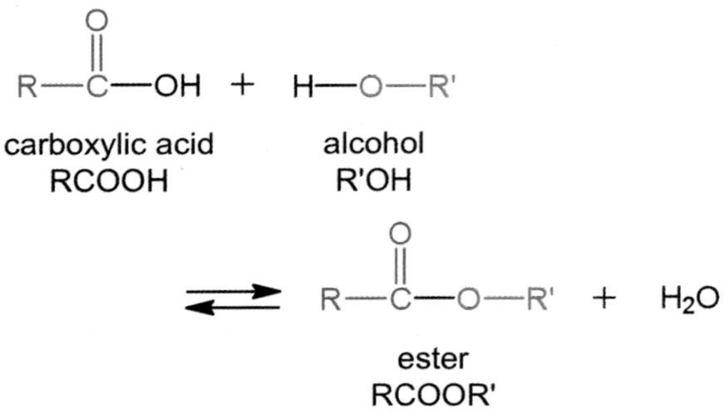

$$R-\overset{\displaystyle O}{\overset{\|}{C}}-OH \; + \; H-O-R'$$

carboxylic acid     alcohol
RCOOH        R'OH

$$\rightleftharpoons \quad R-\overset{\displaystyle O}{\overset{\|}{C}}-O-R' \; + \; H_2O$$

ester
RCOOR'

Hydrogen ions from the sulfuric acid increase the rate of the reaction by acting as a catalyst. The sulfuric acid also increases the yield of ester by removing water from the reaction mixture, causing the position of equilibrium to shift to the right.

The yield of ester can also be increased by adding a large excess of the carboxylic acid or the alcohol to shift the position of equilibrium to the right.

#### Worked Example 4.9ii

Draw the structure of the esters formed by reacting ethanoic acid, $CH_3COOH$ with each of the following alcohols.

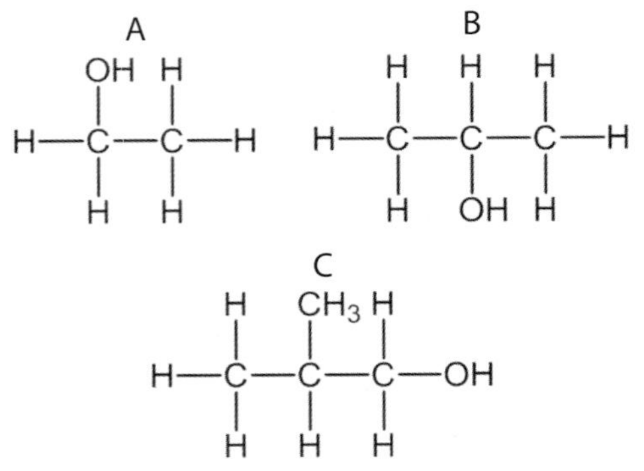

### Strategy

- Ethanoic acid forms ethanoate esters ($CH_3COOR'$)
- The alcohols contain the following alkyl groups (R').

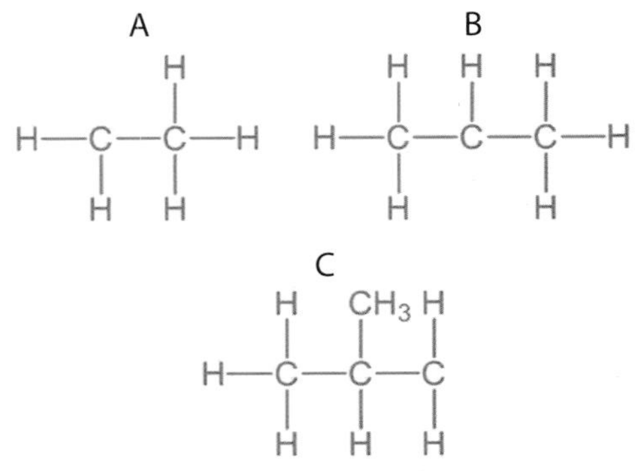

### Solution

The structures of the esters (RCOOR') are:

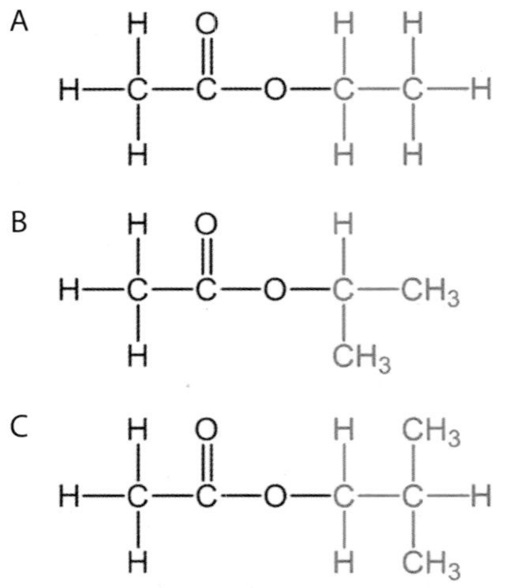

## Exercise 4.9E

1. The fragrance of raspberries is largely due to the ester ethyl methanoate.

   ethanol + methanoic acid
   $$\rightleftharpoons \text{ethyl methanoate} + \text{water}$$

   (a) Explain how the equilibrium yield of the ester could be increased. (b) Draw the structural formula of ethyl methanoate. (c) Draw and name two structural isomers of ethyl methanoate.

   *(CCEA June 2004)*

2. (a) Write an equation for the preparation of methyl propanoate by the reaction of propanoic acid and methanol. (b) Explain why concentrated sulfuric acid is added to the reaction mixture.

   *(CCEA May 2010)*

3. Simple monoesters can be prepared by reacting carboxylic acids with alcohols. (a) Give the systematic names of the carboxylic acid and alcohol used to prepare the ester shown below. (b) Write the equation for the formation of the ester.

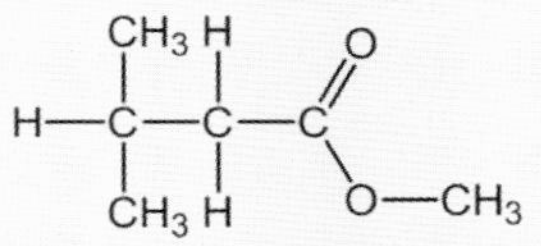

   *(CCEA January 2011)*

4. The ester responsible for the characteristic smell of bananas is formed by the reaction between ethanoic acid and isoamyl alcohol, $C_5H_{11}OH$. Write the equation for the reaction.

   *(CCEA June 2003)*

5. Ethanol undergoes an esterification reaction when refluxed with ethanoic acid in the presence of concentrated sulfuric acid. (a) State two roles of the concentrated sulfuric acid. (b) Draw the structure of the ester formed. (c) Name the ester formed in the reaction.

   *(Adapted from CCEA June 2007)*

6. Butan-2-ol reacts with carboxylic acids to form volatile esters which are used as perfumes or flavourings. Write the equation for the reaction of butan-2-ol with ethanoic acid showing the structures of the reactants and products.

   *(CCEA June 2015)*

7. Which one of the following combinations react to form an ester with the structure shown below?

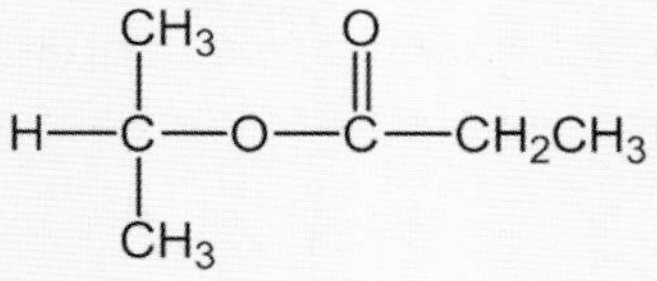

   A  ethanoic acid and propan-1-ol

   B  ethanoic acid and propan-2-ol

   C  propanoic acid and propan-1-ol

   D  propanoic acid and propan-2-ol

   *(CCEA January 2006)*

8. Ester A is one of several compounds responsible for the flavour of beer. In contrast, the presence of ester B in beer indicates that the beer may not have been brewed in sterile conditions. (a) State the reagents needed to form each ester from a carboxylic acid and an alcohol. (b) Write the systematic name for each ester. (c) Write the equation for the formation of each ester from a carboxylic acid and an alcohol.

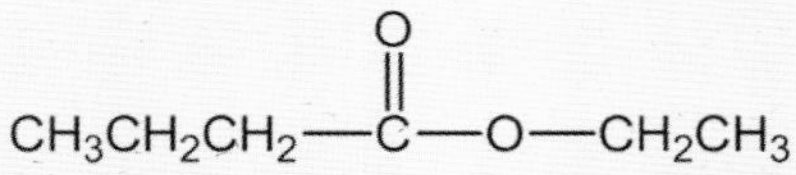

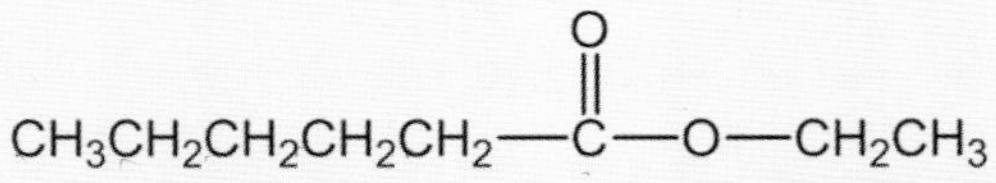

9. 6.0 g of butan-1-ol reacted with an excess of propanoic acid to produce 7.4 g of an ester. Calculate the percentage yield of the ester.

   *(Adapted from CCEA May 2011)*

### Purification of the Ester

A pure, dry sample of the ester is obtained by distilling the reaction mixture and collecting the crude ester at its boiling point. Traces of alcohol and other water soluble impurities are then removed by washing the distillate with dilute sodium hydrogencarbonate. The crude ester is dried by swirling the distillate with a drying agent such as anhydrous sodium sulfate until the distillate is completely clear. The mixture is then filtered to remove the drying agent before being distilled and a pure, dry sample of the ester collected at its boiling point. The principal steps involved in the preparation of a pure, dry sample of an ester from the parent carboxylic acid are summarised in Figure 2.

### Synthesis of an ester from a carboxylic acid and an alcohol

**Stage 1**

**Form** the crude product by refluxing the reactants with concentrated sulfuric acid.

**Stage 2**

**Extract** the crude ester by distilling the reaction mixture and collecting the crude ester at its boiling point.

**Stage 3**

**Purify** the crude product by:
- Washing the crude product with dilute sodium hydrogencarbonate.
- Using anhydrous sodium sulfate to dry the crude product.
- Distilling the crude product and collecting the ester at its boiling point.

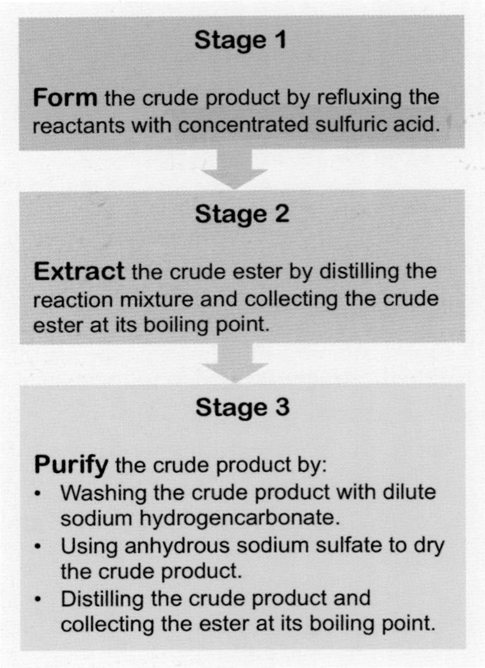

*Figure 2: Flow scheme for the synthesis of a pure, dry sample of an ester from the parent carboxylic acid and an alcohol.*

### Worked Example 4.9iii

Describe, giving experimental details, the preparation of a pure, dry sample of an ester from the reaction between a carboxylic acid and an alcohol.

*(Adapted from CCEA January 2011)*

### Solution

- Slowly add concentrated sulfuric acid to a mixture of the carboxylic acid and the alcohol in a round-bottom flask. Add anti-bumping granules and reflux the mixture for an extended period.
- Distil the mixture and collect the crude ester at its boiling point.
- Add dilute sodium hydrogencarbonate solution to the crude product in a separating funnel. Stopper, invert and shake the separating funnel. Open the tap every few seconds to release any carbon dioxide formed.

- Clamp the separating funnel, remove the stopper, and allow the layers to separate. Collect the upper (organic) layer containing the product.
- Add anhydrous sodium sulfate to the product in a small conical flask and swirl the mixture until the product becomes clear.
- Filter the mixture into a clean, dry round-bottom flask then distil the sample and collect a pure, dry sample of the ester at its boiling point.

### Exercise 4.9F

1. Explain, giving experimental details, the preparation of a pure dry sample of an ester from the corresponding carboxylic acid.

2. Butyl butanoate, $CH_3CH_2CH_2COOCH_2CH_2CH_2CH_3$ is a liquid with a boiling point of 165 °C and a density of 0.87 g cm$^{-3}$. It may be prepared by reaction between butanoic acid and butan-1-ol using concentrated sulfuric acid as a catalyst. (a) Write an equation for the esterification. (b) Calculate the mass of butanoic acid needed to produce 30 cm$^3$ of pure butyl butanoate assuming a 70% yield. (c) The first stage produces a crude sample of the ester. Describe this procedure, including an explanation for any relevant safety precautions, apart from using safety glasses. (d) (i) Describe how the acid impurities are removed. (ii) Suggest a suitable method to dry the butyl butanoate. (iii) Describe how the butyl butanoate is further purified.

*(Adapted from CCEA June 2010)*

---

Before moving to the next section, check that you are able to:

- Write an equation for the esterification of a carboxylic acid, deduce the structure of the ester formed, and account for the reaction conditions.
- Explain, giving experimental details, how a pure, dry sample of an ester is obtained from the corresponding carboxylic acid.

### Esters from Acyl Chlorides

An ester (RCOOR') can also be formed by slowly adding an acyl chloride (RCOCl) to an alcohol (R'OH).

acyl chloride
**RCOCl**

alcohol
**R'OH**

ester
**RCOOR'**

The reaction is generally preferred to forming an ester from the corresponding carboxylic acid as the reaction goes to completion, giving a better yield of the ester. It is also easier to obtain a pure, dry sample of the ester as the only other product of the reaction is a gas.

The reaction is very exothermic and must be carried out in a fume cupboard as acyl chlorides react with water vapour in the air to produce pungent fumes of HCl.

$$RCOCl_{(l)} + H_2O_{(g)} \rightarrow RCOOH_{(l)} + HCl_{(g)}$$

The condensed formulas and systematic names for acyl chlorides with up to six carbon atoms are summarised in Table 2.

| Parent alkane | Acyl chloride (Suffix: -oyl chloride) |
|---|---|
| methane, $CH_4$ (Naming prefix: methan) | HCOCl **methan**oyl chloride |
| ethane, $CH_3CH_3$ (Naming prefix: ethan) | $CH_3COCl$ **ethan**oyl chloride |
| propane, $CH_3CH_2CH_3$ (Naming prefix: propan) | $CH_3CH_2COCl$ **propan**oyl chloride |
| butane, $CH_3CH_2CH_2CH_3$ (Naming prefix: butan) | $CH_3CH_2CH_2COCl$ **butan**oyl chloride |
| pentane, $CH_3CH_2CH_2CH_2CH_3$ (Naming prefix: pentan) | $CH_3CH_2CH_2CH_2COCl$ **pentan**oyl chloride |
| hexane, $CH_3CH_2CH_2CH_2CH_2CH_3$ (Naming prefix: hexan) | $CH_3CH_2CH_2CH_2CH_2COCl$ **hexan**oyl chloride |

*Table 2: Systematic names for acyl chlorides (RCOCl) with up to six carbon atoms.*

### Worked Example 4.9iv

The ester ethyl valerate is used as an artificial flavour and is formed by reacting ethanol with valeric acid. (a) Write the systematic name for valeric acid.

(b) Write the systematic name for the ester ethyl valerate. (c) Name another combination of reagents that could be used to form ethyl valerate. (d) Write an equation for the formation of the ester using the reagents identified in part (c).

ethyl valerate

### Solution

(a) The systematic name for valeric acid, $CH_3CH_2CH_2CH_2COOH$ is pentanoic acid.

(b) The systematic name of the ester is ethyl pentanoate.

(c) The ester can also be made from ethanol, $C_2H_5OH$ and pentanoyl chloride, $CH_3CH_2CH_2CH_2COCl$.

(d) $C_2H_5OH + C_4H_9COCl \rightarrow C_4H_9COOC_2H_5 + HCl$

................................................................

### Exercise 4.9G

1. (a) Name the type of reaction that occurs when ethanoic acid reacts with ethanol to form ethyl ethanoate. (b) Name another reagent which reacts with ethanol to form ethyl ethanoate.

   *(CCEA June 2010)*

2. The compound $CH_3CH_2OH$ reacts with $CH_3COOH$ to form $CH_3COOCH_2CH_3$. (a) Name another compound that will react with $CH_3CH_2OH$ to form the product. (b) Write the equation for the reaction involving the named compound.

   *(Adapted from CCEA June 2006)*

3. What is formed when propanol reacts with ethanoyl chloride?

   A  chloropropane
   B  ethyl propanoate
   C  propanoyl chloride
   D  propyl ethanoate

   *(CCEA June 2005)*

4. Which one of the following combinations can be used to produce methyl ethanoate?

A   ethanoyl chloride and methanoic acid

B   ethanoyl chloride and methanol

C   methane and ethanoic acid

D   methanoic acid and ethanol

*(CCEA January 2008)*

5.  The ester ethyl butanoate is largely responsible for the taste and smell of pineapples. Which two reagents would combine to form this ester?

    A   butan-1-ol and ethanoic acid
    B   butanoyl chloride and ethanoic acid
    C   ethanol and butanoic acid
    D   ethanoyl chloride and butanoic acid

    *(CCEA January 2002)*

6.  (a) Draw the structure of the product formed when propanoyl chloride, $CH_3CH_2COCl$ is added to butan-2-ol. (b) Write an equation for the reaction. (c) Write the systematic name for the product. (d) Explain why the reaction is carried out in a fume cupboard.

7.  The compound formed when methanol is added to $CH_2ClCOCl$ is:

    A  $CH_2OCH_3COCl$
    B  $CH_2OCH_3COCH_3$
    C  $CH_2ClCO_2CH_3$
    D  $CH_2ClCOCH_3$

    *(CCEA May 2015)*

8.  Give two reasons why propanoyl chloride may be used instead of propanoic acid to prepare methyl propanoate.

    *(CCEA May 2010)*

9.  Which one of the following statements about the formation of an ester from ethanoyl chloride and propan-1-ol is correct?

    A  Concentrated sulfuric acid is required.
    B  Heat is required.
    C  The ester produced is called ethyl propanoate.
    D  The reaction goes to completion.

    *(CCEA May 2012)*

10. Cholesterol is concentrated in the brain and spinal cord. It is present both as the free alcohol and as esters of organic acids.

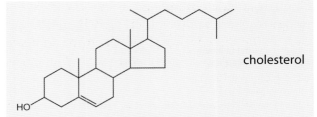

cholesterol

Cholesterol forms an ester with ethanoic acid. (a) Suggest the name of the ester formed. (b) Using the formula ROH for cholesterol write the equation for the formation of the ester. (c) Name a substance that can be used to catalyse the formation of the ester in this reaction. (d) Name another substance that reacts with cholesterol to form the same ester and using the formula ROH for cholesterol write the equation for the reaction.

*(CCEA May 2014)*

**Before moving to the next section, check that you are able to:**

- Write an equation for the esterification of an acyl chloride, deduce the structure of the ester formed, and account for the reaction conditions.
- Recall the advantages of preparing esters from acyl chlorides.

## Esters from Diols and Polyalcohols

If an esterification reaction is carried out using an alcohol that contains two or more hydroxyl (-OH) groups, each hydroxyl group will react to form an ester linkage. For example, diols such as ethane-1,2-diol will react to form a diester that contains two ester linkages.

*Esterification of a diol to form a diester:*

Similarly, if an esterification reaction is carried out using a triol such as glycerol, $CH_2OHCH_2OHCH_2OH$ each of the three hydroxyl groups in the triol will react to form an ester linkage and the product will be a triester.

*Esterification of a triol to form a triester:*

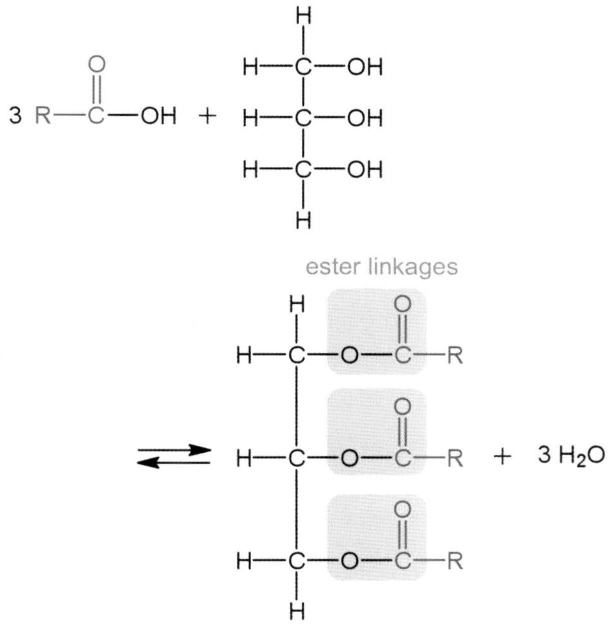

ester linkages

### Exercise 4.9H

1. (a) Write an equation for the reaction of ethane-1,2-diol ($HOCH_2CH_2OH$) with an excess of ethanoic acid, in the presence of concentrated sulfuric acid, to form a diester. (b) Write the equilibrium constant, $K_c$ for the reaction and state its units.

*(CCEA May 2011)*

2. Two molecules of tartaric acid can combine to form an ester. Draw the structure of the ester produced.

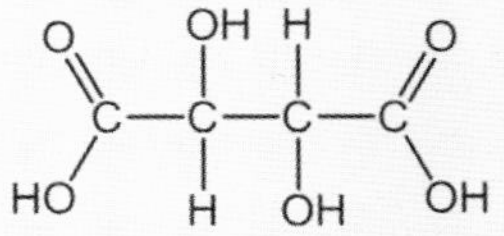

tartaric acid

*(CCEA May 2012)*

3. Fats and oils are triesters of glycerol and long chain carboxylic acids. The fat contained in mutton is predominantly a triester formed from stearic acid, $CH_3(CH_2)_{16}COOH$. Draw the structure of this triester.

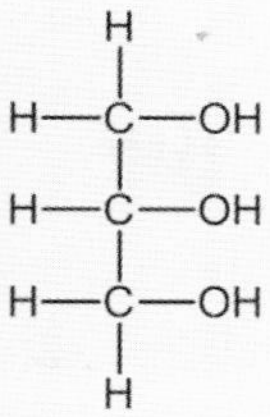

glycerol

*(CCEA January 2010)*

4. Ethylene glycol reacts vigorously with an excess of ethanoyl chloride. (a) Suggest two observations in this reaction. (b) Name the type of reaction occurring. (c) Draw the structure of the organic product. (d) Suggest a test for the inorganic product formed in this reaction.

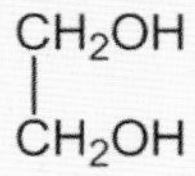

ethylene glycol

*(CCEA June 2014)*

> Before moving to the next section, check that you are able to:
>
> • Deduce the structure of an ester formed from an alcohol with two or more hydroxyl groups and write an equation for the reaction.

## Reactions

> **In this section we are learning to:**
>
> • Deduce the structure of the products formed when an ester undergoes acid or alkaline hydrolysis and write an equation for the reaction.
> • Explain the role of hydrogen ions in the acid hydrolysis of an ester and the role of hydroxide ions in the alkaline hydrolysis of an ester.

### Acid Hydrolysis

When an ester is refluxed with dilute hydrochloric acid the parent carboxylic acid is formed; a process known as acid hydrolysis. The reaction is reversible and results in a dynamic equilibrium.

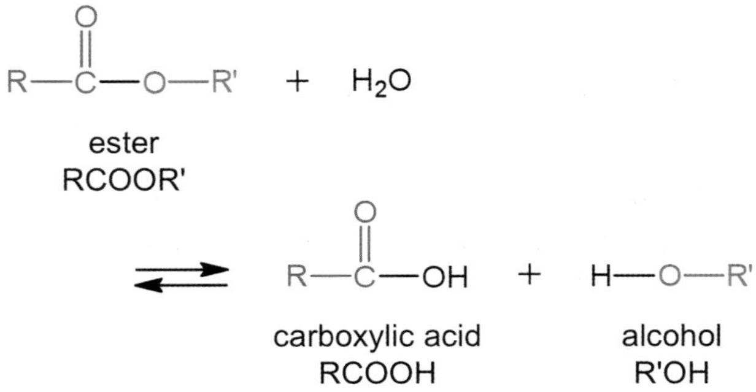

ester
RCOOR'

carboxylic acid
RCOOH

alcohol
R'OH

The reaction is also an example of *acid-catalysed hydrolysis* as the hydrogen ions from the dilute acid function as a catalyst. The hydrogen ions lower the activation energy for the reaction by reacting with the ester to form an intermediate, and are subsequently regenerated as the reaction proceeds.

The extent of hydrolysis can be increased by refluxing the ester with an excess of dilute acid, which provides an excess of water and shifts the position of the equilibrium to the right.

### Exercise 4.9I

1. The acid hydrolysis of methyl ethanoate, $CH_3COOCH_2CH_3$ occurs when a molecule of water uses a lone pair of electrons to bond with the protonated form of methyl ethanoate shown below. (a) Write an equation for the acid hydrolysis of methyl ethanoate. (b) Draw the structure of the intermediate formed when water bonds with the protonated form of ethyl ethanoate shown below. (c) Explain why water can be considered a nucleophile in this reaction.

protonated methyl
ethanoate

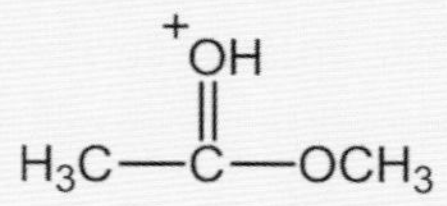

$$\overset{+}{O}H$$
$$H_3C—\overset{\|}{C}—OCH_3$$

2. (a) Write an equation for the acid hydrolysis of ethyl methanoate, $HCOOCH_2CH_3$. (b) The reaction begins when a hydrogen ion combines with the ester to form a protonated ester. The protonated ester then reacts with water to form the intermediate shown below. Draw the structure of the protonated ester. (c) Explain why the reaction is an example of an acid-catalysed reaction.

structure of the
intermediate

$$\overset{OH}{H—\underset{\underset{OH}{|}}{\overset{|}{C}}—OCH_2CH_3}$$

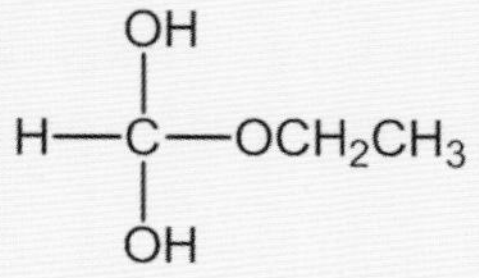

Before moving to the next section, check that you are able to:

• Write an equation for the acid hydrolysis of an ester and deduce the structure of the products formed.

• Explain the role of hydrogen ion as a catalyst.

### Alkaline Hydrolysis

If the hydrolysis is instead carried out by refluxing the ester with an excess of dilute alkali the process is referred to as alkaline hydrolysis.

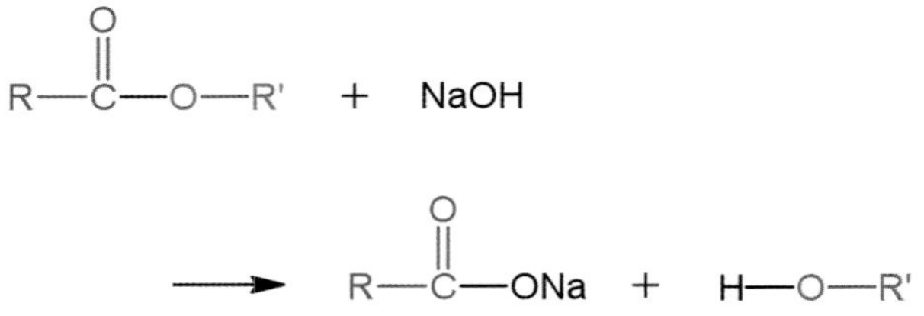

$$R—\overset{\overset{O}{\|}}{C}—O—R' \quad + \quad NaOH$$

$$\longrightarrow \quad R—\overset{\overset{O}{\|}}{C}—ONa \quad + \quad H—O—R'$$

sodium salt of the acid
RCOONa

The alcohol (R'OH) can then be removed by distillation, and the carboxylic acid liberated from its sodium salt by adding an excess of dilute hydrochloric acid to the reaction mixture.

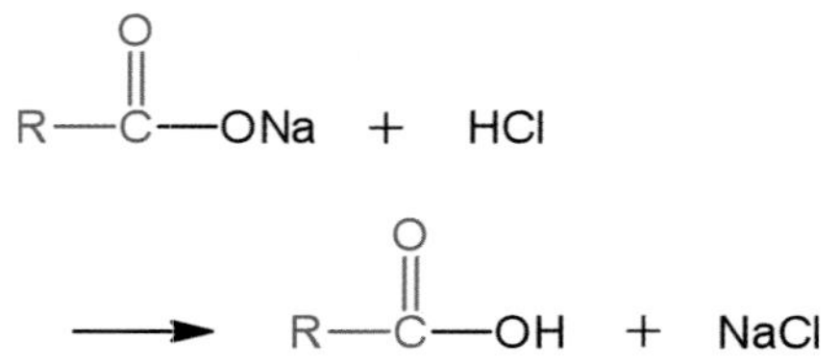

$$R—\overset{\overset{O}{\|}}{C}—ONa \quad + \quad HCl$$

$$\longrightarrow \quad R—\overset{\overset{O}{\|}}{C}—OH \quad + \quad NaCl$$

The reaction is an example of *base-induced hydrolysis* as the hydroxide ions from the dilute alkali increase the rate of the reaction by acting as a nucleophile and attacking the electron deficient carbon atom in the ester linkage.

### Exercise 4.9J

1. A mixture containing sodium ethanoate and propan-2-ol is formed when an ester is refluxed with dilute sodium hydroxide. (a) Draw the structure of the ester. (b) Write an equation for the alkaline hydrolysis of the ester. (c) Explain, with the aid of an equation, how ethanoic acid is liberated from the reaction mixture.

2. (a) Write an equation for the alkaline hydrolysis of the ester isobutyl acetate. (b) Explain how hydroxide ion increases the rate of the reaction by acting as a nucleophile. (c) The reaction begins when hydroxide ion reacts with the ester to form an intermediate. Suggest a structure for the intermediate.

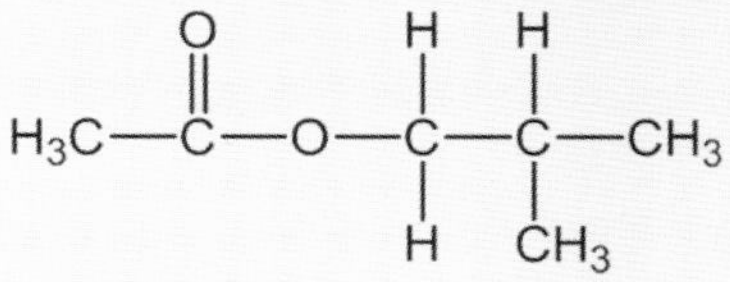

$$H_3C-\underset{\underset{}{\overset{\overset{O}{\|}}{C}}}{}-O-\underset{\underset{H}{|}}{\overset{\overset{H}{|}}{C}}-\underset{\underset{CH_3}{|}}{\overset{\overset{H}{|}}{C}}-CH_3 \quad \text{isobutyl acetate}$$

---

Before moving to the next section, check that you are able to:

- Write equations for the alkaline hydrolysis of an ester, and the liberation of the corresponding carboxylic acid from its salt.

- Deduce the structure of the products of alkaline hydrolysis.

- Explain the role of hydroxide ion as a nucleophile.

# 4.10 Fats and Oils

## Structure and Properties

**In this section we are learning to:**

- Describe fats and oils as mixtures of triglycerides.
- Deduce the structures of triglycerides formed from one or more fatty acids.
- Account for the melting points of fats and oils in terms of molecular structure.

A **triglyceride** *is a triester formed from glycerol and long-chain carboxylic acids* such as stearic acid, $CH_3(CH_2)_{16}COOH$.

$$\text{fatty acids} \quad + \quad \text{glycerol} \longrightarrow \text{triglyceride} \quad + \text{water}$$

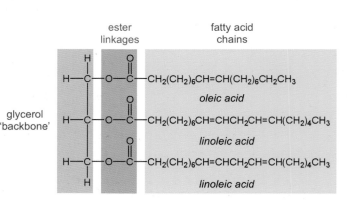

The fats and oils in plants and animals are often complex mixtures of triglycerides. In this context the term **fat** refers to *a solid mixture of triglycerides* and the term **oil** refers to *a liquid mixture of triglycerides*.

Carboxylic acids such as oleic acid and linoleic acid are referred to as **fatty acids** as they are *long-chain carboxylic acids of the type found in triglycerides.*

monounsaturated

$$CH_3(CH_2)_7CH=CH(CH_2)_7COOH$$

oleic acid

polyunsaturated

$$CH_3(CH_2)_4CH=CHCH_2CH=CH(CH_2)_7COOH$$

linoleic acid

Oleic acid is a **monounsaturated** fatty acid as it *contains one C=C bond.* Linoleic acid is an example of a **polyunsaturated** fatty acid as it *contains two or more C=C bonds.* The structure of a triglyceride made from one molecule of oleic acid and two molecules of linoleic acid is shown in Figure 1.

Many of the triglycerides in sunflower oil are formed from oleic acid and linoleic acid. As a result a

ester linkages     fatty acid chains

glycerol 'backbone'

$CH_2(CH_2)_6CH=CH(CH_2)_6CH_2CH_3$

*oleic acid*

$CH_2(CH_2)_6CH=CHCH_2CH=CH(CH_2)_4CH_3$

*linoleic acid*

$CH_2(CH_2)_6CH=CHCH_2CH=CH(CH_2)_4CH_3$

*linoleic acid*

A triglyceride in sunflower oil

*Figure 1: The structure of a triglyceride in sunflower oil formed from one molecule of oleic acid and two molecules of linoleic acid*

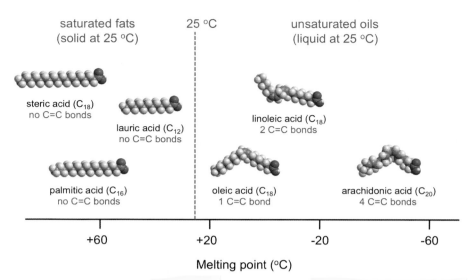

*Figure 2: The effect of unsaturation (C=C bonds) on the melting point of fatty acids.*

high proportion of the fatty acids used to make the triglycerides in sunflower oil are polyunsaturated, and sunflower oil is described as being high in polyunsaturates. In contrast, olive oil is described as being low in polyunsaturates as the triglycerides in olive oil are mostly made from oleic acid which is monounsaturated. Palm oil and coconut oil are also low in polyunsaturates as the triglycerides in the oil are made from **saturated fatty acids** such as lauric acid, $CH_3(CH_2)_{10}COOH$ and palmitic acid, $CH_3(CH_2)_{14}COOH$ that *do not contain C=C bonds.*

The structures in Figure 2 reveal that saturated fatty acids such as lauric acid, palmitic acid and stearic acid have long, straight hydrocarbon chains that pack together efficiently to produce strong van der Waals attraction between neighbouring molecules. As a result saturated fatty acids, and triglycerides containing saturated fatty acids, are often solid at room temperature. In contrast, the C=C bond in oleic acid introduces a substantial 'kink' in the hydrocarbon chain. As a result the hydrocarbon chains in oleic acid, and triglycerides containing oleic acid, pack together less tightly. This reduces the van der Waals attraction between fatty acid molecules to the extent that oleic acid ($C_{18}$) has a lower melting point than lauric acid ($C_{12}$). The relative melting points for linoleic acid and arachidonic acid in Figure 2 suggest that additional C=C bonds in the molecule further reduce the melting point by making it more difficult for the hydrocarbon chains in neighbouring molecules to pack together effectively.

## Exercise 4.10A

1. The percentage composition of three types of oils/fats is shown below. Myristic, palmitic and stearic acids are saturated fatty acid molecules whereas oleic and linoleic acids are unsaturated.

| Oil/fat | Source | Myristic acid | Palmitic acid | Stearic acid | Oleic acid | Linoleic acid |
|---|---|---|---|---|---|---|
| animal fat | butter | 8–15 | 25–29 | 9–12 | 8–33 | 2–4 |
| vegetable oil | olive oil | 0–1 | 5–15 | 1–4 | 67–84 | 8–12 |
| marine oil | whale oil | 5–10 | 10–20 | 2–5 | 33–40 | 0 |

(a) Which one of the oils/fats is likely to be the most unsaturated? (b) Suggest an experimental test that would quickly show that an oil or a fat was unsaturated.

*(CCEA May 2015)*

2. Glycerol reacts with acids to form esters. The reaction with oleic acid, $C_{17}H_{33}COOH$ forms glyceryl trioleate. Draw the structure of glyceryl trioleate.

*(CCEA May 2014)*

3. Triglycerides made from a combination of stearic acid, palmitic acid and oleic acid are a major component of cocoa butter. Draw the structure of a triglyceride made from stearic acid, palmitic acid and oleic acid.

stearic acid, $CH_3(CH_2)_{16}COOH$

palmitic acid, $CH_3(CH_2)_{14}COOH$

oleic acid, $CH_3(CH_2)_7CH=CH(CH_2)_7COOH$

4. (a) Classify the fatty acids shown below as monounsaturated and polyunsaturated. Explain your reasoning. (b) All the double bonds in arachidonic acid are *cis*. Draw the structure of the acid.

$CH_3(CH_2)_7CH=CH(CH_2)_7COOH$
oleic acid

$CH_3(CH_2)_4CH=CHCH_2CH=CH(CH_2)_7COOH$
linoleic acid

$CH_3CH_2CH=CHCH_2CH=CHCH_2CH$
$=CH(CH_2)_7COOH$
linolenic acid

$CH_3(CH_2)_4CH=CHCH_2CH=CHCH_2CH$
$=CHCH_2CH=CH(CH_2)_3COOH$
arachidonic acid

*(Adapted from CCEA January 2012)*

5. The structures of glyceryl tristearate and glyceryl trioleate are shown in the following diagrams. Suggest why glyceryl tristearate is a solid whereas glyceryl trioleate is a liquid.

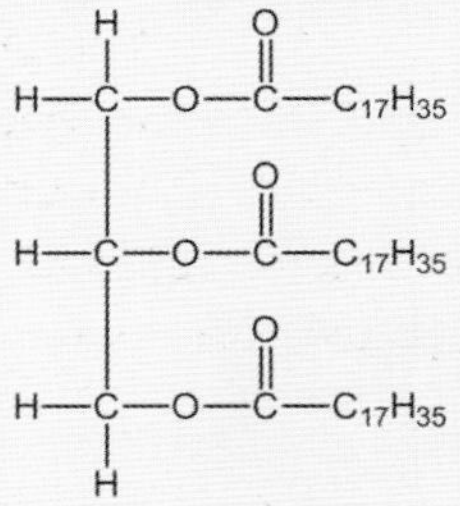

glyceryl tristearate 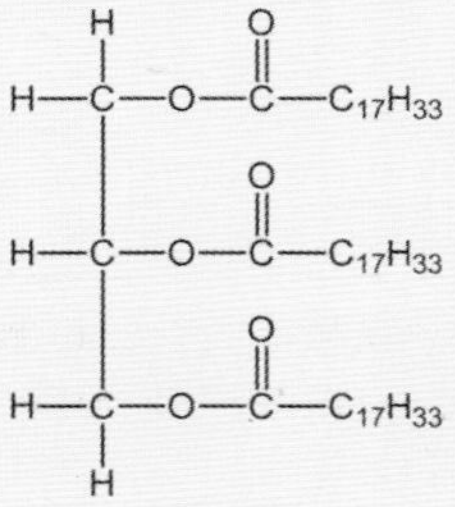    glyceryl trioleate

*(Adapted from CCEA May 2013)*

6. The difference between oils and fats is based upon their melting points. Oils are liquid at room temperature and fats are solid. Describe how you would measure the melting point range of a frozen oil/fat and then explain how you would determine whether the substance was an oil or a fat at 25 °C.

*(CCEA May 2015)*

---

Before moving to the next section, check that you are able to:

- Recall that fats and oils are mixtures of triglycerides.
- Deduce the structure of triglycerides formed from one or more fatty acids.
- Classify fatty acids as saturated, monounsaturated or polyunsaturated according to the number of C=C bonds in the fatty acid molecule.
- Account for the melting points of fats and oils in terms of the number of C=C bonds in the fat or oil.

## Reactions

**In this section we are learning to:**

- Describe the hydrolysis of triglycerides.
- Describe the hydrogenation of unsaturated fats and oils and explain the role of hydrogenation in food production.
- Describe the use of transesterification in the manufacture of fats and oils for food production and the synthesis of biodiesel.

### Saponification

When a fat or oil is refluxed with dilute alkali the triglycerides in the sample undergo alkaline hydrolysis, a process known as **saponification**.

triglyceride + alkali ⟶ salts of fatty acids + glycerol

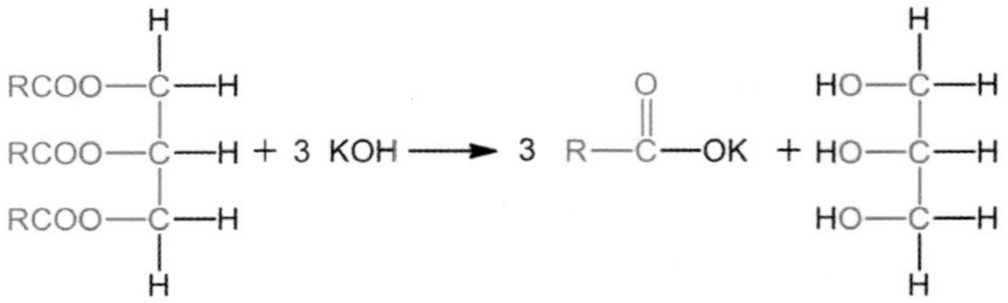

### Worked Example 4.10i

Around one third of the triglycerides in cocoa butter are formed from a combination of stearic acid, palmitic acid and oleic acid. Refluxing the triglycerides with aqueous potassium hydroxide produces a mixture containing potassium stearate, potassium palmitate, potassium oleate and one other product. (a) Write an equation for the hydrolysis of a triglyceride. (b) Write the systematic name for the other product formed in the reaction.

$$CH_3(CH_2)_{16}COOH$$
stearic acid

$$CH_3(CH_2)_{14}COOH$$
palmitic acid

$$CH_3(CH_2)_7CH=CH(CH_2)_7COOH$$
oleic acid

## Strategy

- The triglyceride will react with three equivalents of KOH to form the potassium salt of each fatty acid and glycerol.

## Solution

(a)

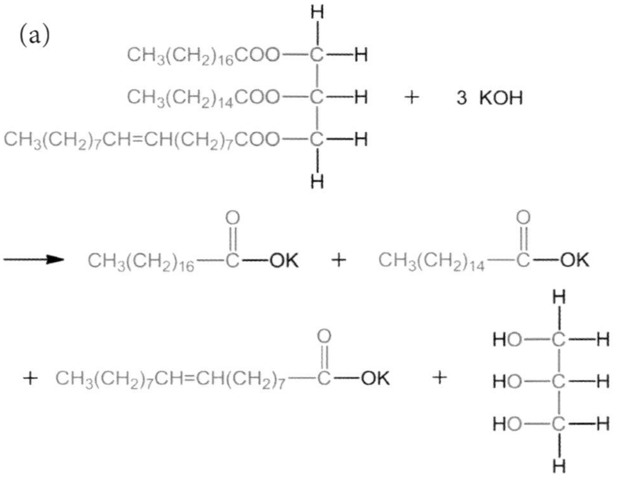

(b) Propane-1,2,3-triol

## Exercise 4.10B

1. Refluxing the fat, stearin with potassium hydroxide produces potassium stearate and one other product. (a) Write an equation for the reaction of stearin with excess potassium hydroxide. (b) State the systematic name of the other product.

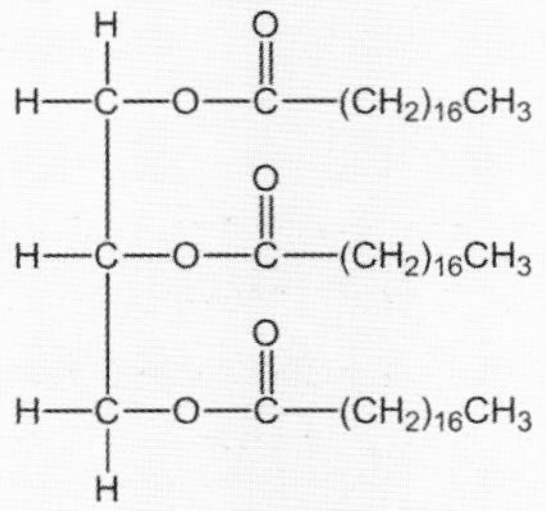

stearin

*(Adapted from CCEA May 2011)*

2. The structure of glyceryl tristearate is shown in the following diagram. Saponification of glyceryl tristearate can be carried out using sodium hydroxide or potassium hydroxide. (a) Write an equation for the saponification of glyceryl tristearate using sodium hydroxide. (b) Write the molecular formula for glyceryl tristearate and calculate its relative molecular mass.

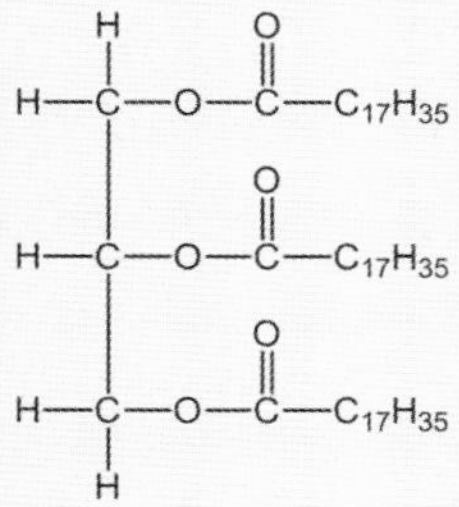

glyceryl tristearate

*(Adapted from CCEA May 2013)*

3. Palmitic acid, $C_{15}H_{31}COOH$ forms the triglyceride palmitin when it reacts with glycerol. Draw the structure of palmitin.

*(Adapted from CCEA January 2013)*

4. Lauric acid triglyceride, the triester formed from lauric acid, $C_{11}H_{23}COOH$ and glycerol is the main constituent in coconut oil. Lauric acid triglyceride has a saponification value of 260. (a) Explain what is meant by the term *saponification*. (b) Write an equation for the saponification of lauric acid triglyceride using aqueous potassium hydroxide.

*(Adapted from CCEA May 2012)*

5. Fats and vegetable oils are triesters of long-chain carboxylic acids. Base catalysed hydrolysis of an oil produces glycerol and the sodium salt of octadeca-9,12-dienoic acid as the only products. (a) Draw the structure of glycerol. (b) State the systematic name for glycerol. (c) Draw the structure of the oil.

$$CH_3(CH_2)_4CH=CHCH_2CH=CH(CH_2)_7COOH$$
octadeca-9,12-dienoic acid

*(CCEA January 2011)*

6. Linoleic acid is one of two essential fatty acids in our diet. Glyceryl esters of the acid are plentiful in sunflower oil. (a) Draw the structure of linoleic acid. The configuration of each double bond is *cis*. (b) Draw the structure of the oil formed when one molecule of glycerol reacts with three molecules of linoleic acid.

Represent the acid as $C_{17}H_{31}COOH$.

$CH_3(CH_2)_4CH=CHCH_2CH=CH(CH_2)_7COOH$
linoleic acid

*(CCEA May 2008)*

7. Hydrolysis of a fat produces two molecules of palmitic acid, $C_{15}H_{31}COOH$ and one molecule of myristic acid, $C_{13}H_{27}COOH$. Draw a structure for the unhydrolysed fat.

*(CCEA January 2014)*

8. The hydrolysis of 1 mole of an oil gave 1 mole of oleic acid and 2 moles of stearic acid together with propane-1,2,3-triol. The oil molecule is optically active. (a) Give the common name for propane-1,2,3-triol. (b) Using the following formulas for the acids draw the structure of the oil and label the asymmetric centre with an asterisk (*).

oleic acid, $R_1COOH$

stearic acid, $R_2COOH$

*(Adapted from CCEA May 2015)*

> **Before moving to the next section, check that you are able to:**
>
> - Explain what is meant by *saponification* and write an equation for the saponification of a triglyceride.

## Hydrogenation

Natural fats and oils used in the production of food are high in polyunsaturates. Many are semi-solid oils that must be **hardened** to form solid fats before they are suitable for use in products such as margarine. An oil is hardened by adding hydrogen ($H_2$) across C=C bonds in the oil until the oil has achieved the desired consistency.

*Adding hydrogen across one C=C bond in a fat or oil:*

unsaturated
fat or oil

The hydrogenation is carried out by bubbling hydrogen gas ($H_2$) through the oil at a temperature of around 150 °C in the presence of finely divided

nickel. The nickel has a large surface area and acts as a catalyst for the reaction. In order for the reaction to occur both reactants must first adsorb on the surface of the nickel. Adsorbed hydrogen molecules ($H_2$) then add across one or more C=C bonds in the oil before the hydrogenated oil desorbs from the nickel surface. The extent to which the oil is hydrogenated depends on the reaction conditions.

> ### Exercise 4.10C
>
> 1. Name the catalyst and state the conditions used to catalytically hydrogenate fats and oils.
>
> *(CCEA January 2012)*
>
> 2. Olive oil may be 'hardened' using a nickel catalyst. Explain the chemistry of 'hardening'.
>
> *(CCEA May 2007)*

> **Before moving to the next section, check that you are able to:**
>
> - Explain why polyunsaturated fats and oils are *hardened* by hydrogenation.
> - Recall the conditions used to hydrogenate fats and oils

## Transesterification

The melting point of fats and oils can also be increased by a process known as **transesterification** in which carboxylate (RCOO-) groups are exchanged between triglycerides (intermolecular exchange), or within the same triglyceride (intramolecular exchange). The exchange occurs on heating the fat or oil to around 120 °C in the presence of dilute sodium hydroxide and glycerol.

*Intermolecular transesterification:*

*Intramolecular transesterification:*

Transesterification is widely used to increase the melting point of sunflower oil for use in the manufacture of margarine and is carried out before the oil is hardened by hydrogenation. Transesterification is also used to produce biodiesel, *a fuel similar to diesel that contains alkyl esters formed from the long chain fatty acids in renewable sources such as vegetable oils*. Biodiesel is formed by heating a fat or oil with an excess of an alcohol, typically methanol or ethanol, in presence of aqueous sodium hydroxide which acts as catalyst.

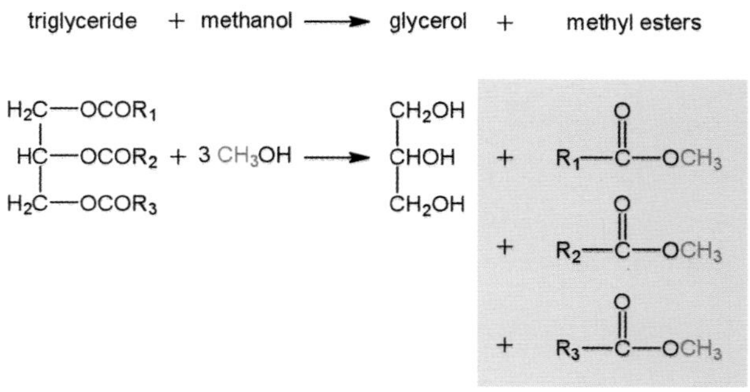

triglyceride + methanol ⟶ glycerol + methyl esters

$$H_2C-OCOR_1$$
$$HC-OCOR_2 + 3\ CH_3OH \longrightarrow$$
$$H_2C-OCOR_3$$

$$CH_2OH$$
$$CHOH$$
$$CH_2OH$$

$$+ \quad R_1-\overset{\overset{\displaystyle O}{\|}}{C}-OCH_3$$

$$+ \quad R_2-\overset{\overset{\displaystyle O}{\|}}{C}-OCH_3$$

$$+ \quad R_3-\overset{\overset{\displaystyle O}{\|}}{C}-OCH_3$$

Biodiesel
(a mixture of esters)

On heating, the glycerol in the triglycerides exchanges with the alcohol to produce a mixture of fatty acid esters. Glycerol is a useful by-product, and can be used in the manufacture of cosmetics, toiletries and other pharmaceuticals.

The mixture of ethyl esters obtained by transesterification with ethanol is less viscous than the mixture of methyl esters obtained by transesterification with methanol, and is therefore more suitable for use as a fuel, particularly at low temperatures. The mixture of esters obtained from rapeseed oil and other oils high in polyunsaturates is also more suitable for use as a fuel as it has a lower melting point than the esters produced from triglycerides high in saturated fatty acids.

Biodiesel is an effective replacement for petrol as it generates a similar amount of energy when burnt, and can be burnt in petrol engines without modifying the engine. Fuels such as ethanol can also be used as an alternative to petrol but are less suitable as ethanol generates less energy than biodiesel, and petrol engines must be modified to burn ethanol.

## Exercise 4.10D

1.  (a) Explain what is meant by the term *biodiesel*. (b) State the conditions used to produce biodiesel from vegetable oil. (c) Explain why biodiesel is considered a more suitable alternative to petrol than ethanol.

2.  Waste sunflower oil recycled from restaurants is used to produce biodiesel. Saponification of the triglycerides in sunflower oil produces oleic acid and linoleic acid. (a) Draw the structure of the esters formed when sunflower oil is heated with ethanol in the presence of a small amount of dilute sodium hydroxide. (b) Explain why dilute sodium hydroxide is added to the reaction mixture.

    $CH_3(CH_2)_7CH=CH(CH_2)_7COOH$
    oleic acid

    $CH_3(CH_2)_4CH=CHCH_2CH=CH(CH_2)_7COOH$
    linoleic acid

3.  The triglycerides in rapeseed oil have the following structure. Write an equation, showing the structure of each reactant and product, for the formation of biodiesel by heating rapeseed oil with an excess of methanol in the presence of a small amount of sodium hydroxide.

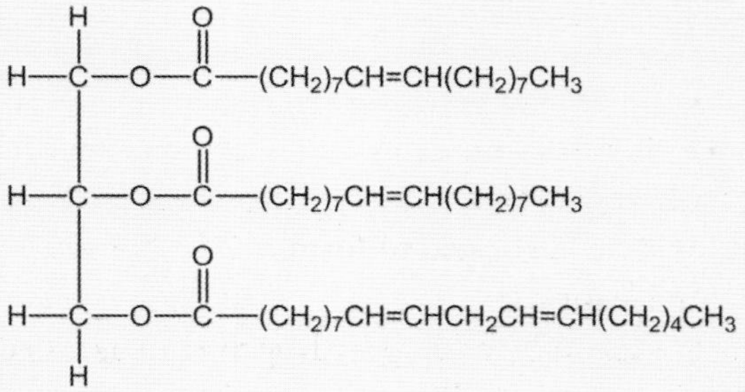

    $$H-\overset{\overset{\displaystyle H}{|}}{C}-O-\overset{\overset{\displaystyle O}{\|}}{C}-(CH_2)_7CH=CH(CH_2)_7CH_3$$
    $$H-\overset{|}{C}-O-\overset{\overset{\displaystyle O}{\|}}{C}-(CH_2)_7CH=CH(CH_2)_7CH_3$$
    $$H-\underset{\underset{\displaystyle H}{|}}{\overset{|}{C}}-O-\overset{\overset{\displaystyle O}{\|}}{C}-(CH_2)_7CH=CHCH_2CH=CH(CH_2)_4CH_3$$

Before moving to the next section, check that you are able to:

*   Explain what is meant by *transesterification* and write equations to describe intermolecular and intramolecular transesterification reactions.
*   Recall what is meant by *biodiesel* and explain why biodiesel is an effective alternative to petrol.
*   Write equations for the production of biodiesel from triglycerides.

# 4.11 Arenes

Many herbs and spices, and other natural fragrances, contain aromatic compounds. The compound vanillin is an aromatic compound, and is a component of the extract obtained from vanilla beans. The structure of vanillin is based on benzene, $C_6H_6$. When an aromatic compound such as vanillin reacts, it does so in a way that preserves the structure of the 'benzene ring' within the molecule.

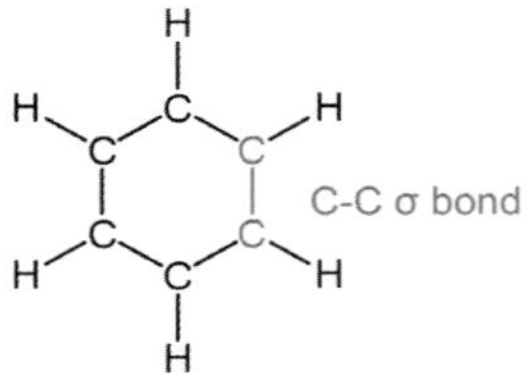

C-C and C-H
σ bonds in benzene

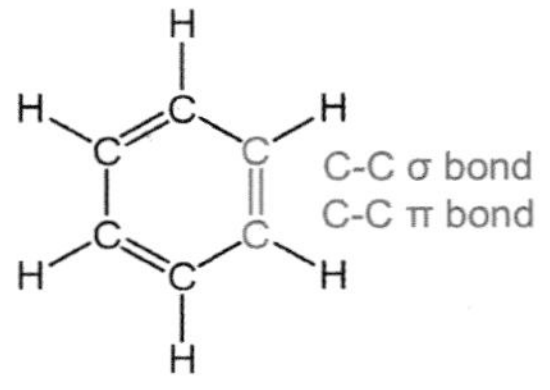

Structural formula
for benzene

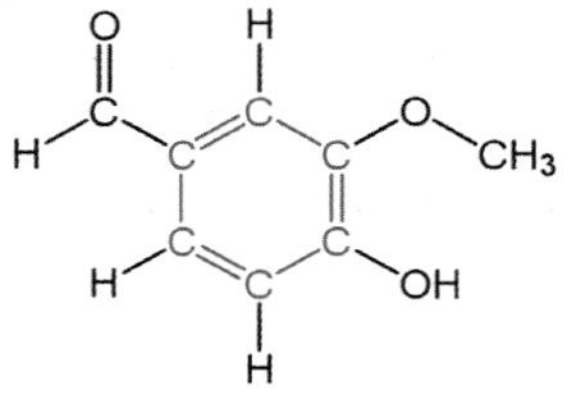

Vanillin
$C_8H_8O_3$

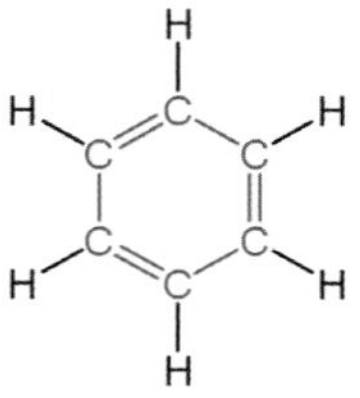

Benzene
$C_6H_6$

## Benzene

**In this section we are learning to:**

- Account for the structure and stability of benzene in terms of the bonding within the molecule.

Benzene is a colourless liquid with the molecular formula $C_6H_6$. The carbon atoms in a molecule of benzene form a six-membered ring with each carbon atom using three of its four outer-shell electrons to sigma bond with a hydrogen atom, and two neighbouring carbon atoms in the ring. The bonding pairs used to form the sigma bonds have a trigonal planar arrangement about the carbon atom. Each carbon atom in the ring then uses its fourth outer-shell electron to form a C-C π-bond with a neighbouring carbon atom.

In theory the set of three C-C π-bonds in a molecule of benzene could be used to construct either of the Kekulé structures shown in Figure 1. In terms of electrons and bonds the Kekulé structures are identical. As a result, benzene is equally likely to exist in either form, and each C-C π-bond will only be present half of the time. This 'spreading out' of the electrons involved in π-bonding around the ring is referred to as **delocalisation,** and is represented by a dashed line (---) as shown in Figure 1.

Delocalisation of the electrons in the C-C π-bonds to form partial C-C π-bonds between neighbouring carbon atoms results in six identical C-C bonds. Each

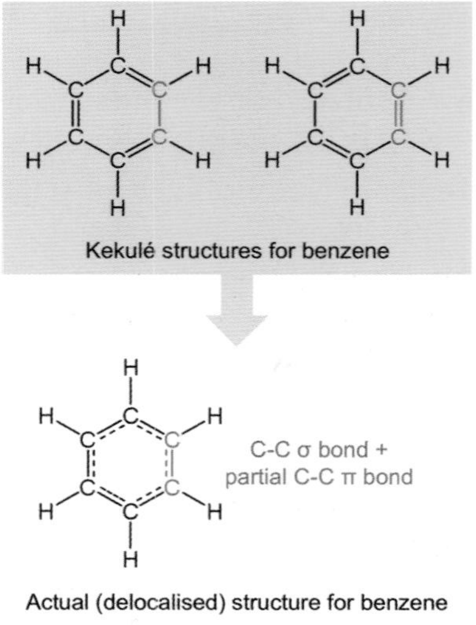

Kekulé structures for benzene

C-C σ bond +
partial C-C π bond

Actual (delocalised) structure for benzene

*Figure 1: Delocalisation of the electrons in the C-C π-bonds around the benzene ring to form partial C-C π-bonds between neighbouring carbon atoms.*

C-C bond consists of a C-C σ-bond and a partial C-C π-bond. As a result the length and strength of a C-C bond in benzene is intermediate between the length and strength of a C-C bond in an alkane and a C=C bond in an alkene.

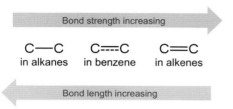

Bond strength increasing

C—C in alkanes   C≡≡C in benzene   C=C in alkenes

Bond length increasing

Delocalisation of the π-electrons in benzene also lowers the energy of benzene, making it considerably less reactive than alkenes; a type of stability referred to as **aromatic character.** Delocalisation of the π-electrons can only occur if the molecule has a flat (planar) shape that makes it possible for the p-orbitals on adjacent carbon atoms to overlap.

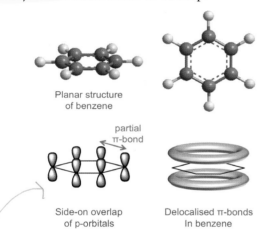

Planar structure of benzene

partial π-bond

Side-on overlap of p-orbitals

Delocalised π-bonds In benzene

**Exercise 4.11A**

1. How many p-orbitals are involved in the delocalisation of π-electrons in a benzene molecule?   *Six*

(CCEA June 2015)

2. The electrons in the π-bonds in benzene are delocalised. Draw two structures for benzene to show the p-orbitals before and after delocalisation.

(CCEA May 2012)

3. In total, how many electrons are involved in bonding in a molecule of benzene? *30 electrons*

(Adapted from CCEA May 2011)

4. Describe the bonding in a molecule of benzene.

(Adapted from CCEA May 2009)

5. State and explain the shape of a benzene molecule. *Planar molecule*

(CCEA June 2004)

6. Which one of the following statements about benzene is incorrect?

A  A total of six electrons per molecule are delocalised.

B  All of the carbon-carbon bonds are the same length.

C  The bond angles are all 120°.

D  The empirical formula is $C_6H_6$.

(CCEA June 2006)

Delocalisation of the π-electrons in benzene can be effectively represented by drawing the skeletal formula for benzene in which only the bonds between the carbon atoms forming the backbone of the structure are shown. The partial C-C π-bonds (---) that result from delocalisation of the π-electrons are represented by a circle in the centre of the ring.

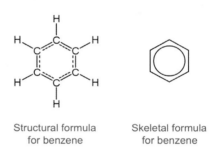

Structural formula for benzene

Skeletal formula for benzene

The stability or 'aromatic character' resulting from the delocalisation of the π-electrons in benzene can be measured by comparing the enthalpy of hydrogenation for the C=C bond in an alkene such as cyclohexene, $C_6H_{10}$ with the enthalpy of hydrogenation for benzene.

Structural formula for cyclohexene

Skeletal formula for cyclohexene

In the absence of delocalisation, each one of the three C=C bonds in one of the Kekulé structures for benzene is equivalent to the C=C bond in cyclohexene.

It therefore follows that the enthalpy of hydrogenation for the Kekulé structure should be three times greater than the enthalpy of hydrogenation for cyclohexene.

cyclohexene $C_6H_{10}$ + $H_2$ → cyclohexane $C_6H_{12}$ ΔH = -120 kJ mol⁻¹

Kekulé structure $C_6H_6$ + 3 $H_2$ → cyclohexane $C_6H_{12}$ ΔH = -360 kJ mol⁻¹

The enthalpy of hydrogenation for benzene ($-208$ kJ mol$^{-1}$) is found to be considerably less than the anticipated enthalpy of hydrogenation for a Kekulé structure ($-360$ kJ mol$^{-1}$), and reflects the additional stability or 'aromatic character' associated with delocalisation of $\pi$-electrons in benzene. This additional stability is also referred to as the resonance energy for benzene ($E_{res}$) and is illustrated by the enthalpy diagram in Figure 2.

benzene $C_6H_6$ + 3 $H_2$ → cyclohexane $C_6H_{12}$ ΔH = -208 kJ mol⁻¹

### Exercise 4.11B

1. Benzene may be catalytically reduced in several steps to cyclohexane using nickel. (a) Write the overall equation for the reduction. (b) Draw a flow scheme showing the structure of all the reduction products. $C_6H_6 + 3H_2 \rightarrow C_6H_{12}$

*(CCEA June 2013)*

2. The enthalpy of hydrogenation for cyclohexene is $-120$ kJ mol$^{-1}$. (a) What does this suggest for the enthalpy of hydrogenation for benzene? (b) The actual value for benzene is $-208$ kJ mol$^{-1}$. Suggest a reason for the difference.

a) -360 Kjmol⁻¹ *(Adapted from CCEA June 2013)*

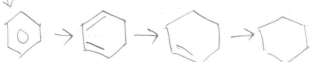

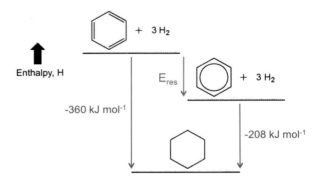

*Figure 2: Enthalpy diagram illustrating the additional stability provided by the delocalisation of the π-electrons in benzene.*

Before moving to the next section, check that you are able to:

- Explain the nature of the bonding within a benzene molecule.
- Account for the planar shape of benzene in terms of bonding.
- Draw structures to explain the delocalisation of electrons in benzene.
- Explain how the properties of the C-C bonds in benzene can be used as evidence for delocalisation.
- Explain how the enthalpy of hydrogenation for cyclohexene can be used to demonstrate the additional stability that results from delocalisation.

## Arenes

**In this section we are learning to:**

- Recognise the structures of arenes.
- Deduce systematic names for arenes whose structure is based on benzene.

The term **arene** refers to *a compound with aromatic character*. Toluene, phenol and benzoic acid are arenes; their structure is based on benzene and retains the aromatic character associated with the delocalisation of the $\pi$-electrons in the benzene ring.

Toluene $C_6H_5CH_3$

Phenol $C_6H_5OH$

Benzoic acid $C_6H_5COOH$

Naphthalene and anthracene are also arenes as their structures are based on two or more benzene rings fused together.

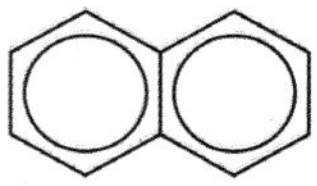

Naphthalene
$C_{10}H_8$

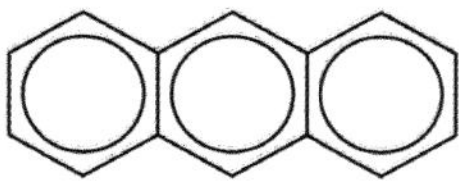

Anthracene
$C_{14}H_{10}$

The systematic name for an arene is based on the name of the parent arene. For example, the compound 1,3-dinitrobenzene is based on benzene. The location of the nitro ($-NO_2$) groups is described by adding the prefix *1,3-dinitro* to the name of the parent arene, where the carbon atoms in the ring are numbered in a way that produces the lowest number prefix.

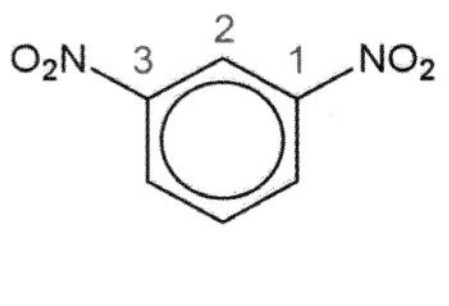

1,3-dinitrobenzene 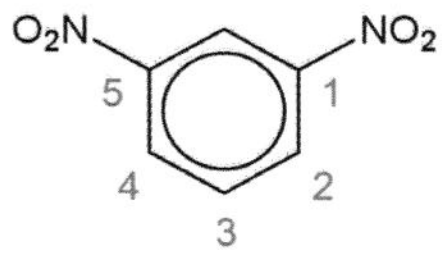 ✓     1,5-dinitrobenzene ✗

If the groups attached to the parent arene are different a separate prefix is added for each group. The prefixes are written in alphabetical order, and the carbon atoms in the parent arene are numbered in a way that produces the lowest number prefixes.

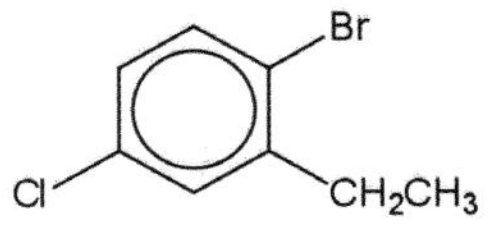

1-bromo-4-chloro-2-ethylbenzene 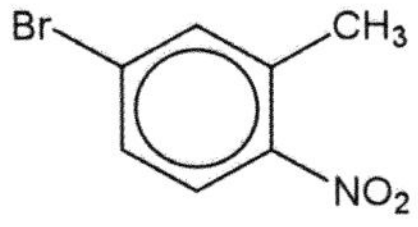   4-bromo-2-methyl-1-nitrobenzene

If the structure is based on a derivative with a common name such as toluene, phenol or benzoic acid, the derivative can also be used to name the compound.

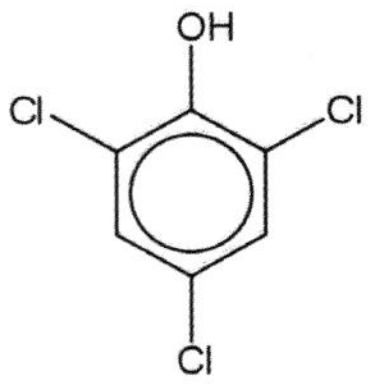

2,4,6-trichlorophenol 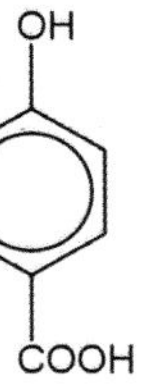     4-hydroxybenzoic acid

### Exercise 4.11C

1. Draw all possible Kekulé structures for naphthalene, $C_{10}H_8$.

2. Draw and name the isomers of dibromobenzene, $C_6H_4Br_2$.

   *(Adapted from CCEA January 2010)*

3. The structure of 4-nitrotoluene is shown in the following diagram. Write the systematic name for 4-nitrotoluene based on benzene.

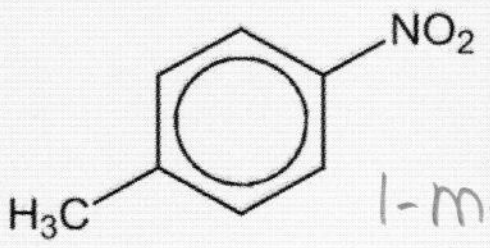

   4-nitrotoluene

   *1-methyl-4-nitrobenzene*

4. The compound 2,4-dinitrophenol is used as an antiseptic and in the industrial production of herbicides. Write the systematic name for 2,4-dinitrophenol based on benzene.

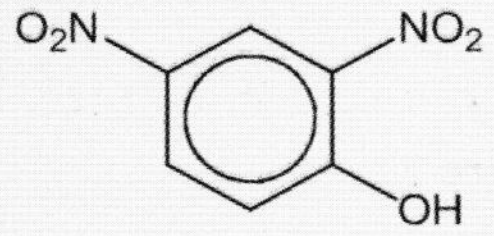

   2,4-dinitrophenol

   *1-hydroxy-2,4-dinitrobenzene*

5. The compound 4-allyl-2-methoxyphenol is commonly known as eugenol and is a major component of clove oil. Write the systematic name for eugenol based on benzene.

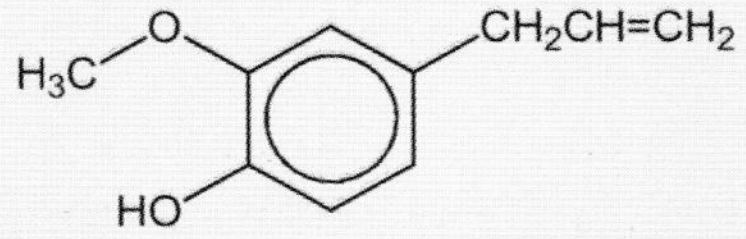

   eugenol

6. Calculate the RMM of 2,4-dichloro-3,5-dimethylphenol.

   *(Adapted from CCEA May 2011)*

7. Benzoic acid is nitrated to produce three products which are shown in the following diagram together with their melting points and their former names. (a) Suggest the systematic names for *ortho, meta* and *para* nitrobenzoic acids. (b) Suggest, using hydrogen bonding, why the melting points of these nitrobenzoic acids increase as the nitro group is further away from the carboxylic acid group.

   *continued overleaf*

COOH
NO₂

**ortho-
nitrobenzoic
acid**

COOH

NO₂

**meta-
nitrobenzoic
acid**

COOH

NO₂

**para-
nitrobenzoic
acid**

*(CCEA June 2014)*

---

Before moving to the next section, check that you are able to:

- Recognise arenes as compounds containing one or more benzene rings.
- Deduce systematic names for arenes with structures based on benzene.

---

## Reactions of Benzene

### Bromination

The term **bromination** refers to *a reaction in which one or more bromine atoms are added to a compound*. When bromine water, $Br_{2\,(aq)}$ is added to a compound containing one or more C=C bonds the bromine water is decolourised as bromine ($Br_2$) adds across each C=C bond in the compound.

$$\underset{}{\text{C=C}} + Br_2 \longrightarrow \underset{}{\overset{Br\ Br}{\text{—C—C—}}}$$

In contrast, bromine will not add across the partial C=C π-bonds in benzene as additional energy is required to overcome the stability associated with the delocalisation of the π-electrons. Bromination is instead accomplished by using a catalyst such as iron to provide an alternative pathway for the reaction with a lower activation energy.

The iron catalyst reacts with bromine to form iron(III) bromide which, once formed, combines with a molecule of bromine to form a complex. As the complex forms the Br-Br bond in the bromine molecule undergoes heterolytic fission to form a bromine cation, $Br^+$. The $Br^+$ ion is a good electrophile and readily attacks the electron rich regions formed by the delocalised π-electrons above and below the benzene ring.

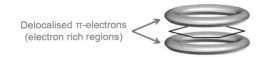

Delocalised π-electrons (electron rich regions)

*Using a catalyst to form bromine ion ($Br^+$):*
$$Br_2 + MBr_3 \rightarrow Br^+ + MBr_4^- \qquad M = Fe, Al$$

When $Br^+$ approaches benzene it forms a coordinate bond with a carbon atom by accepting a pair of delocalised π-electrons from the benzene ring. On forming the coordinate bond the benzene ring acquires a positive charge, and the carbon atom bonded to bromine is no longer able to participate in π-bonding. The resulting break in the delocalisation of the π-electrons at this point in the ring is indicated by a break in the circle representing the delocalisation of the π-electrons at this point as shown in Figure 3.

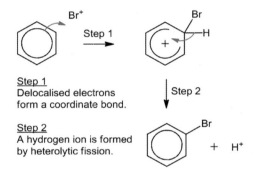

**Step 1**
Delocalised electrons form a coordinate bond.

**Step 2**
A hydrogen ion is formed by heterolytic fission.

*Figure 3: Mechanism for the monobromination of benzene to form bromobenzene, $C_6H_5Br$.*

The addition of $Br^+$ to form an intermediate is then followed by elimination of a hydrogen ion ($H^+$) in a way that restores delocalisation of the π-electrons around the entire benzene ring. In this way the bromination of benzene becomes an example of an **electrophilic substitution** reaction *as it involves the addition of an electrophile followed by the elimination of an atom, molecule or ion.*

The chlorination of benzene occurs by same mechanism, and is accomplished by reacting benzene with chlorine in presence of iron(III) chloride or aluminium chloride.

*Mechanism for the monohalogenation of benzene:*
STEP 1

Forming the electrophile
$$X_2 + MX_3 \rightarrow X^+ + MX_4^-$$
$$X_2 = Cl_2, Br_2 \quad \text{and} \quad M = Fe, Al$$

STEP 2

Electrophilic substitution
$C_6H_6 + X^+ \rightarrow C_6H_5X + H^+$

STEP 3

Reforming the catalyst
$MX_4^- \rightarrow MX_3 + X^-$

The catalyst is reformed when hydrogen ($H^+$) ion is eliminated from the intermediate, and therefore does not appear in the chemical equation for the reaction.

*Chemical equation for the monohalogenation of benzene:*

$C_6H_6 + X_2 \rightarrow C_6H_5X + HX$    where    $X_2 = Cl_2, Br_2$

## Worked Example 4.11i

(a) Draw a flow scheme to show the mechanism for the reaction of bromine with benzene. (b) Draw a flow scheme to show the mechanism for the reaction of bromine with ethene where $Br^+$ is the electrophile. (c) Explain why there are different mechanisms for the reactions.

*(CCEA June 2013)*

### Solution

(a)

(b)

(c) The $\pi$-electrons in benzene are delocalised and are therefore less available to bond with an electrophile than the electrons in the C=C $\pi$-bond in ethene.

## Exercise 4.11D

1. Benzene is more resistant than alkenes to reaction with bromine. (a) What type of reaction do alkenes undergo with bromine? (b) Name a catalyst required for the reaction of benzene with bromine. (c) Draw a flow scheme to show the mechanism for the catalysed reaction of benzene with bromine. (d) Name the mechanism for the reaction of benzene with bromine.

*(CCEA June 2015)*

2. (a) Draw a flow scheme to show the mechanism for the monobromination of methylbenzene to form 4-bromomethylbenzene. (b) Suggest the name of the product formed in the monobromination of 1,4-dimethylbenzene.

*(CCEA June 2011)*

3. Toluene (methylbenzene), $C_6H_5CH_3$ is used to make artificial sweeteners, pharmaceuticals and explosives. (a) Monobromination results in three possible structural isomers. Draw and name all three isomers. (b) Name a suitable catalyst for the bromination of toluene. (c) Explain why toluene undergoes substitution rather than addition with bromine.

*(Adapted from CCEA June 2006)*

Before moving to the next section, check that you are able to:

- Describe the mechanism for the monobromination of benzene.
- Write an equation for the monobromination of benzene and explain why the reaction is an example of electrophilic substitution.
- Explain why benzene undergoes electrophilic substitution in preference to addition.

### Alkylation and Acylation

Aluminium chloride, $AlCl_3$ can also be used to polarise the C-Cl bond in a chloroalkane (RCl) or acyl chloride (RCOCl) to the extent that it undergoes heterolytic fission to form an alkyl cation ($R^+$) or acyl cation ($RCO^+$).

*Forming an alkyl cation ($R^+$):*
$R\text{-}Cl + AlCl_3 \rightarrow R^+ + AlCl_4^-$

*Forming an acyl cation ($RCO^+$):*
$RCOCl + AlCl_3 \rightarrow RCO^+ + AlCl_4^-$

The alkyl and acyl cations are good electrophiles and will form a coordinate bond by accepting a pair of delocalised $\pi$-electrons. As a result the mechanisms for the **alkylation** and **acylation** of benzene in Figure 4 are examples of electrophilic substitution as they involve an electrophile substituting for a hydrogen atom attached to the benzene ring.

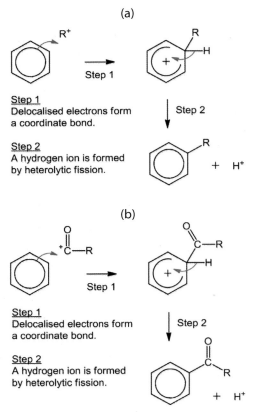

(a)

Step 1
Delocalised electrons form a coordinate bond.

Step 2
A hydrogen ion is formed by heterolytic fission.

(b)

Step 1
Delocalised electrons form a coordinate bond.

Step 2
A hydrogen ion is formed by heterolytic fission.

*Figure 4: Mechanisms for (a) the alkylation of benzene, and (b) the acylation of benzene, using aluminium chloride as a catalyst.*

## Exercise 4.11E

1. The mechanism for the following reaction is very similar to the mechanism for the monobromination of benzene. In the case of bromination the electrophile is $Br^+$, in this case the electrophile is $CH_3CH_2CH_2^+$. Draw a flow scheme for this reaction.

*(Adapted from CCEA June 2013)*

2. Benzene can be converted to methylbenzene by reaction with chloromethane in the presence of aluminium chloride. (a) State the function of the aluminium chloride. (b) Write the formula of the species which attacks the benzene ring.

$$C_6H_6 + CH_3Cl \rightarrow C_6H_5CH_3 + HCl$$

*(Adapted from CCEA May 2009)*

3. Benzene reacts with ethanoyl chloride in the presence of a catalyst to form acetophenone which is used in fragrances. (a) Name the catalyst. (b) Draw the mechanism for the reaction. (c) State the type of mechanism and explain your reasoning.

acetophenone

### Additional Problems

4. The compound 1-methylethylbenzene, also known as cumene, is used to manufacture phenol and propanone on an industrial scale. (a) Write an equation, showing the structure of each reactant and product, for the formation of cumene from a mixture of benzene and propene. (b) A small amount of propylbenzene is also formed in the reaction between benzene and propene. Account for the relative amounts of cumene and propylbenzene formed in terms of the mechanism for the reaction.

1-methylethylbenzene (cumene)

propylbenzene

Before moving to the next section, check that you are able to:

• Describe the mechanisms for the alkylation and acylation of benzene.

• Write equations for the alkylation and acylation of benzene and explain why the reactions are examples of electrophilic substitution.

• Write equations for the formation of the electrophiles.

### Nitration

The term **nitration** refers to *the addition of one or more nitro (-NO₂) groups to a compound*. Benzene undergoes nitration to form nitrobenzene, $C_6H_5NO_2$

when it reacts with a *nitrating mixture* that is made by mixing concentrated nitric acid with concentrated sulfuric acid.

The nitrating mixture contains nitronium ion, $NO_2^+$ which is a good electrophile. The reaction begins when a nitronium ion accepts a pair of electrons from the delocalised π-bonds to form a coordinate bond as shown in Figure 5. As the bond forms the benzene ring acquires a positive charge, and the carbon atom bonded to the nitro group is no longer able to participate in π-bonding. The delocalisation of π-electrons around the ring is subsequently restored by the elimination of a hydrogen ($H^+$) ion from the intermediate to form nitrobenzene.

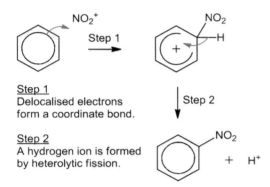

**Step 1**
Delocalised electrons form a coordinate bond.

**Step 2**
A hydrogen ion is formed by heterolytic fission.

*Figure 5: Mechanism for the mononitration of benzene to form nitrobenzene, $C_6H_5NO_2$.*

*Mechanism for the mononitration of benzene:*

STEP 1
Forming the electrophile
$HNO_3 + H_2SO_4 \rightarrow NO_2^+ + HSO_4^- + H_2O$

STEP 2
Electrophilic substitution
$C_6H_6 + NO_2^+ \rightarrow C_6H_5NO_2 + H^+$

The sulfuric acid in the nitrating mixture can be considered a catalyst for the reaction as it is reformed when the hydrogen ($H^+$) ion is eliminated from the intermediate.

*Chemical equation for the mononitration of benzene:*
$C_6H_6 + HNO_3 \rightarrow C_6H_5NO_2 + H_2O$

**Exercise 4.11F**

1. Benzene and its derivatives are nitrated by the nitronium ion which is formed when nitric acid reacts with sulfuric acid. (a) Explain whether the nitronium ion is an electrophile or a nucleophile. (b) Draw a flow scheme to show the mechanism for the reaction of benzene with the nitronium ion to form nitrobenzene. (c) Explain whether this mechanism is addition or substitution.

*(Adapted from CCEA June 2014)*

2. The explosive trinitrotoluene (TNT) is prepared by the nitration of methylbenzene (toluene). The nitrating mixture is the same as the mixture used to nitrate benzene. (a) Suggest a systematic name for TNT. (b) Name the acids in the nitrating mixture. (c) Write an equation for the formation of the nitrating species. (d) Name the nitrating species. (e) What name is given to the mechanism?

trinitrotoluene
(TNT)

*(CCEA June 2010)*

3. A mixture of concentrated nitric and sulfuric acids forms a nitrating mixture which can be used to nitrate benzene. (a) Write the equation for the reaction between nitric acid and sulfuric acid to form a nitronium ion. (b) Explain how nitric acid is acting as a Brønsted base in this reaction. (c) Explain why sulfuric acid may be regarded as a catalyst in this reaction.

*(CCEA May 2008)*

Before moving to the next section, check that you are able to:

- Describe the mechanism for the mononitration of benzene.

- Write an equation for the mononitration of benzene and explain why the reaction is an example of electrophilic substitution.

- Write an equation for the formation of the electrophile.

## Preparation of Methyl 3-nitrobenzoate

Methyl 3-nitrobenzoate is a cream coloured solid (melting point 78 °C) and is prepared by nitrating methyl benzoate. The temperature is maintained below 10 °C during the reaction to prevent the formation of methyl 3,5-dinitrobenzoate.

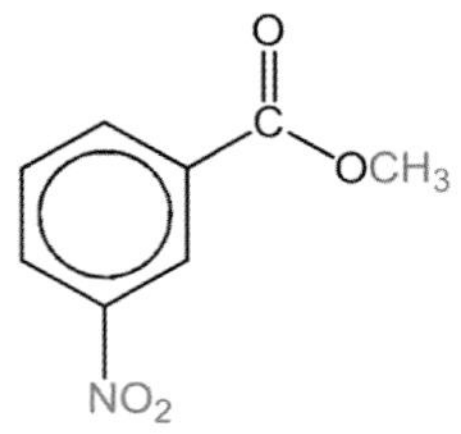

methyl 3-nitrobenzoate 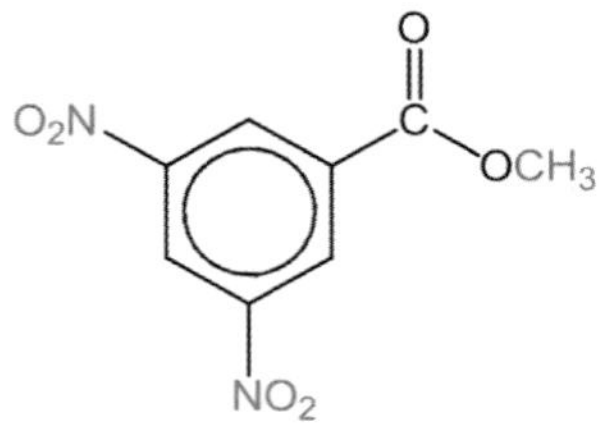    methyl 3,5-dinitrobenzoate

## Worked Example 4.11ii

Describe, giving experimental detail, how you would prepare a pure, dry sample of methyl 3-nitrobenzoate from methyl benzoate.

### Solution

Dissolve solid methyl benzoate in concentrated sulfuric acid and cool the mixture in ice. Prepare a nitrating mixture containing equal amounts of concentrated nitric acid and concentrated sulfuric acid. Cool the nitrating mixture in ice before adding the mixture dropwise to the solution of methyl benzoate, using an ice bath to keep the temperature of the mixture below 10 °C.

The reaction mixture is then allowed to stand at room temperature for several minutes before pouring the mixture over a small amount of crushed ice. The crude methyl 3-nitrobenzoate is obtained by vacuum filtration and washed with cold water to remove traces of the nitrating mixture. The product is then recrystallised using ethanol, separated from the reaction mixture by vacuum filtration, and dried in a dessicator.

### Exercise 4.11G

1. Nitration of methyl benzoate can be achieved using a 'nitrating mixture' of concentrated nitric and sulfuric acids. (a) Draw a flow scheme to show the mechanism for the mononitration of methyl benzoate. (b) State the type of mechanism drawn. (c) Name the organic product of the reaction. (d) Describe the appearance of the product.

   *(CCEA May 2012)*

2. Suggest why the temperature is carefully controlled in the preparation of methyl 3-nitrobenzoate.

   *(CCEA May 2002)*

Before moving to the next section, check that you are able to:

- Describe, giving practical details, the mononitration of methyl benzoate.
- Write an equation for the reaction and explain why the temperature must be controlled during the reaction.

# Unit A2 2:

# Analytical, Transition Metals, Electrochemistry and Organic Nitrogen Chemistry

# 5.1 Chromatography

The term chromatography refers to a range of techniques that are used to separate mixtures. In a chromatography experiment the mixture is first added to a *mobile phase* such as a liquid or gas. The compounds in the mixture are then separated as the mobile phase passes over a *stationary phase* as illustrated by Figure 1. The example in Figure 1 demonstrates that *a substance which spends more time in the mobile phase will travel further than a substance that spends less time in the mobile phase.*

## Paper Chromatography

**In this section we are learning to:**

- Describe how paper chromatography can be used to separate liquid mixtures.
- Use the results of a paper chromatography experiment to identify the compounds in a liquid mixture.

### Simple Chromatography

In a simple chromatography experiment a concentrated spot of the mixture to be separated is placed on a thin pencil baseline drawn on a sheet of chromatography paper as shown in Figure 2. Concentrated spots of additional samples are then added for comparison and the paper hung vertically in a developing tank containing solvent to a depth of 1–2 cm, again shown in Figure 2. As the solvent rises up the paper the compounds in each sample move between the solvent (the mobile phase) and the paper (the stationary phase), and travel up the paper at different speeds. Once the compounds in each sample have separated, the chromatography paper is removed from the developing tank, and a line drawn to mark the **solvent front** which represents *the final position of the solvent in the experiment.*

The outcome of this process is a **chromatogram** that *details the extent of the separation that occurred during the experiment.* The paper chromatogram in Figure 2b reveals that the mixture X may contain the compounds B, C and D, or other compounds that spend the same amount of time in the mobile phase as B, C and D. The analysis also reveals that the mixture X does not contain compound A, or a different compound that spends the same amount of time in the mobile phase as compound A.

If the compounds being separated are not visible the chromatogram must be exposed to a developing

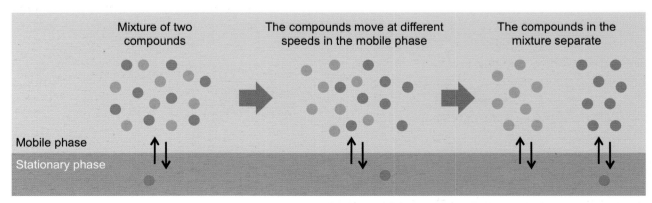

*Figure 1: The separation that results from each substance in a mixture spending different amounts of time in the mobile phase.*

(a)

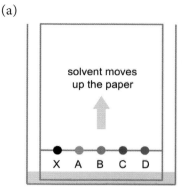

(b)

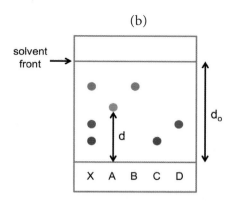

*Figure 2: (a) A simple paper chromatography experiment. (b) Using pure compounds A-D to identify the compounds in a mixture (X).*

agent, or viewed under ultraviolet (UV) light, to locate the compounds on the chromatogram.

The location of a compound on a chromatogram can be specified by calculating the **retardation factor** or '$R_f$ value' for the compound.

$$R_f = \frac{\text{Distance traveled by the compound}}{\text{Distance traveled by the the solvent}} = \frac{d}{d_0}$$

The distances d and $d_0$ used to calculate the $R_f$ value for compound A are shown in Figure 2.

Paper is made of cellulose fibres. The surface of a cellulose fibre is covered in hydroxyl (-OH) groups and is therefore a polar environment. If the mobile phase is a nonpolar solvent such as dichloromethane, $CH_2Cl_2$ or hexane, $C_6H_{14}$ nonpolar compounds will prefer to spend most of their time in the mobile phase (and have high $R_f$ values), while polar compounds such as alcohols will spend most of their time in the stationary phase (and have low $R_f$ values).

### Worked Example 5.1i

Different inks contain unique combinations of dyes such as methyl violet 2b and methyl violet 6b. Describe how simple paper chromatography could be used to demonstrate tthat a bank cheque was forged. The pen used to write the cheque and pure samples of the dyes methyl violet 2b, 6b and 10b are available for use.

### Solution

Using a pencil, draw five crosses along a pencil line that is approximately 2 cm from the bottom of the chromatography paper. Use a clean capillary tube to place a small spot of the ink from the suspect's pen on the first cross. Use a clean capillary tube to place a spot of the ink used to write the cheque on the second cross before placing spots of methyl violet 2b, 6b and 10b on the remaining crosses.

Develop the chromatogram and draw a pencil line to mark the position of the solvent front before exposing the chromatogram to a developing agent, or viewing the chromatogram under UV light, to locate the compounds on the chromatogram. The presence of methyl violet 2b, 6b and 10b in each ink is confirmed by comparing the $R_f$ values for the pure dyes to the $R_f$ values for the compounds in each ink. The cheque is forged if the relative amount of each dye is different in the two inks.

### Exercise 5.1A

1. A mixture of amino acids may be separated using paper chromatography. (a) Explain the term *$R_f$ value* as it applies to paper chromatography. (b) Explain what a low $R_f$ value indicates about a particular amino acid.

*(Adapted from CCEA June 2011)*

2. Use the paper chromatogram to identify which compounds or mixtures are present in Sample 1.

   A  2 + 5                    B  3 + 4

   C  3 + 5                    D  4 + 5

*continued overleaf*

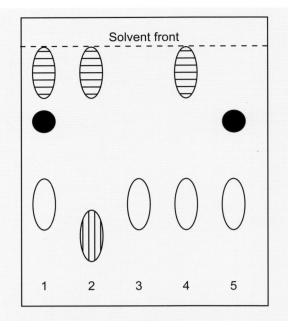

*(Adapted from CCEA June 2014)*

3. Acetaminophen is the active ingredient in paracetamol, a medicine used to reduce mild to moderate pain and fever. Describe, giving experimental details, how you would use paper chromatography to determine if a crude sample of acetaminophen made in a laboratory had been purified.

acetaminophen

Before moving to the next section, check that you are able to:

- Describe how simple paper chromatography can be used to confirm the presence of a compound in a mixture.
- Use the concept of an $R_f$ value to identify compounds in a mixture.

## Two-Way Chromatography

If the compounds in a mixture cannot be effectively separated by a single solvent, a second solvent can be used to advance the separation achieved by the first solvent. This is achieved by conducting a 'two-way' chromatography experiment. In a two-way

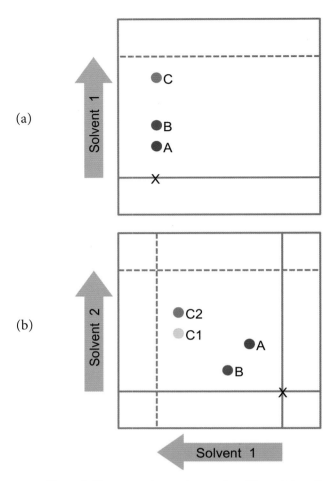

*Figure 3: Two-way chromatography of the mixture X. (a) Separation of the mixture using the first solvent. (b) The chromatogram is rotated and developed using a second solvent.*

experiment the chromatogram obtained using the first solvent is rotated by 90° before being developed using a second solvent as shown in Figure 3. In the example shown in Figure 3 the separation achieved by the first solvent suggests that mixture X contains the compounds A, B and C. Further development using a second solvent reveals that substance C is actually a mixture of the compounds C1 and C2. In this way two-way chromatography can be used to better separate mixtures in which two or more compounds have similar $R_f$ values.

## Worked Example 5.1ii

Hydrolysis of proteins yields amino acids, which can be separated by two-way chromatography. Explain how two-way chromatography could be used to separate a mixture of the amino acids glycine, alanine, threonine and leucine. Describe how the presence of leucine in the mixture could be confirmed.

*(CCEA May 2008)*

### Solution

Using a pencil, draw a small cross 2-3 cm from the corner of the chromatography paper. Use a capillary tube to place a small spot of the mixture on the cross. Repeat several times to produce a concentrated sample.

Develop the chromatogram using the first solvent and draw a pencil line to mark the position of the solvent front. Turn the paper through 90 degrees and develop the chromatogram using the second solvent. Again draw a pencil line to mark the position of the solvent front.

Expose the chromatogram to a developing agent, or view the chromatogram under UV light, to locate the compounds on the chromatogram. The presence of leucine is confirmed by comparing the $R_f$ values from the chromatogram to the $R_f$ values for pure leucine obtained using the same solvents.

### Exercise 5.1B

1. The chromatogram below was produced by two-way paper chromatography of a mixture of amino acids. The table gives the $R_f$ values of some amino acids. Which one of the spots, W, X, Y or Z is glycine?

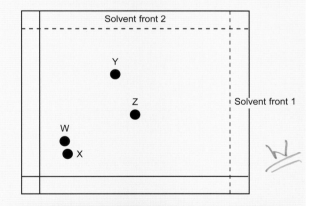

| Amino acid | $R_f$ in solvent 1 | $R_f$ in solvent 2 |
|---|---|---|
| alanine | 0.51 | 0.38 |
| asparagine | 0.63 | 0.21 |
| isoleucine | 0.44 | 0.72 |
| glycine | 0.12 | 0.26 |
| lysine | 0.18 | 0.14 |

*(CCEA June 2015)*

2. A mixture of two amino acids was subjected to 'two-way' chromatography. After elution with solvent 1 the paper was removed, dried, rotated through 90° and eluted with solvent 2. The chromatogram obtained is shown below. Use the $R_f$ values for the amino acids in the table to identify the amino acids in the mixture.

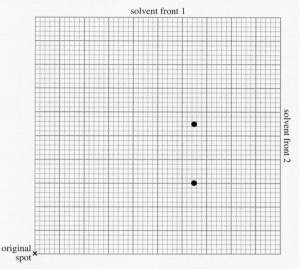

| Amino acid | $R_f$ (solvent 1) | $R_f$ (solvent 2) |
|---|---|---|
| alanine | 0.30 | 0.65 |
| aspartic acid | 0.14 | 0.37 |
| glycine | 0.29 | 0.42 |
| lysine | 0.21 | 0.52 |
| valine | 0.54 | 0.65 |

*(Adapted from CCEA May 2007)*

3. The burning sensation felt when eating chilli peppers is caused by capsaicin. A sample of capsaicin extracted from chilli peppers will contain a large number of organic impurities. Describe how you would use two-way paper chromatography to show that the sample contained capsaicin.

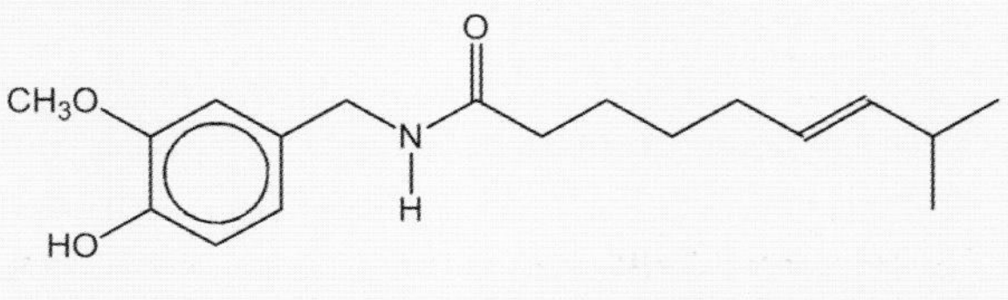

capsaicin

*(CCEA June 2010)*

## Thin-Layer Chromatography

**In this section we are learning to:**

- Describe how thin-layer chromatography can be used to separate liquid mixtures.
- Use the results of a thin-layer chromatography experiment to identify the compounds in a liquid mixture.

In a thin-layer chromatography (TLC) experiment the stationary phase is a thin-layer of solid silica ($SiO_2$) fixed to one side of a plastic strip, and is referred to as a 'TLC plate'. As the solvent rises the compounds in the sample travel up the TLC plate at different speeds as shown in Figure 4a. Once the compounds in each sample have separated, the TLC plate is removed from the developing tank, and a line is drawn to mark the position of the solvent front.

The silica coating on the TLC plate is a polar environment. If the mobile phase is a nonpolar solvent such as dichloromethane, $CH_2Cl_2$ or hexane, $C_6H_{14}$ nonpolar compounds will prefer to spend most of their time in the mobile phase (and have high $R_f$ values), while polar compounds such as alcohols will spend most of their time in the stationary phase (and have low $R_f$ values).

There are several advantages to TLC and paper chromatography; both techniques can be used to quickly separate mixtures using a simple procedure that requires inexpensive materials. However, TLC is generally preferred to paper chromatography as the quality of the separation achieved with TLC is usually much better. For example, the compounds found in natural oils such as eucalyptus oil and orange oil are relatively nonpolar, and can be effectively separated by TLC using a hydrocarbon solvent as shown in Figure 4b.

Often, the quality of the separation achieved with

TLC makes it possible to separate larger quantities of compounds using *preparative TLC*. A preparative TLC plate is significantly larger, and uses a thick layer of silica to separate mixtures. Preparative TLC is routinely used in industry to purify gram amounts of organic compounds made in laboratories.

**Worked Example 5.1iii**

Acetylsalicylic acid is the active ingredient in Aspirin. Describe, giving experimental details, how you would use thin-layer chromatography (TLC) to determine if a crude sample of acetylsalicylic acid made in a laboratory had been purified.

Acetylsalicylic acid

*Solution*

Using a pencil, draw three crosses along a pencil line that is close to the bottom of the TLC plate. Make a concentrated solution by dissolving a small amount of the crude compound, then use a capillary tube to place a small spot of the solution on the first cross. Spot a concentrated solution of the purified compound on the second cross, and a concentrated solution of Aspirin from a pharmacy on the third cross.

Develop the chromatogram and draw a pencil line to mark the position of the solvent front before exposing the chromatogram to a developing agent, or viewing the chromatogram under UV light, to locate the compounds on the chromatogram. The sample is pure if the $R_f$ value for the purified compound matches the $R_f$ value for Aspirin from the pharmacy, and any impurities in the crude sample have been removed.

**Exercise 5.1C**

1. The extract obtained from the leaves of the bearberry plant *arctostaphylos uva-ursi* is used to treat urinary tract infections. The active ingredients in the extract include hydroquinone, and tannins that reduce inflammation. (a) Explain how you would carry out a two-way TLC experiment to show that the extract contained hydroquinone. (b) Suggest why hydroquinone has a higher $R_f$ value than gallic acid.

(a)

Solvent front

*NC State University*

Time

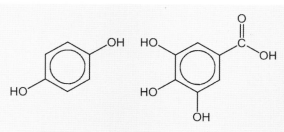

hydroquinone          gallic acid

2. The extract from *guaco*, vine-like climbing plants found in Central and South America, is reported to repel snakes. The extract contains the compounds coumarin and o-coumaric acid. (a) State what is meant by the $R_f$ *value* of a compound. (b) Suggest why coumarin ($R_f = 0.79$) has a higher $R_f$ value than o-coumaric acid ($R_f = 0.39$). (c) Calculate the distance moved by coumarin if the solvent front is marked at a distance of 6.4 cm above the baseline.

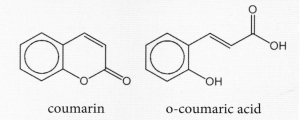

coumarin          o-coumaric acid

Before moving to the next section, check that you are able to:

- Describe how thin-layer chromatography can be used to confirm the presence of a compound in a mixture.

- Recall advantages of thin-layer chromatography and the use of preparative TLC to purify organic compounds.

(b)

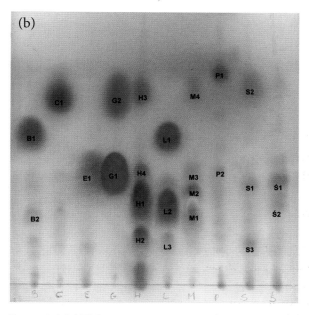

*Figure 4: (a) A TLC experiment using a silica-coated plate. (b) A thin-layer chromatogram of essential oils obtained using a hydrocarbon solvent. The compounds were located by spraying the plate with an acidic solution of the compound vanillin.*

## Gas-Liquid Chromatography

**In this section we are learning to:**

- Describe how gas-liquid chromatography can be used to separate mixtures of volatile liquids and gases.

- Use the results of a gas-liquid chromatography experiment to identify the compounds in a mixture.

A gas-liquid chromatography (GLC) experiment is used to separate mixtures of volatile liquids and gases that can be easily vaporised. In a GLC experiment (Figure 5) several micro-litres (µL) of the sample to be analysed are injected into a heated sample chamber,

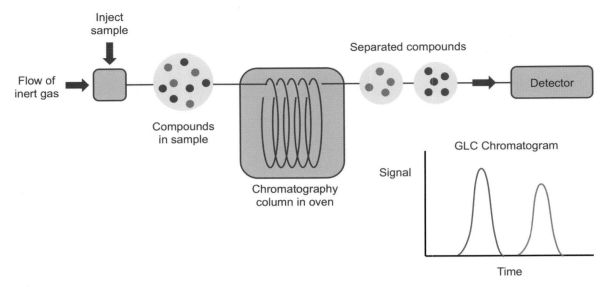

*Figure 5: Schematic illustration of the separation that occurs during a GLC experiment.*

vaporised, and mixed with an inert gas such as nitrogen or argon that acts as the mobile phase. The mobile phase then carries the vaporised sample through a very thin chromatography column packed with fine particles of an inert solid such as silica. The particles in the solid are coated with a thin-layer of a non-volatile liquid that functions as the stationary phase. Compounds that spend more of their time in the stationary (liquid) phase move more slowly through the column. On entering the column the compounds in the sample are partitioned between the mobile phase and the stationary phase. Compounds that spend more of their time in the stationary (liquid) phase move more slowly through the column.

Mixtures of volatile compounds such as hydrocarbons, halogenoalkanes, aldehydes, ketones and esters can be effectively separated using GLC. In contrast non-volatile compounds such as carboxylic acids and amino acids cannot be separated by GLC as they have a very high affinity for the stationary phase and 'stick' to the column.

The **retention time** of a compound, which is *the time taken from injection until the compound is detected*, can be used to confirm the presence of the compound in complex mixtures such as natural oils. The retention times for the most abundant compounds in two samples of English lavender oil are summarised in Table 1. On noting that the area under the signal produced by a compound is proportional to the amount of the compound detected, the data in Table 1 can be used to conclude that Sample 1 contains large amounts of linalool,

**Sample 1: English lavender *Lavandula Angustifolia***

| Compound | Retention time (s) | Area under signal |
|---|---|---|
| cis-ocimene | 742 | 6.00 |
| trans-ocimene | 756 | 2.34 |
| linalool | 819 | 23.78 |
| terpinen-4-ol | 912 | 13.47 |
| a-terpineol | 926 | 4.14 |
| linalyl acetate | 986 | 25.40 |
| lavandulyl acetate | 1019 | 3.35 |

**Sample 2: English lavender *Lavandula Intermedia Lavandin***

| Compound | Retention time (s) | Area under signal |
|---|---|---|
| eucalyptol | 737 | 5.40 |
| linalool | 819 | 31.57 |
| camphor | 877 | 8.46 |
| endo-borneol | 900 | 3.69 |
| terpinen-4-ol | 912 | 2.00 |
| a-terpineol | 926 | 3.55 |
| linalyl acetate | 986 | 26.58 |
| lavandulyl acetate | 1019 | 2.30 |

*Table 1: The principal components identified in a GLC analysis of pure English lavender oils.*

terpinen-4-ol and linalyl acetate. Similarly, the presence of significant amounts of linalool and linalyl acetate in Sample 2 is confirmed by signals with a large area at retention times of 819 s and 986 s.

The amount of a compound in the sample being analysed can be determined by comparing the area under the signal produced by the compound to the total area under the signals in the chromatogram.

Amount of compound in sample

$$= \frac{\text{Area under signal}}{\text{Total area under all signals}} \times 100\,\%$$

According to the data in Table 1 the compound linalyl acetate accounts for 32.4 % of the total molecules in Sample 1 and 31.8 % of the total molecules in Sample 2.

Amount of linalyl acetate in Sample 1

$$= \frac{25.40}{78.48} \times 100\,\% = 32.4\%$$

Amount of linalyl acetate in Sample 2

$$= \frac{26.58}{83.55} \times 100\,\% = 31.8\%$$

**Worked Example 5.1iv**

The identification of many drugs uses the technique of GLC. Explain how this is carried out.

*(CCEA June 2013)*

*Solution*

A drug is present in the sample if its retention time matches the retention time for a pure sample of the drug.

**Exercise 5.1D**

1. The compounds g-terpinene and terpinen-4-ol are the principal components of the oil extracted from the leaves of the narrow-leaved tea-tree. (a) Explain what is meant by the *retention time* of a compound. (b) Calculate the amount of g-terpinene in the extract. (c) Use the data in the table to sketch the chromatogram obtained by GLC analysis of the extract.

| Compound | Retention time (s) | Area under signal |
|---|---|---|
| g-terpinene | 1140 | 15.76 |
| terpinen-4-ol | 1372 | 34.03 |

2. Extracts from the leaves of three varieties of Basil are found to contain varying amounts of the compounds linalool, methyl cinnamate, methyl eugenol and caryophyllene. (a) Use the data in the table to determine which extract contains the greatest amount of methyl eugenol. (b) With reference to the data in the table suggest how GLC could be used to distinguish extracts from the *purple castle* and *clove* varieties.

| | Area under signal | | |
|---|---|---|---|
| | **Purple Castle** | **Purple Ruffle** | **Clove** |
| linalool | 3.1 | 16.5 | 0.9 |
| methyl cinnamate | 42.4 | 61.9 | 8.3 |
| methyl eugenol | 24.3 | 0.4 | 26.0 |
| caryophyllene | 0.8 | 0.7 | 43.0 |

3. Which one of the following is **not** true for gas-liquid chromatography of a mixture?

A The liquid phase is mobile and the gas phase is stationary

B The molecules in the mixture have characteristic retention times

C The molecules in the mixture spend time in the liquid phase and the gas phase

D The percentage composition of the mixture can be determined

*(CCEA June 2015)*

4. Succinic acid can be analysed by converting it to the diethyl ester and submitting the ester to GLC analysis. (a) Explain why it is better to use the ester rather than the acid in GLC analysis. (b) Describe the results expected if the sample of the ester was 90% pure.

$$\text{CH}_2\text{COOH} \\ | \qquad\qquad \text{succinic acid} \\ \text{CH}_2\text{COOH}$$

*(Adapted from CCEA June 2014)*

Before moving to the next section, check that you are able to:

- Explain how gas-liquid chromatography can be used to separate a mixture of compounds.
- Recall the meaning of the term retention time and use retention times to identify compounds in a mixture.
- Use the relative areas under the signals in a GLC chromatogram to determine the relative amount of each compound in the sample.

# 5.2 Volumetric Analysis

In this section the principles and techniques developed previously to conduct acid-base titrations are applied to a range of analyses routinely carried out by chemists working in industry.

## Back Titration Methods

**In this section we are learning to:**

- Determine the amount of an insoluble compound in a sample by back titration.

In a **back titration** *the excess reagent added to a sample that cannot be analysed by titration is titrated to determine the amount of substance in the sample.* For instance, the purity of an insoluble compound such as a metal carbonate or oxide could be determined by reacting a sample of the compound with an excess of acid. The amount of the compound present in the sample could then be determined by using a standard alkali to titrate the remaining acid.

### Worked Example 5.2i

0.80 g of limestone (mostly $CaCO_3$) was allowed to completely react with 40.0 cm$^3$ of 1.00 M hydrochloric acid. The following results were then obtained by titrating the resulting mixture against 1.00 M NaOH. Calculate the % purity of the limestone.

| | Initial Burette Reading (cm$^3$) | Final Burette Reading (cm$^3$) | Titre (cm$^3$) |
|---|---|---|---|
| Rough | 0.00 | 29.00 | 29.00 |
| First Accurate | 0.10 | 28.80 | 28.70 |
| Second Accurate | 0.00 | 28.80 | 28.80 |

**Solution**

The % purity refers to the % by mass of calcium carbonate in the sample. The steps needed to calculate the % purity of the limestone are:

1. Use the accurate titres to calculate the average titre.
2. Calculate the moles of sodium hydroxide used in the titration.
3. Calculate the moles of acid titrated.
4. Calculate the moles of acid that reacted with the carbonate.
5. Calculate the moles of carbonate in the sample.
6. Calculate the % purity of the sample.

**Strategy**

STEP 1: Use the accurate titres to calculate the average titre.
$$\text{Average titre} = \frac{28.70 + 28.80}{2} = 28.75 \text{ cm}^3$$

STEP 2: Calculate the moles of sodium hydroxide used in the titration.

Moles = Volume (in dm$^3$) × Molarity (in mol dm$^{-3}$)

$$\text{Moles} = \frac{\text{Average Titre}}{1000} \times 1.00$$

$$= 2.875 \times 10^{-2} \times 1.00 = 2.88 \times 10^{-2} \text{ mol}$$

STEP 3: Calculate the moles of acid titrated.

Titration reaction:

$$HCl + NaOH \rightarrow NaCl + H_2O$$

Moles of acid = Moles of hydroxide

$$= 2.88 \times 10^{-2} \text{ mol}$$

STEP 4: Calculate the moles of acid that reacted with the carbonate.

Moles of acid in 40.0 cm$^3$ of 1.00 M HCl:

Moles = Volume (in dm$^3$) × Molarity

$$= \frac{40.0}{1000} \times 1.00 = 0.0400 \text{ mol}$$

Moles of acid reacted = $0.0400 - 2.88 \times 10^{-2}$
= 0.0112 mol

STEP 5: Calculate the moles of carbonate in the sample.

$CaCO_3 + 2HCl \rightarrow CaCl_2 + H_2O + CO_2$

Moles of carbonate = $\dfrac{\text{Moles of acid reacted}}{2}$

= $5.60 \times 10^{-3}$ mol

STEP 6: Calculate the % purity of the sample.

Molar mass of $CaCO_3$ = 100 g $mol^{-1}$

Mass of carbonate = Moles × Molar Mass

= $5.60 \times 10^{-3} \times 100$ = 0.560 g

% Purity = $\dfrac{\text{Mass of carbonate}}{\text{Mass of sample}} \times 100$

= $\dfrac{0.560}{0.80} \times 100$ = 70 %

### Exercise 5.2A

1. The amount of magnesium oxide in heartburn tablets can be determined by adding a known excess of hydrochloric acid to the tablets.

$2HCl_{(aq)} + MgO_{(s)} \rightarrow MgCl_{2(aq)} + H_2O_{(l)}$

The amount of unreacted hydrochloric acid is determined by titrating it against sodium hydroxide.

$NaOH_{(aq)} + HCl_{(aq)} \rightarrow NaCl_{(aq)} + H_2O_{(l)}$

(a) What is this method of titration called?

(b) A student added 80 $cm^3$ of 2.0 mol $dm^{-3}$ hydrochloric acid to five crushed heartburn tablets which contained magnesium oxide. The unreacted acid required 25 $cm^3$ of 2.0 mol $dm^{-3}$ sodium hydroxide for complete neutralisation. Use the following bullet points to calculate the mass, in milligrams, of magnesium oxide in each tablet.

- Number of moles of hydrochloric acid added to the tablets.
- Number of moles of unreacted hydrochloric acid.
- Number of moles of hydrochloric acid which reacted with the magnesium oxide.

- Number of moles of magnesium oxide present in five tablets.
- Mass of magnesium oxide per tablet in milligrams.

*(CCEA January 2013)*

2. The percentage of calcium carbonate present in egg shells can be found by back titration. 1.12 g of egg shell was allowed to react with 20.0 $cm^3$ of 2.00 M hydrochloric acid and the solution formed made up to 250 $cm^3$ in a volumetric flask. 25.0 $cm^3$ of this solution completely reacted with 18.6 $cm^3$ of 0.100 M sodium hydroxide. Calculate the percentage of calcium carbonate in the egg shell using the following headings to structure the calculation.

- Moles of hydrochloric acid added to the egg shell.
- Moles of sodium hydroxide used.
- Moles of hydrochloric acid in 250 $cm^3$.
- Moles of hydrochloric acid needed to react with the egg shell.
- Mass of calcium carbonate in the egg shell.
- Percentage of calcium carbonate in the egg shell.

*(CCEA June 2009)*

3. Anhydrous copper(II) chloride, $CuCl_2$ may be prepared by heating copper in chlorine gas. When prepared by dissolving copper(II) oxide in hydrochloric acid, copper(II) chloride crystallises with two molecules of water of crystallisation. (a) Write the equation for the reaction of copper with chlorine. (b) Write the equation for the reaction of copper(II) oxide with hydrochloric acid. (c) Write the formula for hydrated copper(II) chloride. (d) The purity of the copper(II) oxide may be determined by the process of back titration. Explain, without calculations, how this process would be carried out.

*(CCEA January 2012)*

Before moving to the next section, check that you are able to:

- Explain the method of back titration and use the results of a back titration experiment to determine the amount of a compound present in a sample.

## Determination of Reducing Agents

**In this section we are learning to:**

- Determine the amount of a reducing agent present in solution by titration against a standard solution of potassium permanganate.

The amount of a reducing agent such as iron(II), $Fe^{2+}$ or oxalate, $C_2O_4^{2-}$ present in solution can be determined by adding an excess of dilute sulfuric acid and titrating the solution against a standard solution of potassium permanganate, $KMnO_4$. On adding permanganate the manganese in the manganate(VII) ion, $MnO_4^-$ is reduced and the pink colour of the $MnO_4^-$ ion is replaced by a solution containing manganese(II), $Mn^{2+}$ that is essentially colourless as shown in Figure 1. If a drop of permanganate solution is added at the end point, the manganate(VII) in the drop is not reduced, and the solution changes from colourless to pink as shown in Figure 1.

> Equations for the titration of iron(II) by manganate(VII):
>
> *Half-equations*
>
> $Fe^{2+}_{(aq)} \rightarrow Fe^{3+}_{(aq)} + e^-$
>
> $MnO_4^-_{(aq)} + 8H^+_{(aq)} + 5e^- \rightarrow Mn^{2+}_{(aq)} + 4H_2O_{(l)}$
>
> *Ionic equation*
>
> $MnO_4^-_{(aq)} + 5Fe^{2+}_{(aq)} + 8H^+_{(aq)}$
> $\rightarrow Mn^{2+}_{(aq)} + 5Fe^{3+}_{(aq)} + 4H_2O_{(l)}$

### Worked Example 5.2ii

Iron(II) ions are part of the structure of haemoglobin. Many people supplement their diet by taking 'iron tablets', which contain hydrated iron(II) sulfate, $FeSO_4.7H_2O$.

(a) Describe, giving experimental details, how acidified manganate(VII) can be used to determine the amount of iron(II) present in 'iron tablets'.

*Figure 1: Titration of an acidified solution containing iron(II) against a standard solution of potassium permanganate.*

(b) Iron tablets with a total mass of 8.00 g were dissolved in dilute sulfuric acid and the solution made up to 250 cm³ in a volumetric flask. 25.0 cm³ portions of this solution were titrated with 0.020 mol dm⁻³ acidified potassium manganate(VII). The average titre was found to be 24.0 cm³. (i) Write the equation for the reaction of acidified potassium manganate(VII) ions with iron(II) ions. (ii) State the colour change at the end point. (iii) Calculate the percentage of hydrated iron(II) sulfate in the tablets.

*(Adapted from CCEA June 2012)*

### Solution

(a) Use a volumetric flask to prepare a solution containing several crushed iron tablets. Rinse a volumetric pipette with the iron(II) solution before using the pipette and a pipette filler to transfer 25 cm³ of the iron(II) solution to a conical flask. Add an excess of dilute sulfuric acid to the conical flask and swirl to mix.

Rinse and fill the burette with a standard solution of potassium permanganate. Perform a rough titration by adding permanganate solution in 1 cm³ amounts, swirling the contents after each addition, until the solution changes from colourless to pink. Perform an accurate titration by adding permanganate solution dropwise near the end point. Repeat to obtain accurate titres that differ by less than 0.1 cm³.

Use the average of the accurate titres and the 5:1 ratio of iron(II) to manganate(VII) to calculate the amount of iron in each tablet.

(b) (i) $MnO_4^-{}_{(aq)} + 5Fe^{2+}{}_{(aq)} + 8H^+{}_{(aq)}$

$\rightarrow Mn^{2+}{}_{(aq)} + 5Fe^{3+}{}_{(aq)} + 4H_2O_{(l)}$

(ii) Colourless to pink.

(iii) Moles of iron(II) in 250 cm$^3$ = 0.024 mol

Mass of $FeSO_4.7H_2O$ in 8.00 g of tablets

= 0.024 mol × 278 g mol$^{-1}$ = 6.7 g

% $FeSO_4.7H_2O$ = 84 %

- - - - - - - - - - - - - - - - - - - - - - - - - - - - - - - - - -

## Exercise 5.2B

1. Some iron tablets, used to treat anaemia, contain iron(II) fumarate, $FeC_4H_2O_4$. Five of these iron tablets were dissolved in dilute sulfuric acid and the solution made up to 250 cm$^3$ with distilled water. On titration, 25.0 cm$^3$ of this solution reacted with 18.7 cm$^3$ of 0.010 mol dm$^{-3}$ acidified potassium manganate(VII) solution. (a) Write the equation for the reaction of iron(II) ions with acidified manganate(VII) ions. (b) State the colour change at the end point. (c) Calculate the mass of iron(II) fumarate in each tablet. (d) Describe, giving experimental details, how acidified potassium manganate(VII) could be used to determine the amount of iron(II) present in one tablet.

*(Adapted from CCEA June 2010)*

2. A sample of steel (2.0 g) was dissolved in excess dilute sulfuric acid and the solution made up to 250 cm$^3$ with water. 25.0 cm$^3$ samples of this solution were titrated with 0.020 M potassium manganate(VII) solution. The average titre was 33.9 cm$^3$. Calculate the percentage of iron in the sample of steel.

$MnO_4^- + 8H^+ + 5Fe^{2+} \rightarrow Mn^{2+} + 4H_2O + 5Fe^{3+}$

*(Adapted from CCEA January 2010)*

3. Acidified dichromate ions can be used to determine the concentration of iron(II) ions. The half-equations for the reaction are:

$Cr_2O_7^{2-} + 14H^+ + 6e^- \rightarrow 2Cr^{3+} + 7H_2O$

$Fe^{2+} \rightarrow Fe^{3+} + e^-$

(a) Write a balanced ionic equation for the reaction between acidified dichromate and iron(II) ions. (b) Five iron tablets containing iron(II) sulfate, $FeSO_4$ were dissolved in acid and the solution made up to 250 cm$^3$ in a volumetric flask. A 25.0 cm$^3$ portion of this solution required 23.5 cm$^3$ of 0.010 mol dm$^{-3}$ sodium dichromate solution for complete oxidation. Calculate the mass of iron(II) sulfate in an iron tablet.

*(CCEA June 2015)*

4. Iron(II) oxalate, $FeC_2O_4$ is completely oxidised by acidified potassium manganate(VII). The iron(II) ion is oxidised to iron(III), and the oxalate ion is completely oxidised to carbon dioxide:

$Fe^{2+} \rightarrow Fe^{3+} + e^-$

$C_2O_4^{2-} \rightarrow 2CO_2 + 2e^-$

The electrons produced react with the manganate(VII) ion:

$MnO_4^- + 8H^+ + 5e^- \rightarrow Mn^{2+} + 4H_2O$

(a) Write the equation for the reaction of acidified manganate(VII) ions with iron(II) oxalate. (b) Oxalic acid is used to remove iron stains because iron dissolves to form iron(II) oxalate. Calculate the mass of iron, in milligrams, dissolved in a 100 cm$^3$ solution if 20.0 cm$^3$ of the iron(II) oxalate solution reacts with 18.2 cm$^3$ of 0.0020 M potassium manganate(VII) solution.

*(Adapted from CCEA June 2013)*

5. Potassium manganate(VII) oxidises iron(II) ions and ethanedioate ions according to the following equations.

$MnO_4^-{}_{(aq)} + 5Fe^{2+}{}_{(aq)} + 8H^+{}_{(aq)}$
$\rightarrow 5Fe^{3+}{}_{(aq)} + Mn^{2+}{}_{(aq)} + 4H_2O_{(l)}$

$2MnO_4^-{}_{(aq)} + 5C_2O_4^{2-}{}_{(aq)} + 16H^+{}_{(aq)}$
$\rightarrow 2Mn^{2+}{}_{(aq)} + 10CO_{2(g)} + 8H_2O_{(l)}$

25.0 cm$^3$ of an acidified iron(II) ethanedioate

solution required 32.2 cm$^3$ of 0.025 mol dm$^{-3}$ potassium manganate(VII) solution for complete reaction. Calculate the concentration, in mol dm$^{-3}$, of the iron(II) ethanedioate solution.

*(CCEA May 2011)*

Before moving to the next section, check that you are able to:

- Describe, giving experimental details, how the amount of iron(II) or other reducing agent present in solution can be determined by titrating the solution against a standard solution of potassium permanganate.
- Explain the colour change at the end point in terms of the ions formed.
- Deduce the ionic equation for the redox reaction between the reducing agent and manganate(VII).
- Use the manganate(VII) titre to calculate the concentration of the reducing agent.

## Determination of Oxidising Agents

### In this section we are learning to:

- Determine the amount of an oxidising agent present in solution by titration against a standard solution of sodium thiosulfate.

The amount of iodate(V), $IO_3^-$ present in a solution can be determined by adding an excess of potassium

iodide dissolved in dilute sulfuric acid. In acidic solution iodate(V), $IO_3^-$ oxidises iodide, $I^-$ to iodine, $I_2$, which gives the solution a brown colour.

Equations for the oxidation of iodide by iodate(V):

*Half-equations*

$2I^-_{(aq)} \rightarrow I_{2(aq)} + 2e^-$

$2IO_3^-_{(aq)} + 12H^+_{(aq)} + 10e^- \rightarrow I_{2(aq)} + 6H_2O_{(l)}$

*Ionic equation*

$IO_3^-_{(aq)} + 6H^+_{(aq)} + 5I^-_{(aq)} \rightarrow 3I_{2(aq)} + 3H_2O_{(l)}$

The amount of iodine produced or 'liberated' in this way is then titrated against a standard solution of sodium thiosulfate. On adding thiosulfate, $S_2O_3^{2-}$ the iodine in the solution reacts, and the brown colour produced by the iodine fades to give a straw coloured solution as shown in Figure 2a.

Equations for the titration of liberated iodine:

*Half-equations*

$I_{2(aq)} + 2e^- \rightarrow 2I^-_{(aq)}$

$2S_2O_3^{2-}_{(aq)} \rightarrow S_4O_6^{2-}_{(aq)} + 2e^-$

*Ionic equation*

$I_{2(aq)} + 2S_2O_3^{2-}_{(aq)} \rightarrow 2I^-_{(aq)} + S_4O_6^{2-}_{(aq)}$

Several drops of starch solution are then added to form an intensely coloured blue-black complex with the remaining iodine as shown in Figure 2b. On adding thiosulfate dropwise, the iodine in the

**(a)**

**(b)**

**(c)**

*Figure 2: (a) Titration of the iodine formed by the oxidation of iodide. (b) The blue-black complex formed on adding starch indicator. (c) Formation of a colourless solution at the end point.*

complex reacts, and the blue-black colour of the complex is replaced by a colourless solution as shown in Figure 2c. The colour change from blue-black to colourless signals the end point of the titration.

· · · · · · · · · · · · · · · · · · · · · · · · · · · · · · · · · · · · · · · · · · · · · · · · ·

### Worked Example 5.2iii

(a) Describe, giving experimental details, how a standard solution of sodium thiosulfate could be used to determine the % purity of an impure sample of solid potassium iodate(V). (b) Calculate the mass of $KIO_3$ in 1.2 g of an impure sample of $KIO_3$ if an average titre of 21.7 cm$^3$ was obtained when the sample was made up to 250 cm$^3$ in a volumetric flask and 25 cm$^3$ of the potassium iodate(V) solution was titrated against 0.10 mol dm$^{-3}$ sodium thiosulfate solution. (c) Calculate the percentage purity of the $KIO_3$ sample.

*(Adapted from CCEA May 2012)*

### Solution

    (a) Use a volumetric flask to prepare a solution containing the powdered impure sample. Rinse a volumetric pipette with the iodate(V) solution before using the pipette and a pipette filler to transfer 25 cm$^3$ of the iodate(V) solution to a conical flask. Add an excess of potassium iodide dissolved in dilute sulfuric acid to the conical flask and swirl to mix.

    Rinse and fill the burette with a standard solution of sodium thiosulfate. Titrate the sample in the conical flask by adding thiosulfate solution in 1 cm$^3$ amounts, swirling the contents after each addition, until the solution turns a straw colour. Add a few drops of starch indicator and swirl to mix. Add thiosulfate solution dropwise, swirling the contents of the flask after each addition, until the blue-black colour of the iodine-starch complex is replaced by a colourless solution at the end point. Repeat to obtain accurate titres that differ by less than 0.1 cm$^3$.

    Use the average of the accurate titres and the 1:2 ratio of iodine to thiosulfate to calculate the amount of liberated iodine in the conical flask. Then use the 3:1 ratio of iodine to iodate(V) to calculate the amount of iodate(V) in the conical flask. Calculate the amount of iodate(V) in the volumetric flask and use this

amount to calculate the percentage purity of the original sample.

    (b) Moles of thiosulfate used
$$= \text{Molarity} \times \text{Volume} = 2.2 \times 10^{-3} \text{ mol}$$
Moles of $I_2$ liberated
$$= \frac{2.2 \times 10^{-3} \text{ mol}}{2} = 1.1 \times 10^{-3} \text{ mol}$$
Moles of $IO_3^-$ in conical flask
$$= \frac{1.1 \times 10^{-3} \text{ mol}}{3} = 3.6 \times 10^{-4} \text{ mol}$$
Moles of $IO_3^-$ in sample
$$= \text{Moles in volumetric flask} = 3.6 \times 10^{-3} \text{ mol}$$
Mass of $KIO_3$ in sample = Moles of $KIO_3$ in sample × Molar Mass of $KIO_3$
$$= 3.6 \times 10^{-3} \text{ mol} \times 214 \text{ g mol}^{-1} = 0.77 \text{ g}$$

    (c) % purity $= \dfrac{0.77 \text{ g}}{1.2 \text{ g}} \times 100 = 64 \text{ %}$

· · · · · · · · · · · · · · · · · · · · · · · · · · · · · · · · · · · · · · · · · · · · · · · · ·

### Exercise 5.2C

1. 25.0 cm$^3$ of potassium iodate(V) solution were added to excess potassium iodide solution dissolved in sulfuric acid. The iodine liberated required 30.0 cm$^3$ of 0.050 mol dm$^{-3}$ $Na_2S_2O_3$ solution. Calculate the concentration of the potassium iodate(V) solution.

*(Adapted from CCEA May 2012)*

The liberation of iodine can also be used to determine the amount of oxidising agents such as hydrogen peroxide in solution. On adding an excess of potassium iodide dissolved in dilute sulfuric acid to a solution containing hydrogen peroxide, $H_2O_2$ the peroxide is reduced as it oxidises iodide, $I^-$ to iodine, $I_2$.

Equations for the oxidation of iodide by hydrogen peroxide:
*Half-equations*

$2I^-_{(aq)} \rightarrow I_{2(aq)} + 2e^-$

$H_2O_{2(aq)} + 2H^+_{(aq)} + 2e^- \rightarrow 2H_2O_{(l)}$

*Ionic equation*

$H_2O_{2(aq)} + 2I^-_{(aq)} + 2H^+_{(aq)} \rightarrow I_{2(aq)} + 2H_2O_{(l)}$

### Exercise 5.2D

1. 25.0 cm$^3$ of hydrogen peroxide solution were added to excess acidified potassium iodide solution and the resulting solution made up to 500 cm$^3$. 25.0 cm$^3$ of the diluted solution reacted with 36.4 cm$^3$ of 0.10 mol dm$^{-3}$ sodium thiosulfate solution. Calculate the concentration of the undiluted hydrogen peroxide.

*(Adapted from CCEA June 2010)*

Before moving to the next section, check that you are able to:

- Describe, giving experimental details, how the amount of an oxidising agent such as iodate(V) or hydrogen peroxide present in solution can be determined by titrating the solution against a standard solution of sodium thiosulfate.

- Explain the colour change observed on adding thiosulfate, on adding starch indicator, and at the end point.

- Deduce the ionic equation for the redox reactions between iodate(V) and iodide, and hydrogen peroxide and iodide.

- Recall the 2:1 ratio of thiosulfate to iodine and use the thiosulfate titre to calculate the concentration of the oxidising agent.

# 5.3 Mass Spectrometry

**CONNECTIONS**
- Mass spectrometry is used by environmental scientists to detect very small amounts of pollutants such as pesticides in surface waters and in food.
- Crime agencies also use mass spectrometry to detect very small amounts of explosives on criminal suspects and in the environment.

The mass spectrum of a compound is a unique 'signature' that can be used to identify the compound. It can also be used to determine the RMM and structure of the compound. In industry, the technique of mass spectrometry is widely used to confirm the structure of newly developed compounds, and to help identify the presence of even small amounts of a compound in more complex substances.

## Interpreting Mass Spectra

**In this section we are learning to:**

- Identify the molecular ion (M) peak and the base peak in a mass spectrum.
- Account for signals in the mass spectrum of a compound in terms of the formation of fragment ions.
- Explain the use of high resolution mass spectrometry to distinguish between compounds with similar RMM values.

The mass spectrum of a compound is obtained by injecting a small sample of the compound into a mass spectrometer. The sample is then vaporised before being bombarded by high energy electrons. When a high energy electron collides with a molecule in the sample it ionises the molecule (M) by removing an electron from the molecule to form a molecular ion ($M^+$).

*Ionisation to form $M^+$:* $M_{(g)} \rightarrow M^+_{(g)} + e^-_{(g)}$

The signal produced by the molecular ions is referred to as the **molecular ion peak** or 'M peak' as it is *the signal produced by the ion formed when an electron is removed from a molecule of the compound.*

If the molecular ions ($M^+$) are unstable, **fragment ions** ($E^+$) will be formed when some of the molecular ions break apart as they travel through the mass spectrometer; a process known as **fragmentation**.

*Fragmentation of $M^+$:* $M^+_{(g)} \rightarrow E^+_{(g)} + F_{(g)}$

The **mass-to-charge ratio, m/z** for the molecular ion, and any fragment ions formed, is then determined by passing the ions through a magnetic field.

The mass spectrum for propanone in Figure 1 is a plot showing the number of ions detected with each mass-to-charge ratio. In routine mass spectroscopy experiments the charge on each ion (z) is 1+, and the ratio m/z is equal to the mass of the ion (m) as: m/z = m/1 = m. The mass-to-charge ratio m/1 may also be written m/e.

In the case of propanone (Figure 1) the molecular ion, $C_3H_6O^+$ is not stable and fragments to give ions with m/z = 43 and m/z = 15. The signal with m/z = 43 is referred to as the **base peak** as it is *the signal with the greatest abundance in the mass spectrum.* The base peak is assigned a relative abundance of 100%.

Interpreting the mass spectrum for propanone:

*Ionisation to form $M^+$:*
$C_3H_6O_{(g)} \rightarrow C_3H_6O^+_{(g)} + e^-_{(g)}$
    m/z for $C_3H_6O^+$ = 58

*Fragmentation of $M^+$:*
$C_3H_6O^+_{(g)} \rightarrow C_2H_3O^+_{(g)} + CH_{3(g)}$
    m/z for $C_2H_3O^+$ = 43
$C_3H_6O^+_{(g)} \rightarrow C_2H_3O_{(g)} + CH_3^+_{(g)}$
    m/z for $CH_3^+$ = 15

When trying to interpret the mass spectrum for a compound it is helpful to remember that the fragmentation of a large ion ($E^+$) often produces a smaller ion ($R^+$) and a stable molecule (S) such as CO, $H_2$ or $CH_4$.

*Fragmentation of a large ion:*
$E^+_{(g)} \rightarrow R^+_{(g)} + S_{(g)}$

*Examples of fragmentation:*
$CH_3CHCH_3^+_{(g)} \rightarrow CH_3C{=}CH_2^+_{(g)} + H_{2(g)}$
$CH_3CH_2CO^+_{(g)} \rightarrow CH_3CH_2^+_{(g)} + CO_{(g)}$

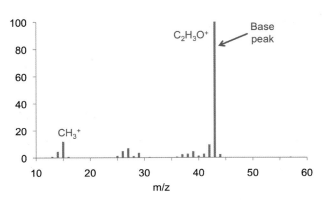

*Figure 1: The mass spectrum of propanone, $CH_3COCH_3$.*

(d) Write an equation to suggest how the signal with m/z = 29 is formed from the ion $CH_3CH_2CO^+$ (m/z = 57).

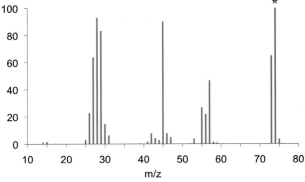

### Worked Example 5.3i

The mass spectrum of propanoic acid is shown opposite. The signal produced by molecular ions (M) is labelled with an asterisk (*) on the spectrum. (a) State the value of m/z for the base peak. Explain your reasoning. (b) Write the formula for the molecular ion. (c) Write an equation to suggest how the signal with m/z = 73 is formed from the molecular ion.

*Solution*

(a) The value of m/z is 74 for the base peak as the base peak has a relative abundance of 100%.

(b) The formula for the molecular ion is $C_3H_6O_2^+$.

(c) $C_3H_6O_2^+ \rightarrow C_3H_5O_2^+ + H$

(d) $CH_3CH_2CO^+ \rightarrow CH_3CH_2^+ + CO$

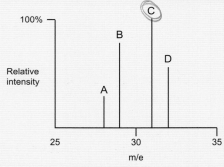

### Exercise 5.3A

1. The mass spectrum of methanol is shown below. Which one of the signals is the base peak?

*(CCEA June 2010)*

2. The mass spectrum of propanamide, $CH_3CH_2CONH_2$ is shown below. (a) Write formulas for the fragment ions with m/e values of 29 and 44. (b) Explain what is meant by the term *fragmentation*. (c) Identify the base peak.

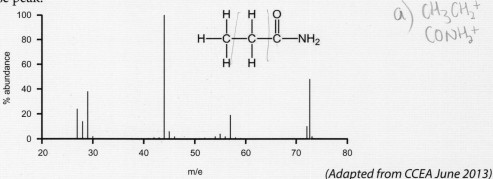

*(Adapted from CCEA June 2013)*

3. The mass spectrum of ethanoic acid shows a distinct peak at m/e = 59. State the formula of the species giving rise to this peak.

*(CCEA May 2011)*

4. Two of the major signals in the mass spectrum of butanone occur at m/e values of 29 and 43. Identify the ions.

*(CCEA June 2005)*

5. The mass spectrum of ethyl methanoate is shown below. Identify the ions responsible for the peaks with m/e values of 28 and 45.

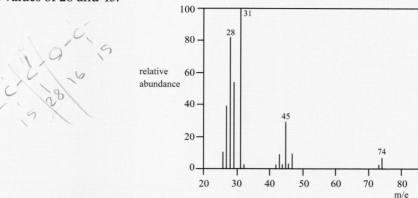

*(CCEA January 2010)*

6. The mass spectrum for methyl propanoate is shown below. (a) What is the m/z value of the base peak? (b) Suggest the formulas of the species responsible for the peaks at 31 and 57. (c) Explain why there is a peak at 89.

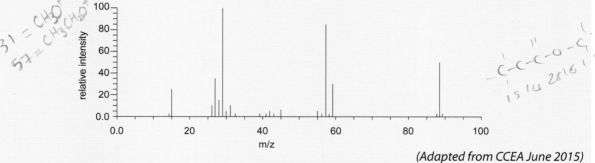

*(Adapted from CCEA June 2015)*

7. The mass spectrum of succinic acid is shown below. (a) Explain the meaning of the term *base peak*. (b) Identify the base peak. (c) Suggest formulas for the fragment ions with m/z values of 45 and 100.

CH₂COOH
|          succinic acid
CH₂COOH

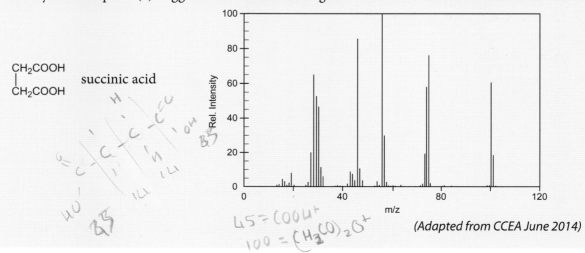

*(Adapted from CCEA June 2014)*

**8.** The mass spectrum of propanal is shown below.
(a) State the value of m/z for the base peak.
(b) Write the formula for the molecular ion.
(c) State the value of m/z for the M peak.
(d) Write an equation to suggest how the signal with m/z = 57 is formed from the molecular ion. (e) Write an equation to suggest how the signal with m/z = 29 is formed from the ion $CH_3CH_2CO^+$.

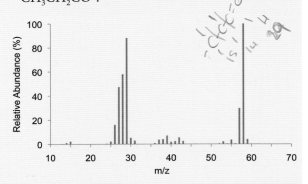

**9.** Ethanol, $C_2H_5OH$ and methoxymethane, $CH_3OCH_3$ are isomers. The mass spectra of ethanol and methoxymethane are shown below but not necessarily in this order. (a) Draw the structures of both compounds showing all of the bonds present. (b) What is the base peak in spectrum X? (c) Identify the M-1 peak in each spectrum and explain how it is formed. (d) Identify the species giving rise to the signals at 31 and 29. (e) Use the fragmentation patterns in the mass spectra to identify X and Y. Explain your reasoning.

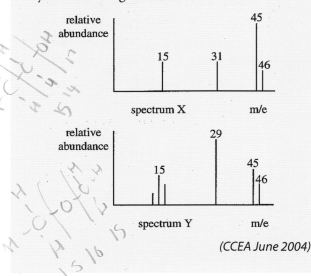

(CCEA June 2004)

## High Resolution Mass Spectrometry

In cases where the value of m/z for an ion could have been produced by two or more different ions, a **high-resolution mass spectrometry** experiment is carried out *to determine the masses of the ions formed to at least one decimal place.* As a result high resolution mass spectrometry can be used to distinguish between ions with similar masses such as $CO^+$ (m/z = 28) and $C_2H_4^+$ (m/z = 28).

| Fragment ion | $CO^+$ | $C_2H_4^+$ |
|---|---|---|
| m/z (low resolution) | $\dfrac{12 + 16}{1} = 28$ | $\dfrac{(2\times12) + (4\times1)}{1} = 28$ |
| m/z (high resolution) | $\dfrac{12.011 + 15.999}{1}$ $= 28.010$ | $\dfrac{(2\times12.011) + (4\times1.008)}{1}$ $= 28.054$ |

> Before moving to the next section, check that you are able to:
>
> - Write the formula for the molecular ion (M⁺) of a compound and locate the molecular ion (M) peak on the mass spectrum of the compound.
> - Recall what is meant by the term *base peak* and locate the base peak on a mass spectrum.
> - Explain what is meant by *fragmentation* and use the concept of fragmentation to account for peaks in the mass spectrum of a compound.
> - Explain how high-resolution mass spectrometry can be used to distinguish between ions with similar mass.

## Applications of Mass Spectrometry

**In this section we are learning to:**

- Use the mass spectrum of a compound to determine the RMM of the compound.
- Explain how mass spectroscopy can be combined with gas-liquid chromatography (GLC) to determine the composition of a mixture.

### Determination of RMM

The value of m/z for the molecular ion (M) peak is equal to the relative molecular mass (RMM) of the compound. In a compound containing several carbon atoms, identification of the M peak is made easier by the presence of ¹³C atoms in the compound.

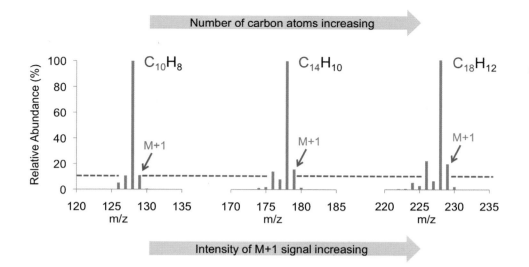

*Figure 2: The relative intensity of the M+1 peak for naphthalene, $C_{10}H_8$ anthracene, $C_{14}H_{10}$ and naphthacene, $C_{18}H_{12}$.*

Approximately 1% of all naturally occurring carbon atoms are $^{13}C$ (RIM = 13); the remainder are $^{12}C$. Thus, if the molecules in a compound each contain one carbon atom, one in every 100 molecules will contain a $^{13}C$ atom and will contribute to **the M+1 peak** on the mass spectrum. Similarly, if a compound contains two carbon atoms, one in every 50 molecules will contain a $^{13}C$ atom and will contribute to the M+1 peak. The relative intensities of the M peak and M+1 peak for naphthalene, $C_{10}H_8$ anthracene, $C_{14}H_{10}$ and naphthacene, $C_{18}H_{12}$ in Figure 2 demonstrate that the intensity of the M+1 peak increases by approximately 1% for every carbon atom in the molecule. As a result the intensity of the M+1 peak can be used to help confirm the identity of the molecular ion (M) peak if the number of carbon atoms in the molecule is known.

Isotopes of other elements can also be used to help identify the molecular ion (M) peak. Chlorine has two naturally occurring isotopes: chlorine-35, $^{35}Cl$ and chlorine-37, $^{37}Cl$. As a result, a molecule of chloromethane, $CH_3Cl$ may be either $CH_3{}^{35}Cl$ (RMM = 50) or $CH_3{}^{37}Cl$ (RMM = 52). The mass spectrum of chloromethane in Figure 3a demonstrates that the 3:1 ratio of $^{35}Cl$ to $^{37}Cl$ in the element gives rise to the molecular ions $CH_3{}^{35}Cl^+$ (m/e = 50) and $CH_3{}^{37}Cl^+$ (m/e = 52) in a 3:1 ratio. The molecular ion signals at m/e = 50 and m/e = 52 are referred to as the M and M+2 peaks.

Bromine also has two naturally occurring isotopes: bromine-79, $^{79}Br$ and bromine-81, $^{81}Br$. As a result, a molecule of bromomethane, $CH_3Br$ may be either

$CH_3{}^{79}Br$ (RMM = 94) or $CH_3{}^{81}Br$ (RMM = 96). Here again, the approximately 1:1 ratio of $^{79}Br$ to $^{81}Br$ in the element gives rise to the molecular ions $CH_3{}^{79}Br^+$ (m/e = 94) and $CH_3{}^{81}Br^+$ (m/e = 96) in the same ratio as shown in Figure 3b.

**Exercise 5.3B**

1. Chlorine has two isotopes, chlorine-35 and chlorine-37. Write the value of m/z and the corresponding formula for each signal in the mass spectrum of chlorine gas.

2. The mass spectrum of 2-chloropropane is shown below. (a) Write the formulas for the ions that give rise to the molecular ion peaks at M and M+2. (b) Write the formulas for the ions that give rise to the peaks at m/z = 63 and 65. (c) Explain, with the aid of an equation, how the peak with an m/z value of 43 is formed.

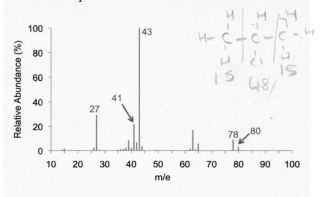

3. The mass spectrum of 2-bromopropane is shown below. (a) Write the formulas for the ions that give rise to the molecular ion peaks at M and M+2. (b) State the value of m/z for the base peak. (c) Explain, with the aid of an equation, how the peak with an m/z value of 43 is formed. (d) Suggest how the peaks with m/z values of 27 and 41 arise from ions with an m/z value of 43.

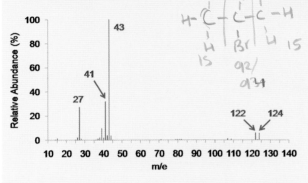

4. The compound 2-chloropropanoic acid produces molecular ion peaks at 108 and 110. It also produces a significant fragment peak at 91. (a) Suggest why there are two molecular ion peaks. (b) Identify the fragment ion.

*(CCEA May 2012)*

Before moving to the next section, check that you are able to:

- Use the intensity of the M+1 and M+2 peaks to confirm the identity of the molecular ion (M) signal.
- Account for the presence and relative intensity of M+1 and M+2 peaks in terms of the presence of $^{13}C$ and the isotopes of chlorine and bromine.

*Figure 3: The mass spectrum of (a) chloromethane, $CH_3Cl$ and (b) bromomethane, $CH_3Br$.*

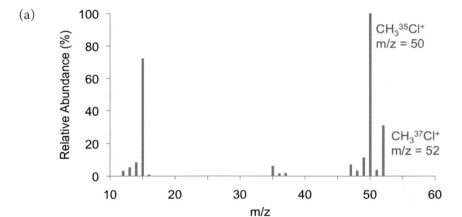

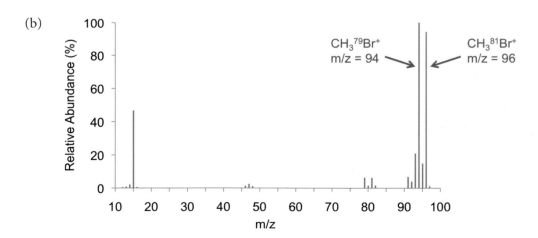

## Combined Techniques

Mass spectrometry (MS) is often used in conjunction with techniques such as chromatography to analyse the composition of mixtures. For example, mixtures of gases and volatile liquids such as hydrocarbons, esters and alcohols are often separated by Gas-Liquid Chromatography (GLC). The identity of each compound is then confirmed by directing a small sample of the compound into a mass spectrometer as it emerges from the GLC experiment.

> Before moving to the next section, check that you are able to:
>
> • Explain how mass spectrometry can be combined with GLC to analyse the composition of mixtures.
>
> • Recall advantages of combining mass spectrometry with separation techniques such as GLC.

### Using GLC and MS to identify the compounds in a mixture

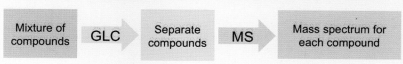

The combined use of GLC and mass spectrometry in a GLC-MS experiment allows for the rapid separation and identification of the compounds in a mixture. This is particularly useful when monitoring chemical processes in real time and is widely used in industry to monitor the large scale production of chemicals.

### Worked Example 5.3ii

In industry butanone is prepared by passing butan-2-ol vapour over copper at 300°C. (a) Explain how mass spectrometry can be linked with GLC to monitor the industrial production of butanone. (b) How would you purify the butanone obtained in this way? FRACTIONAL DISTILLATION

$$CH_3CH(OH)CH_2CH_3 \rightarrow CH_3COCH_2CH_3 + H_2$$

*(Adapted from CCEA Specimen 2010)*

### Solution

(a) Samples of the reaction mixture can be taken at intervals and analysed using GLC. The butanone and butan-2-ol in the mixture are separated and emerge at different times. The area under the signal produced by a compound when it is detected is proportional to the amount of compound present in the mixture. The identity of each compound is confirmed by passing a small amount of each compound to a mass spectrometer as it emerges.

(b) Fractional distillation.

# 5.4 NMR Spectroscopy

**CONNECTIONS**

- The Nobel Prize for Chemistry was awarded to Richard Ernst in 1991 for his contributions to the development of high resolution NMR spectroscopy.
- NMR spectroscopy, in the form of Magnetic Resonance Imaging (MRI), is widely used in medicine to image tissues and organs in the human body.

Nuclear Magnetic Resonance (NMR) spectroscopy is routinely used in chemical research to help deduce the structure of newly synthesised compounds. The results of an NMR experiment are summarised in the form of an NMR spectrum.

## Obtaining an NMR Spectrum

**In this section we are learning to:**

- Describe the use of an internal standard to determine the $^1$H-NMR spectrum of a compound.
- Explain why TMS is used as an internal standard.

**Magnetic Resonance**

Isotopes such as $^1$H, $^{13}$C and $^{31}$P produce a small magnetic field centred on their nucleus. When a molecule containing the isotope is placed in a magnetic field, the magnetic field produced by the nucleus, $H_{nuc}$ may become aligned 'with' or 'against' the applied magnetic field, $H_{app}$ as shown in Figure 1a. The energy of the isotope is lower when the magnetic field produced by the nucleus is aligned 'with' the applied field as shown in Figure 1b. As a result the isotope can absorb energy, and use the energy to align 'against' the applied magnetic field.

The isotope then generates an electrical signal as the magnetic field returns to being aligned 'with' the applied magnetic field. The frequency generated by the isotope depends on the isotope and its location in the molecule. The frequencies produced by the $^1$H isotopes in a molecule are known as the $^1$H-NMR spectrum of the molecule. The $^1$H-NMR spectrum of bromoethane is shown in Figure 2.

(a)

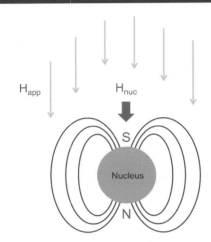

$H_{nuc}$ aligned 'with' the applied field, $H_{app}$

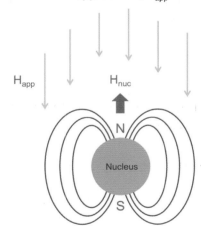

$H_{nuc}$ aligned 'against' the applied field, $H_{app}$

(b)

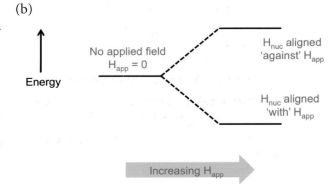

*Figure 1: (a) The magnetic field produced by a nucleus, $H_{nuc}$ may become aligned 'with' or 'against' an applied magnetic field, $H_{app}$. (b) The energy of an isotope is higher when the magnetic field produced by the nucleus, $H_{nuc}$ is aligned against the applied magnetic field, $H_{app}$.*

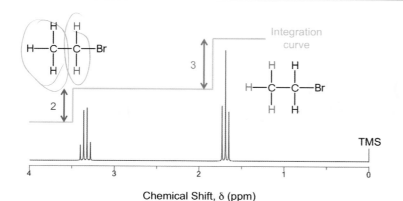

*Figure 2: The ¹H-NMR spectrum of bromoethane, $CH_3CH_2Br$.*

## Chemical Shift

The ¹H-NMR spectrum for bromoethane consists of two signals: one produced by the ¹H atoms in the methyl (-$CH_3$) group, and a second produced by the ¹H atoms in the methylene (-$CH_2$-) group.

The spectrum is obtained by dissolving a few milligrams of bromoethane and a few drops of tetramethylsilane (TMS), $Si(CH_3)_4$ in a solvent that does not give rise to signals in the NMR spectrum. The TMS acts as an **internal standard** as it is part of the sample undergoing analysis and produces a signal that serves as a reference point for the spectrum. The signal produced by the ¹H isotopes in TMS is assigned a **chemical shift** of zero, and allows for a simple scale on which the ¹H atoms in organic compounds produce signals with chemical shift ($\delta$) values in the range 0–15. The chemical shift of a signal is measured in parts-per-million (ppm) of the applied field.

The compound TMS is well-suited for use as an internal standard as it: is miscible with the solvents used in NMR samples, produces a simple signal that is well-separated from the signals produced by other compounds, and will not react with the compounds in the sample.

---

Before moving to the next section, check that you are able to:

- Recall that ¹H isotopes emit radiation with a frequency that reflects the location of the isotope within a compound.
- Recall that the ¹H-NMR spectrum of a compound is obtained by plotting the intensity of the signals produced by the ¹H isotopes in the compound as a function of their chemical shift.
- Recall that the signal produced by the ¹H isotopes in TMS is assigned a chemical shift of zero.
- Recall why TMS is used as an internal standard for ¹H-NMR analysis.

## Interpreting a ¹H-NMR Spectrum

**In this section we are learning to:**

- Use the concept of equivalent atoms to account for the number of signals in the ¹H-NMR spectrum of a compound.
- Explain the chemical shift values of ¹H signals in terms of the extent to which the ¹H isotopes giving rise to the signals are shielded.
- Explain the splitting of ¹H signals in terms of the number of ¹H isotopes bonded to an adjacent atom.

---

### Chemical Equivalence

In bromoethane, $CH_3CH_2Br$ the molecule rotates freely about the C-C bond. This allows each of the hydrogen atoms in the methyl (-$CH_3$) group to interact in the same way with the atoms in the rest of the molecule. As a result the hydrogen atoms in the -$CH_3$ group experience the same chemical environment and are described as being **chemically equivalent**. The chemically equivalent hydrogen atoms in the methyl (-$CH_3$) group give rise to a signal at $\delta$ 1.7 ppm. Similarly the hydrogen atoms in the methylene (-$CH_2$-) group are chemically equivalent and give rise to a signal at $\delta$ 3.3 ppm.

The area under each signal is proportional to the number of hydrogen atoms giving rise to the signal and is obtained directly from the **integration curve** for the spectrum. For example, the integration curve for bromoethane in Figure 2 confirms that the areas under the methyl (-$CH_3$) and methylene (-$CH_2$-) signals are in the ratio 3:2 and therefore reflect the number of hydrogen atoms in each group.

........................................................

### Worked Example 5.4i

The NMR spectrum for pentan-3-one, $CH_3CH_2COCH_2CH_3$ is shown below. (a) The signal at 0 ppm is due to TMS. Explain why TMS is used as a standard. (b) Explain the number of signals. (c) Describe the integration curve. (d) Explain the integration curve.

*Symetry so only 2 different environments*

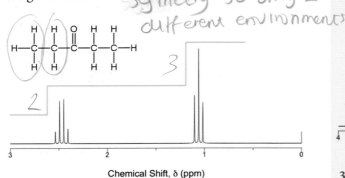

*3*

*2*

Chemical Shift, δ (ppm)

## Solution

(a) TMS produces one signal that is well-separated from the signals produced by the compounds in the sample, and does not react with the compounds in the sample.

(b) The hydrogen atoms in the methyl (-CH₃) groups are equivalent and give rise to one signal. The hydrogen atoms in the methylene (-CH₂-) groups are equivalent and give rise to one signal.

(c) The areas under the signals at δ 2.5 ppm and δ 1.1 ppm are in the ratio 2:3.ˋ

(d) The signal at δ 2.5 ppm was produced by the four equivalent hydrogen atoms in the methylene (-CH₂-) groups. The signal at δ 1.1 ppm was produced by the six equivalent hydrogen atoms in the methyl (-CH₃) groups.

...........................................................

### Exercise 5.4A

1. The NMR spectrum for propanal, $CH_3CH_2CHO$ is shown below. (a) Explain the number of signals. (b) Use the integration curve to explain the origin of each signal in the spectrum.

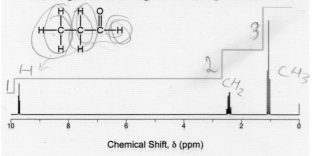

*H*

*3*

*2*  *CH₂*  *CH₃*

Chemical Shift, δ (ppm)

2. The NMR spectrum for one isomer of propanol is shown below. (a) Use the spectrum to identify the isomer. (b) Use the integration curve to justify your reasoning.

*Ratio 1:2:2:3*

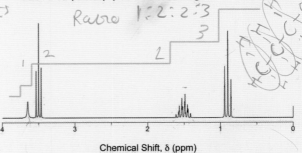

*2*  *3*  *2*

Chemical Shift, δ (ppm)

3. A compound has the molecular formula $C_6H_{12}$ and has only one signal in its NMR spectrum. Draw one possible structure for the compound.

*(Adapted from CCEA May 2012)*

Before moving to the next section, check that you are able to:

- Identify chemically equivalent hydrogen atoms in a compound.
- Interpret the integration curve for a compound in terms of the number of chemically equivalent hydrogen atoms in the compound.

### Shielding

When a $^1H$ isotope is placed in a magnetic field the electrons in the atom produce a magnetic field that opposes the applied field; an effect known as **shielding**.

In bromoethane, $CH_3CH_2Br$ the hydrogen atoms in the methylene (-CH₂-) group are attached to a carbon atom that is adjacent to an electron-withdrawing bromine atom. As a result, the nucleus of each hydrogen atom in the -CH₂- group is less shielded (or *more deshielded*) and has a greater chemical shift (δ 3.3 ppm) than the better shielded hydrogen nuclei in the -CH₃ group (δ 1.7 ppm).

*Integration curve is about number of H⁺.*

*Peaks is the n+1 rule.*

*Ratio 1:2:3*

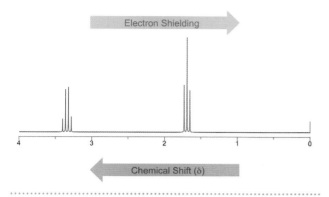

*Electron Shielding*

*Chemical Shift (δ)*

## Worked Example 5.4ii

The NMR spectrum of propanamide, $CH_3CH_2CONH_2$ is shown below. (a) Explain why the signal at 7.2 ppm has the highest chemical shift. (b) Use the integration curve to explain the origin of the remaining signals. (c) Explain why the signal at 2.3 ppm has a higher chemical shift than the signal at 1.0 ppm. (d) State and explain three ways in which this spectrum would differ from the spectrum of the N-methylated compound, $CH_3CH_2CONHCH_3$.

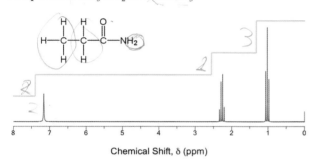

Chemical Shift, δ (ppm)

*(Adapted from CCEA June 2013)*

### Solution

(a) The hydrogen atoms in the amino (-$NH_2$) group at δ 7.2 ppm experience the least shielding as they are attached to the electron-withdrawing nitrogen atom.

(b) The areas under the signals are in the ratio 2:3. In this way the integration shows that the signal at δ 2.3 ppm is produced by the methylene (-$CH_2$-) group, and the signal at δ 1.0 ppm is produced by the methyl (-$CH_3$) group.

(c) The hydrogen atoms in the methylene (-$CH_2$-) group are closer to the electron-withdrawing nitrogen and oxygen atoms than the hydrogen atoms in the methyl (-$CH_3$) group.

(d) The N-methylated compound would produce an additional signal, different chemical shifts, and areas under the signals in the ratio 3:3:2:1.

## Exercise 5.4B

1. The NMR spectrum of 2-chloropropane contains two sets of signals as shown below. (a) Explain the peak integration. (b) Explain the chemical shifts.

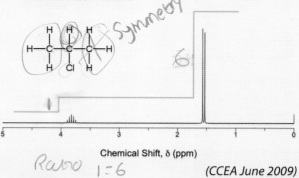

Chemical Shift, δ (ppm)

*(CCEA June 2009)*

2. Ethanoic acid reacts with ethanol to form the ester ethyl ethanoate, $CH_3COOCH_2CH_3$. The NMR spectrum of ethyl ethanoate consists of three signals. (a) Interpret and explain the integration. (b) Explain the chemical shifts.

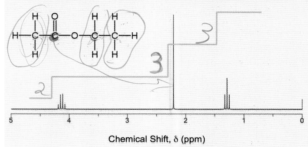

Chemical Shift, δ (ppm)

*(Adapted from CCEA June 2011)*

3. Succinic acid is a dicarboxylic acid. The high resolution NMR spectrum of succinic acid is shown below. (a) Explain why the $CH_2$ groups do not interact with each other. (b) Identify which hydrogen atoms give rise to the signals at δ 11.0 ppm and δ 2.8 ppm. (c) Explain the chemical shift values.

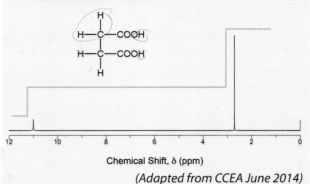

Chemical Shift, δ (ppm)

*(Adapted from CCEA June 2014)*

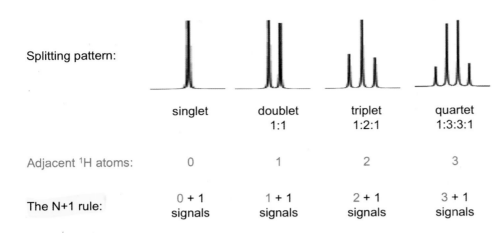

Splitting pattern:

| singlet | doublet 1:1 | triplet 1:2:1 | quartet 1:3:3:1 |
|---|---|---|---|

Adjacent $^1H$ atoms: 0 1 2 3

The N+1 rule:
0 + 1 signals | 1 + 1 signals | 2 + 1 signals | 3 + 1 signals

*Figure 3: The splitting patterns in multiplets produced by hydrogen atoms with up to three hydrogen atoms attached to an adjacent atom.*

---

**Before moving to the next section, check that you are able to:**

- Recall that nuclei are less shielded *(more deshielded)* when they are close to electron-withdrawing atoms such as nitrogen and oxygen.
- Recall that nuclei which experience less shielding (more deshielding) have a greater chemical shift than nuclei that experience more shielding.

## High-Resolution NMR

The NMR spectrum for bromoethane in Figure 2 reveals that the methyl (-CH$_3$) group gives rise to a triplet of signals at δ 1.7 ppm with intensities in the ratio 1:2:1. The 'splitting' of the signal to give a 1:2:1 ratio results from the presence of two chemically equivalent hydrogen atoms on the neighbouring carbon atom. The splitting of a signal by hydrogen atoms on a neighbouring atom is referred to as **spin-spin splitting**. Similarly, the methylene (-CH$_2$-) group in bromoethane gives rise to a quartet of signals at δ 3.3 ppm with intensities in the ratio 1:3:3:1. The 1:3:3:1 ratio results from the presence of three chemically equivalent hydrogen atoms on the neighbouring carbon atom.

A splitting pattern containing two or more signals is referred to as a **multiplet**. The triplet and quartet in the NMR spectrum for bromoethane are examples of multiplets and illustrate the 'N+1' rule which asserts that *the number of signals in the splitting pattern is one more than the number of adjacent hydrogen atoms (N)*. The splitting patterns in multiplets produced by hydrogen atoms with up to three adjacent hydrogen atoms are summarised in Figure 3.

*If an NMR experiment is performed at low-resolution the splitting patterns that result from spin-spin splitting cannot be resolved, and appear as singlets in the NMR spectrum.*

**Worked Example 5.4iii**

The NMR spectrum for butanone, CH$_3$CH$_2$COCH$_3$ is shown below. (a) Explain the splitting pattern for each signal. (b) Explain the integration curve. (c) Draw the low resolution NMR spectrum for butanone. Include an integration curve.

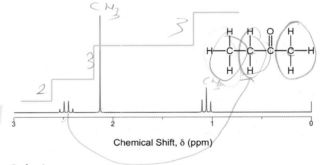

Chemical Shift, δ (ppm)

*Solution*

(a) The signal at δ 2.5 ppm is due to hydrogen atoms adjacent to a set of three equivalent hydrogen atoms; the signal at δ 2.2 ppm is due to hydrogen atoms with no adjacent hydrogen atoms; and the signal at δ 1.1 ppm is due to hydrogen atoms adjacent to a set of two equivalent hydrogen atoms.

(b) The areas under the signals at δ 2.5 ppm, δ 2.2 ppm and δ 1.1 ppm are in the ratio 2:3:3 and are due to the methylene (-CH$_2$-) group, the methyl (-CH$_3$) group adjacent to the carbonyl (CO) group, and the methyl (-CH$_3$) group adjacent to the methylene (-CH$_2$-) group.

(c)

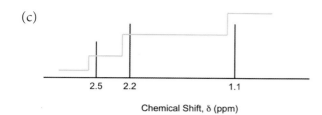

2.5    2.2         1.1

Chemical Shift, δ (ppm)

## Exercise 5.4C

1. The NMR spectrum of ethyl methanoate, $HCOOCH_2CH_3$ is shown below. (a) Name the substance responsible for the signal at δ = 0 and state its formula. (b) Explain the spin-spin splitting. (c) Explain the peak integration. (d) Explain the chemical shifts.

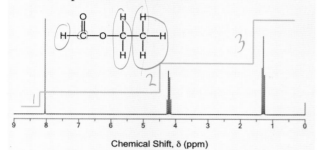

Chemical Shift, δ (ppm)

*(CCEA January 2010)*

2. Sketch the NMR spectrum for methyl propanoate, $CH_3CH_2COOCH_3$ showing the integration curve together with the splitting patterns. Indicate which hydrogen atoms are responsible for each peak.

*(Adapted from CCEA June 2015)*

3. The NMR spectrum of a compound X is shown below. Which of the following compounds is X?

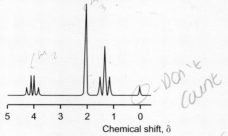

5    4    3    2    1    0
Chemical shift, δ

A  $CH_3CH_2CH_2COOH$
B  $CH_3CH_2COOCH_2CH_3$
C  $CH_3COOCH_2CH_3$
D  $CH_3CH_2COOH$

*(CCEA June 2010)*

4. Complete the table by giving the integration values and the splitting of each signal in the NMR spectrum of 2-chloropropanoic acid.

| | Signal 1 | Signal 2 | Signal 3 |
|---|---|---|---|
| Integration | 3 | 1 | 1 |
| Splitting | Doublet | Quartet | Singlet |

*(CCEA June 2012)*

5. Compounds A and B are isomers with molecular formula $C_4H_8O_2$. Both have a triplet, a singlet and a quartet in their NMR spectrum. Draw possible structures for A and B.

*(Adapted from CCEA June 2012)*

---

Before moving to the next section, check that you are able to:

- Account for the splitting of $^1H$-NMR signals in terms of the number of equivalent hydrogen atoms bonded to an adjacent atom.
- Use the N+1 rule in conjunction with an integration curve to identify the hydrogen atoms giving rise to signals in the NMR spectrum of a compound.

*Integration is about the number of hydrogens on that environment.*

*Splitting is about how many peaks that environment will produce and it depends on the number of hydrogens on the adjacent carbon so use n+1 rule.*

# 5.5 Electrochemistry

## Electrochemical Cells

**In this section we are learning to:**

- Explain how an electrochemical cell produces a voltage.
- Use shorthand notation to describe electrochemical cells.

An **electrochemical cell** can be used to produce a voltage from a chemical reaction. If the **electromotive force (emf)** or 'voltage' generated by the cell is sufficiently large, the chemical reaction in the cell will produce an electric current as soon as the cell is connected to an electric circuit.

Electrochemical Cells
- ➤ Produce a voltage
- ➤ Use a chemical reaction to produce an electric current
- ➤ Are used to construct batteries and power supplies

The apparatus used to construct an electrochemical cell in the laboratory is shown in Figure 1. The copper-zinc cell in Figure 1 consists of two half-cells, each containing an **electrode** that *establishes electrical contact between a half-cell and the external circuit*. The electrodes are constructed by placing a strip of copper in a solution containing copper ions, and a strip of zinc in a solution containing zinc ions. When a metal such as zinc or copper is placed in a solution containing its ions a dynamic equilibrium is established at the metal surface.

*Dynamic equilibrium at the surface of the copper electrode:* $\quad Cu_{(s)} \leftrightarrows Cu^{2+}_{(aq)} + 2e^-$

*Dynamic equilibrium at the surface of the zinc electrode:* $\quad Zn_{(s)} \leftrightarrows Zn^{2+}_{(aq)} + 2e^-$

When the cell is connected to an electric circuit electrons produced at the negative electrode flow around the circuit, and are used at the positive electrode.

*Half-equation for the negative electrode:*
$$Zn_{(s)} \rightarrow Zn^{2+}_{(aq)} + 2e^-$$

*Half-equation for the positive electrode:*
$$Cu^{2+}_{(aq)} + 2e^- \rightarrow Cu_{(s)}$$

The **cell reaction** describes *the overall chemical change that occurs in the cell*, and is obtained by combining the half-equations.

*Cell reaction:*
$$Zn_{(s)} + Cu^{2+}_{(aq)} \rightarrow Zn^{2+}_{(aq)} + Cu_{(s)}$$

**Worked Example 5.5i**

Explain what is meant by *the electromotive force (emf) of a cell.*

**Solution**

The electromotive force (emf) or 'voltage' generated by a cell is the potential difference measured by a voltmeter when the two half-cells making up the cell are connected, and the voltmeter is connected across the cell.

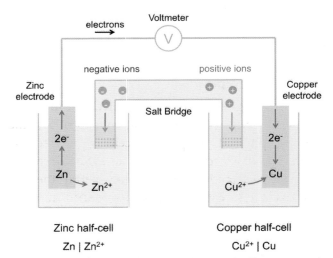

*Figure 1: An electrochemical cell constructed from zinc and copper electrodes.*

The **salt bridge** contains an aqueous salt solution and completes the circuit by allowing ions to move between the salt bridge and the solutions at each electrode. Aqueous potassium nitrate can be used in the salt bridge as the potassium ions and nitrate ions do not react at the electrodes.

On introducing the notation || to represent the salt bridge, the zinc-copper cell in Figure 1 can be represented by the shorthand $Zn|Zn^{2+}||Cu^{2+}|Cu$. The shorthand shows that the salt bridge is in contact with both solutions ($Zn^{2+}||Cu^{2+}$), and describes the nature of oxidation ($Zn|Zn^{2+}$) and reduction ($Cu^{2+}|Cu$) at the electrodes. In this notation a vertical line is used to indicate a boundary between two different physical phases (solid and liquid, liquid and gas, etc.).

The oxidation and reduction processes that occur at the electrodes are referred to as **half-cells**. By convention, when writing the shorthand for a cell, the half-cell in which reduction occurs is written on the right of the salt bridge. Thus, in the zinc-copper cell, the copper half-cell ($Cu^{2+}|Cu$) is written to the right of the salt bridge.

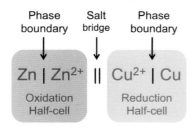

By adopting this convention we can quickly deduce that electrons flow from the zinc half-cell to the copper half-cell as *electrons will always flow from the half-cell in which oxidation occurs (on the left) to the half-cell in which reduction occurs (on the right).*

## Worked Example 5.5ii

The following cell uses a platinum electrode to reduce iron(III) ions. (a) Write half-equations for the $Fe^{3+},Fe^{2+}|Pt$ and $Fe^{2+}|Fe$ half-cells. (b) State the direction of electron flow in the external circuit. (c) Describe the movement of ions within the cell. (d) Explain the role of the platinum electrode.

### Solution

(a) Platinum electrode:
$$Fe^{3+}_{(aq)} + e^- \rightarrow Fe^{2+}_{(aq)}$$

Iron electrode:
$$Fe_{(s)} \rightarrow Fe^{2+}_{(aq)} + 2e^-$$

(b) Electrons flow from the iron electrode to the platinum electrode.

(c) Positive ions move from the salt bridge into the $Fe^{3+},Fe^{2+}|Pt$ half-cell and negative ions flow from the salt bridge into the $Fe^{2+}|Fe$ half-cell.

(d) The platinum electrode provides electrons for the reduction of iron(III) ions.

## Exercise 5.5A

1. (a) Write half-equations for the oxidation and reduction reactions in the cell $Fe|Fe^{2+}||Sn^{2+}|Sn$.
   (b) State the direction of electron flow in the external circuit.

2. The cell shown below is constructed from aluminium and zinc half-cells.

   When the cell is connected to an electric circuit a current flows and the mass of the zinc electrode increases. (a) Write half-equations for the reactions that occur in the $Al^{3+}|Al$ and $Zn^{2+}|Zn$ half-cells. (b) State the direction of electron flow in the external circuit. (c) Write the shorthand for the cell.

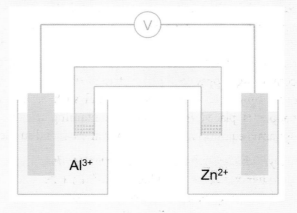

Before moving to the next section, check that you are able to:

- Explain what is meant by the *emf* of a cell.
- Write half-equations for the reactions occurring at the electrodes.
- Explain the role of the salt bridge and deduce the movement of electrons in the external circuit.
- Write the shorthand for an electrochemical cell.

## Calculating the EMF of a Cell

**In this section we are learning to:**

- Deduce the cell reaction and emf for an electrochemical cell.
- Describe the use of a standard hydrogen electrode to measure standard electrode potentials.

### Standard Electrode Potentials

The potential generated by a half-cell when it operates as a reduction under standard conditions is referred to as the **standard electrode potential, E°** for the half-cell.

*Standard electrode potential for a $Zn^{2+}|Zn$ half-cell:*
$Zn^{2+} + 2e^- \rightarrow Zn \qquad E° = -0.76\ V$

*Standard electrode potential for a $Cu^{2+}|Cu$ half-cell:*
$Cu^{2+} + 2e^- \rightarrow Cu \qquad E° = +0.34\ V$

In order to operate a $Zn^{2+}|Zn$ or $Cu^{2+}|Cu$ half-cell under standard conditions the metal must be placed in a solution containing metal ions at a concentration of 1 mol dm$^{-3}$, and the half-cell operated at 25 °C and a pressure of 100 kPa.

If a half-cell is operated under non-standard conditions the potential generated is not equal to E° and is instead referred to as the **electrode potential, E** for the half-cell.

In the copper-zinc cell, $Zn|Zn^{2+}||Cu^{2+}|Cu$ the reduction of copper(II) ions generates a potential equal to E° for the $Cu^{2+}|Cu$ half-cell (+0.34 V), and the potential generated by the oxidation of zinc is the negative of E° for the $Zn^{2+}|Zn$ half-cell (−0.76 V) as the half-cell is operating in reverse. The emf for the cell is is then obtained by adding the potentials generated by reduction ($E_{red}$) and oxidation ($E_{ox}$).

*Potential generated by reduction:*
$Cu^{2+} + 2e^- \rightarrow Cu \qquad E_{red} = +0.34\ V$

*Potential generated by oxidation:*
$Zn \rightarrow Zn^{2+} + 2e^- \qquad E_{ox} = +0.76\ V$

*The emf of the cell:*
$emf = E_{red} + E_{ox} = (+0.34) + (+0.76) = +1.10\ V$

Check by applying the *anticlockwise rule* to the half-equations:

|  | E (V) |
|---|---|
| $Zn^{2+}(aq) + 2e^- \leftrightarrows Zn(s)$ | -0.76 |
| $Cu^{2+}(aq) + 2e^- \leftrightarrows Cu(s)$ | +0.34 |

- The half-equations are written as reductions (with electrons on the left).
- The half-equation with the more negative potential is written first (on top).
- The cell reaction is then obtained by following the blue arrow (Zn is oxidised and Cu$^{2+}$ is reduced): $Zn + Cu^{2+} \rightarrow Zn^{2+} + Cu$
- The emf is calculated by following the red arrow and subtracting the second potential from the first: $emf = (+0.34) - (-0.76) = +1.10\ V$

### Worked Example 5.5iii

Write the equation for the reaction of aluminium with aqueous zinc ions and calculate the emf produced by the reaction.

|  | E° /V |
|---|---|
| $Al^{3+}(aq) + 3e^- \leftrightarrows Al(s)$ | −1.66 |
| $Zn^{2+}(aq) + 2e^- \leftrightarrows Zn(s)$ | −0.76 |

*(CCEA May 2012)*

**Strategy**
- Combine balanced half-equations for the oxidation of aluminium and the reduction of zinc.
- Calculate the emf using the equation: $emf = E_{red} + E_{ox}$.

**Solution**
Balanced half-equations
$2Al(s) \rightarrow 2Al^{3+}(aq) + 6e^-$
$3Zn^{2+}(aq) + 6e^- \rightarrow 3Zn(s)$

Cell reaction
$2Al(s) + 3Zn^{2+}(aq) \rightarrow 2Al^{3+}(aq) + 3Zn(s)$

Emf for the cell reaction
$emf = E_{red} + E_{ox} = (-0.76) + (+1.66) = +0.90\ V$

## Exercise 5.5B

1. (a) Write the ionic equation for the reduction of silver(I) to silver by chromium(II). (b) Calculate the emf for the reduction.

| | $E^\circ$ / V |
|---|---|
| $Cr^{3+}{}_{(aq)} + e^- \rightleftharpoons Cr^{2+}{}_{(aq)}$ | $-0.41$ |
| $Ag^+{}_{(aq)} + e^- \rightleftharpoons Ag_{(s)}$ | $+0.80$ |

*(Adapted from CCEA June 2011)*

2. Electrochemical methods may be used to detect carbon monoxide. The half-equations for the reaction used to detect carbon monoxide are given below. (a) Use the following half-equations to write the equation for the reaction that occurs when carbon monoxide is present. (b) Calculate the emf produced by the reaction.

$$CO + H_2O \rightarrow CO_2 + 2H^+ + 2e^- \quad E = -0.10 \text{ V}$$
$$O_2 + 4H^+ + 4e^- \rightarrow 2H_2O \quad E = +1.23 \text{ V}$$

*(Adapted from CCEA January 2007)*

3. (a) Use the half-equations to write the equation for the reaction between fluorine and a solution of tin(II) ions. (b) Use the electrode potentials to calculate the emf produced by the reaction.

$$2F^-{}_{(aq)} \rightarrow F_2{}_{(g)} + 2e^- \quad E^\circ = -2.87 \text{ V}$$
$$Sn^{2+}{}_{(aq)} \rightarrow Sn^{4+}{}_{(aq)} + 2e^- \quad E^\circ = -0.15 \text{ V}$$

*(CCEA January 2003)*

7. The standard electrode potentials for some half-cells are listed below:

$$Cu^{2+}{}_{(aq)} + 2e^- \rightarrow Cu_{(s)} \qquad +0.34 \text{ V}$$
$$AgCl_{(s)} + e^- \rightarrow Ag_{(s)} + Cl^-{}_{(aq)} \qquad +0.22 \text{ V}$$
$$H^+{}_{(aq)} + e^- \rightarrow \tfrac{1}{2}H_2{}_{(g)} \qquad 0.00 \text{ V}$$
$$Zn^{2+}{}_{(aq)} + 2e^- \rightarrow Zn_{(s)} \qquad -0.76 \text{ V}$$

Which one of the following emf values could be obtained by combining two of these standard electrodes?

|   |   |   |   |
|---|---|---|---|
| A | 0.42 V | B | 0.54 V |
| C | 0.56 V | D | 0.98 V |

*(Adapted from CCEA June 2013)*

Before moving to the next section, check that you are able to:

- Recall the *standard conditions* for an electrochemical cell.
- Deduce a cell reaction from half-equations defining the electrode potentials.
- Use electrode potentials to calculate the emf of an electrochemical cell.

## The Standard Hydrogen Electrode

The standard electrode potential, $E^\circ$ generated by the reaction in a half-cell can be measured by attaching the half-cell to a standard electrode such as a standard hydrogen electrode (SHE). The cell in Figure 2 illustrates the use of a SHE to measure $E^\circ$ for a copper electrode. A standard hydrogen electrode is constructed by placing a platinum electrode in a 1 mol dm$^{-3}$ solution of hydrochloric acid that is in contact with hydrogen gas at a pressure of 100 kPa. If the cell in Figure 2 is operated under standard conditions, $E^\circ$ for the SHE is zero and the emf (+0.34 V) corresponds to $E^\circ$ for the Cu$^{2+}$|Cu half-cell.

*Potential generated by reduction:*
$$Cu^{2+} + 2e^- \rightarrow Cu$$
$$E_{red} = +0.34 \text{ V}$$

*Potential generated by oxidation:*
$$H_2 \rightarrow 2H^+ + 2e^-$$
$$E_{ox} = +0.00 \text{ V}$$

*The emf for the cell:*
$$\text{emf} = E_{red} + E_{ox} = (+0.34) + (+0.00) = +0.34 \text{ V}$$
therefore $E^\circ$ for the Cu$^{2+}$|Cu half-cell
$$= E_{red} = +0.34 \text{ V}$$

The half-cell in the SHE is represented by the shorthand H$^+$|H$_2$|Pt where the vertical lines are again used to separate species in different physical phases.

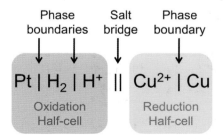

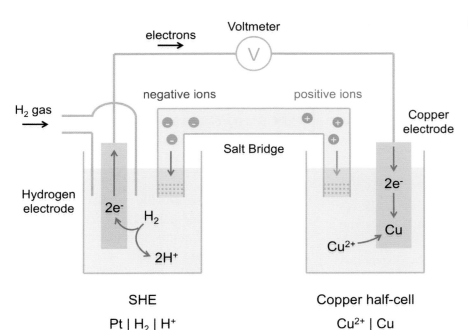

*Figure 2: Using a SHE to measure E° for a Cu²⁺|Cu half-cell.*

SHE

Pt | H₂ | H⁺

Copper half-cell

Cu²⁺ | Cu

If the SHE is instead connected to a zinc half-cell as shown in Figure 3, and the cell operated under standard conditions, zinc is oxidised and the emf (+0.76 V) corresponds to the negative of E° for the $Zn^{2+}|Zn$ half-cell.

*Potential generated by reduction:*
$2H^+ + 2e^- \rightarrow H_2$
$E_{red} = +0.00 \text{ V}$

*Potential generated by oxidation:*
$Zn \rightarrow Zn^{2+} + 2e^-$
$E_{ox} = +0.76 \text{ V}$

*The emf for the cell:*
emf $= E_{red} + E_{ox} = (+0.00) + (+0.76) = +0.76$ V
therefore E° for the $Zn^{2+}|Zn$ half-cell
$= -E_{ox} = -0.76$ V

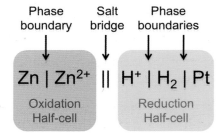

| Phase boundary | Salt bridge | Phase boundaries | |
|---|---|---|---|

Zn | Zn²⁺ || H⁺ | H₂ | Pt

Oxidation Half-cell | Reduction Half-cell

Electron flow (in external circuit)

The SHE is widely used as a reference electrode as the potential generated by the platinum electrode is reproducible. The platinum electrode is also inert,

and is an effective catalyst for the reaction occurring in the half-cell. In practice, an additional layer of platinum is deposited on the surface of the platinum electrode to produce a rougher surface with a much greater surface area. The rougher surface increases the rate of the reaction in the half-cell by lowering the activation energy for the reaction.

**Worked Example 5.5iv**

Define the term *standard electrode potential*.

*(CCEA May 2012)*

*Solution*

The potential difference measured by a voltmeter when a half-cell is connected to a standard hydrogen electrode, and the cell operated under standard conditions with the voltmeter connected across the cell.

**Exercise 5.5C**

1. Electrode potentials can be measured using a hydrogen electrode. Describe a hydrogen electrode and state the conditions under which it operates.

*(Adapted from CCEA June 2014)*

2. (a) State the conditions under which the hydrogen reference electrode operates. (b) What is the purpose of the salt bridge in an electrochemical cell. (c) Describe how a

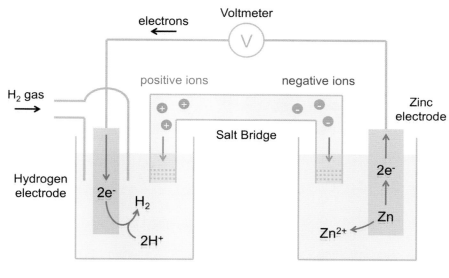

SHE

Pt | H₂ | H⁺

Zinc half-cell

$Zn^{2+}$ | Zn

hydrogen reference electrode could be used to measure the standard electrode potential for the half-cell described by the half-equation: $Cl_{2(g)} + 2e^- \rightarrow 2Cl^-_{(aq)}$.

*(CCEA January 2003)*

3. (a) Use the electrode potentials given below to calculate the emf for an iron-chlorine cell. (b) Write the shorthand for the cell. (c) State the direction of electron flow in the external circuit. (d) Describe how to operate the cell under standard conditions.

| | | |
|---|---|---|
| $Cl_{2(g)} + 2e^- \rightarrow 2Cl^-_{(aq)}$ | $Cl_2\|Cl^-\|Pt$ | +1.36 V |
| $Fe^{3+}_{(aq)} + e^- \rightarrow Fe^{2+}_{(aq)}$ | $Fe^{3+},Fe^{2+}\|Pt$ | +0.77 V |

Before moving to the next section, check that you are able to:

- Explain the term *standard electrode potential* with reference to the use of a standard hydrogen electrode.
- Describe the conditions under which a standard hydrogen electrode operates.
- Explain how a standard hydrogen electrode could be used to determine the standard potential of an electrode.

## Applications of Electrode Potentials

**In this section we are learning to:**

- Use electrode potentials to construct a reactivity series, and determine if a redox reaction is feasible.

### Constructing a Reactivity Series

Less reactive metals such as copper are poor reducing agents and will not form positive ions as readily as more reactive metals such as zinc. As a result, copper is displaced from solution when a better reducing agent such as zinc is added to a solution containing copper ions.

*Displacement of copper ions by zinc:*
$Zn_{(s)} + Cu^{2+}_{(aq)} \rightarrow Zn^{2+}_{(aq)} + Cu_{(s)}$

Similarly magnesium, which is a better reducing agent than zinc, will displace zinc from solution when added to a solution containing zinc ions.

*Displacement of zinc ions by magnesium:*
$Mg_{(s)} + Zn^{2+}_{(aq)} \rightarrow Mg^{2+}_{(aq)} + Zn_{(s)}$

In this way the reactivity of a metal can be associated with its ability to act as a reducing agent, and we can construct a reactivity series by writing the half-equations that define the electrode potentials in order of increasing electrode potential as shown in Figure 4.

According to the reactivity series Fe²⁺ will be displaced from solution by better reducing agents

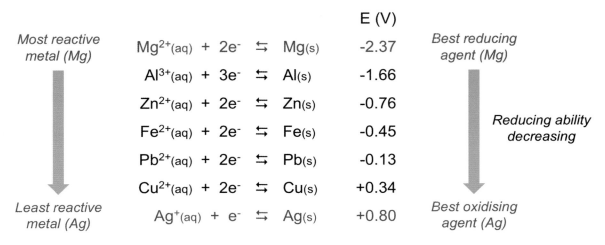

E (V)

Most reactive metal (Mg)

$Mg^{2+}_{(aq)} + 2e^- \rightleftharpoons Mg_{(s)}$    -2.37

$Al^{3+}_{(aq)} + 3e^- \rightleftharpoons Al_{(s)}$    -1.66

$Zn^{2+}_{(aq)} + 2e^- \rightleftharpoons Zn_{(s)}$    -0.76

$Fe^{2+}_{(aq)} + 2e^- \rightleftharpoons Fe_{(s)}$    -0.45

$Pb^{2+}_{(aq)} + 2e^- \rightleftharpoons Pb_{(s)}$    -0.13

$Cu^{2+}_{(aq)} + 2e^- \rightleftharpoons Cu_{(s)}$    +0.34

$Ag^+_{(aq)} + e^- \rightleftharpoons Ag_{(s)}$    +0.80

Least reactive metal (Ag)

Best reducing agent (Mg)

Reducing ability decreasing

Best oxidising agent (Ag)

*Figure 4: Using standard electrode potentials to construct a reactivity series. The electrode potentials increase from top to bottom.*

such as zinc, aluminium and magnesium. Similarly, iron is shown to be a better reducing agent than lead, copper and silver, and will therefore displace $Pb^{2+}$ ions, $Cu^{2+}$ ions and $Ag^+$ ions from solution.

### Worked Example 5.5v

Which one of the following elements will reduce $Fe^{3+}_{(aq)}$ to $Fe^{2+}_{(aq)}$ but not to $Fe_{(s)}$?

A   iodine
B   manganese
C   nickel
D   silver

|  |  |  | $E^{\ominus}$ /V |
|---|---|---|---|
| $Mn^{2+}_{(aq)} + 2e^-$ | $\rightleftharpoons$ | $Mn_{(s)}$ | −1.19 |
| $Fe^{2+}_{(aq)} + 2e^-$ | $\rightleftharpoons$ | $Fe_{(s)}$ | −0.44 |
| $Ni^{2+}_{(aq)} + 2e^-$ | $\rightleftharpoons$ | $Ni_{(s)}$ | −0.25 |
| $I_{2(s)} + 2e^-$ | $\rightleftharpoons$ | $2I^-_{(aq)}$ | +0.54 |
| $Fe^{3+}_{(aq)} + e^-$ | $\rightleftharpoons$ | $Fe^{2+}_{(aq)}$ | +0.77 |
| $Ag^+_{(aq)} + e^-$ | $\rightleftharpoons$ | $Ag_{(s)}$ | +0.80 |

*(CCEA June 2010)*

### Strategy

- The reactivity series can be used to predict that iron(III), $Fe^{3+}$ will be reduced to iron(II), $Fe^{2+}$ by iodide ($I^-$), nickel (Ni), iron (Fe) and manganese (Mn).
- Of these only manganese would reduce the iron(II) ions formed to iron.

### Solution

Answer C

### Exercise 5.5D

1. Standard electrode potentials for two half-cells are shown below. Which one of the following species is the most powerful reducing agent?

| Half-cell |  |  | $E^{\ominus}$ /V |
|---|---|---|---|
| $Ce^{3+}_{(aq)} + 3e^-$ | $\rightleftharpoons$ | $Ce_{(s)}$ | −2.3 |
| $Th^{4+}_{(aq)} + 4e^-$ | $\rightleftharpoons$ | $Th_{(s)}$ | −1.9 |

A   $Ce^{3+}_{(aq)}$    B   $Ce_{(s)}$    C   $Th^{4+}_{(aq)}$    D   $Th_{(s)}$

*(CCEA June 2015)*

2. Select (a) the most powerful reducing agent and (b) the most powerful oxidising agent from the following table.

|  |  |  | $E^{\ominus}$ /V |
|---|---|---|---|
| $Al^{3+}_{(aq)} + 3e^-$ | $\rightleftharpoons$ | $Al_{(s)}$ | −1.66 |
| $Zn^{2+}_{(aq)} + 2e^-$ | $\rightleftharpoons$ | $Zn_{(s)}$ | −0.76 |
| $Fe^{3+}_{(aq)} + e^-$ | $\rightleftharpoons$ | $Fe^{2+}_{(aq)}$ | +0.77 |

*(Adapted from CCEA June 2012)*

3. The iron(III) in iron ore can be reduced to iron(II) by treatment with zinc amalgam. (a) Write the equation for the reaction between the zinc in the amalgam and iron(III) ions. (b) Using zinc amalgam prevents the further reduction of iron(II) to iron. Use the electrode potentials to explain why, in contrast, zinc would further reduce iron(II) to iron.

| | $E^\ominus$ /V |
|---|---|
| $Zn^{2+}_{(aq)} + 2e^- \leftrightarrows Zn_{(s)}$ | −0.76 |
| $Fe^{2+}_{(aq)} + 2e^- \leftrightarrows Fe_{(s)}$ | −0.44 |
| $Fe^{3+}_{(aq)} + e^- \leftrightarrows Fe^{2+}_{(aq)}$ | +0.77 |

*(Adapted from CCEA May 2008)*

4. Use the following standard electrode potentials to determine which one of the statements is correct.

| | $E^\ominus$ /V |
|---|---|
| $Zn^{2+}_{(aq)} + 2e^- \leftrightarrows Zn_{(s)}$ | −0.76 |
| $Fe^{2+}_{(aq)} + 2e^- \leftrightarrows Fe_{(s)}$ | −0.44 |
| $I_{2(aq)} + 2e^- \leftrightarrows 2I^-_{(aq)}$ | +0.54 |
| $Fe^{3+}_{(aq)} + e^- \leftrightarrows Fe^{2+}_{(aq)}$ | +0.77 |

A  Zinc metal is the most powerful oxidising agent

B  Iron metal will displace iodide ions from solution

C  Iron(II) ions will reduce iodine to iodide ions

D  Iodide ions will reduce iron(III) ions to iron(II) ions but not to iron

*(CCEA May 2007)*

5. Use the following standard electrode potentials to determine which one of the statements is correct.

| | $E^\ominus$ /V |
|---|---|
| $Sn^{2+}_{(aq)} + 2e^- \leftrightarrows Sn_{(s)}$ | +0.15 |
| $I_{2(aq)} + 2e^- \leftrightarrows 2I^-_{(aq)}$ | +0.54 |
| $Ag^+_{(aq)} + e^- \leftrightarrows Ag_{(s)}$ | +0.80 |
| $Cl_{2(aq)} + 2e^- \leftrightarrows 2Cl^-_{(aq)}$ | +1.36 |

A  A mixture of chlorine water and silver will produce silver ions

B  Metallic tin is oxidised by aqueous chloride ions

C  Iodine and tin to not react

D  Silver will displace tin from a solution of tin(II) ions

*(CCEA June 2004)*

6. Which one of the following species is reduced by $Sn^{2+}_{(aq)}$?

A  $Br^-_{(aq)}$

B  $Fe^{2+}_{(aq)}$

C  $I_{2(s)}$

D  $Ni^{2+}_{(aq)}$

| | $E^\ominus$ /V |
|---|---|
| $Fe^{2+}_{(aq)} + 2e^- \leftrightarrows Fe_{(s)}$ | −0.44 |
| $Ni^{2+}_{(aq)} + 2e^- \leftrightarrows Ni_{(s)}$ | −0.25 |
| $Sn^{2+}_{(aq)} + 2e^- \leftrightarrows Sn_{(s)}$ | −0.14 |
| $Sn^{4+}_{(aq)} + 2e^- \leftrightarrows Sn^{2+}_{(aq)}$ | +0.15 |
| $I_{2(aq)} + 2e^- \leftrightarrows 2I^-_{(aq)}$ | +0.54 |
| $Br_{2(l)} + 2e^- \leftrightarrows 2Br^-_{(aq)}$ | +1.09 |

*(CCEA May 2009)*

7. Use the following half-equations to determine which one of the following species could oxidise water to oxygen?

A  $Br^-_{(aq)}$    B  $Br_{2(aq)}$    C  $SO_4^{2-}_{(aq)}$    D  $S_2O_8^{2-}_{(aq)}$

| | $E^\ominus$ /V |
|---|---|
| $Br_{2(l)} + 2e^- \leftrightarrows 2Br^-_{(aq)}$ | +1.07 |
| $O_{2(g)} + 4H^+_{(aq)} + 4e^- \leftrightarrows 2H_2O_{(l)}$ | +1.23 |
| $S_2O_8^{2-}_{(aq)} + 2e^- \leftrightarrows 2SO_4^{2-}_{(aq)}$ | +2.01 |

*(CCEA May 2008)*

---

Before moving to the next section, check that you are able to:

- Use electrode potentials to construct a reactivity series.
- Use a reactivity series to determine if a redox reaction is feasible.

---

**Determining if a Redox Reaction is Feasible**

The sign of the emf produced by a redox reaction can be used to determine if the reaction is feasible. For example, the displacement of zinc(II) ions from solution by magnesium *is feasible ($\Delta G < 0$) as the reaction generates a positive emf.*

$$Mg_{(s)} + Zn^{2+}_{(aq)} \rightarrow Mg^{2+}_{(aq)} + Zn_{(s)}$$

*Potential generated by reduction:*
$$Zn^{2+} + 2e^- \rightarrow Zn$$
$$E_{red} = -0.76 \text{ V}$$

*Potential generated by oxidation:*

$Mg \rightarrow Mg^{2+} + 2e^-$

$E_{ox} = +2.37$ V

*The emf produced by the reaction:*

emf = $E_{red} + E_{ox} = (-0.76) + (+2.37) = +1.61$ V

In contrast, the displacement of magnesium ions by zinc *does not occur (ΔG > 0) as the reaction generates a negative emf.*

$Zn_{(s)} + Mg^{2+}_{(aq)} \rightarrow$ No reaction

*Potential generated by reduction:*

$Mg^{2+} + 2e^- \rightarrow Mg$

$E_{red} = -2.37$ V

*Potential generated by oxidation:*

$Zn \rightarrow Zn^{2+} + 2e^-$

$E_{ox} = +0.76$ V

*The emf produced by the reaction:*

emf = $E_{red} + E_{ox} = (-2.37) + (+0.76) = -1.61$ V

## Exercise 5.5E

1. Calculate the emf for the cell based on the following half equations.

| | E° / V |
|---|---|
| $Mn^{2+}_{(aq)} + 2e^- \leftrightarrows Mn_{(s)}$ | −1.18 |
| $Ag^+_{(aq)} + e^- \leftrightarrows Ag_{(s)}$ | +0.80 |

*(Adapted from CCEA January 2008)*

2. Pain is often felt when a piece of aluminium foil touches an amalgam filling in a tooth because an electric current briefly flows. The amalgam contains tin.

| | E° / V |
|---|---|
| $Al^{3+} + 3e^- \leftrightarrows Al$ | −1.66 |
| $Sn^{2+} + 2e^- \leftrightarrows Sn$ | −0.13 |

Which one of the following statements is correct?

A Aluminium ions are produced from the foil

B The aluminium foil acts as the positive electrode

C The emf of the cell is +1.79 V

D Tin ions are discharged into the saliva in the mouth

*(CCEA January 2009)*

3. Under standard conditions, the emf of the cell shown below is +0.32 V. Calculate the standard electrode potential for the iron half-cell.

| | E° / V |
|---|---|
| $Zn^{2+}_{(aq)} + 2e^- \leftrightarrows Zn_{(s)}$ | −0.76 |

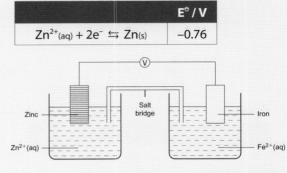

*(CCEA May 2012)*

4. Use the standard electrode potentials given in the table to determine which one of the following reactions will **not** occur.

| | | | E° /V |
|---|---|---|---|
| $Al^{3+}_{(aq)} + 3e^-$ | $\leftrightarrows$ | $Al_{(s)}$ | −1.66 |
| $Fe^{2+}_{(aq)} + 2e^-$ | $\leftrightarrows$ | $Fe_{(s)}$ | −0.44 |
| $Br_{2(l)} + 2e^-$ | $\leftrightarrows$ | $2Br^-_{(aq)}$ | +1.07 |
| $Ce^{4+}_{(aq)} + e^-$ | $\leftrightarrows$ | $Ce^{3+}_{(s)}$ | +1.45 |

A $2Ce^{4+}_{(aq)} + 2Br^-_{(aq)} \rightarrow 2Ce^{3+}_{(aq)} + Br_{2(aq)}$

B $2Al_{(s)} + 3Fe^{2+}_{(aq)} \rightarrow 3Fe_{(s)} + 2Al^{3+}_{(aq)}$

C $Fe_{(s)} + Br_{2(aq)} \rightarrow FeBr_{2(aq)}$

D $3Ce^{3+}_{(aq)} + Al^{3+}_{(aq)} \rightarrow 3Ce^{4+}_{(aq)} + Al_{(s)}$

*(CCEA January 2004)*

5. Use the standard electrode potentials given in the table to determine which one of the following reactions will **not** occur.

| | | | E° /V |
|---|---|---|---|
| $Cr^{3+}_{(aq)} + 3e^-$ | $\leftrightarrows$ | $Cr_{(s)}$ | −0.74 |
| $S_{(s)} + 2H^+_{(aq)} + 2e^-$ | $\leftrightarrows$ | $H_2S_{(aq)}$ | −0.14 |
| $Pb^{2+}_{(aq)} + 2e^-$ | $\leftrightarrows$ | $Pb_{(s)}$ | −0.13 |
| $I_{2(aq)} + 2e^-$ | $\leftrightarrows$ | $2I^-_{(aq)}$ | +0.54 |
| $2NO_3^-_{(aq)} + 4H^+_{(aq)} + 2e^- \leftrightarrows N_2O_{4(aq)} + 2H_2O_{(l)}$ | | | +0.80 |

A $2HNO_{3(aq)} + 2HI_{(aq)} \leftrightarrows I_{2(aq)} + N_2O_{4(aq)} + 2H_2O_{(l)}$

B $2HI_{(aq)} + S_{(s)} \leftrightarrows H_2S_{(aq)} + I_{2(aq)}$

C $2Cr_{(s)} + 3Pb(NO_3)_{2(aq)}$
$$\leftrightharpoons 3Pb_{(s)} + 2Cr(NO_3)_{3(aq)}$$

D $H_2S_{(aq)} + 2HNO_{3(aq)}$
$$\leftrightharpoons N_2O_{4(aq)} + 2H_2O_{(l)} + S_{(s)}$$

*(CCEA January 2006)*

---

**Before moving to the next section, check that you are able to:**

- Use electrode potentials to determine if a redox reaction is feasible.

---

# Green Technology

**In this section we are learning to:**

- Describe the cell reactions in a rechargeable Li-ion cell and an alkaline hydrogen-oxygen fuel cell.
- Explain why Li-ion cells and fuel-cells are considered environmentally friendly technologies and recall examples of their use.

---

### Rechargeable Cells

Modern lightweight batteries such as those used in cameras, laptop computers and mobile devices contain lithium-ion (Li-ion) cells. In a Li-ion cell lithium atoms stored between the layers of carbon in a graphite electrode loose an electron before moving through a non-aqueous electrolyte as $Li^+$ ions as illustrated in Figure 5. The electrolyte is made by dissolving a lithium salt such as $LiPF_6$ or $LiBF_4$ in an organic solvent. The $Li^+$ ions then become incorporated in a second electrode, which is the positive electrode, and is made from a lithium-containing transition metal compound such as $LiCoO_2$ or $LiMnO_2$. The formulas of these compounds are more accurately represented as $Li_{1-x}CoO_2$ and $Li_{1-x}MnO_2$ where x < 1 and increases as $Li^+$ ions move into the compound.

*Production of $Li^+$ ions at the graphite electrode:*
$Li_xC \rightarrow C + xLi^+ + xe^-$

*Incorporation of $Li^+$ ions at the positive electrode:*
$xLi^+ + xe^- + Li_{1-x}CoO_2 \rightarrow LiCoO_2$

Li-ion cells are **rechargeable** as the cell reaction is reversible and the cell can be recharged by operating the cell in reverse. Li-ion cells are particularly well-suited for use in mobile electronic devices as they are lightweight, can be manufactured in a variety of shapes, produce a large emf (around 3 V), and can be recharged hundreds of times, greatly reducing the amount of toxic waste sent for recycling or to landfill

For some applications the relatively high cost of Li-ion cells remains prohibitive and a market still exists for older technologies. For instance, rechargeable lead-acid cells are still widely used in car batteries and wheelchair batteries, in spite of the increased risk of damage to the environment resulting from the recycling and reuse of lead which is toxic in the environment.

---

### Exercise 5.5F

1. (a) Describe the movement of lithium ions in a Li-ion cell containing electrodes made from graphite and $LiMnO_2$. (b) Write a half-equation for the process that occurs at the $LiMnO_2$ electrode.

2. (a) Explain why batteries containing Li-ion cells are well-suited for use in mobile devices. (b) Explain, with the help of a half-equation, why the process that occurs at the graphite electrode is described as oxidation.

3. With reference to environmental issues, explain why wheelchair batteries containing rechargeable lead-acid cells are often used instead of much smaller and lighter batteries containing Li-ion cells.

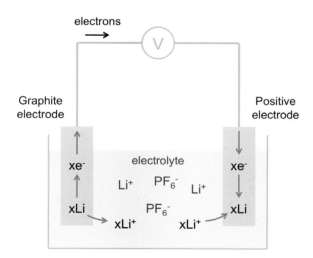

*Figure 5: The movement of ions in a Li-ion cell.*

Before moving to the next section, check that you are able to:

- Describe the movement of lithium ions in a Li-ion cell and write half-equations for the reactions occurring at the electrodes.
- With reference to environmental issues, account for the widespread use of batteries containing Li-ion cells.

## Fuel Cells

In a **fuel cell** the reaction of a fuel with oxygen is used to generate a voltage. The alkaline hydrogen-oxygen fuel cell in Figure 6 was used by NASA to power the electrical systems in spacecraft developed for the Apollo space program of the 1960s and the Space Shuttle program of the 1980s. The cell consists of porous carbon electrodes that allow gases to permeate the electrode and react on finely divided platinum dispersed over the interior and exterior surfaces of the electrode. Hydrogen gas fuels the cell reaction by reacting with hydroxide ions from the electrolyte to form water, the only product of the cell reaction.

*Oxidation at the hydrogen electrode:*
$2H_{2(g)} + 4OH^-_{(aq)} \rightarrow 4H_2O_{(l)} + 4e^-$

The hydroxide ions consumed at the hydrogen electrode are regenerated when oxygen reacts with water from the electrolyte to form hydroxide ions at the other electrode.

*Reduction at the oxygen electrode:*
$O_{2(g)} + 2H_2O_{(l)} + 4e^- \rightarrow 4OH^-_{(aq)}$

In most fuel cells 40–60% of the energy produced by the cell reaction is converted to electrical energy. The efficiency of the cell can be increased to around 85% if some of the heat generated by the cell reaction is also retained and used to generate electrical energy. In contrast only around one-third of the energy generated by the burning of coal in power stations can be harnessed and used to generate electricity. The burning of coal and other fossil fuels also produces very large amounts of carbon dioxide that contribute to global warming.

Fuel cells are also very reliable as there are no moving parts and as such can continue to operate indefinitely if properly maintained and supplied with fuel. Fuel cells can also operate using alternatives to fossil fuels such as methanol and natural gas (mostly methane) from renewable sources such as agricultural waste and landfill sites.

### Exercise 5.5G

1. The half-equations for the cell reaction in an alkaline hydrogen-oxygen fuel cell are given below. (a) Write an equation for the cell reaction. (b) Explain why generating electricity using a hydrogen-oxygen fuel cell poses less risk to the environment than the burning of fossil fuels.

   $2H_2 + 4OH^- \rightarrow 4H_2O + 4e^-$
   $O_2 + 2H_2O + 4e^- \rightarrow 4OH^-$

*Figure 6: An alkaline hydrogen-oxygen fuel cell.*

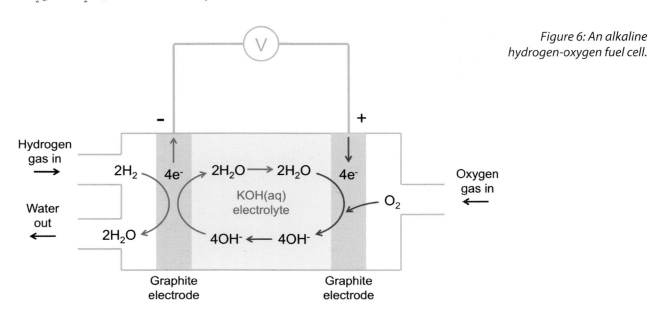

2. (a) Explain why finely divided platinum is present on the interior and exterior surfaces of the electrodes in an alkaline hydrogen-oxygen fuel cell. (b) State two reasons why the electrodes are made of carbon.

3. The half-equations for the cell reaction in an alkaline hydrogen-oxygen fuel cell are given below. (a) Identify species X in the half-equations. (b) Explain, in terms of its role in the fuel cell, why X is generated at one electrode and consumed at the other electrode.

$$2H_2 + 4X \rightarrow 4H_2O + 4e^-$$
$$O_2 + 2H_2O + 4e^- \rightarrow 4X$$

4. In a direct methanol fuel cell an aqueous solution containing 3.00% methanol by mass reacts with oxygen to form carbon dioxide and water. (a) Write an equation for the cell reaction. (b) The half-equations describing the electrode reactions in a direct methanol fuel cell are given below. Identify species A and B in the half-equations. (c) Calculate the molarity of the methanol solution (density = $1.06\,g\,cm^{-3}$).

$$CH_3OH + H_2O \rightarrow 6H^+ + 6e^- + A$$
$$B + 4H^+ + 4e^- \rightarrow 2H_2O$$

---

Before moving to the next section, check that you are able to:

- Recall what is meant by the term *fuel cell*.
- Describe, with the help of half-equations, the reactions that occur at the electrodes in an alkaline hydrogen-oxygen fuel cell.
- Explain why the use of fuel cells to generate electricity is less harmful to the environment than the burning of fossil fuels.

# 5.6 Transition Metals

## Properties

**In this section we are learning to:**

- Recall the characteristic properties of transition metals.
- Describe the composition of transition metal compounds.

The elements in the Groups from Sc-Cu are referred to as **transition metals** as they *have a partly filled d-subshell, or form at least one stable ion with a partly filled d-subshell.*

***Transition metals form brightly coloured compounds and solutions.*** The brightly coloured solutions in Figure 1 are formed by dissolving transition metal compounds in water to form solvated ions. The purple colour of potassium permanganate, $KMnO_4$ is due to the presence of permanganate ions, $MnO_4^-$ in the solid. The permanganate ions are also responsible for the purple colour of aqueous potassium permanganate. Similarly, the orange colour of solid and aqueous potassium dichromate, $K_2Cr_2O_7$ is due to the presence of dichromate ions, $Cr_2O_7^{2-}$.

### The d-block of The Periodic Table

| Sc $4s^23d^1$ | Ti $4s^23d^2$ | V $4s^23d^3$ | Cr $4s^13d^5$ | Mn $4s^23d^5$ | Fe $4s^23d^6$ | Co $4s^23d^7$ | Ni $4s^23d^8$ | Cu $4s^13d^{10}$ | Zn $4s^23d^{10}$ |
|---|---|---|---|---|---|---|---|---|---|
| Y | Zr | Nb | Mo | Tc | Ru | Rh | Pd | Ag | Cd |
| La | Hf | Ta | W | Re | Os | Ir | Pt | Au | Hg |

Transition metal       Non-transition metal

(a)　　　　　(b)　　　　　(c)

KMnO$_4$(aq) *purple*  KMnO$_4$(s)

K$_2$Cr$_2$O$_7$(aq) *orange*  K$_2$Cr$_2$O$_7$(s)

CuSO$_4$(aq) *blue*  CuSO$_4$(s)

*Figure 1: (a) The purple colour produced by permanganate, $MnO_4^-$ ions in solid and aqueous potassium permanganate, $KMnO_4$. (b) The orange colour produced by dichromate, $Cr_2O_7^{2-}$ ions in solid and aqueous potassium dichromate, $K_2Cr_2O_7$. (c) Anhydrous copper(II) sulfate, $CuSO_{4(s)}$ dissolves to form a blue solution, $CuSO_{4(aq)}$.*

*Dissolving potassium permanganate:*

$$KMnO_4(s) \rightarrow K^+(aq) + MnO_4^-(aq)$$

purple solid        purple solution

*Dissolving potassium dichromate:*

$$K_2Cr_2O_7(s) \rightarrow 2K^+(aq) + Cr_2O_7^{2-}(aq)$$

orange solid        orange solution

**Transition metals form complexes.** Anhydrous copper(II) sulfate, $CuSO_4$ is a white solid that dissolves in water to form a blue solution as shown in Figure 1. The blue colour of the solution is due to the formation of hexaaquacopper(II), $[Cu(H_2O)_6]^{2+}$ ions in which copper(II), $Cu^{2+}$ is bonded to six water molecules to form a complex with a charge of 2+. Complexes with a charge, such as the $[Cu(H_2O)_6]^{2+}$ ion, are referred to as **complex ions**.

*Dissolving anhydrous copper(II) sulfate:*

$$CuSO_4(s) \rightarrow Cu^{2+}(aq) + SO_4^{2-}(aq)$$

white solid     blue solution

*Or equivalently:*

$$CuSO_4(s) + 6H_2O(l) \rightarrow [Cu(H_2O)_6]^{2+}(aq) + SO_4^{2-}(aq)$$

white solid          blue solution

In salts such as hexaamminecobalt(III) chloride, $[Co(NH_3)_6]Cl_3$ square brackets are used to indicate that the metal is present in the form of a complex ion. The hexaamminecobalt(III), $[Co(NH_3)_6]^{3+}$ ions and chloride, $Cl^-$ ions in the solid are arranged to form an ionic lattice held together by attractive forces between oppositely charged ions. As in other ionic compounds the ions in the lattice are solvated when the solid dissolves.

*Dissolving hexaamminecobalt(III) chloride:*

$$[Co(NH_3)_6]Cl_3(s) \rightarrow [Co(NH_3)_6]^{3+}(aq) + 3Cl^-(aq)$$

**Transition metals can vary their oxidation state.** Transition metals and their compounds are frequently used as catalysts as the transition metal is able to change its oxidation state in the course of a reaction. For instance palladium, Pd can be used to catalyse the removal of CO from exhaust emissions as the metal can change its oxidation state when CO chemisorbs and reacts on the metal surface. The common oxidation states achieved by the transition

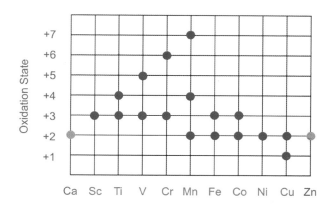

*Figure 2: Common oxidation states achieved by the transition metals Sc-Cu when forming compounds.*

metals Sc-Cu when forming compounds are summarised in Figure 2.

The transition metal compounds in Table 1 demonstrate that transition metals in low oxidation states form simple oxides, sulfides and halides such as chromium(III) oxide, $Cr_2O_3$ and manganese(II) chloride, $MnCl_2$, while transition metals in high oxidation states form molecular ions such as permanganate, $MnO_4^-$ and dichromate, $Cr_2O_7^{2-}$.

**Transition metals form at least one ion with a partly-filled d-subshell**. The oxidation states in Figure 2 demonstrate that the metals Ti-Cu can be considered transition metals as they each form at least one ion with a partly-filled d-subshell. For example, copper readily forms copper(II), $Cu^{2+}$ ions which have a partly-filled 3d-subshell ($3d^9$). In contrast, zinc is not considered a transition metal as it only forms $Zn^{2+}$ ions which have a full d-subshell ($3d^{10}$).

---

### Exercise 5.6A

1. Write the formulas of the ions present in an aqueous solution of the salt $[Co(NH_3)_5Br]SO_4$.

2. Prussian Blue, $KFe[Fe(CN)_6]$ may be prepared by adding potassium ferrocyanide solution, $K_4[Fe(CN)_6]$ to an aqueous iron salt. Identify the ions present in potassium ferrocyanide solution.

   *(CCEA May 2009)*

3. Write the formula for the chloride salt formed by the hexaaquachromium(III) ion, $[Cr(H_2O)_6]^{3+}$.

(a)

| Compound | Ions in Lattice | Oxidation States |
|---|---|---|
| chromium(III) oxide $Cr_2O_3$ | chromium(III), $Cr^{3+}$<br>oxide, $O^{2-}$ | Cr(+3)<br>O(−2) |
| iron(II) sulfide FeS | iron(II), $Fe^{2+}$<br>sulfide, $S^{2-}$ | Fe(+2)<br>S(−2) |
| manganese(II) chloride $MnCl_2$ | manganese(II), $Mn^{2+}$<br>chloride, $Cl^-$ | Mn(+2)<br>Cl(−1) |
| manganese(IV) oxide $MnO_2$ | manganese(IV), $Mn^{4+}$<br>oxide, $O^{2-}$ | Mn(+4)<br>O(−2) |

(b)

| Compound | Ions in Lattice | Oxidation States |
|---|---|---|
| potassium permanganate $KMnO_4$ | potassium, $K^+$<br>permanganate, $MnO_4^-$ | K(+1)<br>Mn(+7), O(−2) |
| sodium chromate $Na_2CrO_4$ | sodium, $Na^+$<br>chromate, $CrO_4^{2-}$ | Na(+1)<br>Cr(+6), O(−2) |
| sodium dichromate $Na_2Cr_2O_7$ | sodium, $Na^+$<br>dichromate, $Cr_2O_7^{2-}$ | Na(+1)<br>Cr(+6), O(−2) |

*Table 1: Transition metal compounds containing transition metals in (a) low oxidation states and (b) high oxidation states.*

4. Write the formula for the chloride salt formed by the pentaaquachlorochromium(III) ion, $[Cr(H_2O)_5Cl]^{2+}$.

5. The compound, $K_3Fe(C_2O_4)_3$ contains a metal in the form of a complex ion. (a) Write the formula for each type of ion present in the compound. (b) Re-write the formula of the compound in a way that more clearly shows the presence of complex ions in the compound.

6. Suggest why the salt $[Cr(NH_3)_6]Cl_3$ is orange while the salt $[Cr(NH_3)_5Cl]Cl_2$ is a dark red colour.

7. Explain, in terms of electronic structure, what is meant by the term *transition metal*.

*(CCEA June 2010)*

Before moving to the next section, check that you are able to:

- Recall that transition metals form coloured compounds and solutions.
- Identify molecular ions and complex ions in the formulas of transition metal compounds.
- Write the formula of a compound containing a complex ion.
- Explain why transition metals and their compounds are used as catalysts.
- Explain, in terms of electronic structure, why an element is a transition metal.

## Electronic Structure

**In this section we are learning to:**

- Deduce ground state electron configurations for transition metals and transition metal cations.

### Transition Metal Atoms

The ground state of a transition metal atom is determined by the Aufbau principle which states that the electron subshells within the atom fill in order of increasing energy. The subshell filling order across Period 4 (from K to Kr) is illustrated in Figure 3 and can be used to quickly determine that the ground state of a scandium (Sc) atom is [Ar] $4s^2 3d^1$ where the shorthand [Ar] represents the electron configuration of argon.

If the electron configurations for vanadium (V) and iron (Fe) are represented using 'electrons-in-boxes' notation, we are reminded that electrons occupy the orbitals in the 3d-subshell singly with spins aligned (↑,↑,...) before 'pairing-up' to form pairs of electrons with opposite spins (↑↓).

V atom     [Ar] $4s^2 3d^3$

4s $\boxed{↑↓}$   3d $\boxed{↑}\boxed{↑}\boxed{↑}\boxed{\phantom{↑}}\boxed{\phantom{↑}}$

Fe atom     [Ar] $4s^2 3d^6$

4s $\boxed{↑↓}$   3d $\boxed{↑↓}\boxed{↑}\boxed{↑}\boxed{↑}\boxed{↑}$

s block        d block        p block

*Figure 3: The subshell filling order across Period 4.*

Period 4    | K | Ca | Sc | Ti | V | Cr | Mn | Fe | Co | Ni | Cu | Zn | Ga | Ge |

4s subshell        3d subshell        4p subshell

**Subshell filling order** →

The ground state electron configurations for chromium (Cr) and copper (Cu) are exceptions, and demonstrate the additional stability associated with half-filled and completely filled subshells.

Cr atom    [Ar] $4s^1$ $3d^5$

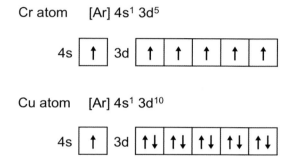

Cu atom    [Ar] $4s^1$ $3d^{10}$

### Exercise 5.6B

1. Use electrons-in-boxes notation to represent the ground state of (a) a manganese atom and (b) a cobalt atom.

2. State the electronic structure of a chromium atom and explain why the arrangement is stable.

*(CCEA May 2011)*

Before moving to the next section, check that you are able to:

- Use electrons-in-boxes notation to represent the electron configurations of transition metal atoms.
- Account for exceptions to the Aufbau principle.

### Transition Metal Ions

The ground state electron configurations for vanadium(II), $V^{2+}$ and vanadium(III), $V^{3+}$ ions demonstrate that when a transition metal atom becomes a cation, the energy of the 3d-subshell decreases to the extent that it fills before the 4s-subshell.

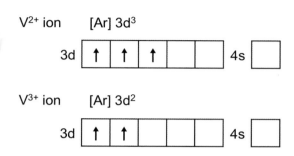

$V^{2+}$ ion    [Ar] $3d^3$

$V^{3+}$ ion    [Ar] $3d^2$

The electron configurations for iron(II), $Fe^{2+}$ and iron(III), $Fe^{3+}$ ions further remind us that electrons paired in the same orbital (↑↓) repel, and are therefore easier to remove than unpaired electrons within the same subshell.

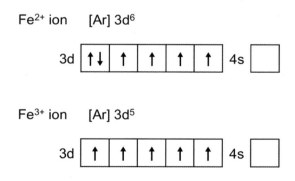

$Fe^{2+}$ ion    [Ar] $3d^6$

$Fe^{3+}$ ion    [Ar] $3d^5$

### Exercise 5.6C

1. Write the electronic structure for a $Ti^{2+}$ ion in its ground state.

     22

     $1s^2 2s^2 2p^6 3s^2 3p^6 3d^2 4s^2$

*(CCEA June 2006)*

2. (a) Represent the ground state of nickel using electrons-in-boxes notation. (b) Explain, in terms of electronic structures, why nickel is a transition metal.

3. In terms of electronic structures, explain why zinc is not a transition metal.

*(CCEA May 2012)*

4. Which one of the following is the electronic structure of a $Co^{2+}$ ion in its ground state?

| | | | | | | | | | |
|---|---|---|---|---|---|---|---|---|---|
| A | [Ar] | 3d | ↑↓ | ↑↓ | ↑ | ↑ | ↑ | 4s | |
| B | [Ar] | 3d | ↑↓ | ↑↓ | ↑↓ | ↑ | | 4s | |
| C | [Ar] | 3d | ↑ | ↑ | ↑ | ↑ | ↑ | 4s | ↑↓ |
| D | [Ar] | 3d | ↑↓ | ↑↓ | ↑ | | | 4s | ↑↓ |

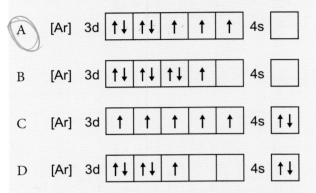

27

*(CCEA May 2009)*

4. Which one of the following gives the ground state electronic configuration for a copper atom and a copper(II) ion?

| | Copper atom | Copper(II) ion |
|---|---|---|
| A | $1s^2 2s^2 2p^6 3s^2 3p^6 3d^9 4s^2$ | $1s^2 2s^2 2p^6 3s^2 3p^6 3d^9$ |
| B | $1s^2 2s^2 2p^6 3s^2 3p^6 3d^9 4s^2$ | $1s^2 2s^2 2p^6 3s^2 3p^6 3d^7 4s^2$ |
| C | $1s^2 2s^2 2p^6 3s^2 3p^6 3d^{10} 4s^1$ | $1s^2 2s^2 2p^6 3s^2 3p^6 3d^8 4s^1$ |
| D | $1s^2 2s^2 2p^6 3s^2 3p^6 3d^{10} 4s^1$ | $1s^2 2s^2 2p^6 3s^2 3p^6 3d^9$ |

*(CCEA May 2012)*

5. Iron(II) ions are readily oxidised to iron(III). (a) Iron(II) ions can be oxidised by bubbling chlorine gas through an aqueous solution of the ions. Write an equation for the reaction. (b) Write the electron configuration for an iron(II) ion and an iron(III) ion. (c) Use the electron structures for iron(II) and iron(III) to explain the relative stabilities of the ions.

$2Fe^{2+} + Cl_2 \rightarrow 2Fe^{3+} + 2Cl^-$

*(Adapted from CCEA May 2007)*

**Before moving to the next section, check that you are able to:**

- Use electrons-in-boxes notation to represent the electron configurations of transition metal ions.
- Account for exceptions to the Aufbau principle.

# 5.7 Metal Complexes

## Bonding and Structure

**In this section we are learning to:**

- Describe the formation of complexes.
- Deduce and explain the shapes of complexes.

### Bonding in Complexes

A molecule of *cis*-platin is formed when two ammonia molecules, and two chloride ions, each form a co-ordinate bond with a platinum(II) ion, $Pt^{2+}$.

*cis*-platin
$Pt(NH_3)_2Cl_2$          Top View          Side View

Each ammonia molecule and chloride ion uses a lone pair to form a coordinate bond with platinum and is referred to as a **ligand** as it is *a molecule or ion that uses one or more lone pairs to form coordinate bonds with a metal atom or ion in a complex*. The resulting compound, cis-platin, is referred to as a **complex** as it consists of *a metal atom or ion with ligands attached by coordinate bonds*.

*Smaller ligands such as water ($H_2O$) and ammonia ($NH_3$) form complexes with up to six ligands bonded to a metal atom or ion. Larger ligands such as chloride ($Cl^-$) and bromide ($Br^-$) tend to form complexes with fewer than six ligands bonded to the metal.*

When anhydrous copper(II) sulfate, $CuSO_4$ dissolves in water, the surrounding water molecules bond with the copper(II) ions from the salt to form the hexaaquacopper(II), $[Cu(H_2O)_6]^{2+}$ complex. Formation of a complex is indicated by enclosing the formula of the complex in square brackets.

$$CuSO_4(s) + 6H_2O(l) \rightarrow [Cu(H_2O)_6]^{2+}(aq) + SO_4^{2-}(aq)$$
blue solution

The complex consists of six water molecules bonded to a copper(II) ion, and gives the resulting solution a blue colour as shown in Figure 1. On adding concentrated hydrochloric acid, chloride ions from the acid replace the water ligands to form the tetrachlorocopper(II), $[CuCl_4]^{2-}$ complex. The complex consists of four chloride ions bonded to a copper(II) ion, and gives the resulting solution a green colour as shown in Figure 1.

$$[Cu(H_2O)_6]^{2+}(aq) + 4Cl^-(aq) \rightleftharpoons [CuCl_4]^{2-}(aq) + 6H_2O(l)$$
blue solution                    green solution

Add concentrated hydrochloric acid

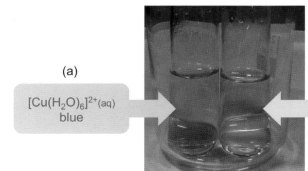

(a)

$[Cu(H_2O)_6]^{2+}(aq)$
blue

(b)

$[CuCl_4]^{2-}(aq)$
green

*Figure 1: (a) Forming aqueous $[Cu(H_2O)_6]^{2+}$ ions by dissolving copper(II) sulfate in water. (b) Forming $[CuCl_4]^{2-}$ ions by adding concentrated hydrochloric acid to aqueous copper(II) sulfate.*

## Exercise 5.7A

1. The $[Mn(H_2O)_6]^{2+}$ ion is formed when manganese(II) sulfate dissolves in water.
   (a) Explain the meaning of the term *complex*.
   (b) Explain why the $[Mn(H_2O)_6]^{2+}$ ion is considered a complex.

2. (a) Explain what is meant by the term *ligand*.
   (b) State the number of ligands in the complex $[NiCl_4]^{2-}$. (c) Explain how the complex is formed.

3. (a) State the number of ligands in the complex $[Cu(NH_3)_4(H_2O)_2]^{2+}$. (b) Explain how the complex is formed.

4. Suggest the formula for the complex formed when cobalt(II) chloride is dissolved in water. Explain your reasoning.

5. (a) Explain why ammonia can act as a ligand.
   (b) Suggest the formula for the complex formed when concentrated ammonia solution is added to a solution containing chromium(III) ions, $Cr^{3+}$. Explain your reasoning.

---

Before moving to the next section, check that you are able to:

- Explain what is meant by the terms *complex* and *ligand*.
- Recall the number of ligands in complexes formed by water, ammonia, chloride and bromide.
- Write formulas for complexes formed with water, ammonia, chloride and bromide ligands.

---

## Shapes of Complexes

Ligands such as water ($H_2O$), ammonia ($NH_3$), and chloride ($Cl^-$) ion each use one lone pair to form a co-ordinate bond with the metal in a complex. According to VSEPR theory the electrons in neighbouring metal-ligand bonds repel and move as far from each other as possible to minimise the repulsion. In this way VSEPR theory can be used to account for the shapes of complexes such as those in Figure 2. In the case of diamminesilver(I), $[Ag(NH_3)_2]^+$ VSEPR theory asserts that the electrons in the Ag-N bonds repel to give a linear arrangement of Ag-N bonds about the metal. Similarly, in

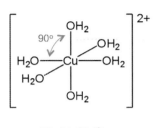

$[Ag(NH_3)_2]^+$
A linear complex

$[CuCl_4]^{2-}$
A tetrahedral complex

$[Cu(H_2O)_6]^{2+}$
An octahedral complex

*Figure 2: Linear, tetrahedral and octahedral shapes resulting from repulsion between the electrons in neighbouring metal-ligand bonds.*

tetrachlorocopper(II), $[CuCl_4]^{2-}$ the electrons in the Cu-Cl bonds repel to give a tetrahedral arrangement of Cu-Cl bonds about the metal, and in hexaaquacopper(II), $[Cu(H_2O)_6]^{2+}$ the electrons in the Cu-O bonds repel to give an octahedral arrangement of Cu-O bonds about the metal.

Thus, according to VSEPR theory, the tetrachloropalladium(II) anion, $[PdCl_4]^{2-}$ would adopt a tetrahedral shape to minimise repulsion between the electrons in the four Pd-Cl bonds. In reality the tetrachloropalladium(II) anion, $[PdCl_4]^{2-}$ is square planar, and reflects the tendency for platinum-group metals (Ni, Pd, and Pt) to form square planar complexes.

Square planar complexes formed by platinum-group metals

## Exercise 5.7B

1. Vanadium(III) sulfate dissolves in water to form a green solution. (a) State the formula of vanadium(III) sulfate. (b) Suggest the formula of hydrated vanadium(III) ions in aqueous solution and state the shape of this complex.

    *(CCEA May 2009)*

2. The salt $K_2PtCl_6$ contains a complex ion. (a) Write the formula for the complex ion. (b) Suggest a shape for the complex ion and explain your reasoning.

3. (a) Write the formulas for the ions in the salt $[(C_4H_9)_4N][FeBr_4]$. (b) Suggest the shape of the iron complex and explain your reasoning.

4. A dark blue solution containing the complex $[Cu(NH_3)_4(H_2O)_2]^{2+}$ is formed when concentrated ammonia solution is added to aqueous copper(II) nitrate. Suggest a shape for the complex and explain your reasoning.

5. Which one of the following complexes is tetrahedral?

    A $MnO_4^-$  B $[PtCl_4]^{2-}$
    C $[Cu(NH_3)_4(H_2O)_2]^{2+}$  D $[CoCl_4]^{2-}$

6. The following complex is formed when dimethylglyoxime is added to a solution of hydrated nickel(II) ions. (a) Suggest the shape of the complex around the nickel(II) ion. (b) What type of bond is represented by (i) a solid line, (ii) a dashed line, and (iii) an arrow.

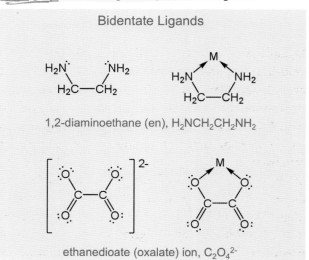

*(Adapted from CCEA June 2010)*

Before moving to the next section, check that you are able to:

- Use VSEPR theory to explain why complexes with two, four and six metal-ligand bonds have linear, tetrahedral and octahedral shapes respectively.
- Recall that the platinum-group metals form square planar complexes in preference to tetrahedral complexes.

## Ligands

**In this section we are learning to:**

- Use the terms monodentate, bidentate and polydentate to classify ligands.
- Determine the number of metal-ligand bonds in a complex.

### Types of Ligand

A **monodentate ligand** is *a molecule or ion that uses a lone pair of electrons to form a coordinate bond with a metal atom or ion in a complex*.

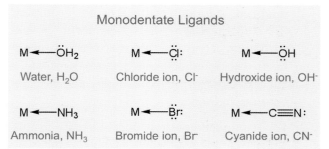

A **bidentate ligand** is *a molecule or ion that uses two lone pairs of electrons to form two coordinate bonds with a metal atom or ion in a complex*. The compound 1,2-diaminoethane, $H_2NCH_2CH_2NH_2$ and oxalate ion, $C_2O_4^{2-}$ are examples of bidentate ligands.

In a molecule of en each nitrogen atom uses its lone pair to form a co-ordinate bond with a metal atom or ion (N→M). The distance between the nitrogen atoms in en makes it possible for one molecule of en to replace two neighbouring monodentate ligands such as $H_2O$ or $NH_3$ in an octahedral complex. For example, the complex $[Ni(en)_3]^{2+}$ is formed when en is added to an aqueous solution of a nickel(II) salt containing $[Ni(H_2O)_6]^{2+}$ ions.

Similarly, the distance between the oxygen atoms makes it possible for oxalate ion, $C_2O_4^{2-}$ to replace two neighbouring monodentate ligands in a complex. For example, the complex $[Fe(C_2O_4)_3]^{3-}$ is formed when an aqueous solution containing oxalate ions is added to an aqueous solution of an iron(III) salt.

## Exercise 5.7C

1. The salt $K_3Fe(CN)_6$ contains a complex ion. (a) Write the formula for the complex ion. (b) Suggest a shape for the complex ion and explain your reasoning.

2. A green solution containing the complex $[Cr(H_2O)_2(OH)_4]^-$ is formed when chromium(III) hydroxide, $Cr(OH)_3$ dissolves in an excess of aqueous sodium hydroxide. Suggest a shape for the complex and explain your reasoning.

3. 1,2-diaminoethane (en) is a bidentate ligand which complexes with nickel(II) ions in aqueous solution. (a) Explain the term *bidentate*. (b) Draw the structure of en. (c) Write the formula for the complex formed.

   *(CCEA June 2006)*

4. Aqueous iron(III) ions form a stable complex with the bidentate ligand ethanedioate, $C_2O_4^{2-}$. The iron(III) ions each combine with three ethanedioate ions. Deduce the formula of the complex formed.

   *(CCEA May 2011)*

5. The complex $[Ru(bpy)_3]^{2+}$ is formed when a solution containing 2,2'-bipyridine (bpy) is added to a solution containing ruthenium(III) chloride and a reducing agent.

   2,2'-bipyridine

(a) Explain why 2,2'-bipyridine is a bidentate ligand. (b) Suggest a shape for the complex and explain your reasoning. (c) Write the formula for the hexahydrate salt formed when the volume of solution is reduced and crystals are allowed to form.

A **hexadentate ligand** is *a molecule or ion that uses six lone pairs of electrons to form six coordinate bonds with a metal atom or ion in a complex*. The ethylenediamminetetraacetate ion, $[(OOCCH_2)_2 NCH_2CH_2N(CH_2COO)_2]^{4-}$ is a hexadentate ligand, and is represented by the shorthand $(edta)^{4-}$ when writing formulas and equations.

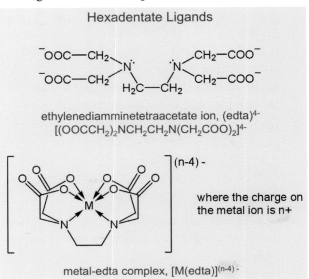

Hexadentate Ligands

ethylenediamminetetraacetate ion, $(edta)^{4-}$
$[(OOCCH_2)_2NCH_2CH_2N(CH_2COO)_2]^{4-}$

$(n-4)-$

where the charge on the metal ion is $n+$

metal-edta complex, $[M(edta)]^{(n-4)-}$

The $(edta)^{4-}$ ion can use the lone pair on each nitrogen atom, and one lone pair from each carboxylate ($COO^-$) group, to form six co-ordinate bonds with a metal. The distance between the lone pairs is sufficient to allow one $(edta)^{4-}$ ion to replace up to six monodentate ligands such as $H_2O$ or $NH_3$ in an octahedral complex. The complex $[Ni(edta)]^{2-}$ is typical of the octahedral complexes formed by $(edta)^{4-}$ in aqueous solution and is formed when an $(edta)^{4-}$ ion bonds with nickel(II), $Ni^{2+}$.

The $(edta)^{4-}$ ligand is also an example of a **polydentate ligand** as it is *a molecule or ion that uses many lone pairs to form more than two coordinate bonds with a metal atom or ion in a complex*. Bidentate and polydentate ligands are also referred to as chelating ligands as they 'grip' a metal atom or ion like a claw to form a 'shell-like' complex known as a **chelate** with the metal at the centre.

## Exercise 5.7D

1. In the Merckoquant test, the amount of iron(II) present in a solution is detected by the addition of 2,2'-bipyridine, which forms a dark red complex with iron(II). Explain why 2,2'-bipyridine is **not** a polydentate ligand.

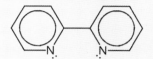

2,2'-bipyridine

*(CCEA June 2004)*

2. Cadaverine, $NH_2(CH_2)_5NH_2$ has chelating properties whereas hydrazine, $NH_2NH_2$ is a monodentate ligand. Suggest why cadaverine is able to chelate metal ions while hydrazine is not.

*(CCEA June 2005)*

3. Ranelic acid and edta are polydentate ligands. (a) Explain what is meant by the term *ligand*. (b) Explain what is meant by the term *polydentate*. (c) Draw a diagram to show the outer electron structure of the nitrile group and use it to suggest why it can or cannot act as a ligand.

NC      CH₂COOH    ranelic
                   acid
HOOCH₂C
       N
HOOCH₂C    S      COOH

*(CCEA June 2014)*

4. Which one of the following nickel complexes contains a chelating ligand?

A  $[Ni(H_2O)_6]^{2+}$      B  $[Ni(NH_3)_6]^{2+}$

C  $[Ni(CN)_4]^{2-}$      D  $[Ni(en)_3]^{2+}$

*(CCEA June 2005)*

Before moving to the next section, check that you are able to:

- Explain what is meant by the terms *monodentate*, *bidentate* and *polydentate* when describing ligands.

- Recognise monodentate, bidentate, and polydentate ligands in complexes.

- Use the terms *chelating ligand* and *chelate* when referring to complexes containing bidentate and polydentate ligands.

### Coordination Number

The **coordination number** *of a metal in a complex is the total number of coordinate bonds formed when the ligands bond with the metal to form the complex.*

In complexes containing only monodentate ligands, the coordination number of the metal in the complex is equal to the number of ligands in the complex. For example, in diamminesilver(I), $[Ag(NH_3)_2]^+$ silver has a coordination number of two as each ammonia molecule forms a co-ordinate bond with the metal. Similarly, in tetrachlorocopper(II), $[CuCl_4]^{2-}$ copper has a coordination number of four as each of the four chloride ligands forms a co-ordinate bond with the metal. And in hexaaquacopper(II), $[Cu(H_2O)_6]^{2+}$ copper has a coordination number of six as each of the six water molecules forms a co-ordinate bond with the metal.

In complexes containing bidentate ligands such as en and oxalate ion, each bidentate ligand increases the coordination number of the metal by two as it forms two co-ordinate bonds with the metal. As a result, the coordination number of nickel in the complex $[Ni(en)_3]^{2+}$ is six as each of the three en ligands increases the coordination number of nickel by two. The coordination number of nickel is also six in the complex $[Ni(edta)]^{2-}$ as the $(edta)^{4-}$ ligand forms six co-ordinate bonds with nickel.

## Exercise 5.7E

1. The complex $[CoCl_4]^{2-}$ is formed when concentrated hydrochloric acid is added to an aqueous solution of cobalt(II) nitrate. State the coordination number of cobalt in the complex and explain your reasoning.

2. The complex $[Cu(NH_3)_4(H_2O)_2]^{2+}$ is formed when concentrated ammonia solution is added to an aqueous solution of copper(II) sulfate. State the coordination number of copper in the complex and explain your reasoning.

3. The platinum salt $(NH_4)_2PtCl_6$ was found to inhibit cell division in several different types of bacteria. (a) Write the formula of the platinum complex in the salt. (b) State the coordination number of platinum in the complex and explain your reasoning.

4. (a) Write the formula for the square planar complex formed when a solution containing oxalate ion is added to aqueous nickel(II) sulfate. (b) State the coordination number of nickel in the complex. (c) State other possible shapes for the complex and explain why the complex is more stable in a square planar arrangement.

---

Before moving to the next section, check that you are able to:

- Explain what is meant by the term *coordination number*.
- Deduce the coordination number of the metal in a complex.

## Geometric Isomerism

**In this section we are learning to:**

- Identify complexes that give rise to geometric isomers.
- Explain the origin of geometric isomerism in complexes and draw the geometric isomers of complexes.

---

Octahedral complexes such as $[Co(NH_3)_4Cl_2]^+$ and $Co(en)_2Cl_2$ give rise to geometric isomers with the same formula but a different arrangement of ligands about the metal. In the complex $[Co(NH_3)_4Cl_2]^+$ the positioning of the chloride ions about the metal gives rise to cis and trans isomers.

Geometric isomers of $[Co(NH_3)_4Cl_2]^+$

$cis$-$[Co(NH_3)_4Cl_2]^+$     $trans$-$[Co(NH_3)_4Cl_2]^+$

---

The isomers can also be distinguished using E-Z notation. The chlorine atom in a chloride ligand has a higher priority than the nitrogen atom in an ammonia ligand. As a result the cis-isomer *becomes the Z-isomer as the high priority (chloride) ligands are on the same side of the complex*, and the trans-isomer becomes the *E-isomer as the high priority ligands are on opposite sides of the complex*.

The positioning of the chloride ions in the complex $Co(en)_2Cl_2$ also gives rise to cis and trans isomers. The cis-isomer gives rise to optical isomers as the bidentate (en) ligands can be arranged to form isomers that are non-superimposable mirror images. In this way the metal at the centre of the cis-isomer becomes an asymmetric centre.

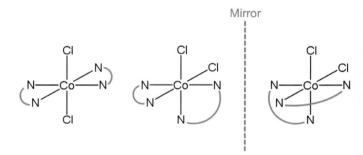

1,2-diaminoethane (en)

$trans$-$[Co(en)_2Cl_2]$     Optical isomers of $cis$-$[Co(en)_2Cl_2]$
(non-superimposable mirror images)

---

## Worked Example 5.7i

Which one of the following is a correct statement about the stereochemistry of the complex $[Pt(NH_3)_2Cl_2]$?

A  It is square planar and has cis-trans isomers

B  It is square planar and has two optical isomers

C  It is tetrahedral and has cis-trans isomers

D  It is tetrahedral and has two optical isomers

*(CCEA June 2012)*

### Strategy

- The complex is square planar as the metal is a platinum-group metal.
- The complex does not exist as optical isomers as it contains only monodentate ligands.

### Solution

Answer A

..........................................................................

### Exercise 5.7F

1. The isomers of the complex ion $[Cr(NH_3)_4Cl_2]^+$ are shown below. (a) Classify each isomer as *cis* or *trans* and explain your reasoning. (b) Classify the isomers as *E* or *Z* and explain your reasoning.

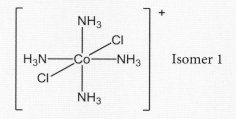

Isomer 1

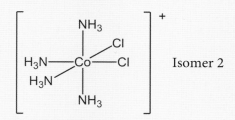

Isomer 2

*(Adapted from CCEA June 2015)*

2. The compound *trans*-$[Co(en)_2Cl_2]Cl$ is a green solid. When a solution of the salt is heated the colour of the solution changes from green to violet as the trans-isomer is converted to the cis-isomer. (a) Draw the structures of the cis and trans isomers. (b) Explain why the complex exists as cis-trans isomers. (c) Classify the isomers as *E* or *Z* and explain your reasoning.

3. Nickel(II) forms the complex $[Ni(en)_3]^{2+}$ when en is added to an aqueous solution of nickel(II) sulfate. (a) Draw the structure of the complex. (b) Explain why the complex can exist as optical isomers.

4. Oxalate ion acts as a bidentate ligand and forms the compound $K_3Fe(C_2O_4)_3$ when it combines with iron(III) ions. The compound contains the trisoxalato anion whose structure is based on an octahedron. (a) Suggest a 3D structure for the trisoxalato anion. (b) Explain why the trisoxalato anion is optically active.

*(Adapted from CCEA June 2013)*

5. The complex $Cr(acac)_3$ is formed when a solution containing acetylacetonate (acac) ions is added to a solution of chromium(III) chloride. (a) State the coordination number of chromium in the complex. (b) Draw the isomers of the complex. (c) Explain the origin of the isomers. (d) Suggest why the complex is soluble in organic solvents.

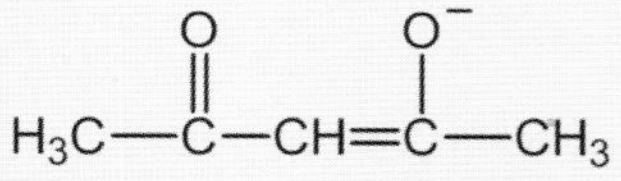

$$H_3C-\overset{\overset{\displaystyle O}{\|}}{C}-CH=\overset{\overset{\displaystyle O^-}{|}}{C}-CH_3$$

acetylacetonate (acac) ion

---

Before moving to the next section, check that you are able to:

- Identify complexes that form cis-trans (E/Z) isomers.
- Draw the cis-trans (E/Z) isomers of a complex.
- Use E/Z notation to name the cis-trans isomers of a complex.
- Draw the optical isomers of a complex and identify the asymmetric centre.
- Explain the origin of optical activity in complexes.

---

## Oxidation State

**In this section we are learning to:**

- Deduce the oxidation state of the metal in a complex.

---

The oxidation state of the metal in a complex is included when naming the complex and can be deduced from the formula of the complex. For example, the designation cobalt(III) is used to indicate that the hexaamminecobalt(III), $[Co(NH_3)_6]^{3+}$ ions in hexaamminecobalt(III) chloride, $[Co(NH_3)_6]Cl_3$ contain cobalt in an oxidation state of +3 ($Cr^{3+}$). In practice the oxidation state of the metal is deduced by remembering that the charges on the metal and ligands add to give the charge on the complex.

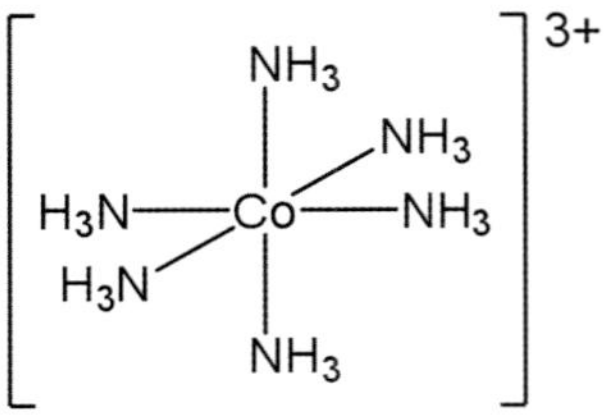

Charge on complex (3+) = Charge on metal (3+) + Charge on ligands (6 x 0 = 0)

**Worked Example 5.7ii**

Deduce the oxidation state and coordination number of cobalt in the complex ion $[Co(NH_3)_4Cl_2]^+$.

**Solution**

Charge on ligands $= (4 \times 0) + (2 \times 1-) = 2-$

Charge on cobalt
= Charge on complex – Charge on ligands
= 3+

Oxidation state of cobalt = +3

All six ligands are monodentate.

Coordination number of cobalt $= 6 \times 1 = 6$

**Exercise 5.7G**

1. State the charge and coordination number of nickel in (a) the complex $[Ni(H_2O)_6]^{2+}$ and (b) the complex $[Ni(edta)]^{2-}$.

2. Potassium cyanide is used to extract gold from its ore by forming the complex anion $[Au(CN)_2]^-$. (a) State the type of bond formed between the gold ions and cyanide ions. (b) State the coordination number of gold in the complex. (c) Deduce the oxidation number of gold in the complex. (d) Suggest the shape of the complex.

$4Au_{(s)} + 8CN^-_{(aq)} + 2H_2O_{(l)} + O_{2(g)}$
$\rightarrow 4[Au(CN)_2]^-_{(aq)} + 4OH^-_{(aq)}$

*(Adapted from CCEA May 2007)*

3. Which one of the following contains a metal in the +2 state?

A $[Ag(NH_3)_2]^+$   B $[Co(NH_3)_5Br]^{2+}$
C $K_4[Fe(CN)_6]$   D $K_2Cr_2O_7$

*(Adapted from CCEA May 2011)*

4. Which one of the following complexes contains a transition metal with an oxidation state of +2?

A $[Co(NH_3)_4Cl_2]Cl$   B $[Cu(CN)_4]^{3-}$
C $K_3[Fe(CN)_6]$   D $[Ni(en)_3]Cl_2$

*(CCEA May 2007)*

5. Which one of the following complexes contains a transition metal with an oxidation state of +2?

A $[Cr(H_2O)_5OH]^{2+}$   B $[CuCl_4]^{2-}$
C $[Fe(SCN)(H_2O)_5]^{2+}$   D $[TiCl_6]^{2-}$

*(CCEA June 2006)*

**Before moving to the next section, check that you are able to:**

- Use the formula of a complex to deduce the oxidation state of the metal in the complex.

## Ligand Replacement

**In this section we are learning to:**

- Explain how ligand replacement results from ligand substitution.
- Account for the relative stability of complexes by considering the changes in entropy and free energy that accompany ligand replacement.

*Figure 3: (a) Forming a precipitate of copper(II) hydroxide, $Cu(OH)_2$ by adding dilute ammonia solution to aqueous copper(II) sulfate. (b) The precipitate dissolves to form a dark blue solution on adding dilute ammonia solution to excess.*

### Ligand Substitution

A solution of copper(II) sulfate contains hexaaquacopper(II) ions, $[Cu(H_2O)_6]^{2+}$ that give the solution a blue colour. On adding ammonia solution a blue precipitate of copper(II) hydroxide, $Cu(OH)_2$ forms. On adding ammonia solution to excess the precipitate dissolves to form a dark blue solution containing the complex $[Cu(NH_3)_4(H_2O)_2]^{2+}$ as shown in Figure 3. The complex is formed by a series of **ligand substitution** reactions in which water ligands are replaced by ammonia molecules (Equations 1–4).

$$[Cu(H_2O)_6]^{2+}{}_{(aq)} + NH_{3(aq)}$$
$$\leftrightarrows [Cu(NH_3)(H_2O)_5]^{2+}{}_{(aq)} + H_2O_{(l)} \quad [1]$$

$$[Cu(NH_3)(H_2O)_5]^{2+}{}_{(aq)} + NH_{3(aq)}$$
$$\leftrightarrows [Cu(NH_3)_2(H_2O)_4]^{2+}{}_{(aq)} + H_2O_{(l)} \quad [2]$$

$$[Cu(NH_3)_2(H_2O)_4]^{2+}{}_{(aq)} + NH_{3(aq)}$$
$$\leftrightarrows [Cu(NH_3)_3(H_2O)_3]^{2+}{}_{(aq)} + H_2O_{(l)} \quad [3]$$

$$[Cu(NH_3)_3(H_2O)_3]^{2+}{}_{(aq)} + NH_{3(aq)}$$
$$\leftrightarrows [Cu(NH_3)_4(H_2O)_2]^{2+}{}_{(aq)} + H_2O_{(l)} \quad [4]$$

The equilibria 1-4 lie to the right as copper bonds more strongly with ammonia, making the complex formed with ammonia more stable. The combined effect of the ligand substitution reactions 1–4 is a **ligand replacement** reaction (Equation 5) in which four water ligands are replaced by four ammonia molecules.

$$[Cu(H_2O)_6]^{2+}{}_{(aq)} + 4NH_{3(aq)}$$
$$\leftrightarrows [Cu(NH_3)_4(H_2O)_2]^{2+}{}_{(aq)} + 4H_2O_{(l)} \quad [5]$$

### Exercise 5.7H

1. A blood-red solution containing the complex $[Fe(SCN)(H_2O)_5]^{2+}$ is formed on adding a few drops of aqueous potassium thiocyanate, $KSCN_{(aq)}$ to an aqueous solution of an iron(III) salt containing the hexaaquairon(III) ion, $[Fe(H_2O)_6]^{3+}$. (a) Write an equation for the reaction that occurs on adding aqueous potassium thiocyanate. (b) Use the nature of the complex formed with iron(III) to explain why thiocyanate ion, $SCN^-$ is a monodentate ligand.

2. A blue solution containing the tetrachlorocobalt(II) ion, $[CoCl_4]^{2-}$ is formed on adding concentrated hydrochloric acid to an aqueous solution containing the hexaaquacobalt(II) ion, $[Co(H_2O)_6]^{2+}$. (a) Write an equation to describe the reaction that occurs on adding concentrated hydrochloric acid. (b) Account for the number of ligands in each complex. (c) State and explain the shape of the tetrachlorocobalt(II) ion.

### Enthalpy Effects

The enthalpy change ($\Delta H$) for the replacement of two water ligands by two ammonia molecules (Equation 6) is very similar to the enthalpy change for the replacement of two water molecules by a molecule of en (Equation 7) as both reactions involve breaking two Cu-O bonds and forming two Cu-N bonds.

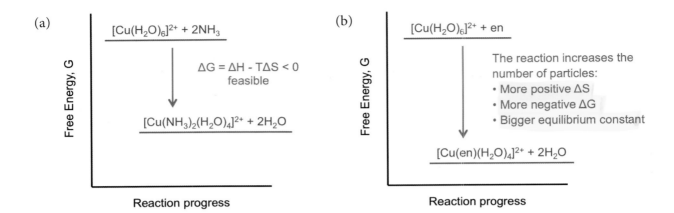

*Figure 4: The change in free energy, ΔG for (a) the replacement of water by ammonia, and (b) the replacement of water by en.*

$[Cu(H_2O)_6]^{2+}_{(aq)} + 2NH_{3(aq)}$
$\leftrightharpoons [Cu(NH_3)_2(H_2O)_4]^{2+}_{(aq)} + 2H_2O_{(l)}$ [6]

$[Cu(H_2O)_6]^{2+}_{(aq)} + en_{(aq)}$
$\leftrightharpoons [Cu(en)(H_2O)_4]^{2+}_{(aq)} + 2H_2O_{(l)}$ [7]

Both reactions are feasible (ΔG < 0), and occur when the reactants are mixed. The entropy change, ΔS for the replacement of water by en (Equation 7) is more positive as the reaction increases the number of particles in the reaction mixture. As a result, the change in free energy for the reaction, ΔG = ΔH – TΔS is more negative, and the position of equilibrium lies further to the right.

### Worked Example 5.7iii

Which one of the following complexes is most likely to be formed in high yield when a ligand replacement reaction is carried out in an aqueous solution containing nickel(II) ions?

A $[Ni(H_2O)_6]^{2+}$     B $[Ni(NH_3)_6]^{2+}$
C $[Ni(en)_3]^{2+}$     D $[Ni(edta)]^{2-}$
*(Adapted from CCEA May 2009)*

### Strategy

- The ligand that produces the biggest increase in the number of particles when it replaces water will produce the complex that is most likely to be formed in high yield.

### Solution

Answer D

### Exercise 5.7I

1. State and explain the change in coordination number, and the sign of ΔS°, for the ligand substitution reaction shown below.

$[Ni(H_2O)_6]^{2+} + 3 \text{ en} \rightarrow [Ni(en)_3]^{2+} + 6 H_2O$
*(Adapted from CCEA May 2012)*

2. Hexaaquanickel(II) ions react with 1,2-diaminoethane (en) in solution. (a) Write the equation for this reaction in which all the water ligands are replaced. (b) Explain why this ligand replacement takes place.
*(CCEA May 2011)*

3. Hydrated chromium(III) ions, $[Cr(H_2O)_6]^{3+}$ readily react with edta$^{4-}$ ions in a ligand replacement reaction. (a) What term is given to ligands such as edta? (b) Write an equation for the reaction taking place between hydrated chromium(III) ions and edta$^{4-}$ ions. (c) Explain, in terms of entropy, why the reaction takes place.
*(CCEA June 2015)*

4. An orange solution containing the tetracyanonickel(II) ion, $[Ni(CN)_4]^{2-}$ is formed on adding aqueous sodium cyanide to an aqueous solution containing hexaaquanickel(II), $[Ni(H_2O)_6]^{2+}$ ions. (a) Write an equation to describe the reaction that occurs on adding aqueous sodium

cyanide. (b) Explain in terms of entropy why the reaction occurs. (c) Suggest the shape of the complex $[Ni(CN)_4]^{2-}$. Explain your reasoning.

5. The following complex is formed when dimethylglyoxime is added to a solution of hydrated nickel(II) ions. Explain in terms of entropy why dimethylglyoxime displaces the water ligands in a hydrated nickel(II) ion to form the nickel(II) dimethylglyoxime complex.

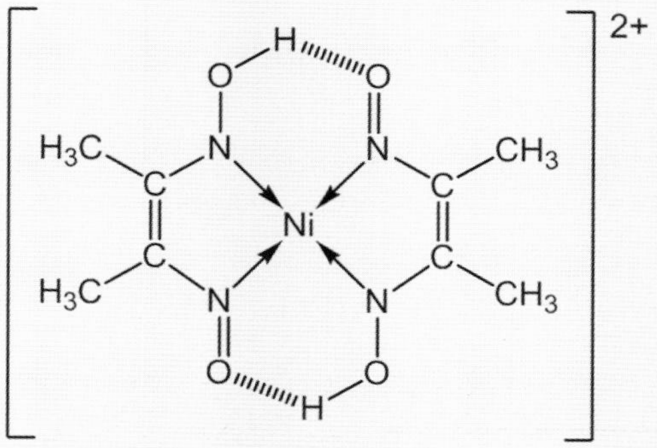

*(CCEA June 2010)*

6. Oxalate ion acts as a bidentate ligand and forms the compound $K_3[Fe(C_2O_4)_3]$ when it combines with iron(III) ions. If a solution of the compound is treated with edta a reaction takes place. Suggest what reaction takes place and explain why it occurs.

*(Adapted from CCEA June 2013)*

7. Edta and ranelic acid form complexes with the ions of Group II metals such as calcium and strontium.

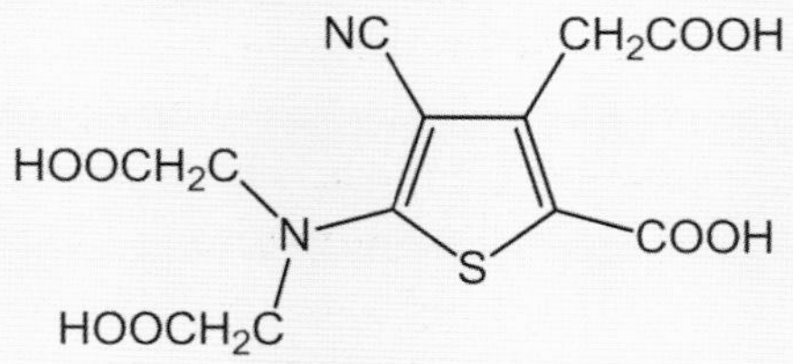

ranelic acid

(a) Write the formula of the monostrontium salt of ranelic acid showing the ions present. (b) Suggest whether edta might be expected to displace ranelic acid from its complex with strontium ions.

*(CCEA June 2014)*

Before moving to the next section, check that you are able to:

- Write equations for ligand substitution reactions and the overall ligand replacement reaction that occurs as a result of ligand substitution.
- Account for ligand substitution in terms of metal-ligand bond strength and the change in entropy that accompanies ligand substitution.

# 5.8 Transition Metal Chemistry

**CONNECTIONS**

- Iron(III) chloride is used to remove suspended solids during the production of drinking water and the treatment of wastewater.
- Chromium(VI) compounds are very toxic to humans. Chromium(III) compounds are much less toxic.

## Transition Metal Ions in Aqueous Solution

**In this section we are learning to:**

- Recall the complexes formed by transition metal ions in aqueous solution.
- Explain, using equations, the nature of ligand replacement reactions involving transition metal complexes in aqueous solution.
- Describe, using equations, how to test for the presence of transition metal ions in aqueous solution.

### Vanadium

*Chemistry of V(II) and V(III)*

Aqueous solutions of vanadium(II) salts such as $VCl_2$ and $VSO_4$ contain the hexaaquavanadium(II) ion, $[V(H_2O)_6]^{2+}$ which gives the solution a violet colour (Equation 1).

$$VCl_{2(s)} + 6H_2O_{(l)} \rightarrow [V(H_2O)_6]^{2+}{}_{(aq)} + 2Cl^-{}_{(aq)} \ [1]$$
$$\text{violet solution}$$

Similarly, aqueous solutions of vanadium(III) salts such as $VCl_3$ and $V_2(SO_4)_3$ contain the hexaaquavanadium(III) ion, $[V(H_2O)_6]^{3+}$ which gives the solution a green colour. (Equation 2).

$$VCl_{3(s)} + 6H_2O_{(l)}$$
$$\rightarrow [V(H_2O)_6]^{3+}{}_{(aq)} + 3Cl^-{}_{(aq)} \ [2]$$
$$\text{green solution}$$

*Chemistry of V(IV) and V(V)*

Vanadium(IV) salts such as oxovanadium(IV) sulfate, $VOSO_4$ dissolve in water to form oxovanadium(IV) ion, $VO^{2+}$ which is more accurately described as a complex with the formula $[VO(H_2O)_5]^{2+}$ and gives the solution a blue colour (Equation 3).

$$VOSO_{4(s)} + 5H_2O_{(l)}$$
$$\rightarrow [VO(H_2O)_5]^{2+}{}_{(aq)} + SO_4{}^{2-}{}_{(aq)} \ [3]$$
$$\text{blue solution}$$

Vanadium(V) is commonly encountered in the form of vanadate(V) salts such as ammonium vanadate(V), $NH_4VO_3$. Vanadate(V) salts contain the vanadate(V) ion, $VO_3^-$ which is colourless in solution and reacts with acid to form dioxovanadium(V) ion, $VO_2^+$. In aqueous solution the $VO_2^+$ ion is more accurately described as a complex with the formula $[VO_2(H_2O)_4]^+$ and gives the solution a yellow colour (Equation 4).

$$VO_3{}^-{}_{(aq)} + 2H^+{}_{(aq)} + 3H_2O_{(l)}$$
$$\text{colourless solution}$$
$$\rightarrow [VO_2(H_2O)_4]^+{}_{(aq)} \ [4]$$
$$\text{yellow solution}$$

**Exercise 5.8A**

1. Complete the table below giving the formula, oxidation number and colour in solution of some vanadium ions.

| Ion | Oxidation number | Colour |
|---|---|---|
| $V^{2+}{}_{(aq)}$ | | |
| | | yellow |
| $VO^{2+}{}_{(aq)}$ | | |
| $V^{3+}{}_{(aq)}$ | | |

*(CCEA June 2015)*

Before moving to the next section, check that you are able to:

- Recall the formula and colour of the ions formed by V(II), V(III), V(IV) and V(V) in compounds and in aqueous solution.
- Explain, with the help of an equation, the formation of the dioxovanadium(V) ion from vanadate(V) ion in acidic solution.

### Chromium

*Chemistry of Cr(III)*

Aqueous solutions of chromium(III) salts such as $CrCl_3$ and $Cr_2(SO_4)_3$ contain the hexaaquachromium(III) ion, $[Cr(H_2O)_6]^{3+}$ which gives the solution a green colour. (Equation 5).

$$CrCl_{3(s)} + 6H_2O_{(l)} \rightarrow [Cr(H_2O)_6]^{3+}_{(aq)} + 3Cl^-_{(aq)} \ [5]$$
green solution

On adding a few drops of aqueous sodium hydroxide a ligand replacement occurs and a green-blue precipitate is formed (Equation 6).

$$[Cr(H_2O)_6]^{3+}_{(aq)} + 3OH^-_{(aq)}$$
green solution

$$\rightarrow [Cr(H_2O)_3(OH)_3]_{(s)} + 3H_2O_{(l)} \ [6]$$
green-blue precipitate

On adding aqueous sodium hydroxide to excess the ligand replacement continues, and the green-blue precipitate reacts to form the soluble complex $[Cr(OH)_6]^{3-}$ (Equation 7).

$$[Cr(H_2O)_3(OH)_3]_{(s)} + 3OH^-_{(aq)}$$
green-blue precipitate

$$\rightarrow [Cr(OH)_6]^-_{(aq)} + 3H_2O_{(l)} \ [7]$$
green solution

### Testing for Cr³⁺ ions in solution:

Chromium(III) ions are present in solution if a green-blue precipitate forms on adding aqueous sodium hydroxide, and then reacts to form a green solution on adding to excess.

$$Cr^{3+}_{(aq)} + 3OH^-_{(aq)} \rightarrow Cr(OH)_{3(s)}$$
green-blue precipitate

$$Cr(OH)_{3(s)} + 3OH^-_{(aq)} \rightarrow [Cr(OH)_6]^{3-}_{(aq)}$$
green solution

### Chemistry of Cr(VI)

The intense yellow colour of chromate(VI) compounds such as sodium chromate(VI), $Na_2CrO_4$ is due to the presence of chromate(VI) ions, $CrO_4^{2-}$ in the solid. Similarly, the intense orange colour of dichromate(VI) compounds such as potassium dichromate(VI), $K_2Cr_2O_7$ is due to the presence of dichromate(VI) ions, $Cr_2O_7^{2-}$ in the solid. In aqueous solution chromate(VI) ion, $CrO_4^{2-}$ is in equilibrium with dichromate(VI) ion, $Cr_2O_7^{2-}$ (Equation 8).

$$2CrO_4^{2-}_{(aq)} + 2H^+_{(aq)} \leftrightharpoons Cr_2O_7^{2-}_{(aq)} + H_2O_{(l)} \ [8]$$
yellow solution       orange solution

At low pH the position of equilibrium lies to the right and the orange colour of dichromate(VI) ion

dominates. On adding alkali the position of equilibrium shifts to the left and the yellow colour of chromate(VI) ion, $CrO_4^{2-}$ dominates.

### Exercise 5.8B

1. Explain how you would use aqueous sodium hydroxide to determine if an aqueous solution contains chromium(III) ions. Write an equation for each reaction that would occur.

2. Chromate(VI) ions and dichromate ions are involved in the following equilibrium. State and explain the colour change when sodium hydroxide solution is added to this equilibrium.

$$2CrO_4^{2-}_{(aq)} + 2H^+_{(aq)} \leftrightharpoons Cr_2O_7^{2-}_{(aq)} + H_2O_{(l)}$$

*(CCEA June 2010)*

3. The oxygen atoms in the dichromate ion are arranged tetrahedrally around both chromium atoms. Draw a diagram to suggest the 3D arrangement of the atoms in the dichromate ion.

*(CCEA June 2015)*

### Before moving to the next section, check that you are able to:

- Recall the formula and colour of the ions formed by Cr(III) and Cr(VI) in compounds and in aqueous solution.
- Describe, with the aid of equations, how to use aqueous sodium hydroxide to test for the presence of Cr(III) in aqueous solution.
- Explain, with the aid of equations, how pH affects the chromate(VI)-dichromate(VI) equilibrium in aqueous solution.

### Manganese

### Chemistry of Mn(II)

Aqueous solutions of manganese(II) salts contain the hexaaquamanganese(II) ion, $[Mn(H_2O)_6]^{2+}$ which gives the solution a pink colour. (Equation 9).

$$MnCl_{2(s)} + 6H_2O_{(l)} \rightarrow [Mn(H_2O)_6]^{2+}_{(aq)} + 2Cl^-_{(aq)} \ [9]$$
pink solution

On adding a few drops of aqueous sodium hydroxide or ammonia solution a ligand replacement occurs and a white precipitate is formed (Equation 10).

$[Mn(H_2O)_6]^{2+}_{(aq)} + 2OH^-_{(aq)}$
pink solution

$$\rightarrow [Mn(H_2O)_4(OH)_2]_{(s)} + 2H_2O_{(l)} \quad [10]$$
white precipitate

The precipitate is insoluble on adding either solution to excess, and turns brown on standing as it reacts with dissolved oxygen to form manganese(IV) oxide, $MnO_2$ (Equation 11).

$2Mn(OH)_{2(s)} + O_{2(aq)} \rightarrow 2MnO_{2(s)} + 2H_2O_{(l)}$ [11]
white precipitate　　　　brown precipitate

### Testing for Mn²⁺ ions in solution:

Manganese(II) ions are present in solution if a white precipitate forms on adding aqueous sodium hydroxide or ammonia solution, turns brown on standing in air, and remains on adding to excess.

$Mn^{2+}_{(aq)} + 2OH^-_{(aq)} \rightarrow Mn(OH)_{2(s)}$
white precipitate

### Chemistry of Mn(VII)

The intense purple colour of permanganate compounds such as potassium manganate(VII), $KMnO_4$ is due to the presence of permanganate ion, $MnO_4^-$ in the solid. Permanganate ion is also known as manganate(VII) ion as it contains manganese in an oxidation state of +7. Permanganate ion is a good oxidising agent and is readily reduced to form manganese(II) in acidic solution (Equation 12).

$MnO_4^-{}_{(aq)} + 8H^+_{(aq)} + 5e^- \rightarrow Mn^{2+}_{(aq)} + 4H_2O_{(l)}$ [12]

The reduction of manganate(VII) in acidic solution (Equation 12) is the basis for redox titrations in which manganate(VII) is used to determine the amount of reducing agents such as iron(II), $Fe^{2+}$ in aqueous solution. The end point is characterised by a colour change from colourless to pink as the purple colour of permanganate persists when there is no reducing agent remaining in the solution.

### Exercise 5.8C

1. Explain how you would use ammonia solution to determine if an aqueous solution contains manganese(II) ions. Include an equation for any reaction that occurs on adding ammonia solution.

2. A solution of potassium manganate(VII) oxidises nitrites to nitrates.

   $6H_2SO_4 + 4KMnO_4 + 5Ca(NO_2)_2$
   $\rightarrow 2K_2SO_4 + 4MnSO_4 + 5Ca(NO_3)_2 + 6H_2O$

   (a) Rewrite this equation as an ionic equation.
   (b) State and explain the colour change observed.

   *(CCEA January 2010)*

3. When heated, potassium manganate(VII) decomposes to form $K_2MnO_4$, $MnO_2$ and oxygen. The compound $K_2MnO_4$ is a soluble green solid. Manganese dioxide, $MnO_2$ is an insoluble black solid. (a) Explain, with experimental details, how you would obtain a pure dry sample of $MnO_2$ from the reaction mixture. (b) Use oxidation numbers to explain the redox changes that occur when $KMnO_4$ decomposes.

   $2KMnO_4 \rightarrow K_2MnO_4 + MnO_2 + O_2$

   *(Adapted from CCEA January 2010)*

---

Before moving to the next section, check that you are able to:

- Recall the formula and colour of the ions formed by Mn(II) and Mn(VII) in compounds and in aqueous solution.

- Describe, with the aid of equations, how to use aqueous sodium hydroxide and ammonia solution to test for the presence of Mn(II) in aqueous solution.

- Explain, with the aid of equations, how aqueous manganate(VII) can be used to determine the amount of a reducing agent in solution.

---

## Iron

### Chemistry of Fe(II)

Aqueous solutions of iron(II) salts contain the hexaaquairon(II) ion, $[Fe(H_2O)_6]^{2+}$ which gives the solution a green colour (Equation 13).

$FeCl_{2(s)} + 6H_2O_{(l)}$
$$\rightarrow [Fe(H_2O)_6]_{(aq)} + 2Cl^-_{(aq)} \quad [13]$$
green solution

On adding a few drops of aqueous sodium hydroxide or ammonia solution a ligand replacement occurs and a green precipitate is formed (Equation 14).

$$[Fe(H_2O)_6]^{2+}{}_{(aq)} + 2OH^-{}_{(aq)}$$
green solution
$$\rightarrow [Fe(H_2O)_4(OH)_2]_{(s)} + 2H_2O_{(l)} \quad [14]$$
green precipitate

The precipitate is insoluble on adding either solution to excess, and turns brown on standing as it reacts with dissolved oxygen to form iron(III) hydroxide, $Fe(OH)_3$.

### Testing for $Fe^{2+}$ ions in solution:
Iron(II) ions are present in solution if a green precipitate forms on adding dilute sodium hydroxide or ammonia solution, turns brown on standing in air, and remains on adding either solution to excess.

$$Fe^{2+}{}_{(aq)} + 2OH^-{}_{(aq)} \rightarrow Fe(OH)_2{}_{(s)}$$
green precipitate

*Chemistry of Fe(III)*

Aqueous solutions of iron(III) salts contain the hexaaquairon(III) ion, $[Fe(H_2O)_6]^{3+}$ which gives the solution a yellow colour (Equation 15).

$$FeCl_3{}_{(s)} + 6H_2O_{(l)} \rightarrow [Fe(H_2O)_6]^{2+}{}_{(aq)} + 3Cl^-{}_{(aq)} \quad [15]$$
yellow solution

On adding a few drops of aqueous sodium hydroxide or ammonia solution a ligand replacement occurs, and a brown precipitate is formed that remains on adding either solution to excess (Equation 16).

$$[Fe(H_2O)_6]^{3+}{}_{(aq)} + 3OH^-{}_{(aq)}$$
yellow solution
$$\rightarrow [Fe(H_2O)_3(OH)_3]_{(s)} + 3H_2O_{(l)} \quad [16]$$
brown precipitate

### Testing for $Fe^{3+}$ ions in solution:
Iron(III) ions are present in solution if a brown precipitate forms on adding dilute sodium hydroxide or ammonia solution, and remains on adding either solution to excess.

$$Fe^{3+}{}_{(aq)} + 3OH^-{}_{(aq)} \rightarrow Fe(OH)_3{}_{(s)}$$
brown precipitate

The presence of trace amounts of iron(III) in aqueous solution can be confirmed by the formation of a blood-red complex when a few drops of potassium thiocyanate solution, KSCN are added to the solution (Equation 17).

$$[Fe(H_2O)_6]^{3+}{}_{(aq)} + SCN^-{}_{(aq)}$$
$$\rightarrow [Fe(SCN)(H_2O)_5]^{2+}{}_{(aq)} + H_2O_{(l)} \quad [17]$$
blood-red solution

### Exercise 5.8D

1. Describe how you would use ammonia solution to test for iron(II) ions in solution.

   *(Adapted from CCEA June 2006)*

2. (a) Write the formulas for iron(II) oxalate and iron(III) oxalate. (b) Oxalate ions are colourless in aqueous solution. State the expected colour for solutions of iron(II) oxalate and iron(III) oxalate. (c) State and explain what would be observed when a solution of sodium hydroxide is added to each of these solutions.

   *(Adapted from CCEA June 2013)*

3. (a) What is observed when sodium hydroxide solution is added to a solution containing $[Fe(H_2O)_6]^{3+}$ ions? (b) Describe a different chemical test, including observations, which can be used to detect the presence of low concentrations of $[Fe(H_2O)_6]^{3+}$ ions. Give the formula of any new complex formed in the test.

   *(CCEA May 2012)*

4. Describe, with observations, how you would confirm the presence of aqueous iron(III) ions without interference from manganese(II) ions.

   *(CCEA June 2011)*

---

**Before moving to the next section, check that you are able to:**

- Recall the formula and colour of the ions formed by Fe(II) and Fe(III) in aqueous solution.
- Describe, with the aid of equations, how to use aqueous sodium hydroxide and ammonia solution to test for the presence of Fe(II) or Fe(III) in aqueous solution.
- Explain, with the aid of equations, how aqueous potassium thiocyanate can be used to test for trace amounts of Fe(III) in aqueous solution.

---

## Cobalt

*Chemistry of Co(II)*

Aqueous solutions of cobalt(II) salts such as $CoCl_2$ and $CoSO_4$ contain the hexaaquacobalt(II) ion, $[Co(H_2O)_6]^{2+}$ which gives the solution a pink colour (Equation 18).

$$CoCl_{2(s)} + 6H_2O_{(l)}$$
$$\rightarrow [Co(H_2O)_6]^{2+}_{(aq)} + 2Cl^-_{(aq)} \ [18]$$
pink solution

On adding concentrated hydrochloric acid to a solution containing aqueous cobalt(II) ions a ligand replacement occurs in which water is replaced by chloride ions to form the tetrachlorocobalt(II) ion, $[CoCl_4]^{2-}$ (Equation 19).

$$[Co(H_2O)_6]^{2+}_{(aq)} + 4Cl^-_{(aq)}$$
pink solution
$$\rightleftharpoons [CoCl_4]^{2-}_{(aq)} + 6H_2O_{(l)} \ [19]$$
blue solution

A ligand replacement also occurs on adding a few drops of aqueous sodium hydroxide or ammonia solution to a solution containing aqueous cobalt(II) ions. On adding aqueous sodium hydroxide a blue precipitate is formed that remains on adding aqueous sodium hydroxide to excess (Equation 20).

$$[Co(H_2O)_6]^{2+}_{(aq)} + 2OH^-_{(aq)}$$
pink solution
$$\rightarrow [Co(H_2O)_4(OH)_2]_{(s)} + 2H_2O_{(l)} \ [20]$$
blue precipitate

On adding ammonia solution the blue precipitate forms and then reacts to give a brown solution on adding ammonia solution to excess (Equation 21).

$$[Co(H_2O)_4(OH)_2]_{(s)} + 6NH_{3(aq)}$$
blue precipitate
$$\rightarrow [Co(NH_3)_6]^{2+}_{(aq)} + 4H_2O_{(l)} + 2OH^-_{(aq)} \ [21]$$
brown solution

### Testing for Co²⁺ ions in solution:

Cobalt(II) ions are present in solution if a blue precipitate forms and then remains on adding aqueous sodium hydroxide to excess, and forms before reacting to give a brown solution on adding ammonia solution to excess.

$$Co^{2+}_{(aq)} + 2OH^-_{(aq)} \rightarrow Co(OH)_{2(s)}$$
blue precipitate

$$Co(OH)_{2(s)} + 6NH_{3(aq)}$$
$$\rightarrow [Co(NH_3)_6]^{2+}_{(aq)} + 2OH^-_{(aq)}$$
brown solution

The hexaaquacobalt(II) ion, $[Co(H_2O)_6]^{2+}$ also forms chelates with ligands such as en (Equation 22) and edta (Equation 23).

$$[Co(H_2O)_6]^{2+}_{(aq)} + 3en_{(aq)}$$
$$\rightarrow [Co(en)_3]^{2+}_{(aq)} + 6H_2O_{(l)} \ [22]$$
orange solution

$$[Co(H_2O)_6]^{2+}_{(aq)} + (edta)^{4-}_{(aq)}$$
$$\rightarrow [Co(edta)]^{2-}_{(aq)} + 6H_2O_{(l)} \ [23]$$
pink solution

### Exercise 5.8E

1. When cobalt(II) oxide is treated with dilute hydrochloric acid a complex ion with formula $[Co(H_2O)_6]^{2+}$ is formed. The colour of the solution changes on adding concentrated hydrochloric acid. (a) State the coordination number of cobalt in the complex $[Co(H_2O)_6]^{2+}$ and the colour of the solution containing this ion. (b) Write the ionic equation for the reaction that occurs on adding concentrated hydrochloric acid.

*(CCEA May 2002)*

2. (a) State the colour of aqueous cobalt(II) chloride. (b) Write the formula for the complex formed in aqueous cobalt(II) chloride. (c) Explain, with the aid of equations, how solutions of aqueous sodium hydroxide and ammonia solution could be used to confirm that a solution contained aqueous cobalt(II) ions.

3. Which one of the following complexes is formed when excess ammonia solution is added to cobalt(II) sulfate solution?

   A $[Co(NH_3)_4(H_2O)_2]^{2+}$
   B $[Co(NH_3)_4]^{2+}$
   C $[Co(NH_3)_6]^{2+}$
   D $[Co(NH_3)_2(H_2O)_4]^{2+}$

*(CCEA June 2007)*

4. An orange solution is formed when 1,2-diaminoethane (en) is added to aqueous cobalt(II) sulfate. (a) Write an equation for the reaction that occurs on adding en. (b) Explain the colour change observed on adding en in terms of the complexes present in solution.

5. A pale pink solid is formed when aqueous sodium oxalate, $Na_2C_2O_4$ is added to a solution containing aqueous cobalt(II) ions. Suggest the formula of the solid. Explain your reasoning.

Before moving to the next section, check that you are able to:

- Recall the formula and colour of the ions formed by Co(II) in aqueous solution.
- Describe, with the aid of equations, how to use aqueous sodium hydroxide and ammonia solution to test for the presence of Co(II) in aqueous solution.

## Nickel

### Chemistry of Ni(II)

Aqueous solutions of nickel(II) salts such as $NiCl_2$ and $NiSO_4$ contain the hexaaquanickel(II) ion, $[Ni(H_2O)_6]^{2+}$ which gives the solution a green colour (Equation 24).

$$NiCl_{2(s)} + 6H_2O_{(l)}$$
$$\rightarrow [Ni(H_2O)_6]^{2+}_{(aq)} + 2Cl^-_{(aq)} \quad [24]$$
green solution

On adding a few drops of aqueous sodium hydroxide to a solution containing aqueous nickel(II) ions a green precipitate is formed that remains on adding aqueous sodium hydroxide to excess (Equation 25).

$$[Ni(H_2O)_6]^{2+}_{(aq)} + 2OH^-_{(aq)}$$
green solution
$$\rightarrow [Ni(H_2O)_4(OH)_2]_{(s)} + 2H_2O_{(l)} \quad [25]$$
green precipitate

On adding ammonia solution to a solution containing aqueous nickel(II) ions the green precipitate forms and then reacts to give a blue solution on adding ammonia solution to excess (Equation 26).

$$[Ni(H_2O)_4(OH)_2]_{(s)} + 6NH_{3(aq)}$$
green precipitate
$$\rightarrow [Ni(NH_3)_6]^{2+}_{(aq)} + 4H_2O_{(l)} + 2OH^-_{(aq)} \quad [26]$$
blue solution

### Testing for $Ni^{2+}$ ions in solution:

Nickel(II) ions are present in solution if a green precipitate forms and then remains on adding aqueous sodium hydroxide to excess, and forms before reacting to give a blue solution on adding ammonia solution to excess.

$$Ni^{2+}_{(aq)} + 2OH^-_{(aq)} \rightarrow Ni(OH)_{2(s)}$$
green precipitate
$$Ni(OH)_{2(s)} + 6NH_{3(aq)}$$
$$\rightarrow [Ni(NH_3)_6]^{2+}_{(aq)} + 2OH^-_{(aq)}$$
blue solution

The hexaaquanickel(II) ion, $[Ni(H_2O)_6]^{2+}$ also forms chelates with ligands such as en (Equation 27) and edta (Equation 28).

$$[Ni(H_2O)_6]^{2+}_{(aq)} + 3en_{(aq)}$$
$$\rightarrow [Ni(en)_3]^{2+}_{(aq)} + 6H_2O_{(l)} \quad [27]$$
violet solution

$$[Ni(H_2O)_6]^{2+}_{(aq)} + (edta)^{4-}_{(aq)}$$
$$\rightarrow [Ni(edta)]^{2-}_{(aq)} + 6H_2O_{(l)} \quad [28]$$
blue solution

## Exercise 5.8F

1. Complete the table below which summarises the results of adding sodium hydroxide solution and ammonia solution to a solution containing nickel(II) ions.

| Solution added | After a few drops | On adding an excess |
|---|---|---|
| sodium hydroxide | | |
| ammonia | | |

*(Adapted from CCEA June 2010)*

2. When an excess of aqueous ammonia is slowly added to a solution of $Ni^{2+}$ ions

 A  a blue solution is formed with no further change

 B  a pale green precipitate is formed with no further change

 C  a blue precipitate is formed which dissolves to form a green solution

 D  a pale green precipitate is formed which dissolves to form a blue solution

*(CCEA May 2003)*

3. (a) State the colour of aqueous nickel(II) sulfate. (b) Write the formula for the complex formed in aqueous nickel(II) sulfate. (c) Explain, with the aid of equations, how solutions of aqueous sodium hydroxide and ammonia solution could be used to confirm that a solution contained aqueous nickel(II) ions.

4. Which one of the following represents the complex formed when excess ammonia solution is added to an aqueous solution containing nickel(II) ions?

*continued overleaf*

A  $[Ni(NH_3)_4(H_2O)_2]^{2+}$

B  $[Ni(NH_3)_6]^{2+}$

C  $[Ni(NH_3)_2(H_2O)_4]^{2+}$

D  $[Ni(NH_3)_4]^{2+}$

*(CCEA May 2002)*

5. Complete the following flow scheme by writing the formula for the nickel compound formed in each reaction.

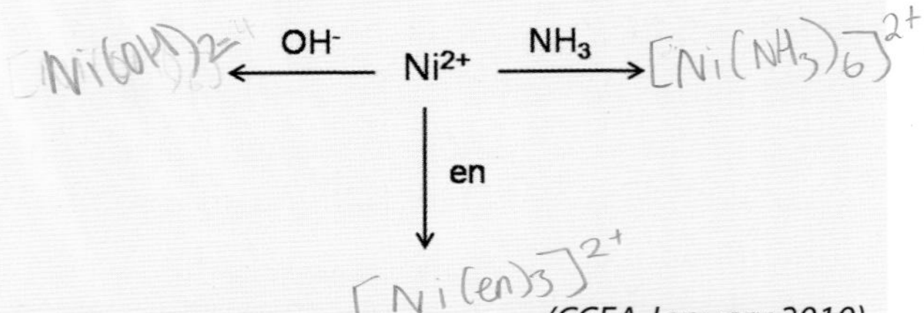

*(CCEA January 2010)*

6. A blue solution is formed when a solution containing the disodium salt of edta, $Na_2H_2(edta)$ is added to aqueous nickel(II) sulfate. (a) Write an equation for the reaction that occurs. (b) Explain the colour change observed in terms of the complexes present in solution.

---

Before moving to the next section, check that you are able to:

- Recall the formula and colour of the ions formed by Ni(II) in aqueous solution.
- Describe, with the aid of equations, how to use aqueous sodium hydroxide and ammonia solution to test for the presence of Ni(II) in aqueous solution.

---

## Copper

*Chemistry of Cu(II)*

Aqueous solutions of copper(II) salts such as $CuCl_2$ and $CuSO_4$ contain the hexaaquacopper(II) ion, $[Cu(H_2O)_6]^{2+}$ which gives the solution a blue colour (Equation 29).

$$CuCl_{2(s)} + 6H_2O_{(l)}$$
$$\rightarrow [Cu(H_2O)_6]^{2+}_{(aq)} + 2Cl^-_{(aq)} \quad [29]$$
blue solution

On adding concentrated hydrochloric acid to a solution containing aqueous copper(II) ions a ligand replacement occurs in which water is replaced by chloride ions to form the tetrachlorocopper(II) ion,

$[CuCl_4]^{2-}$ (Equation 30).

$$[Cu(H_2O)_6]^{2+}_{(aq)} + 4Cl^-_{(aq)}$$
blue solution

$$\leftrightharpoons [CuCl_4]^{2-}_{(aq)} + 6H_2O_{(l)} \quad [30]$$
yellow solution

A ligand replacement also occurs on adding a few drops of aqueous sodium hydroxide or ammonia solution to a solution containing aqueous copper(II) ions. On adding aqueous sodium hydroxide a blue precipitate is formed that remains on adding aqueous sodium hydroxide to excess (Equation 31).

$$[Cu(H_2O)_6]^{2+}_{(aq)} + 2OH^-_{(aq)}$$
blue solution

$$\rightarrow [Cu(H_2O)_4(OH)_2]_{(s)} + 2H_2O_{(l)} \quad [31]$$
blue precipitate

On adding ammonia solution the blue precipitate forms and then reacts to give a dark blue solution on adding ammonia solution to excess (Equation 32).

$$[Cu(H_2O)_4(OH)_2]_{(s)} + 4NH_{3(aq)}$$
blue precipitate

$$\rightarrow [Cu(NH_3)_4(H_2O)_2]^{2+}_{(aq)} + 2H_2O_{(l)} + 2OH^-_{(aq)} \quad [32]$$
dark blue solution

---

### Testing for Cu$^{2+}$ ions in solution:

Copper(II) ions are present in solution if a blue precipitate forms and then remains on adding aqueous sodium hydroxide to excess, and forms before reacting to give a dark blue solution on adding ammonia solution to excess.

$$Cu^{2+}_{(aq)} + 2OH^-_{(aq)} \rightarrow Cu(OH)_{2(s)}$$
blue precipitate

$$Cu(OH)_{2(s)} + 4NH_{3(aq)}$$
$$\rightarrow [Cu(NH_3)_4]^{2+}_{(aq)} + 2OH^-_{(aq)}$$
dark blue solution

---

The hexaaquacopper(II) ion, $[Cu(H_2O)_6]^{2+}$ also forms chelates with ligands such as en (Equation 33) and edta (Equation 34).

$$[Cu(H_2O)_6]^{2+}_{(aq)} + 3en_{(aq)}$$
$$\rightarrow [Cu(en)_3]^{2+}_{(aq)} + 6H_2O_{(l)} \quad [33]$$
violet solution

$$[Cu(H_2O)_6]^{2+}_{(aq)} + (edta)^{4-}_{(aq)}$$
$$\rightarrow [Cu(edta)]^{2-}_{(aq)} + 6H_2O_{(l)} \quad [34]$$
blue solution

## Exercise 5.8G

1. (a) State the colour of each copper complex in the following equilibrium. (b) Name a reagent which could be used to shift the equilibrium to the right.

$$[Cu(H_2O)_6]^{2+}(aq) + 4Cl^-(aq)$$
$$\leftrightarrows [CuCl_4]^{2-}(aq) + 6H_2O(l)$$

*(CCEA June 2006)*

2. Complete the following flow scheme by writing the formula for the copper complex formed in each reaction.

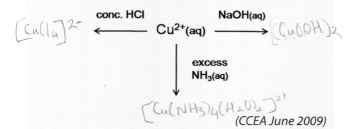

$[CuCl_4]^{2-}$

conc. HCl ← Cu²⁺(aq) → NaOH(aq) $[Cu(OH)_2]$

excess NH₃(aq)

$[Cu(NH_3)_4(H_2O)_2]^{2+}$

*(CCEA June 2009)*

3. (a) State and explain the observations on adding ammonia solution to aqueous copper(II) nitrate dropwise until it is in excess. Give the formula of each copper compound or complex formed. (b) State and explain the colour change observed on adding concentrated hydrochloric acid to the solution containing an excess of ammonia. Give the formula of the copper complex formed. (c) Suggest why the ligand replacement occurs on adding concentrated hydrochloric acid.

*(Adapted from CCEA June 2008)*

Before moving to the next section, check that you are able to:

- Recall the formula and colour of the ions formed by Cu(II) in aqueous solution.
- Describe, with the aid of equations, how to use aqueous sodium hydroxide and ammonia solution to test for the presence of Cu(II) in aqueous solution.

## Redox Chemistry of Vanadium

In this section we are learning to:

- Describe the reduction of aqueous vanadate(V) salts in acidic solution.

In this section the redox chemistry of vanadium is used to illustrate the factors that determine the extent to which transition metal compounds and ions will participate in redox reactions in aqueous solution.

When a small amount of solid ammonium HCl vanadate(V), $NH_4VO_3$ is dissolved in dilute acid, a yellow solution containing the dioxovanadium(V) ion, $VO_2^+$ is formed (Equation 35).

$$VO_3^-(aq) + 2H^+(aq) \rightarrow VO_2^+(aq) + H_2O(l) \quad [35]$$
$$\text{yellow solution}$$

On adding zinc the colour of the solution gradually changes from yellow to blue as dioxovanadium(V) ion, $VO_2^+$ is reduced to oxovanadium(IV) ion, $VO^{2+}$ by the combination of zinc and hydrogen ions in the solution. The sequence of colours in Figure 1 reveals that the colour change from yellow to blue is the first of three colour changes that occur on adding zinc to the solution.

The potential generated by the reduction of $VO_2^+$ ($E_{red}$) can be combined with the potential generated by the oxidation of zinc ($E_{ox}$) to produce a positive emf for the reduction of $VO_2^+$ by zinc.

*Potential generated by reduction:*
$$VO_2^+(aq) + 2H^+(aq) + e^-$$
$$\rightarrow VO^{2+}(aq) + H_2O(l) \quad E_{red} = +1.00 \text{ V} \quad [36a]$$

*Potential generated by oxidation:*
$$Zn(s) \rightarrow Zn^{2+}(aq) + 2e^- \quad E_{ox} = +0.76 \text{ V} \quad [36b]$$

*Emf for the reduction of $VO_2^+$ by zinc in acidic solution:*
$$emf = E_{red} + E_{ox} = (+1.00) + (+0.76) = +1.76 \text{ V}$$

As in an electrochemical cell, the reaction is feasible because the emf generated by the reaction is positive. The equation for the reduction of $VO_2^+$ by zinc (Equation 36c) is obtained by combining the half-equations describing oxidation and reduction (Equations 36a and 36b).

$$2VO_2^+(aq) + 4H^+(aq) + Zn(s)$$
$$\text{yellow solution}$$
$$\rightarrow Zn^{2+}(aq) + 2VO^{2+}(aq) + 2H_2O(l) \quad [36c]$$
$$\text{blue solution}$$

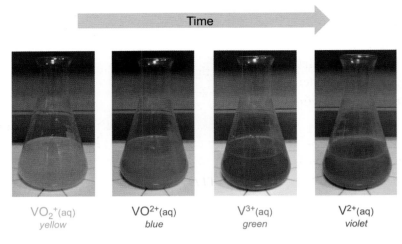

Time

$VO_2^+{(aq)}$
*yellow*

$VO^{2+}{(aq)}$
*blue*

$V^{3+}{(aq)}$
*green*

$V^{2+}{(aq)}$
*violet*

*Figure 1: The sequence of colours that accompany the reduction of dioxovanadium(V), $VO_2^+$ ions on adding zinc to an acidic solution of $VO_2^+$ ions.*

If an excess of zinc and hydrogen ions are present the oxovanadium(IV) ions, $VO^{2+}$ are further reduced to vanadium(III), $V^{3+}$ and the solution changes colour from blue to green as shown in Figure 1. The reaction is feasible as the potential generated by the reduction ($E_{red}$) can be combined with the potential generated by the oxidation of zinc ($E_{ox}$) to produce a positive emf for the reduction of $VO^{2+}$ to $V^{3+}$ by zinc in acidic solution.

*Potential generated by reduction:*
$$VO^{2+}{(aq)} + 2H^+{(aq)} + e^-$$
$$\rightarrow V^{3+}{(aq)} + H_2O{(l)} \qquad E_{red} = +0.34 \text{ V} \quad [37a]$$

*Potential generated by oxidation:*
$$Zn{(s)} \rightarrow Zn^{2+}{(aq)} + 2e^- \qquad E_{ox} = +0.76 \text{ V} \quad [37b]$$

*Emf for the reduction of $VO^{2+}$ by zinc in acidic solution:*
$$emf = E_{red} + E_{ox} = (+0.34) + (+0.76) = +1.10 \text{ V}$$

The equation for the reduction of $VO^{2+}$ by zinc (Equation 37c) is obtained by combining the half-equations describing oxidation and reduction (Equations 37a and 37b).

$$2VO^{2+}{(aq)} + 4H^+{(aq)} + Zn{(s)}$$
blue solution
$$\rightarrow Zn^{2+}{(aq)} + 2V^{3+}{(aq)} + 2H_2O{(l)} \quad [37c]$$
green solution

If zinc and hydrogen ions remain in excess the vanadium(III) ions, $V^{3+}$ are further reduced to vanadium(II), $V^{2+}$ and the solution changes colour from green to violet as shown in Figure 1. Again the reaction is feasible as the potential generated by the reduction of $V^{3+}$ ($E_{red}$) can be combined with the potential generated by the oxidation of zinc ($E_{ox}$) to

produce a positive emf for the reduction of $V^{3+}$ to $V^{2+}$ by zinc in acidic solution.

*Potential generated by reduction:*
$$V^{3+}{(aq)} + e^- \rightarrow V^{2+}{(aq)} \qquad E_{red} = -0.26 \text{ V} \quad [38a]$$

*Potential generated by oxidation:*
$$Zn{(s)} \rightarrow Zn^{2+}{(aq)} + 2e^- \qquad E_{ox} = +0.76 \text{ V} \quad [38b]$$

*Emf for the reduction of $VO^{2+}$ by zinc in acidic solution:*
$$emf = E_{red} + E_{ox} = (-0.26) + (+0.76) = +0.50 \text{ V}$$

The equation for the reduction of $V^{3+}$ by zinc (Equation 38c) is obtained by combining the half-equations describing oxidation and reduction (Equations 38a and 38b).

$$2V^{3+}{(aq)} + Zn{(s)} \rightarrow Zn^{2+}{(aq)} + 2V^{2+}{(aq)} \quad [38c]$$
green solution \qquad violet solution

### Worked Example 5.8i

The following cell was set up to investigate the reaction between an acidic solution of vanadyl ions, $VO^{2+}$ and acidified permanganate ions. The standard electrode potentials for the $VO_2^+|VO^{2+}$ and $MnO_4^-|Mn^{2+}$ half-cells are +1.02 V and +1.51V respectively.

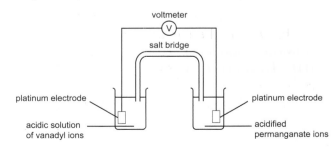

voltmeter

V

salt bridge

platinum electrode

platinum electrode

acidic solution of vanadyl ions

acidified permanganate ions

(a) Write the equations for the reactions taking place in the two half-cells and combine them to obtain the overall equation. (b) Describe the colour change in (i) the vanadyl half-cell and (ii) the permanganate half-cell. (c) Calculate the reading on the voltmeter.

*(Adapted from CCEA June 2014)*

### Strategy

- Vanadyl, $VO^{2+}$ (blue solution) will be oxidised to $VO_2^+$ (yellow solution) and permanganate, $MnO_4^-$ (pink solution) will be reduced to $Mn^{2+}$ (colourless).

- Hydrogen ions $(H^+)$ and water can be included as reactants or products when balancing equations in acidic solution.

### Solution

(a) *Oxidation in the vanadyl half-cell:*

$VO^{2+}{}_{(aq)} + H_2O_{(l)} \rightarrow VO_2^+{}_{(aq)} + 2H^+{}_{(aq)} + e^-$

*Reduction in the permanganate half-cell:*

$MnO_4^-{}_{(aq)} + 8H^+{}_{(aq)} + 5e^- \rightarrow Mn^{2+}{}_{(aq)} + 4H_2O_{(l)}$

*Overall equation:*

$5VO^{2+}{}_{(aq)} + MnO_4^-{}_{(aq)} + H_2O_{(l)}$
$\rightarrow 5VO_2^+{}_{(aq)} + Mn^{2+}{}_{(aq)} + 2H^+{}_{(aq)}$

(b) (i) The solution changes from blue to yellow.
(ii) The solution changes from pink to colourless.

(c) $emf = E_{red} + E_{ox} = (+1.51) + (-1.02) = +0.49$ V

### Exercise 5.8H

1. The following change occurs when a solution containing $VO_2^+$ ions is shaken with zinc amalgam. (a) Deduce the oxidation state of vanadium in each species. (b) State the role of the zinc amalgam in the reaction.

$VO_2^+{}_{(aq)} \rightarrow VO^{2+}{}_{(aq)}$

*(CCEA June 2009)*

2. Chromium will reduce a solution of ammonium vanadate(V). (a) Write an equation for the reaction between chromium and $VO_2^+{}_{(aq)}$ ions. (b) Calculate the emf for the reaction.

| | | | E° /V |
|---|---|---|---|
| $Cr^{3+}{}_{(aq)} + 3e^-$ | ⇌ | $Cr_{(s)}$ | −0.74 |
| $VO_2^+{}_{(aq)} + 2H^+{}_{(aq)} + e^-$ | ⇌ | $VO^{2+}{}_{(aq)} + H_2O_{(l)}$ | +1.00 |

*(CCEA June 2010)*

3. The $VO_2^+$ ion can be reduced to $V^{2+}$ using zinc in the presence of an acid. Zinc is oxidised to form $Zn^{2+}$ ions. (a) Write a half-equation for the reduction of $VO_2^+$ to $V^{2+}$. (b) Combine this half-equation with the half-equation: $Zn \rightarrow Zn^{2+} + 2e^-$ to give the ionic equation for the reaction. (c) When the reaction is carried out in the laboratory a series of colour changes are observed. Complete the following table.

| Ion in solution | Solution colour |
|---|---|
| $VO_2^+$ | |
| | Blue |
| | Green |
| $V^{2+}$ | |

*(CCEA May 2012)*

4. Use the standard electrode potentials given in the table to determine which one of the following reagents will convert $V^{3+}{}_{(aq)}$ to $VO^{2+}{}_{(aq)}$.

| | | | E° /V |
|---|---|---|---|
| $V^{3+}{}_{(aq)} + e^-$ | ⇌ | $V^{2+}{}_{(aq)}$ | −0.26 |
| $SO_4^{2-}{}_{(aq)} + 2H^+{}_{(aq)} + 2e^-$ | ⇌ | $SO_3^{2-}{}_{(aq)} + H_2O_{(l)}$ | +0.17 |
| $VO^{2+}{}_{(aq)} + 2H^+{}_{(aq)} + e^-$ | ⇌ | $V^{3+}{}_{(aq)} + H_2O_{(l)}$ | +0.34 |
| $Fe^{3+}{}_{(aq)} + e^-$ | ⇌ | $Fe^{2+}{}_{(aq)}$ | +0.77 |
| $VO_2^+{}_{(aq)} + 2H^+{}_{(aq)} + e^-$ | ⇌ | $VO^{2+}{}_{(aq)} + H_2O_{(l)}$ | +1.00 |

A  Aqueous iron(II) ions
B  Aqueous iron(III) ions
C  Aqueous sulfate ions in acidic solution
D  Aqueous sulfite $(SO_3^{2-})$ ions

*(Adapted from CCEA May 2011)*

Before moving to the next section, check that you are able to:

- Explain, in terms of the ions formed, the colour changes that occur when vanadate(V) salts are reduced using zinc in acidic solution.

- Deduce half-equations, and the overall equation, for redox reactions involving vanadium in acidic solution.

- Use potentials for oxidation and reduction to determine if a reaction is feasible.

# 5.9 Organic Nitrogen Chemistry: Amines

**CONNECTIONS**

- Amines such as trimethylamine, $N(CH_3)_3$ are abundant in living things and give fish their characteristic 'fishy' smell.
- Azo compounds (RN=NR') are used as indicators and dyes and are synthesised by coupling reactions involving amines with aromatic character.

## Structure and Properties

$C_nH_{2n+1}NH_2$

**In this section we are learning to:**

- Classify the structures of amines as primary, secondary or tertiary.
- Account for the properties of amines in terms of their structure, and the nature of the bonding between amine molecules.
- Use systematic (IUPAC) rules to name amines.

### Structure

An amine is a derivative of ammonia, $NH_3$ in which one or more of the hydrogen atoms have been replaced by an alkyl group (R). Amines are classified as primary, secondary or tertiary amines according to the number of alkyl groups bonded to the nitrogen atom.

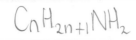

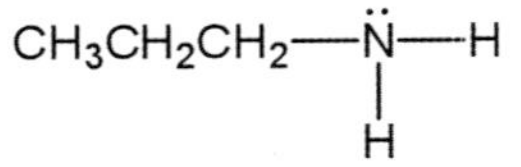

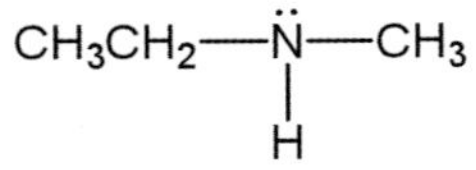

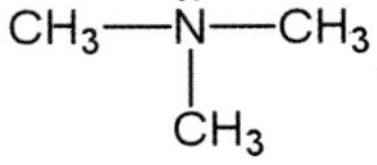

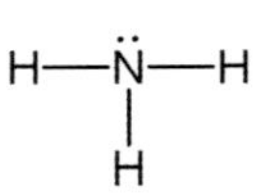

ammonia

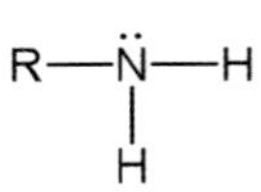

primary amine

ammonia

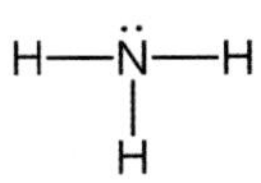

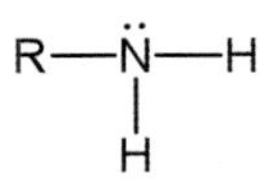

primary amine

The compound propylamine, $C_3H_7NH_2$ is an example of a **primary amine** as *the nitrogen atom is bonded to one carbon atom and the compound has the structure $RNH_2$.* The compound ethylmethylamine is a structural isomer of propylamine. It is a **secondary amine** as *the nitrogen atom is bonded to two carbon atoms and the compound has the structure RNHR' where R and R' are different groups*. Similarly, the compound trimethylamine is a structural isomer of propylamine and is a **tertiary amine** as *the nitrogen atom is bonded to three carbon atoms and the compound has the structure RNR'R'' where R, R' and R'' are different groups.*

propylamine

ethylmethylamine

trimethylamine

**Exercise 5.9A**

1. Phenylethylamine is a 'chemical cousin' of the amphetamines. It is found in chocolate and to a lesser extent in the brain. In terms of brain chemistry, the effects of eating chocolate and taking amphetamines are similar. The structures of phenylethylamine and amphetamine are shown below. (a) Which of these molecules is chiral? Explain your answer. (b) Which of these molecules is a primary amine? Explain your reasoning.

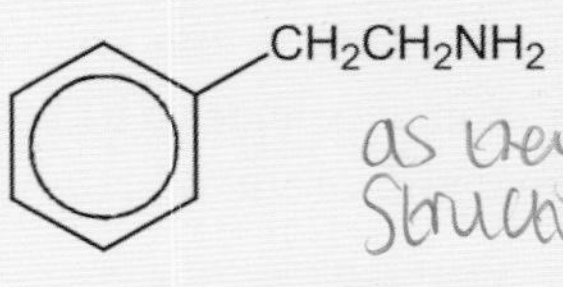

Both compounds are primary as they both have the structure $RNH_2$

phenylethylamine
$C_6H_5CH_2CH_2NH_2$

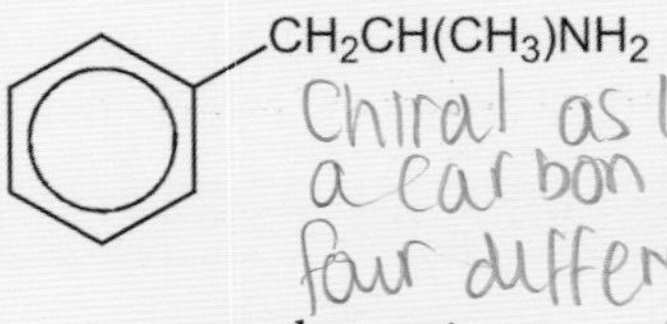

Chiral as it contains a carbon bonded to four different groups of atoms.

amphetamine
$C_6H_5CH_2CH(CH_3)NH_2$

*(Adapted from CCEA June 2004)*

2. Ephedrine is a decongestant and is a component of many cold and flu remedies. (a) Write the condensed formula for ephedrine. (b) Classify ephedrine as a primary, secondary or tertiary amine. Explain your reasoning.

ephedrine

3. Salbutamol is an active ingredient in some inhalers used to treat asthma. (a) Write the molecular formula for salbutamol. (b) Classify salbutamol as a primary, secondary or tertiary amine. Explain your reasoning.

salbutamol

4. Draw all possible structural isomers of butanamine, $C_4H_9NH_2$ and classify each as a primary, secondary or tertiary amine.

5. Compound D is a tertiary amine with a molecular formula $C_5H_{13}N$. The NMR spectrum of compound D reveals three types of chemically equivalent hydrogen atom in the ratio 6:6:1. Draw one possible structure for compound D.

*(CCEA June 2012)*

---

Before moving to the next section, check that you are able to:

- Write structural and condensed formulas for amines.
- Classify the structures of amines as primary, secondary or tertiary.

---

### Solubility

The molecular formulas of amines can be obtained by setting n = 1, 2, 3 … in the general formula, $C_nH_{2n+1}NH_2$. Small amines such as methylamine, $CH_3NH_2$ (n=1) and ethylamine, $CH_3CH_2NH_2$ (n=2)

are gases. Larger amines such as butan-1-amine, $CH_3CH_2CH_2CH_2NH_2$ are colourless liquids with a characteristic 'fishy' smell.

Smaller amines such as ethylamine are miscible in water as they can use the lone pair of electrons on the nitrogen atom to bond with hydrogen atoms on neighbouring water molecules as shown in Figure 1a. The molecules in primary and secondary amines ($RNH_2$ and $RNHR'$) can also hydrogen bond with each other as shown in Figure 1b. As the molecular mass of the amine (n) increases, the attraction between neighbouring molecules becomes increasingly dominated by van der Waals' attraction between the alkyl groups on neighbouring molecules. As a result amines with longer alkyl groups such as hexan-1-amine, $CH_3(CH_2)_5NH_2$ are miscible in nonpolar solvents such as hexane, but are only sparingly soluble in polar solvents such as water.

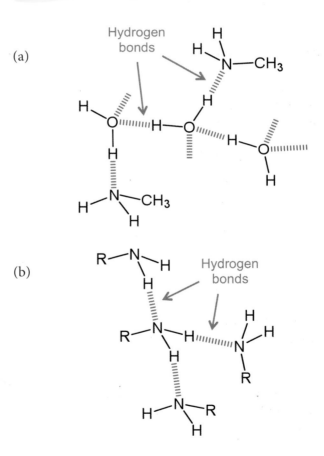

*Figure 1: Hydrogen bonding between (a) methylamine and water in aqueous methylamine, and (b) the molecules in a primary amine (RNH$_2$).*

## Exercise 5.9B

1. Explain, in terms of intermolecular forces, why amines become less soluble in water as their molecular mass increases.

2. Cadaverine, $H_2N(CH_2)_5NH_2$ is soluble in water.
   (a) Which part of the molecule aids solvation?
   (b) What type of bond is formed when cadaverine dissolves in water?

   *(CCEA June 2005)*

---

**Before moving to the next section, check that you are able to:**

- Recall the characteristic odour and physical states of amines.
- Use the general formula $C_nH_{2n+1}NH_2$ to generate molecular formulas for amines.
- Describe the nature of the attraction between molecules in smaller amines.
- Explain why amines become less soluble in polar solvents as they get larger.

---

### Boiling Point

The boiling points of primary amines ($RNH_2$) are significantly lower than the boiling points of the corresponding alcohols (ROH) as oxygen is more electronegative than nitrogen and forms stronger hydrogen bonds between molecules.

The ability of amines to form hydrogen bonds is determined by the amount of contact between the nitrogen atom on one molecule and the hydrogen atoms attached to the nitrogen atoms on neighbouring molecules. The compounds butan-1-amine and butan-2-amine are structural isomers of butanamine, $C_4H_9NH_2$. The boiling point of butan-2-amine is lower than the boiling point of butan-1-amine as it has a more branched structure which reduces the amount of contact between the amino (-NH₂) groups on neighbouring molecules.

butan-1-amine
$CH_3CH_2CH_2CH_2NH_2$

Boiling point 78 °C

butan-2-amine
$CH_3CH_2CH(NH_2)CH_3$

Boiling point 63 °C

The compounds diethylamine and methylisopropylamine are also structural isomers of butanamine, $C_4H_9NH_2$. Both are secondary amines and have lower boiling points than the primary isomers of butanamine as the nitrogen atom is bonded to two alkyl groups, making it less available to hydrogen bond with neighbouring molecules.

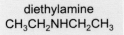

### Secondary Amines

diethylamine
$CH_3CH_2NHCH_2CH_3$

Boiling point 56 °C

methylisopropylamine
$CH_3CH(CH_3)NHCH_3$

Boiling point 52 °C

It therefore follows that the boiling point of dimethylethylamine, a tertiary amine and structural isomer of butanamine, is lower than the boiling points of the secondary isomers of butanamine as the nitrogen atom is bonded to three alkyl groups and is even less available to form hydrogen bonds with neighbouring molecules.

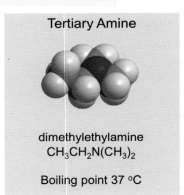

### Tertiary Amine

dimethylethylamine
$CH_3CH_2N(CH_3)_2$

Boiling point 37 °C

### Exercise 5.9C

1. The boiling point of methylamine, $CH_3NH_2$ is –6°C, the boiling point of ethylamine, $CH_3CH_2NH_2$ is 18 °C, and the boiling point of dimethylamine, $NH(CH_3)_2$ is 8 °C. Explain the relative boiling points in terms of intermolecular forces.

2. The boiling point of dimethylamine, $NH(CH_3)_2$ is 8°C and the boiling point of trimethylamine, $N(CH_3)_3$ is 2 °C. Explain the relative boiling points in terms of intermolecular forces.

3. The boiling point of aniline is 110 °C, the boiling point of phenylethylamine is 195 °C, and the boiling point of propylbenzene is 159 °C. Explain the relative boiling points in terms of intermolecular forces.

aniline   110°C

propylbenzene   159°C

phenylethylamine   195°C

*(Adapted from CCEA January 2010)*

---

**Before moving to the next section, check that you are able to:**

- Recall that the boiling point of an amine is lower than the boiling point of the corresponding alcohol.
- Explain how the ability of an amine to form hydrogen bonds is determined by its structure.
- Explain how the boiling point of an amine is determined by its structure.

---

## Naming

The systematic name for an amine consists of a prefix that describes the parent alkane, followed by the suffix *amine*. For example, propan-1-amine and propan-2-amine are structural isomers, and are named using the prefix *propan* as their structure is based on the three carbon chain in propane, $C_3H_8$. The suffix 1-amine or 2-amine is then added to locate the amino ($-NH_2$) group on the carbon chain. As in other organic compounds the carbon atoms are numbered in a way that produces the smallest number prefixes.

propan-1-amine
$CH_3CH_2CH_2NH_2$

propan-2-amine
$CH_3CH(NH_2)CH_3$

**Non-systematic** names constructed using the prefix *amino* to locate the $-NH_2$ group in the parent alkane can also be used. The carbon atoms are again numbered in a way that produces the lowest number prefixes.

1-aminopropane

2-aminopropane

The compounds N-methylethanamine and N,N-dimethylmethanamine are structural isomers of propan-1-amine and propan-2-amine. In the case of N-methylethanamine the prefix *ethan* is used as its structure is based on ethane, $CH_3CH_3$. The additional prefix *N-methyl* is then added to locate the methyl group bonded to the nitrogen atom. Similarly in N,N-dimethylmethanamine the prefix *methan* is used as the structure is based on methane, $CH_4$ and the additional prefix N,N-dimethyl is added to locate the two methyl groups bonded to the nitrogen atom.

N-methylethanamine
$CH_3CH_2NHCH_3$

N,N-dimethylmethanamine
$CH_3N(CH_3)_2$

**Non-systematic** names constructed by listing the alkyl groups attached to the nitrogen atom can also be used. The number prefixes *di*, *tri* ... describe how many of each group are present.

methylethylamine

trimethylamine

**Exercise 5.9D**

1. Write the systematic name for the following amines.

   $CH_3CH_2CH_2CH_2CH_2NH_2$
   (a)

   $CH_3CH_2CH(CH_3)NH_2$  $CH(CH_3)_2NH_2$
   (b)                     (c)

2. Write the systematic name for each of the following structural isomers of butanamine, $C_4H_9NH_2$.

   $CH_3CH_2CH_2NHCH_3$   $CH_3CH_2NHCH_2CH_3$
   (a)                    (b)

   $CH_3CH_2N(CH_3)_2$
   (c)

   As with other types of organic compound, prefixes can then be added to locate additional groups attached to carbon chain and the nitrogen atom. For example, in 3-bromo-2chloropropan-1-amine the prefixes *3-bromo* and *2-chloro* are used to locate a bromine atom on the third carbon and a chlorine atom on the second carbon in the chain. Here, again, the amino (-NH$_2$) group is described using the smallest possible number prefix, and the prefixes describing additional groups on the carbon chain are listed in alphabetical order.

   3-bromo-2-chloropropan-1-amine
   $CH_2BrCHClCH_2NH_2$

   4-chloro-2,2-diphenylbutan-1-amine
   $CH_2ClCH_2C(C_6H_5)_2CH_2NH_2$

   Similarly, in 4-chloro-2,2-diphenylbutan-1-amine, the carbon atoms are numbered from the carbon bonded to the amino (-NH$_2$) group. The prefixes *2,2-diphenyl* and *4-chloro* are then added to locate a pair of phenyl (-C$_6$H$_5$) groups on the second carbon, and a chlorine atom on the fourth carbon in the chain.

**Exercise 5.9E**

1. (a) Write the systematic name for the following amine. (b) Classify the amine as primary, secondary or tertiary.

2. (a) Write the systematic name for the following amine. (b) Classify the amine as primary, secondary or tertiary.

**Diamines**

The term **diamine** refers to *a compound containing two amino (-NH$_2$) groups*. The compound butane-1,4-diamine is a diamine and is named using the prefix *butane* as its structure is based on the four carbon chain in butane, $CH_3CH_2CH_2CH_3$. The suffix 1,4-diamine is then added to locate amino (-NH$_2$) groups on the first and fourth carbon atoms in the chain.

   butane-1,4-diamine
   $H_2NCH_2CH_2CH_2CH_2NH_2$

   Similarly the compound 2,2-dimethylpropane-1,3-diamine is a propane as its structure is based on the three carbon chain in propane. The suffix 1,3-diamine is used to locate amino (-NH$_2$) groups on first and third carbon atoms, and the prefix 2,2-dimethyl is added to locate two methyl groups on the second carbon atom.

$$H_2N-\overset{\underset{|}{H}}{C}-\overset{\overset{CH_3}{|}}{\underset{\underset{CH_3}{|}}{C}}-\overset{\underset{|}{H}}{C}-NH_2$$

2,2-dimethylpropane-1,3-diamine

$H_2NCH_2C(CH_3)_2CH_2NH_2$

## Exercise 5.9F

1. The compound 1,2-PDA is used as a building block in the synthesis of many different types of compounds including medicines, pesticides, and pigments. Write the systematic name for 1,2-PDA.

$$H_3C-\overset{\underset{\underset{NH_2}{|}}{H}}{C}-\overset{\underset{\underset{H}{|}}{H}}{C}-NH_2$$

1,2-PDA

2. The compound 2-methylcadaverine is used in the synthesis of low viscosity plastics and adhesives, and is a derivative of cadaverine, $H_2N(CH_2)_5NH_2$ a foul-smelling compound produced during the breakdown of amino acids in dead animal tissue. Write the systematic name for 2-methylcadaverine.

$$H_3C-\overset{\underset{\underset{NH_2}{|}}{H}}{C}-CH_2CH_2CH_2CH_2NH_2$$

2-methylcadaverine

3. The alcohol hydroxyputrescine is produced by *Pseudomonas* bacteria and is a derivative of the diamine putrescine, $H_2N(CH_2)_4NH_2$. Write the systematic name for (a) putrescine and (b) hydroxyputrescine.

$$H-\overset{\underset{\underset{NH_2}{|}}{H}}{C}-\overset{\overset{OH}{|}}{C}HCH_2CH_2NH_2$$

hydroxyputrescine

**Rules** for naming amines:
- The name consists of a prefix that is based on the name of the parent alkane followed by the suffix *amine*.

- The number of amino ($-NH_2$) groups is indicated by using the number prefixes *di, tri, tetra,* ... to generate suffixes such as *diamine* and *triamine*.
- The location of each amino group is then added to generate suffixes such as *2-amine* and *1,2-diamine* where the carbon atoms are numbered in a way that generates the lowest numbers.
- The location of additional functional groups is then described by adding additional prefixes in alphabetical order.

Before moving to the next section, check that you are able to:

- Deduce systematic names for amines, diamines and N-substituted amines with up to six carbon atoms in the longest carbon chain.

## Preparation

In this section we are learning to:

- Recall the conditions for the preparation of amines from the corresponding halogenoalkanes, nitriles and nitro compounds.
- Write equations for the preparation of amines, and deduce the structure of the product formed.

### Halogen Substitution

Primary amines ($RNH_2$) can be prepared by heating the corresponding halogenoalkane (RX) with a large excess of concentrated ammonia in a sealed tube to prevent ammonia vapour escaping from the reaction mixture.

$$\overset{\underset{|}{|}}{\underset{|}{C}}-X \;+\; NH_3 \;\longrightarrow\; \overset{\underset{|}{|}}{\underset{|}{C}}-NH_2 \;+\; HX$$

halogenoalkane          primary amine
(X = Cl, Br, I)          $RNH_2$

The reaction is an example of nucleophilic substitution in which ammonia acts as a nucleophile by attacking the electron deficient carbon atom ($C^{\delta+}$) forming the C-X bond. The acid formed by the reaction (HX) then reacts with a second molecule of ammonia to form the corresponding ammonium salt, $NH_4X$.

If ammonia is not in large excess a significant amount of the primary amine formed by the reaction will react further to form a mixture of secondary and tertiary amines.

*Forming a secondary amine:*

RX + RNH$_2$ → NHR$_2$ + HX

*Forming a tertiary amine:*

RX + NHR$_2$ → NR$_3$ + HX

### Worked Example 5.9i

1-bromobutane reacts with ammonia to form 1-aminobutane. (a) Name the mechanism. (b) Write an equation for the reaction. (c) Describe the mechanism for the reaction.

*(CCEA May 2008)*

### Solution

(a) Nucleophilic substitution

(b) CH$_3$CH$_2$CH$_2$CH$_2$Br + 2NH$_3$
   → CH$_3$CH$_2$CH$_2$CH$_2$NH$_2$ + NH$_4$Br

(c) Ammonia is attracted to the electron deficient carbon atom in the C-Br bond. The C-Br bond then begins to break as the nitrogen atom in ammonia uses its lone pair to form a co-ordinate bond with the electron deficient carbon atom in the C-Br bond.

### Exercise 5.9G

1. (a) Draw and name the major product formed when 1-bromopropane, CH$_3$CH$_2$CH$_2$Br is heated with concentrated ammonia in a sealed tube. (b) Draw and name the minor products formed in the reaction.

2. 2-bromobutane reacts with ammonia to form 2-aminobutane. (a) Write a balanced equation for the reaction of 2-bromobutane with an excess of ammonia. (b) Write the systematic name for 2-aminobutane.

---

Before moving to the next section, check that you are able to:

- Recall the conditions for the formation of an amine from the corresponding halogenoalkane and write an equation for the reaction.
- Describe the mechanism for the reaction.

---

### Reduction of Nitriles

Primary amines (RNH$_2$) can also be prepared by refluxing the corresponding nitrile (RCN) with a solution of lithal, LiAlH$_4$ dissolved in dry ether. Lithal is a strong reducing agent and can be represented by a single hydrogen atom, [H] when writing the equation for the reaction.

nitrile          primary amine
RCN              RCH$_2$NH$_2$

If a cyano (-CN) group is needed to form an amine it can be introduced by refluxing a halogenoalkane with a solution of sodium cyanide (NaCN) or potassium cyanide (KCN) dissolved in ethanol.

halogenoalkane                           nitrile
(X = Cl, Br, I)

Adding a cyano group to the molecule introduces an additional carbon atom into the molecule and is an effective way to increase the number of carbon atoms in a compound.

### Worked Example 5.9ii

Iodoethane may be converted to propylamine by reaction with:

A  ammonia

B  ammonia followed by lithal, LiAlH$_4$

C  potassium cyanide followed by ammonia

D  potassium cyanide followed by lithal, LiAlH$_4$

*(CCEA May 2009)*

### Strategy

- The reaction between iodoethane, CH$_3$CH$_2$I and cyanide ion could be used to form propanenitrile, CH$_3$CH$_2$CN.
- The propanenitrile formed could then be reduced with lithal to form propylamine, CH$_3$CH$_2$CH$_2$NH$_2$.

### Solution

Answer D

## Exercise 5.9H

1. 1-aminobutane can be prepared by the reduction of butanenitrile. (a) Name a suitable reducing agent. (b) Using [H] to represent the reducing agent write an equation for the reduction of butanenitrile.

*(CCEA June 2008)*

2. The following scheme can be used to increase the length of the carbon chain in a simple alcohol. State the name and formula for the reagents used in steps A and B.

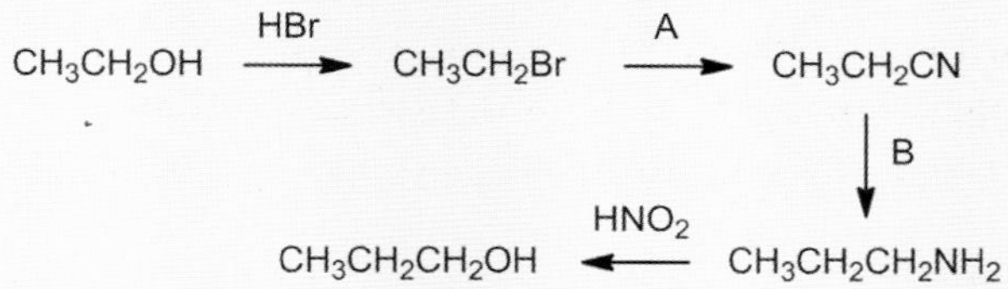

$$CH_3CH_2OH \xrightarrow{HBr} CH_3CH_2Br \xrightarrow{A} CH_3CH_2CN$$

$$\downarrow B$$

$$CH_3CH_2CH_2OH \xleftarrow{HNO_2} CH_3CH_2CH_2NH_2$$

*(Adapted from CCEA June 2006)*

3. Cadaverine, $H_2N(CH_2)_5NH_2$ is a poisonous syrupy liquid formed by the putrefaction of proteins. Cadaverine may be prepared in the laboratory by following Route 1 or Route 2. State the name and formulas for reagents A, B and C.

*Route 1*

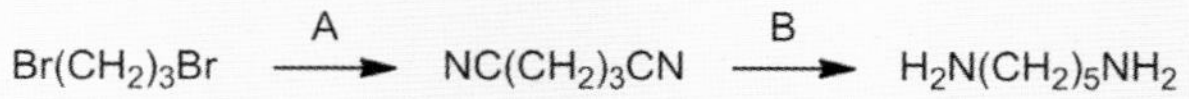

$$Br(CH_2)_3Br \xrightarrow{A} NC(CH_2)_3CN \xrightarrow{B} H_2N(CH_2)_5NH_2$$

*Route 2*

$$Br(CH_2)_5Br \xrightarrow{C} H_2N(CH_2)_5NH_2$$

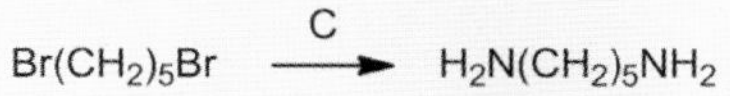

*(Adapted from CCEA June 2005)*

---

**Before moving to the next section, check that you are able to:**

- Recall the conditions for the formation of an amine from the corresponding nitrile and write an equation for the reaction.
- Explain how to prepare an amine from a halogenoalkane with one less carbon atom and write equations for the reactions.

---

### Reduction of Nitro Compounds

Aromatic amines such as phenylamine, $C_6H_5NH_2$ in which the amino (-NH$_2$) group is directly attached to a group with aromatic character, can be prepared by refluxing the corresponding nitro compound (RNO$_2$) with a mixture of tin and concentrated hydrochloric acid. The combination of tin and hydrochloric acid reduces the nitro (-NO$_2$) group to an amino (-NH$_2$) group, and can be represented by a hydrogen atom, [H] when writing an equation for the reaction.

nitrobenzene    phenylamine
$C_6H_5NO_2$     $C_6H_5NH_2$

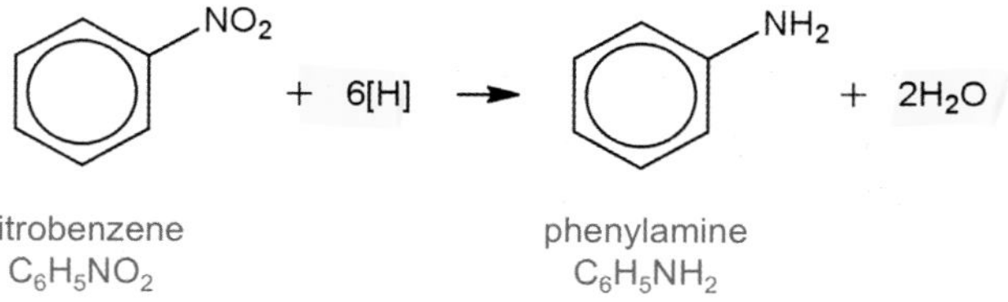

The reaction produces the amine (RNH$_2$) in the form of the corresponding ammonium salt (RNH$_4$Cl), which is then reacted with an excess of dilute alkali to liberate the amine from its salt. The amine is then obtained from the reaction mixture by distillation.

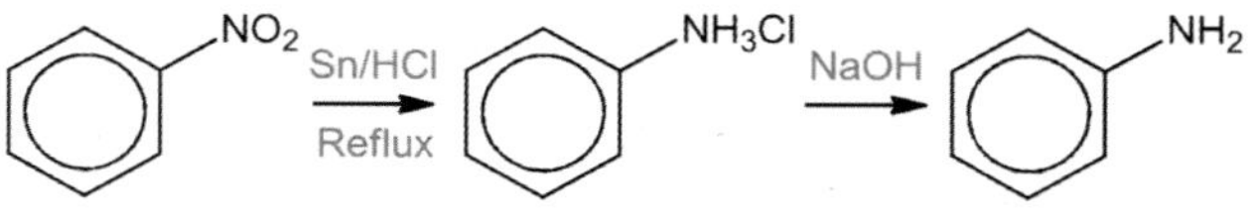

### Exercise 5.9I

1. Write the equation for the reduction of nitrobenzene to aniline using [H] to represent the reducing agent.

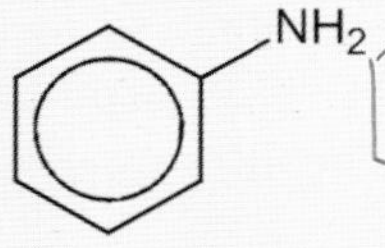

aniline

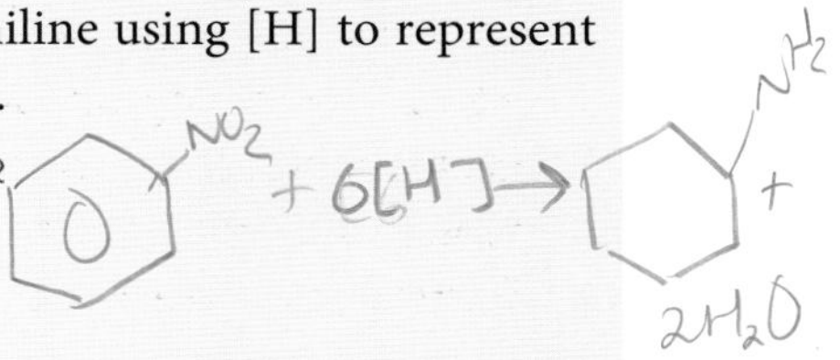

*(CCEA January 2010)*

2. (a) Name the reagents used to convert 4-nitrotoluene to toluidine. (b) A salt of toluidine is formed during the reaction. How can toluidine be liberated from this salt?

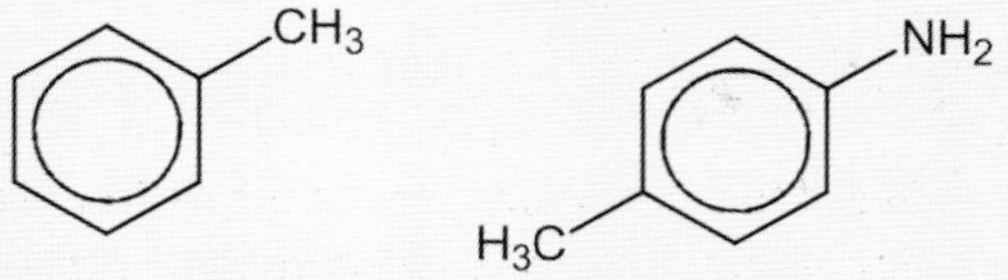

toluene          toluidine

*(CCEA June 2010)*

3. State the reagents and conditions for the reduction of nitrobenzene to phenylamine.

*(CCEA June 2009)*

Before moving to the next section, check that you are able to:

- Recall the conditions for the formation of an amine with aromatic character from the corresponding nitro compound and write an equation for the reaction.
- Recall how the amine is obtained from the reaction mixture.

## Reactions

### In this section we are learning to:

- Describe the formation of salts from amines.
- Account for the basic character of amines in terms of structure.
- Explain how the formation of an amide can be used to deduce the identity of the corresponding amine.

### Salt Formation

The reactions of amines are similar to the reactions of ammonia, $NH_3$. For example, ammonia is a Brønsted-Lowry base, and will accept a hydrogen ($H^+$) ion from an acid to form the corresponding ammonium salt.

*Forming ammonium salts:*
$NH_3 + HCl \rightarrow NH_4Cl$
$2NH_3 + H_2SO_4 \rightarrow (NH_4)_2SO_4$

Amines ($RNH_2$) are also Brønsted-Lowry bases and will accept a hydrogen ($H^+$) ion from an acid to form the corresponding **alkylammonium salt**.

*Forming alkylammonium salts:*
$RNH_2 + HCl \rightarrow RNH_3Cl$
$2RNH_2 + H_2SO_4 \rightarrow (RNH_3)_2SO_4$

Reacting an alkylammonium salt with an excess of dilute sodium hydroxide produces the corresponding amine. The amine is then obtained from the reaction mixture by distillation.

*Liberating an amine from its salt:*
$(RNH_3)_2SO_4 + 2NaOH \rightarrow 2RNH_2 + Na_2SO_4 + 2H_2O$

### Worked Example 5.9iii

Cadaverine, $H_2N(CH_2)_5NH_2$ reacts with hydrochloric acid to form a crystalline salt. (a) Write an equation for the reaction of cadaverine with an excess of hydrochloric acid. (b) Explain why the hydrochloride salt is a solid while cadaverine is a liquid.

*(CCEA June 2005)*

### Solution

(a) $H_2N(CH_2)_5NH_2 + 2HCl \rightarrow ClH_3N(CH_2)_5NH_3Cl$

(b) The ionic bonding between the alkyl-ammonium ions and chloride ions in the salt is stronger than the hydrogen bonding between molecules in cadaverine.

### Exercise 5.9J

1. Name the type of reaction represented by the following equation.

$CH_3CH_2CH_2Cl + NH_3 \rightarrow CH_3CH_2CH_2NH_3^+ + Cl^-$

*(Adapted from CCEA June 2004)*

2. Amphetamine is a liquid, and is administered as a drug in the form of amphetamine sulfate, a solid. (a) Amphetamine sulfate is formed by the reaction of amphetamine with sulfuric acid. Write an equation for this reaction. (b) Explain why amphetamine sulfate is a solid whereas amphetamine is a liquid. (c) Explain how amphetamine can be reformed from amphetamine sulfate, and obtained as a pure liquid.

amphetamine

*(CCEA June 2004)*

Before moving to the next section, check that you are able to:

- Deduce the structure of the salts formed by amines.
- Write equations for the formation of salts from amines.
- Explain, in terms of bonding, why the salts of amines are solids.

### Basic Character

The alkyl groups in an amine are electron donating, and increase the electron density around the nitrogen atom as illustrated by Figure 2. As the electron density around the nitrogen atom increases, the compound becomes a stronger base as the lone pair on the nitrogen atom is more able to form a

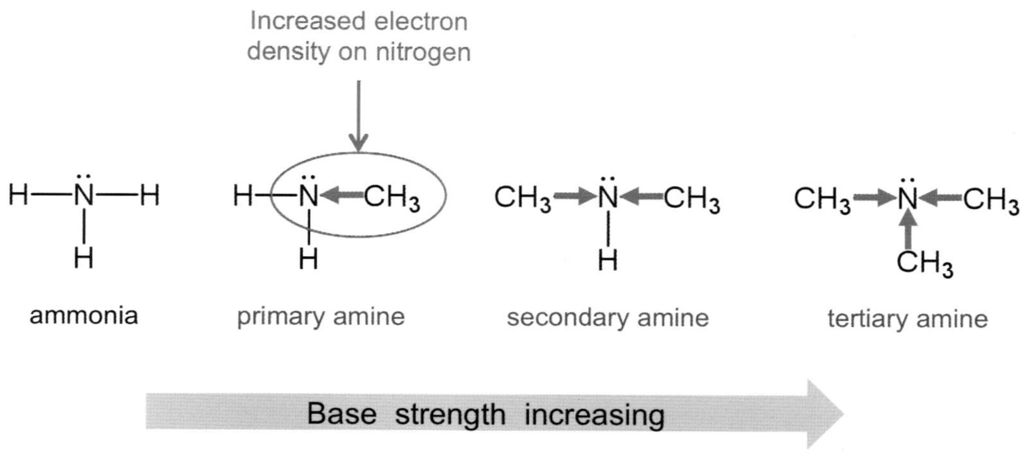

Figure 2: Amines become stronger bases as the number of alkyl groups attached to the nitrogen atom increases.

coordinate bond with a hydrogen ($H^+$) ion.

In contrast, phenylamine, $C_6H_5NH_2$ is a weaker base than ammonia as the lone pair on the nitrogen becomes delocalised, and is therefore less able to accept a hydrogen ($H^+$) ion than the lone pair in ammonia.

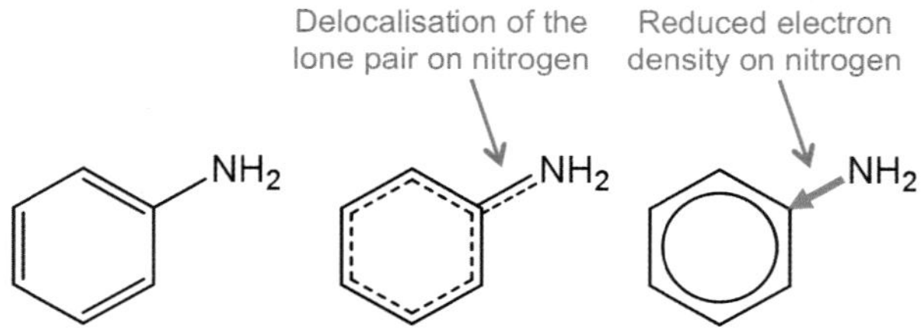

phenylamine
$C_6H_5NH_2$

- The lone pair on the nitrogen in aniline is delocalised making it a weaker base than ammonia.

**Solution**

(a) Phenylethylamine is a stronger base than ammonia, and ammonia is a stronger base than aniline.

(b)

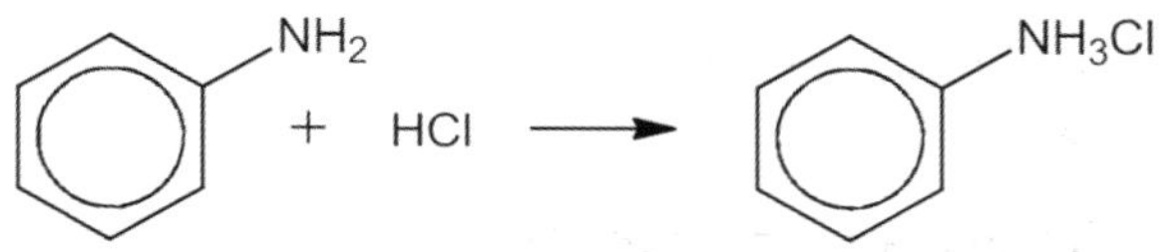

(c) Phenylethylamine is a primary amine as it has the structure $RNH_2$.

**Worked Example 5.9iv**

Aniline is basic and reacts with strong acids to form crystalline salts. (a) State the basicity of aniline compared to ammonia and phenylethylamine. (b) Write an equation for the reaction of aniline with hydrochloric acid. (c) Explain why phenylethylamine is a primary amine.

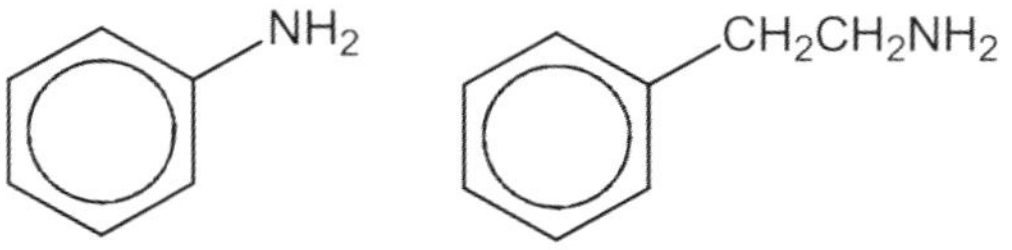

aniline                phenylethylamine

*(CCEA January 2010)*

**Strategy**

- Phenylethylamine is a primary amine ($RNH_2$) and is therefore a stronger base than ammonia.

**Exercise 5.9K**

1. Phenylamine (aniline) is basic and reacts with strong inorganic acids to form crystalline salts. (a) Compare the basicity of aniline to that of ammonia and 1-aminobutane. (b) Write the equation for the reaction of excess aniline with sulfuric acid.

   *(CCEA May 2003)*

2. Patients suffering from Parkinson's disease have a deficiency of the brain neurones that produce the neurotransmitter dopamine. (a) Explain why dopamine should be very soluble in water. (b) Compare the relative base strength of dopamine, ammonia and phenylamine. Explain your reasoning.

(c) Write an equation for the reaction of dopamine with hydrochloric acid.

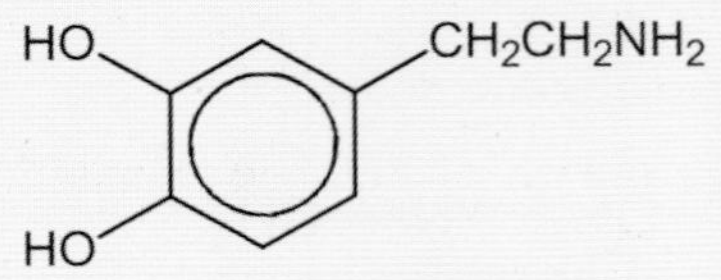

dopamine

*(CCEA May 2007)*

3. Which one of the following is the strongest base?

A $NH_3$      B $NH_4^+$

C $CH_3NH_2$      D $CH_3NH_3^+$

*(CCEA June 2008)*

4. Benzedrine is a stimulant. (a) Deduce whether benzedrine is a primary, secondary or tertiary amine. Explain your reasoning. (b) Explain its strength as a base by comparison with phenylamine.

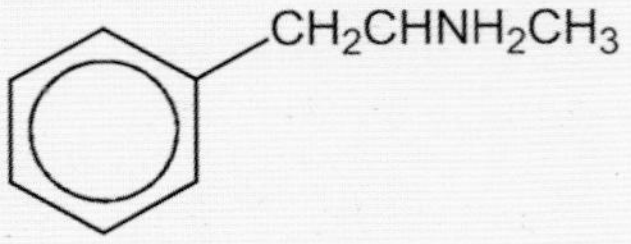

benzedrine

*(CCEA June 2013)*

---

Before moving to the next section, check that you are able to:

- Explain why amines are stronger bases than ammonia.
- Explain how delocalisation of the lone pair on nitrogen affects base strength.

---

### Formation of Amides

A primary amine ($RNH_2$) reacts vigorously with ethanoyl chloride ($CH_3COCl$) to form the corresponding **N-substituted amide** ($CH_3CONHR$).

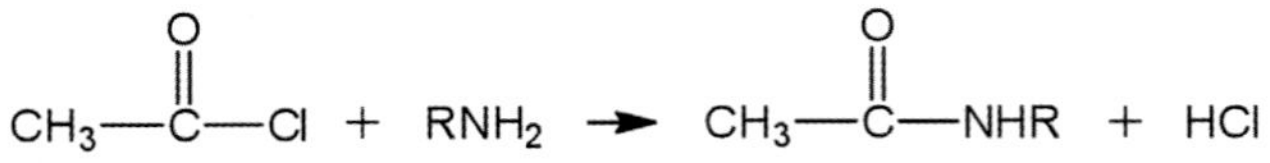

ethanoyl chloride
$CH_3COCl$

N-substituted amide
$CH_3CONHR$

Similarly, a secondary amine ($RNHR'$) reacts with ethanoyl chloride to form the corresponding N,N-disubstituted amide ($CH_3CONRR'$).

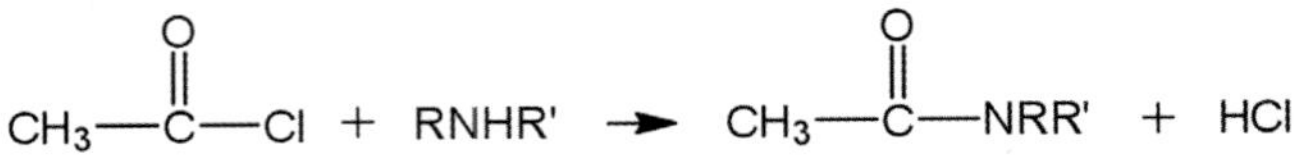

N,N-disubstituted amide
$CH_3CONRR'$

The reaction goes to completion and produces a single product that can be easily isolated from the reaction mixture as the only other product, HCl is a gas. As a result the reaction can be used to identify an unknown amine by determining the melting point of the amide formed in the reaction and comparing it to the melting points of known amides.

......

**Worked Example 5.9v**

(a) Write the equation for the reaction of an unknown amine, $RNH_2$ with ethanoyl chloride. (b) Describe how you would identify the unknown amine using the pure N-substituted amide. Include relevant practical steps.

*(CCEA May 2011)*

**Solution**

(a) $CH_3COCl + RNH_2 \rightarrow CH_3CONHR + HCl$

(b) React the unknown amine with ethanoyl chloride to form the corresponding N-substituted amide, then filter the mixture to obtain the crude product.

Recrystallise the crude product before slowly heating a small sample of the pure, dry product in a capillary tube sealed at one end.

The identity of the amine is confirmed by matching the range of temperature over which the sample melts to the melting points of known amides.

......

## Exercise 5.9L

1. The identity of phenylamine (aniline) may be confirmed using ethanoyl chloride. Outline, giving practical details, how this may be carried out.

*(Adapted from CCEA May 2003)*

2. 6.00 g of N-methylethanamide is produced when 4.24 g of methylamine reacts with an excess of ethanoyl chloride. Calculate the percent yield for the reaction.

$$CH_3COCl + CH_3NH_2 \rightarrow CH_3CONHCH_3 + HCl$$

*(CCEA June 2006)*

3. Putrescine, $H_2N(CH_2)_4NH_2$ reacts in a similar way to ethylamine. (a) Write an equation for the reaction of putrescine with excess ethanoyl chloride. (b) Explain how the purified product of the reaction could be used to identify putrescine.

*(Adapted from CCEA June 2015)*

4. The reaction of 4-hydroxyphenylamine to produce paracetamol is shown below. If the reaction has an 80% yield, calculate the amount of paracetamol produced when 10.9g of 4-hydroxyphenylamine reacts.

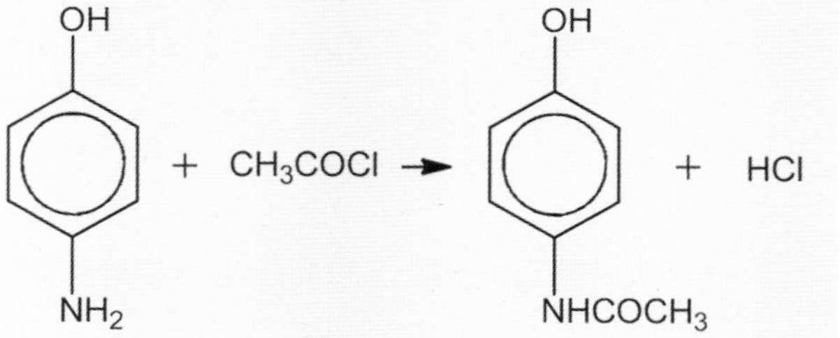

*(CCEA June 2012)*

---

**Before moving to the next section, check that you are able to:**

- Write an equation for the reaction of an amine with ethanoyl chloride to form the corresponding amide.

- Describe, giving practical details, how an amine can be identified by forming the corresponding amide.

## Azo Compounds

**In this section we are learning to:**

- Describe the reactions of amines with nitrous acid to form diazonium salts.
- Describe the use of coupling reactions to form azo compounds.

---

### Forming Diazonium Salts

Nitrous acid, $HNO_2$ is a weak acid and is formed by dissolving sodium nitrite, $NaNO_2$ in hydrochloric acid that is being kept below 10 °C in an ice bath.

$$NaNO_{2(s)} + HCl_{(aq)} \rightarrow HNO_{2(aq)} + NaCl_{(aq)}$$

The solution is kept in the ice bath until needed as the nitrous acid decomposes rapidly when the temperature of the solution rises.

Adding a primary amine ($RNH_2$) to a solution of nitrous acid produces a burst of colourless gas as the amine reacts to form the corresponding alcohol (ROH) and nitrogen gas.

$$RNH_2 + HNO_2 \rightarrow ROH + H_2O + N_2$$

The amine reacts with nitrous acid, $HNO_2$ to form the corresponding **diazonium ion** ($RN_2^+$) which is unstable, and quickly decomposes to form nitrogen gas, $N_2$.

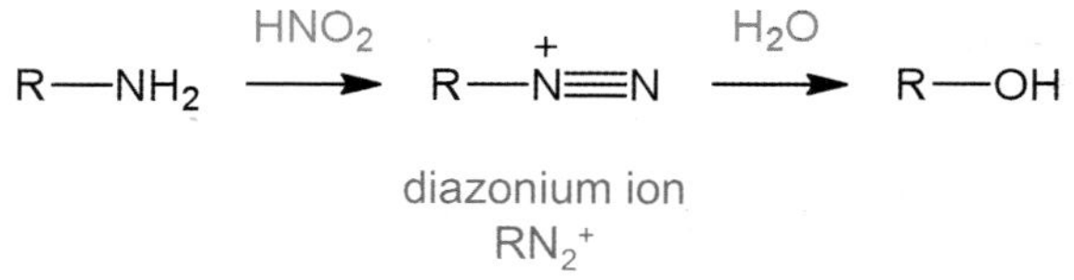

diazonium ion
$RN_2^+$

If the nitrogen atom is adjacent to a group with aromatic character, as in phenylamine, $C_6H_5NH_2$, the diazonium ion formed is more stable and will form a salt such as benzenediazonium chloride if the temperature of the solution is kept in the range 0-10 °C.  5°C

phenylamine
$C_6H_5NH_2$

benzenediazonium chloride
$C_6H_5N_2Cl$

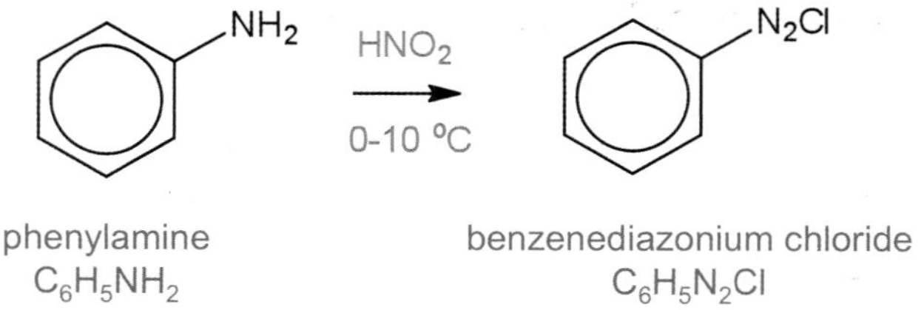

## Exercise 5.9M

1. The amino acid group is found in amines. Phenylamine is used in the synthesis of azo compounds. (a) Name the reagents used in steps A, B and C. (b) State the conditions used in step C and name the product.

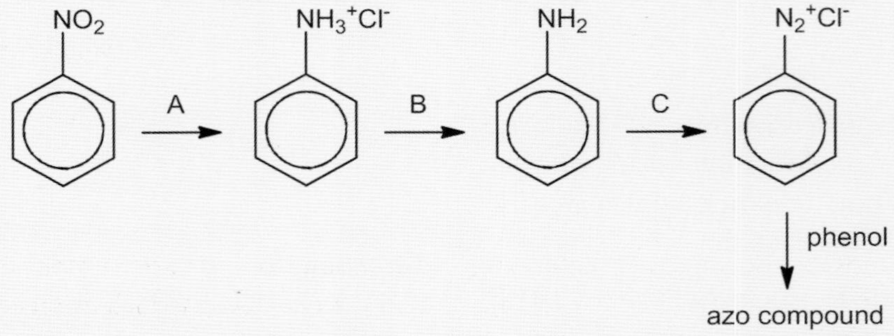

*(Adapted from CCEA June 2012)*

2. Phenylamine reacts with a mixture of sodium nitrite and hydrochloric acid to form benzene diazonium chloride. (a) Sodium nitrite and hydrochloric acid react to form nitrous acid *in-situ*. Write the equation for this reaction. (b) Draw the structure of the benzene diazonium ion. (c) Explain why ethylamine does not form a diazonium ion.

*(CCEA June 2009)*

3. Putrescine, $H_2N(CH_2)_4NH_2$ reacts in a similar way to ethylamine, $CH_3CH_2NH_2$. Write an equation for the reaction of putrescine with excess nitrous acid.

*(Adapted from CCEA June 2015)*

4. Toluidine is used in the manufacture of dyes. The first step in the process is to convert toluidine to its diazonium salt using nitrous acid. (a) Write an equation for the formation of nitrous acid from sodium nitrite. (b) What conditions are necessary for the reaction? (c) Write an equation for the conversion of toluidine to its diazonium ion.

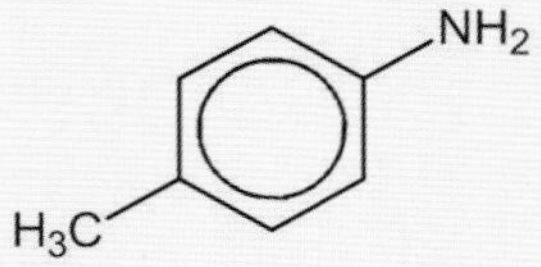

toluidine

*(CCEA June 2010)*

**Before moving to the next section, check that you are able to:**

- Recall the conditions for the reaction of an amine with nitrous acid.
- Describe the reaction of a primary amine with nitrous acid and write an equation for the reaction.
- Deduce the structures of diazonium salts formed by aromatic amines.

### Coupling Reactions

The relatively stable diazonium ion formed by an aromatic amine such as phenylamine, $C_6H_5NH_2$ will 'couple' with an aromatic compound such as phenol, $C_6H_5OH$ to form an **azo compound** with the structure R-N=N-R'. This type of reaction is known as a **coupling reaction** as it is *a reaction in which two benzene rings become linked by an azo (-N=N-) group*. The structure of the azo compound formed on adding phenol to a solution containing benzenediazonium chloride is shown in Figure 3.

Azo compounds are intensely coloured and are used as dyes, food colourings and indicators. The

Figure 3: The coupling reaction between benzenediazonium chloride and phenol to produce an azo compound.

indicator methyl orange, and the food colouring E110 are azo compounds.

methyl orange

Food colouring E110 'sunset yellow'

Altering the functional groups attached to the azo compound can make it better suited for its purpose by altering its colour, its solubility or its ability to bond with other compounds.

Azo compounds are intensely coloured as electrons are delocalised across the entire molecule, and can move to a higher energy level by absorbing visible light. The wavelengths of visible light that are not absorbed give the compound its colour.

azobenzene

delocalisation of electrons

In a smaller aromatic compound such as benzene, $C_6H_6$ the delocalised electrons are confined in a smaller space and more energy is needed to excite a delocalised electron to a higher energy level. As a result smaller aromatic compounds do not absorb visible light and are not coloured.

benzene
$C_6H_6$

delocalisation of electrons

### Worked Example 5.9vi

The dye Prontosil is prepared by the following reaction sequence. (a) Name the reagents required for step A. (b) State and explain the conditions necessary for the first step. (c) Suggest a structure for the dye Prontosil which is formed by a coupling reaction. (d) Explain why Prontosil is coloured.

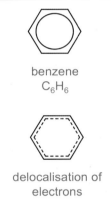

(CCEA June 2011)

## Strategy

- Nitrous acid, $HNO_2$ is needed to form the diazonium salt in step A.
- The diazonium ion formed in step A may replace any one of the hydrogen atoms when it couples with 1,3-diaminobenzene to form prontosil.

## Solution

(a) Sodium nitrite and hydrochloric acid.

(b) The temperature must be kept in the range 0–10 °C during the reaction.

(c)

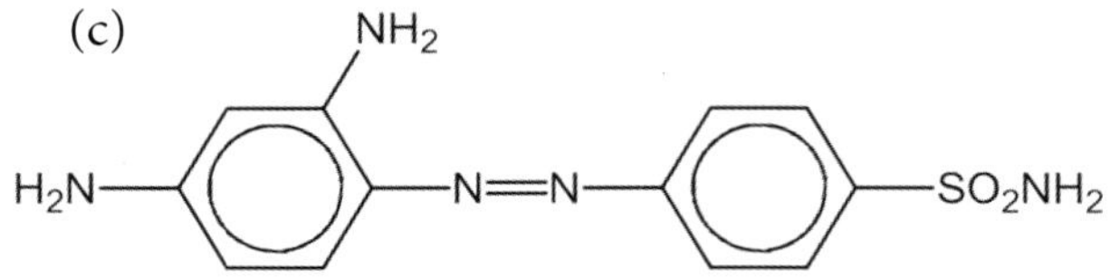

(d) Electrons are delocalised across the entire molecule. As a result the delocalised electrons can be excited to a higher energy level by absorbing visible light. The wavelengths of visible light that are not absorbed give the dye its colour.

## Exercise 5.9N

1. Benzenediazonium chloride forms a yellow dye when coupled with dimethylaminobenzene. Write the equation for the reaction and circle the azo group.

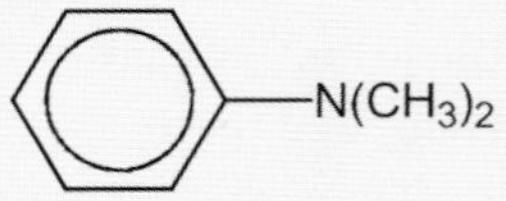

dimethylaminobenzene

*(CCEA June 2015)*

2. (a) Anthranilic acid is diazotised to form a diazonium ion. State the condition necessary for this reaction. (b) Suggest the structure of the product when the diazotised anthranilic acid is coupled with phenol.

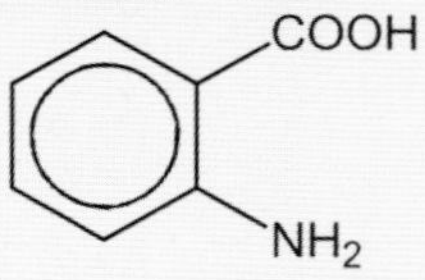

anthranilic acid

*(CCEA June 2014)*

3. Chrysoidine was the first commercially useful azo dye. It was produced by the reaction of 1,3,5-triaminobenzene and benzene diazonium chloride. (a) Draw the structure of chrysoidine, circling the azo group. (b) Explain why chrysoidine is coloured. (c) Suggest why adding and altering the functional groups attached to the azo compound may be useful in the dyestuffs industry.

*(Adapted from CCEA June 2006)*

4. The benzenediazonium ion, $C_6H_5N_2^+$ forms a scarlet precipitate of azo-2-naphthol when added to an alkaline solution of 2-naphthol. (a) Name the type of reaction that has occurred. (b) Deduce the molecular formula of azo-2-naphthol. (c) Explain, in terms of electron transitions, why azo dyes are coloured.

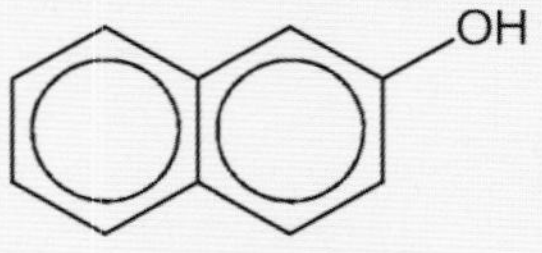

2-naphthol

*(CCEA May 2009)*

5. Para red is a dye that can be detected in cayenne pepper sourced from Uzbekistan. The scheme used to prepare the dye is shown below. (a) Name the reagents used in step A. (b) Explain why a low temperature must be used in step A. (c) Deduce a possible structure for para red. (d) Explain why para red is coloured.

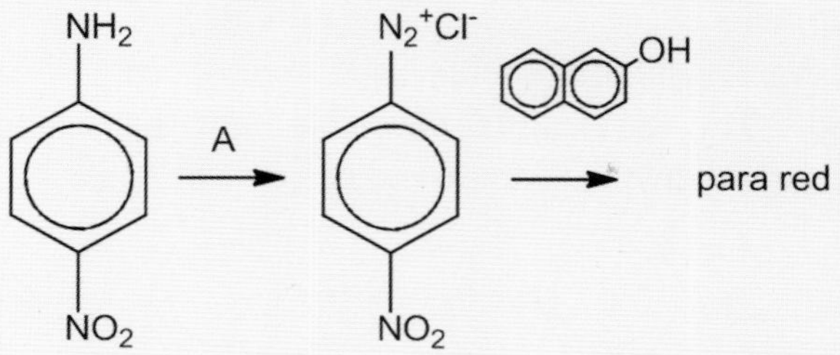

para red

*(Adapted from CCEA June 2007)*

Before moving to the next section, check that you are able to:

- Deduce the structure of the azo compound formed when a diazonium salt is coupled with an aromatic compound.
- Recall the uses of azo compounds, and suggest how the functional groups attached to an azo compound determine the properties of the compound.
- Explain why azo compounds are coloured.

# 5.10 Organic Nitrogen Chemistry: Amides

## CONNECTIONS

- The amide N,N-dimethylformamide (DMF) is used widely in industry as a solvent as it is miscible with water and many organic liquids.
- The 1945 Nobel Prize in Medicine was awarded for the discovery of penicillin; the first antibiotic belonging to a class of cyclic amides known as β-lactams.

## Structure and Properties  $R\,CONH_2$

**In this section we are learning to:**

- Account for the properties of amides in terms of their structure, and the nature of the bonding between amide molecules.

**Amides** are *compounds with the general formula, $RCONH_2$ where R represents an alkyl group*.

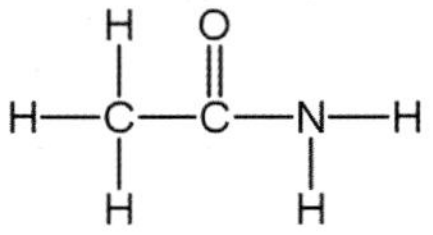

ethanamide
$CH_3CONH_2$

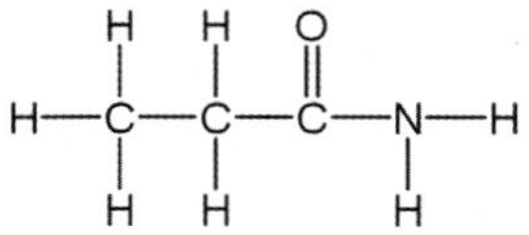

propanamide
$CH_3CH_2CONH_2$

The properties of amides are due to the presence of an **amide linkage** in the molecule.

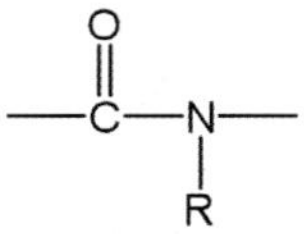

amide linkage
(-CONR-)

An amide can use the oxygen atom in the amide linkage, and any hydrogen atoms attached to the nitrogen atom, to hydrogen bond with neighbouring molecules as shown in Figure 1a. As a result, even smaller amides such as ethanamide and propanamide are crystalline solids, and are very soluble in water as they can effectively hydrogen bond with water as shown in Figure 1b.

### Exercise 5.10A

1. Propanamide, $CH_3CH_2CONH_2$ is a colourless crystalline solid. (a) Explain, in terms of structure, why propanamide is considered an amide. (b) Write the general formula for an amide. (c) Use the general formula to obtain the molecular formula for the amide with the lowest molecular mass.

2. Chlorobutane, $C_4H_9Cl$ and butanamide, $CH_3CH_2CH_2CONH_2$ have similar molar masses. With reference to the type of forces between molecules, explain why butanamide is a crystalline solid while chlorobutane is a liquid.

3. Butanamide, $CH_3CH_2CH_2CONH_2$ is a crystalline solid. Explain, in terms of the interactions between molecules, why butanamide is soluble in water.

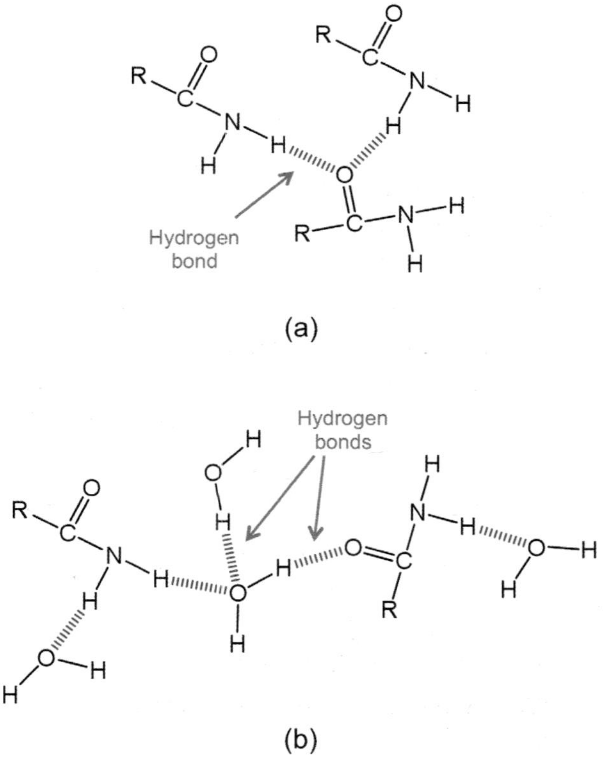

(a)

(b)

*Figure 1: Hydrogen bonding between (a) the molecules in ethanamide, and (b) the molecules in an aqueous solution of ethanamide.*

An amide is a base as it can use the lone pair of electrons on the nitrogen atom to form a coordinate bond with a hydrogen ($H^+$) ion. As in phenylamine,

$C_6H_5NH_2$ the lone pair of electrons on the nitrogen atom is delocalised, and is therefore less able to form a coordinate bond than the lone pair on the nitrogen atom in ammonia, $NH_3$.

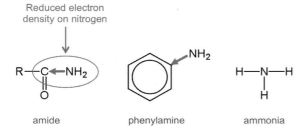

The extent of the delocalisation is such that the lone pair is less available for coordinate bonding than the lone pair in phenylamine and, as a result, amides are weaker bases than phenylamine.

### Exercise 5.10B

1. Which one of the following lists the compounds in order of increasing base strength?

   A  ethanamide, methylamine, phenylamine

   B  ethanamide, phenylamine, methylamine

   C  methylamine, ethanamide, phenylamine

   D  phenylamine, ethanamide, methylamine

   *(CCEA May 2012)*

2. Explain why propanamide, $CH_3CH_2CONH_2$ is a weaker base than ammonia.

---

Before moving to the next section, check that you are able to:

- Recall the general formula $RCONH_2$.
- Write structural and condensed formulas for amides.
- Account for the high melting points of amides, and the high solubility of smaller amides in water, in terms of their ability to form hydrogen bonds.
- Explain, in terms of delocalisation, why amides are weaker bases than ammonia and recall that amides are weaker bases than phenylamine.

---

## Naming Amides

**In this section we are learning to:**

- Use systematic (IUPAC) rules to name amides.

---

The systematic name for an amide consists of a prefix that describes the parent alkane, followed by the suffix *amide*. For example, the amide butanamide is named using the prefix *butan* as its structure is based on butane.

butanamide
$CH_3CH_2CH_2CONH_2$

The compounds N-methylpropanamide and 2-methylpropanamide are structural isomers of butanamide. Both are named using the prefix *propan* as their structure is based on propane. In N-methylpropanamide the additional prefix *N-methyl* is added to locate a methyl (-$CH_3$) group bonded to the nitrogen atom in the amide linkage. Similarly, in 2-methylpropanamide, the prefix *2-methyl* is used to locate a methyl group on the second carbon atom in the chain that begins with the amide linkage (-CONR-).

N-methylpropanamide
$CH_3CH_2CONHCH_3$

2-methylpropanamide
$CH_3CH(CH_3)CONH_2$

Additional prefixes can then be added to locate groups attached to both the carbon chain, and the nitrogen atom in the amide linkage. In 2-amino-N-ethyl-3-methylpentanamide the prefix *2-amino* is used to locate an amino (-$NH_2$) group on the second carbon from the end of the chain that begins with the amide linkage.

2-amino-N-ethyl-3-methylpentanamide
$CH_3CH_2CH(CH_3)CH(NH_2)CONHCH_2CH_3$

The prefixes *3-methyl* and *N-ethyl* are then added to locate a methyl (-$CH_3$) group on the third carbon atom in the chain, and an ethyl (-$CH_2CH_3$) group bonded to the nitrogen atom in the amide linkage. As with other types of compound the prefixes are listed in alphabetical order.

## Exercise 5.10C

1. (a) Name the amides A and B. (b) Explain, in terms of structure, why both compounds are named as amides.

A           B

2. Draw the structures of 3-chloro-N-methyl-propanamide and N,N-dimethylethanamide.

3. Name the following compound as an amide.

4. Draw the structures of the compounds 2-ethyl-3-methylpentanamide and 4-amino-N-phenyl-butanamide.

---

Before moving to the next section, check that you are able to:

- Deduce systematic names for amides with up to six carbon atoms in the longest carbon chain.

## Preparation

In this section we are learning to:

- Describe the preparation of amides from carboxylic acids and acyl chlorides.

---

An amide ($RCONH_2$) can be prepared from the corresponding carboxylic acid ($RCOOH$) by adding solid ammonium carbonate, $(NH_4)_2CO_3$ to an excess of the acid to form the ammonium salt of the acid, $RCOONH_4$.

$$2RCOOH + (NH_4)_2CO_3 \rightarrow 2RCOONH_4 + CO_2 + H_2O$$

An excess of concentrated acid is used to reduce the extent to which the ammonium salt dissociates to reform the acid.

$$RCOONH_4 \leftrightharpoons RCOOH + NH_3$$

When the mixture containing the ammonium salt ($RCOONH_4$) is refluxed, the ammonium salt decomposes to form the corresponding amide ($RCONH_2$).

$$RCOONH_4 \rightarrow RCONH_2 + H_2O$$

The amide is then obtained in solid form by distilling the reaction mixture to remove excess acid.

## Exercise 5.10D

1. Ethanoic acid can be converted to ethanamide by thermal decomposition of its ammonium salt. (a) Write the equation for the reaction of ethanoic acid with ammonia. (b) Write the equation for the thermal decomposition.

*(CCEA May 2011)*

2. Succinic acid reacts with excess ammonia to form a diammonium salt which, when heated, is dehydrated to form a diamide. Draw the flow scheme for the formation of the diamide from succinic acid.

*(Adapted from CCEA June 2014)*

An amide ($RCONH_2$) can also be prepared by slowly adding the corresponding acyl chloride ($RCOCl$) to concentrated ammonia solution. The reaction is very vigorous and produces a colourless solution containing the amide. The reaction also produces hydrogen chloride that reacts with the vapour from excess ammonia to form a white smoke of solid ammonium chloride, $NH_4Cl$.

*Formation of the amide:*
$$RCOCl + NH_3 \rightarrow RCONH_2 + HCl$$

*Formation of ammonium chloride:*
$$HCl + NH_3 \rightarrow NH_4Cl$$

## Exercise 5.10E

1. Polyacrylamide gels made from acrylamide are widely used in water treatment and other industries such as paper making to separate solid particles from liquid mixtures. (a) Write an equation for the formation of acrylamide from the corresponding acyl chloride. (b) Draw the structure of the acyl chloride.

$$H-\overset{\overset{\displaystyle H}{|}}{C}=\overset{\overset{\displaystyle H}{|}}{C}-\overset{\overset{\displaystyle |}{\underset{\underset{\displaystyle O}{||}}{C}}}-NH_2 \quad \text{acrylamide}$$

2. Lidocaine is a local anaesthetic that is widely used to manage pain during dental surgery and other minor surgical procedures. (a) Explain, in terms of structure, why lidocaine is considered an amide. (b) Write an equation for the formation of lidocaine from an acyl chloride, clearly showing the structure of the acyl chloride.

$$CH_3 \quad H \\ \text{(structure of lidocaine with } N(CH_2CH_3)_2) \quad \text{lidocaine} \\ CH_3$$

Before moving to the next section, check that you are able to:

- Explain, with the aid of equations, the preparation of amides from carboxylic acids and acyl chlorides.
- Deduce the structure of the amide formed, or the reactants needed to form a particular amide.

## Reactions

**In this section we are learning to:**

- Describe the hydrolysis and dehydration of amides.

### Hydrolysis

Amides ($RCONH_2$) can be converted to the corresponding carboxylic acid ($RCOOH$) by refluxing the amide with dilute hydrochloric acid. The reaction is an example of acid catalysed hydrolysis as the hydrogen ($H^+$) ions in the acid lower the activation energy by reacting with the amide to form

an intermediate, and are regenerated in the form of a salt as the reaction proceeds.

ACID CATALYSED

$$RCONH_2 + H_2O + HCl \rightarrow RCOOH + NH_4Cl$$

Refluxing an amide ($RCONH_2$) with dilute sodium hydroxide produces a solution containing the sodium salt of the corresponding carboxylic acid ($RCOONa$).

ALKALI CATALYSED

$$RCONH_2 + NaOH \rightarrow RCOONa + NH_3$$

The carboxylic acid can then be liberated from its salt by adding an excess of dilute hydrochloric acid to the reaction mixture.

$$RCOONa + HCl \rightarrow RCOOH + NaCl$$

The reaction is an example of base-induced hydrolysis. The hydroxide ions from the dilute alkali increase the rate of the reaction by acting as a nucleophile and attacking the electron deficient carbon atom in the amide linkage.

### Worked Example 5.10i

Explain how the reaction between an amide and dilute sodium hydroxide can be used to test for the presence of an amide.

### Solution

Heating a mixture of an amide and dilute sodium hydroxide produces ammonia gas. The ammonia vapour produces a colour change from red to blue when a piece of damp red litmus paper is held over the mixture as it is heated. The presence of ammonia vapour can then be confirmed by observing a white smoke of solid ammonium chloride when it contacts the fumes from a glass rod dipped in concentrated hydrochloric acid.

### Dehydration

Distilling a mixture of an amide ($RCONH_2$) and phosphorus(V) oxide, $P_4O_{10}$ produces the corresponding nitrile ($RCN$). The reaction is described as **dehydration** as the nitrile is formed by removing a molecule of water from the amide.

$$RCONH_2 \rightarrow RCN + H_2O$$

**Exercise 5.10F**

1. Which one of the following is produced when $CH_3CONHCH_3$ is refluxed with excess dilute hydrochloric acid?

   A  $CH_3COOH$ and $CH_3NH_2$
   B  $CH_3COO^-$ and $CH_3NH_3^+$
   C  $CH_3COOH$ and $CH_3NH_3^+$
   D  $CH_3COO^-$ and $CH_3NH_2$

   *(CCEA June 2015)*

2. State the formula of the organic product formed when ethanamide is hydrolysed by reaction with (a) hydrochloric acid, and (b) sodium hydroxide.

   *(CCEA May 2011)*

3. (a) Write the equation for the reaction of propanamide with aqueous sodium hydroxide.
   (b) An amide linkage is hydrolysed slowly by water, rapidly by acids and much more rapidly by alkalis. Suggest, with reference to the species present in solution, why the reaction with dilute alkali is much faster than the reaction with dilute acid.

   *(Adapted from CCEA June 2013)*

4. Recent research has revealed that a single vanadium(V) oxide particle on the surface of an inert solid functions as a highly efficient catalyst for the dehydration of amides. (a) Write an equation for the dehydration of *ortho*-toluamide, clearly showing all of the bonds formed in the product. (b) State the reagent and conditions used for the reaction.

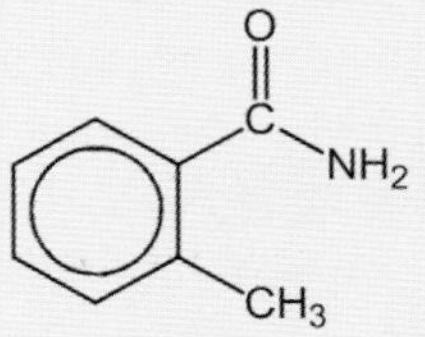

   *ortho*-toluamide

5. Which one of the following statements about propanamide is not correct?

   A  It produces an M+1 peak at 73 in its mass spectrum.
   B  It can be dehydrated to form propane-nitrile.
   C  It has the molecular formula $C_3H_7NO$.
   D  It is a weaker base than ammonia.

   *(CCEA May 2012)*

---

Before moving to the next section, check that you are able to:

- Write equations for the hydrolysis of amides using dilute acid and dilute alkali, and recall the conditions for the reactions.
- Describe how to test for the presence of an amide.
- Recall the reagent and method used for the dehydration of an amide, and deduce the structure of the product formed.

# 5.11 Amino Acids

## Structure and Properties

**In this section we are learning to:**

• Recognise the structure of amino acids and account for the physical properties of amino acids in terms of their structure.

Amino acids are the building blocks of proteins. Each of the 20 amino acids commonly found in proteins are α-amino acids. The term **α-amino acid** is used to describe *a carboxylic acid with an amino (-NH₂) group bonded to the carbon atom adjacent to the carboxyl (-COOH) group.*

General structure of an α-amino acid

$$R—\overset{\displaystyle H}{\underset{\displaystyle NH_2}{C}}—COOH$$

α-carbon atom

The α-amino acids in proteins differ only in the nature of the side-chain (R) attached to the α-carbon atom. The simplest amino acids found in proteins are glycine (R = H) and alanine (R = CH₃).

Glycine (R = H)
$CH_2(NH_2)COOH$

Alanine (R = CH₃)
$CH_3CH(NH_2)COOH$

With the exception of glycine, the α-carbon in an α-amino acid is an asymmetric centre. As a result all α-amino acids, with the exception of glycine, can form optical isomers.

### Worked Example 5.11i

The amino acid lysine has the formula, $H_2N(CH_2)_4CH(NH_2)COOH$. Lysine is optically active. (a) Explain the term *optically active*. (b) Draw the 3D structure of lysine labelling the asymmetric carbon with an asterisk (*).

*(CCEA May 2011)*

*Solution*

(a) A substance is optically active if it rotates the plane of plane polarised light.

(b)

$$HOOC\cdots\overset{\displaystyle H}{\underset{\displaystyle H_2N}{C}}{}^*\!CH_2(CH_2)_3NH_2$$

### Exercise 5.11A

1. Serine, $CH_2(OH)CH(NH_2)COOH$ is an α-amino acid. (a) Explain, in terms of structure, why serine is an α-amino acid. (b) Draw the molecular structure of serine, clearly showing the arrangement of the groups about the asymmetric carbon atom.

2. Anthranilic acid could be described as an amino acid but is not part of any protein. Suggest an explanation for this contradictory statement.

anthranilic acid

*(CCEA June 2014)*

In solid glycine the molecules exist in the form of zwitterions. A **zwitterion** is formed when a hydrogen (H⁺) ion is transferred from the carboxyl group of the amino acid to the amino group to form *a dipolar ion that contains positively and negatively charged groups, and has an overall charge of zero.*

Structure of the zwitterion formed by glycine

$$H-\underset{\underset{\overset{+}{N}H_3}{|}}{\overset{\overset{H}{|}}{C}}-COO^-$$

Amino acids have high melting points as the zwitterions are held together by strong attractive forces between oppositely charged functional groups on neighbouring ions.

Glycine and other amino acids are very soluble in water and other polar solvents as the zwitterions form ion-dipole bonds with surrounding solvent molecules when the solid dissolves as shown in Figure 1. In contrast, amino acids with large nonpolar side-chains such as phenylalanine and tryptophan are much less soluble in water as van der Waals attraction accounts for a greater proportion of the attractive forces between molecules.

phenylalanine

tryptophan

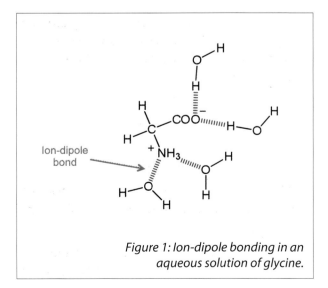

Figure 1: Ion-dipole bonding in an aqueous solution of glycine.

## Exercise 5.11B

1. Research has shown that some organisms use an amino acid called selenocysteine. (a) Explain why selenocysteine, like other amino acids, has a high melting point. (b) Is selenocysteine optically active? Explain your reasoning.

$$H_2N-\underset{\underset{CH_2SeH}{|}}{\overset{\overset{H}{|}}{C}}-COOH$$

selenocysteine

*(CCEA June 2006)*

2. Draw the zwitterion formed by the amino acid asparagine.

$$H_2N-\underset{\underset{CH_2CONH_2}{|}}{\overset{\overset{H}{|}}{C}}-COOH$$

asparagine

*(CCEA June 2010)*

3. Valine, $CH_3CH(CH_3)CH(NH_2)COOH$ is an amino acid. (a) Amino acids form zwitterions. What is a *zwitterion*? (b) Draw the zwitterion formed by valine. (c) Valine is optically active. Draw the 3D representations of the optical isomers.

*(CCEA June 2015)*

4. Monosodium glutamate (MSG) is an additive used in many spicy foods. It is the sodium salt of glutamic acid. (a) Explain why MSG is very soluble in water. (b) Glutamic acid is optically active. Draw the structures of the optical isomers of glutamic acid. (c) Explain why glutamic acid has a high melting point.

$$H_2N-\underset{\underset{CH_2CH_2COOH}{|}}{\overset{\overset{H}{|}}{C}}-COONa$$

monosodium glutamate

*(CCEA May 2003)*

5. Which one of the following statements about glycine is not correct?

   A It has a relatively high melting point
   B It contains 32% carbon by mass
   C It exists as optical isomers
   D It is soluble in water

*(CCEA May 2012)*

Before moving to the next section, check that you are able to:

- Recall the structures of glycine and alanine and explain why compounds such as glycine and alanine are $\alpha$-amino acids.
- Explain why $\alpha$-amino acids are optically active and draw the optical isomers of $\alpha$-amino acids.
- Account for the high melting point and solubility of amino acids in water in terms of the ability of amino acids to form zwitterions.

## Reactions

### In this section we are learning to:

- Describe the reaction of amino acids with acids, alkalis, sodium carbonate, nitrous acid and aqueous copper(II) ions.

### Reaction with Acids and Alkalis

When an amino acid is dissolved in a strongly acidic solution each amino ($-NH_2$) group in the molecule forms a coordinate bond with a hydrogen ($H^+$) ion from the solution to form an alkylammonium ($-NH_3^+$) salt.

$\alpha$-amino acid          alkylammonium salt

In contrast, if an amino acid is dissolved in a strong alkali each carboxyl ($-COOH$) group reacts with a hydroxide ion from the solution to form a carboxylate ($-COO^-$) salt.

$\alpha$-amino acid          carboxylate salt

At an intermediate pH, known as the **isoelectric point**, the amino acid molecules exist as zwitterions. The pH at which an amino acid forms zwitterions depends on the nature of the side-chain (R) and is therefore different for every amino acid.

Solution pH increasing

alkylammonium cation          zwitterion          carboxylate anion

Neutral charge

### Worked Example 5.11ii

Amino acids such as lysine contain more than one amino ($-NH_2$) group. Draw the structure of lysine when it is dissolved in an excess of a strong acid.

lysine

*(Adapted from CCEA June 2012)*

### Strategy

- In an excess of strong acid each amino ($-NH_2$) group will accept a hydrogen ion to form an $-NH_3^+$ group.

### Solution

### Exercise 5.11C

1. Write the formula for the organic ion that is formed when alanine is dissolved in an acidic solution.

2. (a) Explain, in terms of structure, why aspartic acid is an $\alpha$-amino acid. (b) Draw the structure of aspartic acid when it is dissolved in an excess of a strong alkali.

aspartic acid

3. Which one of the following describes the nature of glycine in a solution with a pH of 1?

   A  anions                B  cations
   C  dipolar ions          D  neutral molecules

*(CCEA May 2002)*

## Reaction with Sodium Carbonate

When solid sodium carbonate is added to an aqueous solution containing an amino acid, the solid reacts to form a colourless solution of the corresponding carboxylate salt and carbon dioxide gas is evolved.

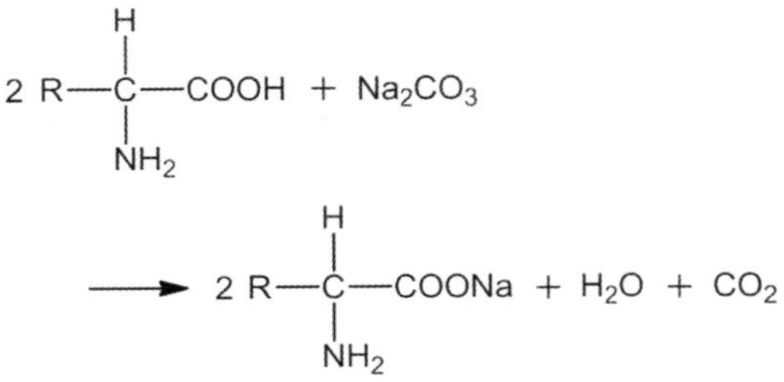

$$2\ R\!-\!\underset{\underset{NH_2}{|}}{\overset{\overset{H}{|}}{C}}\!-\!COOH\ +\ Na_2CO_3$$

$$\longrightarrow\ 2\ R\!-\!\underset{\underset{NH_2}{|}}{\overset{\overset{H}{|}}{C}}\!-\!COONa\ +\ H_2O\ +\ CO_2$$

*Observations: Fizzing, solid disappears, colourless solution formed.*

## Reaction with Nitrous Acid

When a solution containing nitrous acid is added to an aqueous solution of an amino acid the amino (-$NH_2$) group reacts to form the corresponding diazonium (-$N_2^+$) ion. The diazonium ion is unstable and decomposes to form the corresponding alcohol (-OH) and nitrogen gas.

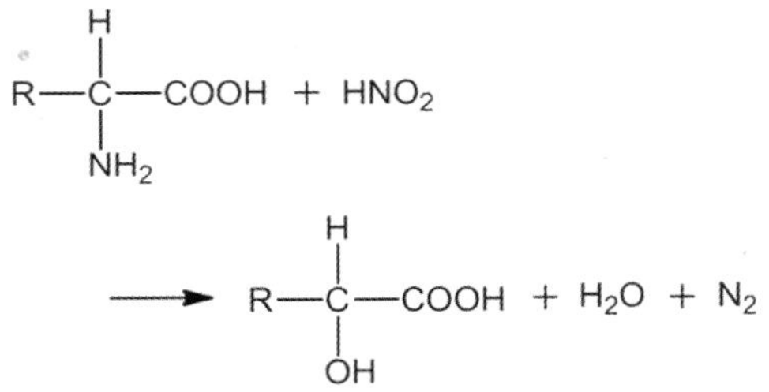

$$R\!-\!\underset{\underset{NH_2}{|}}{\overset{\overset{H}{|}}{C}}\!-\!COOH\ +\ HNO_2$$

$$\longrightarrow\ R\!-\!\underset{\underset{OH}{|}}{\overset{\overset{H}{|}}{C}}\!-\!COOH\ +\ H_2O\ +\ N_2$$

*Observations: Bubbles of colourless gas, colourless solution formed.*

## Complex Formation with Copper(II) Ions

Adding aqueous copper(II) sulfate to an aqueous solution of glycine produces a blue coloured solution. Amino acids are bidentate ligands and will combine with copper(II) ions to form a blue coloured complex ion in which the copper(II) ion has a coordination number of four.

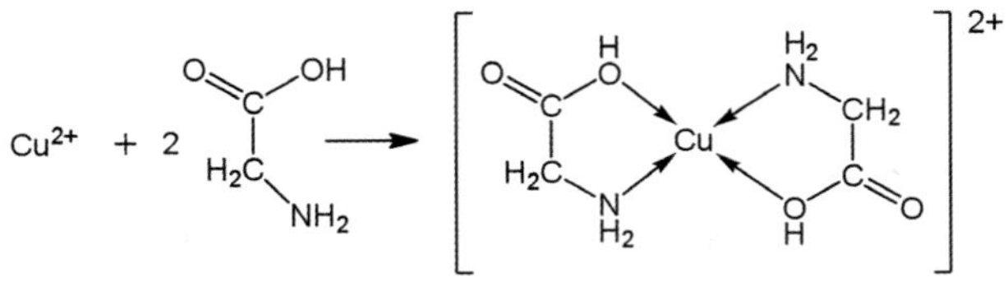

Copper(II) ion    Glycine    Copper-glycine complex ion
$[Cu(CH_2(NH_2)COOH)_2]^{2+}$

*Observations: Dark blue solution formed.*

## Exercise 5.11D

1. (a) Write an equation for the reaction of glycine with sodium carbonate. (b) Esterification of glycine removes its acidity. Write an equation for the reaction of glycine with methanol.

   *(CCEA June 2004)*

2. The amino acid selenocysteine reacts with sodium carbonate. Write an equation for the reaction.

$$H_2N\!-\!\underset{\underset{CH_2SeH}{|}}{\overset{\overset{H}{|}}{C}}\!-\!COOH$$

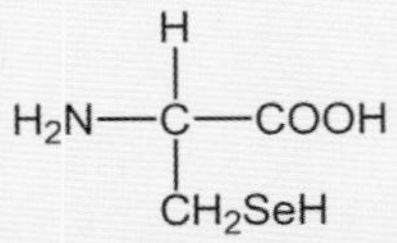

   selenocysteine

   *(CCEA June 2006)*

3. The structure of the zwitterion formed by the amino acid threonine is shown below. (a) Mark any chiral centres in the zwitterion with an asterisk (*). (b) Explain how the zwitterion is formed. (c) Explain why threonine has a high melting point. (d) Write an equation for the reaction between threonine and nitrous acid. (e) Suggest what would be observed if a solution of threonine is added to nitrous acid.

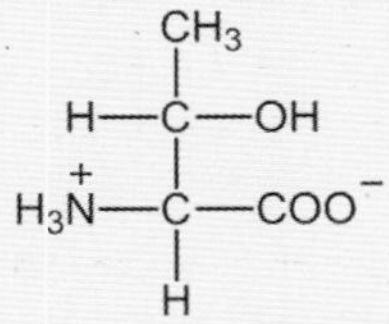

$$\underset{\underset{H}{|}}{\overset{\overset{CH_3}{|}}{\underset{}{H\!-\!C\!-\!OH}}}$$

$$H_3\overset{+}{N}\!-\!C\!-\!COO^-$$

   *(Adapted from CCEA May 2008)*

4. Draw the structural formula for the complex ion that forms when aqueous copper(II) sulfate is added to an aqueous solution containing alanine.

5. Which one of the following is not true for glycine?

   A   It forms a blue solution with $Cu^{2+}$(aq) ions
   B   It is optically active
   C   It reacts with sodium carbonate forming carbon dioxide
   D   It reacts with nitrous acid forming nitrogen

   *(CCEA June 2015)*

## Proteins

**In this section we are learning to:**

- Explain what is meant by the primary, secondary and tertiary structure of a protein.
- Describe the structure and action of an enzyme.

Amino acids are the building blocks of proteins such as haemoglobin, a globular protein found in red blood cells that transports oxygen in the bloodstream. A single molecule of haemoglobin consists of four subunits, each containing over one hundred amino acids. The arrangement of the subunits within haemoglobin can be illustrated by combining the subunits to form a molecule of haemoglobin as shown in Figure 2.

Within each subunit the amino acids are bonded together to form a chain. The **primary structure** of a protein is *the sequence of the amino acids joined by peptide links in a chain*, where the term **peptide link** refers to the -CONH- linkage formed when the amino (-NH$_2$) group on one amino acid reacts with the carboxyl (-COOH) group on a second amino acid. The compound formed by reacting two amino acids is referred to as a **dipeptide**.

*Forming a dipeptide:*

$$H_2N-\overset{\overset{H}{|}}{\underset{\underset{R_1}{|}}{C}}-COOH \ + \ H_2N-\overset{\overset{H}{|}}{\underset{\underset{R_2}{|}}{C}}-COOH$$

$$\longrightarrow \ H_2N-\overset{\overset{H}{|}}{\underset{\underset{R_1}{|}}{C}}-\overset{\overset{O}{||}}{C}-\overset{|}{\underset{\underset{H}{|}}{N}}-\overset{\overset{H}{|}}{\underset{\underset{R_2}{|}}{C}}-COOH \ + \ H_2O$$

peptide linkage

Dipeptide formed from two amino acids

### Exercise 5.11E

1. Draw the structure of the dimer formed when two molecules of the amino acid lysine, H$_2$N(CH$_2$)$_4$CH(NH$_2$)COOH react.

   *(CCEA May 2011)*

2. Draw the structures of the two dipeptides which can be formed from one molecule of glycine and one molecule of alanine. Circle the peptide link in each structure.

   *(CCEA May 2012)*

3. Which one of the following compounds is a peptide?

   A     CH$_3$CONH$_2$

   B     NH$_2$CHCONHCHCOOH
               |         |
              CH$_3$    CH$_3$

   C     HOOC(CH$_2$)$_6$CONH(CH$_2$)$_4$NH$_2$

   D
   $$\overset{H_3N^+}{\diagdown}\overset{\displaystyle H_2C-CH_2}{}\overset{\diagup}{\underset{\displaystyle COO^-}{}}$$
   $$^-OOC\diagdown\quad\diagup NH_3^+$$
   $$\overset{\displaystyle H_2C-C}{\underset{\displaystyle H_2}{}}$$

   *(CCEA June 2014)*

**Combine subunits** →

*Figure 2: Constructing a molecule of haemoglobin by combining four subunits, each containing over one hundred amino acids.*

One subunit of haemoglobin

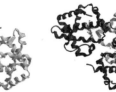

One molecule of haemoglobin (four subunits)

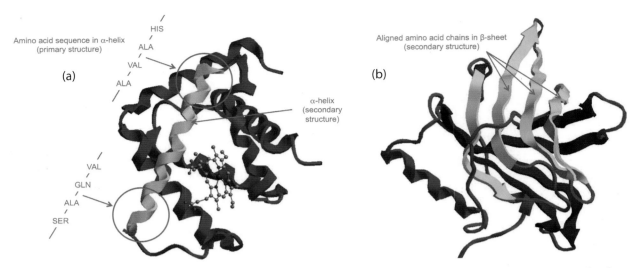

*Figure 3: (a) An α-helix in one subunit of human haemoglobin. (b) Sections of the amino acid chain arranged to form a β-sheet in human retinol binding protein.*

In many proteins, one or more sections of the amino acid chain are arranged to form an α-helix. One of several α-helices in a subunit of human haemoglobin is highlighted in Figure 3a. Parts of the amino acid sequence in the α-helix are also shown, with three-letter abbreviations such as ALA and GLY being used to represent individual amino acids.

Sections of the amino acid chain in a protein may also become arranged in parallel strands to form a β-sheet. The β-sheet in human retinol binding protein in shown in Figure 3b. The **secondary structure** of a protein refers to *the twisting and coiling of the amino acid chain to form α-helices and β-sheets that results from intramolecular hydrogen bonding between the side-chains (R groups) of amino acids in the chain.*

In many proteins folding of the secondary structures to give the protein its 3D shape is governed by van der Waals' attraction between the side-chains of the amino acids. The formation of hydrogen bonds and disulfide (-S-S-) bonds between side-chains, and attractive (ionic) forces between oppositely charged groups on the side-chains ($-NH_3^+$, $-COO^-$, etc), also play a role in the folding of the protein. The term **tertiary structure** refers to *the precise three-dimensional shape produced when the secondary structure folds as a result of van der Waals attraction, hydrogen bonding, ionic interactions, and disulfide bonds in the protein.* The 'barrel' structure in Figure 4 results from folding of the β-sheet in human retinol binding protein and is an example of a tertiary structure.

### Exercise 5.11F

1. Which one of the following statements describes the primary structure of a protein?

   A  The folding of the α-helix

   B  The formation of a β-pleated sheet

   C  The sequence of amino acids

   D  The coiling of the chains

   *(CCEA May 2009)*

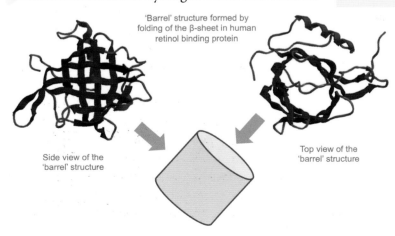

*Figure 4: The tertiary 'barrel' structure formed by the folding of the β-sheet in human retinol binding protein.*

2. Which one of the following statements describes the secondary structure of a protein?

   A  The formation of the α-helix
   B  The folding of the α-helix
   C  The sequence of the amino acids
   D  The sequence of the peptide links

   *(CCEA January 2010)*

3. Describe the primary, secondary and tertiary structure of proteins.

   *(CCEA June 2010)*

4. The following diagram shows a section of a protein chain. The three-letter words represent the names of amino acids.

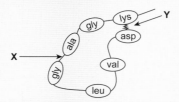

   Different types of bonds are formed at X and Y. Which one of the following represents the bonds X and Y?

|   | X | Y |
|---|---|---|
| A | hydrogen bond | hydrogen bond |
| B | hydrogen bond | ionic bond |
| C | peptide bond | hydrogen bond |
| D | peptide bond | ionic bond |

   *(CCEA June 2014)*

---

**Before moving to the next section, check that you are able to:**

- Associate the primary structure of a protein with the amino acid sequence.
- Deduce the structures of the dipeptides formed from two amino acids.
- Recognise an α-helix and a β-sheet as secondary structures that primarily result from hydrogen bonding between amino acid side-chains.
- Recall that the tertiary structure of a protein results from folding of the secondary structure, and the nature of the attractive forces that direct the folding process.

## Enzymes

**In this section we are learning to:**

- Describe how enzymes catalyse biological reactions.
- Explain the effect of pH and temperature on enzymes.

---

**Enzymes** are *globular proteins with a 'rounded' shape that catalyse reactions in living systems.* For example, the carbonic anhydrases are a family of enzymes that catalyse the interconversion of hydrogencarbonate ion and carbon dioxide in cells.

*Inter-conversion of $HCO_3^-$ and $CO_2$:*
$$CO_2 + H_2O \leftrightarrows H^+ + HCO_3^-$$

The reaction occurs in the **active site** of the enzyme, *a small region close to the surface of the enzyme into which one or more of the reactants bind.* The space-filling model of carbonic anhydrase in Figure 5 reveals the very limited space within the active site. The 'ribbon' model of the enzyme in Figure 5 reveals the presence of a zinc ion within the active site that plays a key role in catalysing the reaction.

The arrangement of the amino acids within the active site is such that an enzyme will only bond with the reactants for a particular reaction. The uniqueness of the fit between the reactants and the active site is described by the *induced fit hypothesis* which asserts that *when the reactants and the enzyme interact, the structures of the reactants and the structure of the active site change in way that lowers the activation energy for the reaction catalysed by the enzyme.*

Once the reactants are 'locked' into place by bonding with functional groups in the active site, they are transformed into products and released from the active site. Any changes in the secondary and tertiary structure of the enzyme that occur during the reaction are temporary, and the enzyme returns to its original configuration when the products are released from the active site.

In many biological reactions the enzyme catalysing the reaction is even more selective and will only catalyse the reaction if a particular isomer is used. *Enzymes requiring a particular isomer for a reaction to occur are described as stereoselective.*

The enzymes found in living organisms have evolved to operate at the temperature and pH of their surroundings. For example, the protease enzymes in the stomach are most effective at a pH of around 2

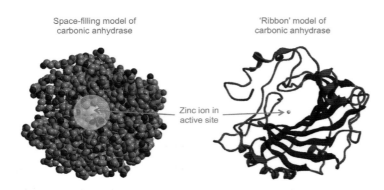

*Figure 5: Space-filling and 'ribbon' models of the carbonic anhydrase found in human red blood cells.*

that reflects the strongly acidic conditions in the stomach. In contrast, the carbonic anhydrases operate most effectively at a pH of around 7 that reflects the neutral conditions within cells.

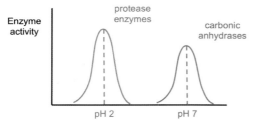

The activity of the enzymes found in humans is also optimal at temperatures close to body temperature (38 °C). Increasing the temperature to around 60 °C alters the tertiary structure of an enzyme to the extent that the active site can no longer facilitate the reaction, and rate of reaction decreases rapidly.

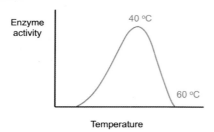

## Worked Example 5.11iii

Some enzymes formed by proteins are used in biological washing powders. (a) Describe how these enzymes act as catalysts. (b) Explain why biological washing powders do not work at high temperatures.

*(Adapted from CCEA June 2015)*

### Solution

(a) The molecules in substances such as sweat and food stains bind in the active site. Binding to the active site provides a reaction pathway with a lower activation energy that makes it possible for the molecules to be broken down quickly into simpler molecules that can be removed by the washing process.

(b) As temperature increases the atoms in an enzyme can overcome the forces responsible for the tertiary structure to the extent that the active site can no longer facilitate the reactions catalysed by the enzyme.

## Exercise 5.11G

1. (a) Explain why some proteins can act as enzymes. (b) Explain why the efficiency of most enzymes is lowered at 60 °C.

   *(CCEA June 2010)*

2. (a) Explain the mechanism by which an enzyme acts. (b) Sketch how the activity of an enzyme is affected by pH.

   *(Adapted from CCEA June 2006)*

3. Benzedrine is optically active and exists in two forms, one of which is more biologically active than the other. This variation in activity is explained in a similar way to that of enzyme activity. Explain why one structure is more biologically active than the other.

   *(CCEA June 2013)*

Before moving to the next section, check that you are able to:

- Recall that enzymes are proteins that catalyse reactions in living organisms.
- Use the induced fit hypothesis to explain how enzymes catalyse reactions, and why some enzymes are stereoselective.
- Describe the effect of pH and temperature on the activity of an enzyme.

# 5.12 Polymer Chemistry

**CONNECTIONS**
- Many of the structural materials in living organisms are polymers.
- In 2000 the Nobel Prize for Chemistry was awarded for the development of conductive polymers.

A **polymer** is *a large molecule formed from many identical molecules known as monomers.* **Addition polymers** such as polythene and PVC *are formed by addition reactions between monomers*. In contrast, polyesters and polyamides such as nylon are referred to as **condensation polymers** as they *are formed by condensation reactions between monomers that each eliminate a small molecule from the polymer.*

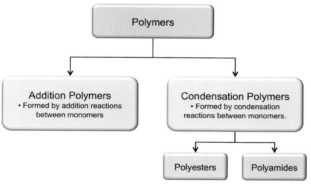

## Polyesters

**In this section we are learning to:**

- Explain why PET is a polyester and recall its structure and uses.
- Identify compounds capable of forming polyesters.
- Account for the strategies used to dispose of polyesters.

The polymer poly(ethylene terephthalate), or PET, is formed when benzene-1,4-dicarboxylic acid (A) reacts with ethane-1,2-diol (B) to form a polymer with the structure -A-B-A-B-A-B-. In a molecule of PET neighbouring monomers are connected by an ester linkage (-COO-). As a result, a molecule of PET contains many ester linkages and is referred to as a **polyester**.

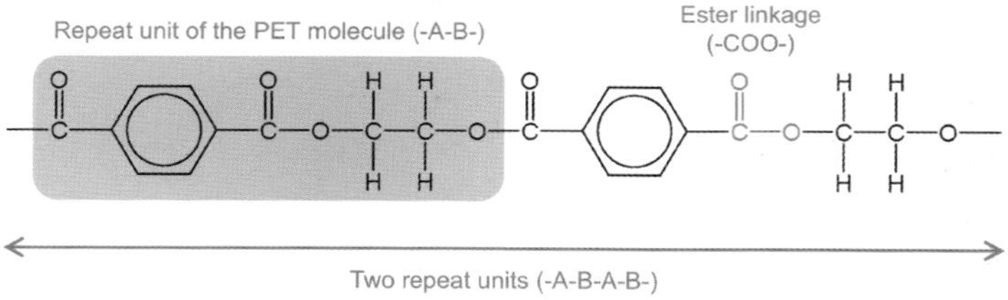

Repeat unit of the PET molecule (-A-B-)   Ester linkage (-COO-)

Two repeat units (-A-B-A-B-)

Formation of a molecule of PET begins when a carboxyl (-COOH) group in monomer (A) reacts with a hydroxyl (-OH) group in monomer B to form a dimer (A-B).

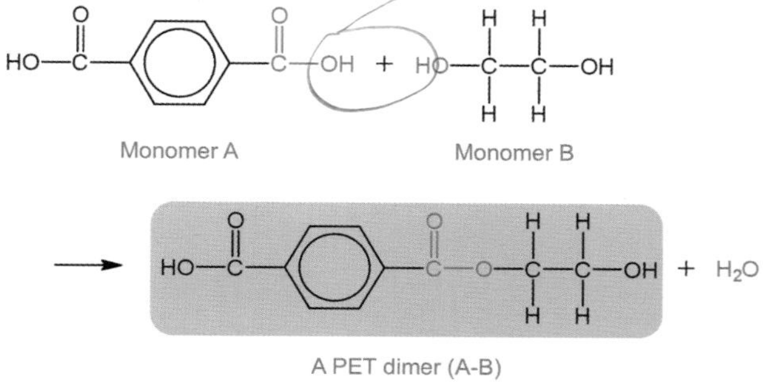

water

Monomer A        Monomer B

A PET dimer (A-B)

Formation of the dimer (A-B) is an example of a condensation reaction as a molecule of water is produced when the ester linkage (-COO-) is formed between the monomers. The polymerisation reaction can then proceed by using the functional groups at each end of the dimer to react with more monomers

*Reaction of the dimer (A-B) with a molecule of the diacid (A):*

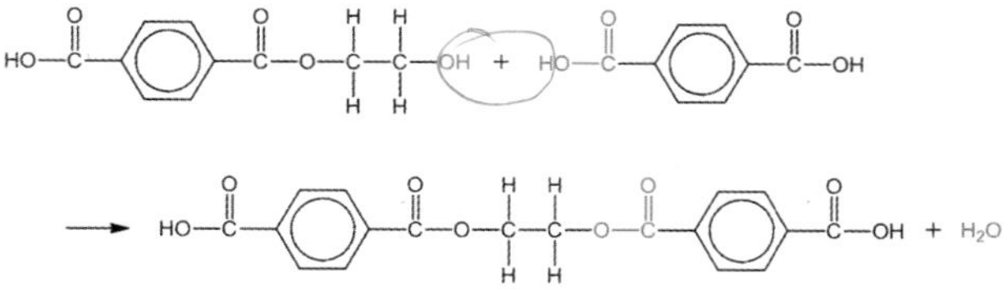

*Reaction of the dimer (A-B) with a molecule of the diol (B):*

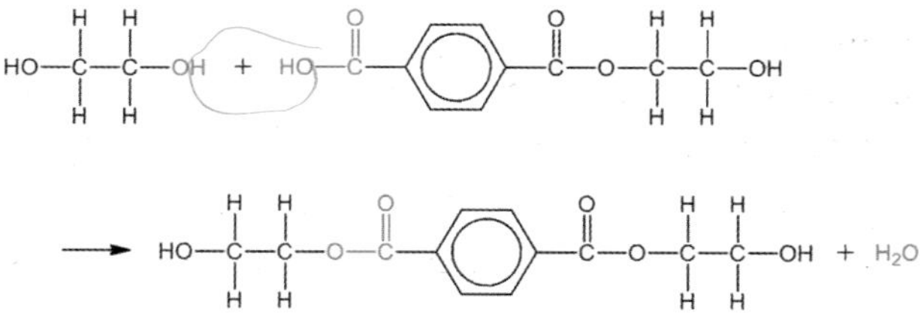

Polyesters such as PET are examples of condensation polymers as a molecule of water is produced each time a monomer is added and a new ester linkage is formed.

*Forming a molecule of PET:*

A large number (n) of repeat units
in one PET molecule

Most of the PET produced in industry is used to manufacture polyester fibres for use in clothing. A significant amount is also used to manufacture plastic bottles.

Polyesters such as PET are **biodegradable** as the ester linkages between the monomers can be hydrolysed by the action of microorganisms in the environment. As a result materials made from PET and other polyesters can be disposed of by placing them in a landfill. In contrast, materials made from addition polymers such as polythene are non-biodegradable as they cannot be broken down by microorganisms in the soil. The amount of non-biodegradable waste sent to landfill can instead be reduced by incinerating the waste. Incineration is an effective method for the management of non-biodegradable waste as it reduces the amount of non-biodegradable waste sent to landfill sites, and heat from the incineration process can be used to produce electricity.

### Exercise 5.12A

1. The wing of a hang glider is made from sheets of polyethylene terephthalate (PET). The frame is an alloy of magnesium and aluminium. (a) Draw the structures of the two monomers used to make PET. (b) Draw the structure for one repeating unit of PET.

   *(CCEA May 2009)*

2. Explain why the disposal of polyesters in landfill sites is more environmentally acceptable than the similar disposal of polythene.

   *(CCEA May 2011)*

3. When succinic acid is heated with ethane-1,2-diol it forms a polymer known as an alkyd resin. (a) Draw the structure of the polymer showing the repeating unit. (b) What is the name given to this type of polymerisation? (c) Suggest why the polymer is acidic. (d) Explain why this polymer is biodegradable.

   $CH_2COOH$
   $|$
   $CH_2COOH$    succinic acid

   *(CCEA June 2014)*

---

Before moving to the next section, check that you are able to:

- Draw the repeating unit of PET and recall the monomers used to form PET.
- Explain why PET is a condensation polymer.
- Deduce the structure of polyesters such as PET and the structure of the monomers used to form polyesters.
- Recall major uses of PET and explain why polyesters such as PET are biodegradable.

## Polyamides

### In this section we are learning to:

- Explain why nylon is a polyamide and recall its structure and uses.
- Identify compounds capable of forming polyamides.
- Account for the strategies used to dispose of polyamides.

---

In industry the polymer nylon is formed when hexane-1,6-dicarboxylic acid (A) reacts with hexane-1,6-diamine (B) to form a polymer with the structure -A-B-A-B-A-B-. In a molecule of nylon neighbouring monomers are connected by an amide linkage (-CONH-). As a result, a molecule of nylon contains many amide linkages and is referred to as a **polyamide.**

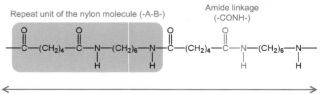

Repeat unit of the nylon molecule (-A-B-)

Amide linkage (-CONH-)

Two repeat units (-A-B-A-B-)

Formation of a molecule of nylon begins when a carboxyl (-COOH) group in monomer (A) reacts with an amine (-NH₂) group in monomer B to form a dimer (A-B).

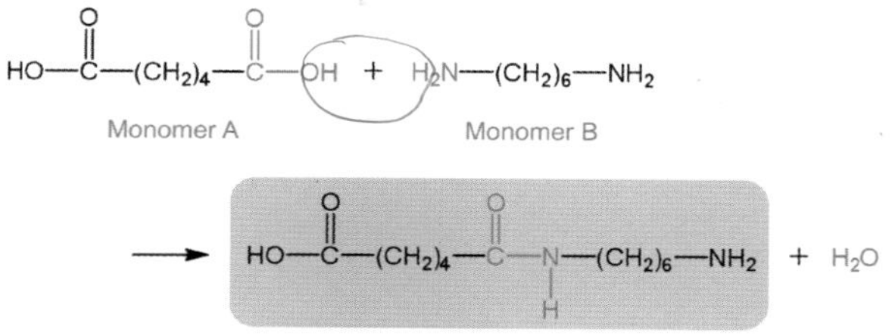

Formation of the dimer (A-B) is an example of a condensation reaction as a molecule of water is produced when the amide linkage (-CONH-) is formed between the monomers. The polymerisation reaction can then proceed by using the functional groups at each end of the dimer to react with more monomers.

*Reaction of the dimer (A-B) with a molecule of the diacid (A):*

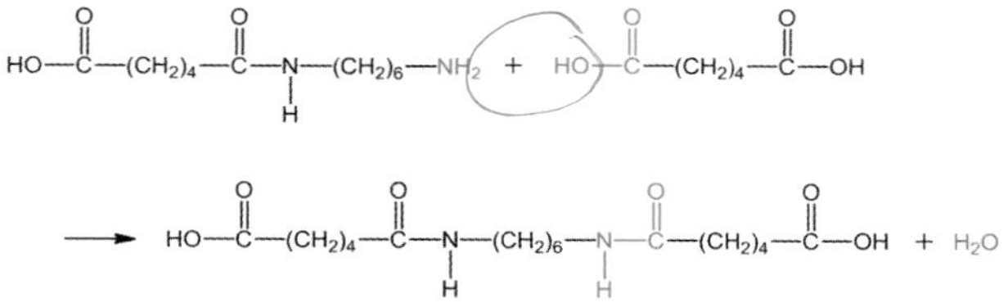

*Reaction of the dimer (A-B) with a molecule of the diamine (B):*

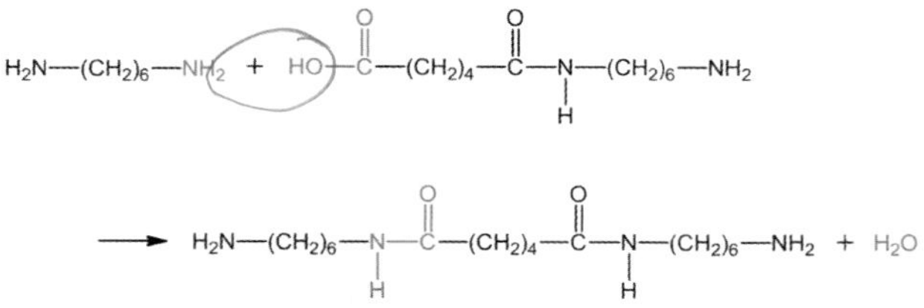

Polyamides such as nylon are also examples of condensation polymers as a molecule of water is produced each time a monomer is added and a new amide linkage is formed.

*Forming a molecule of nylon:*

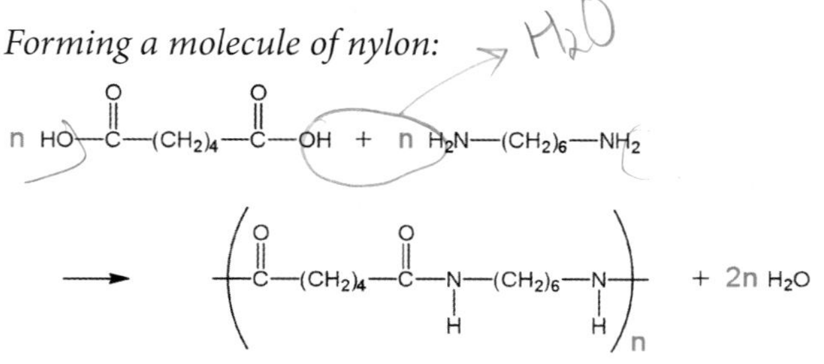

A large number (n) of repeat units in one nylon molecule

Nylon can also be formed in the laboratory by reacting an acyl chloride (A) with an amine (B). The reaction produces a molecule of hydrogen chloride each time an amide linkage is formed between monomers.

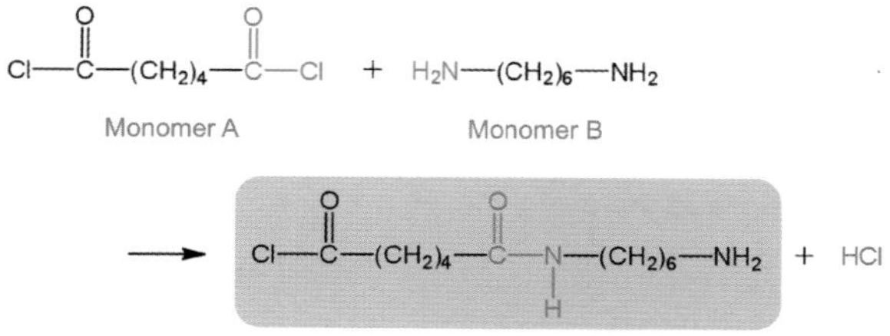

Much of the nylon produced in industry is used in the manufacture of ropes, fishing nets and items of clothing such as tights.

Polyamides such as nylon are biodegradable as the amide linkages between the monomers can be hydrolysed by the action of microorganisms in the environment. As a result nylon and other polyamides can be disposed of by placing them in a landfill.

### Exercise 5.12B

1. The polyamide nylon-6,6 is made by a condensation reaction between 1,6-diamino-hexane and hexanedioic acid. (a) Explain the term *condensation polymer*. (b) Draw a section of the polymer showing two repeating units.

*(Adapted from CCEA May 2012)*

2. Polyamides such as nylon are important industrial chemicals. (a) Write an equation to show the formation of a section of the nylon molecule using the industrial monomers. (b) State two major uses of nylon. (c) Explain, in terms of chemical structure, why nylon is far more easily disposed of than polythene.

*(Adapted from CCEA June 2013)*

3. Kevlar is a polyamide used in bulletproof vests. A section of the polymer chain is shown below. (a) How many repeating units are shown? (b) Draw the structures of the monomers used to produce Kevlar.

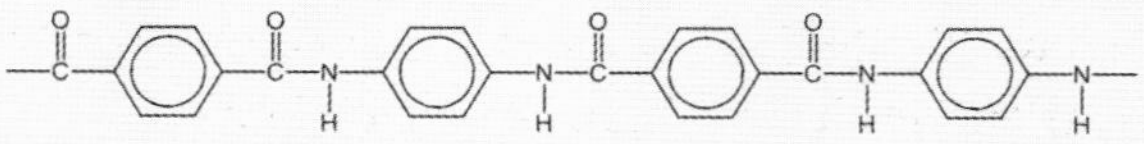

*(CCEA June 2012)*

4. Which one of the following pairs of monomers will **not** combine to form a polymer?

A  $HOOC(CH_2)_4COOH$ and $H_2N(CH_2)_6NH_2$

B  $H_2N(CH_2)_6NH_2$ and $H_2N(CH_2)_6NH_2$

C  $CH_2CH_2$ and $CH_2CH_2$

D  $HOOC(CH_2)_4COOH$ and $HO(CH_2)_2OH$

*(CCEA June 2010)*

**Additional Problems**

5. Polyurethane is made in a two-step process. In step 1 ethane-1,2-diol and hexanedioic acid are polymerised to form a polyester. (a) What type of polymers are polyesters? (b) Draw a diagram of one repeating unit of the polyester.

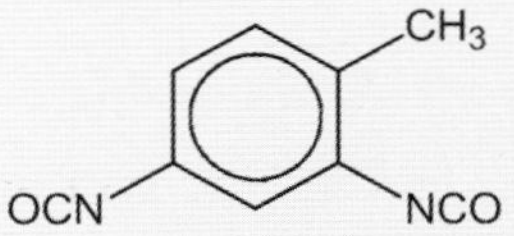

di-isocyanate

In step 2 the polyester is reacted with a di-isocyanate forming an amide linkage. (c) Draw a diagram for the isocyanate group, -NCO showing all the bonds present. (d) Explain why polyurethanes are biodegradable.

*(CCEA June 2015)*

Before moving to the next section, check that you are able to:

- Draw the repeating unit of nylon and recall the monomers used to form nylon.

- Explain why nylon is a condensation polymer.

- Deduce the structure of polyamides such as nylon and the structure of the monomers used to form polyamides.

- Recall major uses of nylon and explain why polyamides such as nylon are biodegradable.

# 5.13 Chemistry in Medicine

Many of the treatments administered by GPs and hospital doctors make use of basic chemical principles, and rely on medicines developed by chemists working in the pharmaceutical industry. In the following sections we examine the chemistry behind several minor medical treatments, the development of medicines, and the role of metal complexes in the human body.

## Treatments Based on Chemical Principles

**In this section we are learning to:**

- Recall the use of specific compounds to treat a range of medical conditions.
- Explain the chemical basis for each treatment.

### Indigestion Remedies

Indigestion remedies containing bases such as $CaCO_3$ and $Mg(OH)_2$ can be purchased without a prescription, and can be used to reduce the effects of excess stomach acid. On reaching the stomach the base in the indigestion remedy neutralises a portion of the hydrochloric acid in the stomach, reducing the amount of stomach acid present to normal levels.

*Antacid tablets contain $CaCO_3$:*

$$CaCO_{3(s)} + 2HCl_{(aq)} \rightarrow CaCl_{2(aq)} + H_2O_{(l)} + CO_{2(g)}$$

*Milk of Magnesia solution contains $Mg(OH)_2$:*

$$Mg(OH)_{2(aq)} + 2HCl_{(aq)} \rightarrow MgCl_{2(aq)} + 2H_2O_{(l)}$$

Only some of the ingredients in an indigestion remedy are soluble. As a result a back titration method must be used to determine the amount of base in the remedy. The back titration is carried out by first reacting a known amount of the remedy with an excess of hydrochloric acid. The remaining acid is then titrated against standard sodium hydroxide solution using phenolphthalein indicator to locate the end point.

### Exercise 5.13A

1. Indigestion tablets with a combined mass of 10.0 g are crushed and reacted with 50.0 cm³ of 1.0 M HCl which is in excess. The resulting solution is then made up to 250 cm³ in a volumetric flask. (a) Explain why the tablets are crushed. (b) Calculate the percentage of magnesium carbonate in the tablets if 25 cm³ of the diluted solution require an average titre of 30.1 cm³ when titrated against 1.0 M NaOH. (c) Explain why a back titration method is used.

$$MgCO_3 + 2HCl \rightarrow MgCl_2 + H_2O + CO_2$$

### Maintaining Skin pH

The outermost layer of human skin is covered by an oily layer with a pH of around 5.5 that is referred to as the 'acid mantle'. The fatty acids in the acid mantle are secreted by glands near the surface of the skin and are immiscible in water. As a result the acid mantle is waterproof, and lubricates the skin when it comes into contact with other objects. The acid mantle is also an effective barrier to bacteria and viruses as it is too acidic an environment.

Frequent washing with soap and other alkaline cleaning agents removes fatty acids from the acid mantle, leaving the skin dry and vulnerable to infection by bacteria and viruses that give rise to skin conditions such as acne and warts. The structure of the acid mantle can be restored and preserved by using mildly acidic cleaners that contain fatty acids.

## Exercise 5.13B

1. (a) Explain why human skin is able to act as a waterproof barrier that resists the growth of bacteria and viruses. (b) Explain why human skin can become dry after repeated use of alkaline soaps and cleansers with a high pH value.

2. (a) Describe how the properties of skin are affected by the repeated use of alkaline soaps and cleansers with high pH value. (b) Explain, in terms of the compounds present, how the use of mildly acidic cleansers containing fatty acids can reverse the damage done to skin by the repeated use of alkaline soaps and cleansers.

### Wart Removal

The term wart is used to describe a rough growth of skin caused by the human papilloma virus (HPV). Warts are common on hands and feet, and can be removed by the repeated application of creams and gels containing salicylic acid, a weak acid that can be safely applied to the skin as it is only mildly corrosive. Solutions containing silver nitrate, $AgNO_3$ can also be used to remove warts as silver nitrate is corrosive when concentrated and care should be taken to avoid surrounding healthy skin as silver nitrate is also toxic.

salicylic acid, $C_7H_6O_3$
(2-hydroxybenzoic acid)

## Exercise 5.13C

1. (a) Explain why a weak acid such as salicylic acid is used as the active ingredient in creams and gels used to treat warts. (b) Explain why treatments containing salicylic acid should not be applied to healthy skin.

### Preventing Eye Disease

Eye drops containing a very dilute solution of silver nitrate have antibacterial properties and can be used to both prevent and treat eye infections in newborn babies. In recent years the use of silver nitrate eye drops has been discontinued in favour of antibiotics such as erythromycin.

## Exercise 5.13D

1. The antibiotic erythromycin is used to prevent eye infections in newborn babies. (a) Use the following skeletal formula to deduce the value of x in the molecular formula for erythromycin. (b) Suggest why erythromycin replaced the use of silver nitrate.

erythromycin, $C_{37}H_{67}NO_x$

Before moving to the next section, check that you are able to:

- Recall the use of bases in indigestion remedies and use back titration methods to determine the amount of base in an indigestion remedy.
- Account for the effect of alkaline soaps and cleansers on the structure and properties of skin.
- Explain how to maintain normal pH levels in skin.
- Account for the use of salicylic acid in creams and gels used to remove warts.
- Recall the use of silver nitrate to prevent and treat eye infections.

## Drug Development

In this section we are learning to:

- Recall the preparation of aspirin and explain the need for new remedies to replace aspirin.
- Explain how cisplatin and related platinum complexes prevent cell-division in cancerous cells.

New compounds with the potential to be used as medicines are developed by chemists working in the pharmaceutical industry. Before a compound can be approved for use a series of clinical studies must be conducted to determine if the compound has the desired effect, and to determine the nature of any side-effects.

## Aspirin

Aspirin is used to relieve mild to moderate pain, reduce fever, and reduce inflammation. Clinical trials have also demonstrated that low doses taken over an extended period can lower the risk of blood clots. The active ingredient in aspirin, acetylsalicylic acid, is an ethanoate ester of salicylic acid.

acetylsalicylic acid, $C_9H_8O_4$
(active ingredient in aspirin)

Salicylic acid is the active ingredient in natural pain relief remedies containing extracts from willow bark. Acetylsalicylic acid is used as the active ingredient in aspirin as it is less soluble than salicylic acid and therefore causes less irritation to the lining of the mouth and stomach when swallowed. The potential for irritation can be further reduced by taking 'soluble aspirin' containing the sodium salt of acetylsalicylic acid. The sodium salt is less acidic than acetylsalicylic acid, and being soluble, is more quickly absorbed by the digestive system.

Acetylsalicylic acid is prepared by heating a mixture of salicylic acid and ethanoic anhydride, $(CH_3CO)_2O$ in the presence of a few drops of concentrated phosphoric acid, $H_3PO_4$.

salicylic acid          ethanoic anhydride

acetylsalicylic acid

The mixture is placed in a round-bottom flask fitted with a reflux condenser and heated using a water bath.

The reaction mixture is then allowed to cool before cold water is added, and the flask placed in an ice bath. On cooling, the acetylsalicylic acid formed in the reaction precipitates, is collected by vacuum filtration, washed with cold water, and left to dry in air.

In the event that TLC analysis of the product reveals a small amount of unreacted salicylic acid, the product can be purified by recrystallisation using ethanol as a solvent. Pure acetylsalicylic acid melts over the narrow range 138–140 °C.

The percentage purity of the acetylsalicylic acid used to make aspirin must be very close to 100% and can be determined by back titration. The back titration is carried out by reacting a known mass of aspirin with an excess of sodium hydroxide solution, and titrating the remaining alkali against standard hydrochloric acid using phenolphthalein indicator.

*Reacting aspirin with excess alkali:*
$$C_9H_8O_{4(s)} + NaOH_{(aq)} \rightarrow C_9H_7O_4Na_{(aq)} + H_2O_{(l)}$$

*Titrating the remaining alkali:*
$$NaOH_{(aq)} + HCl_{(aq)} \rightarrow NaCl_{(aq)} + H_2O_{(l)}$$

## Exercise 5.13E

1. Explain, giving experimental details, how you would prepare a pure, dry sample of acetylsalicylic acid and determine its purity by reacting 2-hydroxybenzoic acid with ethanoic anhydride.

acetylsalicylic acid

2. The sodium salt of acetylsalicylic acid is the active ingredient in soluble aspirin tablets. (a) Draw the structure of the salt showing the bonds between the atoms in each group attached to the ring. (b) State two advantages of using aspirin containing the sodium salt of acetylsalicylic acid instead of aspirin containing acetylsalicylic acid.

acetylsalicylic acid

3. Acetylsalicylic acid, $C_9H_8O_4$ is the active ingredient in aspirin. Aspirin tablets with a total mass of 6.0 g are crushed and reacted with 50.0 cm³ of 0.10 M NaOH which is in excess. The resulting solution is made up to 250 cm³ in a volumetric flask. (a) Write an equation for the reaction. (b) Calculate the percentage of acetylsalicylic acid by mass in the tablets if the average titre is 22.3 cm³ when 25.0 cm³ of the diluted solution is titrated against 0.10 M NaOH. (c) Explain why a back titration method is used.

acetylsalicylic acid

4. Acetaminophen is the active ingredient in paracetamol which, like aspirin, reduces mild to moderate pain and fever. Paracetamol can be used by adults with stomach ulcers as it causes less irritation to the digestive system than aspirin, which contains acetylsalicylic acid. (a) What type of compound is acetaminophen? (b) Explain, in terms of molecular structure, why paracetamol is safer than aspirin for people with stomach ulcers and other digestive problems.

acetaminophen, $C_8H_9NO_2$

5. The compound 2-(4-isobutylphenyl)propanoic acid exists as optical isomers. One of these isomers is the active ingredient in ibuprofen which, like aspirin, relieves pain and fever. (a) Mark each asymmetric centre in the molecule with an asterisk(*). (b) Write the molecular formula for 2-(4-isobutylphenyl) propanoic acid. (c) Suggest, in terms of molecular structure, why ibuprofen causes less irritation to the digestive system than aspirin.

2-(4-isobutylphenyl)propanoic acid

Before moving to the next section, check that you are able to:

- Recall the advantages of acetylsalicylic acid and its sodium salt over salicylic acid.
- Explain how to prepare acetylsalicylic acid from ethanoic anhydride and write an equation for the reaction.
- Use back titration methods to determine the percentage of acetylsalicylic acid in aspirin.

## Cisplatin

Platin, $Pt(NH_3)_2Cl_2$ is a square planar complex of platinum(II) that exists as *cis* and *trans* isomers. The *cis* isomer, known as cisplatin, is used to treat a variety of cancers in humans. A cancer occurs when cells begin to divide and produce new tissue in a way that does not result in the normal growth or regeneration of tissue. The resulting growths are referred to as tumours and may disrupt the normal function of surrounding tissues in the body.

Geometric isomers of platin, [$Pt(NH_3)_2Cl_2$]

*cis*-platin          *trans*-platin

Once inside a cell the cisplatin enters the nucleus of the cell and forms a complex with a guanine side-chain on a strand of DNA as shown in Figure 1a. The cisplatin then introduces a 'kink' in the DNA strand by binding to a second guanine side-chain further along the DNA strand as shown in Figure 1b. Once formed the 'kink' in the DNA is recognised by proteins that bind to the damaged strand and initiate a repair. In a normal cell damage to the DNA caused by the binding of cisplatin can be repaired before **DNA replication** and cell division occurs. In contrast, the damage caused by the binding of cisplatin to DNA in a cancerous cell cannot be repaired in time as the cell divides more quickly than a normal (non-cancerous) cell. This results in cell death as the cancerous cell cannot replicate the damaged DNA and divide, and cisplatin is seen to prevent the growth of tumours by inhibiting cell division.

The toxic side-effects associated with the use of cisplatin in humans include damage to the kidneys and a weakening of the immune system due to a

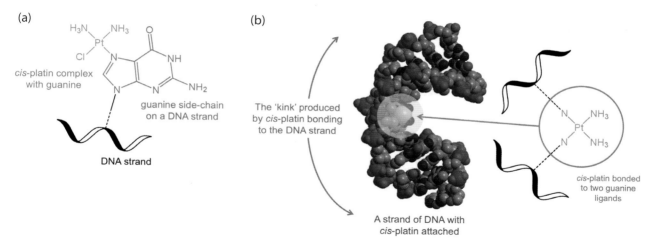

Figure 1: (a) The binding of cisplatin to a guanine side-chain attached to a strand of DNA.
(b) A 'kink' in a strand of DNA produced by the binding of cisplatin to two guanine side-chains.

reduction in the rate at which blood cells are produced. As a result it becomes necessary to allow sufficient time for normal tissues to recover between doses.

A great deal of research is presently focussed on the development of less toxic alternatives to cisplatin. Scientific studies have shown that the compound carboplatin is less toxic than cisplatin, and is effective against a range of cancers in humans. The compound oxaliplatin has also been approved in the UK for the treatment of specific cancers.

carboplatin                                     oxaliplatin

The ability of all three platin-based compounds to treat cancer is attributed to the square planar arrangement about platinum with two amine ligands ($NH_3$ or $NH_2R$) in a *cis* arrangement. Carboplatin and oxaliplatin are less toxic than cisplatin as they are more stable and are therefore less likely to react when they encounter compounds other than DNA in the body. The increased stability of carboplatin and oxaliplatin is due to the presence of bidentate ligands which make the complexes more stable and less likely to undergo ligand replacement than cisplatin.

**Exercise 5.13F**

1. (a) Draw the structures of the *cis* and *trans* isomers of $Pt(NH_3)_2Cl_2$. (b) Explain why these isomers are not chiral. (c) Which of these isomers is used as a drug and for what purpose? (d) Suggest why the drug is extremely expensive.

   *(CCEA May 2002)*

2. The complex $[Pt(NH_3)_2Cl_4]$ has been shown to inhibit cell division in bacteria. (a) Draw and label the E-Z isomers of the complex. (b) Suggest which isomer is more likely to be effective at inhibiting cell division. Explain your reasoning.

3. The complex AMD473 has proven effective in the treatment of cancer in cells that are resistant to treatment by cisplatin. The resistance results from the binding of cisplatin to sulfur-containing compounds present in the cells. (a) Explain how the presence of sulfur-containing compounds makes the cells resistant to treatment by cisplatin. (b) Suggest why the compound AMD473 is a more effective treatment than cisplatin for these cells.

cisplatin                    AMD473

Before moving to the next section, check that you are able to:

- Explain how cisplatin inhibits cell division in cancerous cells.
- Describe how the chelate effect influences the toxicity of the metal complexes used to treat cancer.

## Biological Roles of Metal Complexes

**In this section we are learning to:**

- Recognise that metal complexes play a role in many biological processes.
- Explain the role of metal complexes in oxygen transport and treatments to prevent blood clotting.

Many of the proteins and enzymes in the human body contain one or more metal ions. As a result dietary supplements such as multivitamin tablets contain trace amounts of iron, zinc, manganese, copper and other metals required to maintain the proper function of proteins and enzymes.

### Oxygen Transport in Blood

In humans oxygen from the lungs dissolves in the blood and enters red blood cells where it forms a complex with haemoglobin (Hb), a globular protein that gives blood its characteristic colour. A molecule of haemoglobin consists of four subunits, each containing an iron-haem complex. The complex is formed when a haem ligand chelates iron(II) by forming four Fe-N coordinate bonds in a square planar arrangement as shown in Figure 2. When an oxygen molecule enters a red blood cell it bonds to

haemoglobin by using a lone pair to form a coordinate bond with iron(II). The bond formed between iron(II) and oxygen is relatively weak and can be easily broken to release the oxygen molecule when it is needed in the surrounding tissue.

Other small molecules such as carbon monoxide, CO can also use a lone pair to form a coordinate bond with the iron(II) in the iron-haem complex. Carbon monoxide is particularly toxic to humans as it bonds much more strongly with haemoglobin than oxygen, effectively preventing oxygen transport around the body.

### Exercise 5.13G

1. Explain the role of iron(II) in haemoglobin.

    *(CCEA June 2011)*

2. With reference to the iron(II) in haemoglobin, explain why breathing carbon monoxide can result in death.

    *(Adapted from CCEA June 2012)*

Before moving to the next section, check that you are able to:

- Describe how the formation of an iron complex with oxygen facilitates the transport of oxygen in human blood.
- Explain why carbon monoxide inhibits oxygen transport in human blood.

## Sequestering Calcium Ions in Blood

Polydentate ligands such as (edta)$^{4-}$ can sequester the metal ions in a mixture by forming a stable complex

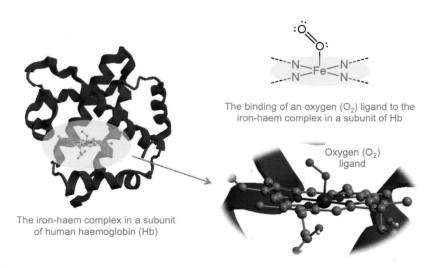

The binding of an oxygen (O$_2$) ligand to the iron-haem complex in a subunit of Hb

Oxygen (O$_2$) ligand

The iron-haem complex in a subunit of human haemoglobin (Hb)

*Figure 2: A molecule of oxygen binding to the iron-haem complex in a subunit of human haemoglobin.*

that prevents the metal ions from reacting with other molecules or ions in the mixture. For instance, solutions containing the disodium salt of edta, $Na_2H_2(edta)$ are used to prevent blood clotting. The $H_2(edta)^{2-}$ ion in the salt acts as a **sequestering agent** by forming the stable complex, $[Ca(edta)]^{2-}$ with any calcium ($Ca^{2+}$) ions present in the bloodstream, preventing the $Ca^{2+}$ ions from participating in clot formation.

*Using an edta salt to sequester $Ca^{2+}$ ions:*

$$Ca^{2+}_{(aq)} + H_2(edta)^{2-}_{(aq)} \rightarrow [Ca(edta)]^{2-}_{(aq)} + 2H^+_{(aq)}$$

**Exercise 5.13H**

1. (a) Explain the role of edta in treating blood.
   (b) State the formula of any complex ions formed.

   *(Adapted from CCEA June 2014)*

2. Aqueous solutions containing edta salts are used to treat cases of heavy metal poisoning. (a) Suggest how the $H_2(edta)^{2-}$ ions from an edta salt sequester toxic metal ions such as mercury(II), $Hg^{2+}$ and lead(II), $Pb^{2+}$ circulating in the body. (b) Write an equation for the reaction that occurs when a $[Pb(H_2O)_6]^{2+}$ ion is sequestered.

Before moving to the next section, check that you are able to:

- Explain what is meant by the term *sequestering agent*.
- Describe how edta can be used as a sequestering agent to soften water and prevent blood from clotting.

# Unit A2 3:

# Further Practical Chemistry

# 6: Practical Assessment

## Introduction

The format of the A2 Practical Assessment is familiar from AS Chemistry and consists of two parts. The first part of the assessment is laboratory-based, and is focussed on making and recording observations. The second part is timetabled for a different day, and is focussed on the analysis of experimental data and the evaluation of experimental techniques.

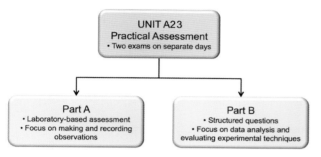

The tasks in Part A afford candidates an opportunity to demonstrate their knowledge of practical chemistry, including the tasks listed in the A2 3 Section of the specification. The Worked Examples and Problems in the following sections exemplify the level of detail expected when making observations, analysing data, and evaluating experimental techniques, and should be used in conjunction with the Specimen Assessment Materials (SAMs)

published by CCEA to gain insight into the likely format and scope of questions in both parts of practical assessment.

## Volumetric Analysis

### In this section we are learning to:

- Identify the knowledge and skills required to complete volumetric analysis questions as part of the practical assessment.

The format of a titration exercise is familiar from AS Chemistry. In the first part of the assessment candidates may be asked to perform a titration and record their results in a suitable table. In the second part, candidates may be asked to analyse the results of a titration, and to describe relevant procedures such as: how to prepare a solution, how to perform a titration, or how to ensure that the results of a titration experiment are accurate.

Worked Example 6i demonstrates how the determination of iron(II) by acidified manganate(VII) could be used to assess understanding of the various aspects of titrations. The laboratory-based tasks in Parts (a) and (b) would be conducted in the first part of the assessment.

---

### Worked Example 6i

You are required to dissolve a weighed sample of ammonium iron(II) sulfate in dilute sulfuric acid and make the solution up to 250 cm³ in a volumetric flask. You will then titrate 25.0 cm³ portions of this solution with acidified potassium manganate(VII). You will use your results to calculate the concentration of the acidified potassium manganate(VII) solution.

You are provided with:

- Hydrated ammonium iron(II) sulfate, $(NH_4)_2Fe(SO_4)_2.6H_2O$
- Dilute sulfuric acid
- Deionised water
- A 250 cm³ volumetric flask
- An acidified solution of potassium manganate(VII).

*(CCEA June 2014)*

(a) Weigh out between 7.80 g and 7.90 g of ammonium iron(II) sulfate. Record the mass to two decimal places.

   7.84 g

Dissolve the weighed sample in approximately 100 cm³ of dilute sulfuric acid and make the solution up to 250 cm³ in the volumetric flask using deionised water. Calculate the concentration of the solution in mol dm⁻³.

$$\text{Moles in 250 cm}^3 = \frac{\text{Mass}}{\text{Molar Mass}} = \frac{7.84 \text{ g}}{392 \text{ g mol}^{-1}} = 2.00 \times 10^{-2} \text{ mol}$$

$$\text{Concentration} = \frac{2.00 \times 10^{-2} \text{ mol}}{0.250 \text{ dm}^3} = 8.00 \times 10^{-2} \text{ mol dm}^{-3}$$

(b) Titrate 25.0 cm³ portions of your solution with acidified potassium manganate(VII). Record your results in a suitable table. Calculate the average titre.

| | Initial Burette Reading (cm³) | Final Burette Reading (cm³) | Titre (cm³) |
|---|---|---|---|
| **Rough** | 0.0 | 23.0 | 23.0 |
| **First Accurate** | 0.4 | 23.1 | 22.7 |
| **Second Accurate** | 0.2 | 23.0 | 22.8 |

$$\text{Average titre} = \frac{22.7 + 22.8}{2} = 22.75 \text{ cm}^3$$

(c) Describe how you ensured the end point of your titration was accurate.

The acidified manganate(VII) was added dropwise with swirling near the end point. The sides of the conical flask were washed with deionised water after each addition to ensure that there were no drops of the solution on the sides of the flask.

State the colour change at the end point of your titration.

Colourless to pink.

(d) Write the half-equation for the reduction of acidified manganate(VII) ions to form manganese(II) ions.

$$MnO_4^-{}_{(aq)} + 8H^+{}_{(aq)} + 5e^- \rightarrow Mn^{2+}{}_{(aq)} + 4H_2O_{(l)}$$

Write the half-equation for the oxidation of iron(II) ions to iron(III) ions.

$$Fe^{2+}{}_{(aq)} \rightarrow Fe^{3+}{}_{(aq)} + e^-$$

Write the ionic equation for the reaction.

$$MnO_4^-{}_{(aq)} + 5Fe^{2+}{}_{(aq)} + 8H^+{}_{(aq)} \rightarrow Mn^{2+}{}_{(aq)} + 5Fe^{3+}{}_{(aq)} + 4H_2O_{(l)}$$

Calculate the concentration of the acidified manganate(VII) solution in g dm⁻³.

Moles of $Fe^{2+}$ in 25 cm³ = $8.00 \times 10^{-2}$ mol dm⁻³ × $2.50 \times 10^{-3}$ dm³
= $2.00 \times 10^{-3}$ mol

$$\text{Moles of KMnO}_4 \text{ in 25 cm}^3 = \frac{\text{Moles of Fe}^{2+} \text{ in 25 cm}^3}{5} = 4.00 \times 10^{-4} \text{ mol}$$

$$\text{Concentration of KMnO}_4 = \frac{\text{Moles of KMnO}_4 \text{ in 25 cm}^3}{\text{Average Titre}} = 0.0176 \text{ mol dm}^{-3}$$

Concentration of $KMnO_4$ = 0.0176 mol dm⁻³ × 158 g mol⁻¹ = 2.78 g dm⁻³

The following examples demonstrate how aspects of the titrations encountered in the A2 course may be examined in the second part of the practical assessment.

## Exercise 6A

1. Crystalline ammonium iron(II) sulfate has the formula $Fe(NH_4)_2(SO_4)_2.nH_2O$. The symbol n represents the number of molecules of water of crystallisation. Assuming that all the apparatus is clean and dry, you are required to carry out a titration and use your results to determine the value of n. You are provided with the following solutions:

   - A solution of ammonium iron(II) sulfate of concentration 31.4 g dm$^{-3}$.

   - A solution of potassium permanganate of concentration 0.020 mol dm$^{-3}$.

   - Solutions of 2.0 mol dm$^{-3}$ sulfuric acid.

   (a) Give details of the procedure you intend to use. The potassium permanganate solution should be placed in a burette. (b) State the colour change at the end point of the titration. (c) Write the equation for the reaction of iron(II) ions with acidified permanganate ions. (d) Calculate the molarity of the ammonium iron(II) sulfate solution if the average titre was 20.3 cm$^3$. (e) Determine the molar mass of ammonium iron(II) sulfate and deduce the value of n.

   *(Adapted from CCEA June 2011)*

2. People with anaemia are often advised to take 'iron' tablets which contain hydrated iron(II) sulfate, $FeSO_4.6H_2O$. The composition of these tablets can be analysed by titration with acidified potassium manganate(VII) solution. (a) Write the ionic equation for this reaction. (b) State the colour observed at the end point of this titration. (c) Give the formula of the ion responsible for the colour observed at the end point of this reaction. (d) One of the major sources of error in this titration is overshooting the end point. State two practical techniques used to minimise this error. (e) 6.00 g of crushed iron tablets were dissolved in deionised water, and the solution was made up to 250 cm$^3$ in a volumetric flask. Describe how the solution

containing the iron tablets was prepared. (f) Titration of 25.0 cm$^3$ samples of the iron tablets solution with 0.0200 mol dm$^{-3}$ potassium manganate(VII) solution resulted in an average titre value of 22.4 cm$^3$. Calculate the percentage of $FeSO_4.6H_2O$ in the tablets.

*(CCEA May 2015)*

3. An acidified solution of potassium iodate(V) acts as an oxidising agent. You are required to carry out a titration and use your results to calculate the concentration of potassium iodate(V). You are provided with:

   - A solution of potassium iodate(V) of unknown concentration.

   - Four 20 cm$^3$ portions of sulfuric acid.

   - Four 1.5 g samples of potassium iodide.

   - Sodium thiosulfate solution of concentration 0.050 mol dm$^{-3}$.

   - Starch indicator.

   (a) Assuming that all the apparatus is clean and dry, give details of the procedure you intend to use. (b) Calculate the number of moles of iodine liberated in the conical flask if the average titre was 24.6 cm$^3$. (c) Balance the half-equation: $IO_3^- + H^+ \rightarrow I_2 + H_2O$ (d) Combine the half-equation with the half-equation: $2I^- \rightarrow I_2 + 2e^-$ to produce a balanced redox equation. (e) Calculate the concentration of the potassium iodate(V) solution in g dm$^{-3}$.

*(Adapted from CCEA May 2010)*

---

**Before moving to the next section, check that you are able to:**

- Describe the methods used to prepare and titrate solutions.

- Deduce the equations needed to analyse the titration results.

- Use the average titre to calculate the concentration of the solution being titrated.

## Observation-Deduction

**In this section we are learning to:**

- Record appropriate observations and deductions during the analysis of inorganic compounds and organic compounds.

### Testing for Ions

If an unknown compound is identified as a salt or other inorganic compound the observation-deduction exercise will likely involve one or more of the following:

- describing the compound and an aqueous solution of the compound,
- using dilute sodium hydroxide solution and/or ammonia solution to test for the presence of transition metal cations,
- forming complexes by adding solutions containing ligands to a solution of the compound, and
- testing for a hydrated salt by heating a solid sample of the unknown.

The observation-deduction exercise may also involve tests for anions such as chloride and sulfate, and in the case of a mixture, tests for cations such as barium ion, $Ba^{2+}$ and ammonium ion, $NH_4^+$ that are familiar from AS level.

### Worked Example 6ii

The following table details the results of tests conducted on a salt, labelled A.

(a) Record appropriate deductions in the table.

| Test | Observations | Deductions |
|---|---|---|
| 1. Describe the appearance of A. | Blue solid. | Transition metal compound. |
| 2. Dissolve 1 spatula measure of A in approximately 50 cm³ of water. | The solid dissolves to form a blue solution. | The compound is soluble. Copper(II) ion present. |
| 3. Add a few drops of barium chloride solution to 2 cm³ of the solution of A. | White precipitate formed. Blue solution remains. | Sulfate ion present. |
| 4. Add a few drops of sodium hydroxide solution to 2 cm³ of the solution of A. | Blue precipitate formed. | Copper(II) hydroxide formed. |
| 5. In a fume cupboard, add excess concentrated ammonia solution dropwise, until present in excess, to 2 cm³ of the solution of A. | Blue precipitate formed. Precipitate dissolves in excess ammonia. Dark blue solution formed. | Copper(II) hydroxide formed. Confirms copper(II) ion present. |
| 6. Add an equal volume of concentrated hydrochloric acid to 2 cm³ of the solution of A. | Yellow solution formed. | Copper(II) complex with chloride formed. |

(b) Write formulas for the complexes formed in tests 2, 5 and 6.

Test 2 $[Cu(H_2O)_6]^{2+}$
Test 5 $[Cu(NH_3)_4(H_2O)_2]^{2+}$
Test 6 $[CuCl_4]^{2-}$

(c) Use your deductions to identify compound A.

Hydrated copper(II) sulfate

*(Adapted from CCEA June 2010)*

## Exercise 6B

1. The following table details the results of tests conducted on a salt, labelled A.
(a) Record appropriate deductions in the table. (b) Give the formula of salt A.

| Test | Observations | Deductions |
|---|---|---|
| 1. Dissolve A in 20 cm³ of water. | Orange solution formed. | Transition metal compound possibly $Fe^{3+}$ compound |
| 2. Add a few drops of concentrated ammonia solution to 2 cm³ of the solution of A in a test tube. | Brown precipitate formed. | Confirms $Fe^{3+}$ present |
| 3. Add 1 cm³ of barium chloride solution to 2 cm³ of the solution of A in a test tube. Allow the mixture to settle. | White precipitate formed.  Orange solution remains. | Sulfate ion present |

*(Adapted from CCEA May 2015)*

(B) Iron(III) Sulfate
$Fe_2(SO_4)_3$

2. The following table details the results of tests conducted on a salt, labelled A.
(a) Record appropriate deductions in the table. (b) Use your deductions to identify compound A.

| Test | Observations | Deductions |
|---|---|---|
| 1. Describe the appearance of A. | Pink solid. | Transition metal compound |
| 2. Add 1 spatula measure of A to approximately 50 cm³ of water and stir. | The solid dissolves to form a pink solution. | Possibly cobalt(II) or manganese(II) solution |
| 3. Add 10 drops of silver nitrate solution to 2 cm³ of the solution of A in a test tube. Allow to stand. | White precipitate formed.  Pink solution remains. | Chloride ion present |
| 4. Add 5 drops of sodium hydroxide solution to 2 cm³ of the solution of A in a test tube. | Blue precipitate formed.  Precipitate turns brown on standing. | Insoluble hydroxide  confirms cobalt present |
| 5. In a fume cupboard, add 6 cm³ of concentrated ammonia, slowly, to 2 cm³ of the solution of A in a test tube. | Blue precipitate formed.  Precipitate dissolves in excess ammonia. Brown solution formed. | Cobalt(II) hydroxide formed  Cobalt(II) complex with ammonia formed |
| 6. Add 4 cm³ of concentrated hydrochloric acid to 2 cm³ of the solution of A in a test tube. | Blue solution formed. | Cobalt(II) complex with chloride formed |

*(Adapted from CCEA May 2011)*

3. The following table details the results of tests conducted on a salt, labelled X.
(a) Record appropriate deductions in the table. (b) Use your deductions to identify compound X.

| Test | Observations | Deductions |
|---|---|---|
| 1. Describe the appearance of X. | Green solid. | |
| 2. Add 1 spatula measure of X to approximately 50 cm³ of water. | The compound dissolves to form a green solution. | |
| 3. Add 10 drops of silver nitrate solution to 2 cm³ of the solution of X in a test tube. Allow to stand. | White precipitate formed. Green solution remains. | |
| 4. Add 5 drops of sodium hydroxide solution to 2 cm³ of the solution of X in a test tube. | Green precipitate formed. | |
| 5. In a fume cupboard, add 6 cm³ of concentrated ammonia, slowly, to 2 cm³ of the solution of X in a test tube. | Green precipitate formed. Precipitate dissolves in excess ammonia. Blue solution formed. | |
| 6. Add 2 cm³ of edta solution to 2 cm³ of the solution of X in a test tube. | Blue solution formed. | |

*(Adapted from CCEA June 2011)*

4. The following table details the results of tests conducted on a salt, labelled X.
(a) Record appropriate deductions in the table. (b) Use your deductions to identify X.

| Test | Observations | Deductions |
|---|---|---|
| 1. Describe the appearance of X. | Green solid. | |
| 2. Add a spatula measure of X to 50 cm³ of deionised water and stir until there is no further change. | The compound dissolves to form a green solution. | |
| 3. Add 5 drops of silver nitrate solution to a test tube containing 2 cm³ of the solution of X. Allow the mixture to stand. | White precipitate formed. Green solution remains. | |
| 4. Put 2 cm³ of the solution of X into a test tube. (a) Add 5 drops of sodium hydroxide solution. (b) Add a further 5 cm³ of sodium hydroxide solution. | (a) Green-blue precipitate formed. (b) Precipitate dissolves to form a green solution. | |
| 5. Place a spatula measure of solid X in a dry boiling tube and heat gently. | Colourless liquid formed on the side of the boiling tube. Solid changes colour. | |

*(Adapted from CCEA May 2013)*

5. The following table details the results of tests conducted on a salt, labelled R. (a) Record appropriate deductions in the table. (b) Use your deductions to identify R.

| Test | Observations | Deductions |
|---|---|---|
| 1. Describe the appearance of R. | Pink solid. | |
| 2. Add a spatula measure of R to 50 cm$^3$ of deionised water and stir until there is no further change. | The compound dissolves to form a pink solution. | |
| 3. Add 5 drops of silver nitrate solution to a test tube containing 2 cm$^3$ of the solution of R. Allow the mixture to stand. | White precipitate formed. Pink solution remains. | |
| 4. Put 2 cm$^3$ of the solution of R into a test tube. (a) Add 5 drops of sodium hydroxide solution and allow to stand. (b) Add a further 5 cm$^3$ of sodium hydroxide solution. | White precipitate formed. Precipitate turns brown on standing. Precipitate remains. | |
| 5. Place a spatula measure of solid R in a dry boiling tube and heat gently. | Colourless liquid formed on the side of the boiling tube. Solid changes colour. | |

*(Adapted from CCEA May 2013)*

6. The following table details the results of tests conducted on an inorganic compound, labelled A. (a) Record appropriate deductions in the table. (b) Use your deductions to identify A. (c) Suggest the formulas of the complex ions formed in tests 2, 3, 4 and 6. (d) Give the formulas of the precipitates formed in tests 5 and 7.

| Test | Observations | Deductions |
|---|---|---|
| 1. Describe the appearance of A. | Blue solid. | |
| 2. Dissolve two spatula measures of A in 50 cm$^3$ of water. Keep this solution for use in further tests. | The compound dissolves to form a blue solution. | |
| 3. Place 4 cm$^3$ of the solution from test 2 in a test tube. Add an equal volume of concentrated hydrochloric acid. | Yellow solution formed. | |
| 4. Place 4 cm$^3$ of the solution from test 2 in a test tube. Add an equal volume of 1,2-diaminoethane solution. | Violet solution formed. | |
| 5. (a) Place 4 cm$^3$ of the solution from test 2 in a test tube. Slowly add an equal volume of sodium hydroxide solution. (b) Add a further 5 cm$^3$ of sodium hydroxide solution. | Blue precipitate formed. Blue precipitate remains. | |

| Test | Observations | Deductions |
|---|---|---|
| 6. Place 4 cm³ of the solution from test 2 in a test tube. In a fume cupboard, add an equal volume of concentrated ammonia solution. | Blue precipitate forms.<br><br>Blue precipitate dissolves to form a dark blue solution on mixing. | |
| 7. Place 4 cm³ of the solution from test 2 in a test tube. Add 1 cm³ of barium chloride solution dropwise. | White precipitate formed. | |

*(Adapted from CCEA June 2014)*

7. The following table details the results of tests conducted on an inorganic compound, labelled A. (a) Record appropriate deductions in the table. (b) Use your deductions to identify compound A. (c) Complex ions are formed in tests 4, 5(a) and 5(b). Write the formulas of the complex ions formed in these tests. (d) Explain why a reaction occurs in test 5(b).

| Test | Observations | Deductions |
|---|---|---|
| 1. Describe the appearance of A. | Green solid. | |
| 2. Dissolve three spatula measures of A in 15 cm³ of deionised water.<br><br>Keep this solution for tests 3(a), 4, 5(a) and 6. | The compound dissolves to form a green solution. | |
| 3. (a) Place 2 cm³ of the solution from test 2 in a test tube and add an equal volume of sodium hydroxide solution.<br><br>(b) Add a further 5 cm³ of sodium hydroxide solution to the test tube. | Green precipitate formed.<br><br><br><br>Green precipitate remains. | |
| 4. Place 2 cm³ of the solution from test 2 in a test tube and add 4 cm³ of edta solution. | Blue solution formed. | |
| 5. (a) Place 2 cm³ of the solution from test 2 in a test tube and add 5 cm³ of dilute ammonia solution.<br><br>(b) Place 2 cm³ of the solution from test 5(a) in another test tube and add 2 cm³ of 1,2-diaminoethane (en) solution. | Blue solution formed.<br><br><br><br>Violet solution formed. | |
| 6. Place 2 cm³ of the solution from test 2 in another test tube and add 2 cm³ of barium chloride solution. Allow to stand. | White precipitate formed. | |

*(Adapted from CCEA May 2012)*

8. The following table details the results of tests conducted on an inorganic compound, labelled B. (a) Record appropriate deductions in the table. (b) Use your deductions to identify compound B. (c) Complex ions are formed in tests 4(b), 5(a) and 5(b). Write the formulas of the complex ions formed in these tests. (d) Explain why a reaction occurs in test 5(b).

| Test | Observations | Deductions |
|---|---|---|
| 1. Describe the appearance of B. | Pink solid. | *Transition metal compound* |
| 2. Dissolve three spatula measures of B in 15 cm³ of deionised water. Keep this solution for tests 3(a), 4(a), 5(a) and 6. | The compound dissolves to form a pink solution. | *The compound is soluble* |
| 3. (a) Place 3 cm³ of the solution from test 2 in a test tube and add 5 drops of sodium hydroxide solution. | Blue precipitate formed. | *Copper hydroxide* |
| (b) Add a further 5 cm³ of sodium hydroxide solution to the test tube. | Blue precipitate remains. Precipitate turns brown on standing. | *Possibly manganese or cobalt ions* |
| 4. (a) In a fume cupboard place 2 cm³ of the solution from test 2 in a test tube and add 3 drops of concentrated ammonia solution. | Blue precipitate formed. | *Cobalt hydroxide* |
| (b) Add a further 5 cm³ of concentrated ammonia solution to the test tube. | Precipitate dissolves in excess ammonia. Brown solution formed. | *Confirms cobalt* |
| 5. (a) Place 3 cm³ of the solution from test 2 in a test tube and in a fume cupboard, add 5 cm³ of concentrated hydrochloric acid. | Blue solution formed. | |
| (b) Place 3 cm³ of the solution from test 5(a) in another test tube and add 5 cm³ of edta solution. | Pink solution formed. | |
| 6. Place 3 cm³ of the solution from test 2 in another test tube and add 3 cm³ of barium chloride solution. | White precipitate formed. | |

*(Adapted from CCEA May 2012)*

Before moving to the next section, check that you are able to:

- Record appropriate observations and deductions when testing for the presence of ions in transition metal compounds and mixtures of inorganic compounds containing a transition metal compound.
- Write ionic equations for any reactions which occur.
- Deduce formulas for any complexes formed and explain why ligand replacement occurs.

## Testing for Functional Groups

If an unknown compound is identified as an organic compound, or a mixture of organic compounds, it may contain compounds familiar at AS or A2 level, and the observation-deduction exercise may involve one or more of the following:

- describing the physical properties of the unknown,
- burning a sample of the unknown,
- using bromine water to test for unsaturation,
- using acidified dichromate to oxidise the unknown, and
- using a base to test for acidity.

The deductions may then be used in conjunction with the mass spectrum, NMR spectrum or IR spectrum of a compound, to deduce the structure of the unknown.

### Worked Example 6iii

The following table details the results of tests conducted on an aqueous solution of an organic compound, labelled B. (a) Record appropriate deductions in the table.

| Test | Observations | Deductions |
|---|---|---|
| 1. Describe the solution. Include a description of its smell. | Colourless liquid. Vinegar smell. | The liquid contains ethanoic acid. |
| 2. Place 4 cm³ of the solution in a test tube. Add an equal volume of potassium dichromate solution and acidify with 1 cm³ of dilute sulfuric acid. Heat in a water bath for five minutes. | The orange colour of dichromate ion remains after heating. No change in smell. | The liquid cannot be oxidised. Confirms ethanoic acid is present. |
| 3. Place 4 cm³ of the solution in a test tube. Add half a spatula measure of sodium hydrogencarbonate. | The solid disappears. Colourless solution formed. Fizzing. Colourless gas produced. Turns limewater milky. | Confirms that the liquid is acidic. Carbon dioxide is produced. |

(b) Identify the functional group present in B.

A carboxyl (-COOH) group.

(c) Suggest how the infrared spectrum of B could confirm the presence of this functional group.

The infrared spectrum would contain strong absorption due to the C=O bond in the carboxyl group and strong absorption due to the O-H bond in the carboxyl group.

(d) Suggest how the mass spectrum of B could confirm its identity.

The mass spectrum may contain a molecular ion signal with an m/z value equal to the RMM of the compound. The relative abundance of each fragment ion in the mass spectrum would also be unique and could be used to identify the compound.

*(Adapted from CCEA May 2014)*

### Exercise 6C

1. The following table details the results of tests conducted on an organic liquid containing one functional group, labelled Y. The mass spectrum of Y is also provided. (a) Record appropriate deductions in the table. (b) Identify the homologous series Y belongs to. (c) Deduce the structure of Y. Explain your reasoning.

| Test | Observations | Deductions |
|---|---|---|
| 1. (a) Place 2 cm³ of Y into a boiling tube. Place in a test tube rack. Cautiously add a very small measure of phosphorus(V) chloride in a fume cupboard. | Solid disappears. Steamy fumes. Mixture warms up. | |
| (b) In a fume cupboard, hold the stopper of a bottle of concentrated ammonia solution over the boiling tube used in test 1(a). | White fumes of solid ammonium chloride. | |
| 2. Place 2 cm³ of Y into a test tube. Add 1 cm³ of sodium carbonate solution. | Solid disappears. Colourless solution formed. Fizzing. Colourless gas produced. | |

Mass spectrum of Y:

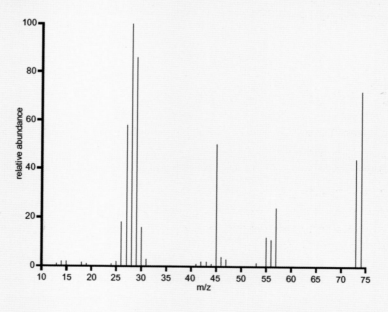

*(Adapted from CCEA May 2013)*

2. Use the following data to deduce the structural formula of the organic compound B, which has the *empirical formula* $C_2H_4O$. (a) Record appropriate deductions in the table. (b) Identify the homologous series B belongs to. (c) Draw a structure for B showing all the bonds present. (d) Identify the species responsible for the base peak in the mass spectrum.

| Test | Observations | Deductions |
|---|---|---|
| 1. Describe the appearance of B. | Colourless liquid. Pungent smell. | |
| 2. Add 2 cm³ of deionised water to 2 cm³ of B in a test tube. | One layer formed. | |
| 3. Add 10 drops of B to 2 cm³ of acidified potassium dichromate solution in a test tube. Place the test tube in a hot water bath. | The orange colour of dichromate ion remains after heating. No change in smell. | |
| 4. Place 2 cm³ of B into a test tube. In a fume cupboard cautiously add 1 very small spatula measure of phosphorus(V) chloride to the test tube. | Solid disappears. Steamy fumes. Mixture warms up. | |
| 5. Place 5 cm³ of B in a boiling tube. Add 5 cm³ of ethanol, and then 1 cm³ of concentrated sulfuric acid. Heat the boiling tube in a water bath. Cautiously smell the contents of the boiling tube. | Sweet smell produced on heating the mixture. | |
| 6. Add a spatula measure of sodium carbonate to 2 cm³ of B in a test tube. | The solid disappears. Colourless solution formed. Fizzing. Colourless gas produced. | |

Mass spectrum of B:

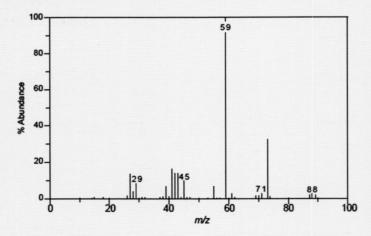

*(Adapted from CCEA May 2015)*

3. Compounds B and C both have the molecular formula $C_3H_6O$. They both produce an orange solid when reacted with 2,4-dinitrophenylhydrazine. (a) Use the observations given to record appropriate deductions in the table. (b) Deduce the structural formula of B. (c) Deduce the structural formula of C.

| Test | Observations | Deductions |
|---|---|---|
| Mix 1 cm³ of Fehling's No 1 solution with an equal volume of Fehling's No 2 solution. Add about 1 cm³ of B and heat in a water bath for at least 5 minutes. | Red precipitate formed on heating. | |

*(Adapted from CCEA May 2010)*

4. Compounds D and E have the molecular formula $C_3H_6O_2$. They both produce a triplet, quartet and singlet in their NMR spectra. (a) Use the observations given to record appropriate deductions in the table. (b) Deduce the structural formula of D. (c) Deduce the structural formula of E.

| Test | Observations | Deductions |
|---|---|---|
| Add a spatula measure of sodium carbonate to about 1 cm³ of D in a test tube. | The solid disappears. Colourless solution formed. Fizzing. Colourless gas produced. | |

*(Adapted from CCEA May 2010)*

5. The following table details the results of tests conducted on an aqueous mixture of two organic compounds, labelled Y. Both compounds in the mixture contain a carbonyl group. (a) Record appropriate deductions in the table. (b) State the two types of organic compound in the mixture Y.

| Test | Observations | Deductions |
|---|---|---|
| 1. Describe the appearance of Y. Cautiously smell Y and give a description of its smell. | Colourless liquid. Pungent smell. | |
| 2. Place 3 cm³ of Y in a test tube and add 10 drops of acidified potassium dichromate solution. Warm in a water bath. | The solution changes from orange to green on heating. Change in smell. | |
| 3. Place 3 cm³ of Y in another test tube and add half a spatula measure of sodium hydrogencarbonate. | The solid disappears. Colourless solution formed. Fizzing. Colourless gas produced. The temperature of the solution decreases. | |

*(Adapted from CCEA May 2012)*

6. The following table details the results of tests conducted on an aqueous mixture of two organic compounds, labelled Z. Both compounds in the mixture contain a carbonyl group. (a) Record appropriate deductions in the table. (b) State the two types of organic compound in the mixture Z.

| Test | Observations | Deductions |
|---|---|---|
| 1. Describe the appearance of Z. Cautiously smell Z and give a description of its smell. | Colourless solution. Pungent smell. | |
| 2. Place 3 cm³ of Z in a test tube and add 10 drops of acidified potassium dichromate solution. Warm in a water bath. | The orange colour of dichromate ion remains after heating. No change in smell. | |
| 3. Place 3 cm³ of Z in another test tube and add half a spatula measure of sodium hydrogencarbonate. | The solid disappears. Colourless solution formed. Fizzing. Colourless gas produced. The temperature of the solution decreases. | |

*(Adapted from CCEA May 2012)*

7. The following table details the results of tests conducted on an organic compound with two functional groups, labelled B. The infrared and NMR spectra of B are also given, and correspond to molecules of B that have made an internal structural rearrangement. (a) Record appropriate deductions in the table. (b) Draw the structure of B. Explain your reasoning.

| Test | Observations | Deductions |
|---|---|---|
| 1. Describe the appearance of B. | White crystalline solid. | |
| 2. Heat one spatula measure of B in a test tube. Heat gently at first and then more strongly. Test any fumes with a glass rod dipped in concentrated hydrochloric acid. | Pungent smelling gas produced. White fumes of solid ammonium chloride. | |
| 3. (a) Dissolve 2 spatula measures of B in approximately 20 cm³ of water. (b) Use Universal Indicator paper to determine the pH of the solution of B. | Solid disappears. Colourless solution formed. Indicator paper turns green. | |
| 4. Add 6 drops of copper(II) sulfate solution, dropwise, to a test tube half-full of a solution of B. | Blue solution formed. | |
| 5. To 3 cm³ of acidified potassium dichromate solution add one spatula measure of B and warm gently. | The orange colour of dichromate ion remains after heating. No change in smell. | |

Infrared spectrum of B:

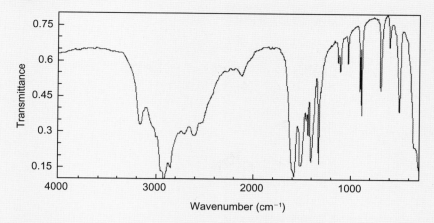

Hydrogen atoms attached to electronegative atoms such as N or O absorb in the region above 3000 cm$^{-1}$. The actual absorption region is affected by acidity and whether the IR spectrum is obtained for the solid or a solution of the substance.

The carbonyl group in ketones absorbs at 1720 cm$^{-1}$. All other compounds containing C=O groups absorb from 1580 to 1800 cm$^{-1}$.

NMR spectrum of B:

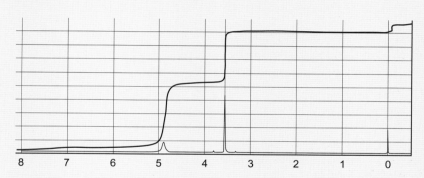

*(Adapted from CCEA May 2011)*

| Before moving to the next section, check that you are able to: |
| --- |

- Record appropriate observations and deductions when testing for functional groups in organic compounds.
- Use the mass spectrum, NMR spectrum or IR spectrum of a compound to help identify the compound.

## Structured Questions

### In this section we are learning to:

- Use practical knowledge to account for the techniques used in the preparation and purification of compounds.
- Use practical knowledge to analyse experimental data and evaluate the experimental techniques used to acquire data.

The structured questions test understanding of how practical techniques such as reflux, distillation, vacuum filtration, recrystallisation, and melting point determination, are used in the preparation and purification of compounds. The questions may also test understanding of the techniques used to collect and analyse the data needed to determine physical quantities such as: the rate of a reaction, the solubility of a compound, and enthalpy changes.

### Exercise 6D

1. Tin(IV) iodide is a solid which can be prepared by reaction of excess tin with iodine by refluxing in a suitable solvent such as dichloromethane, $CH_2Cl_2$ which is toxic and flammable. (a) Write an equation for the reaction. (b) Calculate the mass of iodine needed to produce 6.0 g of tin(IV) iodide assuming a 90% yield. (c) State and explain the relevant safety precautions apart from using safety glasses and a fume cupboard. (d) Explain the term *refluxing*. (e) How would you know when all the iodine has reacted? (f) How is the unreacted tin removed from the reaction mixture? (g) How would you obtain crude tin(IV) iodide from the reaction mixture? (h) Explain how the crude tin(IV) iodide could be purified using the solvent.

*(Adapted from CCEA June 2010)*

2. Ethyl methanoate, $HCOOCH_2CH_3$ exists as a liquid at room temperature and pressure. Its boiling point is 55 °C and its density is 0.9 g $cm^{-3}$. (a) Write the equation for the formation of ethyl methanoate from methanoic acid and ethanol. (b) Assuming a 60 % yield, calculate the minimum mass of each reactant required to produce 4.44 g of ethyl methanoate.

(c) Describe the laboratory preparation of ethyl methanoate up to and including the removal of the crude product from the reaction mixture. (d) The crude product can be purified using an aqueous solution of sodium carbonate followed by anhydrous calcium chloride. (i) Explain why and how the sodium carbonate is used. (ii) Explain why and how the anhydrous calcium chloride is used. (e) Part of the NMR spectrum of ethyl methanoate is shown below. Complete the spectrum showing details of the integration and splitting.

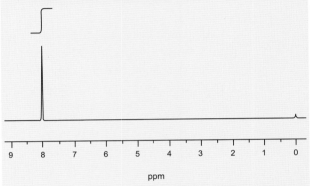

*(Adapted from CCEA May 2014)*

3. Ethyl 3-nitrobenzoate exists as a solid at room temperature and pressure. Its melting point is 42 °C.

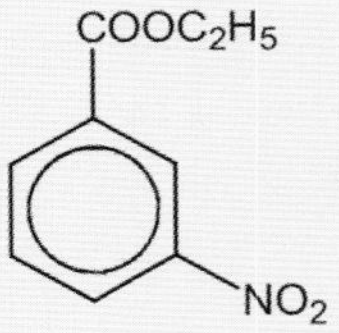

ethyl 3-nitrobenzoate

(a) Write the equation for the formation of ethyl 3-nitrobenzoate from ethyl benzoate. (b) Assuming a 60 % yield, calculate the minimum mass of the organic reactant required to produce 5.85 g of ethyl 3-nitrobenzoate. (c) Describe the laboratory preparation of ethyl 3-nitrobenzoate up to and including the removal of the crude product from the reaction mixture. (d) The crude product is recrystallised before its melting point is determined. Explain why recrystallisation is carried out and, giving experimental details, describe the process of recrystallisation. (e) State one method that could be used to dry the crystals before their melting point is determined. (f) Explain how you would use the melting point to determine if the crystals of ethyl 3-nitrobenzoate are pure. (g) Part of the NMR spectrum of ethyl 3-nitrobenzoate is shown below. The aromatic protons are shown. Complete the spectrum showing details of the integration and splitting.

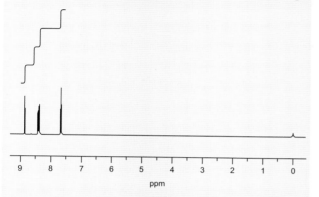

*(Adapted from CCEA May 2014)*

4. Benzene is used to prepare nitrobenzene (bpt 211 °C), which is then used to make phenylamine (bpt 184 °C).

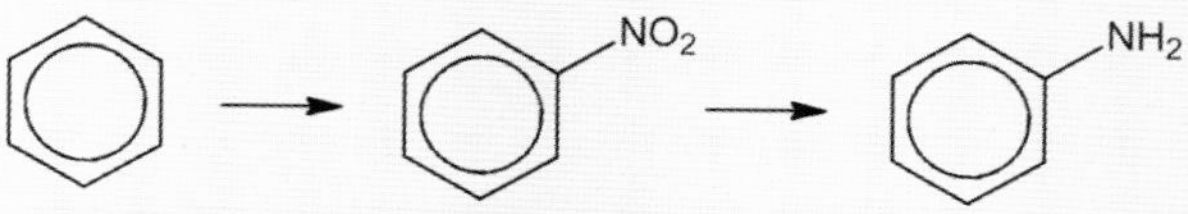

Nitrobenzene is prepared from benzene as follows:

*Concentrated nitric acid, concentrated sulfuric acid and benzene (density 0.88 g cm⁻³) are mixed slowly in a round-bottomed flask, ensuring the temperature does not rise above 60 °C. A reflux condenser is attached and the mixture is heated on a water bath for 30 minutes. The mixture is poured into 100 cm³ of water and the acidic impurities are removed. The organic layer is run off, dried with anhydrous sodium sulfate and placed in a round-bottomed flask. The apparatus is rearranged for distillation and the contents of the round-bottomed flask are distilled using an air condenser (a condenser where no water flows through the outside jacket), collecting the fraction boiling between 207–211 °C.*

(a) Suggest why ammonia will not react with benzene. (b) Define the term *reflux*. (c) Draw a labelled diagram of the apparatus used for this distillation. (d) Calculate the volume of benzene

required to synthesise 7.0 g of nitrobenzene assuming a 90 % yield. (e) Outline, giving practical details, how acidic impurities can be removed from the crude liquid prior to distillation. (f) Phenylamine can be converted to iodobenzene, according to the following flow scheme. Draw the structure of the benzenediazonium ion formed in the process.

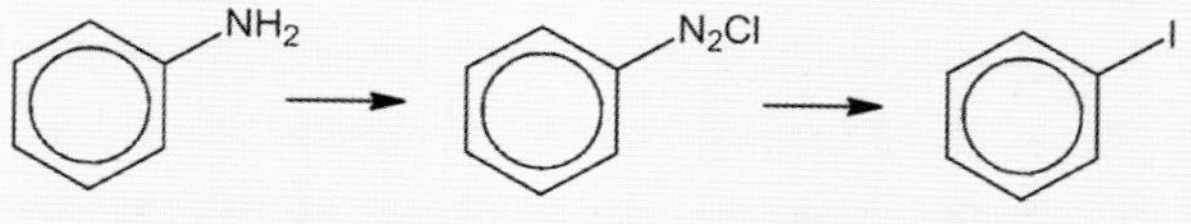

*(Adapted from CCEA May 2015)*

5. Aspirin can be prepared by reacting 2-hydroxy-benzoic acid with ethanoic anhydride in the presence of concentrated phosphoric(V) acid. The product has a melting point of 135 °C.

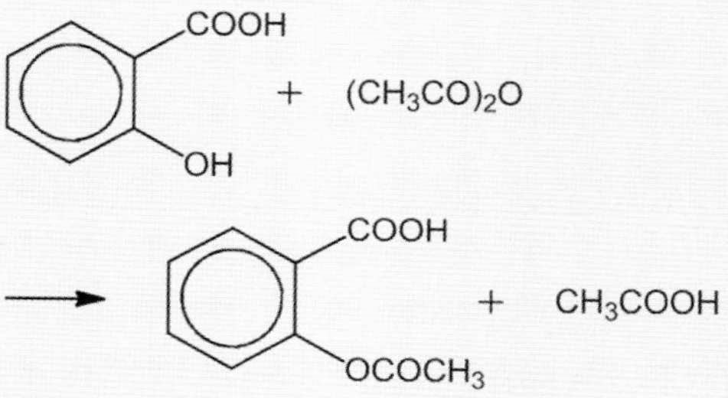

The following method is used:

*Place 20.0 g of 2-hydroxybenzoic acid in a pear-shaped flask and add 40 cm³ of ethanoic anhydride. Safely add 5 cm³ of concentrated phosphoric(V) acid to the mixture. Heat under reflux. Add water to hydrolyse any unreacted ethanoic anhydride to form ethanoic acid. Pour the mixture onto 400 g of crushed ice in a beaker. The product is removed by suction filtration, recrystallised from water, and dried in a desiccator. The melting point is then determined.*

(a) Suggest the role of the concentrated phosphoric(V) acid. (b) Explain how you would *safely* add the concentrated phosphoric(V) acid. (c) Explain what is meant by the term *reflux*. (d) Draw a labelled diagram showing the apparatus used for refluxing. (e) Write an equation for the hydrolysis of ethanoic anhydride. (f) Explain why the mixture is poured onto ice. (g) Explain why suction filtration is used. (h) Describe how the impure product is recrystallised. (i) Assuming a 65% yield, calculate the mass of 2-hydroxybenzoic acid required to form 5.0 g of pure aspirin.

(Adapted from CCEA May 2013)

6. Urea, $(NH_2)_2CO$, was first synthesised by Friedrich Wöhler in 1828. Today some 7 million tons of urea are produced per year, mainly for use as a fertiliser. Urea can be prepared in the laboratory by reacting lead(II) cyanate, $Pb(CNO)_2$ with ammonia and water to produce lead(II) hydroxide and ammonium cyanate, $NH_4CNO$. The ammonium cyanate then rearranges when heated to form urea, which has a melting point of 133 °C.

urea

(a) Write an equation for the reaction of lead(II) cyanate with ammonia and water. (b) Assuming a 70 % yield, calculate the mass of lead(II) cyanate required to produce 450 g of ammonium cyanate. (c) Ammonium cyanate rearranges to form urea as per the equation: $NH_4CNO \rightarrow (NH_2)_2CO$. (i) The crude product is purified by dissolving in the minimum amount of hot ethanol, filtering the mixture, and cooling. Name this process. (ii) Explain how a suitable solvent is chosen. (iii) Explain why the minimum amount of hot solvent is used. (iv) Explain how the pure, dry product is obtained from the filtrate. (d) Giving practical details, describe how you would determine whether or not the crystals of urea produced are pure. (e) Explain how you could use the following data to follow the progress of the rearrangement.

| Bond | Wavenumber ($cm^{-1}$) |
| --- | --- |
| C=O | 1650 |
| C≡N | 2100 |
| N-H (in amines) | 3200–3500 |

(CCEA May 2013)

7. Sodium peroxide, $Na_2O_2$ may be prepared by passing dry oxygen over sodium in a 'boat' made of aluminium foil which is placed in a combustion tube. The tube is heated until the sodium melts. It is further heated until the sodium burns. At this stage the heating can be turned down. After reaction a stream of dry air is passed through the combustion tube. The resulting sodium peroxide is placed in a stoppered bottle and weighed. The sodium peroxide is obtained as a white solid with a slightly yellow appearance. It reacts readily with water to produce hydrogen peroxide or oxygen depending on the temperature at which the reaction is carried out.

(a) Write an equation, including state symbols, for the reaction of sodium with oxygen to produce sodium peroxide. (b) Calculate the mass of sodium needed to form 1.3 g of sodium peroxide assuming an 80% yield. (c) Explain why it is essential that the oxygen, which is passed over the sodium, is dry. (d) Draw a labelled diagram of the apparatus used to prepare sodium peroxide, showing how the oxygen gas may be dried. (e) Sodium peroxide may be used to prepare hydrogen peroxide by reacting it with acids at low temperatures. Adding phosphoric(V) acid to sodium peroxide produces disodium hydrogenphosphate, $Na_2HPO_4$, which recrystallises with 12 molecules of water. (i) Write an equation for the reaction of phosphoric(V) acid with sodium peroxide. (ii) Suggest why this method is better than using hydrochloric acid producing sodium chloride, which crystallises without molecules of water, to prepare a *concentrated* solution of hydrogen peroxide. (f) Sodium peroxide reacts with water at higher temperatures to form sodium hydroxide and oxygen. Describe how you would use GLC to show that oxygen was given off.

(CCEA June 2011)

8. Sodium thiosulfate, $Na_2S_2O_3$, may be prepared by boiling a mixture of powdered roll sulfur and aqueous sodium sulfate(IV) for 30–40 minutes. Excess sulfur is removed. The resulting solution is concentrated by evaporation. The evaporated solution, on cooling, produces crystals of sodium thiosulfate

pentahydrate which are removed by vacuum filtration. The crystals are washed with ethanol and dried using filter paper. The purity of the crystals can be measured by titration with a standard solution of iodine (in potassium iodide solution).

(a) Write an equation, including state symbols, for the reaction of sodium sulfate(IV) solution with sulfur to produce sodium thiosulfate. (b) Write the formula of sodium thiosulfate pentahydrate. (c) Calculate the volume of $0.060 \ mol \ dm^{-3}$ sodium sulfate(IV) needed to prepare 2.5 g of sodium thiosulfate pentahydrate assuming an 80% yield. (d) Draw a labelled diagram of the apparatus used to carry out vacuum filtration. (e) Explain the purpose of washing the sodium thiosulfate with ethanol. (f) The purity of the sodium thiosulfate may be determined using iodine solution. (i) Write an equation for the reaction. (ii) Calculate the percentage purity of a sample of sodium thiosulfate, if 1.2 g of sodium thiosulfate, $Na_2S_2O_3$ required 25.0 $cm^3$ of 0.10 mol $dm^{-3}$ iodine, $I_2$ solution.

*(Adapted from CCEA May 2011)*

Before moving to the next section, check that you are able to:

- Describe and explain the application of standard laboratory techniques to the preparation and purification of compounds.

- Use practical data including percentage yield, atom economy and percentage purity to calculate reacting amounts.

# Answers

## 4.1 Energetics

### Exercise 4.1A

1. Lattice enthalpy is the enthalpy change when one mole of an ionic compound is converted to gas phase ions.

2. Answer D

3. Answer D

4. (a) Energy is required to separate the ions in the lattice.

   (b) The attraction between the calcium ions and halide ions in the lattice decreases as the halide ions get bigger down Group VII.

5. The Group I cations in the lattice become bigger down the group.

6. The Group VII anions in the lattice become bigger down the group.

7. (a) $MgCl_{2(s)} \rightarrow Mg^{2+}_{(g)} + 2Cl^-_{(g)}$

   (b) The attractive forces between oppositely charged ions in $MgCl_2$ are greater as magnesium ions have a bigger charge than sodium ions.

### Exercise 4.1B

1. Answer D

2. Answer D

3. Answer C

4. (a)(i) The enthalpy of atomisation of the halogen (C), (ii) The first electron affinity of the halogen (D), and (iii) The enthalpy of formation of the compound (E).

   (b) (i) The enthalpy of atomisation for chlorine is greater because the Cl-Cl bond enthalpy is greater. (ii) The electron affinity for chlorine is greater because the outermost electrons are closer to the nucleus and less shielded. (iii) The enthalpy of formation is greater for KCl because chloride (Cl⁻) is smaller than bromide (Br⁻) and forms stronger ionic bonds.

5. Answer B

### Exercise 4.1C

1. (a)

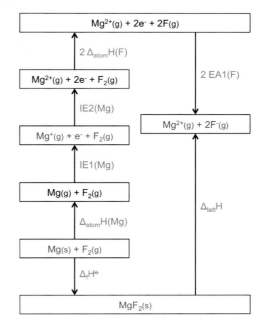

   (b) $\Delta_{atoms}H = \Delta_{atom}H(Mg) + 2\Delta_{atom}H(F)$

   $= 150 + 2(79) = 308 \text{ kJ mol}^{-1}$

   $\Delta_{ions}H = IE1(Mg) + IE2(Mg) + 2EA1(F)$

   $= 736 + 1450 + 2(-348) = 1490 \text{ kJ mol}^{-1}$

   $\Delta_{latt}H = \Delta_{atoms}H + \Delta_{ions}H - \Delta_f H^{\ominus}$

   $= 308 + 1490 - (-1123) = 2921 \text{ kJ mol}^{-1}$

2. (a) Born-Haber cycle

   (b) Step 1 is the enthalpy of formation for magnesium chloride. Step 2 is the enthalpy of atomisation for magnesium. Step 3 is twice the first electron affinity for chlorine.

   (c) $\Delta_{latt}H = +2545 \text{ kJ mol}^{-1}$

3. (a) (i) E  (ii) D  (iii) B  (iv) A

   (b) $\Delta_{atoms}H = \Delta_{atom}H(K) + \Delta_{atom}H(I) = A + C$
   $= 196.1 \text{ kJ mol}^{-1}$

   $\Delta_{ions}H = IE1(K) + EA1(I) = B + D$
   $= 124.6 \text{ kJ mol}^{-1}$

   $\Delta_{latt}H = \Delta_{atoms}H + \Delta_{ions}H - \Delta_f H^{\ominus}$
   $= 196.1 + 124.6 - (-327.6)$
   $= 648.3 \text{ kJ mol}^{-1}$

## Exercise 4.1D

1. (a)

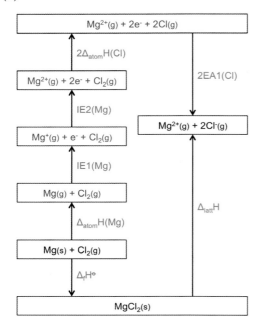

(b) $\Delta_{atom}H = \Delta_{atom}H(Mg) + 2\Delta_{atom}H(Cl)$
= 150 + 2(121) = 392 kJ mol$^{-1}$

$\Delta_{ion}H = IE1(Mg) + IE2(Mg) + 2EA1(Cl)$
= 736 + 1450 + 2EA1(Cl) kJ mol$^{-1}$

$\Delta_{latt}H = \Delta_{atoms}H + \Delta_{ions}H - \Delta_{f}H^{\ominus}$
= 392 + 2186 + 2EA1(Cl) − (−642)
= 2493 kJ mol$^{-1}$

EA1(Cl) = −363.5 kJ mol$^{-1}$

2. (a) $\Delta_{f}H = +1464$ kJ mol$^{-1}$

(b) The enthalpy of formation for an ionic compound is negative.

(c) The attraction between the calcium ions and chloride ions in the lattice increases as the charge on the calcium ions increases.

## Exercise 4.1E

1. (a)

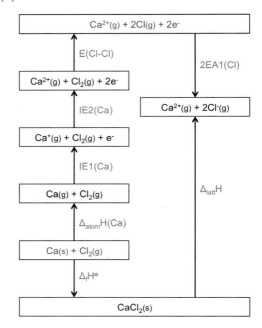

(b) The second ionisation energy of calcium.

(c) $\Delta_{atoms}H = \Delta_{atom}H(Ca) + E(Cl\text{-}Cl)$
= 190 + 242 = 432 kJ mol$^{-1}$

$\Delta_{ions}H = IE1(Ca) + IE2(Ca) + 2EA1(Cl)$
= 590 + 1146 + 2(−348) = 1040 kJ mol$^{-1}$

$\Delta_{latt}H = \Delta_{atoms}H + \Delta_{ions}H - \Delta_{f}H^{\ominus}$
= 432 + 1040 − (−795) = 2267 kJ mol$^{-1}$

2. (a)

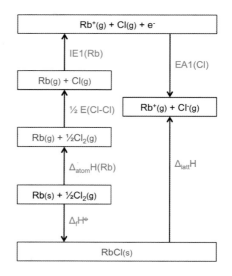

(b) $\Delta_{atoms}H = \Delta_{atom}H(Rb) + \frac{1}{2}E(Cl\text{-}Cl)$
= 81 + $\dfrac{242}{2}$ = 202 kJ mol$^{-1}$

$\Delta_{ions}H = IE1(Rb) + EA1(Cl) = 403 + (−348)$
= 55 kJ mol$^{-1}$

$\Delta_f H^\ominus = \Delta_{atoms}H + \Delta_{ions}H - \Delta_{latt}H$
$= 202 + 55 - 685 = -428 \text{ kJ mol}^{-1}$

3. (a) $\Delta H_{diss}$ is the bond enthalpy for the O=O bond in oxygen, $\Delta H_{atom}$ is the enthalpy of atomisation for magnesium and $I_{Mg}$ is the sum of the first and second ionisation energies for magnesium.

   (b) Applying Hess's law: $\Delta H_f + U = \Delta H_{atom} + \frac{1}{2}\Delta H_{diss} + E_o + I_{Mg}$. Solving gives U $= 3845 \text{ kJ mol}^{-1}$.

   (c) The lattice energy, U is very high. A large amount of energy is needed to separate the ions in MgO.

   (d) Phosphorus(V) oxide is not an ionic compound.

4. (a) Calcium, $Ca^{2+}$ ion: $1s^2 2s^2 2p^6 3s^2 3p^6$

   Hydride, $H^-$ ion: $1s^2$

   (b) $436 \text{ kJ mol}^{-1}$

   (c) IE1 + IE2 = $1740 \text{ kJ mol}^{-1}$. Solving gives IE1 $= 1150 \text{ kJ mol}^{-1}$.

   (d) Applying Hess's law: $-189 + \Delta_{latt}H$
   $= 193 + 1740 + 436 - 144$.
   Solving gives $\Delta_{latt}H = 2414 \text{ kJ mol}^{-1}$.

5. Answer C

6. Iodine has the lowest atomisation energy as the bond between the atoms is the longest and weakest.

7. Answer B

**Exercise 4.1F**

1. (a) The lattice enthalpy of sodium chloride.

   (b) The hydration enthalpy of sodium chloride.

   (c)

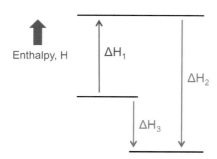

2. The enthalpy of solution is the enthalpy change when one mole of solute dissolves.

3. Answer B

4. (a)

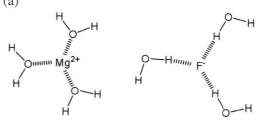

   (b) $\Delta_{hyd}H = \Delta_{hyd}H(Mg^{2+}) + 2\Delta_{hyd}H(Cl^-)$
   $= (-1920) + 2(-364) = -2648 \text{ kJ mol}^{-1}$
   $\Delta_{latt}H = \Delta_{soln}H - \Delta_{hyd}H = (-155) - (-2648)$
   $= 2493 \text{ kJ mol}^{-1}$

5. (a) $KCl_{(s)} \rightarrow K^+_{(aq)} + Cl^-_{(aq)}$

   (b) $\Delta_{hyd}H = \Delta_{hyd}H(K^+) + \Delta_{hyd}H(Cl^-)$
   $= (-305) + (-384) = -689 \text{ kJ mol}^{-1}$
   $\Delta_{soln}H = \Delta_{latt}H + \Delta_{hyd}H = 710 + (-689)$
   $= 21 \text{ kJ mol}^{-1}$

6. $\Delta_{hyd}H = \Delta_{hyd}H(Ca^{2+}) + 2\Delta_{hyd}H(Cl^-)$
   $= (-1651) + 2(-364) = -2379 \text{ kJ mol}^{-1}$
   $\Delta_{soln}H = \Delta_{latt}H + \Delta_{hyd}H = 2267 + (-2379)$
   $= -112 \text{ kJ mol}^{-1}$

## 4.2 Entropy and Free Energy

**Exercise 4.2A**

1. (a) $CH_{4(g)} + 2O_{2(g)} \rightarrow CO_{2(g)} + 2H_2O_{(g)}$

   (b) $\Delta S$ is small as the reaction does not change the number of molecules or the amount of gas in the reaction mixture.

2. Answer D

3. $\Delta S > 0$ as the reaction increases the number of molecules in the reaction mixture and produces a gas from a solution.

4. $\Delta S > 0$ as the reaction produces solvated ions that are free to move from ions with fixed positions in a solid.

5. (a) $Ag^+_{(aq)} + Cl^-_{(aq)} \rightarrow AgCl_{(s)}$

   (b) $\Delta S < 0$ as the reaction transforms solvated ions that are free to move into ions with fixed positions in a solid.

6. Answer A

## Exercise 4.2B

1. (a) $\Delta S^\circ = 2(240.0) - 304.2 = 175.8 \text{ J K}^{-1}$

   (b) $\Delta S^\circ > 0$ as the reaction increases the number of molecules and the amount of gas in the reaction mixture.

2. (a) $\Delta S^\circ = 2(213.6) - 2(197.6) - 205.0 = -173.0 \text{ J K}^{-1}$

   (b) $\Delta S^\circ < 0$ as the reaction reduces the number of molecules and the amount of gas in the reaction mixture.

3. (a) $\Delta S^\circ = 50.9 + 2(27.3) - 87.4 - 2(28.3) = -38.5 \text{ J K}^{-1}$

   (b) $\Delta S^\circ$ is small as the reaction transforms three moles of solid into three moles of solid.

## Exercise 4.2C

1. $\Delta G = \Delta H - T\Delta S = -795 - (298)(-0.152)$
   $= -749.7 \text{ kJ mol}^{-1}$

   The reaction is feasible at 298 K because $\Delta G < 0$.

2. (a) $(NH_4)_2CO_3 + 2CH_3COOH$
   $\rightarrow 2CH_3COONH_4 + H_2O + CO_2$

   (b) A reaction is feasible if $\Delta G < 0$.

   (c) The reaction is endothermic as the temperature drops, which means that $\Delta H^\circ > 0$. The reaction is feasible as $\Delta S^\circ > 0$, and $T\Delta S^\circ$ is bigger than $\Delta H^\circ$, which makes $\Delta G^\circ = \Delta H^\circ - T\Delta S^\circ < 0$.

3. $\Delta S = 220 - 214 - 2(192) - 70 = -448 \text{ J K}^{-1} \text{ mol}^{-1}$
   $= -0.448 \text{ kJ K}^{-1} \text{ mol}^{-1}$

   $T = \dfrac{\Delta H - \Delta G}{\Delta S} = \dfrac{-170 - (-25)}{-0.448} = 324 \text{ K}$

4. (a) Methane is obtained from natural gas or from the cracking of hydrocarbons.

   Ammonia is obtained from the Haber-Bosch process.

   (b) $\Delta H = 217 \text{ kJ mol}^{-1}$

   (c) $\Delta S > 0$ as the reaction increases the amount of gas.

   $T = \dfrac{\Delta H}{\Delta S} = \dfrac{217}{0.125} = 1736 \text{ K}$

5. (a) $\Delta H = -440 \text{ kJ}$

   (b) The entropy change for the reaction is small as the reactants and products are solids.

6. Answer D

## Exercise 4.2D

1. Answer D

2. Answer D

3. (a) $\Delta H^\circ = 3(-393.5) - 2(-824.2) = 467.9 \text{ kJ}$

   $\Delta S^\circ = 4(27.3) + 3(213.6) - 2(87.4) - 3(5.7)$
   $= 558.1 \text{ J K}^{-1}$

   $\Delta G^\circ = \Delta H^\circ - T\Delta S^\circ = 467.9 - (298)(0.5581)$
   $= 301.6 \text{ kJ}$

   (b) The reaction is not feasible as $\Delta G^\circ > 0$.

   (c) $T = \dfrac{\Delta H}{\Delta S} = \dfrac{467.9}{0.5581} = 838.4 \text{ K}$

4. (a) $\Delta H = -766 - 3(-286) = 92 \text{ kJ}$

   Molar enthalpy change $= \dfrac{92}{2} = 46 \text{ kJ mol}^{-1}$

   (b) $\Delta H = 6(388) - 944 - 3(436) = 76 \text{ kJ}$

   Molar enthalpy change $= \dfrac{76}{2} = 38 \text{ kJ mol}^{-1}$

   (c) $\Delta S = 191.6 + 3(130.7) - 2(192.8) = 198.1 \text{ J K}^{-1}$

   Molar enthalpy change $= \dfrac{198.1}{2}$
   $= 99.05 \text{ J K}^{-1} \text{ mol}^{-1}$

   (d) $\Delta G = \Delta H - T\Delta S$

   (e) A process is feasible if $\Delta G < 0$ for the process.

   (f) $T = \dfrac{\Delta H}{\Delta S} = \dfrac{92}{0.1981} = 464 \text{ K}$

5. (a) $\Delta H^\circ = -418 + 3(-394) - 2(-493) = -614 \text{ kJ}$

   (b) $\Delta S^\circ = 115 + 191 + 3(214) - 2(172) - 32 - 3(5.7)$
   $= 554.9 \text{ J K}^{-1}$

   (c) $\Delta G < 0$ at all temperatures because $\Delta H < 0$ and $\Delta S > 0$.

6. (a) Hydrogen is an element.

   (b) $\Delta H^\circ = -393.5 - (-110.5) - (-241.8)$
   $= -41.2 \text{ kJ mol}^{-1}$

   (c) $\Delta S^\circ = 213.6 + 114.6 - 197.9 - 188.7$
   $= -58.4 \text{ J K}^{-1} \text{ mol}^{-1}$

   (d) $T = \dfrac{\Delta H}{\Delta S} = \dfrac{-41.2}{-0.0584} = 705 \text{ K}$

7. (a) $NH_4NO_3 \rightarrow N_2O + 2H_2O$

   (b) $\Delta G = \Delta H - T\Delta S < 0$ at all temperatures because

ΔG is obtained by subtracting a positive number (TΔS) from a negative number (ΔH).

8. (a) The reaction is feasible as $T\Delta S^{\ominus}$ and $\Delta H^{\ominus}$ are positive numbers and $T\Delta S^{\ominus}$ is bigger than $\Delta H^{\ominus}$, making $\Delta G^{\ominus} = \Delta H^{\ominus} - T\Delta S^{\ominus} < 0$.

(b) $\Delta S^{\ominus}$ is the standard entropy change for the reaction.

9. (a) The entropy of a substance is a measure of the amount of disorder in the substance.

(b) $2CH_3COOH + (NH_4)_2CO_3$
   $\rightarrow 2CH_3COONH_4 \ H_2O + CO_2$

(c) $\Delta G < 0$ as $\Delta H$ and $T\Delta S$ are both positive and $T\Delta S$ is bigger than $\Delta H$.

(d) The reaction is not feasible ($\Delta G > 0$) at all temperatures as $\Delta H$ and $-T\Delta S$ are both positive.

## 4.3 Chemical Kinetics

### Exercise 4.3A

1. (a) $\dfrac{1.5 \times 10^{-3}}{2} = 7.5 \times 10^{-4} \ mol \ dm^{-3} \ s^{-1}$

(b) $7.5 \times 10^{-4} \ mol \ dm^{-3} \ s^{-1}$

2. (a) $2.94 \times 10^{-5} \ mol \ dm^{-3} \ s^{-1}$

(b) $2.94 \times 10^{-5} \ mol \ dm^{-3} \ s^{-1}$

3. (a) $\dfrac{1.2 \times 10^{-4}}{5} = 2.4 \times 10^{-5} \ mol \ dm^{-3} \ s^{-1}$

(b) $2.4 \times 10^{-5} \ mol \ dm^{-3} \ s^{-1}$

(c) $3 \times 2.4 \times 10^{-5} = 7.2 \times 10^{-5} \ mol \ dm^{-3} \ s^{-1}$

### Exercise 4.3B

1. Answer A

2. (a) Take a small sample from the reaction mixture at regular intervals. Add an excess of water to quench the reaction, then titrate the sample against standard sodium thiosulfate solution using starch indicator. Plot a graph of iodine concentration against time. Determine the rate of reaction by drawing a tangent to the curve and calculating the slope of the tangent.

(b) Take a small sample from the reaction mixture at regular intervals. Add an excess of silver nitrate solution to quench the reaction. Wash and dry the silver iodide precipitate formed. Use the mass of silver iodide from each sample to plot a graph of iodide concentration against

time. Determine the rate of reaction by drawing a tangent to the curve and calculating the slope of the tangent.

### Exercise 4.3C

1. (a) The rate doubles.

(b) The rate increases by a factor of $2 \times 2 = 4$.

2. (a) (i) The rate doubles. (ii) No change in rate. (iii) The rates doubles.

(b) The rate doubles.

### Exercise 4.3D

1. Answer A

2.

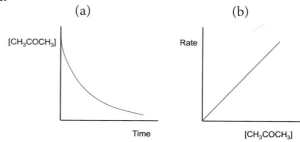

3. (a) Adding starch gives a blue-black colour.

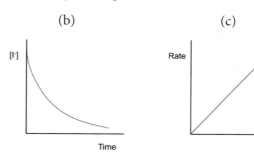

4.

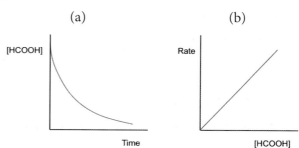

5. Use a gas syringe to measure the volume of oxygen gas produced during the reaction. Plot a graph of the volume of oxygen against time. Determine the initial rate of the reaction by constructing a tangent to the curve at t=0 and measuring the slope of the tangent. The order of reaction with respect to hydrogen peroxide is determined by

the shape of a graph of initial rate against concentration of hydrogen peroxide.

## Exercise 4.3E

1. (a) (i) First order. (ii) First order.

   (b) Rate = k [RCl] [NaOH]

2. (a) First order as the rate doubles when the concentration of $C_4H_9Br$ doubles.

   (b) Zero order as the rate increases by a factor of three when the concentration of $C_4H_9Br$ increases by a factor of three and the concentration of $OH^-$ doubles.

   (c) Rate = k $[C_4H_9Br]$

3. (a) First order with respect to hydrogen peroxide and zero order with respect to hydrogen ion.

   (b) Rate = k $[H_2O_2]$ $[I^-]$

4. (a) First order with respect to persulfate ion and first order with respect to iodide ion.

   (b) Rate = k $[S_2O_8^{2-}]$ $[I^-]$

   (c) The reaction is second order overall as the orders with respect to persulfate ion and iodide ion add to two.

5. Rate = k $[CH_3COCH_3]$ $[H^+]$

6. Rate = k [A] [C]

## Exercise 4.3F

1. Answer C

2. Answer D

3. $k = \dfrac{Rate}{[S_2O_8^{2-}][I^-]} = \dfrac{0.36}{(0.100)(0.050)} = 72 \text{ mol}^{-1} \text{ dm}^3 \text{ s}^{-1}$

## Exercise 4.3G

1. (a)

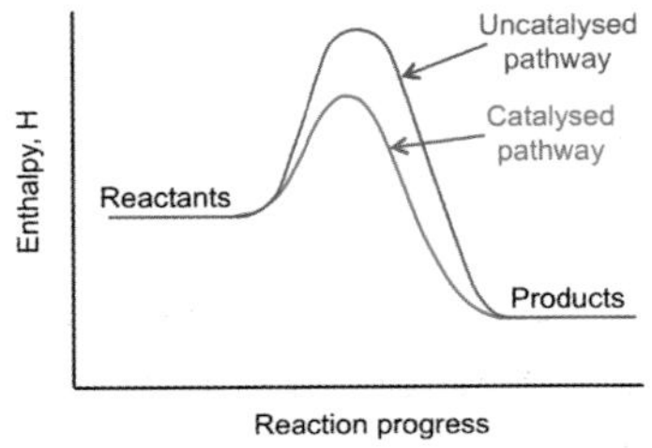

   (b) Adding a catalyst would increase the rate constant, k.

## Exercise 4.3H

1. Answer C

2.

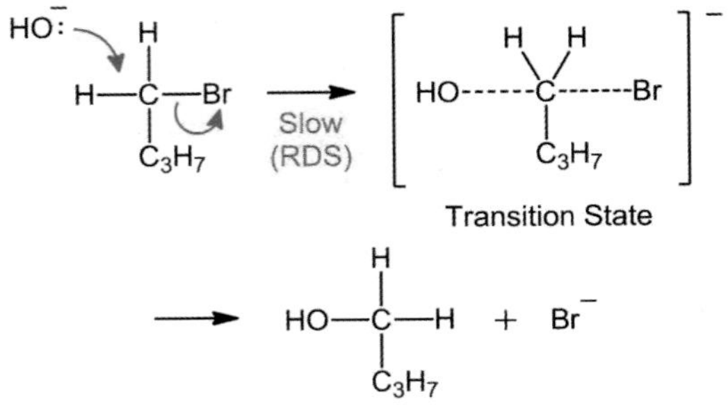

3. (a) Nucleophilic substitution.

   (b) RCl is a primary halogenoalkane as RCl and NaOH are both involved in the rate determining step.

4. (a)

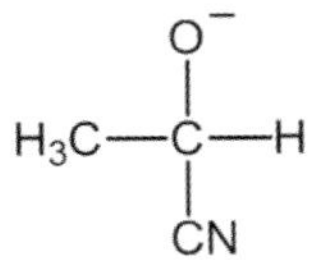

   (b) The rate determining step is the slowest step in the mechanism.

   (c) Rate = k $[CH_3CHO]$ $[CN^-]$

   The symbol k represents the rate constant for the reaction.

   (d) Second order

5.

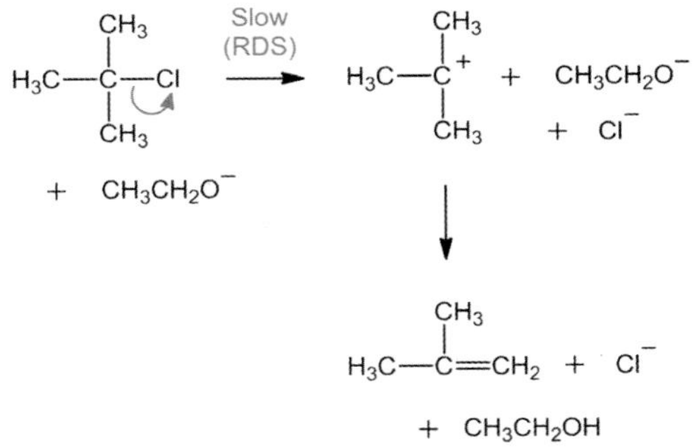

6. Answer B

7. $BrO_3^- + 6H^+ + 5Br^- \rightarrow 3Br_2 + 3H_2O$

8. (a) The slowest step in the reaction.

   (b) $I^- + 2H^+ + IO^- \rightarrow I_2 + H_2O$

## Exercise 4.3I

1. (a) The rate equation reveals that step 1 is slow and step 2 is fast.

   (b) The $OBr^-$ ion is a reactive intermediate as it is formed during the reaction and consumed in a subsequent step.

   (c) Second order

   (d) $Br^-$ ion is a catalyst as it is a reactant in the

rate determining step and is regenerated in the course of the reaction.

(e) Add an excess of silver nitrate solution, filter the mixture and weigh the amount of solid silver bromide formed.

## 4.4 Chemical Equilibrium

### Exercise 4.4A

1. (a) $K_c = \dfrac{[H][H]}{[H_2]} = \dfrac{[H]^2}{[H_2]}$

(b) $K_c = \dfrac{1}{1 \times 10^{40}} = 1 \times 10^{-40}$

(c) $mol\ dm^{-3}$

2. (a) $K_c = \dfrac{[CO_2][H_2]}{[CO][H_2O]}$  No units

(b) $K_c = \dfrac{1}{0.23} = 4.3$

### Exercise 4.4B

1. $K_c = \dfrac{\left(\dfrac{1.1}{10}\right)\left(\dfrac{1.1}{10}\right)}{\left(\dfrac{3.9}{10}\right)} = 0.031\ mol\ dm^{-3}$

2. $K_c = \dfrac{\left(\dfrac{1.5}{5}\right)\left(\dfrac{1.5}{5}\right)}{\left(\dfrac{0.5}{5}\right)} = 0.9\ mol\ dm^{-3}$

3. $K_c = \dfrac{\left(\dfrac{0.08}{5}\right)\left(\dfrac{0.16}{5}\right)^2}{\left(\dfrac{0.04}{5}\right)^2} = 0.25\ mol\ dm^{-3}$

4. $K_c = \dfrac{\left(\dfrac{150}{200}\right)^2}{\left(\dfrac{25}{200}\right)\left(\dfrac{75}{200}\right)^3} = 85\ mol^{-2}\ dm^6$

5. $K_c = \dfrac{(0.1)(0.3)^3}{(0.1)(0.1)} = 0.27\ mol^2\ dm^{-6}$

### Exercise 4.4C

1. (a) $K_c = \dfrac{(0.70)}{(0.55)(0.55)} = 2.3$

(b) $mol^{-1}\ dm^3$

2. $K_c = \dfrac{\left(\dfrac{0.067}{V}\right)\left(\dfrac{1.067}{V}\right)}{\left(\dfrac{0.133}{V}\right)\left(\dfrac{0.133}{V}\right)} = 4.04$

3. $K_c = \dfrac{\left(\dfrac{5.5}{10}\right)\left(\dfrac{16.5}{10}\right)^3}{\left(\dfrac{2.0}{10}\right)\left(\dfrac{0.5}{10}\right)} = 2.5 \times 10^2\ mol^2\ dm^{-6}$

### Exercise 4.4D

1. (a) $K_c = \dfrac{\left(\dfrac{1.50}{V}\right)^2}{\left(\dfrac{0.25}{V}\right)\left(\dfrac{0.25}{V}\right)} = 36$

(b) The volume terms in the expression for $K_c$ cancel.

(c) $K_c' = \dfrac{1}{K_c} = 0.028$

### Exercise 4.4E

1. $[NO_2] = \sqrt{K_c[N_2O_4]} = 3.9 \times 10^{-3}\ mol\ dm^{-3}$

2. $[NH_3] = \sqrt{K_c[N_2][H_2]^3} = 0.022\ mol\ dm^{-3}$

### Exercise 4.4F

1. (a) $K_c = \dfrac{[CH_3COOCH_2CH_3][H_2O]}{[CH_3COOH][CH_3CH_2OH]}$

(b) $K_c = \dfrac{\left(\dfrac{2.0}{V}\right)\left(\dfrac{2.0}{V}\right)}{\left(\dfrac{x-2.0}{V}\right)\left(\dfrac{0.5}{V}\right)} = 3.2$

Initial moles of $CH_3COOH$, $x = 4.5$

## 4.5 Acid-Base Equilibria

### Exercise 4.5A

1. A Brønsted-Lowry acid is a molecule or ion that can donate one or more hydrogen ions to another molecule or ion.

2. Answer A

3. Answer A

4. Answer C

5. Answer D

6. Answer C

7. (a) Acid-base pair 1: $H_2O_2$ and $HO_2^-$ Acid-base pair 2: $H_2O$ and $H_3O^+$.

   (b) Adding water shifts the position of equilibrium to the right increasing the concentration of hydronium ion in the solution.

## Exercise 4.5B

1. Answer C

2. (a) $K_w = [H^+][OH^-]$

   (b) The dissociation of water is endothermic as $K_w$ increases when the temperature increases.

## Exercise 4.5C

1. (a) $[H^+] = 0.1$ mol dm$^{-3}$

   (b) $[OH^-] = 1 \times 10^{-13}$ mol dm$^{-3}$

2. (a) $[OH^-] = 0.05$ mol dm$^{-3}$

   (b) $[H^+] = 2 \times 10^{-13}$ mol dm$^{-3}$

3. $[H^+] = 0.05$ mol dm$^{-3}$; pH = 1.3

4. $[H^+] = 0.011$ mol dm$^{-3}$; pH = 1.96

## Exercise 4.5D

1. (a) $[H^+] = \text{antilog}_{10}(-7.35) = 4.5 \times 10^{-8}$ mol dm$^{-3}$

   (b) $[H^+] = 3.6 \times 10^{-8}$ mol dm$^{-3}$

## Exercise 4.5E

1. $[H^+] = 5 \times 10^{-14}$ mol dm$^{-3}$; pH = 13.3

## Exercise 4.5F

1. (a) $K_a = \dfrac{[H^+][CH_3CH_2COO^-]}{[CH_3CH_2COOH]}$

   (b) $[H^+] = 1.8 \times 10^{-3}$ mol dm$^{-3}$; pH = 2.74

2. (a) $HCOO^-$

   (b) $[H^+] = 4.0 \times 10^{-3}$ mol dm$^{-3}$; pH = 2.40

3. (a) $[H^+] = 2.0$ mol dm$^{-3}$; pH = −0.30

   (b) $[H^+] = 8.9$ mol dm$^{-3}$; pH = −0.95

   (c) The concentration of hydrogen ions differs as one calculation assumes the acid is fully dissociated and the other does not.

## Exercise 4.5G

1. (a) A polybasic acid is a molecule or ion that can dissociate to form more than one hydrogen ion.

   (b) $H_2SO_3(aq) \rightleftharpoons H^+(aq) + HSO_3^-(aq)$

   (c) $K_{a1} = \dfrac{[H^+][HSO_3^-]}{[H_2SO_3]}$

2. (a) Sulfuric acid is a strong acid as it dissociates completely to form hydrogensulfate(VI), $HSO_4^-$ ions.

   (b) $HSO_4^-(aq) \rightleftharpoons H^+(aq) + SO_4^{2-}(aq)$

   (c) $K_{a2} = \dfrac{[H^+][SO_4^{2-}]}{[HSO_4^-]}$

3. (a) 1.57

   (b) $HPO_4^{2-}(aq) \rightleftharpoons H^+(aq) + PO_4^{3-}(aq)$

   (c) $K_{a3} = \dfrac{[H^+][PO_4^{3-}]}{[HPO_4^{2-}]}$

4. (a) $C_6H_8O_7(aq) \rightleftharpoons H^+(aq) + C_6H_7O_7^-(aq)$

   (b) $K_a = \dfrac{[H^+][RCOO^-]}{[RCOOH]}$

   (c) $[H^+] = 9 \times 10^{-3}$ mol dm$^{-3}$; pH = 2.0

## Exercise 4.5H

1. $K_a = 40$ mol dm$^{-3}$; $pK_a = -1.60$

2. $[H^+] = 8 \times 10^{-4}$ mol dm$^{-3}$; pH = 3.1

3. $2.9 \times 10^{-7}$ mol dm$^{-3}$ = 0.026 mg dm$^{-3}$

## Exercise 4.5I

1. Propanoic acid is a weak acid that partially dissociates to form hydrogen ions:

   $CH_3CH_2COOH(aq) \rightleftharpoons H^+(aq) + CH_3CH_2COO^-(aq)$

   Sodium propanoate dissociates to form propanoate ions:

   $CH_3CH_2COONa(aq) \rightarrow Na^+(aq) + CH_3CH_2COO^-(aq)$

   Propanoate ions from sodium propanoate combine with added hydrogen ions to form propanoic acid:

   $CH_3CH_2COO^-(aq) + H^+(aq) \rightarrow CH_3CH_2COOH(aq)$

2. (a) $CH_3COO^-(aq) + H^+(aq) \rightarrow CH_3COOH(aq)$

   (b) $CH_3COOH(aq) + OH^-(aq) \rightarrow CH_3COO^-(aq) + H_2O(l)$

3. (a) $C_4H_5O_6^-(aq) + H^+(aq) \rightarrow C_4H_6O_6(aq)$

   (b) $C_4H_6O_6(aq) + OH^-(aq) \rightarrow C_4H_5O_6^-(aq) + H_2O(l)$

4. The solution behaves as a buffer as it contains $HCN_{(aq)}$ and its conjugate base, $CN^-_{(aq)}$.

On adding acid: $H^+_{(aq)} + CN^-_{(aq)} \rightarrow HCN_{(aq)}$.

On adding alkali: $HCN_{(aq)} + OH^-_{(aq)} \rightarrow H_2O_{(l)} + CN^-_{(aq)}$. Alternatively, on adding alkali: $NH_4^+_{(aq)} + OH^-_{(aq)} \rightarrow NH_{3(aq)} + H_2O_{(l)}$

### Exercise 4.5J

1. (a) A buffer solution resists changes in pH when small amounts of acid or alkali are added.

(b) $[H^+] = 3.4 \times 10^{-5}$ mol dm$^{-3}$; pH = 4.47

2. $[H^+] = 7.3 \times 10^{-5}$ mol dm$^{-3}$; pH = 4.14

3. $[H^+] = 3.2 \times 10^{-4}$ mol dm$^{-3}$; pH = 3.49

4. Answer B

5. 4.9 g

### Exercise 4.5K

1. (a) The molecule can dissociate to produce three hydrogen ions.

(b)
$$2\ HO-\underset{\underset{CH_2COOH}{|}}{\overset{\overset{CH_2COOH}{|}}{C}}-COOH\ +\ 3CaCO_3$$

$$\longrightarrow\ Ca_3\left(HO-\underset{\underset{CH_2COO}{|}}{\overset{\overset{CH_2COO}{|}}{C}}-COO\right)_2\ +\ 3H_2O\ +\ 3CO_2$$

(c)
$$Ca_3\left(HO-\underset{\underset{CH_2COO}{|}}{\overset{\overset{CH_2COO}{|}}{C}}-COO\right)_2\ +\ 3H_2SO_4$$

$$\longrightarrow\ 2\ HO-\underset{\underset{CH_2COOH}{|}}{\overset{\overset{CH_2COOH}{|}}{C}}-COOH\ +\ 3CaSO_4$$

2. (a) $SO_3 + H_2O \rightarrow H_2SO_4$

(b) $H_2SO_4 + 2NaOH \rightarrow Na_2SO_4 + 2H_2O$

3. (a) $SO_2 + H_2O \rightarrow H_2SO_3$

(b) $H_2SO_3 + 2NaOH \rightarrow Na_2SO_3 + 2H_2O$

4. 25 cm$^3$

### Exercise 4.5L

1. Answer B

2. Answer D

3. (a) $NH_3 + HNO_3 \rightarrow NH_4NO_3$

(b) A solution of ammonium nitrate is acidic as ammonium nitrate is an acidic salt formed from a strong acid and a weak base.

4. The pH is close to 7 as calcium chloride is a neutral salt formed from a strong acid and a strong base.

5. A solution of sodium ethanoate is alkaline as sodium ethanoate is a basic salt formed from a weak acid and a strong base.

6. (a) $$H-O-\underset{\underset{O}{||}}{\overset{\overset{O}{||}}{S}}-O-O-\underset{\underset{O}{||}}{\overset{\overset{O}{||}}{S}}-O-H$$

(b) A solution of potassium persulfate is alkaline as potassium persulfate is the salt of a weak acid and a strong base.

7. Aqueous sodium nitrate is neutral as sodium nitrate is the salt of a strong acid and a strong base. Aqueous aluminium nitrate is slightly acidic as aluminium nitrate is the salt of a strong acid and a weaker base. Aqueous ammonium nitrate is acidic as ammonium nitrate is the salt of a strong acid and a weak base.

8. Answer A

### Exercise 4.5M

1. Answer D

2.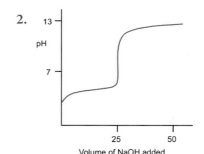

3. (a)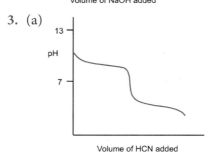

(b) The change in pH at the equivalence point is too small to produce a colour change with an indicator.

## Exercise 4.5N

1. (a) The $In^-$ ion is the conjugate base of the weak acid HIn.

   (b) Adding hydroxide ions produces a colour change from yellow to blue as the position of equilibrium moves to the right.

   Adding hydrogen ions produces a colour change from blue to yellow as the position of equilibrium moves to the left.

2. Answer C

3. (a) The pH of the acid increases as it becomes more dilute.

   (b) The indicator must change colour over a range of pH that lies within the range pH 5 to pH 8.

4. (a) $CH_3CH_2COOH + NaOH \rightarrow$ $CH_3CH_2COONa + H_2O$

   (b) Phenolphthalein is a suitable indicator as it changes colour from colourless to pink over a range of pH that lies within the vertical portion of the titration curve.

   (c) $0.15$ mol dm$^{-3}$

5. (a) $H_2SO_4 + 2NH_3 \rightarrow (NH_4)_2SO_4$

   (b) Ammonia accepts a hydrogen ion to form an ammonium ion.

   (c) Methyl orange is a suitable indicator.

   (d) The indicator changes colour over a range of pH below pH 7 that lies within the vertical portion of the titration curve.

6. (a) $NH_3 + CH_3COOH \rightarrow CH_3COONH_4$

   (b) Ammonia is a weak base and ethanoic acid is a weak acid. The change in pH at the equivalence point is too small to produce a colour change with an indicator.

7. (a) Phenolphthalein is a suitable indicator as it changes colour over a range of pH that lies within the vertical portion of the titration curve.

   (b) $4.5$ g

## 4.6 Isomerism

### Exercise 4.6A

1. Structural isomers are compounds with the same molecular formula that have different structural formulas.

2. Ethyl ethanoate and butanoic acid are structural isomers as they have the same molecular formula but different structural formulas.

### Exercise 4.6B

1. Fumaric acid forms E and Z isomers as the molecule cannot rotate about the C=C bond and each carbon atom forming the C=C bond is attached to two different groups.

2. The compound $CH_2=CHCH_3$ does not form geometric isomers as each carbon forming the C=C bond must be bonded to two different groups.

3.

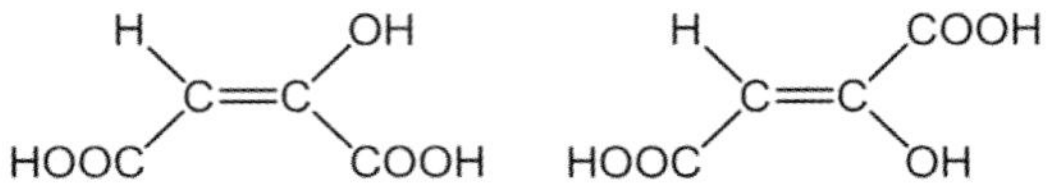

4.

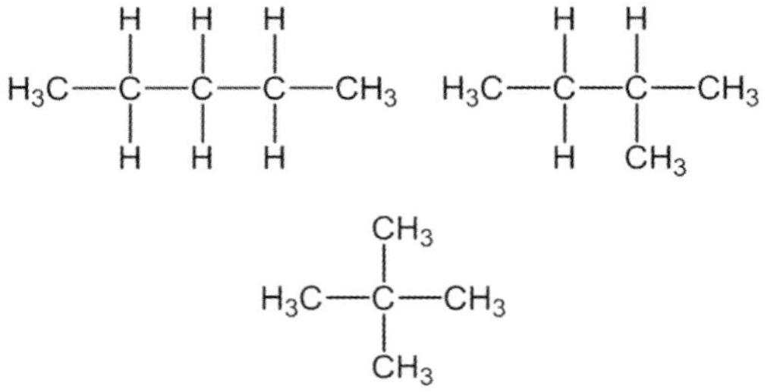

5. $CH_2=CHCH_2CH_2CH_3$
   $CH_2=CHCH(CH_3)_2$   $CH_3CH=CHCH_2CH_3$

6.

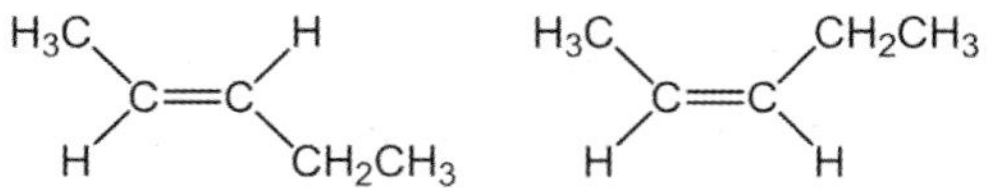

### Exercise 4.6C

1. Answer B

2. Answer D

3. Answer B

4. None

5. Answer A

6.

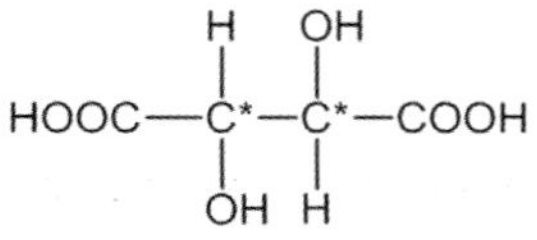

## Exercise 4.6D

1. (a) An optically active substance rotates the plane of plane-polarised light.

   (b)

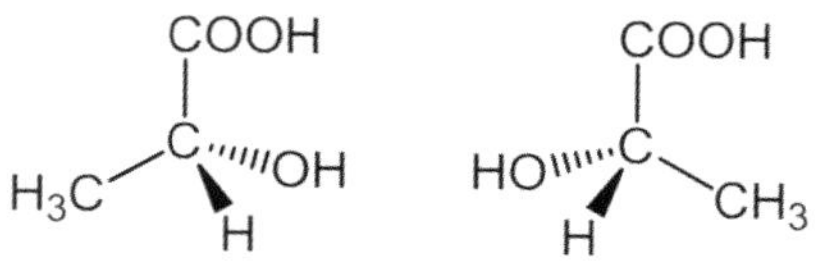

2. The optical isomers of a compound rotate the plane of plane-polarised light in opposite directions.

3. (a) An optically active substance rotates the plane of plane-polarised light.

   (b) The molecule contains a carbon atom that is bonded to four different groups of atoms.

   (c)

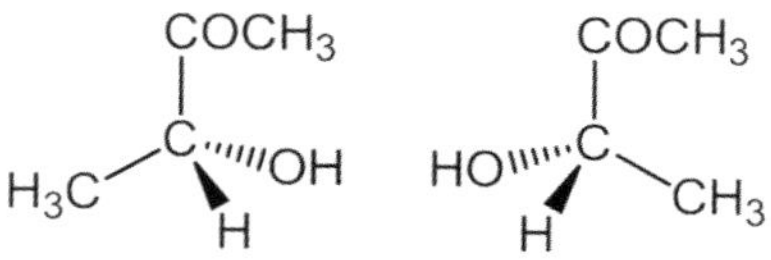

   (d) If the mixture contained an equal amount of both isomers the mixture would be optically inactive as the net rotation of the plane of plane-polarised light would be zero.

4. (a) An optically active substance rotates the plane of plane-polarised light.

   (b)

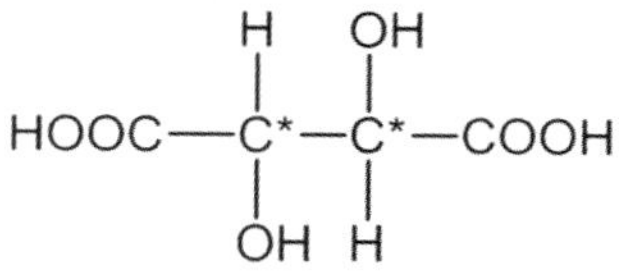

   (c) The samples contain the same amount of both optical isomers.

5. The lactic acid produced by the hydrolysis is a racemic mixture and contains the same amount of both optical isomers.

## Exercise 4.6E

1. (a) A racemic mixture contains the same amount of both optical isomers.

   (b)

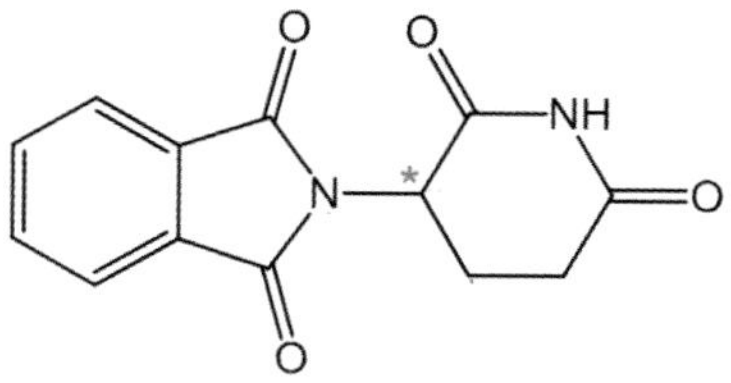

   (c) Only one isomer may have the correct shape to bond with the receptors in the body.

2. (a)

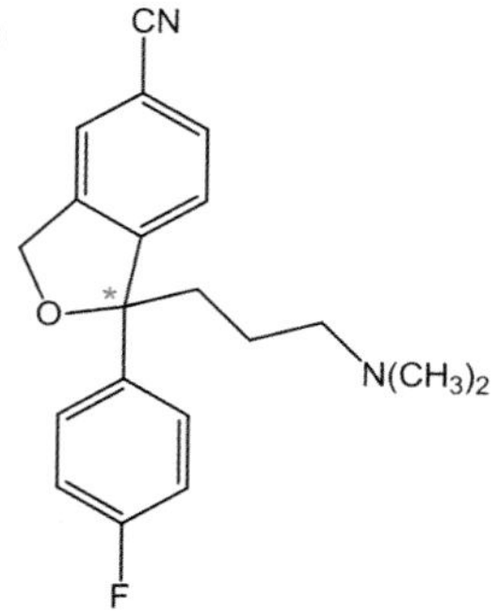

   (b) Only one isomer has the correct shape to bond with the receptors in the body.

## 4.7 Carbonyl Compounds

### Exercise 4.7A

1.

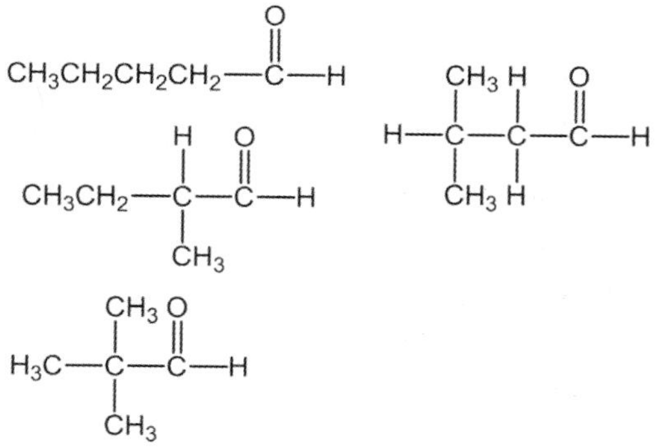

2. 8

### Exercise 4.7B

1.

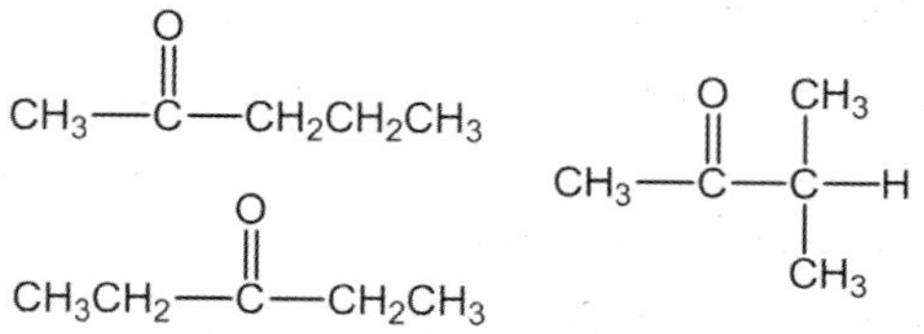

2. 6

### Exercise 4.7C

1. The oxygen atom in formaldehyde can form a hydrogen bond with a hydrogen atom in water.

2. The $-CH_3$ group attached to one side of the carbonyl group in propanone is much smaller than the $-C_5H_{11}$ group attached to the same location in heptan-2-one, which makes it easier for propanone to form hydrogen bonds with water molecules.

3. The oxygen atom in the carbonyl group and the oxygen atom in the hydroxyl group can hydrogen bond with a hydrogen atom in water. The

hydrogen atom belonging to the hydroxyl group can also hydrogen bond with an oxygen atom in water.

## Exercise 4.7D

1. (a) 2-chloro-2-methylpropanal

   (b) 3-bromo-2,2-dimethylpropanal

2. (a)   (b)

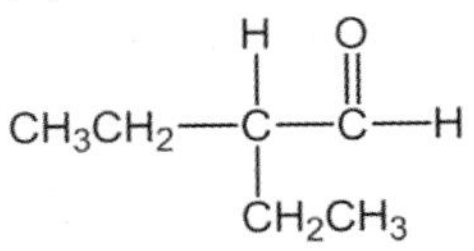

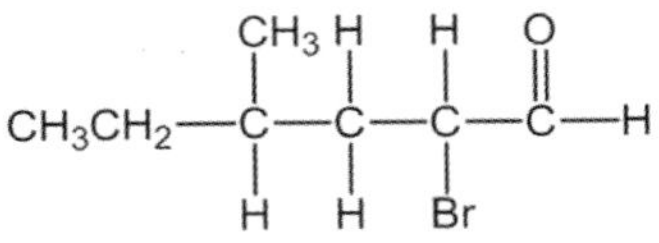

3. (a) Pent-3-enal

   (b) 2-ethylhex-2-enal

4. (a) 3-chloro-2-methylbut-2-enal

   (b) 4-bromo-2-ethylpent-4-enal

5.

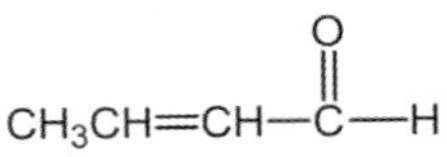

   but-2-enal 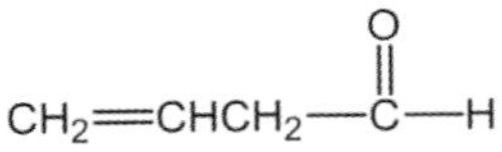          but-3-enal

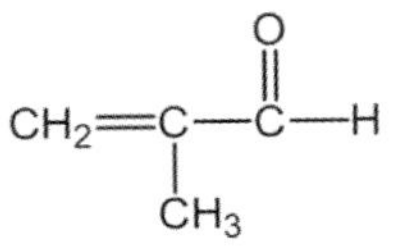

   2-methylpropenal

## Exercise 4.7E

1. 3-hydroxybutanone

2. (a) 3-ethylpentan-2-one

   (b) 2,2-dimethylpentan-3-one

3. (a)   (b)

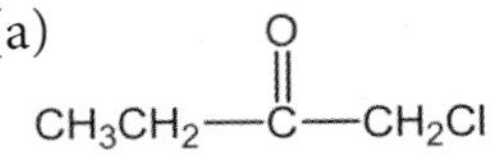

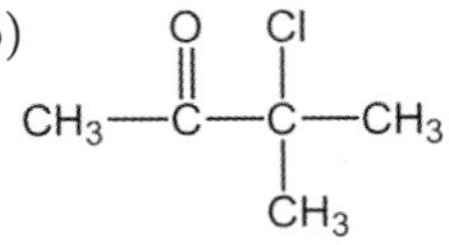

4. (a) pent-3-en-2-one

   (b) hex-1-en-3-one

5. (a) hex-5-en-2-one

   (b) 4-methylpent-4-en-2-one

6. (a)   (b)

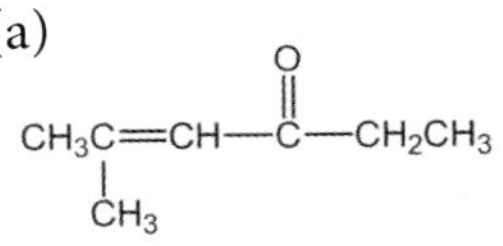

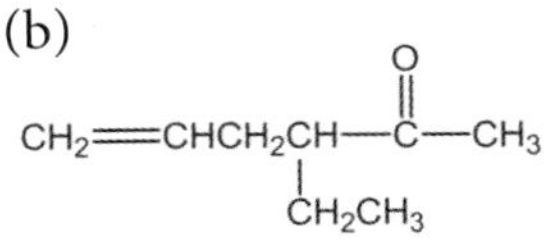

## Exercise 4.7F

1. Answer C

2. (a) $CH_3CH_2CH_2CH_2OH + [O]$
   $\rightarrow CH_3CH_2CH_2CHO + H_2O$

   (b) Distillation ensures that the aldehyde formed in the reaction is not oxidised to the corresponding carboxylic acid.

   (c)   butanal

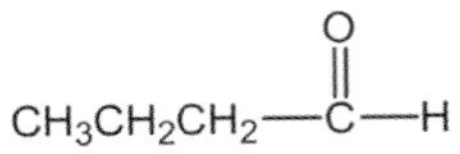

   (d) The orange colour of dichromate ion, $Cr_2O_7^{2-}$ is replaced by the green colour of chromium(III) ion, $Cr^{3+}$.

3. (a)   2-methylpentan-3-ol

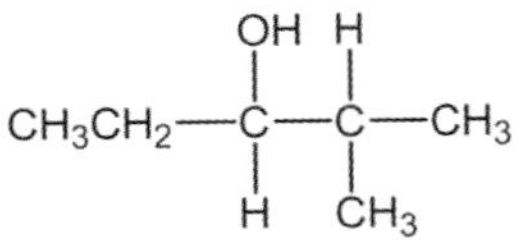

   (b) $CH_3CH_2CH(OH)CH(CH_3)_2 + [O]$
   $\rightarrow CH_3CH_2COCH(CH_3)_2 + H_2O$

4. (a) $Ag_2O$

   (b) $CH_3CH(OH)COOH + [O]$
   $\rightarrow CH_3COCOOH + H_2O$

## Exercise 4.7G

1. Add acidified potassium dichromate to samples of propanal and propanone in separate boiling tubes. Heat the mixtures gently using a water bath. The solution containing propanal will change colour from orange to green. The solution containing propanone will remain orange.

## Exercise 4.7H

1. (a) Silver(I) ion

   (b) Carbonyl group

   (c) To speed up the reaction.

   (d) (i) A silver mirror forms on the side of the boiling tube. (ii) A silver mirror does not form.

2. (a) $HCHO + [O] \rightarrow HCOOH$

   (b) $Ag^+ + e^- \rightarrow Ag$

   (c) A silver mirror forms.

3. (a) Add Tollens' reagent to methanoic acid in a boiling tube. Heat the mixture gently using a water bath until a silver mirror forms on the side of the boiling tube.

   (b) $Ag^+ + e^- \rightarrow Ag$

**Exercise 4.7I**

1. (a) Pentan-2-one

   (b) Add Fehling's solution to samples of A (a ketone) and B (an aldehyde) in separate boiling tubes. Heat the solutions gently using a water bath. When the mixture containing B is heated a red precipitate forms. When the mixture containing A is heated no change is observed.

   (c) $7.2 \times 10^8$ molecules

2. (a) Both contain a carbonyl (C=O) group and hydroxyl (-OH) groups.

   (b) Both have primary and secondary alcohol groups, and will reduce Fehling's solution to form a red precipitate.

   (c) $2Cu^{2+} + 2OH^- + 2e^- \rightarrow Cu_2O + H_2O$

3. Answer B

4. (a)

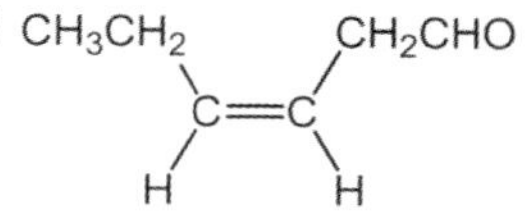

   (b) A red precipitate forms.

**Exercise 4.7J**

1. (a) $CH_3CH_2COCH_3 + 2[H]$
       $\rightarrow CH_3CH_2CH(OH)CH_3$

   (b) Butan-2-ol

2. Hexan-2-ol

3.

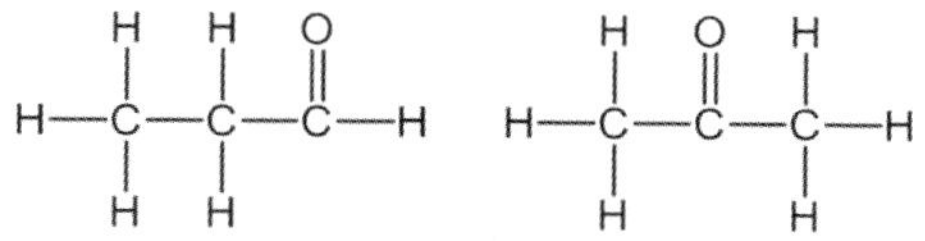

4. Answer B

5. (a) $CH_3CH_2COCH_3 + 2[H]$
       $\rightarrow CH_3CH_2CH(OH)CH_3$

   (b) Butan-2-ol

   (c) Does not rotate the plane of plane-polarised light.

   (d) The product contains equal amounts of two optical isomers.

6. (a) A monohydric alcohol contains one hydroxyl (-OH) group.

   (b) Cholesterol is a secondary alcohol as the hydroxyl group is bonded to a carbon atom that has two carbon atoms attached.

   (c) Reagent A is hydrogen gas, reagent B is acidified potassium dichromate, and reagent C is lithal.

   (d) Both molecules are not very soluble in water as the force between neighbouring molecules is dominated by van der Waals attraction. Cholesterol is slightly more soluble as the O and H atoms in the hydroxyl group can hydrogen bond with water. Cholestan-3-one is less soluble as it can only use the O atom in the carbonyl group to hydrogen bond with water.

**Exercise 4.7K**

1 (a) The nucleophile is attracted to the electron deficient carbon atom in the carbonyl group.

   (b)

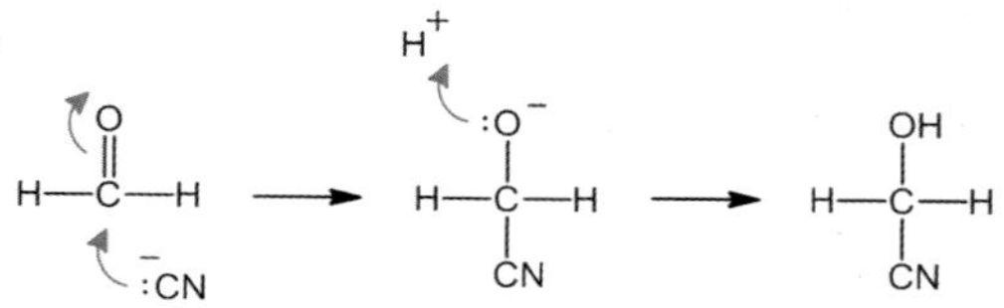

2. Answer B

3.

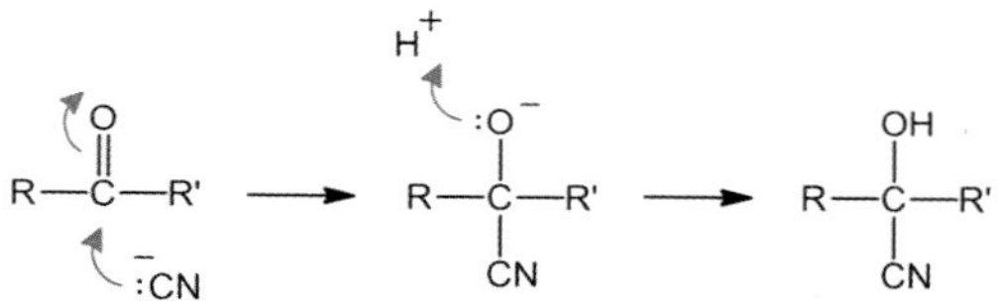

4. (a) 2-hydroxy-2-methylbutanenitrile

   (b) Optical isomerism

   (c)

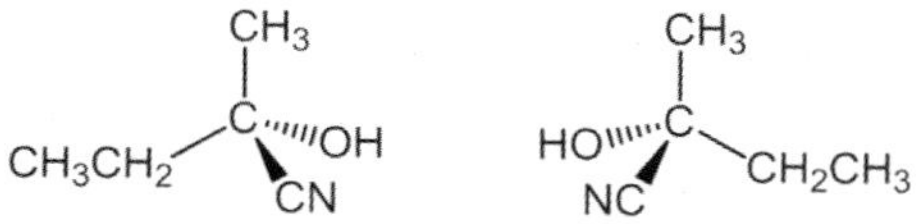

   (d) Nucleophilic addition

   (e)

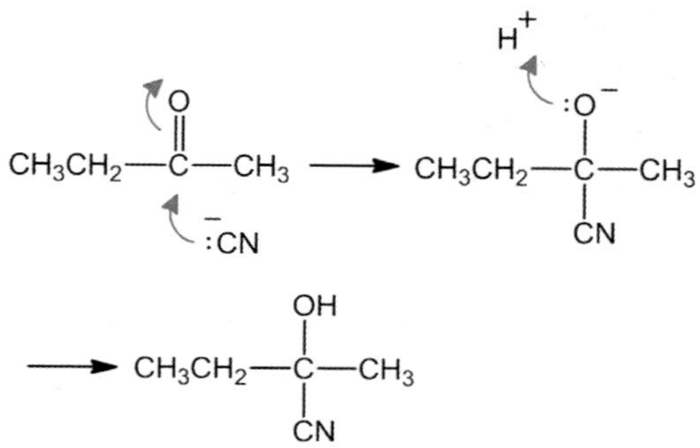

5. (a) They are geometric isomers.

(b) 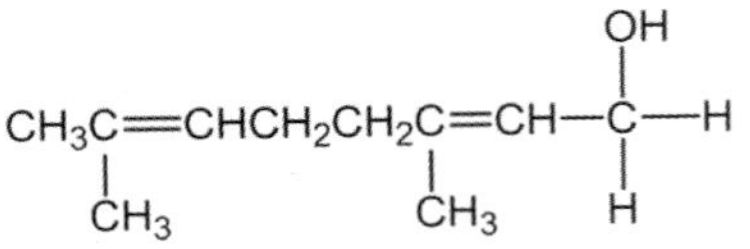 CH₃C=CHCH₂CH₂C=CH—C—H with CH₃, CH₃, H and OH groups

(c) CH₃C=CHCH₂CH₂C=CH—C—H with CH₃, CH₃, CN and OH groups

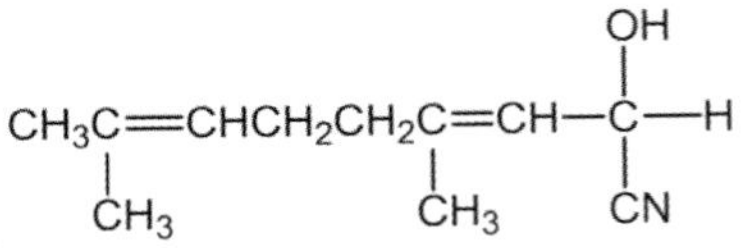

(d) 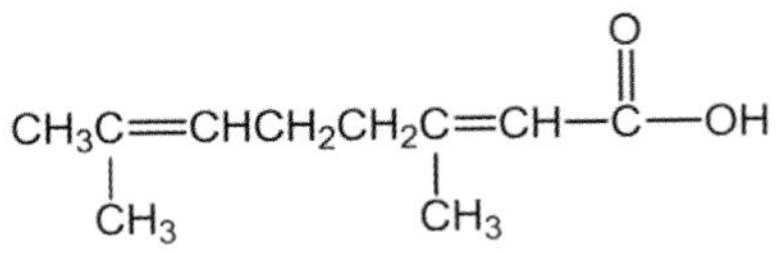 CH₃C=CHCH₂CH₂C=CH—C—OH with CH₃, CH₃ and =O group

## Exercise 4.7L

1. (a) 

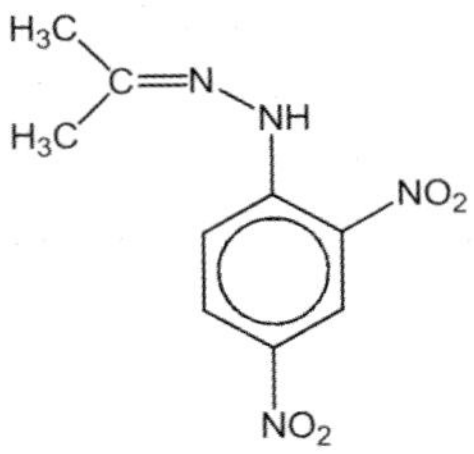

(b) 238

2. Answer A

3. (a) 

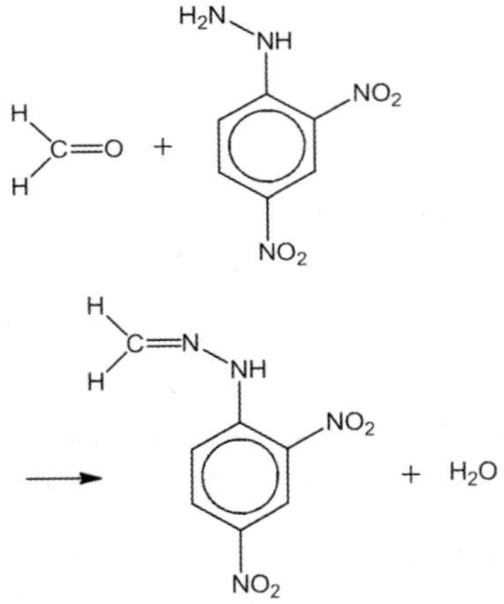

(b) Mass of methanal = 0.21 g
Mass of methanal solution = 0.57 g

4. 2,4-dinitrophenylhydrazine: 

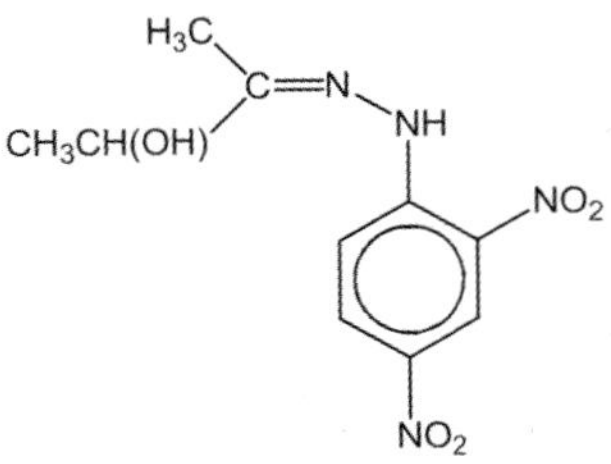

HCN: 

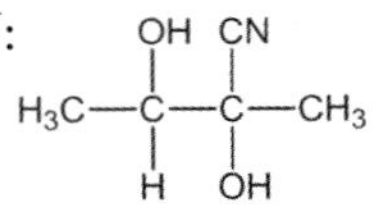

PCl₅: 

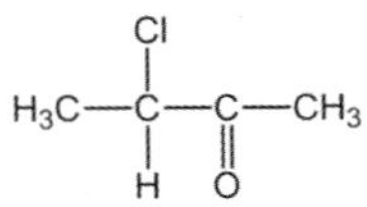

LiAlH₄: 

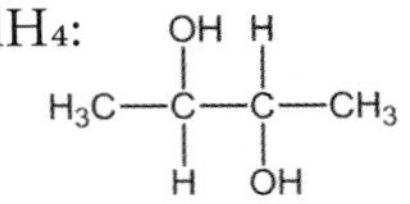

5. (a) 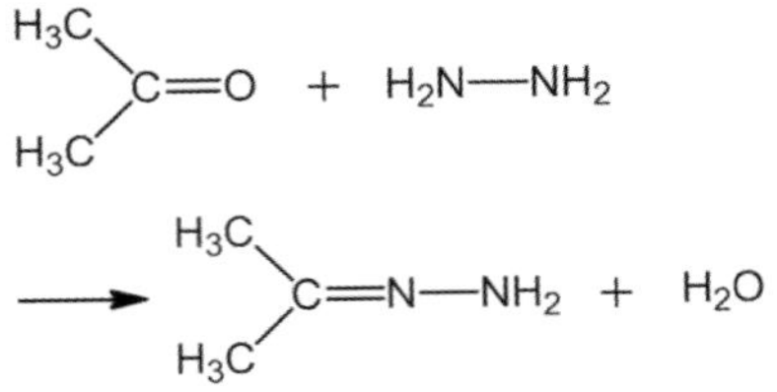 H₃C, H₃C C=O + H₂N—NH₂

H₃C, H₃C C=N—NH₂ + H₂O

(b) 

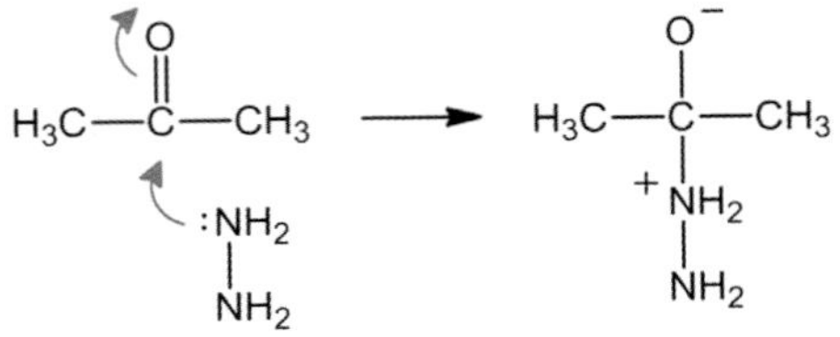

(c) The derivative must be a solid at room temperature if its melting point is to be determined. The derivative formed by hydrazine has a lower molar mass, less van der Waals attraction between molecules, and therefore has a lower melting point, making it less likely to be a solid at room temperature.

6. 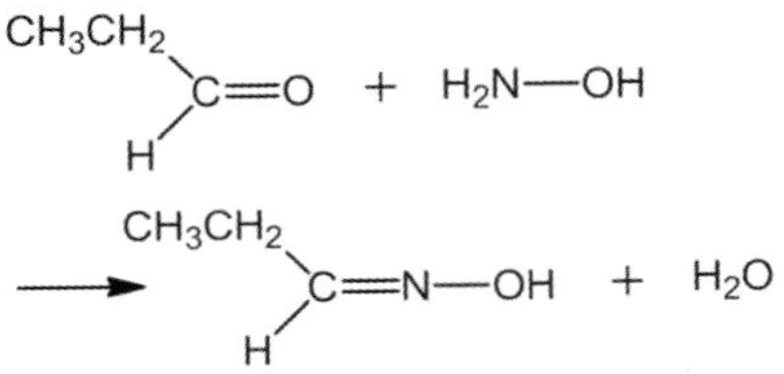 CH₃CH₂, H C=O + H₂N—OH

CH₃CH₂, H C=N—OH + H₂O

7. The molecular ion peak in the mass spectrum of a compound can be used to determine the relative molecular mass of the compound. The frequencies absorbed in the infrared spectrum of the compound can be used to determine the types of bond present in the compound.

## Exercise 4.7M

1. (a) The hydrazone is soluble in ethanol as the oxygen atoms in the nitro groups can hydrogen bond with the hydrogen atom in the -OH group of ethanol. The hydrazone cannot hydrogen bond with hexane.

(b) See Worked Example 4.7vii (a).

2. See Worked Example 4.7vii (b).

**3.** (a)

(b) Add a few drops of cinnamaldehyde to a solution of 2,4-dinitrophenylhydrazine in a test tube. If crystals do not form add dilute sulfuric acid and warm the mixture. Cool the mixture using an iced-water bath then use vacuum filtration to obtain a crude sample of the hydrazone. Recrystallise the crude hydrazone using ethanol as the solvent. Compare the melting point of the pure hydrazone to the melting points of hydrazones in data tables.

**4.** (a)

(b) Moles of hydrazone $= \dfrac{5.4 \text{ g}}{252 \text{ g mol}^{-1}} = 0.021 \text{ mol}$

Moles of butanone $= 0.021 \times \dfrac{100}{90} = 0.023 \text{ mol}$

Volume of butanone $= \dfrac{1.7 \text{ g}}{0.8 \text{ g cm}^{-3}} = 2.1 \text{ cm}^3$

(c) (i) See Worked Example 4.7vi (b).

(ii) See Worked Example 4.7vi (c).

(d) (i) The hydrazone is soluble in methanol as the oxygen atoms in the nitro groups can hydrogen bond with the hydrogen atom in the -OH group of methanol. The hydrazone cannot hydrogen bond with octane. (ii) See Worked Example 4.7vii (a).

## 4.8 Carboxylic Acids

**Exercise 4.8A**

1. Answer C

2. $C_5H_{10}O_2$

**Exercise 4.8B**

1. (a) The term miscible refers to liquids that mix in all proportions. (b) The oxygen atoms in the carboxyl group, and the oxygen atom in the carbonyl group, can form hydrogen bonds with hydrogen atoms in surrounding water molecules.

2. The alkyl chain is much shorter in ethanoic acid. As a result the oxygen atoms belonging to the carboxyl group in ethanoic acid can effectively form hydrogen bonds with the hydrogen atoms in surrounding water molecules.

**Exercise 4.8C**

1. The van der Waals attraction between neighbouring molecules in the acid increases as the molar mass of the acid increases.

2. The attractive forces between the molecules are greater in ethanoic acid as the molecules can hydrogen bond with each other. The molecules in ethanal cannot hydrogen bond with each other.

3. The attractive forces between the molecules are greater in propanoic acid as the molecules can hydrogen bond with each other. The molecules in the ester cannot hydrogen bond with each other.

**Exercise 4.8D**

1. (a) Butanoic acid

   (b) 2-methylpropanoic acid

2. (a) Pentanoic acid

   (b) 3-methylbutanoic acid

3. (a) 2-amino-3-hydroxypropanoic acid

   (b) 2-amino-3-hydroxybutanoic acid

(c) 2,5-diaminopentanoic acid

(d) 2,6-diaminohexanoic acid

4. (a) 2-amino-4-cyanobutanoic acid

(b) 3-bromo-2-oxobutanoic acid

5. (a) 4-methyl-3-oxopentanoic acid

(b) 5-amino-5-oxopentanoic acid

6. $CH_3CH=CHCOOH$     $CH_2=CHCH_2COOH$

    but-2-enoic acid         but-3-enoic acid

7.

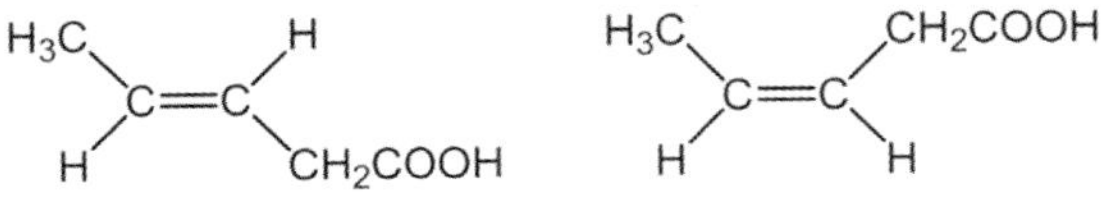

8. Answer D

## Exercise 4.8E

1.

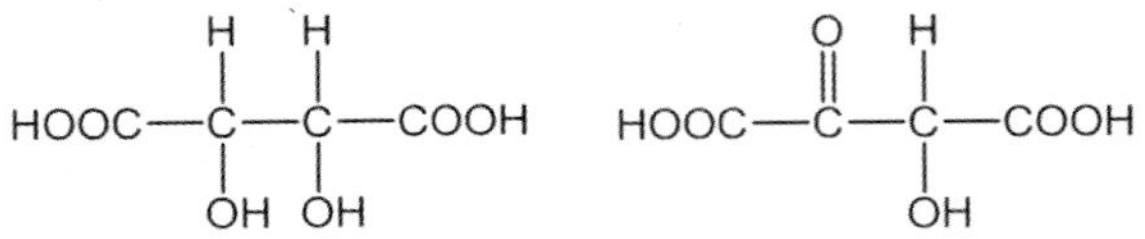

          (a)                (b)

2. (a) 2-amino-3-methylpentanedioic acid

(b) 2-methyl-4-oxopentanedioic acid

3. $HOOCCH=CHCH_2CH_2COOH$

    hex-2-enedioic acid

    $HOOCCH_2CH=CHCH_2COOH$

    hex-3-enedioic acid

4. (a) 3-chlorohexa-2,4-dienedioic acid

(b)

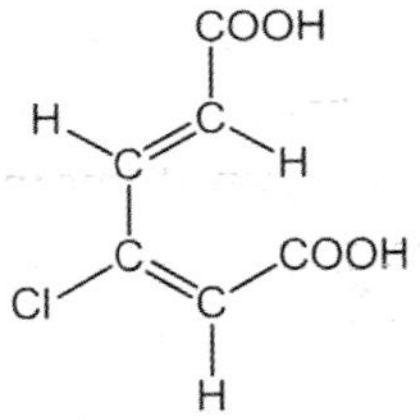

## Exercise 4.8F

1. (a) $CH_3CH_2CH_2OH + 2[O]$

    $\longrightarrow CH_3CH_2COOH + H_2O$

(b)

2. Answer C

3. (a)

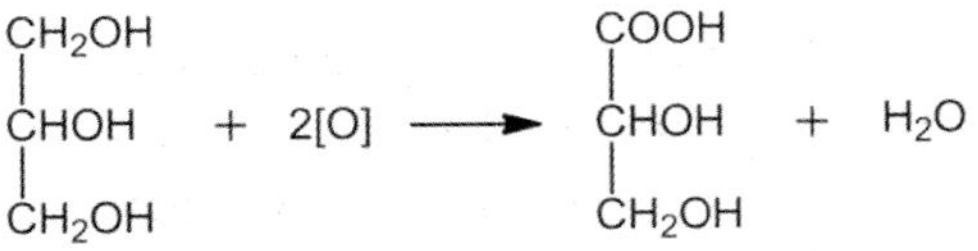

(b) 2,3-dihydroxypropanoic acid

4. (a) See Worked Example 4.8i.

(b)

## Exercise 4.8G

1. (a) $CH_3COCH_2CN + 2H_2O + HCl$
    $\rightarrow CH_3COCH_2COOH + NH_4Cl$

(b)

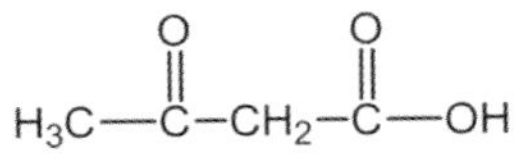

2. (a) $CH_3COCN + H_2O + NaOH$
    $\rightarrow CH_3COCOONa + NH_3$

(b)

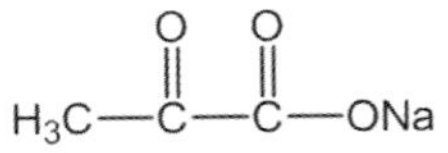

(c) Pyruvic acid is liberated from the salt by adding an excess of dilute hydrochloric acid to the reaction mixture.

## Exercise 4.8H

1. (a) Fizzing, the solid disappears, a colourless solution is formed, and bubbles of colourless gas are produced:
$2HCOOH + Na_2CO_3 \rightarrow 2HCOONa + H_2O + CO_2$

(b) Bubble the gas produced through limewater. If the limewater turns milky the gas was carbon dioxide and the liquid added to the aqueous sodium carbonate was a carboxylic acid.

2. (a) 3-methylbutanoic acid

(b) $2CH_3(CH_2)_3COOH + Na_2CO_3$
    $\rightarrow 2CH_3(CH_2)_3COONa + H_2O + CO_2$

(c) Add an excess of dilute hydrochloric acid.

3.

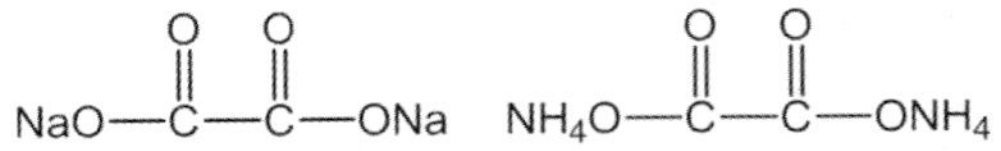

    (a)            (b)

## Exercise 4.8I

1. (a) $CH_3(CH_2)_3COOH + CH_3CH_2OH$
    $\leftrightharpoons CH_3(CH_2)_3COOCH_2CH_3 + H_2O$

(b) The rate can be increased by adding concentrated sulfuric acid and refluxing the reaction mixture.

2. (a) 2-methylpropenoic acid

(b) *Reactant:* Methanol
    *Catalyst:* Concentrated sulfuric acid

(c) Esterification

3. (a) The hydroxyl (-OH) group combines with the carboxyl (-COOH) group on a neighbouring molecule to form an ester linkage (-COO-).

(b) $2CH_3CH(OH)COOH$
$\rightleftharpoons (OCH(CH_3)CO)_2 + 2H_2O$

4. (a) $HOOCCH=CHCOOH + 2CH_3CH_2OH \rightleftharpoons CH_3CH_2OOCCH=CHCOOCH_2CH_3 + 2H_2O$

(b) The reaction mixture must be refluxed.

(c) Concentrated sulfuric acid.

## Exercise 4.8J

1. $CH_3COOH + PCl_5 \rightarrow CH_3COCl + POCl_3 + HCl$

2. (a) The reaction is exothermic and produces a pungent smelling gas.

(b) $CH_3CH(CH_3)CH_2COOH + PCl_5$
$\rightarrow CH_3CH(CH_3)CH_2COCl + POCl_3 + HCl$

3.

## Exercise 4.8K

1. (a) $CH_3COCl + NaCN \rightarrow CH_3COCN + NaCl$

(b) Cyanide ion, $CN^-$, acts as a nucleophile by using a lone pair of electrons on the carbon atom to form a coordinate bond with the electron deficient carbon atom in the carbonyl group.

2. (a) $CH_3CH_2COCl + CH_3CH_2OH$
$\rightarrow CH_3CH_2COOCH_2CH_3 + HCl$

(b) Ethanol acts as a nucleophile by using a lone pair of electrons on the oxygen atom to form a coordinate bond with the electron deficient carbon atom in the carbonyl group.

3. (a) $CH_3COCl + 2NH_3 \rightarrow CH_3CONH_2 + NH_4Cl$

(b) Ammonia acts as a nucleophile by using a lone pair of electrons on the nitrogen atom to form a coordinate bond with the electron deficient carbon atom in the carbonyl group. The ammonia then substitutes for the chlorine to form the corresponding amide.

## Exercise 4.8L

1. (a) $CH_3CH_2COOH + 4[H]$
$\rightarrow CH_3CH_2CH_2OH + H_2O$

(b)

2. Answer B

3. (a) $CH_3COCOOH + 6[H]$
$\rightarrow CH_3CH(OH)CH_2OH + H_2O$

(b)

(c) propane-1,2-diol

4. Answer A

5. (a) Dissolve the solid in a nonpolar solvent then add solid sodium carbonate to the solution. A colourless gas is produced. The gas turns limewater milky.

(b) $C_{11}H_{23}COOH + 4[H] \rightarrow C_{11}H_{23}CH_2OH + H_2O$

(c) Lithium aluminium hydride.

## 4.9 Esters

### Exercise 4.9A

1. Answer C.

2.

### Exercise 4.9B

1. (a) Ethyl lactate is miscible with water as the oxygen atom in the hydroxyl group can hydrogen bond with hydrogen atoms in water. Ethyl propanoate has a low solubility as it cannot hydrogen bond with water.

(b) The term miscible refers to liquids that mix in all proportions.

2. Compound A is miscible as it can use both oxygen atoms to hydrogen bond with hydrogen atoms in water. Compound B is insoluble as a much larger portion of the molecule cannot get involved in hydrogen bonding with water.

### Exercise 4.9C

1. The boiling point of pentyl hexanoate is higher as it has a greater molar mass and, as a result, stronger van der Waals attraction between molecules.

2. The van der Waals attraction between molecules is similar in dihydrofuranone and ethyl ethanoate as they have similar molar masses. The boiling point of dihydrofuranone is greater due to more effective dipole attraction between molecules.

3. The van der Waals attraction between molecules of compound B is greater as compound B has a higher molar mass. The boiling point of compound A is greater due to more effective dipole attraction between molecules.

## Exercise 4.9D

1. Answer A
2. Answer D
3. (a) Pentyl ethanoate
   (b) 3-methylbutyl ethanoate

4. Answer D

5.

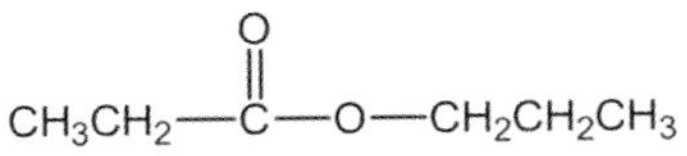

propyl propanoate

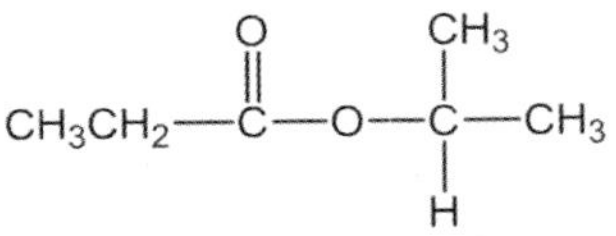

1-methylethyl propanoate

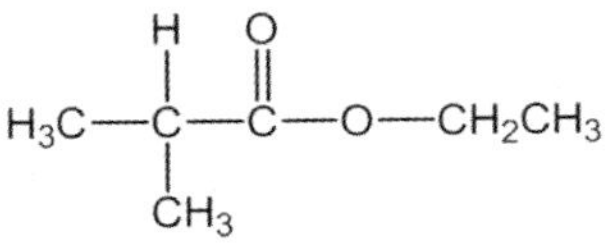

ethyl 2-methylpropanoate

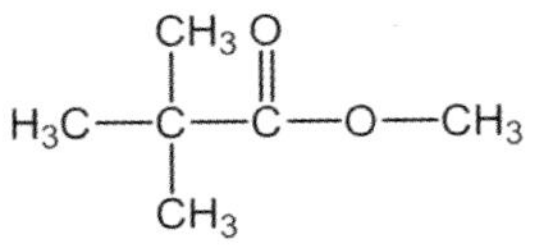

methyl 2,2-dimethylpropanoate

6.

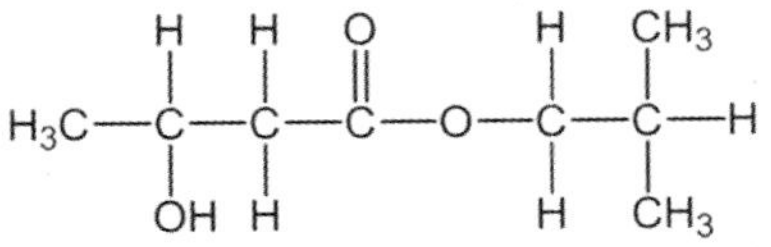

7. Methyl 2-hydroxy-4-methylpentanoate

## Exercise 4.9E

1. (a) Using an excess of ethanol or methanoic acid would increase the yield of ethyl methanoate by shifting the position of equilibrium to the right.

(b)

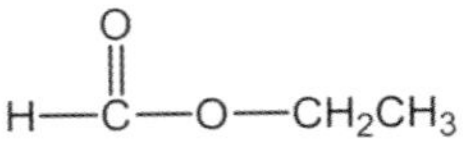

(c)

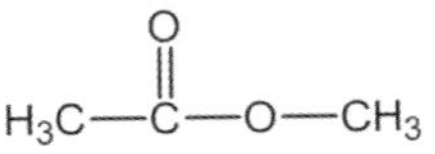

methyl ethanoate

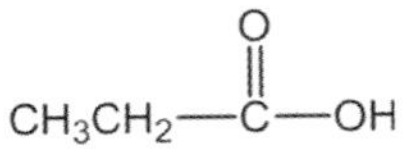

propanoic acid

2. (a) $CH_3CH_2COOH + CH_3OH$
   $\leftrightarrows CH_3CH_2COOCH_3 + H_2O$

(b) Concentrated sulfuric acid increases the rate of reaction by acting as a catalyst and increases the yield of ester by removing water from the reaction mixture.

3. (a) 3-methylbutanoic acid and methanol
   (b) $CH(CH_3)_2CH_2COOH + CH_3OH$
   $\leftrightarrows CH(CH_3)_2CH_2COOCH_3 + H_2O$

4. $CH_3COOH + C_5H_{11}OH$
   $\leftrightarrows CH_3COOC_5H_{11} + H_2O$

5. (a) The concentrated acid acts as a catalyst and increases the yield by absorbing water formed in the reaction.

(b)

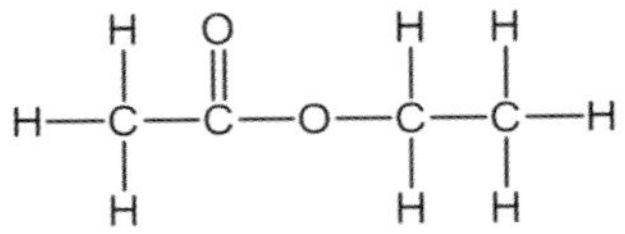

(c) The ester is ethyl ethanoate.

6.

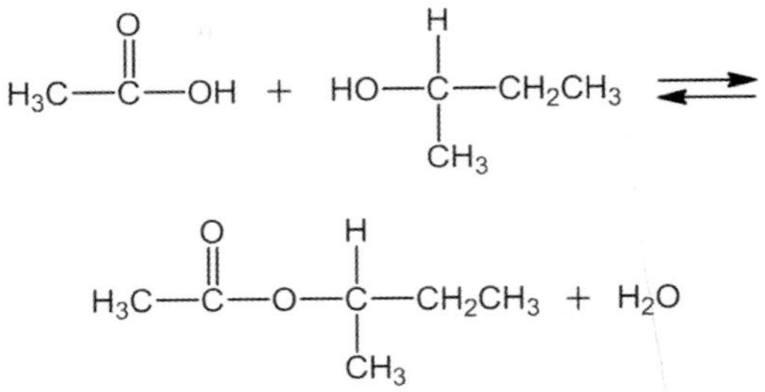

7. Answer D

8. (a) Ester A is formed by reacting ethanol ($HOCH_2CH_3$) with butanoic acid ($CH_3CH_2CH_2COOH$). Ester B is formed by reacting ethanol ($HOCH_2CH_3$) with hexanoic acid ($CH_3CH_2CH_2CH_2CH_2COOH$).

(b) Ester A is ethyl butanoate and ester B is ethyl hexanoate.

(c) Ester A: $C_3H_7COOH + C_2H_5OH$
   $\leftrightarrows C_3H_7COOC_2H_5 + H_2O$

Ester B: $C_5H_{11}COOH + C_2H_5OH$
$\leftrightarrows C_5H_{11}COOC_2H_5 + H_2O$

9.  70 %

## Exercise 4.9F

1.  See Worked Example 4.9iii.

2.  (a) $CH_3CH_2CH_2COOH + CH_3CH_2CH_2CH_2OH$
    $\rightarrow CH_3CH_2CH_2COOCH_2CH_2CH_2CH_3 + H_2O$

    (b) Mass of ester formed
    $= 30 \ cm^3 \times 0.87 \ g \ cm^{-3} = 26 \ g$

    Moles of ester formed = 0.18 mol

    Moles of acid needed
    $= 0.18 \ mol \times \dfrac{100}{70} = 0.26 \ mol$

    Mass of acid needed
    $= 0.26 \ mol \times 88 \ g \ mol^{-1} = 23 \ g$

    (c) Slowly add concentrated sulfuric acid to a mixture of butanoic acid and butan-1-ol in a round-bottom flask. Add anti-bumping granules and reflux the mixture for an extended period. Distil the mixture and collect the crude ester at 165 °C.

    (d) (i) Add dilute sodium hydrogencarbonate solution to the crude product in a separating funnel. Stopper, invert and shake the separating funnel. Open the tap every few seconds to release any carbon dioxide formed. Clamp the separating funnel, remove the stopper, and allow the layers to separate. Collect the upper (organic) layer containing the product.

    (ii) Add anhydrous sodium sulfate to the product in a small conical flask and swirl the mixture until the product becomes clear. Filter the mixture into a clean, dry round-bottom flask.

    (iii) Distil the filtrate and collect a pure sample of the ester at 165 °C.

## Exercise 4.9G

1.  (a) Esterification

    (b) Ethanoyl chloride

2.  (a) Ethanoyl chloride

    (b) $CH_3COCl + CH_3CH_2OH$
    $\rightarrow CH_3COOCH_2CH_3 + HCl$

3.  Answer D

4.  Answer B

5.  Answer C

6.  (a)

    (b) $CH_3CH_2COCl + CH_3CH(OH)CH_2CH_3$
    $\rightarrow CH_3CH_2COOCH(CH_3)CH_2CH_3 + HCl$

    (c) 1-methylpropyl propanoate

    (d) Hydrogen chloride gas is produced.

7.  Answer C

8.  The reaction with propanoyl chloride gives a higher yield as it goes to completion, and the other product is a gas making it easier to obtain methyl propanoate from the reaction mixture.

9.  Answer D

10. (a) cholesteryl ethanoate

    (b) $CH_3COOH + ROH \leftrightarrows CH_3COOR + H_2O$

    (c) Concentrated sulfuric acid.

    (d) Reaction with ethanoyl chloride:
    $CH_3COCl + ROH \leftrightarrows CH_3COOR + HCl$

## Exercise 4.9H

1.  (a) $HOCH_2CH_2OH + 2CH_3COOH$
    $\leftrightarrows CH_3COOCH_2CH_2OOCCH_3 + 2H_2O$

    (b) $K_c = \dfrac{[CH_3COOCH_2CH_2OOCCH_3][H_2O]^2}{[HOCH_2CH_2OH][CH_3COOH]^2}$

    No units.

2.

3.

4. (a) Steamy fumes are produced and the reaction mixture warms up.

(b) Esterification

(c)

$$H_3C-\overset{O}{\underset{}{C}}-O-\overset{H}{\underset{H}{C}}-\overset{H}{\underset{H}{C}}-O-\overset{O}{\underset{}{C}}-CH_3$$

(d) White fumes are formed when the hydrogen chloride gas produced in the reaction contacts a glass rod dipped in concentrated ammonia solution.

### Exercise 4.9I

1. (a) $CH_3COOCH_3 + H_2O \rightleftharpoons CH_3COOH + CH_3OH$

(b)

$$H_3C-\overset{OH}{\underset{\overset{+}{O}H_2}{C}}-OCH_3$$

(c) A water molecule uses a lone pair of electrons to form a coordinate bond with the electron deficient carbon atom in the ester linkage.

2. (a) $HCOOCH_2CH_3 + H_2O$
   $\rightleftharpoons HCOOH + CH_3CH_2OH$

(b)

$$H-\overset{\overset{+}{O}H}{\underset{}{C}}-OCH_2CH_3$$

(c) Hydrogen ions from the dilute acid increase the rate of reaction by reacting with the ester and are not consumed by the reaction.

### Exercise 4.9J

1. (a)

$$H_3C-\overset{O}{\underset{}{C}}-O-\overset{H}{\underset{CH_3}{C}}-CH_3$$

(b) $CH_3COOCH(CH_3)_2 + NaOH$
   $\rightarrow CH_3COONa + CH_3CH(OH)CH_3$

(c) Ethanoic acid is liberated by the addition of dilute hydrochloric acid to the reaction mixture: $CH_3COONa + HCl \rightarrow CH_3COOH + NaCl$

2. (a) $CH_3COOCH_2CH(CH_3)_2 + NaOH$
   $\rightarrow CH_3COONa + CH(CH_3)_2CH_2OH$

(b) Hydroxide ion is attracted to the electron deficient carbon atom in the ester linkage and uses a lone pair of electrons to form a coordinate bond with the electron deficient carbon atom.

(c)

$$H_3C-\overset{O^-}{\underset{OH}{C}}-O-\overset{H}{\underset{CH_3}{C}}-\overset{H}{\underset{CH_3}{C}}-CH_3$$

### 4.10 Fats and Oils

### Exercise 4.10A

1. (a) Vegetable oil

(b) Shake a solution of the fat/oil with bromine water. If the fat/oil is unsaturated the bromine water will be decolourised.

2.

$$H-\overset{H}{\underset{}{C}}-O-\overset{O}{\underset{}{C}}-C_{17}H_{33}$$
$$H-\overset{}{\underset{}{C}}-O-\overset{O}{\underset{}{C}}-C_{17}H_{33}$$
$$H-\overset{H}{\underset{H}{C}}-O-\overset{O}{\underset{}{C}}-C_{17}H_{33}$$

3. One possible structure is:

$$H-\overset{H}{\underset{}{C}}-O-\overset{O}{\underset{}{C}}-(CH_2)_{16}CH_3$$
$$H-\overset{}{\underset{}{C}}-O-\overset{O}{\underset{}{C}}-(CH_2)_{14}CH_3$$
$$H-\overset{H}{\underset{H}{C}}-O-\overset{O}{\underset{}{C}}-(CH_2)_7CH=CH(CH_2)_7CH_3$$

Other triglycerides may be formed by attaching the $(CH_2)_{16}CH_3$, $(CH_2)_{14}CH_3$ and $(CH_2)_7CH=CH(CH_2)_7CH_3$ groups in a different order.

4. (a) Oleic acid is monounsaturated as it contains one C=C bond. Linoleic acid, linolenic acid and arachidonic acid are polyunsaturated acids as they contain more than one C=C bond.

(b)

$$CH_3(CH_2)_4-\overset{H}{\underset{}{C}}=\overset{H}{\underset{}{C}}-CH_2-\overset{H}{\underset{}{C}}=\overset{H}{\underset{}{C}}-CH_2-\overset{H}{\underset{}{C}}=\overset{H}{\underset{}{C}}-CH_2-\overset{H}{\underset{}{C}}=\overset{H}{\underset{}{C}}-(CH_2)_3COOH$$

5. The hydrocarbon chains in glyceryl trioleate are unsaturated and pack together less efficiently. This reduces the van der Waals attraction between neighbouring triglycerides and lowers the melting point of glyceryl trioleate.

6. Put the frozen sample in a capillary tube sealed at

one end and slowly heat the sample using a melting point apparatus. Record the temperature when the sample starts to melt and the temperature when the sample finishes melting. If the sample is solid at 25 °C it is a fat. If the sample is liquid at 25 °C it is an oil.

## Exercise 4.10B

1. (a)

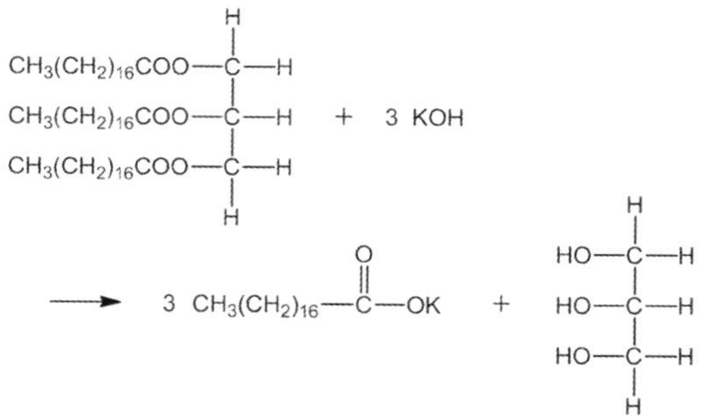

(b) Propane-1,2,3-triol

2. (a)

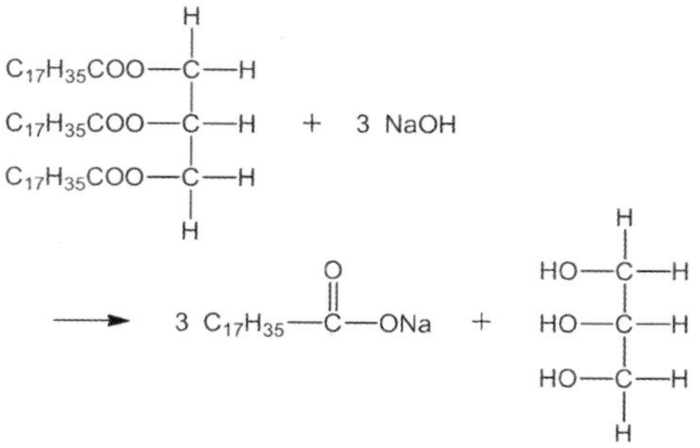

(b) $C_{57}H_{110}O_6$  RMM = 890

3.

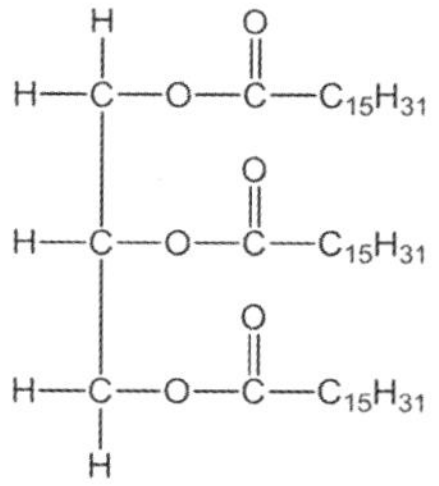

4. (a) Saponification refers to the alkaline hydrolysis of a fat or oil.

(b)

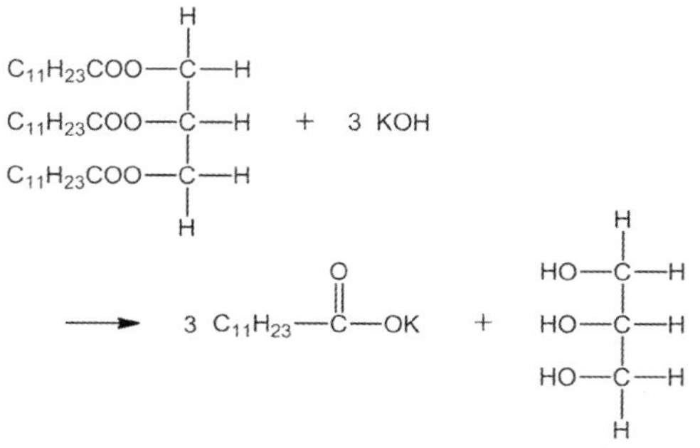

5. (a)

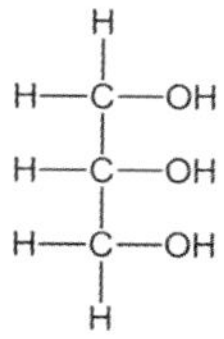

(b) Propane-1,2,3-triol

(c)

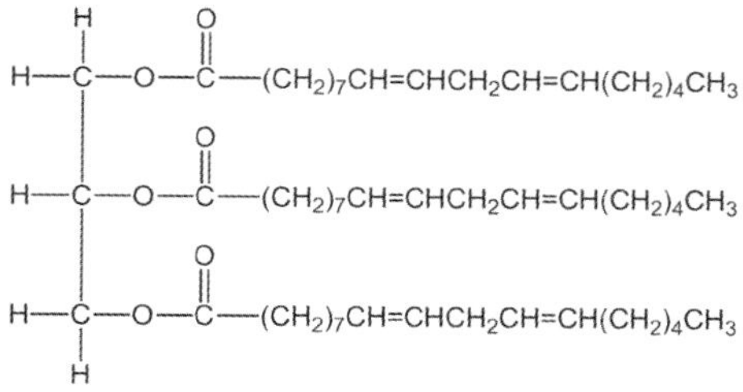

6. (a)

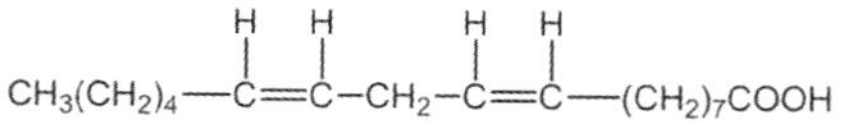

$$CH_3(CH_2)_4-C=C-CH_2-C=C-(CH_2)_7COOH$$

(b)

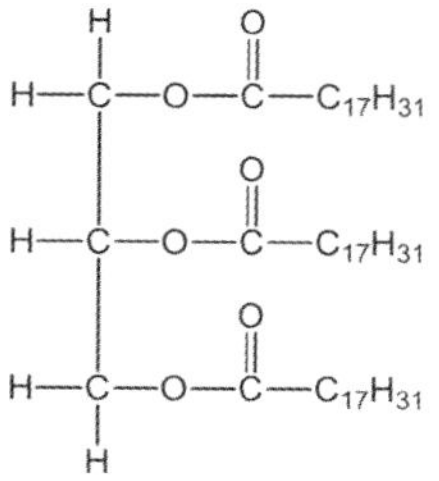

7. One possible structure is:

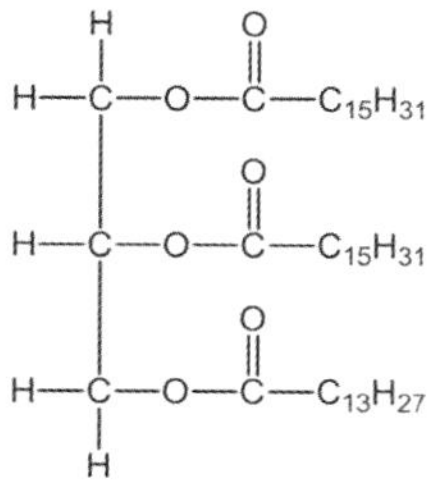

A triglyceride with the $C_{13}H_{27}$ group attached in-between the $C_{15}H_{31}$ groups could also be formed.

8. (a) Glycerol

(b)

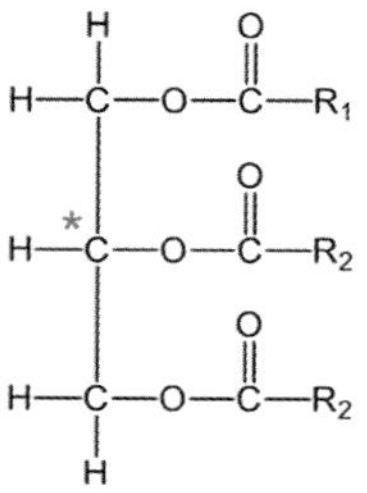

## Exercise 4.10C

1. Fats and oils are heated to around 180 °C before being reacted with hydrogen gas in the presence of a catalyst made from finely divided nickel.

2. Olive oil is hardened when hydrogen ($H_2$) adds across some or all of the C=C bonds in the oil.

## Exercise 4.10D

1. (a) Biodiesel is a fuel similar to diesel that contains alkyl esters formed from the long chain fatty acids in renewable sources such as vegetable oils.

   (b) Biodiesel is formed by heating a fat or oil with an excess of an alcohol in the presence of aqueous sodium hydroxide.

   (c) Biodiesel is more suitable as it produces more energy than ethanol when burnt, and petrol engines do not have to be modified to burn biodiesel.

2. (a) $CH_3(CH_2)_7CH=CH(CH_2)_7COOCH_2CH_3$

   $CH_3(CH_2)_4CH=CHCH_2CH=CH(CH_2)_7COOCH_2CH_3$

   (b) The sodium hydroxide acts as a catalyst.

3.
$H_2C-OCO(CH_2)_7CH=CH(CH_2)_7CH_3$
$HC-OCO(CH_2)_7CH=CH(CH_2)_7CH_3$   $+$   $3 CH_3OH$
$H_2C-OCO(CH_2)_7CH=CHCH_2CH=CH(CH_2)_4CH_3$

$\longrightarrow$
$CH_2OH$
$CHOH$   $+$   $2 CH_3(CH_2)_7CH=CH(CH_2)_7-\overset{O}{\overset{\|}{C}}-OCH_3$
$CH_2OH$

$+$   $CH_3(CH_2)_4CH=CHCH_2CH=CH(CH_2)_7-\overset{O}{\overset{\|}{C}}-OCH_3$

### 4.11 Arenes

## Exercise 4.11A

1. Six

2.

**Before**          **After**

3. 30 electrons

4. Each carbon atom uses three of its four outer-shell electrons to sigma bond with a hydrogen atom and two neighbouring carbon atoms in the ring. The fourth outer-shell electron is used to form a π-bond with a neighbouring carbon atom. The C-C bonds in the ring are identical as the electrons involved in π-bonding are delocalised around the ring.

5. Benzene is a planar molecule as the sigma bonding pairs are arranged in a trigonal planar arrangement about each carbon, and the electrons involved in π-bonding are delocalised around the ring.

6. Answer D

## Exercise 4.11B

1. (a) $C_6H_6 + 3H_2 \rightarrow C_6H_{12}$

   (b)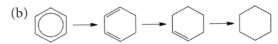

2. (a) $-360 \text{ kJ mol}^{-1}$

   (b) Benzene is more stable than expected as the electrons involved in π-bonding are delocalised around the benzene ring.

## Exercise 4.11C

1.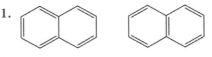

2.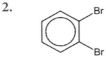

   **1,2-dibromobenzene**   **1,3-dibromobenzene**

   **1,4-dibromobenzene**

3. 1-methyl-4-nitrobenzene

4. 1-hydroxy-2,4-dinitrobenzene

5. 4-allyl-1-hydroxy-2-methoxybenzene

6. 191

7. (a) The ortho-, meta- and para- isomers are named as 2-, 3- and 4-nitrobenzoic acid.

   (b) In 2-nitrobenzoic acid the COOH group hydrogen bonds with the $NO_2$ group in the same molecule. In 4-nitrobenzoic acid the COOH group hydrogen bonds with the $NO_2$ group in a neighbouring molecule.

## Exercise 4.11D

1. (a) Electrophilic addition

   (b) Iron

   (c) See Worked Example 4.11i (a)

   (d) Electrophilic substitution

**2. (a)**

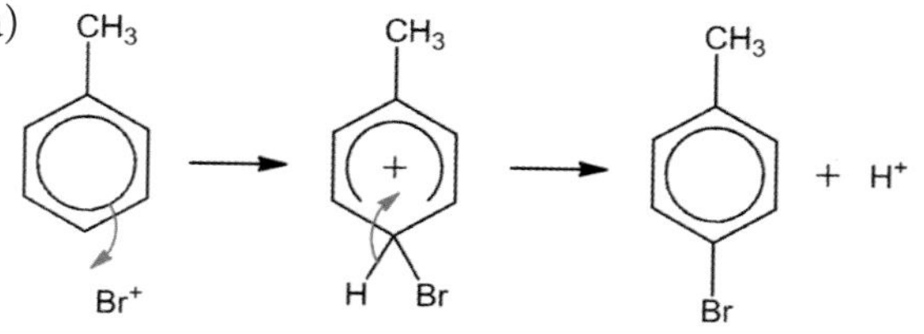

**(b)** 2-bromo-1,4-dimethylbenzene

**3. (a)**

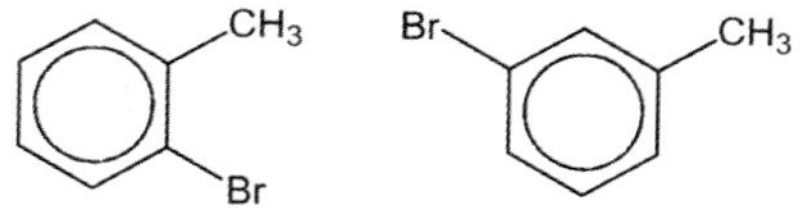

2-bromotoluene     3-bromotoluene

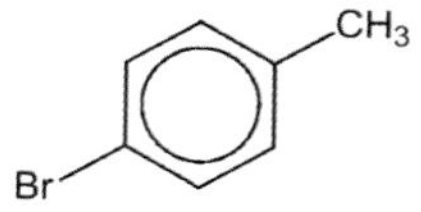

4-bromotoluene

**(b)** Iron or iron(III) bromide or aluminium or aluminium bromide.

**(c)** Addition would remove the additional stability associated with the delocalisation of the $\pi$-electrons around the benzene ring.

## Exercise 4.11E

**1.**

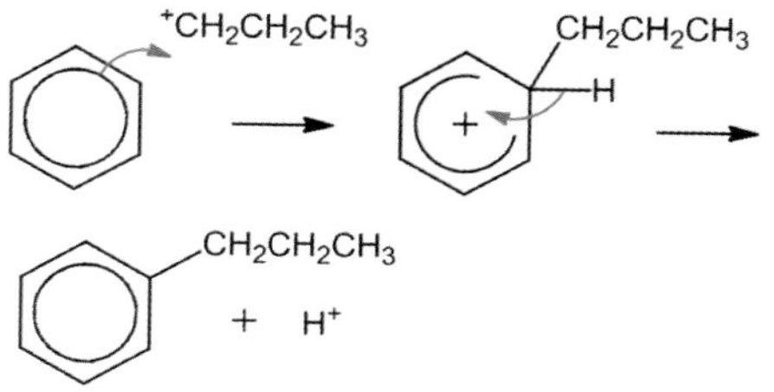

**2. (a)** Catalyst

**(b)** $CH_3^+$

**3. (a)** Aluminium chloride

**(b)**

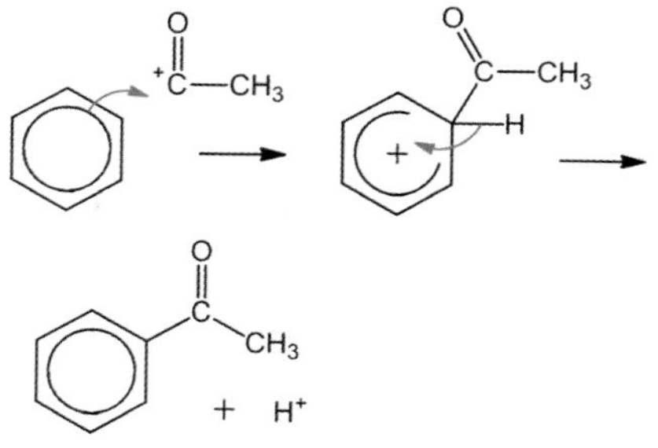

**(c)** Electrophilic substitution as the acyl cation acts as an electrophile and substitutes for a hydrogen atom attached to the benzene ring.

**4. (a)**

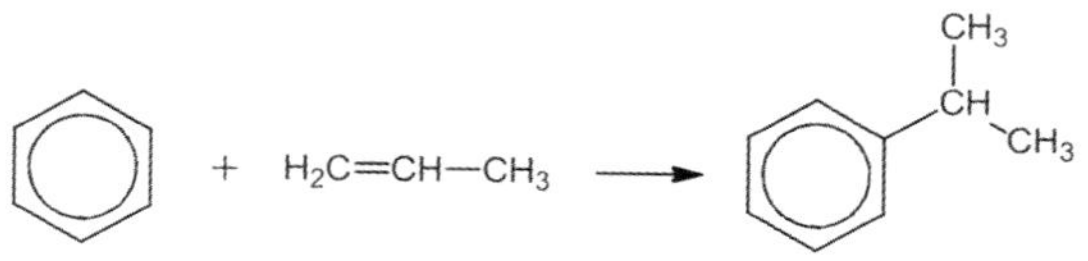

**(b)** The alkyl cation used to form propylbenzene is less stable than the alkyl cation used to form cumene.

## Exercise 4.11F

**1. (a)** The nitronium ion is an electrophile as it attacks a region of high electron density in the benzene molecule.

**(b)**

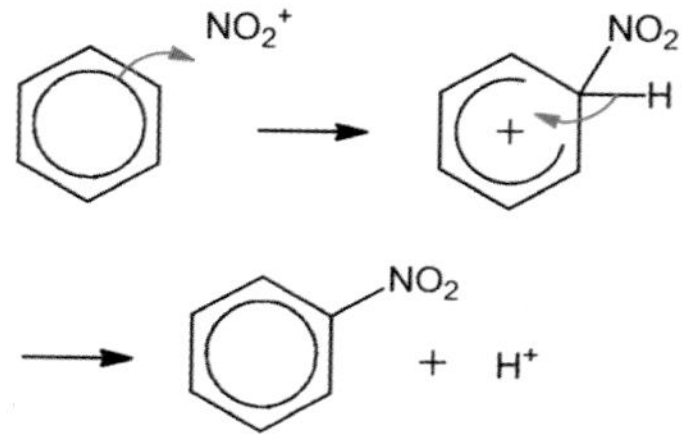

**(c)** The reaction is an example of substitution as it involves the addition of a nitronium ion followed by the elimination of a hydrogen ion.

**2. (a)** 2-methyl-1,3,5-trinitrobenzene or 2,4,6-trinitrotoluene.

**(b)** Concentrated nitric acid and concentrated sulfuric acid.

**(c)** $HNO_3 + H_2SO_4 \rightarrow NO_2^+ + HSO_4^- + H_2O$

**(d)** Nitronium ion

**(e)** Electrophilic substitution

**3. (a)** $HNO_3 + H_2SO_4 \rightarrow NO_2^+ + HSO_4^- + H_2O$

**(b)** Nitric acid accepts a hydrogen ion from sulfuric acid.

**(c)** Sulfuric acid ($H^+ + HSO_4^-$) is regenerated when nitronium ion adds to benzene and a hydrogen ion is eliminated.

## Exercise 4.11G

**1. (a)**

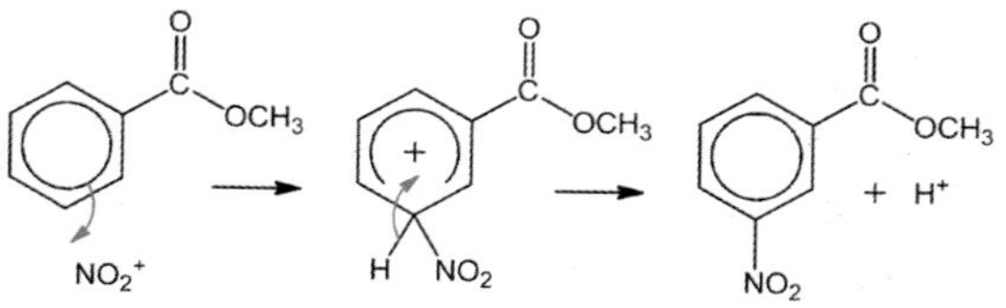

**(b)** Electrophilic substitution

**(c)** Methyl 3-nitrobenzoate

**(d)** Cream solid

**2.** A low temperature is maintained to prevent nitration of methyl 3-nitrobenzoate.

## 5.1 Chromatography

### Exercise 5.1A

1. (a) The distance travelled by the solute divided by the distance travelled by the solvent.

   (b) The amino acid spends most of its time in the stationary phase.

2. Answer D

3. See Worked Example 5.1i.

### Exercise 5.1B

1. Spot W

2. Alanine and valine

3. Using a pencil, draw a small cross 2-3 cm from the corner of the chromatography paper. Use a capillary tube to place a small spot of the mixture on the cross. Repeat several times to produce a concentrated sample.

   Develop the chromatogram using the first solvent and draw a pencil line to mark the position of the solvent front. Turn the paper through 90 degrees and develop the chromatogram using the second solvent. Again draw a pencil line to mark the position of the solvent.

   Expose the chromatogram to a developing agent, or view the chromatogram under UV light, to locate the compounds on the chromatogram. The presence of capsaicin is confirmed by comparing the $R_f$ values from the chromatogram to the $R_f$ value for pure capsaicin obtained using the same solvents.

### Exercise 5.1C

1. (a) See question 3 in Exercise 5.1B.

   (b) Hydroquinone spends more time in the mobile phase as it is less polar than gallic acid.

2. (a) The distance travelled by the solute divided by the distance travelled by the solvent.

   (b) Coumarin spends more time in the mobile phase as it is less polar than o-coumaric acid.

   (c) Distance = 0.79 × 6.4 = 5.1 cm

### Exercise 5.1D

1. (a) The retention time is the time taken from injection until the compound is detected.

(b) $\dfrac{15.76}{49.79} \times 100 = 31.65\%$

(c)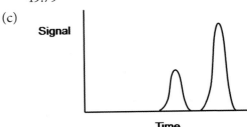

2. (a) Purple castle which is $\dfrac{24.3}{70.6} \times 100 = 34.4\%$ methyl eugenol.

   (b) The signal with the third largest area produced by the clove variety has the same retention time as the signal with the largest area produced by the purple castle variety.

3. Answer A

4. (a) The ester is more volatile and will not 'stick' to the chromatography column.

   (b) The area under the signal produced by the ester would account for 90% of the total area under the signals in the chromatogram. Other signals due to impurities would account for 10% of the total area under the signals.

## 5.2 Volumetric Analysis

### Exercise 5.2A

1. (a) Back titration

   (b) Moles of HCl added = 0.16 mol

   Moles of HCl remaining = Moles of NaOH used = 0.050 mol

   Moles of HCl reacted = 0.16 – 0.050 = 0.11 mol

   Moles of MgO in 5 tablets = $\dfrac{0.11 \text{ mol}}{2}$

   = 0.055 mol

   Mass of MgO per tablet
   = 0.011 mol × 40 g mol$^{-1}$ = 0.44 g = 440 mg

2. Moles of HCl added = 0.0400 mol

   Moles of NaOH used = 0.00186 mol

   Moles of HCl in 250 cm$^3$

   = 0.00186 mol × $\dfrac{250 \text{ cm}^3}{25 \text{ cm}^3}$ = 0.0186 mol

   Moles of HCl reacted = 0.0400 – 0.0186

   = 0.0214 mol

Mass of $CaCO_3$ in egg shell

= 0.0107 mol × 100 g mol$^{-1}$ = 1.07 g

Percentage $CaCO_3 = \dfrac{1.07\ g}{1.12\ g} \times 100 = 95.5\ \%$

3. (a) $Cu + Cl_2 \rightarrow CuCl_2$

(b) $CuO + 2HCl \rightarrow CuCl_2 + H_2O$

(c) $CuCl_2.2H_2O$

(d) Add a known mass of copper oxide to a known volume of hydrochloric acid that is in excess. Titrate the remaining acid against standard sodium hydroxide solution using phenolphthalein indicator. Repeat to obtain two accurate titres.

## Exercise 5.2B

1. (a) $MnO_4^-{}_{(aq)} + 5Fe^{2+}{}_{(aq)} + 8H^+{}_{(aq)}$

$\rightarrow Mn^{2+}{}_{(aq)} + 5Fe^{3+}{}_{(aq)} + 4H_2O_{(l)}$

(b) Colourless to pink.

(c) Moles of iron(II) in 250 cm$^3$ = 0.0095 mol

Mass of $FeC_4H_2O_4$ in five tablets

= 0.0095 mol × 170 g mol$^{-1}$ = 1.6 g

Mass in one tablet = 0.32 g

(d) See Worked Example 5.2ii.

2. Moles of iron(II) in 25 cm$^3$

= 6.8 × 10$^{-4}$ mol × 5 = 3.4 × 10$^{-3}$ mol

Mass of Fe in sample

= 3.4 × 10$^{-2}$ mol × 56 g mol$^{-1}$ = 1.9 g

% Fe in steel = 95 %

3. (a) $Cr_2O_7^{2-} + 6Fe^{2+} + 14H^+ \rightarrow 2Cr^{3+} + 6Fe^{3+} + 7H_2O$

(b) Moles of iron(II) in 25 cm$^3$

= 2.4 × 10$^{-4}$ mol × 6 = 1.4 × 10$^{-3}$ mol

Mass of $FeSO_4$ in 250 cm$^3$

= 1.4 × 10$^{-2}$ mol × 152 g mol$^{-1}$ = 2.1 g

Mass of $FeSO_4$ per tablet = 0.42 g

4. (a) $3MnO_4^- + 5Fe^{2+} + 5C_2O_4^{2-} + 24H^+$

$\rightarrow 3Mn^{2+} + 5Fe^{3+} + 10CO_2 + 12H_2O$

(b) Moles of manganate(VII) = 3.6 × 10$^{-5}$ mol

Moles of $FeC_2O_4$ in 20 cm$^3$

= 3.6 × 10$^{-5}$ mol × $\dfrac{5}{3}$ = 6.0 × 10$^{-5}$ mol

Moles of iron in 100 cm$^3$

= 6.0 × 10$^{-5}$ mol × 5 = 3.0 × 10$^{-4}$ mol

Mass of iron dissolved

= 3.0 × 10$^{-4}$ mol × 56 g mol$^{-1}$ × 1000 = 17 mg

5. Moles of manganate(VII) = 8.1 × 10$^{-4}$ mol

Moles of $FeC_2O_4$ in 25 cm$^3$

= 8.1 × 10$^{-4}$ mol × $\dfrac{5}{3}$ = 1.4 × 10$^{-3}$ mol

Molarity of $FeC_2O_4$ = 1.4 × 10$^{-3}$ mol × 40

= 0.056 mol dm$^{-3}$

## Exercise 5.2C

1. Moles of $I_2$ liberated = 7.5 × 10$^{-4}$ mol

Concentration of iodate = 2.5 × 10$^{-4}$ mol × 40

= 0.010 mol dm$^{-3}$

## Exercise 5.2D

1. Moles of $I_2$ liberated = 1.8 × 10$^{-3}$ mol

Moles of $H_2O_2$ in 500 cm$^3$ = 1.8 × 10$^{-3}$ mol × 20

= 3.6 × 10$^{-2}$ mol

Molarity of undiluted $H_2O_2$

= 3.6 × 10$^{-2}$ mol × 40 = 1.4 mol dm$^{-3}$

## 5.3 Mass Spectrometry

## Exercise 5.3A

1. Answer C

2. (a) $CH_3CH_2^+$ (m/e = 29) and $CONH_2^+$ (m/e = 44)

(b) Fragmentation refers to the breaking apart of a molecular ion to form a smaller ion with a positive charge.

(c) m/e = 44

3. $CH_3COO^+$

4. $CH_3CH_2^+$ (m/e = 29) and $CH_3CO^+$ (m/e = 43)

5. $CO^+$ or $C_2H_4^+$ (m/e = 28) and $HCOO^+$ or $C_2H_5O^+$ (m/e = 45)

6. (a) m/z = 29

(b) $CH_3O^+$ (m/z = 31) and $CH_3CH_2CO^+$ (m/z = 57)

(c) The signal at m/z = 89 is produced by molecules that contain a $^{13}C$ atom.

7. (a) The signal with the greatest abundance.

(b) m/z = 55

(c) $COOH^+$ (m/z = 45) and $(CH_2CO)_2O^+$ (m/z = 100)

8. (a) 58

   (b) $CH_3CH_2CHO^+$

   (c) 58

   (d) $CH_3CH_2CHO^+ \rightarrow CH_3CH_2CO^+ + H$

   (e) $CH_3CH_2CO^+ \rightarrow CH_3CH_2^+ + CO$

9. (a)

   (b) $m/e = 45$

   (c) The signal at $m/e = 45$ is formed when the molecular ion loses a hydrogen atom.

   (d) $CH_3O^+$ ($m/e = 31$) and $CH_3CH_2^+$ ($m/e = 29$)

   (e) The signal at $m/e = 29$ is due to the fragmentation of ethanol:

   $CH_3CH_2OH^+ \rightarrow CH_3CH_2^+ + OH$.

   Compound Y is ethanol.

## Exercise 5.3B

1. $^{35}Cl^+$ ($m/z = 35$); $^{37}Cl^+$ ($m/z = 37$); $^{35}Cl^{35}Cl^+$ ($m/z = 70$); $^{35}Cl^{37}Cl^+$ ($m/z = 72$); $^{37}Cl^{37}Cl^+$ ($m/z = 74$)

2. (a) *M signal:* $CH_3CH^{35}ClCH_3^+$
   *M+2 signal:* $CH_3CH^{37}ClCH_3^+$

   (b) $CH_3CH^{35}Cl^+$ ($m/z = 63$) and $CH_3CH^{37}Cl^+$ ($m/z = 65$)

   (c) Loss of a chlorine atom from the molecular ion: $C_3H_7Cl^+ \rightarrow C_3H_7^+ + Cl$

3. (a) *M signal:* $CH_3CH^{79}BrCH_3^+$
   *M+2 signal:* $CH_3CH^{81}BrCH_3^+$

   (b) $m/z = 43$

   (c) Loss of a bromine atom from the molecular ion: $C_3H_7Br^+ \rightarrow C_3H_7^+ + Br$

   (d) The signal at $m/z = 27$ results from the loss of methane, $CH_4$ and the signal at $m/z = 41$ results from the loss of hydrogen, $H_2$.

4. (a) The signal at $m/z = 108$ is due to $CH_3CH^{35}ClCOOH^+$ ions and the signal at $m/z = 110$ is due to $CH_3CH^{37}ClCOOH^+$ ions.

   (b) The signal at $m/z = 91$ is due to $CH_3CH^{35}ClCO^+$ ions.

## 5.4 NMR Spectroscopy

### Exercise 5.4A

1. (a) The hydrogen atoms in the methyl (-$CH_3$) group, the methylene (-$CH_2$-) group and the aldehyde (-CHO) group each give rise to one signal.

   (b) The areas under the signals at $\delta$ 9.8 ppm, $\delta$ 2.4 ppm and $\delta$ 1.1 ppm are in the ratio 1:2:3, and are produced by hydrogen atoms in the -CHO, -$CH_2$- and -$CH_3$ groups.

2. (a) The isomer is propan-1-ol as the spectrum contains four signals produced by hydrogen atoms in four different chemical environments.

   (b) The areas under the signals are in the ratio 1:2:2:3, and are produced by hydrogen atoms in the -OH, -$CH_2$- (beside OH), -$CH_2$- (beside -$CH_3$), and -$CH_3$ groups.

3.

   or

### Exercise 5.4B

1. (a) The areas under the signals are in the ratio 1:6. The hydrogen atom attached to the second carbon (CH) gives rise to one signal. The six hydrogen atoms in the methyl (-$CH_3$) groups give rise to one signal.

   (b) The signal produced by the CH group has a greater chemical shift as the hydrogen is adjacent to the electron-withdrawing chlorine atom and is less shielded.

2. (a) The areas under the signals at $\delta$ 4.2 ppm, $\delta$ 2.4 ppm and $\delta$ 1.7 ppm are in the ratio 2:3:3, and are produced by the -$CH_2$-, -$CH_3$ beside -COO-, and -$CH_3$ beside -$CH_2$- groups.

   (b) The signal produced by the -$CH_2$- group at $\delta$ 4.2 has the greatest chemical shift as the -$CH_2$- group is adjacent to an electron-withdrawing oxygen atom. The signal produced by the -$CH_3$ group beside -COO- has a greater chemical shift than the signal produced by the -$CH_3$ group beside -$CH_2$- as it is adjacent to a carbon atom bonded to electron-withdrawing oxygen atoms.

3. (a) The hydrogen atoms in the -CH$_2$- groups are chemically equivalent.

   (b) The signal at δ 11.0 ppm is produced by hydrogen atoms in the -COOH groups. The signal at δ 2.8 ppm is produced by hydrogen atoms in the -CH$_2$- groups.

   (c) The -COOH signal has a greater chemical shift as the hydrogen atoms in the -COOH groups are attached to an electron-withdrawing oxygen atom and are less shielded than the hydrogen atoms in the -CH$_2$- groups.

## Exercise 5.4C

1. (a) Tetramethylsilane, Si(CH$_3$)$_4$

   (b) The signals at δ 8.0 ppm, δ 4.3 ppm and δ 1.4 ppm are produced by hydrogen atoms with zero, three, and two equivalent hydrogen atoms bonded to an adjacent atom.

   (c) The areas under the signals at δ 8.0 ppm, δ 4.3 ppm and δ 1.4 ppm are in the ratio 1:2:3, and are produced by the hydrogen atom beside -COO-, the -CH$_2$- group, and the -CH$_3$ group.

   (d) The signal produced by the HCOO- group has the greatest chemical shift as the hydrogen atom is adjacent to two electron-withdrawing oxygen atoms. The signal produced by the -CH$_2$- group has a greater chemical shift than the signal produced by the -CH$_3$ group as it is adjacent to an electron-withdrawing oxygen atom.

2.

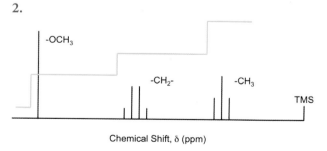

3. Answer C

4.

| | Signal 1 | Signal 2 | Signal 3 |
|---|---|---|---|
| Integration: | 3 | 1 | 1 |
| Splitting: | Doublet | Quartet | Singlet |

5. Possible structures for A and B:

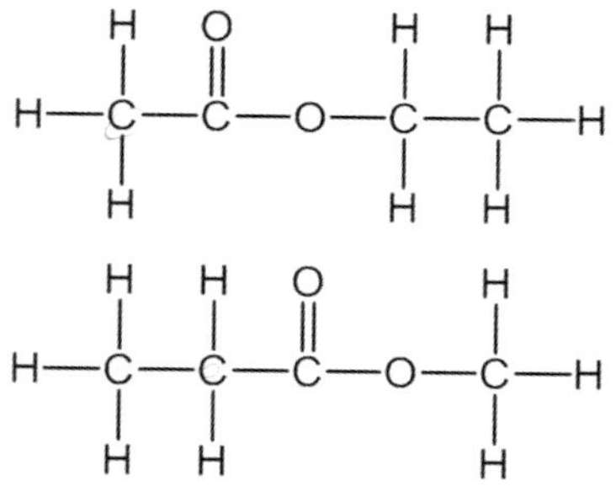

## 5.5 Electrochemistry

### Exercise 5.5A

1. (a) Oxidation  Fe$_{(s)}$ → Fe$^{2+}$$_{(aq)}$ + 2e$^-$
      Reduction  Sn$^{2+}$$_{(aq)}$ + 2e$^-$ → Sn$_{(s)}$

   (b) Electrons flow from the iron electrode to the tin electrode.

2. (a) Al$_{(s)}$ → Al$^{3+}$$_{(aq)}$ + 3e$^-$  Zn$^{2+}$$_{(aq)}$ + 2e$^-$ → Zn$_{(s)}$

   (b) Electrons flow from the aluminium electrode to the zinc electrode.

   (c) Al|Al$^{3+}$||Zn$^{2+}$|Zn

### Exercise 5.5B

1. (a) Ag$^+$$_{(aq)}$ + Cr$^{2+}$$_{(aq)}$ → Ag$_{(s)}$ + Cr$^{3+}$$_{(aq)}$

   (b) emf = E$_{red}$ + E$_{ox}$ = (+0.80) + (+0.41) = +1.21 V

2. (a) 2CO + O$_2$ → 2CO$_2$

   (b) emf = E$_{red}$ + E$_{ox}$ = (+1.23) + (−0.10) = +1.13 V

3. (a) F$_{2(g)}$ + Sn$^{2+}$$_{(aq)}$ → 2F$^-$$_{(aq)}$ + Sn$^{4+}$$_{(aq)}$

   (b) emf = E$_{red}$ + E$_{ox}$ = (+2.87) + (−0.15) = +2.72 V

4. Answer D

### Exercise 5.5C

1. A hydrogen electrode is constructed by placing a platinum electrode in 1 mol dm$^{-3}$ hydrochloric acid ([H$^+$] = 1 mol dm$^{-3}$) that is in contact with hydrogen gas at a pressure of 100 kPa. The electrode is then operated at 25 °C.

2. (a) The cell operates at 25 °C with hydrogen ions at a concentration of 1 mol dm$^{-3}$ and hydrogen gas at a pressure of 100 kPa.

   (b) The salt bridge completes the circuit by allowing ions to flow between the salt bridge and the solutions at each electrode.

   (c) Connect the chlorine half–cell to a standard hydrogen electrode, then connect the cell to a voltmeter and record the emf produced by the cell when the cell operates under standard conditions.

3. (a) emf $= E_{red} + E_{ox} = (+1.36) + (-0.77) = +0.59$ V

(b) $Pt|Fe^{2+},Fe^{3+}||Cl^-|Cl_2|Pt$

(c) The electrons flow from the iron electrode to the chlorine electrode.

(d) The cell operates at 25 °C with all ions at a concentration of 1 mol $dm^{-3}$ and chlorine gas at a pressure of 100 kPa.

## Exercise 5.5D

1. Answer B

2. (a) Al          (b) $Fe^{3+}$

3. (a) $2Fe^{3+} + Zn \rightarrow 2Fe^{2+} + Zn^{2+}$

(b) The emf for the reduction of iron(II) by zinc is positive:
$emf = E_{red} + E_{ox} = (-0.44) + (0.76) = 0.32$ V

4. Answer D

5. Answer A

6. Answer C

7. Answer D

## Exercise 5.5E

1. $emf = E_{red} + E_{ox} = (+0.80) + (+1.18) = +1.98$ V

2. Answer A

3. Zinc is more reactive and displaces iron.
$emf = E_{red} + E_{ox} = E^{\ominus}_{Fe} + (+0.76) = +0.32$ V
Solving gives $E^{\ominus}_{Fe} = -0.44$ V

4. Answer D

5. Answer B

## Exercise 5.5F

1. (a) Lithium ions are produced at the graphite electrode and move through the electrolyte before becoming part of the $LiMnO_2$ electrode.

(b) $Li_{1-x}MnO_2 + xLi^+ \rightarrow LiMnO_2$

2. (a) Batteries containing Li-ion cells are lightweight, rechargeable, generate a large emf, and can be manufactured in a variety of shapes.

(b) Lithium atoms stored in the graphite electrode lose an electron to form lithium ions:
$Li_xC \rightarrow C + xLi^+ + xe^-$

3. Lead-acid cells are much cheaper to manufacture than Li-ion cells, and are used in-spite of the risk posed by the recycling and reuse of lead which is toxic in the environment.

## Exercise 5.5G

1. (a) $2H_2 + O_2 \rightarrow 2H_2O$

(b) A greater proportion of the energy produced by the fuel cell is used to generate electricity and the only product is water which is non-polluting.

2. (a) Platinum is a catalyst for the half-reaction at each electrode.

(b) Carbon is an electrical conductor and is inert.

3. (a) X is hydroxide ion.

(b) Hydroxide ion is present in the electrolyte and is not produced or consumed by the cell reaction.

4. (a) $CH_3OH + \dfrac{3}{2}O_2 \rightarrow CO_2 + 2H_2O$

(b) A is $CO_2$ and B is $O_2$

(c) Mass of 1 $dm^3$ of solution = 1060 g
Mass of methanol in 1 $dm^3$
$= 1060 \text{ g} \times \dfrac{3.00}{100} = 31.8$ g
Molarity of solution $\dfrac{31.8 \text{ g}}{32 \text{ g mol}^{-1}} = 0.99$ mol $dm^{-3}$

## 5.6 Transition Metals

### Exercise 5.6A

1. $[Co(NH_3)_5Br]^{2+}$   $SO_4^{2-}$

2. $K^+$   $[Fe(CN)_6]^{4-}$

3. $[Cr(H_2O)_6]Cl_3$

4. $[Cr(H_2O)_5Cl]Cl_2$

5. (a) $K^+$ and $[Fe(C_2O_4)_3]^{3-}$

(b) $K_3[Fe(C_2O_4)_3]$

6. The orange salt contains the complex $[Cr(NH_3)_6]^{3+}$ while the dark red salt contains the $[Cr(NH_3)_5Cl]^{2+}$ complex.

7. A transition metal has a partly filled d-subshell or forms at least one stable ion with a partly filled d-subshell.

## Exercise 5.6B

1. Mn atom    [Ar] $4s^2 3d^5$

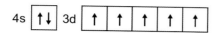

Co atom    [Ar] $4s^2 3d^7$

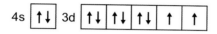

2. The electron configuration of a chromium atom is [Ar] $4s^1 3d^5$, and is stable as it contains a half-filled d-subshell.

## Exercise 5.6C

1. [Ar] $3d^2$

2. (a) Ni atom    [Ar] $4s^2 3d^8$

   4s ↑↓  3d ↑↓ ↑↓ ↑↓ ↑ ↑

   (b) Nickel has a partly filled d-subshell: [Ar] $3d^8 4s^2$, and nickel(II) ions, $Ni^{2+}$ have a partly filled d-subshell: [Ar] $3d^8$.

3. Zinc does not have a partly filled d-subshell: [Ar] $3d^{10} 4s^2$, and does not form a stable ion with a partly filled d-subshell. The electron configuration of a $Zn^{2+}$ ion is [Ar] $3d^{10}$.

4. Answer A

5. Answer D

6. (a) $2Fe^{2+} + Cl_2 \rightarrow 2Fe^{3+} + 2Cl^-$

   (b) $Fe^{2+}$ [Ar] $3d^6$   $Fe^{3+}$ [Ar] $3d^5$

   (c) Iron(III) is more stable as it has a half-filled d-subshell.

### 5.7 Metal Complexes

## Exercise 5.7A

1. (a) A complex consists of a metal atom or ion with ligands attached by coordinate bonds.

   (b) Each water molecule uses a lone pair on the oxygen atom to form a coordinate bond with the metal.

2. (a) A ligand is a molecule or ion that uses one or more lone pairs to form coordinate bonds with a metal atom or ion in a complex.

   (b) Four

   (c) Each chloride ion uses a lone pair to form a coordinate bond with nickel.

3. (a) Six

   (b) Each of the four ammonia ligands and two water ligands use a lone pair to form a coordinate bond with the copper.

4. *Formula:* $[Co(H_2O)_6]^{2+}$ *Explanation:* Six water molecules can bond with cobalt as water is a small ligand.

5. (a) The nitrogen atom has a lone pair that can be used to form a coordinate bond with a metal.

   (b) *Formula:* $[Cr(NH_3)_6]^{3+}$    *Explanation:* Six ammonia molecules can bond with chromium as ammonia is a small ligand.

## Exercise 5.7B

1. (a) $V_2(SO_4)_3$

   (b) *Formula:* $[V(H_2O)_6]^{3+}$ *Shape:* Octahedral

2. (a) $[PtCl_6]^{2-}$

   (b) The complex adopts an octahedral shape to minimise repulsion between the electrons in the Pt-Cl bonds.

3. (a) $[(C_4H_9)_4N]^+$ and $[FeBr_4]^-$

   (b) The complex $[FeBr_4]^-$ adopts a tetrahedral shape to minimise repulsion between the electrons in the Fe-Br bonds.

4. The complex adopts an octahedral shape to minimise repulsion between the electrons in the six bonds formed between copper and the ligands.

5. Answer D

6. (a) Square planar

   (b) A covalent bond. (ii) A hydrogen bond. (iii) A coordinate bond.

## Exercise 5.7C

1. (a) $[Fe(CN)_6]^{3-}$

   (b) The complex adopts an octahedral shape to minimise repulsion between the electrons in the six bonds formed between iron and the ligands.

2. The complex adopts an octahedral shape to minimise repulsion between the electrons in the six bonds formed between chromium and the ligands.

3. (a) A bidentate ligand is a molecule or ion that uses two lone pairs of electrons to form two coordinate bonds with a metal atom or ion in a complex.

(b) $H_2\ddot{N}$—$CH_2$—$CH_2$—$\ddot{N}H_2$

(c) $[Ni(en)_3]^{2+}$

4. $[Fe(C_2O_4)_3]^{3-}$

5. (a) It can use the lone pair on each nitrogen atom to form two coordinate bonds with a metal.

(b) The complex adopts an octahedral shape to minimise repulsion between the electrons in the six Ru-N bonds.

(c) $[Ru(bpy)_3]Cl_2.6H_2O$

## Exercise 5.7D

1. The molecule can use the lone pair on each nitrogen atom to form two coordinate bonds with a metal atom or ion. A polydentate ligand forms more than two coordinate bonds with a metal atom or ion.

2. The greater distance between the nitrogen atoms in cadaverine allows both nitrogen atoms to use their lone pair to form a coordinate bond with the same metal atom or ion.

3. (a) A ligand is a molecule or ion that uses one or more lone pairs to form coordinate bonds with a metal atom or ion in a complex.

(b) A polydentate ligand is a molecule or ion that uses many lone pairs of electrons to form more than two coordinate bonds with a metal atom or ion in a complex.

(c) The nitrile group ·C≡N: can act as a ligand as the nitrogen atom has a lone pair.

4. Answer D

## Exercise 5.7E

1. The coordination number of cobalt is four as each of the four ligands uses a lone pair to form a coordinate bond with cobalt.

2. The coordination number of copper is six as each of the six ligands uses a lone pair to form a coordinate bond with copper.

3. (a) $[PtCl_6]^{2-}$

(b) The coordination number of platinum is six as each of the six ligands uses a lone pair to form a coordinate bond with platinum.

4. (a) $[Ni(C_2O_4)_2]^{2-}$

(b) Four

(c) The complex could also adopt a tetrahedral arrangement. Platinum-group metals form square planar complexes in preference to

tetrahedral complexes.

## Exercise 5.7F

1. (a) Isomer 1 is the trans-isomer as the chloride ligands are on opposite sides of the complex. Isomer 2 is the cis-isomer as the chloride ligands are on the same side of the complex.

(b) Isomer 1 is the E-isomer as the high priority chloride ligands are on opposite sides of the complex. Isomer 2 is the Z-isomer as the high priority chloride ligands are on the same side of the complex.

2. (a)

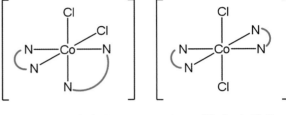

cis-$[Co(en)_2Cl_2]^+$        trans-$[Co(en)_2Cl_2]^+$

(b) The relative positioning of the chlorine atoms about the metal gives rise to cis and trans isomers.

(c) The cis-isomer is also the Z-isomer as the high priority chloride ligands are on the same side of the complex. The trans-isomer is also the E-isomer as the high priority chloride ligands are on opposite sides of the complex.

3. (a)

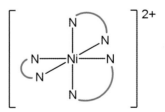

(b) The arrangement of the bidentate ligands about the metal turns the metal into an asymmetric centre.

4. (a)

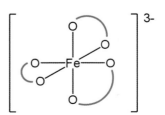

(b) The complex cannot be superimposed on its mirror image.

5. (a) Six

(b)

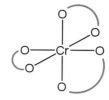 

(c) The arrangement of the bidentate acac ligands about the metal turns the metal into an asymmetric centre.

(d) The complex does not have a charge.

## Exercise 5.7G

1. (a) Charge 2+; Coordination number 6

(b) Charge 2+; Coordination number 6

2. (a) Coordinate bond

(b) Two

(c) +1

(d) Linear

3. Answer C

4. Answer D

5. Answer B

## Exercise 5.7H

1. (a) $[Fe(H_2O)_6]^{3+}$ (aq) + SCN$^-$ (aq)
$\leftrightarrows [Fe(SCN)(H_2O)_5]^{2+}$ (aq) + $H_2O$ (l)

(b) Thiocyanate ion, SCN$^-$ is a monodentate ligand as it replaces one water molecule in the complex.

2. (a) $[Co(H_2O)_6]^{2+}$ (aq) + 4Cl$^-$ (aq)
$\leftrightarrows [CoCl_4]^{2-}$ (aq) + $6H_2O$ (l)

(b) The complex $[Co(H_2O)_6]^{2+}$ has six ligands as water is a small ligand. The complex $[CoCl_4]^{2-}$ has four ligands as chloride ion is a large ligand.

(c) The complex $[CoCl_4]^{2-}$ adopts a tetrahedral shape to minimise repulsion between the electrons in the Co-Cl bonds.

## Exercise 5.7I

1. The coordination number of nickel is six in both complexes and therefore does not change. $\Delta S° > 0$ as the reaction increases the number of particles in the reaction mixture.

2. (a) $[Ni(H_2O)_6]^{2+}$ (aq) + 3en (aq)
$\leftrightarrows [Ni(en)_3]^{2+}$ (aq) + $6H_2O$ (l)

(b) The entropy change for the reaction is positive as three en ligands replace six water ligands, increasing the number of particles in the reaction mixture.

3. (a) Polydentate ligand

(b) $[Cr(H_2O)_6]^{3+}$ (aq) + (edta)$^{4-}$ (aq)
$\rightarrow [Cr(edta)]^-$ (aq) + $6H_2O$ (l)

(c) The entropy change for the reaction is positive as one edta ligand replaces six water ligands, increasing the number of particles in the reaction mixture.

4. (a) $[Ni(H_2O)_6]^{2+}$ (aq) + 4CN$^-$ (aq)
$\leftrightarrows [Ni(CN)_4]^{2-}$ (aq) + $6H_2O$ (l)

(b) The entropy change for the reaction is positive as four cyanide ligands replace six water ligands, increasing the number of particles in the reaction mixture.

(c) The complex $[Ni(CN)_4]^{2-}$ is square planar as nickel is a platinum-group metal.

5. The entropy change for the reaction is positive as two dimethylglyoxime ligands replace six water ligands, increasing the number of particles in the reaction mixture.

6. The three oxalate ligands bonded to iron are replaced by one edta ligand, increasing the number of particles in the reaction mixture. The reaction occurs as the entropy change for the reaction is positive.

7. (a) $Sr^{2+} (C_{12}H_8O_8N_2S)^{2-}$

(b) Edta would displace ranelic acid as it would form more coordinate bonds with a strontium ion.

## 5.8 Transition Metal Chemistry

### Exercise 5.8A

1.

| ion | oxidation number | colour |
|---|---|---|
| | +2 | violet |
| VO$_2$$^+$ (aq) | +5 | |
| | +4 | blue |
| | +3 | green |

## Exercise 5.8B

1. Chromium(III) ions are present if a green-blue precipitate forms on adding aqueous sodium hydroxide: $Cr^{3+}_{(aq)} + 3OH^-_{(aq)} \rightarrow Cr(OH)_{3(s)}$, and then reacts to form a green solution on adding to excess: $Cr(OH)_{3(s)} + 3OH^-_{(aq)} \rightarrow [Cr(OH)_6]^{3-}_{(aq)}$.

2. The orange colour of dichromate ion is replaced by the yellow colour of chromate ion as the added hydroxide ions react with the hydrogen ions and shift the position of equilibrium to the left.

3.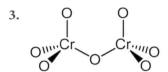

## Exercise 5.8C

1. Manganese(II) ions are present if a white precipitate forms on adding ammonia solution: $Mn^{2+}_{(aq)} + 2OH^-_{(aq)} \rightarrow Mn(OH)_{2(s)}$, remains on adding to excess, and turns brown on standing in air.

2. (a) $2MnO_4^- + 6H^+ + 5NO_2^-$
   $\rightarrow 2Mn^{2+} + 5NO_3^- + 3H_2O$

   (b) The solution changes from pink to colourless as manganate(VII) ion is reduced to manganese(II).

3. (a) Add water and swirl the mixture to dissolve the $K_2MnO_4$. Filter the mixture using a glass funnel, wash the residue with deionised water, then dry the residue in a low temperature oven.

   (b) Manganese is reduced to an oxidation state of +6 in $K_2MnO_4$ and an oxidation state of +4 in $MnO_2$. Oxygen is oxidised from an oxidation state of −2 in $KMnO_4$ to an oxidation state of zero in $O_2$.

## Exercise 5.8D

1. Iron(II) ions are present if a green precipitate forms on adding ammonia solution: $Fe^{2+}_{(aq)} + 2OH^-_{(aq)} \rightarrow Fe(OH)_{2(s)}$, and remains on adding to excess.

2. (a) *Iron(II) oxalate:* $FeC_2O_4$
   *Iron(III) oxalate:* $Fe_2(C_2O_4)_3$

   (b) *Iron(II) oxalate:* Green
   *Iron(III) oxalate:* Yellow

   (c) A green precipitate of $Fe(OH)_2$ is formed on adding sodium hydroxide solution to aqueous iron(II) oxalate. A brown precipitate of $Fe(OH)_3$ is formed on adding sodium hydroxide solution to aqueous iron(III) oxalate. Both precipitates remain on adding to excess.

3. (a) A brown precipitate of iron(III) hydroxide is formed, and remains on adding to excess.

   (b) A blood-red solution containing the complex $[Fe(SCN)(H_2O)_5]^{2+}$ is formed on adding a few drops of aqueous potassium thiocyanate, KSCN.

5. A blood-red solution containing the complex $[Fe(SCN)(H_2O)_5]^{2+}$ is formed on adding a few drops of aqueous potassium thiocyanate, KSCN. Manganese(II) ions do not form a coloured complex with thiocyanate ions.

## Exercise 5.8E

1. (a) Six; pink

   (b) $[Co(H_2O)_6]^{2+}_{(aq)} + 4Cl^-_{(aq)}$
   $\leftrightarrows [CoCl_4]^{2-}_{(aq)} + 6H_2O_{(l)}$

2. (a) Pink

   (b) $[Co(H_2O)_6]^{2+}$

   (c) Cobalt(II) ions are present if a blue precipitate forms and remains on adding aqueous sodium hydroxide to excess:

   $Co^{2+}_{(aq)} + 2OH^-_{(aq)} \rightarrow Co(OH)_{2(s)}$.

   The blue precipitate also forms before reacting to give a brown solution on adding ammonia solution to excess: $Co(OH)_{2(s)} + 6NH_{3(aq)}$
   $\rightarrow [Co(NH_3)_6]^{2+}_{(aq)} + 2OH^-_{(aq)}$.

3. Answer C

4. (a) $[Co(H_2O)_6]^{2+}_{(aq)} + 3en_{(aq)}$
   $\rightarrow [Co(en)_3]^{2+}_{(aq)} + 6H_2O_{(l)}$

   (b) The pink colour of the $[Co(H_2O)_6]^{2+}$ complex is replaced by the orange colour of the $[Co(en)_3]^{2+}$ complex.

5. The complex $[Co(C_2O_4)(H_2O)_4]$ is formed when two water ligands in the $[Co(H_2O)_6]^{2+}$ complex are replaced by an oxalate ion. The resulting complex is insoluble as it does not have a charge.

## Exercise 5.8F

1.

| Solution added | After a few drops | On adding an excess |
|---|---|---|
| sodium hydroxide | green precipitate | precipitate remains |
| ammonia | green precipitate | blue solution |

2. Answer D

3. (a) Green

   (b) $[Ni(H_2O)_6]^{2+}$

   (c) Nickel(II) ions are present if a green precipitate forms and remains on adding aqueous sodium hydroxide to excess:

   $Ni^{2+}_{(aq)} + 2OH^-_{(aq)} \rightarrow Ni(OH)_{2(s)}$.

   The green precipitate also forms before reacting to give a blue solution on adding ammonia solution to excess:   $Ni(OH)_{2(s)} + 6NH_{3(aq)}$

   $\rightarrow [Ni(NH_3)_6]^{2+}_{(aq)} + 2OH^-_{(aq)}$.

4. Answer B

5.

$$Ni(OH)_2 \xleftarrow{OH^-} Ni^{2+} \xrightarrow{NH_3} [Ni(NH_3)_6]^{2+}$$

$$\downarrow en$$

$$[Ni(en)_3]^{2+}$$

6. (a) $[Ni(H_2O)_6]^{2+}_{(aq)} + H_2(edta)^{2-}_{(aq)}$

   $\rightarrow [Ni(edta)]^{2-}_{(aq)} + 6H_2O_{(l)} + 2H^+_{(aq)}$

   (b) The green colour of the $[Ni(H_2O)_6]^{2+}$ complex is replaced by the blue colour of the $[Ni(edta)]^{2-}$ complex.

## Exercise 5.8G

1. (a) $[Cu(H_2O)_6]^{2+}$: Blue  $[CuCl_4]^{2-}$: Yellow

   (b) Concentrated hydrochloric acid

2.

$$[CuCl_4]^{2-} \xleftarrow{conc. HCl} Cu^{2+}_{(aq)} \xrightarrow{NaOH_{(aq)}} Cu(OH)_2$$

$$\downarrow \begin{array}{c} excess \\ NH_{3(aq)} \end{array}$$

$$[Cu(NH_3)_4(H_2O)_2]^{2+}$$

3. (a) The blue colour of the $[Cu(H_2O)_6]^{2+}$ complex is replaced by a blue precipitate of $Cu(OH)_2$.

On adding to excess the blue precipitate reacts to form a dark blue solution containing the complex $[Cu(NH_3)_4(H_2O)_2]^{2+}$.

   (b) The dark blue solution containing the complex $[Cu(NH_3)_4(H_2O)_2]^{2+}$ is replaced by a yellow solution containing the complex $[CuCl_4]^{2-}$.

   (c) The entropy change for the reaction is positive as the substitution of six ligands by four increases the number of particles in the reaction mixture.

## Exercise 5.8H

1. (a) +5 in $VO_2^+$ and +4 in $VO^{2+}$

   (b) Reducing agent

2. (a) $3VO_2^+{}_{(aq)} + 6H^+_{(aq)} + Cr_{(s)}$

   $\rightarrow 3VO^{2+}_{(aq)} + 3H_2O_{(l)} + Cr^{3+}_{(aq)}$

   (b) emf = +1.74 V

3. (a) $VO_2^+{}_{(aq)} + 4H^+_{(aq)} + 3e^- \rightarrow V^{2+}_{(aq)} + 2H_2O_{(l)}$

   (b) $2VO_2^+{}_{(aq)} + 8H^+_{(aq)} + 3Zn_{(s)}$

   $\rightarrow 2V^{2+}_{(aq)} + 4H_2O_{(l)} + 3Zn^{2+}_{(aq)}$

   (c)

| Ion in solution | Solution colour |
|---|---|
| | Yellow |
| $VO^{2+}$ | |
| $V^{3+}$ | |
| | Violet |

4. Answer B

## 5.9 Amines

## Exercise 5.9A

1. (a) Amphetamine is chiral as it contains a carbon atom bonded to four different groups of atoms.

   (b) Both compounds are primary amines as they have the structure $RNH_2$.

2. (a) $C_6H_5CH(OH)CH(CH_3)NHCH_3$

   (b) Ephedrine is a secondary amine as it has the structure RNHR′.

3. (a) $C_{13}H_{21}O_3N$

   (b) Salbutamol is a secondary amine as it has the structure RNHR′.

4.

| primary | secondary |
|---|---|
| $CH_3CH_2CH_2CH_2NH_2$ | $CH_3CH_2CH_2NHCH_3$ |

$CH_3CH_2\overset{\overset{\displaystyle NH_2}{|}}{C}HCH_3$

$CH_3\overset{\overset{\displaystyle CH_3}{|}}{C}HNHCH_3$

$CH_3\overset{\overset{\displaystyle CH_3}{|}}{C}HCH_2NH_2$

$CH_3CH_2NHCH_2CH_3$

$CH_3\overset{\overset{\displaystyle CH_3}{|}}{\underset{\underset{\displaystyle NH_2}{|}}{C}}CH_3$

tertiary

$CH_3CH_2\overset{\overset{\displaystyle CH_3}{|}}{N}CH_3$

5.

$H_3C-\overset{\overset{\displaystyle CH_3}{|}}{\underset{\underset{\displaystyle H}{|}}{C}}-\overset{\overset{\displaystyle }{}}{\underset{\underset{\displaystyle CH_3}{|}}{N}}-CH_3$

## Exercise 5.9B

1. As molar mass increases the hydrogen bonding between molecules becomes less effective, making the amine molecules less able to hydrogen bond with surrounding water molecules.

2. (a) The amino ($-NH_2$) groups

   (b) Hydrogen bonds

## Exercise 5.9C

1. The molecules in ethylamine and dimethylamine experience greater van der Waals attraction than the molecules in methylamine as they have a greater molar mass than methylamine. The van der Waals attraction between molecules in dimethylamine is less than in ethylamine as dimethylamine has a more branched structure than ethylamine.

2. The molecules in trimethylamine experience greater van der Waals attraction but are not able to form hydrogen bonds. The absence of hydrogen bonding results in weaker attractive forces between molecules.

3. The molecules in phenylethylamine experience greater van der Waals attraction than the molecules in aniline, and the lone pair on the nitrogen is more available for hydrogen bonding than in aniline. The boiling point of propylbenzene is lower than the boiling point of phenylethylamine as propylbenzene cannot form hydrogen bonds between molecules.

## Exercise 5.9D

1. (a) pentan-1-amine

   (b) butan-2-amine

   (c) propan-2-amine

2. (a) N-methylpropan-1-amine

   (b) N-ethylethanamine

   (c) N,N-dimethylethanamine

## Exercise 5.9E

1. (a) 1-chloropropan-1-amine

   (b) primary

2. (a) 1-bromo-2-methylpropan-2-amine

   (b) primary

## Exercise 5.9F

1. propane-1,2-diamine

2. 2-methylpentane-1,5-diamine

3. (a) butane-1,4-diamine

   (b) 1,4-diaminobutan-2-ol

## Exercise 5.9G

1. (a)

$CH_3CH_2CH_2-\overset{\overset{\displaystyle }{}}{\underset{\underset{\displaystyle H}{|}}{N}}-H$

propan-1-amine

   (b)

$CH_3CH_2CH_2-\overset{\overset{\displaystyle }{}}{\underset{\underset{\displaystyle CH_2CH_2CH_3}{|}}{N}}-H$

N-propylpropan-1-amine

$CH_3CH_2CH_2-\overset{\overset{\displaystyle }{}}{\underset{\underset{\displaystyle CH_2CH_2CH_3}{|}}{N}}-CH_2CH_2CH_3$

N,N-dipropylpropan-1-amine

2. (a) $CH_3CH_2CHBrCH_3 + 2NH_3$
   $\rightarrow CH_3CH_2CH(NH_2)CH_3 + NH_4Br$

   (b) butan-2-amine

## Exercise 5.9H

1. (a) lithal

   (b) $CH_3CH_2CH_2CN + 4[H]$
   $\rightarrow CH_3CH_2CH_2CH_2NH_2$

2. A is sodium cyanide, NaCN
   B is lithal, $LiAlH_4$

3. A is sodium cyanide, NaCN
   B is lithal, $LiAlH_4$
   C is concentrated ammonia solution, $NH_3$

## Exercise 5.9I

1.

$$\text{(benzene ring)-}NO_2 + 6[H] \longrightarrow \text{(benzene ring)-}NH_2 + 2H_2O$$

2. (a) Tin and concentrated hydrochloric acid.

   (b) Add dilute sodium hydroxide.

3. Reflux nitrobenzene with a mixture of tin and concentrated hydrochloric acid. Then add dilute sodium hydroxide to form phenylamine from its ammonium salt.

## Exercise 5.9J

1. Nucleophilic substitution

2. (a)

   (b) The ionic bonding in amphetamine sulfate is stronger than the combination of van der Waals attraction and hydrogen bonding between molecules of amphetamine.

   (c) Add dilute sodium hydroxide then distil the mixture and collect crude amphetamine at its boiling point. Wash the distillate with water in a separating funnel to remove traces of alkali before adding anhydrous sodium sulfate to dry the distillate. Filter the mixture then distil the filtrate and collect pure amphetamine at its boiling point.

## Exercise 5.9K

1. (a) Phenylamine is less basic than ammonia and 1-aminobutane is more basic than ammonia.

   (b)

2. (a) Dopamine can use its amino ($-NH_2$) group and hydroxyl ($-OH$) groups to form hydrogen bonds with neighbouring water molecules.

   (b) Dopamine is more basic than ammonia as it is a primary amine and the lone pair on the nitrogen atom is more available to form coordinate bonds. Phenylamine is less basic than ammonia as the lone pair on the nitrogen atom in phenylamine is delocalised and less available to form coordinate bonds.

   (c)

3. Answer C

4. (a) Benzedrine is a primary amine as it has the structure $RNH_2$.

   (b) Benzedrine is a stronger base as the lone pair on the nitrogen atom is not delocalised and is therefore more available to form coordinate bonds.

## Exercise 5.9L

1. See Worked Example 5.9v.

2. 60.0%

3. (a) $H_2N(CH_2)_4NH_2 + 2CH_3COCl$
   $\rightarrow CH_3CONH(CH_2)_4NHCOCH_3 + 2\ HCl$

   (b) Compare the melting point of the pure product with the melting points of amides in data tables.

4. Mass of paracetamol formed
   $= 0.080\ mol \times 151\ g\ mol^{-1} = 12\ g$

## Exercise 5.9M

1. (a) Step A requires tin and concentrated hydrochloric acid. Step B requires dilute sodium hydroxide. Step C requires sodium nitrite and hydrochloric acid.

   (b) Step C is carried out at 0–10 °C. The product formed in step C is benzenediazonium chloride.

2. (a) $NaNO_{2(s)} + HCl_{(aq)} \rightarrow HNO_{2(aq)} + NaCl_{(aq)}$

(b)

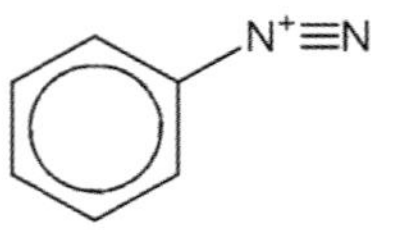

(c) The diazonium ion formed by ethylamine is very unstable as ethylamine does not have aromatic character.

3. $H_2N(CH_2)_4NH_2 + 2HNO_2$
   $\rightarrow HO(CH_2)_4OH + 2H_2O + 2N_2$

4. (a) $NaNO_{2(s)} + HCl_{(aq)} \rightarrow HNO_{2(aq)} + NaCl_{(aq)}$

   (b) Temperature in the range 0–10 °C.

   (c)

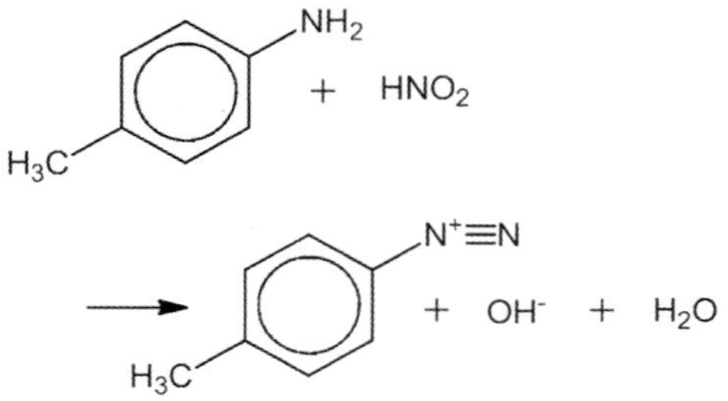

### Exercise 5.9N

1.

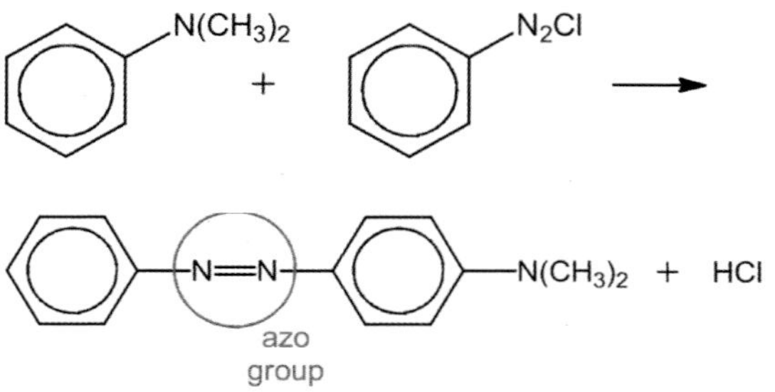

2. (a) Temperature in the range 0–10 °C.

   (b)

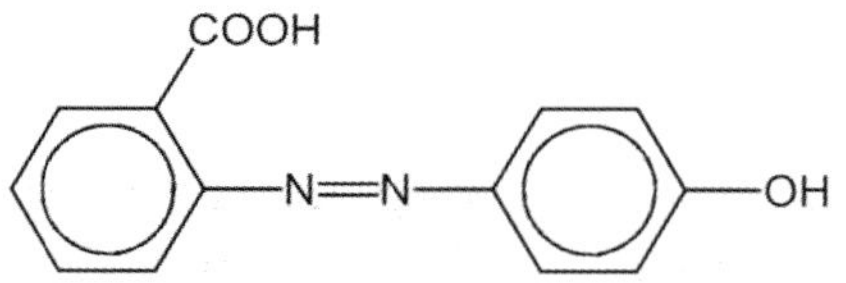

3. (a)

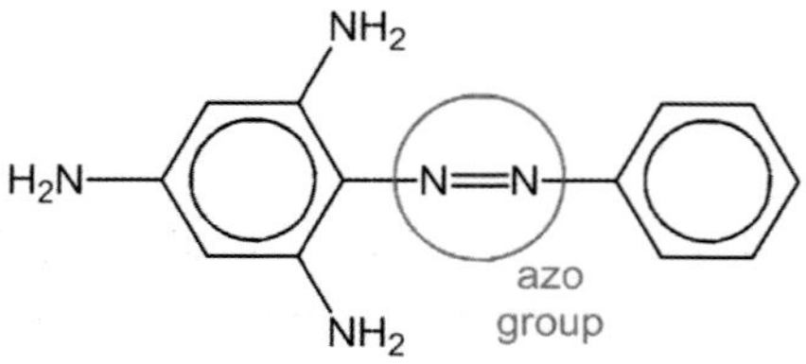

   (b) See worked example 5.9vi (d).

   (c) The colour, solubility and other physical properties of the dye can be altered by modifying the functional groups.

4. (a) Coupling reaction

   (b) $C_{16}H_{12}N_2O$

(c) See worked example 5.9vi (d).

5. (a) Sodium nitrite and hydrochloric acid.

   (b) The diazonium ion formed in step A is unstable and will decompose if the temperature rises above 10 °C.

   (c)

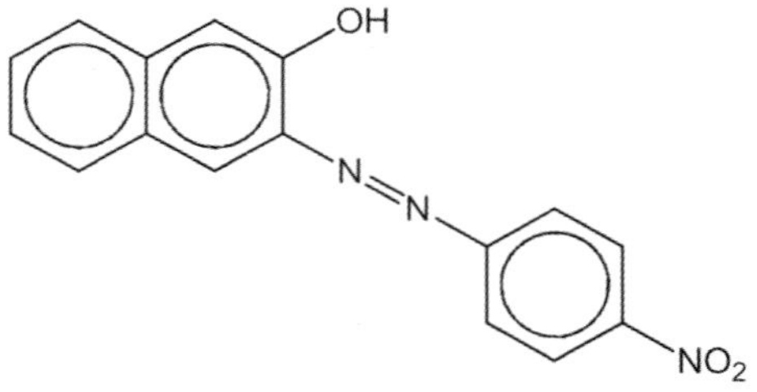

   (d) See worked example 5.9vi (d).

### 5.10 Amides

### Exercise 5.10A

1. (a) Propanamide contains a -$CONH_2$ group.

   (b) $RCONH_2$

   (c) $HCONH_2$

2. The magnitude of the van der Waals attraction between molecules is similar in both compounds. The melting point of butanamide is higher as the hydrogen bonds between the molecules in butanamide are stronger than the attractive dipole forces between the molecules in chlorobutane.

3. The oxygen or nitrogen atom in a molecule of butanamide can form a hydrogen bond with a hydrogen atom in a neighbouring water molecule. Similarly, a hydrogen atom bonded to the nitrogen in butanamide can hydrogen bond with the oxygen atom in a neighbouring water molecule.

### Exercise 5.10B

1. Answer B

2. The lone pair on the nitrogen atom in propanamide is delocalised and is therefore less available for coordinate bonding than the lone pair on the nitrogen atom in ammonia.

### Exercise 5.10C

1. (a) Compound A is 2-bromo-4-methyl-pentanamide and compound B is N-chloro-N-methylbutanamide.

   (b) A and B are amides as they contain an amide linkage (-CONR-).

**2.**

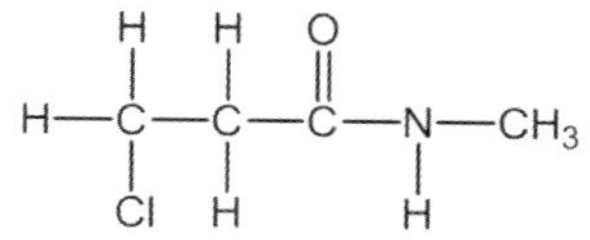

3-chloro-N-methylpropanamide

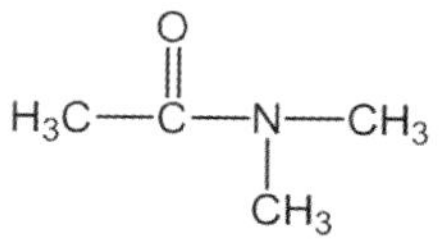

N,N-dimethylethanamide

**3.** 2-amino-3-chloro-N-hydroxypropanamide

**4.**

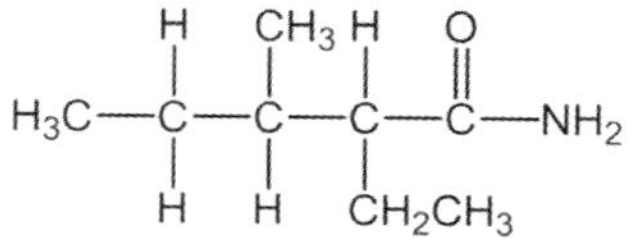

2-ethyl-3-methylpentanamide

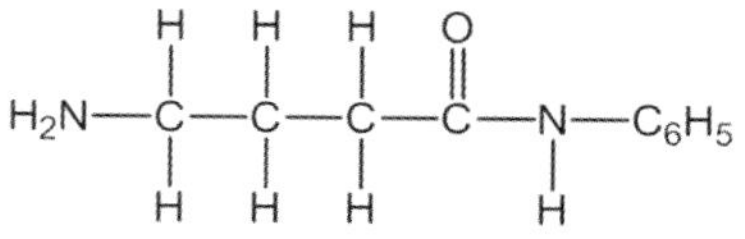

4-amino-N-phenylbutanamide

## Exercise 5.10D

**1.** (a) $CH_3COOH + NH_3 \rightarrow CH_3COONH_4$

(b) $CH_3COONH_4 \rightarrow CH_3CONH_2 + H_2O$

**2.**

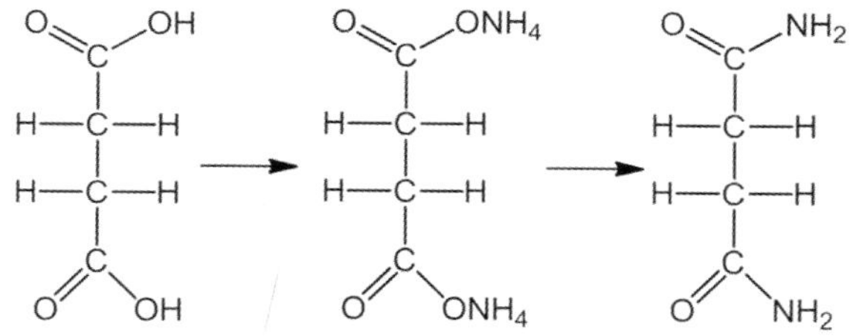

## Exercise 5.10E

**1.** (a) $CH_2CHCOCl + NH_3$

$\rightarrow CH_2CHCONH_2 + HCl$

(b)

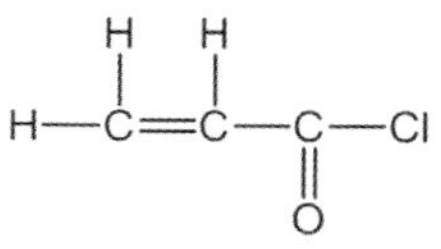

**2.** (a) Lidocaine is an amide as it contains an amide linkage (-CONR-).

**(b)**

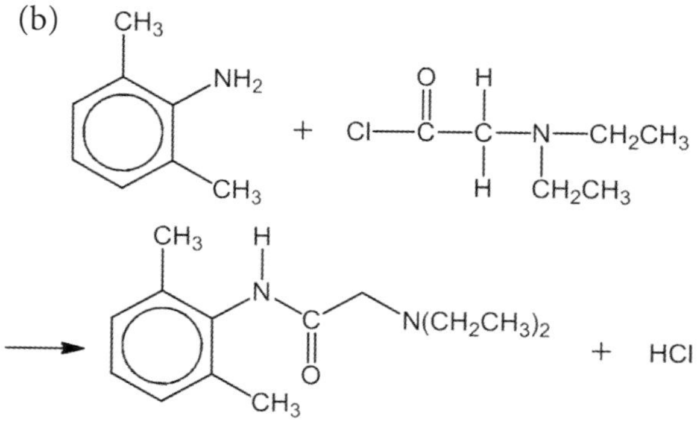

## Exercise 5.10F

**1.** Answer C

**2.** (a) $CH_3COOH$  (b) $CH_3COONa$

**3.** (a) $CH_3CH_2CONH_2 + NaOH$

$\rightarrow CH_3CH_2COONa + NH_3$

(b) Hydroxide ion is a good nucleophile as it has a lone pair, and is attracted to the electron-deficient carbon atom in the amide linkage. Hydrogen ion is not a nucleophile.

**4.** (a)

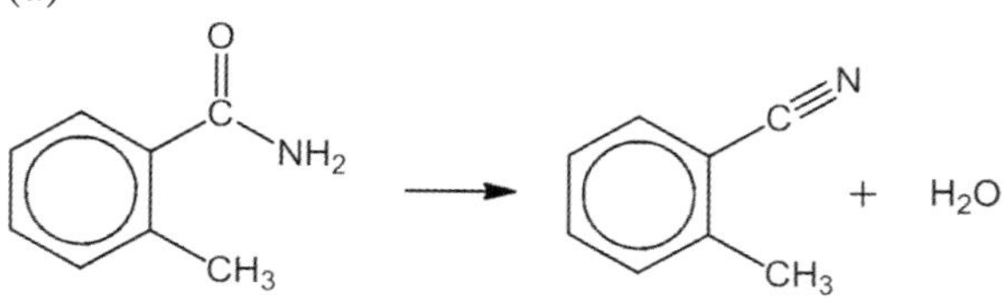

(b) Distil a mixture of the amide and solid phosphorus(V) oxide.

**5.** Answer A

## 5.11 Amino Acids

### Exercise 5.11A

**1.** (a) Serine has an amino group and a carboxyl group bonded to the same carbon atom.

(b)

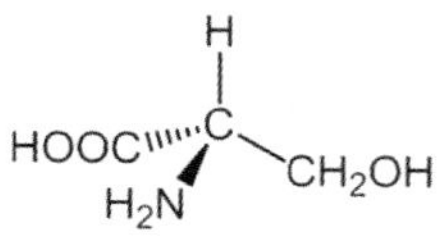

**2.** Anthranilic acid is not an $\alpha$-amino acid as the amino group and the carboxyl group are not bonded to the same carbon atom.

### Exercise 5.11B

**1.** (a) The compound exists as zwitterions held together by strong attractive forces.

(b) Selenocysteine is optically active as four different groups are bonded to the carbon atom adjacent to the carboxyl group.

303

**2.**

$$H_3N^+-\overset{\overset{\displaystyle H}{|}}{\underset{\underset{\displaystyle CH_2CONH_2}{|}}{C}}-COO^-$$

**3.** (a) A zwitterion is a dipolar ion with positive and negative charges that add to give a charge of zero.

(b)

$$H_3N^+-\overset{\overset{\displaystyle H}{|}}{\underset{\underset{\displaystyle CH(CH_3)_2}{|}}{C}}-COO^-$$

(c)

$$\underset{NH_2}{\overset{CH(CH_3)_2}{\underset{H}{C''''COOH}}} \qquad \underset{H_2N}{\overset{CH(CH_3)_2}{HOOC''''C\underset{H}{}}}$$

**4.** (a) MSG is a sodium salt and is therefore soluble in water.

(b)

$$HOOCCH_2CH_2-\overset{\overset{\displaystyle H}{|}}{\underset{NH_2}{C''''COOH}}$$

$$HOOC''''\overset{\overset{\displaystyle H}{|}}{\underset{H_2N}{C}}-CH_2CH_2COOH$$

(c) Glutamic acid exists as zwitterions that are held together by strong attractive forces.

**5.** Answer C

**Exercise 5.11C**

**1.**

$$H_3N^+-\overset{\overset{\displaystyle H}{|}}{\underset{\underset{\displaystyle CH_3}{|}}{C}}-COOH$$

**2.** (a) Aspartic acid has an amino group and a carboxyl group bonded to the same carbon atom.

(b)

$$H_2N-\overset{\overset{\displaystyle H}{|}}{\underset{\underset{\displaystyle CH_2COO^-}{|}}{C}}-COO^-$$

**3.** Answer B

**Exercise 5.11D**

**1.** (a)

$$2\ H-\overset{\overset{\displaystyle H}{|}}{\underset{\underset{\displaystyle NH_2}{|}}{C}}-COOH\ +\ Na_2CO_3$$

$$\longrightarrow 2\ H-\overset{\overset{\displaystyle H}{|}}{\underset{\underset{\displaystyle NH_2}{|}}{C}}-COONa\ +\ H_2O\ +\ CO_2$$

(b)

$$H-\overset{\overset{\displaystyle H}{|}}{\underset{\underset{\displaystyle NH_2}{|}}{C}}-COOH\ +\ CH_3OH$$

$$\longrightarrow H-\overset{\overset{\displaystyle H}{|}}{\underset{\underset{\displaystyle NH_2}{|}}{C}}-COOCH_3\ +\ H_2O$$

**2.** (a)

$$2\ H-\overset{\overset{\displaystyle CH_2SeH}{|}}{\underset{\underset{\displaystyle NH_2}{|}}{C}}-COOH\ +\ Na_2CO_3$$

$$\longrightarrow 2\ H-\overset{\overset{\displaystyle CH_2SeH}{|}}{\underset{\underset{\displaystyle NH_2}{|}}{C}}-COONa\ +\ H_2O\ +\ CO_2$$

**3.** (a)

$$H_3N^+-\overset{\overset{\displaystyle CH_3}{|}\overset{*}{}}{\underset{\underset{\displaystyle H}{|}}{\underset{*}{C}}}-COO^-$$
(with $H-\overset{*}{C}-OH$ above)

(b) The zwitterion is formed by the transfer of a hydrogen ($H^+$) ion from the carboxyl group to the amine group.

(c) Threonine exists as zwitterions that are held together by strong attractive forces.

(d)

$$H-\overset{\overset{\displaystyle CH(OH)CH_3}{|}}{\underset{\underset{\displaystyle NH_2}{|}}{C}}-COOH\ +\ HNO_2$$

$$\longrightarrow R-\overset{\overset{\displaystyle CH(OH)CH_3}{|}}{\underset{\underset{\displaystyle OH}{|}}{C}}-COOH\ +\ H_2O\ +\ N_2$$

(e) A colourless solution is formed and bubbles of a colourless gas are produced.

**4.**

**5.** Answer B

**Exercise 5.11E**

**1.**

$$H_2N(CH_2)_4-\overset{\overset{\displaystyle H}{|}}{\underset{\underset{\displaystyle NH_2}{|}}{C}}-\overset{\overset{\displaystyle O}{\|}}{C}-\overset{\displaystyle N}{\underset{\underset{\displaystyle H}{|}}{}}-\overset{\overset{\displaystyle COOH}{|}}{\underset{\underset{\displaystyle H}{|}}{C}}-(CH_2)_4NH_2$$

**2.**

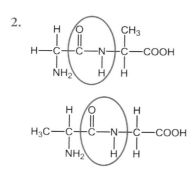

**3.** Answer B

## Exercise 5.11F

**1.** Answer C

**2.** Answer A

**3.** The primary structure refers to the sequence of amino acids joined by peptide links. Secondary structure refers to the twisting and coiling of the chain to form α-helices and β-sheets as a result of intramolecular hydrogen bonding between amino acid side-chains. Folding of the secondary structures produces the tertiary structure and results from a combination of van der Waals attraction, hydrogen bonding, ionic interactions, and the formation of disulfide (-S-S-) bonds.

**4.** Answer C

## Exercise 5.11G

**1. (a)** The protein has an active site within which the reactants can bind.

**(b)** At 60 °C the structure of the enzyme is altered to the extent that the active site can no longer facilitate the reaction.

**2. (a)** The structures of the reactants and the structure of the active site change as they interact, lowering the activation energy for the reaction catalysed by the enzyme.

**(b)**

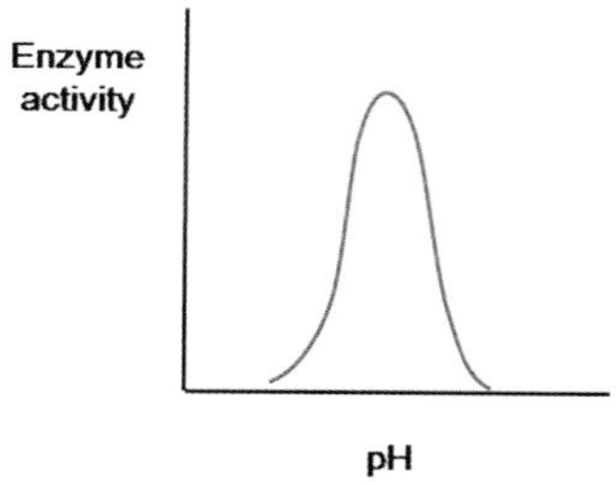

Enzyme activity vs pH graph

**3.** Only one isomer can bond with the 'active site' of the host molecule in the human body.

## 5.12 Polymer Chemistry

### Exercise 5.12A

**1. (a)**

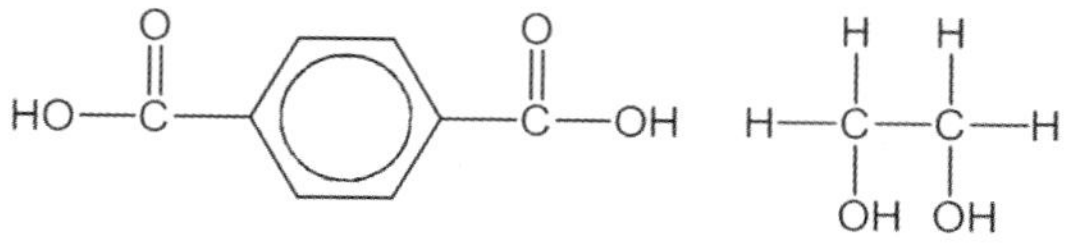

**(b)**

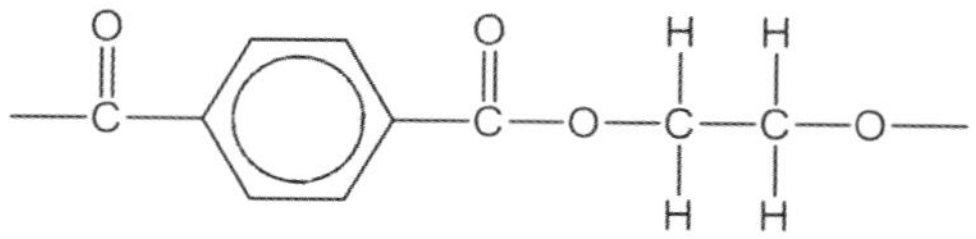

**2.** The molecules in polythene are non-biodegradable as the C-C bonds in addition polymers such as polythene cannot be hydrolysed by the action of microorganisms in the environment. Landfill is more suitable for the disposal of polyesters as the ester linkages between monomers can be hydrolysed by the action of microorganisms in the environment.

**3. (a)**

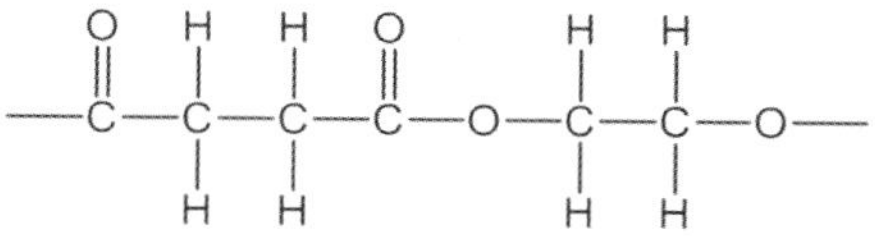

**(b)** Condensation polymerisation

**(c)** There is a carboxyl (-COOH) group at one end of each polymer molecule.

**(d)** The ester linkages between monomers can be hydrolysed by the action of microorganisms in the environment.

### Exercise 5.12B

**1. (a)** A condensation polymer is a large molecule formed by condensation reactions between monomers that each eliminate a small molecule from the polymer.

**(b)**

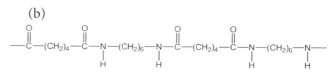

**2. (a)**

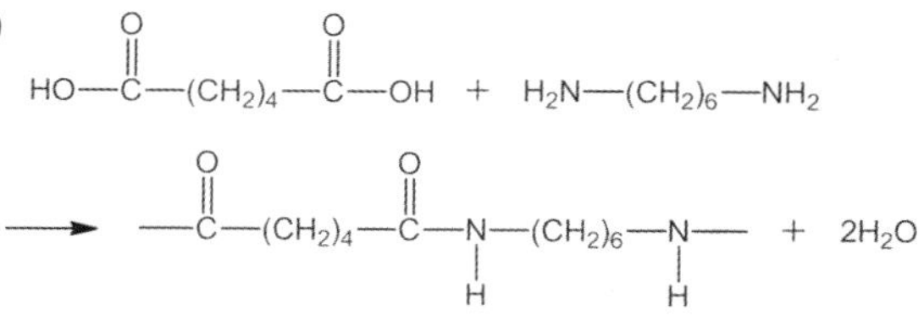

**(b)** Any two of: ropes, fishing nets, clothes.

**(c)** Nylon is biodegradable as the amide linkages between the monomers can be hydrolysed by the action of microorganisms in the environment. In contrast, polythene is non-biodegradable as the C-C bonds in polythene cannot be hydrolysed by the action of microorganisms in the environment.

3. (a) Two repeating units.

(b)

HO—C(=O)—⟨benzene ring⟩—C(=O)—OH

H₂N—⟨benzene ring⟩—NH₂

4. Answer B

5. (a) Condensation polymers

(b)

—C(=O)—(CH₂)₄—C(=O)—O—CH₂—CH₂—O—

(c) —N̈=C=Ö:

(d) The ester linkages between the monomers in each polyester molecule, and the amide linkages between the polyester molecules, can be hydrolysed by the action of microorganisms in the environment.

## 5.13 Chemistry in Medicine

### Exercise 5.13A

1. (a) To speed up the reaction.

(b) Moles of HCl added
= $0.0500 \ dm^3 \times 1.0 \ mol \ dm^{-3} = 0.050 \ mol$

Moles of HCl remaining
= $0.0301 \ dm^3 \times 1.0 \ mol \ dm^{-3} = 0.030 \ mol$

Moles of HCl reacted = 0.020 mol

Mass of $MgCO_3$ in 25 cm³
= $0.010 \ mol \times 84 \ g \ mol^{-1} = 0.84 \ g$

% $MgCO_3$ in the tablets

= $\dfrac{8.4 \ g}{10.0 \ g} \times 100 \ \% = 84 \ \%$

(c) Back titration is used as the base is insoluble and may not fully react each time acid is added.

### Exercise 5.13B

1. (a) Skin acts as a waterproof layer as the fatty acids and triglycerides in the acid mantle are not miscible with water. The pH of the acid mantle is low enough to prevent the growth of bacteria and viruses that thrive at higher pH values.

(b) Skin becomes dry as fatty acids are removed from the acid mantle.

2. (a) Skin becomes dry and more vulnerable to infection.

(b) Fatty acids in the mild cleanser can replace fatty acids removed from the acid mantle by the use of alkaline soaps and cleansers.

### Exercise 5.13C

1. (a) A strong acid cannot be used as it is too corrosive. Weak acids such as salicylic acid are mildly corrosive and will destroy warts after several applications.

(b) Weak acids such as salicylic acid will also corrode healthy skin.

### Exercise 5.13D

1. (a) x = 13

(b) Even dilute silver nitrate solution is corrosive and may damage eyes.

### Exercise 5.13E

1. Add a few drops of concentrated phosphoric acid to a mixture of 2-hydroxybenzoic acid and ethanoic anhydride in a round-bottom flask fitted with a reflux condenser. Heat the mixture using a water bath. Allow the mixture to cool before adding cold water and continuing to cool the mixture using an ice bath. Acetylsalicylic acid precipitates on cooling. The crude product then is removed by vacuum filtration, washed with cold water and dried in air before being recrystallised using ethanol as the solvent and dried in a low temperature oven.

2. (a)

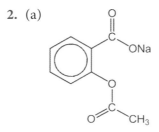

(b) The sodium salt causes less irritation to the

digestive system as it is less acidic and, being soluble, is more quickly absorbed.

3. (a) $C_9H_8O_4 + NaOH \rightarrow C_9H_7O_4Na + H_2O$

(b) Moles of NaOH added
$= 0.0500 \text{ dm}^3 \times 0.10 \text{ mol dm}^{-3} = 0.0050 \text{ mol}$

Moles of NaOH remaining
$= 0.0223 \text{ dm}^3 \times 0.10 \text{ mol dm}^{-3} = 0.0022 \text{ mol}$

Moles of NaOH reacted $= 0.0028 \text{ mol}$

Mass of $C_9H_8O_4$ in 25 cm$^3$
$= 0.0028 \text{ mol} \times 180 \text{ g mol}^{-1} = 0.50 \text{ g}$

$C_9H_8O_4 = \dfrac{5.0 \text{ g}}{6.0 \text{ g}} \times 100 = 83\%$

(c) Back titration is used as acetylsalicylic acid is only slightly soluble and may not fully react each time alkali is added.

4. (a) Acetaminophen is an N-substituted amide.

(b) Acetaminophen causes less irritation to the digestive system as it is less acidic than acetylsalicylic acid.

5. (a)

(b) $C_{13}H_{18}O_2$

(c) Ibuprofen causes less irritation to the digestive system as it is less soluble than acetylsalicylic acid.

## Exercise 5.13F

1. (a)

cis-isomer      trans-isomer

(b) The cis and trans isomers are not chiral as they can be superimposed on their mirror image.

(c) The cis-isomer is used to treat a variety of cancers in humans by preventing DNA replication and cell division.

(d) The drug is very expensive because platinum is expensive and large sums of money must be invested to research and develop new drugs.

2. (a)

E-isomer (trans)      Z-isomer (cis)

(b) The Z-isomer is more likely to prevent DNA replication and cell division as the arrangement of the ammonia ligands about platinum is similar to cisplatin.

3. (a) The cells become resistant to cisplatin as some or all of the cisplatin forms a complex with the sulfur-containing compounds in the cells before it can form a complex with the DNA in the cells.

(b) The large ligand in AMD473 may prevent the complex from bonding with the sulfur-containing compounds, making it more available to form a complex with the DNA in the cells.

## Exercise 5.13G

1. Oxygen, $O_2$ forms a coordinate bond with iron(II) in haemoglobin and is then transported around the body.

2. Carbon monoxide binds strongly to the iron(II) in haemoglobin forming a stable complex. Formation of a stable complex prevents oxygen being transported around the body.

## Exercise 5.13H

1. (a) Edta forms a stable complex with the calcium ions in blood, preventing them from participating in the formation of blood clots.

(b) $[Ca(edta)]^{2-}$

2. (a) The metal ions form stable complexes with the $H_2(edta)^{2-}$ ion, rendering the metal ions unreactive, and reducing their toxic effect on the body.

(b) $[Pb(H_2O)_6]^{2+}{}_{(aq)} + H_2(edta)^{2-}{}_{(aq)}$
$\rightarrow [Pb(edta)]^{2-}{}_{(aq)} + 6H_2O_{(l)} + 2H^+{}_{(aq)}$

### 6: Practical Assessment

## Exercise 6A

1. (a) Rinse a volumetric pipette with the iron(II) solution before using the pipette and a pipette

filler to transfer 25 cm³ of the iron(II) solution to a conical flask. Add sulfuric acid to the conical flask and swirl to mix.

Rinse and fill the burette with the permanganate solution. Perform rough titration by adding permanganate solution in 1 cm³ amounts, swirling the contents after each addition, until the solution changes from colourless to pink. Perform an accurate titration by adding permanganate solution dropwise near the end point. Repeat to obtain accurate titres that differ by less than 0.1 cm³.

(b) Colourless to pink.

(c) $MnO_4^{-}{}_{(aq)} + 5Fe^{2+}{}_{(aq)} + 8H^{+}{}_{(aq)}$
$\rightarrow Mn^{2+}{}_{(aq)} + 5Fe^{3+}{}_{(aq)} + 4H_2O_{(l)}$

(d) Moles of permanganate = $4.1 \times 10^{-4}$ mol
Moles of iron(II) in 25 cm³ = $2.1 \times 10^{-3}$ mol

Molarity of iron(II) sulfate
= $2.1 \times 10^{-3}$ mol $\times 40 = 0.084$ mol dm⁻³

(e) Molar mass of $Fe(NH_4)_2(SO_4)_2.nH_2O$
$= \dfrac{31.4 \text{ g dm}^{-3}}{0.084 \text{ mol dm}^{-3}} = 374$ g mol⁻¹

Molar mass of $Fe(NH_4)_2(SO_4)_2 = 284$ g mol⁻¹

Moles of water, $n = \dfrac{374 - 284}{18} = 5$

2. (a) $MnO_4^{-}{}_{(aq)} + 5Fe^{2+}{}_{(aq)} + 8H^{+}{}_{(aq)}$
$\rightarrow Mn^{2+}{}_{(aq)} + 5Fe^{3+}{}_{(aq)} + 4H_2O_{(l)}$

(b) Pink

(c) $MnO_4^{-}$

(d) Add acidified manganate(VII) dropwise near the end point, using deionised water to wash any drops of solution on the side of the conical flask into the solution being titrated.

(e) Dissolve the tablets in deionised water and transfer the solution to a volumetric flask. Use a wash bottle filled with deionised water to wash any drops remaining into the volumetric flask. Add deionised water to the flask until the bottom of the meniscus lies on the fill line. Stopper the flask and invert several times to mix.

(f) Moles of iron(II) in 250 cm³ = 0.0224 mol

Mass of $FeSO_4.6H_2O$ in 6.00 g
= 0.0224 mol $\times$ 260 g mol⁻¹ = 5.82 g

% $FeSO_4.7H_2O$ = 97.0 %

3. (a) Rinse a volumetric pipette with the iodate(V) solution before using the pipette and a pipette filler to transfer 25 cm³ of the solution to a conical flask. Add a sample of potassium iodide dissolved in sulfuric acid to the conical flask and swirl to mix.

Rinse and fill the burette with the thiosulfate solution. Add thiosulfate solution in 1 cm³ amounts, swirling the contents of the flask after each addition, until the solution turns a straw colour. Add a few drops of starch indicator and swirl to mix. Add thiosulfate solution dropwise, swirling the contents of the flask after each addition, until the blue-black colour of the iodine-starch complex is replaced by a colourless solution at the end point. Repeat to obtain accurate titres that differ by less than 0.1 cm³.

(b) $6.0 \times 10^{-4}$ mol

(c) $2IO_3^{-}{}_{(aq)} + 12H^{+}{}_{(aq)} + 10e^{-} \rightarrow I_2{}_{(aq)} + 6H_2O_{(l)}$

(d) $IO_3^{-}{}_{(aq)} + 6H^{+}{}_{(aq)} + 5I^{-}{}_{(aq)} \rightarrow 3I_2{}_{(aq)} + 3H_2O_{(l)}$

(e) Moles of iodate(V) in 25 cm³ = $2.0 \times 10^{-4}$ mol

Molarity of $KIO_3 = 2.0 \times 10^{-4}$ mol $\times 40$
= $8.0 \times 10^{-3}$ mol dm⁻³

Mass of $KIO_3$ in 1 dm³
= $8.0 \times 10^{-3}$ mol dm⁻³ $\times$ 214 g mol⁻¹ = 1.7 g

### Exercise 6B

1. (a)

| Test | Observations | Deductions |
|---|---|---|
| 1. Dissolve A in 20 cm³ of water. | Orange solution formed. | Transition metal compound. Possibly iron(III) ion present. |
| 2. Add a few drops of concentrated ammonia solution to 2 cm³ of the solution of A in a test tube. | Brown precipitate formed. | Confirms iron(III) ion present. |
| 3. Add 1 cm³ of barium chloride solution to 2 cm³ of the solution of A in a test tube, allow the mixture to settle. | White precipitate formed. Orange solution remains. | Sulfate ion present. |

(b) Salt A is iron(III) sulfate.

**2.** (a)

| Test | Observations | Deductions |
|---|---|---|
| 1. Describe the appearance of A. | Pink solid. | Transition metal compound. |
| 2. Add 1 spatula measure of A to approximately 50 cm$^3$ of water and stir. | The solid dissolves to form a pink solution. | The compound is soluble. Possibly cobalt(II) ion or manganese(II) ion present. |
| 3. Add 10 drops of silver nitrate solution to 2 cm$^3$ of the solution of A in a test tube. Allow to stand. | White precipitate formed. Pink solution remains. | Chloride ion present. |
| 4. Add 5 drops of sodium hydroxide solution to 2 cm$^3$ of the solution of A in a test tube. | Blue precipitate formed. Precipitate turns brown on standing. | Insoluble metal hydroxide formed. Confirms cobalt(II) ion present. |
| 5. In a fume cupboard, add 6 cm$^3$ of concentrated ammonia, slowly, to 2 cm$^3$ of the solution of A in a test tube. | Blue precipitate formed. Precipitate dissolves in excess ammonia. Brown solution formed. | Cobalt(II) hydroxide formed. Cobalt(II) complex with ammonia formed. |
| 6. Add 4 cm$^3$ of concentrated hydrochloric acid to 2 cm$^3$ of the solution of A in a test tube. | Blue solution formed. | Cobalt(II) complex with chloride formed. |

(b) Compound A is cobalt(II) chloride.

**3.** (a)

| Test | Observations | Deductions |
|---|---|---|
| 1. Describe the appearance of X. | Green solid. | Transition metal compound. |
| 2. Add 1 spatula measure of X to approximately 50 cm$^3$ of water. | The compound dissolves to form a green solution. | The compound is soluble. Nickel(II) ion present. |
| 3. Add 10 drops of silver nitrate solution to 2 cm$^3$ of the solution of X in a test tube. Allow to stand. | White precipitate formed. Green solution remains. | Chloride ion present. |
| 4. Add 5 drops of sodium hydroxide solution to 2 cm$^3$ of the solution of X in a test tube. | Green precipitate formed. | Nickel(II) hydroxide formed. |

| 5. In a fume cupboard, add 6 cm$^3$ of concentrated ammonia, slowly, to 2 cm$^3$ of the solution of X in a test tube. | Green precipitate formed. Precipitate dissolves in excess ammonia. Blue solution formed. | Nickel(II) hydroxide formed. Nickel(II) complex with ammonia formed. |
|---|---|---|
| 6. Add 2 cm$^3$ of edta solution to 2 cm$^3$ of the solution of X in a test tube. | Blue solution formed. | Nickel(II) complex with edta formed. |

(b) Compound X is nickel(II) chloride.

**4.** (a)

| Test | Observations | Deductions |
|---|---|---|
| 1. Describe the appearance of X. | Green solid. | Transition metal compound. |
| 2. Add 1 spatula measure of X to 50 cm$^3$ of deionised water and stir until there is no further change. | The compound dissolves to form a green solution. | The compound is soluble. Possibly chromium(III) ion, iron(II) ion, or nickel(II) ion present. |
| 3. Add 5 drops of silver nitrate solution to a test tube containing 2 cm$^3$ of the solution of X. Allow the mixture to stand. | White precipitate formed. Green solution remains. | Chloride ion present. |
| 4. Put 2 cm$^3$ of the solution of X into a test tube. (a) Add 5 drops of sodium hydroxide solution. (b) Add a further 5 cm$^3$ of sodium hydroxide solution. | (a) Green-blue precipitate formed. (b) Precipitate dissolves to form a green solution. | Chromium(III) hydroxide formed. Confirms chromium(III) ion present. |
| 5. Place 1 spatula measure of solid X in a dry boiling tube and heat gently. | Colourless liquid formed on the side of the boiling tube. Solid changes colour. | The solid is a hydrated salt. |

(b) Compound X is hydrated chromium(III) chloride.

**5.** (a)

| Test | Observations | Deductions |
|---|---|---|
| 1. Describe the appearance of R. | Pink solid. | Transition metal compound. |

| | | |
|---|---|---|
| 2. Add a spatula measure of R to 50 cm$^3$ of deionised water and stir until there is no further change. | The compound dissolves to form a pink solution. | The compound is soluble.<br><br>Possibly manganese(II) ion or cobalt(II) ion present. |
| 3. Add 5 drops of silver nitrate solution to a test tube containing 2 cm$^3$ of the solution of R. Allow the mixture to stand. | White precipitate formed.<br><br>Pink solution remains. | Chloride ion present. |
| 4. Put 2 cm$^3$ of the solution of R into a test tube.<br><br>(a) Add 5 drops of sodium hydroxide solution and allow to stand.<br><br>(b) Add a further 5 cm$^3$ of sodium hydroxide solution. | White precipitate formed. Precipitate turns brown on standing.<br><br><br>Precipitate remains. | Manganese(II) hydroxide formed.<br><br><br><br>Confirms manganese(II) ion present. |
| 5. Place a spatula measure of solid R in a dry boiling tube and heat gently. | Colourless liquid formed on the side of the boiling tube.<br><br>Solid changes colour. | The solid is a hydrated salt. |

(b) Compound R is hydrated manganese(II) chloride.

**6.** (a)

| Test | Observations | Deductions |
|---|---|---|
| 1. Describe the appearance of A. | Blue solid. | Transition metal compound. |
| 2. Dissolve two spatula measures of A in 50 cm$^3$ of water. Keep this solution for use in further tests. | The compound dissolves to form a blue solution. | The compound is soluble.<br><br>Copper(II) ion present. |
| 3. Place 4 cm$^3$ of the solution from test 2 in a test tube. Add an equal volume of concentrated hydrochloric acid. | Yellow solution formed. | Copper(II) complex with chloride formed. |
| 4. Place 4 cm$^3$ of the solution from test 2 in a test tube. Add an equal volume of 1,2-diaminoethane solution. | Violet solution formed. | Copper(II) complex with en formed. |

| | | |
|---|---|---|
| 5. (a) Place 4 cm$^3$ of the solution from test 2 in a test tube. Slowly add an equal volume of sodium hydroxide solution.<br><br>(b) Add a further 5 cm$^3$ of sodium hydroxide solution. | Blue precipitate formed.<br><br><br><br>Blue precipitate remains. | Copper(II) hydroxide formed. |
| 6. Place 4 cm$^3$ of the solution from test 2 in a test tube. In a fume cupboard, add an equal volume of concentrated ammonia solution. | Blue precipitate forms.<br><br>Blue precipitate dissolves to form a dark blue solution on mixing. | Copper(II) hydroxide formed.<br><br>Copper(II) complex with ammonia formed. |
| 7. Place 4 cm$^3$ of the solution from test 2 in a test tube. Add 1 cm$^3$ of barium chloride solution dropwise. | White precipitate formed. | Sulfate ion present. |

(b) Compound A is hydrated copper(II) sulfate.

(c) Test 2 $[Cu(H_2O)_6]^{2+}$   Test 3 $[CuCl_4]^{2-}$
Test 4 $[Cu(en)_3]^{2+}$   Test 6 $[Cu(NH_3)_4(H_2O)_2]^{2+}$

(d) Test 5 $Cu(OH)_2$   Test 7 $BaSO_4$

**7.** (a)

| Test | Observations | Deductions |
|---|---|---|
| 1. Describe the appearance of A. | Green solid. | Transition metal compound. |
| 2. Dissolve three spatula measures of A in 15 cm$^3$ of deionised water.<br><br>Keep this solution for tests 3(a), 4, 5(a) and 6. | The compound dissolves to form a green solution. | The compound is soluble.<br><br>Possibly chromium(III) ion, iron(II) ion, or nickel(II) ion present. |
| 3. (a) Place 2 cm$^3$ of the solution from test 2 in a test tube and add an equal volume of sodium hydroxide solution.<br><br>(b) Add a further 5 cm$^3$ of sodium hydroxide solution to the test tube. | Green precipitate formed.<br><br><br><br>Green precipitate remains. | Insoluble metal hydroxide formed.<br><br><br><br>Confirms iron(II) ion or nickel(II) ion present. |
| 4. Place 2 cm$^3$ of the solution from test 2 in a test tube and add 4 cm$^3$ of edta solution. | Blue solution formed. | Nickel(II) complex with edta formed. |

| | | |
|---|---|---|
| 5. (a) Place 2 cm³ of the solution from test 2 in a test tube and add 5 cm³ of dilute ammonia solution. | Blue solution formed. | Nickel(II) complex with ammonia formed. |
| (b) Place 2 cm³ of the solution from test 5(a) in another test tube and add 2 cm³ of 1,2-diaminoethane (en) solution. | Violet solution formed. | Nickel(II) complex with en formed. |
| 6. Place 2 cm³ of the solution from test 2 in another test tube and add 2 cm³ of barium chloride solution. Allow to stand. | White precipitate formed. | Sulfate ion present. |

(b) Compound A is nickel(II) sulfate.

(c) Test 4 $[Ni(edta)]^{2-}$    Test 5a $[Ni(NH_3)_6]^{2+}$

Test 5b $[Ni(en)_3]^{2+}$

(d) The ligand replacement reaction produces an increase in entropy because three en ligands replace six ammonia ligands.

**8.** (a)

| Test | Observations | Deductions |
|---|---|---|
| 1. Describe the appearance of B. | Pink solid. | Transition metal compound. |
| 2. Dissolve three spatula measures of B in 15 cm³ of deionised water.  Keep this solution for tests 3(a), 4(a), 5(a) and 6. | The compound dissolves to form a pink solution. | The compound is soluble.  Possibly manganese(II) ion or cobalt(II) ion present. |
| 3. (a) Place 3 cm³ of the solution from test 2 in a test tube and add 5 drops of sodium hydroxide solution. | Blue precipitate formed. | Cobalt(II) hydroxide formed. |
| (b) Add a further 5 cm³ of sodium hydroxide solution to the test tube. | Blue precipitate remains. Precipitate turns brown on standing. | Confirms cobalt(II) ion present. |
| 4. (a) In a fume cupboard place 2 cm³ of the solution from test 2 in a test tube and add 3 drops of concentrated ammonia solution. | Blue precipitate formed. | Cobalt(II) hydroxide formed. |
| (b) Add a further 5 cm³ of concentrated ammonia solution to the test tube. | Precipitate dissolves in excess ammonia. Brown solution formed. | Cobalt(II) complex with ammonia formed. |
| 5. (a) Place 3 cm³ of the solution from test 2 in a test tube and in a fume cupboard, add 5 cm³ of concentrated hydrochloric acid. | Blue solution formed. | Cobalt(II) complex with chloride formed. |
| (b) Place 3 cm³ of the solution from test 5(a) in another test tube and add 5 cm³ of edta solution. | Pink solution formed. | Cobalt(II) complex with edta formed. |
| 6. Place 3 cm³ of the solution from test 2 in another test tube and add 3 cm³ of barium chloride solution. | White precipitate formed. | Sulfate ion present. |

(b) The compound B is cobalt(II) sulfate.

(c) Test 4b $[Co(NH_3)_6]^{2+}$
Test 5a $[CoCl_4]^{2-}$
Test 5b $[Co(edta)]^{2-}$

(d) The ligand replacement reaction produces an increase in entropy because one edta ligand replaces four chloride ligands.

## Exercise 6C

**1.** (a)

| Test | Observations | Deductions |
|---|---|---|
| 1. (a) Place 2 cm³ of Y into a boiling tube. Place in a test tube rack. Under supervision, cautiously add a very small measure of phosphorus(V) chloride in a fume cupboard. | Solid disappears. Steamy fumes. Mixture warms up. | Hydroxyl (-OH) group present. |
| (b) In a fume cupboard, hold the stopper of a bottle of concentrated ammonia solution over the boiling tube used in test 1(a). | White fumes of solid ammonium chloride. | Hydrogen chloride gas evolved. |
| 2. Place 2 cm³ of Y into a test tube. Add 1 cm³ of sodium carbonate solution. | Solid disappears. Colourless solution formed. Fizzing. Colourless gas produced. | The liquid is acidic. |

(b) Compound Y is a carboxylic acid.

(c) Compound Y is propanoic acid, $CH_3CH_2COOH$. The molecular ion at m/z = 74 can fragment to give signals due to $CH_3CH_2CO^+$ at m/z = 57, $COOH^+$ ions at m/z = 45 and $CH_3CH_2^+$ ions at m/z = 29.

**2.** (a)

| Test | Observations | Deductions |
|---|---|---|
| 1. Describe the appearance of B. | Colourless liquid. Pungent smell. | |
| 2. Add 2 cm³ of deionised water to 2 cm³ of B in a test tube. | One layer formed. | Compound B can form hydrogen bonds. |
| 3. Add 10 drops of B to 2 cm³ of acidified potassium dichromate solution in a test tube. Place the test tube in a hot water bath. | The orange colour of dichromate ion remains after heating. No change in smell. | Compound B is not oxidised by acidified dichromate. |

| Test | Observations | Deductions |
|---|---|---|
| 4. Place 2 cm³ of B into a test tube. In a fume cupboard cautiously add a very small spatula measure of phosphorus(V) chloride to the test tube. | Solid disappears. Steamy fumes. Mixture warms up. | Hydroxyl (-OH) group present. |
| 5. Place 5 cm³ of B in a boiling tube. Add 5 cm³ of ethanol, and then 1 cm³ of concentrated sulfuric acid. Heat the boiling tube in a water bath. Cautiously smell the contents of the boiling tube. | Sweet smell produced on heating the mixture. | Ester formed. Compound B is a carboxylic acid. |
| 6. Add 1 spatula measure of sodium carbonate to 2 cm³ of B in a test tube. | The solid disappears Colourless solution formed. Fizzing. Colourless gas produced. | Compound B is acidic. Confirms B is a carboxylic acid. |

(b) Compound B is a carboxylic acid.

(c)

(d) The base peak at m/z = 59 is due to an ion with the formula $C_2H_3O_2^+$.

**3.** (a)

| Test | Observations | Deductions |
|---|---|---|
| Mix 1 cm³ of Fehling's No 1 solution with an equal volume of Fehling's No 2 solution. Add about 1 cm³ of B and heat in a water bath for at least 5 minutes. | Red precipitate formed on heating. | Compound B is oxidised. Compound B is propanal. |

(b)

(c)

**4.** (a)

| Test | Observations | Deductions |
|---|---|---|
| Add a spatula measure of sodium carbonate to about 1 cm³ of D in a test tube. | The solid disappears. Colourless solution formed. | Compound D is acidic. |
| | Fizzing. Colourless gas produced. | Compound D is propanoic acid. |

(b) 

(c) 

**5.** (a)

| Test | Observations | Deductions |
|---|---|---|
| 1. Describe the appearance of Y. Cautiously smell Y and give a description of its smell. | Colourless liquid. Pungent smell. | |
| 2. Place 3 cm³ of Y in a test tube and add 10 drops of acidified potassium dichromate solution. Warm in a water bath. | The solution changes from orange to green on heating. Change in smell. | A compound in the mixture is oxidised. The mixture contains an aldehyde. |
| 3. Place 3 cm³ of Y in another test tube and add half a spatula measure of sodium hydrogencarbonate. | The solid disappears. Colourless solution formed. Fizzing. Colourless gas produced. The temperature of the solution decreases. | The mixture is acidic. Confirms the presence of a carboxylic acid. |

(b) The mixture contains an aldehyde and a carboxylic acid.

**6.** (a)

| Test | Observations | Deductions |
|---|---|---|
| 1. Describe the appearance of Z. Cautiously smell Z and give a description of its smell. | Colourless solution. Pungent smell. | |
| 2. Place 3 cm³ of Z in a test tube and add 10 drops of acidified potassium dichromate solution. Warm in a water bath. | The orange colour of dichromate ion remains after heating. No change in smell. | The compounds in the mixture are not oxidised by acidified dichromate. The mixture may contain ketones, carboxylic acids, esters or amides. |
| 3. Place 3 cm³ of Z in another test tube and add half a spatula measure of sodium hydrogencarbonate. | The solid disappears. Colourless solution formed. Fizzing. Colourless gas produced. The temperature of the solution decreases. | The mixture is acidic. Confirms the presence of a carboxylic acid. The mixture does not contain an ester or an amide. |

(b) The mixture contains a ketone and a carboxylic acid.

**7.** (a)

| Test | Observations | Deductions |
|---|---|---|
| 1. Describe the appearance of B. | White crystalline solid. | Amino acid or amide. |
| 2. Heat one spatula measure of B in a test tube. Heat gently at first and then more strongly. Test any fumes with a glass rod dipped in concentrated hydrochloric acid. | Pungent smelling gas produced. White fumes of solid ammonium chloride. | Ammonia gas evolved. Compound B contains nitrogen. |
| 3. (a) Dissolve 2 spatula measures of B in approximately 20 cm³ of water. | Solid disappears. Colourless solution formed. | |
| (b) Use Universal Indicator paper to determine the pH of the solution of B. | Indicator paper turns green. | pH 7 |

| 4. Add 6 drops of copper(II) sulfate solution, dropwise, to a test tube half-full of a solution of B. | Blue solution formed. | Amino acid complex with copper(II) formed. |
|---|---|---|
| 5. To 3 cm³ of acidified potassium dichromate solution add one spatula measure of B and warm gently. | The orange colour of dichromate ion remains after heating. No change in smell. | Compound B is not oxidised by acidified dichromate. Compound B is not a primary/secondary alcohol. |

(b) The 3:2 ratio obtained from the NMR integration is evidence for the $NH_3^+$ and $CH_2$ groups in the zwitterion formed by glycine, $CH_2(NH_2)COOH$. Compound B is glycine.

## Exercise 6D

1. (a) $Sn + 2I_2 \rightarrow SnI_4$

   (b) Moles of $SnI_4$ formed = 0.0096 mol

   Amount of $I_2$ needed = 0.021 mol = 5.3 g

   (c) Use gloves since dichloromethane is toxic. Use an electrical heater since dichloromethane is flammable.

   (d) The continuous boiling and condensing of a mixture using a flask fitted with a condenser in the vertical position.

   (e) The colour produced by the iodine in solution has disappeared.

   (f) Filter the reaction mixture.

   (g) Distil the solution to remove the solvent. Solid tin(IV) iodide will form in the flask.

   (h) Recrystallise the crude solid by dissolving it in the minimum amount of hot solvent, filtering the hot solution, and leaving the filtrate to cool so crystals can form.

2. (a) $HCOOH + CH_3CH_2OH$
   $\rightarrow HCOOCH_2CH_3 + H_2O$

   (b) Moles of ethyl methanoate formed = 0.060 mol

   Amount of each reactant needed = 0.10 mol

   Reactants have the same molar mass

   Amount of each reactant needed = 4.6 g

   (c) Slowly add concentrated sulfuric acid to a mixture of ethanol and methanoic acid in a round-bottom flask. Add anti-bumping granules and reflux the mixture for an extended period. Distil the mixture and collect the crude ester at its boiling point.

(d) (i) Aqueous sodium carbonate removes acidic impurities when it is shaken with the crude product in a separating funnel. The tap on the funnel is opened every few seconds to release any carbon dioxide formed. The funnel is then used to separate the product from the aqueous layer.

(ii) Anhydrous calcium chloride removes any water present when it is added to the product in a small conical flask and the mixture swirled until the product becomes clear. The dry product is then obtained by filtering the mixture.

(e)

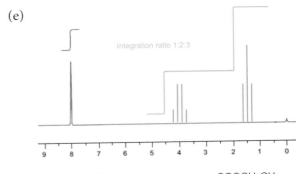

Integration ratio 1:2:3

3. (a)

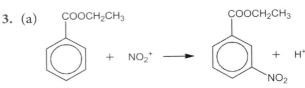

   (b) 7.50 g

   (c) Dissolve ethyl benzoate in concentrated sulfuric acid. Add a mixture containing equal amounts of concentrated sulfuric acid and concentrated nitric acid dropwise, cooling both solutions in an ice bath to ensure that the temperature remains below 10 °C during the addition. Allow the mixture to stand at room temperature for several minutes before pouring the mixture over a small amount of crushed ice. The crude ethyl 3-nitrobenzoate is then obtained by vacuum filtration, and washed with cold water to remove traces of the nitrating mixture.

   (d) The crude product is recrystallised to remove impurities. The crude ethyl 3-nitrobenzoate is dissolved in the minimum amount of hot ethanol. The solution is filtered while hot and the filtrate left to cool, allowing time for crystals to form. The crystals are then obtained from the filtrate by vacuum filtration.

(e) The crystals can be dried in a low temperature oven.

(f) The product is pure if it melts over a narrow range (typically 1–2 °C) that includes the melting point (42 °C).

(g)

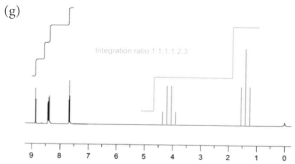

Integration ratio 1:1:1:1 2.3

4. (a) Ammonia is not a good electrophile.

(b) Reflux is the continuous boiling and condensing of a mixture using a flask fitted with a condenser in the vertical position.

(c)

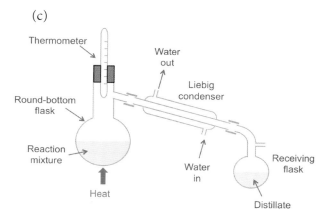

(d) Moles of nitrobenzene formed = 0.057 mol

Amount of benzene needed = 0.063 mol = 4.9 g = 5.6 cm$^3$

(e) The crude product is shaken with aqueous sodium hydrogencarbonate in a separating funnel. The tap on the funnel is opened every few seconds to release any carbon dioxide formed. The funnel is then used to separate the product from the aqueous layer.

(f)

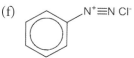

5. (a) Catalyst

(b) Add dropwise using a dropping funnel. Wear gloves.

(c) Reflux is the continuous boiling and condensing of a mixture using a flask fitted with a condenser in the vertical position.

(d)

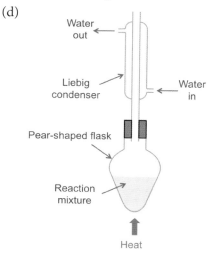

(e) $(CH_3CO)_2O + H_2O \rightarrow 2CH_3COOH$

(f) To form the solid product by reducing the solubility of the product.

(g) To speed up the filtration process and produce a drier product.

(h) The crude aspirin is dissolved in the minimum amount of hot water. The solution is filtered while hot and the filtrate left to cool, allowing time for crystals to form. Crystals of pure aspirin are then obtained from the filtrate by vacuum filtration.

(i) Moles of aspirin formed = 0.028 mol

Amount of acid needed = 0.043 mol = 5.9 g

6. (a) $Pb(CNO)_2 + 2NH_3 + 2H_2O$
$$\rightarrow Pb(OH)_2 + 2NH_4CNO$$

(b) Amount of $NH_4CNO$ formed = 7.50 mol

Amount of $Pb(CNO)_2$ needed
$$= \frac{10.7 \text{ mol}}{2} = 5.35 \text{ mol} = 1.56 \text{ kg}$$

(c) (i) Recrystallisation. (ii) The product should be soluble in hot solvent and not very soluble at room temperature. (iii) To create a saturated solution. (iv) The solution is filtered and the product dried in a low temperature oven.

(d) Place a sample of urea in a capillary tube sealed at one end. Heat the sample slowly using an oil bath. Record the temperature at which the sample starts melting and the temperature at which the sample stops melting. If the sample is pure it will melt over a narrow range of 1–2 °C that includes the melting point of urea (133 °C).

(e) Infrared spectroscopy could be used to monitor the reduction in absorption at 2100 cm$^{-1}$ as C≡N bonds in $NH_4CNO$ are broken, and the accompanying increase in absorption at 1650 cm$^{-1}$ and 3200–3500 cm$^{-1}$ as the C=O and N-H bonds in urea are formed.

7. (a) $2Na_{(l)} + O_{2(g)} \rightarrow Na_2O_{2(s)}$

(b) Amount of $Na_2O_2$ formed = 0.017 mol

Amount of Na needed = 2 × 0.021 mol

= 0.042 mol = 0.97 g

(c) Water vapour in the oxygen would reduce the yield by reacting with any sodium and/or sodium peroxide present.

(d)

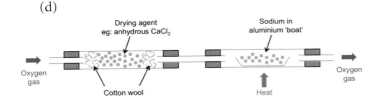

(e) (i) $Na_2O_2 + H_3PO_4 \rightarrow Na_2HPO_4 + H_2O_2$

(ii) The hydrated salt concentrates the solution by removing water as it forms.

(f) The retention time for the oxygen formed by the reaction would be the same as the retention time for a pure sample of oxygen gas.

8. (a) $8Na_2SO_{3(aq)} + S_{8(s)} \rightarrow 8Na_2S_2O_{3(aq)}$

(b) $Na_2S_2O_3.5H_2O$

(c) Amount of $Na_2S_2O_3.5H_2O$ formed = 0.010 mol

Amount of $Na_2SO_3$ needed = 0.013 mol

Volume of $Na_2SO_3$ needed

$= \dfrac{0.013 \text{ mol}}{0.060 \text{ mol dm}^{-3}} = 0.22 \text{ dm}^3 = 220 \text{ cm}^3$

(d)

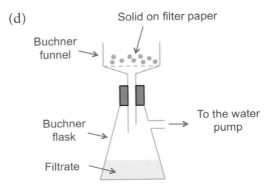

(e) To dissolve impurities that are insoluble in water.

(f) (i) $2Na_2S_2O_{3(aq)} + I_{2(aq)} \rightarrow 2NaI_{(aq)} + Na_2S_4O_{6(aq)}$

(ii) Amount of $I_2$ used = 2.50 × 10$^{-3}$ mol

Amount of $Na_2S_2O_3$ in 1.2 g

= 5.00 × 10$^{-3}$ mol = 0.790 g

% purity $= \dfrac{0.790 \text{ g}}{1.2 \text{ g}} \times 100 \% = 66 \%$

# Glossary

## 4.1 Lattice Enthalpy

- The **lattice enthalpy** of an ionic compound is the enthalpy change when one mole of an ionic compound is converted to gas phase ions.

### Born-Haber Cycles

- A **Born-Haber cycle** is an enthalpy diagram that can be used to relate enthalpy changes associated with the formation of an ionic compound.

- The **standard enthalpy of formation** of a compound is the enthalpy change when one mole of the compound is formed from its elements under standard conditions.

- The **enthalpy of atomisation** of an element is the enthalpy change when one mole of gas phase atoms are formed from the element in its standard state.

- The **first electron affinity** of an element is the enthalpy change when one mole of electrons is added to one mole of gas phase atoms to form gas phase ions with a charge of 1–.

- The **second electron affinity** of an element is the enthalpy change when one mole of electrons is added to one mole of gas phase ions with a charge of 1– to form gas phase ions with a charge of 2–.

### Working with Born-Haber Cycles

- The **enthalpy of vaporisation** of a compound is the enthalpy change when one mole of a liquid is converted to vapour.

- The **enthalpy of sublimation** of a compound is the enthalpy change when one mole of a solid is converted to vapour.

### Dissolving Ionic Compounds

- A **solvated ion** is an ion that has dissolved in a solvent and bonded with the surrounding solvent molecules.

- An **ion-dipole bond** results from the attraction between an ion and the oppositely charged ends of neighbouring dipoles.

- The **enthalpy of solution** for a solute is the enthalpy change when one mole of the solute dissolves in a solvent.

- The **enthalpy of hydration for a compound** is the enthalpy change when the gas phase ions formed from one mole of the compound bond with water to form solvated ions.

- The **enthalpy of hydration for an ion** is the enthalpy change when one mole of gas phase ions bond with water to form solvated ions.

## 4.2 Entropy and Free Energy

### Why Reactions Occur

- The **entropy** of a substance is a measure of the amount of disorder in the substance.

- The **standard entropy** of a substance is the amount of entropy in one mole of the substance under standard conditions.

- The **standard entropy change** for a reaction is the change in entropy when the reaction is carried out under standard conditions.

### Determining if a Reaction Occurs

- A reaction is **feasible** if the free energy change for the reaction, $\Delta G$ is negative ($\Delta G < 0$).

- The **standard free energy change** for a reaction is the free energy change when the reaction is carried out under standard conditions.

## 4.3 Chemical Kinetics

### Rate of Reaction

- The **rate of a reaction** is a positive number that describes how quickly the concentrations of the reactants and products change during the reaction.

- The **rate of formation** of a product is the speed at which the product is formed and is a multiple of the rate of the reaction.

- The **rate of removal** of a reactant is the speed at which the reactant is used and is a multiple of the rate of the reaction.

- The **initial rate** of a reaction is the rate when the reactants are mixed and the reaction begins (the rate at time, $t = 0$).

- The **average rate** of a reaction is the average speed at which the reactants are converted to products during the reaction.

### Rate Equations

- A **rate equation** defines the relationship between the rate of a reaction and the composition of the reaction mixture.

- The **rate constant** for a reaction is a positive number that varies with temperature, and is the proportionality constant that defines the relationship between the rate of the reaction and the concentrations in the rate equation.

- The **order of a reaction** is the sum of the powers to which the concentration terms are raised in the rate equation.

### Determining Reaction Mechanisms

- The **rate determining step (RDS)** for a reaction is the slowest step in the mechanism for the reaction.

- A **transition state** is the highest energy structure on the reaction pathway and cannot be isolated from the reaction mixture.

- A **nucleophile** is a molecule or ion that attacks regions of low electron density by using a lone pair to form a coordinate bond with an electron-deficient atom.

### Catalysis

- A **catalyst** is a substance that speeds up a reaction by lowering the activation energy, and is not consumed by the reaction.

- A **reaction intermediate** is formed during a reaction and subsequently consumed by the reaction as it proceeds.

## 4.4 Chemical Equilibrium

### Properties of $K_c$

- The **equilibrium constant, $K_c$** for a reaction defines the position of equilibrium at a particular temperature in terms of the concentrations of the reactants and products at equilibrium.

- The term **homogeneous reaction** describes a reaction in which all of the reactants and products are in the same physical state.

## 4.5 Acid-Base Equilibria

### Brønsted-Lowry Theory

- A **Brønsted-Lowry acid** is a molecule or ion that can donate a hydrogen ion.

- A **Brønsted-Lowry base** is a molecule or ion that can accept a hydrogen ion.

- The **conjugate acid** of a Brønsted-Lowry base is formed when the base accepts a hydrogen ion.

- The **conjugate base** of a Brønsted-Lowry acid is formed when the acid donates a hydrogen ion.

### Aqueous Solutions

- The **ionic product of water, $K_w$** describes the extent to which water dissociates in an aqueous solution and is defined by the product $K_w = [H^+][OH^-]$.

### Acid and Base Strength

- The **acid dissociation constant, $K_a$** of a weak acid (HA) describes the extent to which the acid dissociates and is defined by the quotient

$$K_a = \frac{[H^+][A^-]}{[HA]}.$$

### Polybasic Acids

- A **monobasic acid** is a molecule or ion that dissociates to form one hydrogen ion.

- A **polybasic acid** is a molecule or ion that dissociates to form more than one hydrogen ion.

### Buffer Solutions

- A **buffer solution** is a solution that resists changes in pH that result from the addition of small amounts of acid or alkali.

### Neutralisation Reactions

- A **neutralisation** reaction occurs when an acid reacts with a base to form a salt.

- **Salt hydrolysis** occurs when an aqueous ion reacts with water in the solution to form $H^+$ or $OH^-$ ions.

### Acid-Base Titrations

- The **equivalence point** of an acid-base titration is the point at which the acid or alkali in the solution being titrated has been completely neutralised.

- The **titration curve** for an acid-base titration is a plot showing the pH of the solution being titrated against the volume of solution added from the burette.

## 4.6 Isomerism

### The Origins of Isomerism

- **Isomers** are compounds with the same formula that have a different arrangement of atoms within the compound.

- **Structural isomers** are compounds with the same molecular formula that have different structural formulas.

- **Geometric isomers** are compounds with the same structural formula but a different arrangement of atoms in space as the molecule cannot rotate about the C=C bonds in the compound.

- **Stereoisomerism** gives rise to isomers with the same structural formula that have a different arrangement of atoms in space.

## Optical Isomerism

- An **asymmetric centre** is an atom bonded to four different groups of atoms in a tetrahedral arrangement.
- **Optical isomers** are molecules which exist as non-superimposable mirror images of each other.

## Optical Activity

- A substance is **optically active** if it rotates the plane of plane-polarised light.
- A substance is **optically inactive** if it does not rotate the plane of plane-polarised light.
- A **racemic mixture** is an equimolar mixture of optical isomers.

## 4.7 Carbonyl Compounds

### Structure and Properties

- An **aldehyde** contains a carbonyl (C=O) group in the form of a functional group with the structure RCHO.
- A **ketone** contains a carbonyl (C=O) group in the form of a functional group with the structure RCOR'.
- An **enal** is an aldehyde that contains a C=C bond.
- A **dienal** is an aldehyde that contains two C=C bonds.
- An **enone** is a ketone that contains a C=C bond.
- A **dienone** is a ketone that contains two C=C bonds.

### Reactions

- The term **nucleophilic addition** describes a reaction in which addition occurs as the result of a reactant behaving as a nucleophile.

### Identifying Aldehydes and Ketones

- A **condensation reaction** is a reaction in which a small molecule is formed when the reactants combine to form the product.
- **Vacuum filtration** is the process of filtering a mixture into a flask that is maintained at a reduced pressure.
- **Recrystallisation** is a process used to remove impurities from a substance by filtering a hot saturated solution of the substance before allowing the substance to recrystallise as the filtrate cools.

## 4.8 Carboxylic Acids

### Structure and Bonding

- A **carboxylic acid** contains a carboxyl (–COOH) functional group.
- A **dicarboxylic acid** contains two carboxyl (–COOH) groups.

### Reactions

- A **carboxylate ion** (RCOO$^-$) is formed when a carboxylic acid (RCOOH) reacts with a base.
- The term **esterification** is used to describe a reaction in which an ester (RCOOR') is formed.
- An **ester** (RCOOR') is a derivative of a carboxylic acid (RCOOH).
- An **acyl chloride** (RCOCl) is a derivative of a carboxylic acid (RCOOH).

## 4.10 Fats and Oils

### Structure and Properties

- A **triglyceride** is a triester formed from glycerol and long-chain carboxylic acids.
- A **fat** is a mixture of triglycerides that is solid at 25 °C.
- An **oil** is a mixture of triglycerides that is liquid at 25 °C.
- A **fatty acid** is a long-chain carboxylic acid of the type found in triglycerides.
- A **monounsaturated fatty acid** is a fatty acid that contains one C=C bond.
- A **polyunsaturated fatty acid** is a fatty acid that contains two or more C=C bonds.
- A **saturated fatty acid** is a fatty acid that does not contain a C=C bond.

### Reactions

- **Saponification** is the alkaline hydrolysis of triglycerides in a fat or oil.
- Fats and oils are **hardened** by catalytic hydrogenation using a finely divided nickel catalyst.
- **Transesterification** is a reaction in which the alkyl group attached to an ester linkage (-COOR) is replaced by the alkyl group from a different alcohol.
- **Biodiesel** is a fuel similar to diesel that contains alkyl esters formed from the long chain fatty acids in renewable sources such as vegetable oils.

## 4.11 Arenes

**Benzene**

- The term **delocalisation** refers to the formation of partial $\pi$-bonds by the sharing of the electrons in a $\pi$-bond between three or more atoms.
- The **aromatic character** of a compound refers to the stability associated with the delocalisation of $\pi$-electrons within the compound.

**Arenes**

- An **arene** is a compound with aromatic character.

**Reactions of Benzene**

- In a **bromination** reaction a bromine atom is added to a compound.
- An **electrophilic substitution** reaction involves the addition of an electrophile followed by the elimination of an atom, molecule or ion.
- In an **alkylation** reaction an alkyl (-R) group is added to a compound.
- In an **acylation** reaction an acyl (-COR) group is added to a compound.
- In a **nitration** reaction a nitro ($-NO_2$) group is added to a compound.

## 5.1 Chromatography

**Paper Chromatography**

- The **solvent front** is the final position of the solvent in a chromatography experiment.
- A **chromatogram** details the extent of the separation that occurred during a chromatography experiment.
- The **retardation factor** or '$R_f$ value' of a compound is the distance travelled by the compound divided by the distance travelled by the solvent.

**Gas-Liquid Chromatography**

- The **retention time** of a compound is the time taken from injection until the compound is detected.

## 5.2 Volumetric Analysis

**Back titration Methods**

- In a **back titration** the excess reagent added to a sample that cannot be analysed by titration is titrated to determine the amount of substance in the sample.

## 5.3 Mass Spectrometry

**Interpreting Mass Spectra**

- The **molecular ion (M) peak** is the signal produced by the ion formed when an electron is removed from a molecule of the compound.
- A **fragment ion** is a positive ion that is formed when the molecular ion breaks apart.
- **Fragmentation** is the breaking apart of a molecular ion to form a smaller ion with a positive charge.
- The **mass-to-charge ratio (m/z)** for an ion is equal to the RMM of the ion divided by the charge on the ion.
- The **base peak** is the signal with the greatest abundance in a mass spectrum.
- In **high-resolution mass spectrometry** the masses of the ions formed are determined to at least one decimal place.
- The **M+1 peak** is the signal produced by molecular ions that contain a carbon-13 atom.

## 5.4 NMR Spectroscopy

**Obtaining an NMR Spectrum**

- An **internal standard** is a substance that is part of the mixture being analysed, and provides reference data for the analysis.
- The **chemical shift** of an NMR signal is the difference in frequency, in units of parts-per million, between the signal and the signal produced by an internal standard.

**Interpreting an NMR Spectrum**

- The term **chemically equivalent** is used to describe atoms that contribute to the same NMR signal.
- The **integration curve** for an NMR spectrum details the area under each signal in the spectrum.
- The term **shielding** refers to the magnitude of the magnetic field produced by the electrons in the atom when the atom is placed in a magnetic field.
- The term **spin-spin splitting** refers to the action of one or more adjacent atoms on the signal produced by a set of chemically equivalent atoms.
- The term **multiplet** refers to the group of signals produced when an NMR signal is subject to spin-spin splitting.

## 5.5 Electrochemistry

### Electrochemical Cells

- An **electrochemical cell** produces a voltage from a chemical reaction.
- The **electromotive force (emf)** produced by a cell is the potential difference measured by a voltmeter when the half-cells are connected, and the voltmeter is connected across the cell.
- An **electrode** is used to establish electrical contact between a half-cell and the external circuit.
- The **cell reaction** describes the overall chemical change taking place in the cell.
- A **salt bridge** maintains electrical contact between the electrodes by allowing ions to move between the salt bridge and the electrode solutions.
- A **half-cell** is a process that takes place at an electrode and is described by a half-reaction.

### Standard Electrode Potentials

- The **standard electrode potential** for a half-cell is the potential difference measured by a voltmeter when the half-cell is connected to a standard hydrogen electrode, and the cell operated under standard conditions with the voltmeter connected across the cell.

### Other Types of Cells

- In a **rechargeable cell** the cell reaction is reversible and the cell can be recharged by operating the cell reaction in reverse.
- In a **fuel cell** the reaction of a fuel with oxygen is used to generate a voltage.

## 5.6 Transition Metals

### Properties

- A **transition metal** is an element that has a partly filled d-subshell, or forms at least one stable ion with a partly filled d-subshell.
- A **complex ion** is a complex with a positive or negative charge.

## 5.7 Metal Complexes

### Bonding and Structure

- A **ligand** is a molecule or ion that uses one or more lone pairs to form coordinate bonds with a metal atom or ion in a complex.
- A **complex** consists of a metal atom or ion with ligands attached by coordinate bonds.

### Ligands

- A **monodentate ligand** is a molecule or ion that uses one lone pair of electrons to form a coordinate bond with a metal atom or ion in a complex.
- A **bidentate ligand** is a molecule or ion that uses two lone pairs of electrons to form two coordinate bonds with a metal atom or ion in a complex.
- A **hexadentate ligand** is a molecule or ion that uses six lone pairs of electrons to form six coordinate bonds with a metal atom or ion in a complex.
- A **polydentate ligand** is a molecule or ion that uses many lone pairs of electrons to form more than two coordinate bonds with a metal atom or ion in a complex.
- A **chelate** is formed when a metal atom or ion forms a complex with a bidentate or polydentate ligand.
- The **coordination number** of a metal in a complex is the total number of coordinate bonds formed when the ligands bond with the metal to form the complex.

### Ligand Replacement

- **Ligand substitution** occurs when a ligand is displaced from a complex by a different ligand.
- **Ligand replacement** occurs when the ligands in a complex are replaced as the result of one or more ligand substitution reactions.

## 5.9 Amines

### Structure and Properties

- In a **primary amine** the nitrogen atom is bonded to one carbon atom and the compound has the structure $RNH_2$.
- In a **secondary amine** the nitrogen atom is bonded to two carbon atoms and the compound has the structure $RNHR'$.
- In a **tertiary amine** the nitrogen atom is bonded to three carbon atoms and the compound has the structure $RNR'R''$.
- A **diamine** is a compound that contains two amino ($-NH_2$) groups.

### Reactions

- An **alkylammonium salt** is the salt of an amine in which the nitrogen atom is bonded to one or more alkyl groups.

- An **N-substituted amide** is a compound with the structure RCONHR'.

### Azo Compounds

- A **diazonium ion** is an ion with the structure R-N$^+\equiv$N.

- An **azo compound** is a compound with the structure R-N=N-R'.

- A **coupling reaction** is a reaction in which two benzene rings become linked by an azo (-N=N-) group.

## 5.10 Amides

### Structure and Properties

- An **amide** is a compound with the structure RCONH$_2$ whose properties are due to the presence of an amide linkage (-CONR-).

### Reactions

- A **dehydration** is a reaction that involves the elimination of a molecule of water from a compound.

## 5.11 Amino Acids

### Structure and Properties

- An **α-amino** acid is a carboxylic acid with an amino group attached to the carbon atom adjacent to the carboxyl group.

- A **zwitterion** is a dipolar ion that contains positively and negatively charged groups, and has an overall charge of zero.

### Reactions

- The **isoelectric point** of an amino acid is the pH at which the amino acid exists as zwitterions.

### Proteins

- The **primary structure** of a protein is the sequence of amino acids joined by peptide links in a chain.

- The term **peptide link** refers to the -CONH- linkage formed when the amino (-NH$_2$) group on one amino acid reacts with the carboxyl (-COOH) group on a second amino acid.

- A **dipeptide** is formed when two amino acids react to form a molecule containing a peptide (-CONH-) linkage.

- The **secondary structure** of a protein refers to the twisting and coiling of the amino acid chain to form α-helices and β-sheets that results from intramolecular hydrogen bonding between amino acid side-chains.

- The **tertiary structure** of a protein is the precise three-dimensional shape produced when the secondary structure folds as a result of van der Waals attraction, hydrogen bonding, ionic interactions and disulfide bonds in the protein.

### Enzymes

- **Enzymes** are proteins that catalyse reactions in living systems.

- The **active site** of an enzyme is the small region on the surface of the enzyme into which one or more of the reactants bind.

## 5.12 Polymer Chemistry

- A **polymer** is a large molecule formed from many identical molecules known as monomers.

- An **addition polymer** is a polymer formed by addition reactions between monomers.

- A **condensation polymer** is a polymer formed by condensation reactions between monomers that each eliminate a small molecule from the polymer.

### Polyesters

- **Polyester** is a polymer in which the monomers in the polymer molecules are joined by ester linkages.

- A polymer is **biodegradable** if the linkages between the monomers can be hydrolysed by the action of microorganisms in the environment.

### Polyamides

- A **polyamide** is a polymer in which the monomers in the polymer molecules are joined by amide linkages.

## 5.13 Chemistry in Medicine

### Drug Development

- **DNA replication** is the process by which double stranded DNA is copied to produce two identical DNA molecules.

### Biological Roles of Metal Complexes

- A **sequestering agent** is a substance that renders an ion inert by forming a stable complex with it.

# Copyright

Copyright has been acknowledged to the best of our ability. If there are any inadvertent errors or omissions, we shall be happy to correct them in any future editions.

## Acknowledgements

CCEA past paper questions are included with the permission of the Northern Ireland Council for the Curriculum, Examinations and Assessment. All content © CCEA 2002-16.

## Credits

All diagrams in questions taken from, or adapted from, CCEA past papers are © CCEA unless otherwise stated.

Figure 4(a) on page 145 is used with the kind permission of Dr Maria T. Gallardo-Williams, NC State University. Figure 4(b) on page 145 is reproduced under the terms of the Creative Commons Attribution-ShareAlike 3.0 Unported (CC BY-SA 3.0) license (WikiPremed).

Unless otherwise stated, all other images are ©Wingfield Glassey and Colourpoint Creative Limited.